ROBERT STEPHENSON – THE EMINENT E

1850 portrait of Robert Stephenson and the Britannia Tubular Bridge by John Lucas (Courtesy of Institution of Mechanical Engineers)

Robert Stephenson
– The Eminent Engineer

Edited by Michael R. Bailey

Published in association with
The Institution of Civil Engineers
The Institution of Mechanical Engineers
The Newcomen Society

ASHGATE

Published by

Ashgate Publishing	Ashgate Publishing
Limited	Company
Gower House	Suite 420
Croft Road	101 Cherry Street
Aldershot	Burlington,
Hants GU11 3HR	VT 05401-4405
England	USA

Ashgate website: http://www.ashgate.com

British Library Cataloguing in Publication Data
Robert Stephenson : the eminent engineer
   1. Stephenson, Robert, 1803-1859 2. Railroad
  engineers - Great Britain - Biography
  I. Bailey, Michael R. (Michael Reeves)
  625.1'0092

Library of Congress Cataloging-in-Publication Data
Robert Stephenson-the eminent engineer / edited by
  Michael R. Bailey.
    p. cm.
  Includes bibliographical references and index.
  ISBN 0-7546-3679-8 (alk. paper)
   1. Stephenson, Robert, 1803–1859. 2. Civil
  engineers--Great Britain--Biography. 3. Civil
  engineering--Great Britain--History--19th century.
  I. Bailey, Michael R. (Michael Reeves)

  TA140.S72.R63 2003
  624'.092--dc21
  [B]

                          2003052124

ISBN 0 7546 3679 8

Typeset in Garamond by Bookcraft Ltd, Stroud,
Gloucestershire
Printed and bound in Great Britain by Biddles Ltd,
Guildford and Kings Lynn.

Robert Stephenson (1803–1859)
MP, FRS, Hon. MA (Durham), Hon. DCL (Oxford)
Knight of the Order of Leopold (Belgium)
Légion d'Honneur (France)
Grand Cross of the Order of St Olaf (Norway)
President of the Institution of Civil Engineers
President of the Institution of Mechanical Engineers

Mr. Robert Stephenson … this eminent engineer, distinguished not more for his professional skill than for his unassuming disposition and benevolence as a man, and for the part he played for upwards of a quarter of a century in connexion with gigantic public works

The Times, 22 October 1859

Contents

List of Illustrations

Colour plates

Black and white illustrations

List of Contributors

Michael Bailey MA, DPhil, Past-President of the Newcomen Society, Associate of the Institute of Railway Studies and Transport History, Associate Trustee of the Museum of Science & Industry in Manchester

Mike Chrimes BA, MLS, ALA, Head Librarian, Institution of Civil Engineers

Julia Elton BA, Vice-President of the Newcomen Society

Ted Ruddock MBE, BA, MAI, MSc(Eng), MICE, member of the Institution of Civil Engineers' Panel for Historical Engineering Works

Denis Smith PhD, MSc, DIC, CEng, Past-President of the Newcomen Society, member of the Institution of Civil Engineers' Panel for Historical Engineering Works and their Archives Panel

James Sutherland BA, FICE, FIStructE, Past-President of the Newcomen Society

Robert Thomas BA(Hons), MCLIP, Assistant Librarian, Institution of Civil Engineers

Foreword

It is timely for this new biography of Robert Stephenson to be published in 2003, the bicentenary of his birth. As a senior and most respected member of the engineering profession in the nineteenth century, his many prominent achievements have made a major impact not only on the lives of Victorian society, but on subsequent generations through to the present day. The economies of Britain and several overseas countries were stimulated by the provision of many hundreds of miles of railway for which he was the responsible engineer. The building of large and pioneering bridges and other structures, and his remarkable contribution to steam locomotion, made possible this transport revolution, whilst his wider pursuits included urban water supply and drainage, together with dock, river and coastal improvements.

Stephenson's influence over the development of the engineering profession was profound. Whilst following in the footsteps of his illustrious forebears, such as Smeaton and Telford, in forming an influential consulting firm, the sheer scale of its operations and the breadth of its influence were altogether on a new plane. From this time began the prominence of the British consulting engineering movement that continues to form such an important part of the profession today.

Stephenson played a major part in the affairs of both the Institution of Civil Engineers and the Institution of Mechanical Engineers. He took over from his late father, George Stephenson, as the second president of the newly formed 'Mechanicals', then based in Birmingham, and served in that capacity between 1849 and 1853. He contributed much to the affairs of the 'Civils' and was a regular contributor to the papers and 'conversaziones' at its Great George Street premises in Westminster, adjacent to his consultancy chambers. His strong relationship with the other leading engineers of the day, particularly with Isambard Kingdom Brunel and Joseph Locke, allowed the profession to enjoy an influential status in the nation's affairs. Stephenson's two-year term as the President of the Institution of Civil Engineers in 1856 and 1857 was, in many ways, the pinnacle of his career, serving as an exemplar for those who have succeeded him.

The wider public perception of Robert Stephenson today does not accord with the great admiration and respect in which he was held in his own time. There has long been a need for a biography to raise the profile of this engineering pioneer, which seeks to redress the balance between the importance and impact of his contributions with those of his father. We must therefore be grateful for all the efforts of Michael Bailey and his co-authors in undertaking the comprehensive and daunting task of researching Stephenson's life and works. Their findings in this volume have allowed us to be so much better informed of one of the greatest engineers, and his contribution to the world's development.

Professor Adrian Long, President, Institution of Civil Engineers
Professor Christopher Taylor, President, Institution of Mechanical Engineers
Sir Neil Cossons, President, The Newcomen Society

Acknowledgements

A volume of this size, containing so much detail about the life of Robert Stephenson, whose career was so diverse and whose impact on society was so profound, has required a level of research beyond the scope of a normal biography. The considerable efforts on the part of the authors have been made possible only through the extensive cooperation of many people and institutions both in Britain and in other countries.

Particular acknowledgement is addressed to the Institution of Civil Engineers, whose Archives Panel took the initiative to pursue a biography that most would acknowledge to be long overdue. The Panel's invitation to me to take on the daunting task of driving a large multi-author biography through to publication was a major but welcome challenge. I am pleased to acknowledge the particular role of Professor Sir Alec Skempton, 'Skem' to his wide circle of friends and colleagues, whose death during the early stages of the research was a major blow to us all. His long-standing interest in Stephenson's pioneering geotechnical work helped to stimulate the wider research programme for this volume.

The Newcomen Society is not only the world's oldest society for the study of the history of engineering and technology; it remains the forum that allows so many leading engineering historians of the day to discuss and debate their findings. Whilst being closely associated with the Institution of Civil Engineers and the Institution of Mechanical Engineers, the authors of this biography are prominent and active members of the Society, and include three past presidents and a vice-president. This close association through the Society has enabled the team to come together, each contributing knowledge and expertise in their particular subjects, and to assist each other in so many ways during the writing and editing phases.

Other members of the Society have assisted in many ways. I am grateful in particular to Bob Rennison and E. F. Clark, past presidents, and John Rapley for their observations and suggestions during both the gathering of the material and the editing phases. Much gratitude is also due to John Liffen who, with tireless enthusiasm and intimate knowledge of the Science Museum's comprehensive collections, has been helpful throughout.

The librarians of many academic and professional institutions and smaller archive collections have, as always, been immensely helpful in making it possible for the authors to consult large quantities of primary source material. I should like to acknowledge in particular the considerable help of the Head

Librarians of the Institution of Civil Engineers, Mike Chrimes, and the Institution of Mechanical Engineers, Keith Moore, and their respective members of staff, who have offered every facility to allow the authors to trawl through their extensive archives, and made available so many illustrations.

Great Britain has a good record, not only for having retained so much archival material, but also for having such a well-structured network of libraries and record offices through which it is made available for research. Robert Stephenson's letters, for example, may be found in over two dozen collections in libraries and record offices around the country, to which may be added the several further examples retained in private ownership. Only by bringing copies together into one large collection of correspondence has it been possible to interrelate the many themes they address. To the custodians of all the libraries and record offices who assisted with this biography, my colleagues and I offer our sincere thanks.

My fellow-authors and I are pleased to acknowledge with gratitude those many other individuals who gave their advice or permission to use material for the book. Their contributions are recorded in the footnotes throughout the book.

Michael Bailey, June 2003

Reference Sources

Archives and Archive Collections

Airy	G. B. Airy Collection, Manuscript Library, Cambridge University
BL	British Library
Brunel	Brunel Collection, Special Collections, Bristol University Library
CCL	Canterbury Cathedral Library
DRO	Derbyshire Record Office
Forbes	J. D. Forbes Collection, St Andrews University Library
ICE	Institution of Civil Engineers
IMechE	Institution of Mechanical Engineers
LRO	Liverpool Record Office
NRM	National Railway Museum
NRO	Northumberland Record Office
OIOC	Oriental and India Office Collection, British Library
Pease–Stephenson	Pease–Stephenson Collection, Durham County Record Office, Darlington Public Library
PRO	Public Record Office
RSA	Royal Society of Arts
Salford	Salford Museum and Heritage Service
ScM	Science Museum Library
Starbuck	Starbuck Collection, Tyne and Wear Record Office
Stephenson	Robert Stephenson & Co. Collection, National Railway Museum
V&A	Victoria and Albert Museum

Periodicals and Proceedings

Art	*The Artizan*
CEAJ	*The Civil Engineer and Architect's Journal*
IAR	*Industrial Archaeology Review*
ILN	*Illustrated London News*
JRCHS	*Journal of the Railway & Canal Historical Society*
JTH	*Journal of Transport History*
MM	*Mechanic's Magazine*
PM	*The Penny Magazine*

Proc. ICE	*Minutes of the Proceedings of the Institution of Civil Engineers*
Proc. IMechE	*Proceedings of the Institution of Mechanical Engineers*
RC	*Railway Chronicle*
RM	*Herapath's Railway Magazine* 1835
	The Railway Magazine and Annals of Science (NS) 1836–1839
	Railway Magazine and Commercial Journal (1840–)
RR	*The Railway Record*
RT	*The Railway Times*
TNS	*Transactions of the Newcomen Society*

Introduction

On Friday, 21 October 1859, thousands of people packed Westminster Abbey and thousands more thronged the streets of London to witness the funeral of Robert Stephenson. The cortège passed through Hyde Park, a privilege, 'for which no precedent exists', being made possible by the express permission of Queen Victoria:[1]

Her Majesty considers that as the late Mr. Stephenson is to be buried in Westminster Abbey, in acknowledgment of the high position he occupied, and the world-wide reputation he had won for himself as an engineer, his funeral, though strictly speaking private partakes of the character of a public ceremony; and being anxious, moreover, to show that she fully shares with the public in lamenting the loss which the country has sustained by his death – she cannot hesitate for a moment in giving her entire sanction [to this request].

Robert Stephenson, the country's most famous engineer, was also internationally renowned, and is one of only two engineers, with Thomas Telford, to be buried in the Abbey. When he died, aged only 56, *The Times* described him as:[2]

… this eminent engineer, distinguished not more for his professional skill than for his unassuming disposition and benevolence as a man, and for the part he played for upwards of a quarter of a century in connexion with gigantic public works.

His influence in City boardrooms and Parliament was profound. He was President of the Institution of Mechanical Engineers in 1849–1853, and of the Institution of Civil Engineers in 1856–1857. He was made a Knight of the Order of Leopold in Belgium, and was awarded the Légion d'Honneur from France and Grand Cross of the Order of St Olaf from Norway, but declined a British knighthood. He received an Honorary MA from the University of Durham and an Honorary DCL from the University of Oxford and was a Fellow of the Royal Society.

Robert Stephenson was born of humble origins in the Northumbrian coalfield two hundred years ago in 1803. To rise from obscurity to such fame is an outstanding achievement under any circumstances, but in early nineteenth-century British society it was truly remarkable. His story has been told before,

---

1 Letters, J. Macdonald to Charles Manby, 19 and 20 October 1859, **ScM**, GPB 5/12/3.
2 *The Times*, 22 October 1859.

most recently in 1960 when L. T. C. Rolt combined his history with that of his father in *George and Robert Stephenson*. This father and son combination echoed the work of Samuel Smiles, who dedicated a complete volume to their biography in his *Lives of the Engineers* of 1862. J. C. Jeaffreson, as far back as 1864, is the only major author to have written a biography devoted to Robert Stephenson alone. That such a time has elapsed since this last endeavour may be considered regrettable given the disproportionate attention given to the life of George Stephenson, the progenitor of the steam-powered main-line railway system.

Robert Stephenson deserves a specific enquiry into his life and works. This long-overdue biography addresses his crucial contribution to railways, and to civil, structural, mechanical and water engineering, and examines his involvement in the world of railway promotion in the free-market climate of nineteenth-century Britain, and the political and business connections that produced great wealth and influence for him.

The biography of a man whose life was so active, and encompassed so many disciplines, requires a similarly wide enquiry and interpretation. This has been provided here by a team of authors whose experience enables them to understand and interpret Stephenson's many strengths and weaknesses. The extraordinary diversity of his achievements necessitated a series of separate studies that clearly illustrate each of his many attributes.

Technology is the engine of social change and, as the leading engineer of his day, Stephenson had more impact on society than most of his contemporaries. The expansion of main-line railways, for which he was largely responsible, both stimulated and was stimulated by the industrial revolution and the immense growth in the country's prosperity during Stephenson's lifetime. Cheaper transport costs led to expansion in manufacturing through cheaper movement of raw materials and products, and made foodstuffs affordable to meet the demands of the rapidly growing cities. The greatest social change, however, came about with the ability of the railways to fulfil an unexpected latent demand for personal travel. Stephenson was a champion of travel opportunities for all, and believed that 'the true and full effect of railways would not take place until they were made so cheap in their fares that a poor man could not afford to walk'.[3]

Stephenson's 'fame and future' were 'built upon a rock',[4] that is, the first trunk railway from London to Birmingham. In his assessment of its construction, Mike Chrimes shows that it was achieved through Stephenson's selection and supervision of a large and reliable team of engineers. In overseeing and motivating them, and often taking the necessary difficult decisions, he earned their respect as the 'Chief'.

---

3 Speech by Robert Stephenson on the occasion of a dinner and presentation of plate to George Bidder by the shareholders of the Northern & Eastern Railway, Blackwall, *RT*, **VII**, 1 June 1844, p. 622.

4 Letter, Michael Longridge to Robert Stephenson, Bedlington Iron Works, 4 February 1835, **Pease–Stephenson**, D/PS/2/67.

As the railway network expanded, Stephenson was constantly in demand to represent new companies and schemes. His consulting practice provided professional opportunities to many associates who remained loyal to him throughout their careers. The most senior of these, George Parker Bidder, became a close confidant as well as colleague. The Westminster practice was more akin to barristers' chambers, with opportunities for individual professional engagement, than to a hierarchical partnership. Stephenson directed and monitored design policies, whilst his associates, who undertook the detailing of individual structural designs, pooled their knowledge within the practice.

By 1850 he had been involved in the provision of a third of the nation's railway network, and his role focused on the strategy and tactics of promotion, in which he had an influential, if enigmatic, involvement with the proprietors. Stephenson detested the British free-market system, which he regarded as wasteful, and he railed against the 'anomalies, incongruities, irreconcilabilities, and absurdities which pervade the entire mass of legislation' for railway promotion.[5] The more he campaigned against the system, however, the more he was drawn into it, and during the 'mania' years of the mid-1840s he allowed himself to become entangled in the manoeuvrings of the railway proprietors – especially George Hudson, the 'Railway King'.

During the 'mania' years the applications for him to represent railway projects were more than time would allow. Proprietors scrambled to include his name on their prospectuses to attract investment from an eager capital market. He accepted more than 160 assignments for over 60 different railway companies. Because of his involvement in so many schemes, he gave evidence to parliamentary committees on 150 occasions. He gained a reputation for considerable ability in dealing with the close and often hostile questioning by barristers representing rival schemes.

The frustrations of the 'mania' years were compounded for Stephenson by the very public disagreements over track gauge, atmospheric propulsion and the internecine battles between the Great Western and London & North Western railways. It was a great tribute to the characters of both Robert Stephenson and Isambard K. Brunel that in spite of their confrontations, they never ceased to enjoy a strong personal regard for each other. Brunel wrote of Stephenson: 'In spite of our very bitter contests I have a great regard [for him].'[6]

Stephenson made a conscious decision from 1847 to withdraw from the British railway scene. Although he fulfilled his remaining commitments, especially the Chester & Holyhead Railway, his reduced involvement with British railways was matched by a growing involvement in consultations for railway development overseas. Such consultations ranged from strategic planning of

5 Robert Stephenson, Presidential Address, *Proc. ICE*, **XV**, 1855/6, p. 136.
6 Copy letter, Isambard K. Brunel to H. Robertson (for the Shrewsbury & Chester Railway), 11 January 1848, **Brunel**, Letter Book 5, pp. 334–5.

whole networks for Switzerland, Sweden and Denmark, to supervision of major railway schemes in Belgium, Norway, Egypt and India.

Stephenson's railway construction work was characterized by innovation rather than invention. The impact of the London & Birmingham Railway can be likened to the works of John Smeaton, whose published record had guided the previous generation of engineers. In discussing Stephenson's railway-building techniques, Mike Chrimes notes that neither Brunel nor Joseph Locke served as such exemplars to the profession. Stephenson's growing experience was reflected in papers and discussions at the Institution of Civil Engineers and elsewhere. The drawings and specifications for his railways formed major sections of published works that were made available to the civil engineering profession, providing 'time-saver' standards for the railway age.

The high reputation of the Stephenson team in railway building reflects the delegation and close communication developed between him and his associates. It was Stephenson too who was largely responsible for developing a system of railway construction relying on delegation and cooperation with client and contractor. This system enabled a network of railways to be built in many countries.

Stephenson and his associates also played a leading role in the transition from cast-iron to wrought-iron bridge designs. His confidence in the trussed compound girder bridge was reflected in the large number built in the 1840s, until the failure and collapse of the bridge carrying the Chester & Holyhead Railway across the River Dee near Chester in May 1847. This disaster sent shock waves throughout the engineering profession and was a traumatic time for Stephenson himself. He characteristically fulfilled his responsibilities as Chief Engineer at the subsequent enquiry. As James Sutherland concludes, however, it would be wrong to blame a single individual for the misconception over the behaviour of these girders. It was a case of group myopia suffered by many of the most distinguished engineers of the day.

Stephenson's enduring reputation will surely rest on the spectacular tubular bridges in North Wales, even though their history was marred by controversy. In his discussion of Stephenson's iron bridge development, however, James Sutherland notes that, though innovative in its conception, this type of bridge was redundant almost before the Britannia Bridge was completed. Within ten years the design was overtaken by several forms of open truss girder, and the accompanying analytical knowledge.

He was also responsible for hundreds of masonry bridges and other types of iron bridges during his career. Two masterpieces, however, were those that carried the York, Newcastle & Berwick Railway across the rivers Tyne and Tweed. The wrought-iron High Level Bridge across the Tyne was the crowning example of his bowstring designs that had evolved during the previous decade. Its six majestic spans carry the railway 100 feet above the river Tyne, with a road tucked beneath the tracks.

The Royal Border Bridge at Berwick was an outstanding example of masonry bridge design and construction in the mid-nineteenth century. However, Ted Ruddock concludes that Stephenson's masonry structures were less technically innovative than his large iron bridges. It was the quantity and scale of masonry structures and the speed with which they were completed that was astonishing, particularly when compared with the works of the busiest engineers of the previous generation, such as John Rennie and Thomas Telford.

Stephenson also made considerable contributions to water engineering. Denis Smith reveals that he was extensively involved in dock, river and estuarial projects, and in pioneering water supply and drainage schemes. He was central to the protracted debate about sewerage that brought about major social change in the years following his death. However, his participation in the 1850s debate over the Suez Canal was controversial. He believed that a canal was unnecessary, but compounded this by claiming that such a canal was also impractical. His opinion had a far-reaching impact because it kept the Canal, opened a decade after his death, away from the sphere of British political influence.

Among his many other responsibilities, Stephenson was the managing partner of the Newcastle-upon-Tyne factory that bore his name and that supplied large numbers of steam locomotives to the growing railway network around the world. He pursued his remarkable talents as a mechanical engineer in parallel with his railway-building and civil engineering activities. In the late 1820s, while his father was building the Liverpool & Manchester Railway, the world's first main-line railway, he undertook a major development programme for the steam locomotive. Locomotive design advanced from the crude mineral engines of the Stockton & Darlington Railway to the *Planet* class of 1830, suitable for main-line operation, in the astonishingly short period of 33 months. The resourceful innovation of the Newcastle team under Stephenson's direction continued to improve materials, designs and manufacturing techniques that kept the factory in the forefront of manufacturing throughout the 1830s and 1840s.

Stephenson's involvement with manufacturing, however, presented him with conflicts of interest that at first he found hard to handle. His expectation that he could supply locomotives to clients for whom he was the chief engineer resulted in major disagreements that threatened his authority and future. He was initially naive in business, but learned from his partners about profitable manufacture. Prompted by the economic depression of the late 1840s, his growing experience led to a development strategy that saw the firm's activities diversify into marine, factory and agricultural engines.

Stephenson never saw himself as an entrepreneurial businessman. Having been brought to near-bankruptcy by accepting shares in lieu of payment in the unlimited Stanhope & Tyne Railroad, he was circumspect about business ventures. However, from the 1840s his increasing wealth, from his consultancy work and royalty payments, led him to invest in some profitable ventures. Other investments were all too often made to bail out friends and colleagues, rather than being sound in themselves. He also inherited large shareholdings on his father's death in 1848, and maintained a close association with the Electric Telegraph Company founded through the energies of George Bidder. He was for some time its Chairman.

Stephenson's frustration with the free-market system led him towards a political career as an old school 'Tory'. Paradoxically, as Julia Elton has shown, it was his close association with George Hudson that gave him the opportunity to run for Parliament in the 1847 general election. During his twelve unbroken years as MP for Whitby, he participated in a number of parliamentary committees. No doubt he would have found the violence that accompanied his re-election in 1852 distasteful. The importance of Stephenson's role in setting up and planning the Great Exhibition of 1851 is also highlighted by Julia Elton. In the hesitant transfer of the planning from the Society of Arts to Prince Albert's Royal Commission, Stephenson was replaced as Chairman of the Executive Committee to become a Commissioner; 'a man in whom all parties would have confidence'.[7]

Stephenson was widely admired across the whole spectrum of nineteenth-century society. Integrity was perhaps his greatest quality, demonstrated by the extraordinary number of contentious issues of a business, financial and engineering nature that were presented to him for arbitration. He argued strongly in favour of arbitration against litigation, and disputants accepted often unpalatable resolutions through the clear logic of his findings.

He was immensely sociable, and frequently attended dinners and society meetings with parliamentarians, financiers and men of learning. Above all, Stephenson was respected by his peers. He was one of the nation's 'triumvirate' of senior engineers, with his close colleagues Isambard K. Brunel and Joseph Locke, and the death of all three within such a short time was a major blow to the profession. The loss from Stephenson's death was, however, mitigated by the talents of his associates, who perpetuated his innovative approach and organizational skills.

Engineers, parliamentarians, statesmen, financiers, men of learning, and the working men whose cause he often championed: to them all Robert Stephenson was the 'Eminent Engineer'.

---

7 Letter, Stafford Northcote to Colonel Grey, 2 February 1850, **Royal Archives at Windsor**, on permanent loan to the Royal Commission for the Exhibition of 1851.

Poem by J. H. Eccles[8]

Entomb'd amid the noble ones
The great illustrious dead,
Where sleep the chosen of our land,
Now rests his honoured head.
Endow'd with genius rich and rare
A deep conceptive mind;
How full of thought and enterprise,
The works he's left behind.

Along our valleys, speeding forth,
Upon their iron ways,
The very engines seem to breathe,
Their triumph in his praise;
While distant lands in gratitude,
His deeds of worth can tell,
How he has laboured for their sake –
How truly and how well.

Great must have been his power of thought,
And noble his design,
Who formed the bridge o'er Menai's Straits,
And crossed the troubled Tyne;
Who raised up works on every hand
By his consummate skill;
And made the greatest obstacles
Yield to his ardent will.

Now he is gone, and we have lost
One of our greatest men,
Who toiled alike with head and hand,
And laboured with his pen;
Whose name shall live on history's page,
While progress holds it sway,
The first and foremost of his time,
The greatest of his day.

---

8 J. H. Eccles, published in 1859 or 1860, unattributed clipping, in album, **IMechE**, IMS/173.

Part I

Influence and achievement

Portrait of Robert
Stephenson by
George
Richmond
(J. C. Jeaffreson,
1864, frontispiece)

George Richmond 1844   Henry Adlard 1863

London: Longman & Cº

The early years

Michael Bailey

I can engineer matter very well, but my great difficulty is in engineering men
George Stephenson, as recalled by Robert Stephenson[1]

Robert Stephenson was appointed as engineer-in-chief of the London &
Birmingham Railway on 19 September 1833. The railway's directors were
'persuaded that to no one could this charge be more safely or more properly
confided'.[2] For Stephenson, born into a humble Northumbrian mining
community nearly 30 years earlier, his appointment to the largest civil engineering undertaking the country had yet experienced was a remarkable achievement that begs many questions about his qualities as an engineer, manager and
diplomat.

To oversee such a major project required considerable understanding of
surveying, material behaviour and structural design. It also required leadership
to recruit, motivate and maintain the respect of a team of design and resident
engineers, and negotiating skills to appoint and monitor the performance of
contractors. Furthermore, the appointment would need to heed the pressures
of divided opinion amongst factions both within and external to the board of
directors, for which diplomacy and persuasion were prerequisite.

Stephenson demonstrated that he had sufficient experience, skills and qualities to 'persuade' the country's leading businessmen to place in him the
responsibility of overseeing the execution of this major venture. That he could
demonstrate this, before reaching the age of 30, prompts enquiry into the
influences and experiences in his early career.

Education and apprenticeship

Robert Stephenson's upbringing was dominated by the Tyneside mining
community. From his birth at Willington on 16 October 1803, through the
family's move to Killingworth, until the age of 19, Stephenson was raised,
educated and apprenticed in a region dominated by the mining, leading and

---

1 Speech by Robert Stephenson, in Memoir of James John Berkley, *Proc. ICE*, **XXII**, 1862/3, p. 621.
2 Minute Book of the Board of Directors of the London & Birmingham Railway, 1833–1837, **PRO,**
RAIL 384/2, p. 17.

shipping of coal, and by the developing technology that allowed the industry to grow. Following the loss of his mother and infant sister, his father George Stephenson (1781–1848) dominated his early years, and a strong bond developed between them that was sustained throughout their professional life.[3]

George Stephenson's influence over his son's character was profound. His strong personality and tenacity were traits that engaged all those with whom he worked. His friends allied themselves in the expectation that his strong views would largely prevail, whilst his enemies regarded him as arrogant and motivated by self-interest. The young Stephenson, influenced by his father's character and the responses of his father's contemporaries, formed his character with similar tenacity, but appreciating the necessity for a less provocative manner. He was to become only too aware in his professional life that winning arguments needed a combination of knowledge, self-belief and persuasive dialogue. Notwithstanding the inevitable disagreements that he would face, he never earned the label of arrogance that dogged his father's career.

Stephenson received a good education. This was his father's firm resolve, recognizing that lack of education was limiting his own career. George Stephenson's income as a brakesman at the West Moor pit, Killingworth, was insufficient to pay for his son's schooling, so he used his clock and watch repair skills to earn extra money, as he later recalled:[4]

… in his early days, when that son [Robert] was a little boy, he saw how deficient he himself was in education; and though he was a poor man, he set to work and made up his mind to educate his son at some of the best schools. He was determined to give his son a liberal education. … after he had worked a hard day's work, he applied himself to clock and watch repairing in his spare hours. By this means he saved money, which he put by.

Although lacking a formal education, George Stephenson demonstrated considerable practical skill in maintaining and improving the machinery at the Killingworth pits. Having gained the respect of the Viewer, Ralph Dodds (1792–1874), he was promoted to engine-wright in 1812. He also gained the trust of the colliery's trainee Viewer, Nicholas Wood (1795–1865), with whom he formed a lifelong friendship. Stephenson's endeavours gained the attention of his employers, Lord Strathmore, Sir Thomas Liddell (afterwards Lord Ravensworth) and Stuart Wortley (afterwards Lord Wharncliffe), the so-called 'Grand Allies', because of both the cost savings he made and his tenacious pursuit of improvements for which they approved funding. From 1814, these improvements included the building of 'travelling engines'.

Robert Stephenson therefore had a growing familiarity with mining engines and machinery, and witnessed his father's ventures into locomotive

3 A narrative of Stephenson's earliest years is set out in Jeaffreson, chapters 1 to 3.
4 'The Hengist of Railways', report of speech by George Stephenson at the opening of the Newcastle & Darlington Junction Railway, *RT*, **VII**, 6 July 1844, p. 735.

building and improvements. He also witnessed the development of the colliery safety lamp in 1815, and the extraordinary events surrounding the rival claims for priority following its simultaneous development with that of Sir Humphry Davy.[5] The episode brought his father to public notice, and Robert Stephenson learned at close quarters that public disputes could become vitriolic, requiring the robust character that his father undoubtedly had.

Stephenson's secondary education was at the Percy Street Academy in Newcastle. The school was highly regarded, being attended by the sons of professional men, traders and 'minor gentry'.[6] Stephenson's character, quite apart from his education, was clearly matured by his attendance there. Although a 'working class' child in a school whose pupils were largely 'middle class', he apparently adapted well in his four-year attendance. Although he had not shown 'any remarkable signs of talent',[7] his education had clearly been of a standard sufficient to earn him a pupillage with the prospect of a professional career.

However, Stephenson's close identification with the mining world and his awareness of the pioneering work in the Northumberland and Durham coal-fields, not least through acquaintance with his father's techniques and innovations, had laid the foundation of his interest in engineering. George Stephenson later recalled that 'having got the assistance of his son, who became a companion to him while quite a boy, his son worked for him at night when he came home'.[8] When Stephenson was 13, he copied a drawing of a sundial from Ferguson's *Astronomy*, prompting the two Stephensons to construct one, bearing the date 'August 11th MDCCCXVI', which was placed above the doorway of the family home.[9]

From 1819 Stephenson was apprenticed to Nicholas Wood, then Viewer of Killingworth Colliery. His training included mine surveying, and the design and operation of colliery and wagonway machinery. He also had responsibilities towards some miners, later recalling that he 'had a body of them under my control, and I may say in my employ'.[10] In addition, he assisted his father in improving the five-mile Killingworth wagonway.[11] Stephenson also exhibited something of his father's practical capabilities, and made himself a circumferentor (instrument for taking angles) to assist with his survey work. It was inscribed 'Robert Stephenson *fecit*'.[12] As events in his father's career accelerated, Stephenson was needed to assist him, and his apprenticeship lasted less than three years.

5 Alan Smith, 'George Stephenson, Sir Humphry Davy and the Miners' Safety Lamp', *Bulletin of the Newcomen Society*, 172, December 1998, pp. 14–16.

6 Jeaffreson, p. 34.

7 Ibid.

8 Op. cit. (n. 4)

9 Jeaffreson, p. 43.

10 Letter, Robert Stephenson to R. S. Illingworth, 8 December 1825, in Jeaffreson, p. 90.

11 Robert Stephenson evidence, 27 March 1829, in *Copy of the Evidence &c on the Newcastle & Carlisle Railway Bill*, Newcastle-upon-Tyne, 1829, p. 127.

12 Jeaffreson, p. 48.

In 1819 George Stephenson was asked to prepare plans and sections for a wagonway to serve a new colliery at Hetton in County Durham. His previous wagonway experience had been on the Killingworth 'new' line, and short extensions, such as that to Burradon Colliery.[13] The undulating eight-mile line between Hetton Colliery and Bishopwearmouth was laid out with inclines adopting self-acting and stationary winding engine haulage, with two stretches to be worked by locomotives.[14] The building and equipping of the line commenced in March 1821, but for George Stephenson to maintain his other commitments, he appointed his younger brother, Robert (1788–1837), as the line's resident engineer.

After work on the line had commenced, George Stephenson accepted the invitation of Edward Pease (1767–1858), the successful businessman and leading Quaker of Darlington, and his fellow directors of the Stockton & Darlington Railway to undertake a re-survey of that railway's parliamentary route and branch lines.[15] George Overton (fl. 1795–1827) had originally surveyed the line, but the potential economy of using locomotives prompted the invitation. In October 1821 Stephenson was authorized to proceed, assisted by his son and by John Dixon (1796–1865).[16] Dixon was a surveyor, with knowledge of the original alignment, whose career diversified thereafter as part of the Stephenson team.[17]

Robert Stephenson effectively transferred his apprenticeship to his father and to Dixon by assisting with this re-survey. In January 1822, George Stephenson recommended to the directors significant improvements to the route's gradients and alignment, reducing it by almost three miles to nearly 25 miles. The directors accepted the deviations and submitted a further bill to Parliament, simultaneously appointing Stephenson as engineer to build the unaltered parts of the route.[18]

The building of the Stockton & Darlington line, as well as the Hetton line opened in November 1822, attracted the attention of other colliery proprietors, engineers and surveyors, who visited the north-east to meet George Stephenson, who began to take on the role of a consulting engineer. Robert Stephenson assisted his father in this role, both to relieve him of some of the workload and because he could write clearly.

An early example of his assistance followed a visit by Thomas Brewin of Halesowen, who had been accompanied by Lord Dudley's engineer, possibly to discuss the building of the Shutt End Railway in Staffordshire.[19] Stephenson

---

13 Evidence by George Stephenson to House of Commons Committee for the Liverpool & Manchester Railroad Bill, 25 April 1825.

14 'Cast-Iron Railway from Hetton Colliery to Sunderland', in von Oeynhausen and von Dechen, pp. 33–42.

15 Letter, Edward Pease to George Stephenson, Darlington, 7 mo. 28 [28 July] 1821, and reply, 2 August 1821 (in *Sunderland Herald*, 15 March 1857).

16 Minutes of the Sub Committee of Management, Stockton & Darlington Railway, 27 September and 15 October 1821, **PRO**, RAIL 667/30.

17 Evidence of John Dixon, 30 March 1829, in op. cit. (n. 11), p. 167.

18 Minutes of the Committee of the Stockton & Darlington Railway, **PRO**, RAIL 667/8, pp. 11–13.

19 Letter, George Stephenson to William James, 16 February 1822, in Warren, pp. 30–1.

wrote to Brewin with recommendations for planning the operation of the line based on the performance of the Killingworth locomotives. At the end of the letter he added:[20]

P.S. After shewing the above to my father he advised me to say he did not recommend his Engines to move on a Railway that ascended with the Load more than 3/16 pr yd. so that they may work with their Load in any kind of weather excepting when the Roads are blocked up with Snow. I may add I dont recollect our Engines being stoped with Snow this some years

One of the surveyors and engineers who made themselves known to the Stephensons was William James (1771–1837).[21] James had considerable experience as a land agent and surveyor, and for nearly 20 years had been advocating longer-distance rail routes. He had made a preliminary survey for a route between Liverpool and Manchester as early as 1803. He visited Killingworth and, after seeing the locomotives in action, became enthusiastic for their use. Many years later he reflected: 'Mr. Stephenson must remember my opinion emphatically expressed on first viewing and reflecting upon his locomotive engines, "that its powers were so transcendent, it would work a complete revolution in society".'[22] James struck up a good relationship with the Stephensons, and agreed to promote the use of locomotives for the several railway schemes on which he was engaged.

James's Liverpool and Manchester route gained the interest of several potential promoters from Liverpool. He invited Robert Stephenson to assist him with a comprehensive survey of the line. This was a good opportunity for Stephenson to develop further his knowledge and experience of surveying by assisting James and the rest of his team, namely his eldest son, William, his brother-in-law, Paul Padley, George Hamilton and Hugh Greenshields. Although the junior, Stephenson struck up a strong rapport with his colleagues. His relationship with James, a man ten years older than his father, was remarkably cordial and confident:[23]

My Dr. Sir
  Hugh [Greenshields] & I set off last night to see you but we were so unfortunate as to lose our guide. I am sorry we can not meet your expectations in arriving at Manchester with the survey it is utterly impossible – had the weather been favourable to us, we might have accomplished it. In our present situation we may arrive on Wednesday evening but no sooner, and with regard to finishing Survey & Plan on or before the 16th it is quite impracticable and let me assure you (however it may derange your business) that no effort has been spared by Mr. Padley or myself: we even by ourselves surveyed the greater part of Sunday – for God sake! don't depreciate Mr. P.'s exertions he is very much concerned at your request. I should be glad to see you if convenient at the Canteen this evening when we may talk matters over. Mr. P. went

20 Letter, Robert Stephenson to Thomas Brewin, Killingworth Colliery, 13 February 1822, **ScM**, MSL 257. This is the earliest known surviving letter written by Stephenson.
21 *Biographical Notice of William James, Projector of the Railway System in England*, London, 1840.
22 Published letter, 'The Origin of the Brighton Railway and Waterloo Bridge', W. James, 15 October 1836, *RM*, NS, **I**, November 1836, pp. 363–7.
23 Letter, Robert Stephenson to William James, 'Canteen', 3 September 1822, **LRO**, 385 JAM 1/6/1.

over (yesterday afternoon) Mr. Bradshaw's land and just as they were leaving the last field three men came running up to dismiss them but fortunately we had got finished. We commence at the Canal today and shall make every effort in our power to arrive at Manchester tomorrow evening – from there I should wish very much to go over the other end of the line with you – I am quite delighted with this part of the line for I feel confident by care in setting it out after the act is got it may be made a very complete line of Railway.

Should you be under the necessity of having the plans finished by the 16th I should advise another assistant (a competent surveyor) to be procured immediately … .

I remain Dr. Sir

Yours sincerely

Rt. Stephenson

During Stephenson's several weeks' absence from Killingworth, his father's consulting workload continued to grow. George Stephenson wrote to James: 'I am very much in want of Robert, you will send him off as soon as possible as I want him to go to Knaresburgh and also to do business on the Darlington Railway … .'[24]

Robert Stephenson was particularly upset to learn, in the summer of 1823, that James, for whom he had high regard, had got into serious financial difficulties. He wrote to him in a style that reflected both maturity and loyalty to his mentor:[25]

It gives rise to feelings of true regret when I reflect on your situation; but yet a consolation springs up when I consider your persevering spirit will for ever bear you up in the arms of triumph, instances of which I have witnessed of too forcible a character to be easily effaced from my memory. It is these thoughts, and these alone, that could banish from my soul feelings of despair for one; the respect I have for him can be easier conceived than described. Can I ever forget the advice you have afforded me in your last letters? and what a heavenly inducement you pointed before me at the close, when you said that attention and obedience to my dear father would afford me music at midnight.

William James' financial problems were serious enough in 1824 for him to lose the confidence of the promoters of the two most promising railway schemes that he had pursued, the Liverpool & Manchester and the Canterbury & Whitstable. George Stephenson was invited to replace him as engineer for both projects. James was aggrieved at being stood down and felt betrayed when George Stephenson accepted the positions. As this situation unfolded, Robert Stephenson experienced conflicting loyalties.

In spite of this conflict, Stephenson maintained faith with James and in 1838, the year after James died, Stephenson met his widow, Elizabeth, to discuss a memorial to her husband. He subsequently wrote: 'With [regard to] the memorial I wrote to him [Joseph Sandars] expressing my willingness to

24 Letter, George Stephenson to William James, Killingworth Colliery, 17 September 1822, **LRO**, 385 JAM 1/5/3.
25 Letter, Robert Stephenson to William James, Newcastle-upon-Tyne, 29 August 1823, in E. M. S. P[aine], p. 55.

give any aid in my power.'[26] As a result of Stephenson's intercession, the Liver-pool & Manchester Railway made retrospective recognition of James' pioneering role and a grant of £250 towards the memorial.[27]

At the conclusion of the Liverpool and Manchester survey in early October 1822, Stephenson returned to Killingworth. He only had a couple of weeks in which to assist his father, however, before taking up a place at Edinburgh University – a remarkable step for a young man from the Tyneside mining community. Stephenson no doubt went to Edinburgh with his father's encouragement and funding, even though he had been anxious for continuing help with his consultancy work. Stephenson himself was no doubt keen to gain further knowledge, stimulated by the realization during his survey work of his limited understanding of the 'natural sciences'.

It was uncommon for Edinburgh University students to graduate at this time. It was more usual for them to select subjects they wished to study, and to acquire 'class tickets' of particular professors that they could use as a reference for future engagements. Students would depart after a relatively short time once they felt they had gained sufficient learning.[28] Stephenson spent six months at the university, during which time he studied natural philosophy, natural history (including meteorology, geology and zoology) and chemistry. Whilst some of the subjects he found relevant and interesting, others, notably zoology, he did not.[29] He won one of the periodic prizes 'for some mathemat-ical questions given by Professor Leslie relative to various branches of Natural Philosophy'.[30] This was a copy of Charles Hutton's *Tracts on Mathematical and Philosophical Subjects*, the first seven chapters of which related to 'The Principles of Bridges' (Fig. 1.1).[31]

Shortly after Stephenson began in Edinburgh, William James reported to George Stephenson some inappropriate comments made about Northumbrian engineering by the Scottish engineer Robert Stevenson (1772–1850). Stevenson was at that time seeking to play a part in the developing interest in railways, including the Liverpool and Manchester line. George Stephenson's response was caustic:[32]

With respect to Mr Stephenson [Stevenson] of Edinburgh giving such a rash opinion on our Railroad and Engines is because the knowledge of machinery has not yet entered his head at least I have not seen any marks of it when in his company and if not now its unlikely ever will. I have heard him make some remarks on Railways which I hardly could have expected from a child he has collected news like other book makers and setting it of for his own [as] if we are just rising from darkness. I hope he means we

26 Letter, Robert Stephenson to Mrs. Elizabeth James, [London & Birmingham] R.[ail] W.[ay] Office, Camden Town, 4 October 1838. Copy letter, **Stephenson**, Folder 19.
27 Copy letter, Joseph Sandars to Robert Stephenson, Liverpool, 12 October 1838, **Stephenson**, Folder 19.
28 The author is grateful to the University Archivist for these background details.
29 Letter, Robert Stephenson to Michael Longridge, Edinburgh, December 1822, in Jeaffreson, p. 58.
30 Letter, Robert Stephenson to Michael Longridge, Edinburgh, 11 April 1823, in Jeaffreson, p. 59.
31 Hutton (1812).
32 Letter, George Stephenson to William James, Killingworth Colliery, 25 November 1822, **LRO**, 385 JAM 1/5/5.

1.1 Inscription to 'Roberto Stephenson' inserted in his presentation copy of Charles Hutton's *Tracts on Mathematical and Philosophical Subjects* and signed by Professor Leslie (Courtesy of Prof. Roland Paxton)

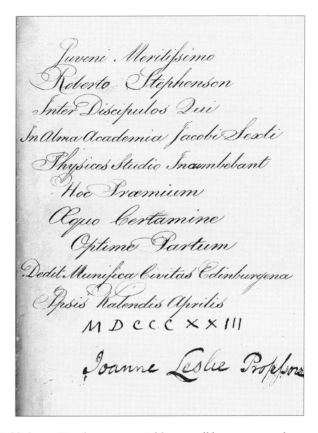

are the first, and if so it is likely our North country neighbours will have to grope there way by the refracted rays from our light.

In December 1822, Robert Stephenson took time off from his studies to meet Robert Stevenson. He reported his meeting to William James in a letter that succinctly summarizes his knowledge and understanding of railways at the outset of his career:[33]

… I was with him [Robert Stevenson] this morning we had some talk about Mr. James and the Liverpool line of Railway – he said he had some correspondence with some gentlemen in which he had mentioned that the Northumbrians were only emerging out of darkness: he said he did not mean to say that the Engineers such as Chapman <u>Buddle</u> & Stephenson were; but the northumbns in general. I think he said you had wrote him regarding it. His views and my fathers differ materially in the construction of Railways: he thinks my fathers Engines will answer very well on a Colliery but not on a public Railroad for this reason viz that they require the Rails much stronger. I told him they were not so injurious as a common chaldron waggon – 'true' says he but I would advise waggons of smaller size to be used. I immediately asked him whether he thought it better to lay a strong Railway down and enjoy the advantage of Locomotive Engines (for no doubt they were an advantage over every mode hitherto used) or lay a slight Railway down to save capital and suffer the continued disadvantage of horses – again when small waggons are employed the friction is considerably augmented from the greater number of axletrees; likewise a greater number of wheels are employed hence the wear and tear will be much more – when all these circumstances are candidly considered more especially on a Public Railroad where an immense quantity of heavy goods are passing over: they cannot fail (in my opinion) in making every Engineer a convert to a strong Railroad.

One of Stephenson's fellow students was George Parker Bidder (1806–1878), a Devonian lad three years his junior. Bidder had shown extraordinary arithmetical talents as the 'Calculating Boy', and in 1819, at the age of 13, he had begun studying at Edinburgh, where he remained for three years.[34] Bidder's career paralleled that of Stephenson in the field of engineering until, in 1834, he joined him as a member of his London & Birmingham Railway staff. Bidder became a loyal and close colleague of Stephenson, and was himself a much respected and talented engineer.

Stephenson's return from Edinburgh marked the conclusion of his education and the commencement of his professional life. Then 19½ years of age, he had achieved a good theoretical and mathematical grounding to add to the practical experience he had gained in surveying techniques. He still had much to learn about materials and structures, and had yet to develop his talents in mechanical engineering that he had displayed as a youth assisting his father. He always recognized that his opportunities for training and education resulted directly from his father's endeavours. These allowed him both to develop his talents and to make the first contacts that would carry him forward with his career.

Engineering assistant

Shortly after Stephenson returned from Edinburgh, in May 1823, the Stockton & Darlington Railway Bill received the royal assent.[35] This not only confirmed George Stephenson's reputation as a railway surveyor, it also provided for the use of 'travelling engines'. The passage of the bill had been delayed, however, by objections from the Trustees of Lord Strathmore, who sought the addition of a branch line to allow passage of coals from his Norwood Colliery. To avoid further delay, the objections were withdrawn, by agreement, which was subject to an application for a further bill to authorize the branch, from St. Helen's Auckland to Hagger Leases Lane, to serve the colliery.

George Stephenson delegated to his son the survey of the 4¾-mile branch, and preparation of plans, sections and cost estimates. This was thus the first route for which Robert Stephenson had responsibility as engineer, albeit under his father's guidance. Stephenson undertook the work with John Dixon's assistance. The parliamentary plan was endorsed 'R. STEPHENSON, ENGINEER' and 'J. DIXON, SUR.[veyo]R' (Fig. 1.2).[36] Stephenson travelled to

34 Clark (1983), chapter 2.
35 *4 Geo. IV, c. 33.*
36 A Plan of the RAILWAY or TRAMROAD from the River Tees at Stockton to Witton Park Colliery and of the Several BRANCHES therefrom .... and also a Plan and Sections of Several New or Additional Branch Railway or Tramroads Proposed to be made from the said Main Railway, **ScM**, MSL 259.

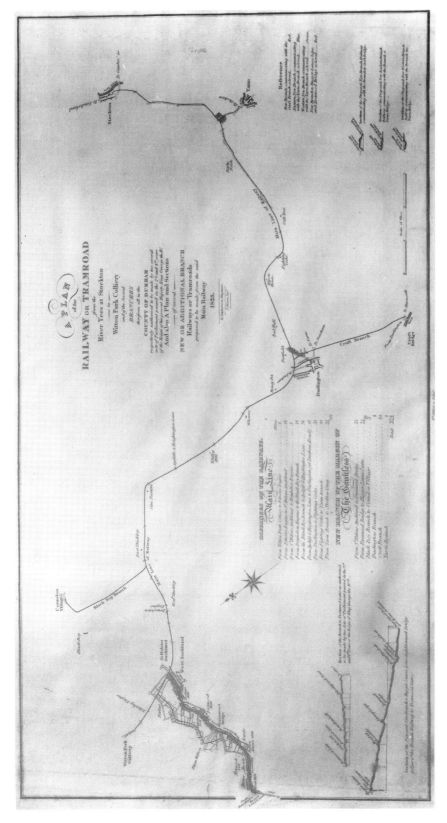

1.2 1824 plan of the Stockton & Darlington Railway, showing the Hagger Leases branch from West Auckland, with Stephenson's name as engineer (Science & Society Picture Library)

London in early 1824 to give evidence in connection with the bill should this be required.[37] He was not called upon, however, and the bill received royal assent in May.[38]

The opportunity for Robert Stephenson to develop his mechanical engineering interests arose in 1823. The passing of the Stockton & Darlington Railway Act that year significantly increased awareness of and interest in railways and steam engines, and there was much discussion in the City of London about the potential for investment and dividends in railway ventures. It suggested to Edward Pease and George Stephenson that an opportunity would quickly open up for the manufacture of equipment, particularly steam engines, to meet the requirements of the burgeoning railway industry, and they set up a firm for this purpose.

The firm was established on 23 June 1823 with five partners: George and Robert Stephenson; Edward Pease, together with Pease's cousin and fellow-Quaker, Thomas Richardson (1771–1853), a leading London banker and founder of the financial house of Overend Gurney & Co.; and Michael Longridge (1785–1858), the efficient and paternalistic manager of the Bedlington Iron Works, 12 miles north of Newcastle. The Stephensons had been on cordial terms with Longridge since 1820, when first consideration had been given to the use of wrought iron rails, following their development at Bedlington by John Birkinshaw, the ironworks' Agent. Longridge had, furthermore, become a mentor and confidant of Robert Stephenson from that year.

The firm was called Robert Stephenson & Co., reflecting the partners' wish for the young Stephenson to be its managing partner. This arrangement was an extraordinary risk by the partners, as he lacked any experience in manufacturing and business affairs, which they clearly expected him to learn as he went, under their guiding hand.[39] However, Pease and Richardson were non-executive partners, and George Stephenson was so taken up with railway consulting, surveying and building work that he had too little time for the firm's affairs. It was thus left to Longridge to oversee the firm's start-up and Robert Stephenson's contribution to that endeavour. He had at first been reluctant to join the Stephensons because of their lack of business experience, and later wrote:[40]

It was against my wish they commenced Engine Builders, but after they had begun, considering it beneficial to the Bedlington Iron Co. & that Geo. & Robert would benefit from my habits of Business, in which they were both deficient, I offerred to take a part with them.

37 Letter, Robert Stephenson to Michael Longridge, Lombard Street [London], 27 February 1824. Letter auctioned June 1997, now privately owned.
38 5 *Geo. IV, c. 48.*
39 Robert Stephenson & Co. Partners' Memorandum of Agreement, 23 June 1823, Partners' Minute Book, **ScM**, 1947-134, pp. 1–5.
40 Letter, Michael Longridge to Thomas Richardson, Bedlington Iron Works, 7 March 1825, **Pease–Stephenson**, U415J, vol. III, Item 7.

Robert Stephenson was thus pitched straight into the unfamiliar responsibilities of investment and employment, in addition to product development. Whilst dependent upon Longridge and his father for these attributes, he had clearly demonstrated confidence, authority and presence of mind for his partners to risk their opening capital commitments. Whilst his father had no doubt instilled in him a strong sense of self-belief, he would also have gained further confidence and communication skills from his activities and contacts at Edinburgh University.

Pease and Richardson were able to use their contacts and influence to generate business for the fledgling firm, an important role in its first six years as it struggled for survival. The firm began trading in July 1823, using spare capacity at the Bedlington Iron Works,[41] but arrangements were soon made to establish new premises in South Street, just off Forth Street in an expanding area on the west side of the Newcastle city wall. The site was adjacent to an iron foundry operated by two brothers, Isaac and John Burrell, with whom George Stephenson had entered into partnership in 1821.[42]

In addition to arranging for new buildings to be erected and equipped, and recruiting staff to work at the new site, Robert Stephenson embarked on a round of visits with his father to gain business for the company, including London, Dublin and Cork. Richardson provided a number of introductions, and through him the firm won orders for machinery, including drying equipment for banknote paper production that provided Stephenson with his first opportunity to demonstrate mechanical competence (see Chapter 6).

Richardson's many financial involvements in the City of London included a directorship of the Colombian Mining Association, which, together with a sister company, the Mexican Mining Association, was established to exploit the mineral wealth of central America, abandoned by the Spaniards in the wake of the wars of independence. The two associations were thus potential clients for the Stephenson Company, and Richardson was anxious for Stephenson to meet the engineers for both companies, to pursue orders for steam engines and mining machinery.

Arising out of these discussions, it was suggested early in 1824 that Stephenson should go to Mexico to ascertain directly what the requirements would be. His partners were apparently content with the proposal, and Longridge wrote to him in London:[43]

You would learn from your Fathers letter that we are making arrangements for your going out to Mexico …

In the meantime – consider

1.   if you would like to go
2.   how long you would probably be from home
3   what you should have for salary
& 4 how are we to do at home for want of you

41 Accounting Day Book, **Stephenson**, p. 1.
42 Bailey (1984), pp. 13–30.
43 Copy letter, Michael Longridge to Robert Stephenson, B.[edlington] I.[ron] W.[orks], 14 February 1824. Letter auctioned June 1997, now privately owned.

A fortnight later, however, Stephenson wrote 'my uncle [Robert] is likely to come to an agreement with the Mexican mining association.'[44] The firm lost the Mexican engine order to the Neath Abbey Iron Works, however, and Richardson insisted to Stephenson that as his uncle should 'pay a visit to Neath Abbey Manufactory to examine the Engines that I should accompany him and that we should extend our journey to Cornwall in order to take an example (if superior) from their Herculanian Steam Engines'.[45] Stephenson accompanied his uncle on a tour of South Wales and the West Country to examine steam engines and factories. After much consideration, however, Robert Stephenson senior subsequently withdrew from his Mexican commitments 'in consequence of the great disapprobation of my Wife and large family'.[46]

Stephenson returned to London in mid-March 1824 and met with J. D. Powles, the chairman of the Colombian Mining Association. Colombia and neighbouring countries were then emerging from the turmoil of the wars of independence. The initiative by the City of London investors was therefore a rapid response to exploit the vacated gold and silver workings for which the Association had obtained concessions. Stephenson was enthused by what Powles had to say and with the Association's aims, as he agreed to visit Colombia as its agent or engineer, to survey a rail or road route. The first indication that his partners knew of this intention came in letters to his father and Longridge:[47]

There are some new prospects here in agitation, which I look forward to with great satisfaction. It is the making of a road in Colombia. What a place London is for prospects! This new scheme of the road or railway is also connected with four silver mines at Mariquita. The road is projected between La Guayra [La Guaira] and the city of Caraccas. You may find La Guayra on the coast, I believe, of the Gulf of Mexico. The climate, from Humboldt, is not quite so salubrious as that of Mexico. Mr. Powles is the head of the concern, and he assures me there is no one to meddle with us. We are to have all the machinery to make, and we are to construct the road in the most advisable way we may think, after making surveys and levellings.

There is a hint of justification in the last two sentences, as if Stephenson expected some disagreement. Disagreement there clearly was from his father, and Stephenson felt obliged to write to him:[48]

But now let me beg of you not to say anything against my going out to America, for I have already ordered so many instruments that it would make me look extremely foolish to call off. Even if I had not ordered any instruments, it seems as if we were all working one against another. You must recollect I will only be away for a time; and in the mean time you could manage with the assistance of Mr. Longridge, who, together

44 Letter, Robert Stephenson to Michael Longridge, Lombard Street [London], 27 February 1824. Letter auctioned June 1997, now privately owned.
45 Ibid.
46 Letter Robert Stephenson (senior) to William James, Newcastle, 18 April 1824, **LRO**, 385/JAM 1/7/1.
47 Letter, Robert Stephenson to Michael Longridge, Covent Garden [London], 9 March (error for 19 March) 1824, in Jeaffreson, p. 73.
48 Letter, Robert Stephenson to George Stephenson, Newcastle, April 1824, in Jeaffreson, p. 70.

with John Nicholson [error for Thomas Nicholson, the Stephenson Company clerk], would take the whole of the business part off your hands. And only consider what an opening it is for me as an entry into business; and I am informed by all who have been there that it is a very healthy country. I must close this letter, expressing my hope that you will not go against me for this time.

Stephenson was clearly sensitive to the reactions of his partners, and it would seem that, at first, he refrained from informing them of the full extent of the responsibilities he had agreed to take on, or of the expected duration of his absence. It is uncertain whether he was first offered a three-year contract as a mining agent, or whether this developed as plans for his expedition were being prepared. Longridge had not known of the extent of Stephenson's absence before his departure and was clearly upset when he wrote of his[49]

regret that you had signed an Agreement for <u>three years</u> with Messrs. Graham & Coy. [Colombian Mining Association].

When your Father & your other Partners consented that you should go out to Colombia it was with the clear understanding that your engagement was only of a temporary nature: and that as soon as you had informed yourself about the practicability of forming a Rail Way & had made your Geological enquiries you should then return to England to make your Report.

<u>On no account</u> would we ever have consented that you should become <u>the Agent of Messrs. Graham & Co. for three</u> <u>years</u>.

I have spoken to our friend Mr. Thomas Richardson upon the subject and He has promised me to use his influence with Mr. Powles so that you may be released from your Agreement as soon as you have satisfied yourself upon the subject for which you are gone out and I do hope that you will be able to return to us in the course of the year 1825 ...

Stephenson's reasoning in agreeing to go to Colombia is complex. His decision went against his father's known wishes for assistance at a time when his railway activities were becoming more numerous and widespread, especially the invitation to take over the reins of the Liverpool and Manchester line from William James. Stephenson presumed, but without consultation, that Michael Longridge would somehow manage the affairs at the Newcastle factory, then in its critical start-up phase, together with the Bedlington Iron Works. He was also to forego the opportunity to supervise the building of the Hagger Leases branch, royal assent for which was obtained just three weeks before his departure.

Jeaffreson considered that Stephenson's 'threatening symptoms of pulmonary disease' was a major factor,[50] but in the absence of evidence, it is not possible to substantiate this view. A more likely explanation reflects that stage in his life when manhood and education combined to seek individual responsibility. Stephenson was clearly enthusiastic about his venture, and there was a sense of anticipation that reflected his youth.

Although he was nominally the managing partner of Robert Stephenson & Co., in practice each endeavour and decision was subject to the monitoring

---

49 Letter, Michael Longridge to Robert Stephenson, Glasgow, 17 August 1824, **IMechE**, IMS/164/1.
50 Jeaffreson, p. 68.

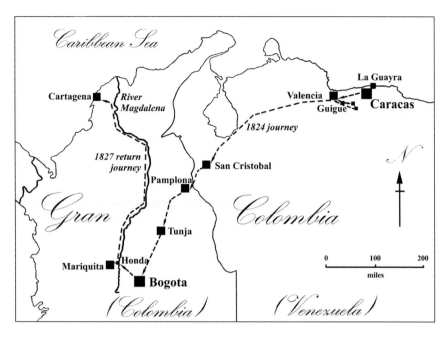

and criticism of his partners, including his father. The opportunity to become an agent of a major London company with the large annual salary of £500, plus expenses,[51] and to head up an expedition of miners to survey and exploit silver and gold mines in Colombia, offered an opportunity for independent responsibility. Just prior to his departure he wrote to his stepmother:[52]

Glad would I have been to have joined my father in his undertaking at Liverpool but I do not even now despair of taking the chief part of his engagements on myself in a year or two and if I was returned home again this work will always be an important crisis in my life to reflect upon

A few days later, he was still exercizing his conscience: 'many will say that I am wrong but I will never say that: I know the experience which I shall gain is worth all the trouble … '[53]

Colombia

Robert Stephenson sailed from Liverpool in June 1824[54] and arrived the following month at La Guayra (La Guaira), then in the 'Federation of Gran Colombia' that included Venezuela and Ecuador (Fig.1.3).[55] He was accompanied by an assistant, Charles Empson (1792–1861), and several miners. Reporting   to   the   Colombian   Mining   Association's   representative

51 Jeaffreson, p. 69.
52 Letter, Robert Stephenson to Elizabeth Stephenson, London, 4 June 1824, **ScM**, MSL 8/1.
53 Letter, Robert Stephenson to Elizabeth Stephenson, Liverpool, n.d. but June 1824, **ScM**, MSL 8/2.
54 Letter, Robert Stephenson to Elizabeth Stephenson, Liverpool, 18 June 1824, **ScM**, MSL 8/3.
55 Logbook of Robert Stephenson, in Jeaffreson, pp. 76–7.

R. S. Illingworth in Bogotá, his first task was to consider the expediency of improving the port's ability to load ships without lighters, for which he recommended a stone pier be built (see Chapter 12).[56]

His main project, however, was to survey a seven-mile rail route between La Guaira and Caracas. His experience being limited to the gentle rise and fall of British rail routes, it must have been a shock to witness the Venezuelan terrain, which rose steeply up to Caracas, 3000 feet above sea level. He wrote of the survey: ' … it is quite incredible the difficulties I have had to contend with and after all it will require an enormous sum of money to complete it and make it all feasible.'[57] He estimated a cost of £160,000 for an annual traffic of less than 6000 tons, and concluded: 'I think it would not be prudent at the present moment to commence the speculation.'[58]

Stephenson's subsequent instructions were to find, survey and report on the several mines in Venezuela and Colombia, the information for which was limited. Having dispatched the miners and their equipment, under Empson's supervision, by water transport, he undertook a four-month trek from Caracas to Bogotá to find and investigate each of the mines. The roads were just tracks requiring mule transport.[59]

By April 1825, Stephenson and Empson had established themselves at the Santa Ana silver mine near Mariquita, on the eastern slopes of the Andes about 65 miles north-west of Bogotá.[60] The miners prepared the mine for working whilst waiting for the main group of miners being sent out from England.

Stephenson left Empson in charge of this work whilst he undertook a second extended tour, of over 1100 miles, again on mule-back, investigating further potential mine workings. He was then feeling homesick: 'you may easily conceive how often I think of an English fireside and all the joys that spring around it.'[61] These trips enhanced his interest in geology, first aroused by his studies in Edinburgh, and in flora and fauna. He collected samples of rock, seeds, flowers and fruit, with the intention of returning them to England.

The main group of miners, from Cornwall, arrived in October 1825 to begin extracting the silver ore.[62] By the end of 1826, there were nearly 200 miners, under the supervision of Stephenson in Mariquita and a Mr. Harker in Pamplona.[63] Stephenson was now obliged to develop management skills, particularly the motivation of a large workforce. Although his upbringing in the Tyneside mining community and his apprenticeship with Nicholas Wood

56 Jeaffreson, p. 79.
57 Letter, Robert Stephenson to George and Elizabeth Stephenson, Caracas, 29 September 1824, **ScM**, MSL 8/4.
58 Jeaffreson, p. 81.
59 Robert Stephenson's report to Messrs. Herring, Graham and Powles, Bogotá, 7 January 1825, **IMechE**, IMS 166/1 (part only).
60 Letter, Robert Stephenson to Elizabeth Stephenson, Mariquita, 28 April 1825, **ScM**, MSL 8/5.
61 Letter, Robert Stephenson to Elizabeth Stephenson, Bogotá, 7 August 1825, **ScM**, MSL 8/6.
62 Jeaffreson, p. 87.
63 Report, 'Colombian Mining Association', The Times, 8 February 1827.

had taught him how a workforce responds to supervision, he now needed to exercise authority and respect. These were attributes that would be hard-earned, as he wrote to Illingworth:[64]

I have no idea of letting [the miners] linger out another week without some work being done. Indeed, some of them are anxious to get on with something. Many of them, however, are ungovernable. I dread the management of them. They have already commenced to drink in the most outrageous manner, Their behaviour in Honda [nearby town] has, I am afraid, incurred for ever the displeasure of the Governor ... I hope when they are once quietly settled at Santa Ana and the works regularly advancing, that some improvement may take place ...

It appears remarkable that having been all my life accustomed to deal with miners, and having had a body of them under my control, and I may say in my employ, that I should now find it difficult to contribute to their comfort and welfare.

Late 1825 and early 1826 was a trying time for Stephenson. Working at Santa Ana was unpleasant because, although he gradually improved relations with the men, he was unable to encourage more than an average of half a day's work from each one, with generally a third of them being disabled through drink. His only company was Empson, with whom, fortunately, he got on well. He was also under pressure, firstly from his partners to return to England and, secondly, from the Mining Association to extend his stay in Colombia to four years:[65]

Nothing but the fullest consent of my partners could induce me to stay in this country and an assurance that an important necessity existed to call me home.

To remain in my present situation untill the expiration of the term of my Engagement I cannot urge any reasonable objection since a legal agreement binds me –

Stephenson had mastered the different geological, extraction, chemical, equipment and refining characteristics of gold and silver mining so much to his employers' satisfaction that his stay at Mariquita was prolonged. Indeed, his assessment of the potential profitability of mine working must have pleased the Mining Association:[66]

The mines in this country I believe will turn out very advantageous, if carefully & skilfully conducted. Many of the Silver Mines are exceedingly rich, but they are much inferior to some Gold mines which are now in the possession of the Association: they have been examined carefully and the produce of them is enormous, and should they be followed up with attention & skill; they will produce to the satisfaction of the most avaricious –

Through his involvement with both the Colombian Mining Association and Robert Stephenson & Co., Thomas Richardson's role was clearly important in deciding how long Stephenson should remain in Colombia. Although Stephenson might have returned to England in the second half of 1826, the Association's directors were anxious to maintain output from the mine,

---

64 Letters, Robert Stephenson to R. S. Illingworth, October and 8 December 1825, in Jeaffreson, pp. 87–90.
65 Letter, Robert Stephenson to R. S. Illingworth, Santa Ana, March 1826, **IMechE**, IMS 166/2.
66 Letter, Robert Stephenson to George and Elizabeth Stephenson, Mariquita, 11 June 1826, **ScM**, MSL 8/7.

leading him to write: ' … for my own credit I am almost obliged to stay till I receive consent from the Directors to leave … .'[67] His sense of duty prevailed, and it was not until the end of July 1827 when, having completed the three years' service to which he had contracted, he concluded his affairs at Mariquita and passed over responsibility for the mines to Illingworth.[68] Stephenson's stay had been made the more bearable by his good relationship with Illingworth, to whom he gave the microscope that he had brought out from London.[69]

Stephenson and Empson went to the coastal town of Cartagena to seek passage for England. Whilst there, came an extraordinary meeting with the Cornish engineer Richard Trevithick (1771–1833), who was returning to England after ten years as a mining engineer in Peru. He had diverted to pursue mining opportunities in Costa Rica, but had the misfortune to be ship-wrecked. He was rescued by Bruce Hall, 'an officer in the Venezuelan and Peruvian services', who took him, without belongings or funds, to Stephenson's hotel.[70]

Hall later recalled that when the two engineers met 'I know not the cause, but they were not so cordial as I could have wished'.[71] This strange event is hard to explain, as it might have been expected that Stephenson would have been delighted to meet a fellow countryman and engineer. That Trevithick had known George Stephenson over 20 years earlier, when Robert Stephenson was an infant, made the lack of cordiality even harder to explain. Stephenson provided funds for Trevithick's homeward passage, but, although both were destined for England, they parted at Cartagena, Stephenson and Empson bound for New York, whilst Trevithick waited for an alternative ship.

Their passage was eventful, the ship being wrecked off the American coast in hurricane-force winds. Stephenson and Empson reached the shore in a life-boat, leaving behind most of their possessions, including money, with the exception of Stephenson's much-prized collection of mineral specimens.[72]

They made their way to New York and spent a few days there during September 1827. Stephenson could then have sailed for Britain, but knew that within hours of his return, he would be plunged into a career whose demands on his time would provide all too little opportunity to see more of the world. He therefore took the opportunity to travel to Niagara and Montreal. Making comparisons between the United States and Colombia, he was impressed by what he witnessed, later recording that the country[73]

67 Letter, Robert Stephenson to Elizabeth Stephenson, Santa Ana Silver Mines, Mariquita, 28 June 1826, **ScM**, MSL 8/8.

68 Letter, Robert Stephenson to Michael Longridge, [Santa Ana] 16 July 1827, in Jeaffreson, pp. 101–4.

69 Now in possession of his great-great-granddaughter, and brought in for assessment to the BBC's *Antiques Roadshow* programme from Fort William, broadcast 15 February 1998.

70 Dickinson and Titley, pp. 203–6.

71 Account of Bruce Napier Hall, in letter from Carlisle, 16 December 1864, contained in *Enys Papers, Life of Richard Trevithick &c*, 2 vols., 1872, vol. II, p. 273; quoted in Dickinson and Titley, p. 205.

72 Jeaffreson, p. 107.

73 Letter, Robert Stephenson to R. S. Illingworth, n.d., but 1827, in Jeaffreson, p. 110.

… affords to an attentive observer a wonderful example of human industry; and it is gratifying to a liberal-minded Englishman to observe how far the sons of his own country have outstripped the other European powers which have transatlantic possessions.

After several weeks, Stephenson and Empson returned to New York and made passage for Liverpool.

Stephenson sailed into Liverpool at the end of November 1827, after an absence of nearly 3½ years. The son that George Stephenson met had gained maturity and independence, having adapted to the rigours and responsibilities of the foreign environment. Without opportunity to refer to others, he had developed strategic and tactical decision-making abilities that would benefit him on his return to a civil engineering career in England. Although his largely unwilling workforce had been difficult, he had developed management skills, especially the ability to motivate a workforce and to earn their respect, which would serve him throughout his career.

Now 24, he was ready to pick up the threads of his domestic life as well as an engineering career at the very birth of the main-line railway era. He re-established his acquaintance with Fanny Sanderson, daughter of a London merchant. They were wed on 17 June 1829, and began their married life in No. 5 Greenfield Place, Newcastle.

Stephenson's time in Colombia had been overshadowed by the knowledge that his father's business was expanding quickly and he was required to take his share of the railway projects. This was in addition to resuming his role of managing the Newcastle factory, the financial health of which was giving much cause for concern. Therein lay the issue that Stephenson knew he would have to deal with throughout his busy life; how to balance the demands of a growing civil engineering career with the requirements of managing a manufacturing business. His absence from Newcastle had required the patient understanding of his partners, particularly Michael Longridge, to whom he could no longer assume continuing delegation.

George Stephenson & Son

In the six years between his return from Colombia and the commencement of the building of the London & Birmingham Railway, Stephenson pursued the joint roles of civil engineer and factory manager. The business development of the factory and the extraordinary design progress that the new railway industry required were achieved only through his reliance on delegation to reliable subordinates, backed up by frequent correspondence and visits to the factory as often as his activities permitted. Even then, it was necessary to rely on Longridge's continuing involvement, as Stephenson's railway surveying and building activities prevented a comprehensive involvement in the business affairs of the factory.

In 1824 and 1825, although the economy was in recession, a network of railways around the country had been proposed as offering opportunities for profitable investment. The building of the Stockton & Darlington Railway sparked this first railway 'mania', and the speed with which City of London interests were proposing trunk railway schemes suggested Richardson's particular involvement. The projection of George Stephenson as the country's leading railway engineer was extraordinary for a man who was supervising the building of only his second mineral-railway route, and who had no experience of major earthworks or bridge design. The City investors thrived on recommendation and rumour, and George Stephenson's sudden high profile must have puzzled, if not angered, more established engineers.

To meet the demand for so many rail projects, the Stephenson partners established a new firm, George Stephenson & Son, from January 1825. It was also based in Newcastle in an office 'adjoining to RS & Co where the two businesses may be distinctly transacted'.[74] In expectation of Stephenson's early return to England, he and his father were appointed as 'Chief Engineers' of the firm. A further 18 employees were engaged, including John Dixon and a youthful team of former and present apprentices including Joshua Richardson (1799–1886), Joseph Locke (1805–1860), Thomas Longridge Gooch (1808–1882), William Allcard (1809–1861) and the young John Cass Birkinshaw (1811–1867). It is notable that older engineers, experienced in civil engineering, were not engaged. The most obvious omission was William James, who could have contributed much to the railway-building endeavour, based on his lifelong experience.

Their omission suggests that George Stephenson sought to develop railway-building technology in his own empirical way, uninfluenced by the experience of others. He thereby avoided the necessity of relying on that experience, with its perception of undermining his and his son's authority as 'Chief Engineers'. The youthful team would develop George Stephenson's limited experience in soil and rock excavation and deposit techniques, and bridge design and construction, by their own empirical endeavours, whilst he in turn would learn from them. As soon as Robert Stephenson returned to Britain, the burden of learning could be shared between father and son, and their joint authority secured.

The grand schemes of 1824–1825 were soon seen to be premature and too speculative, with the exception of the Liverpool & Manchester proposal that was brought to Parliament.[75] Its rejection, under pressure from affected landowners and canal interests, was a severe blow to the fledgling George Stephenson & Son, not least because of errors by the young surveyors.[76] However, the assent to the second Liverpool & Manchester Bill and George Stephenson's subsequent appointment as engineer, as well as for the Bolton & Leigh Railway, had restored the firm's standing.

---

74 Letter, Michael Longridge to Edward Pease, Edin[burgh], 18 January 1825, **Pease–Stephenson**, U415J, vol. III, Item 4.
75 Ibid.
76 Thomas, pp. 24–7.

When Stephenson met his father in Liverpool in November 1827, two major issues were high on their agenda. First was the urgent need to attend to the affairs of Robert Stephenson & Co., and to pursue major improvements in locomotive design to meet the more demanding requirements of the inter-urban Liverpool & Manchester Railway. Second was the need for him to take on a large share of the new railway project and consulting work, to which George Stephenson himself could apply little time because '…he finds that all his attention must be devoted to this [Liverpool & Manchester] road alone'.[77]

Having concluded his responsibilities to the Colombian Mining Association,[78] Robert Stephenson resumed his railway-engineering career from the beginning of 1828. He first assisted his father with 'laying down' and building work on the Liverpool & Manchester and Bolton & Leigh railways, for which he 'superintended a great many [excavations]'.[79] Although relatively inexperienced, he soon began an intensive programme supervising route planning, surveying, levelling, soil sampling, structural design and cost estimation for proposed rail routes, supplying plans and sections and giving evidence before Parliamentary Committees, and supervising the building and equipping of railway routes.

Stephenson had become used to working on his own initiative and taking decisions; attributes that stood him well in his new role. He was, however, less experienced in selecting and supervising reliable subordinates on several diverse projects. Furthermore, his experience in dealing with contractors was limited to the few weeks he had been assisting his father. He was also inexperienced in the design and building of bridges and tunnels, these being skills that he would have to develop, project by project, in consultation with his father and other associates. He also maintained a close involvement with the affairs of the Newcastle factory, and particularly with the development of the steam locomotive. As his duties expanded, he spent much time travelling and covered thousands of miles annually.

Early rail projects

Robert Stephenson appointed Joshua Richardson and John Cass Birkinshaw to help him with surveying and levelling work, and preparation of plans. Richardson had joined the Stephenson firm in about 1825, having spent two years paying 'attention to subjects connected with civil engineering'.[80] Birkinshaw, the son of John Birkinshaw, the Bedlington Iron Works agent, continued his apprenticeship under Stephenson, who trained him in the role of resident engineer on some early railway projects. He became a reliable and

77 Letter, Robert Stephenson to Michael Longridge, Liverpool, 1 January 1828, in Jeaffreson, p. 114.
78 Accounting day book, **Stephenson**, folios 126 and 149.
79 Op. cit. (n. 11), pp. 128–9. Jeaffreson, p. 130.
80 Obituary, Joshua Richardson, *Proc. ICE*, **LXXXVI**, 1885/6, pp. 358–63. Also op. cit. (n. 11), p. 112.

competent engineer with several rail projects under Stephenson in the 1830s and 1840s.

Stephenson took over responsibility for completing the six-mile Canterbury & Whitstable Railway from the spring of 1828. The railway had been surveyed and costs estimated by William James, but it required a lot more capital than had been allowed for in its 1825 Act.[81] In the wake of James' own financial problems, and with Thomas Richardson also a director of the company, George Stephenson had been appointed its Chief Engineer.[82] The company ran into further financial difficulties, however, and, with building work halted, a lease was obtained by Lister Ellis, a Liverpool businessman. This required a further Act, obtained in May 1828,[83] which allowed Stephenson to resume building work.

The line had been partly built under Locke's and Dixon's supervision, including the 828-yard Tyler Hill tunnel excavation, which had already broken through before work ceased. In resuming the work, Robert Stephenson was well aware of the railway's parlous financial position, and he appointed Joshua Richardson to be both resident engineer and chief clerk 'on the outset, in order to effect economy as far as practicable'.[84] The appointment of the inexperienced Richardson indicated the extent to which George Stephenson & Son was being stretched. The work of building the engine-houses, and installing and commissioning the winding engines and ropes, was given to Thomas Cabry (1801–1873), one of the talented foremen at the Newcastle works, assisted by Birkinshaw.

As far as time allowed, Stephenson took a close interest in the line, and he wrote in December 1828: 'I have got up a proposal in my father's name, which is now before the directors of the Canterbury Railway Co.'[85] He made occasional visits to monitor progress, whilst, through correspondence with Richardson, he was briefed on progress and difficulties arising. The building of the railway was slow, however, and the directors were concerned at the delays. Although they subsequently felt 'much pleasure in testifying their approbation of the conduct and ability of Mr. Richardson',[86] his inexperience and Stephenson's protracted absences caused concern, which he acknowledged:[87]

The Directors I fear have already charged me with negligence; if I had not been perfectly well informed respecting every thing that was going on through the detailed reports of my assistant I should have been <u>down</u> ere this, notwithstanding the urgent engagements I have had in this neighbourhood [the north-west].

81 *6 Geo. IV, c. 120.*
82 Letter, Messrs. Curtis & Kingsford, for the Canterbury & Whitstable Railway, to George Stephenson, Canterbury, 18 July 1825, letter book, Canterbury & Whitstable Railway, **CCL**, CC/W9/5.
83 *9 Geo. IV, c. 29.*
84 Letter, Robert Stephenson to Messrs. Curtis & Kingsford, Liverpool, 20 January 1830, **ScM**, MS1370.
85 Letter, Robert Stephenson & Co. to Michael Longridge, Liverpool, 1 December 1828, in Jeaffreson, p. 122.
86 Minute Book, Canterbury & Whitstable Railway, 2 November 1830, **CCL**, CC/W9/1.
87 Op. cit. (n. 84).

Stephenson was called upon to offer advice on managing the railway when operations commenced, to which he responded: 'If the Directors look forward with confidence to the traffic being realized to as great a degree as was represented in the report which I examined, and which was drawn up with great care by Mr. Richardson, there can be little doubt of an Engineer being well employed.'[88] Thomas Cabry was appointed as the railway's engineer.[89] Richardson subsequently worked on the Leicester & Swannington line but, in August 1831, he applied for the post of Manager of the Canterbury & Whitstable Railway. No doubt citing his previous experience as Chief Clerk, he was appointed for a one-year term shortly afterwards.[90]

The Canterbury & Whitstable line included two structures, the Tyler Hill tunnel (Plate 1) and a brick under-bridge across Church Street, Whitstable. Just over a year after the opening, the bridge bulged and became unstable. Cabry undertook to rebuild it but, after remedial work, the basic structure stabilized and the bridge stood until demolition in 1969.[91] The responsibility for the bridge lay with Robert Stephenson through his supervision of Richardson. However, when George Stephenson was later questioned about its condition he diverted criticism from his son onto Richardson when he stated: 'I recollect going down when the bridge was finishing and I told them it would come down. However, the engineer had done the best he could, he was a beginner, but the bridge is still standing and it has not come down.'[92]

In contrast to his extraordinary contributions to locomotive design during this period, Robert Stephenson's first venture into railway building was of limited success. Not only did the line take a long time to complete; he had failed, through lack of experience, to detect either a design weakness with the Church Street bridge or the poor standard of its construction. Against the background of an intensive work programme in the north-west, his reliance on delegation to an inexperienced assistant was also called into question. He no doubt resolved thereafter to satisfy himself better regarding design, suitability of materials, and standard of bridge building, whilst balancing delegation with adequate supervision.

At the opening of the Canterbury & Whitstable Railway on 3 May 1830, Stephenson was invited to make a speech, the content of which needed to be both professional and diplomatic. His shyness meant that he 'spoke so low that we could not hear distinctly what he said'.[93] Such festivities soon became a feature of the opening of rail routes but, unlike his father, he never felt comfortable at such events, and would refrain, if possible, from speech-making.

88 Ibid.
89 Op. cit. (n. 86), first reference to Cabry on 26 October 1830.
90 Ibid., 18 August 1831.
91 Lewis, p. 15.
92 George Stephenson's evidence to the House of Lords Committee for the Great Western Railway Bill, June/July 1835, p. 273 ff., quoted in Fellows, p. 41.
93 Article, 'Opening of the Canterbury and Whitstable Railway', *Kent Herald*, 6 May 1830.

In the summer of 1828 Stephenson surveyed two short routes feeding into the Liverpool & Manchester Railway. The first was the Kenyon & Leigh Junction Railway, ' … a short line of railway which I have got the management of near Bolton'.[94] This 2½-mile branch line linked the Liverpool & Manchester line at Kenyon Junction with the Bolton & Leigh Railway, which terminated on the north bank of the Leeds & Liverpool Canal. His first submission of plans, sections and cost estimate were rejected by the railway's Liverpool-based directors as being too expensive, and he was asked to undertake a fresh survey 'even at the risk of having a less advisable line'. Stephenson was clearly put out by this request and, albeit in private correspondence, he showed some petulance, reminiscent of his father's character:[95]

This is one way of doing things, but proud as I am I must submit. I have tried in my cool solitary moments to look with patience on such proceedings, but, by heavens, it requires a greater store than I have. I would patiently bear this alteration if they did it from principle; but knowing, and indeed hearing, them say from what the alteration does really spring, I cannot but consider it unworthy of Liverpool merchants.

The only structures of consequence along the route were at Leigh for the crossing of the Leeds & Liverpool Canal and a nearby road, and it was probably the cost of these bridges and attendant embankments that gave rise to the directors' reservations. Referring to the embankments, Stephenson wrote to his uncle, Robert, then engaged on the Bolton & Leigh line:[96]

Mr. Boardman wants the precise quantity of land occupied by the Railway in approaching the canal at Leigh … .
    The section will be required, to get the breadths at the different points you will please to bring the section or book of hights so that we may get at the necessary particulars

With the design of the canal crossing agreed, the Kenyon & Leigh Junction Railway obtained its Act in May 1829.[97] Stephenson did not supervise the building of the line, however, because of his many other commitments. With George Stephenson & Son so fully committed on other projects, John Rastrick (1780–1856) was appointed to undertake the building of the line, which was opened in January 1831.[98]
    It is possible, however, that Stephenson had first considered the design of the bridge across the Leeds & Liverpool Canal. With limited headroom, it was decided to erect a cast iron beam bridge, no doubt similar to the bridge being installed across Water Street, Manchester for the Liverpool & Manchester Railway. This bridge was, itself, a technological breakthrough, following

94 Letter, Robert Stephenson to 'an intimate friend', Liverpool, 27 August 1828, in Jeaffreson, p. 131.
95 Ibid.
96 Letter Robert Stephenson to Robert Stephenson (senior), Liverpool, 4 October 1828, **Salford**, U405 C2.
97 The Liverpool & Manchester Act was *10 Geo. IV, c. 35*; the Kenyon & Leigh Junction was *10 Geo. IV, c. 36*, both receiving royal assent on 14 May 1829.
98 John Rastrick's evidence to the Committee on the London & Brighton Railway Bill, London, 1836, p. 20.

several months of testing different beam forms by the innovative physicist, Eaton Hodgkinson (1789–1861). Trial beams were cast and test facilities made freely available at the Ancoats, Manchester, foundry of William Fairbairn and James Lillie.[99]

William Fairbairn (1789–1874) had known George Stephenson since their days as young men in the north-east, and would also have known Robert Stephenson as an infant.[100] There would thus have been a good line of communication between Fairbairn and the Stephensons in respect of both the Water Street and Leigh bridges. Stephenson's association with Fairbairn and Hodgkinson was renewed in the 1840s when designs and testing for the tubular bridges at Conway and Menai were undertaken (see Chapter 10).

Stephenson's second route in the north-west was the 4¼-mile Warrington & Newton Railway (Plate 2). There were no major earthworks or bridges required for this line, which linked the Liverpool & Manchester line at Newton-le-Willows to Warrington. At Warrington the line was to have been divided into four branches, although only that serving Bank Quay alongside the river Mersey and one of the town centre lines were built.[101]

The Warrington & Newton Railway Bill also received royal assent in May 1829.[102] Thomas Gooch, who had briefly been employed on the Bolton & Leigh Railway, became Stephenson's resident engineer. However, at the beginning of 1830 he was recalled to become resident engineer for the completion of the Liverpool end of the Liverpool & Manchester Railway.[103] The line was completed in July 1831.

In December 1829 the railway's directors asked Stephenson to survey an extension across the Mersey and southwards 'towards Birmingham'.[104] This would turn a short feeder route into a strategic inter-urban main line, with ramifications far beyond a simple expansion of the rail network. The Warrington & Newton directors were largely Lancashire-based entrepreneurs, rather than the Liverpool financiers who dominated the Liverpool & Manchester Board. In Stephenson's words their ambition 'did not meet the views of the Liverpool people'.[105] Thus, nine months before the opening of the Liverpool & Manchester line, the first clash of interests between rival groups of main-line railway promoters took place. The 'Liverpool people' were the wealthy and influential financiers of that city who had taken the extraordinary risk of investing in the Liverpool & Manchester line, in anticipation of good

99 Eaton Hodgkinson, 'Theoretical and Experimental Researches to Ascertain the Strength and Best Forms of Iron Beams', read 2 April 1830 and published in *Memoirs of the Literary and Philosophical Society of Manchester*, second series, vol. 5, London, 1831, pp. 407–544.

100 Smiles, 1862, pp. 41–2.

101 'A Plan and Section of an Intended Railway or Tram Road from the Liverpool and Manchester Railway ... to Warrington ...', **ICE**, 385 (084.3) (427.2).

102 *10 Geo. IV, c. 37*. A short supplementary Act was passed on 29 May 1830 (*11 Geo. IV, c. 57*) for an additional short south to east curve with the Liverpool & Manchester line at Newton-le-Willows.

103 Memoir for Thomas Longridge Gooch, *Proc. ICE*, **LXXII**, 1882/3, p. 302.

104 Letter, Robert Stephenson to Thomas Richardson, Newcastle-upon-Tyne, 17 December 1829, in Jeaffreson, pp. 151–3.

105 Ibid.

returns, and with the expectation of an expanding network of routes providing further investment and profit opportunities.

The Stephensons did not anticipate the potential conflict of interest, and quickly found themselves caught up in circumstances that could have led to professional embarrassment. In November 1829 Robert Stephenson agreed, with Gooch's assistance, to carry out a preliminary survey of a route between Warrington and Sandbach. The Liverpool community again interpreted this route as being a precursor to a full Birmingham route, and strong objections were quickly expressed. Having 'lodged the plans in the customary manner', Stephenson then found himself in trouble with the Liverpool financiers:[106]

The Liverpool directors were not agreeable that my father or I should be concerned in the Sandbach line, as it would be opposed by the Marquis of Stafford; and as my father might be employed to oppose the line in Parliament, he and I would thus be brought into direct collision, which would certainly not be very pleasant. Having made this survey I was of course bound in honour to sign the plan and section. What will be the result in Parliament I cannot guess. There will doubtless be a strong opposition, and perhaps a fatal one. It is averse to my feelings to be concerned with any undertaking which might interfere with Mr. [Joseph] Locke's views, as his kindness to my father has been very great. Being however, engineer for the Warrington directors, I could not refuse with any appearance of consistency to attend to an extension of this line – an extension which, if made, will be of immense benefit to that which I am now executing.

Stephenson stood his ground, and, although he had 'lodged the plans' by the November 1829 deadline, preparatory work remained before Parliament was petitioned. In early January 1830 he was 'engaged in getting up the parliamentary plans and estimate' for the line,[107] but the considerable opposition that was mounted against the project resulted in no petition for the bill being made in the 1830/31 parliamentary year.

After several months of negotiation between the Warrington & Newton directors and the Liverpool caucus, Stephenson prepared a truncated scheme for a line from Warrington only as far as Norton, where it would have formed a junction with a proposed Liverpool to Birmingham railway then being promoted in Liverpool. The bill was petitioned to Parliament in February 1831, and provided for a diversion of the Bank Quay branch from its first-planned terminus on the bank of the river Mersey to an alignment within a loop of the river that allowed for an inclined embankment to elevate the line for the crossing of the river and the adjacent Mersey & Irwell Canal. Stephenson would only have prepared a general scheme for the Mersey bridge for cost estimation purposes. The bill had a tortuous passage through Parliament and failed in the House of Lords in October 1831.[108]

Stephenson had acquitted himself well and, in spite of the pressure put upon him, had the strength of character to pursue what he believed to be the

106 Ibid.
107 Letter, Robert Stephenson to Thomas Richardson, Liverpool, 3 January 1830, in Jeaffreson, p. 153.
108 *Journal of the House of Commons*, **86**, Session 1831, pp. 275–927, *passim*, and *Journal of the House of Lords*, **63** (Part the Second), Session 1831, pp. 916–1089, *passim*.

proper course of action. It was, however, a salutary lesson that being a leading engineer in the main-line railway era was as much concerned with handling personalities and the profit drive of a free-market society as it was about engineering. He had quickly to learn about diplomacy and the manoeuvrings of factional interests, whilst maintaining professional integrity – lessons that would later stand him in good stead, particularly during the mid-1840s railway 'mania'.

Since 1825, George Stephenson & Son had been involved with a scheme for a railway between Newcastle and Carlisle, having been engaged by the governors of Greenwich Hospital, the largest landowners in the Tyne valley. Joseph Locke had carried out a partial survey in that year.[109] The project, which was abandoned, had been a response by the hospital governors to a railway project proposed by a group of businessmen from both cities. Benjamin Thompson (1779–1867), who had experience of mineral railways, was appointed engineer.[110] The bill for the Newcastle & Carlisle line eventually came before Parliament in March 1829, where it met strong opposition.[111] George Stephenson & Son was retained by the objectors to give evidence to the House of Commons Committee against Thompson's line, which, it was argued, carried a risk of flooding. Robert Stephenson, Joseph Locke and Joshua Richardson, who had all undertaken part surveys of the proposed route, gave evidence to the Committee, as also did John Dixon. Their collective concerns were however overruled, and the Newcastle & Carlisle Railway Act was passed in May.[112]

Stephenson's work continued to expand during 1829, in tandem with his growing involvement with locomotive development. In February, the provisional committee of the Leicester & Swannington Railway appointed him as their engineer. Together with a Leicester surveyor, Thomas Miles, he surveyed and prepared a cost estimate of the proposed 16-mile route.[113] Their recommended route was from West Bridge, Leicester, to Swannington, with three branches to serve collieries, and a fourth to extend the line to the river Soar in Leicester (Fig. 1.4). In addition to a mile-long tunnel at Glenfield, the route included the 1 in 29 self-acting Bagworth incline, and the 1 in 17 Swannington incline, to be worked by stationary engines and ropes. The layout and cost estimation for these would have been based on the current Canterbury & Whitstable experience. The Committee adopted Stephenson's plans and sections, and the railway's act was obtained in May 1830.[114]

Also, in May 1830 George Stephenson & Son was appointed as engineers to the proposed Sheffield & Manchester Railway. In addition to committee members from both cities, there was a strong contingent from Liverpool, who were also directors of the Liverpool & Manchester line. The project had,

109 Maclean, pp. 13–22.
110 Rennison (2000/1), p. 205.
111 Op. cit. (n. 11) p. 1.
112 10 Geo. IV, c. 72.
113 Leicester Journal, 13 February 1829, quoted in Clinker, p. 5.
114 11 Geo. IV, c. 58.

1.4 Leicester &
Swannington
Railway

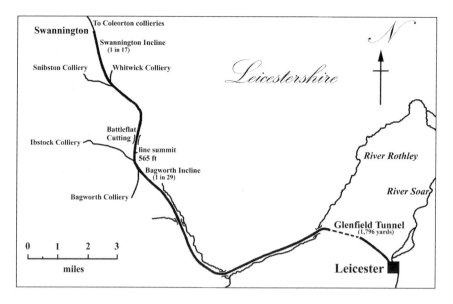

however, long been the brainchild of the Sheffield land surveyor, Henry Sanderson, whom the Committee appointed to take levels and prepare the sections. George Stephenson preferred his own team of surveyors, however, and tactlessly proceeding without Sanderson, selected a route across the Pennines that, in the wake of all that he had recently proved on the Liverpool & Manchester route, seemed inappropriate for an inter-urban line. It included inclined planes as steep as 1 in 18, requiring stationary engine and rope haulage.[115]

George Stephenson appointed his assistant, John Gillespie, to take the levels and prepare the sections for the western end of the route. Sanderson undertook the survey for the Yorkshire stretch, and noted a ten-foot discrepancy in Gillespie's levels at the summit. Sanderson's irritation with both the choice of route and the error led to his publishing a pamphlet in January 1831, in which he spoke out against Stephenson's route.[116]

The principal opposition to the Sheffield & Manchester Bill was from the Duke of Bridgewater's Trustees, who feared a considerable loss of canal traffic. It was significant that Robert Stephenson rather than his father gave evidence to the House of Lords Committee, suggesting that he demonstrated a better ability at presenting evidence and responding to adverse questioning. The bill was passed in August 1831,[117] but the railway was not built, as Sanderson kept up his vociferous opposition to the scheme and, to George Stephenson's humiliation, the project was abandoned in June 1833.

Good progress was, however, being made with the Leicester & Swannington Railway project as, in July 1830, George Stephenson & Son had been appointed to undertake the building of the line, with Robert Stephenson as

115 Dow, pp. 6–17.
116 Pamphlet dated 25 January 1831, printed by Platt & Todd of Sheffield.
117 *1 & 2 Will. IV, c. 59.*

engineer and Thomas Miles as the company's agent.[118] The project, including the tunnel and two inclines, was the longest and most difficult Stephenson had yet attempted. He appointed as his resident assistant Joshua Richardson, whose experience had been limited to the Canterbury line. Stephenson therefore needed to monitor both Richardson's work and that of the six contractors, none of whom was experienced with this type of work. A series of regrettable events brought sharply home to him the pitfalls of delegation and dealing with contractors.

In February 1831, Stephenson was appalled to receive a letter of complaint about Richardson, from the railway's chairman, alleging 'a material variation in the measurement [of spoil] from the quantities stated by Mr. Joshua Richardson' in at least one location.[119] After assessing the situation, Stephenson had no hesitation in dismissing his resident engineer and 'offered to send another competent Assistant Engineer in place of Mr. Joshua Richardson and promised to investigate the accuracy of the other admeasurements stated in the Pay Bills on which advancements had been made to Mr. Thomas Richardson the contractor'.[120]

John Gillespie was quickly drafted in as resident engineer, shortly after completing his erroneous survey on the Sheffield and Manchester line. He 'reported that the result of his measurement shewed that the Contractor had received considerably more than was due to him'.[121] The contractor was then obliged to abandon the contract, which was re-awarded to another firm working on the line. In the same month a contractor was criticized for using poor mortar.[122] Two months later another contractor was killed after a fall down one of the tunnel shafts, leaving his partners unable to continue and withdrawing from their contract.[123] The following month yet another contractor was so far behind time he 'consented to abandon his contract'.[124]

Stephenson's main problem, however, was with the Glenfield tunnel (Fig. 1.5). He wrote in March 1831 that the trial borings for the tunnel 'were wrong described and that instead of Rock (which we expected would stand for a great Portion of the Tunnel without arching) it is actually sand'.[125] This was, no doubt, a situation that Stephenson would reflect upon five years later with Kilsby tunnel on the London and Birmingham line (see Chapter 8). The situation was not helped when Gillespie informed the directors that the cost of the tunnel would double, to which Stephenson was quick to respond 'nor is Mr Gillespie justified in stating that without consulting either my Father or myself.'

---

118 Minute Book of the Directors of the Leicester & Swannington Railway, 9 July 1830, **PRO**, RAIL
      359/2, pp. 1–2.
119 Ibid, 5 February 1831, p. 38.
120 Ibid, 12 February 1831, p. 39.
121 Ibid, 18 February 1831, p. 41.
122 Ibid, 12 February 1831, p. 39.
123 Ibid, 12 and 15 April 1831, pp. 53 and 55.
124 Ibid, 13 May 1831, p. 63.
125 Letter, Robert Stephenson to the Directors of the Leicester & Swannington Railway, London, 31
      March 1831, reproduced in op. cit. (n. 118), 4 April 1831, pp. 51–3.

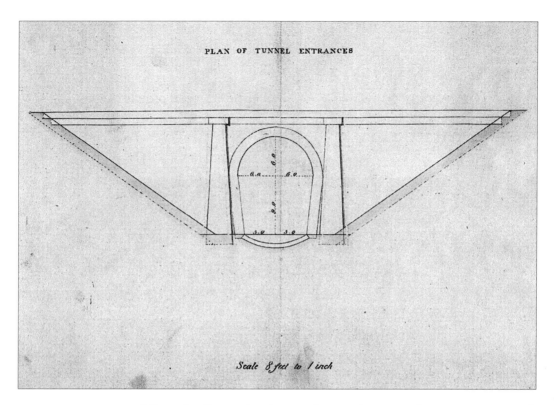

PLAN OF TUNNEL ENTRANCES

Scale 8 feet to 1 inch

1.5 Pre-construction elevation of Glenfield Tunnel portal (Public Record Office)

Gillespie's ill-considered remarks, resulting in this open reprimand, worried the directors, who sought the advice of George Stephenson, suggesting two further rope-worked inclines might be built over the Glenfield Ridge instead. He firmly backed his son's decision, however, in his direct style: 'I do not know that I can express myself more distinctly than I did in my last letter as to the propriety of proceeding with the Tunnel in preference to inclined Planes over Glenfield Ridge … .'[126]

Robert Stephenson advised that a brick lining of 14 inches (18 inches in part) would be required to contain the sand. The tunnel and its contractor, however, continued to require regular attention, particularly through the difficulty of obtaining satisfactory bricks. Gillespie frequently monitored their quality and the standard of bricklaying, but even by the June of 1832 when Stephenson inspected the tunnel, it was clear that the quality of the lining was far from adequate.[127] Remedial work was required before the first 11¾ miles of line from Leicester to Bagworth could be opened a few weeks later.[128]

The opening of the remaining 4¼ miles to Swannington was much delayed by the slow completion of Battleflat cutting. Gillespie made matters worse when he sought to mislead the directors by understating the amount of work

126 Letter, George Stephenson to the Directors of the Leicester & Swannington Railway, London, 14 April 1831, reproduced in op. cit. (n. 118), 15 April 1831, p. 54.
127 Op. cit. (n. 118), 21 June 1832.
128 *Leicester Journal*, 20 July 1832, quoted in Clinker, p. 13.

remaining to be undertaken. Stephenson, who learned of the problem from his father, was furious:[129]

What a grievous thing it is to witness such a wanton breach of faith on the part of Gillespie – Why did he not let me know before it was discovered by the Directors that the cutting was likely to be behind hand – Means might have been taken to avoid the unpleasant triumph which our enemies will have – But it is no use talking to him, he is quite incurable, I never will depend upon him in future – … The receipt of the letter about Gillespie actually unhinged me, by the anxiety which it occasioned –

Gillespie was withdrawn from the line and his career with the Stephensons appears to have terminated. To complete the line, Stephenson brought in John Birkinshaw – his first appointment as resident engineer – and through his endeavours the remainder of the line was opened in three stretches during 1833.[130]

In the final stages of the line's construction, a second Act was obtained by the railway company for a 1/3-mile long branch across the Leicester Navigation to Soar Lane, Leicester, alongside the river Soar itself, and a short branch to Snibston Colliery.[131] The Soar Lane branch, opened in October 1834, required a small lifting bridge to allow passage of canal craft. Stephenson designed a timber structure, the rail platform for which was slung from four pillars, and lifted by counterbalance weights and chains.[132]

The London & Birmingham surveys

Four days prior to the opening of the Liverpool & Manchester Railway, on 11 September 1830, two groups of businessmen joined forces to promote the London & Birmingham Railway.[133] They approached George Stephenson & Son, and an agreement appointing the firm as engineers was signed seven days later.[134] Robert Stephenson was appointed to undertake an immediate preliminary survey of the 112-mile route.[135]

The resources of the firm were severely stretched at this time, however, as Locke, Dixon, Allcard, Swanwick and Gooch all continued their engagement on the Liverpool & Manchester line and its extensions, whilst Cabry and Richardson continued with their duties at Canterbury and Leicester. Robert

129 Letter, Robert Stephenson to George Stephenson, London, 15 November 1832, **Stephenson**, Folder 18.
130 Last reference to Gillespie's involvement was 7 December 1832; first reference to Birkinshaw was 11 January 1833; both in op. cit. (n. 118), pp. 245–52.
131 *3 & 4 Will. IV, c. 69*.
132 Clinker, p. 21.
133 Minute Book of the Board of Directors of the London & Birmingham Railway, 1830–1833, **PRO**, RAIL 384/1, p. 1.
134 Memorandum of Agreement between Messrs. George Stephenson & Son … and the Committee of the London & Birmingham Railway Company, in Jeaffreson, pp. 166–8.
135 Letter from Robert Stephenson, unaddressed but probably to Michael Longridge, Daventry, 20 October 1830. Letter privately owned.

Stephenson therefore recruited two further young engineers, who had some experience in surveying, to assist him. John Brunton (1812–1899) was first recruited to be the 'resident engineer at the London end'.[136] Thomas Elliot Harrison (1808–1888) who had served a pupillage under William Chapman (1749–1832), was recruited later in the year. Both Brunton and Harrison went on to become accomplished railway engineers.

Both Stephensons and Brunton immediately travelled between London and Birmingham to establish 'the most desirable line' and just a month later reported to the railway's 'Committee of Survey'.[137] The directors had asked them to consider a route out of London via Chipping Barnet and South Mimms to Hemel Hempstead, but the engineers recommended the route via Watford. The survey committee also asked for surveys of a route between Stonebridge and Wednesbury along the Tame valley to link the route with the proposed 'Birmingham and Liverpool Railway'.[138] After these extra preliminary surveys, however, the directors were persuaded of the benefits of the Watford route, and also postponed consideration of the Tame valley link.[139]

The engineers then carried out a line survey, with levels being taken. Although Stephenson had been set a demanding schedule, even with Brunton and Harrison's assistance, he reported to the directors in December 1830 and 'exhibited the plan and section of the line of Railway from London to Birmingham and of the Northampton Branch'.[140] He was authorized to undertake a detailed examination of the most difficult parts of the route through the Meriden Ridge, Kilsby Ridge and between Watford and London, about which he reported to the Board in February 1831.[141] The Board accepted the route (Fig. 2.1, p. 41) and instructed him to proceed to a detailed route design and cost estimate, and to prepare plans and sections to form the basis of an application to Parliament. The major task of drawing up detailed route plans and preparing lithographed copies, showing each plot of land to be acquired, was to take nine months.

By 1831, the Stephensons' growing reputation for railway work stimulated enquiries for assistance with other schemes, including one from Berlin, to which Stephenson responded:[142]

I may add that both my father & myself are engaged in business so important that it would be impracticable for us to leave it for so long a period as would be required for going abroad and making an examination that would enable us to make a report on the feasibility of the undertaking –

136 Op. cit. (n. 134).
137 Report, Geo Stephenson and Robt. Stephenson to the Directors of the London and Birmingham Railway, Birmingham, 23 October 1830, and Minutes of the Committee of Survey, same date, **PRO**, RAIL 384/27, pp. 1–2.
138 Op. cit. (n. 137), 25 October 1830, p. 5.
139 Op. cit. (n. 133), 5 and 6 November 1830, pp. 13–16.
140 Minutes, op. cit. (n. 137), Appendix No. 5, Meeting of Directors, 17 December 1830.
141 Op. cit. (n. 133), 18 and 21 February 1831, pp. 48–54.
142 Letter, Robert Stephenson to ' – Woless Esqre', Birmingham, 19 June 1831, Deutsche Museum Archive, Ref. 3454.

Stephenson, Brunton and Harrison, together with a team of surveyors, concluded their task in November 1831: ' ... the whole of Tuesday night [29 November] was spent by the Engineer and Surveyors in collating and finally revising the plans.'[143] This ensured that the railway company met the 30 November parliamentary deadline for the deposition of private bills. A further six weeks were required to complete trial borings and to prepare estimates of excavation and structure quantities and costs.[144]

The bill had its first reading on 20 February 1832, after which petitions were submitted against it from several landowners and road and canal interests, requiring evidence to be heard by the House of Commons Committee. In a lengthy interrogation of Stephenson, the legal representatives of the opposing bodies tried hard to challenge the accuracy of the plans and sections. By 1 June, the last day of the enquiry, however, Stephenson wrote that 'Our opponents have admitted the correctness of our plans & levels ... ' and that the committee approved the bill by 24 votes to 9.[145] He was elated by this 'capital majority. It seems doubtful whether our opponents will persist in pursuing us to the Lords.'[146]

Stephenson was, however, quite wrong about the opposition in the House of Lords, where in committee he was again subjected to three days of intensive questioning. Experienced opposing counsel challenged him on a number of basic principles in the hope of undermining his reputation. Although he steadfastly stood his ground, the barristers caught him out on the subject of the material of the Tring ridge and the angle of slope of the proposed cutting.[147] The main opposition, however, was from major landowners unwilling to allow the route through their estates, and the committee concluded[148]

That the case for the promoters of the Bill having been concluded, it does not appear to the Committee that they have made out such a case as would warrant the forcing of the proposed railway through the lands and property of so great a proportion of the dissentient landowners and proprietors.

Although Stephenson had put up such a resolute performance, he was devastated that the bill had been lost partly through his account. Although 29 years old and gaining experience and maturity with each new project, he did not yet have his father's strength of character in dealing with such determined opposition. Jeaffreson records (without reference) that Lord Wharncliffe, the Committee Chairman, offered friendly advice to Stephenson: 'My young friend, don't take this to heart. The decision is against you; but you have made such a display of power that your fortune is made for life.'[149]

143 Minute Book, op. cit. (n. 133), 2 December 1831, p. 113.
144 Minute Book, op. cit. (n. 133), 12 January 1832, p. 124.
145 Letter, Robert Stephenson to T. E. Harrison, London, 30 May 1832. Letter privately owned.
146 Ibid.
147 Jeaffreson, pp. 177–8.
148 Jeaffreson, p. 172.
149 Jeaffreson, p. 178.

Stephenson's extraordinary exertions in preparing for the Bill, whilst maintaining supervision of the other railway construction work and the Newcastle factory, proved too much for him. He was unwell through the summer and autumn, although he struggled to maintain his high level of work.[150]

The bill had failed for political rather than engineering reasons, as was immediately demonstrated by a determined effort of supporting MPs and peers to stimulate a further bill in the next parliamentary session.[151] Intensive lobbying by the caucus amongst the opposing landowners resulted in large sums of money being agreed for the required land in return for the withdrawal of their opposition.[152] The canvassing intensified towards the 30 November parliamentary deadline, with Stephenson assisting the directors wherever necessary. He wrote on 15 November 1832:[153]

Our Canvass amongst the Landowners has so far been pretty favorable – Thornton of Brockhall & Sir Wm Wake have both become neuter – The Duke of Grafton & Earl of Essex have also withdrawn their opposition – Negotiations are pending with Lady Bridgwater & Ld Southampton and it is hoped they will terminate favorably – if they do not I am afraid our success is very doubtful if they give way the Bill is quite safe –

The negotiations and large payments were, however, sufficient to avoid a repetition of the opposition to the new bill and, in spite of further arguments against it in committee, it received royal assent in May 1833.[154] The whole parliamentary process had been a learning experience for Stephenson that would prepare him for the many contentious issues in his long career of over 150 attendances before parliamentary committees.

Conclusion

Stephenson had acted for the London & Birmingham company in his capacity as joint chief engineer, with his father, of George Stephenson & Son. George Stephenson had assisted with the work, and had signed the revised estimates for the line's construction.[155] On 19 September 1833, however, Robert Stephenson was appointed as the railway's engineer-in-chief in his own name. The directors' minute book records:[156]

The Directors, considering it indispensable, that in the execution of the works, one Engineer should have the entire direction, and that his time and services should be

150 Four letters, Robert Stephenson to George Stephenson, September to December 1832, **Stephenson**, Folder 18.
151 Jeaffreson, p. 178. Also *Extracts from the Minutes of Evidence Given Before the Committee of the Lords on the London and Birmingham Railway Bill*, London, 1832, p. vi.
152 Jeaffreson, p. 180.
153 Letter, Robert Stephenson to George Stephenson, London, 15 November 1832, **Stephenson**, Folder 18.
154 *3 Will. IV, c. 36*.
155 Report 'Estimate of the Engineers', Newcastle Upon Tyne, 2 February 1833, op. cit. (n. 133), p. 270.
156 Op. cit. (n. 2), 19 September 1833, p. 17.

devoted exclusively to the Company, have, under these conditions, appointed Mr. Robert Stephenson Engineer in Chief for the whole line ...

This was a remarkable appointment with Stephenson still several weeks short of his thirtieth birthday. The directors had clearly been impressed by his technical competence and his performance in the intense cross-examination of the parliamentary committees, but would he be a competent chief engineer in the demanding world of long-distance railway construction, requiring extraordinary abilities in leadership, delegation, supervision, motivation, negotiation and tenacity, quite apart from technical competence?

Whereas three years earlier his father had achieved a remarkable success in completing the Liverpool & Manchester line, which required all of these abilities, Stephenson's building experience had been limited to shorter routes, for all of which he had been absent for long periods and dependent upon his resident engineers. In completing them he demonstrated his talents in supervising multiple projects, but not without significant problems, delays and cost over-runs. Whilst his experiences with Richardson and Gillespie had demonstrated that delegation required particular supervisory skills, his engagement of Harrison and Brunton showed also that he could recruit reliable subordinates.

His experiences during his apprenticeship, his time in Colombia, his factory workforce and his more recent railway-building work demonstrated his maturing abilities to motivate and lead a large workforce. He had, however, gained only limited experience in selecting contractors and negotiating terms with them, and his experiences on the Leicester & Swannington line showed how many pitfalls there were in this process.

Quite apart from the knowledge and understanding of materials and structures gained from his father and William James, and at Edinburgh University, he had developed his own experience from the fieldwork in Colombia and his recent railway-building work. However, excepting some brick under-bridges, albeit with the embarrassment of the partial failure of the Church Street bridge in Whitstable, his direct involvement in bridge specification and design had been limited. His experience in tunnelling had begun with his mine survey work at Killingworth and his time in Colombia, but the Glenfield railway tunnel had given him a foretaste of the hazards of over-reliance on trial borings.

Stephenson had yet to develop the political understanding and skills that would be required for the high-profile position of engineer-in-chief. He was clearly more comfortable in engineering pursuits than in dealing with the conflicting advocacy of railway proprietors and the personal agendas that went with it. The London & Birmingham Railway Act had been obtained at an extraordinary price, however, requiring a broader base of proprietors to provide the additional capital that was required. Capitalists from Liverpool were keen to invest in the project and, in providing that extra capital, obtained representation on the board of directors. The strong Liverpool caucus was to exert a considerable influence over the affairs of both the London & Birmingham and Grand Junction Railways.

It took the London & Birmingham Railway proprietors four months after obtaining their Act to elect their new board and appoint their engineer-in-chief. The board was made up of directors from London, sitting as the 'London Committee', and from Birmingham and Liverpool, sitting as the 'Birmingham Committee'.[157] A number of the influential Liverpool directors, particularly Edward Cropper, Theodore Rathbone and Robert Garnett, had also been directors of the Liverpool & Manchester Railway and had often clashed with George Stephenson.[158] It was therefore notable that, notwithstanding its collective experience in locomotive railways, George Stephenson & Son, per se, was not appointed to undertake the building of either the London & Birmingham or Grand Junction Railways.

The directors of both railways acknowledged the collective experience, but looked for direct accountability from their respective engineers-in-chief. Whilst George Stephenson was appointed to the Grand Junction Railway, Robert Stephenson was appointed to the London & Birmingham line. The directors anticipated that should conflicts arise, particularly over motive-power issues, they had better opportunity to exert authority over their engineer, a judgement that was put to the test in the bruising battles of 1835–1836 (see Chapter 6). The appointments spelled the end for George Stephenson & Son.

157 Ibid, p. 22, minutes 28/9.
158 Correspondence, **PRO**, RAIL 384/276. Also Bailey (1984), pp. 194–200.

2

London and Birmingham

Mike Chrimes

Let nothing deter you from executing the work in the most substantial manner, and on the most scientific principles so that it may serve as a model for all future railways and become the wonder and admiration of posterity. There is not anything but what a Large Spirited Company like yours can accomplish. Remember that faint heart never won fair lady. Therefore let me conclude with the advice of Queen Elizabeth to one of her courtiers: 'Climb Boldly Then'

John U. Rastrick to the directors of the London & Birmingham Railway, 1833[1]

Robert Stephenson's appointment as engineer-in-chief of the London & Birmingham Railway in September 1833 marked a new stage not only in his career, but also in the general development of civil engineering in the British Isles.[2] In his statement, John Rastrick reflected the historical significance of the project, his anticipation of the risks, and the possibility that the shareholders might take fright before the project was completed. That the directors sought peer endorsement of his scheme was a reminder that Stephenson's appointment would be closely monitored. Both Rastrick and Henry Palmer (1795–1844) had been recruited to support the parliamentary process, and both were invited to make recommendations on how to proceed with construction. If they had been critical, Stephenson might not have been appointed, despite his sterling work in the field and parliamentary committees.

In the early 1830s civil engineering was 'a profession moving to maturity'.[3] John Smeaton had coined the term seventy-five years earlier and, following its foundation in 1818, the Institution of Civil Engineers had secured a Royal Charter in 1828. There had been skills shortages in years of high demand, and not until the 1820s did the majority of practitioners receive training explicitly as civil engineers. By the standards of the time therefore, Stephenson, with his training and university education, was well prepared for the task.

1 Report, John Rastrick to London & Birmingham Railway, 13 May 1833, **PRO**, RAIL 384/101, p. 69.
2 Minute Book, Birmingham Committee, London & Birmingham Railway, 13 September 1833, **PRO**, RAIL 384/65.
3 Watson (1979) and Skempton (1996 and 2002). Also M. M. Chrimes, 'Civil Engineering 1500–1830: the biographical dimension', *Proc. ICE, Civil Engineering*, in press, 2003.

George Stephenson & Son had risen rapidly to prominence from the mid-1820s, and the successful completion of the Liverpool & Manchester Railway had considerably strengthened its hand because of the demonstrable success of locomotive traction. By 1833, this experience was considered essential, thus discounting other experienced engineers, notably the Rennies, James Walker, Jesse Hartley and Francis Giles.

Company directors played an active role in their projects and the engineer was seen as a source of technical expertise, to be hired and dismissed as needs changed. This active role of directors continued throughout Stephenson's lifetime. Some directors, particularly those from Liverpool, apparently felt that George Stephenson's appointment as Engineer to the Grand Junction Railway, assisted by Joseph Locke, and Robert Stephenson's appointment to the London & Birmingham line would make it easier to monitor their progress. For this individual appointment, therefore, Stephenson was the obvious person.

The route

The earliest proposal for a railway between London and Birmingham was 'the line of the Central Junction Railway or Tramroad' projected by William James in 1820. It ran from London via Uxbridge, Thame and Oxford to the Stratford and Moreton-in-Marsh railway (Fig. 2.1).[4] Surveys for the 'Birmingham and London Railroad Company', which issued its prospectus in early September 1824,[5] were organized by (Sir) John Rennie (1794–1874) following his appointment as engineer in February 1825.[6] The route originated in the West and East India Docks and, skirting central London, followed much of the eventual route before diverting towards Banbury and Bicester.[7] The Rennies' proposal was prepared for the 1825–1826 parliamentary session.[8]

Francis Giles (1787–1847) proposed an alternative route for a rival company in the late 1820s,[9] and it was his route that formed the basis of that developed by the Stephensons. Robert Stephenson and George Hennet resurveyed Giles' route,[10] and the company secretary, Richard Creed, also surveyed the route, making recommendations for modifications.[11] Once the route had been agreed, surveying teams made detailed surveys indicating the

4 E.M.S.P[aine] (1861).

5 *Aris & Birmingham Gazette*, 6, 13 and 20 September 1824.

6 *Aris & Birmingham Gazette*, 14 March 1825.

7 *Aris & Birmingham Gazette*, 5 December 1825. Also, [Sir] John Rennie, Report, 1 April 1826, Reports, vol. 2, **ICE**. Also letter from Edward Grantham, *MM*, **XXII**, 1834, pp. 436–8.

8 *RM*, NS, **I & II**, 1836–7.

9 Lecount (1839a), pp. 4–11.

10 Minutes of the directors of the London & Birmingham Railway, 13 May and 2 September 1831 and 5 January 1832, **PRO**, RAIL 384/1. Hennet was paid c.£2500 for his surveys, and produced the deposited plans. He later became a contractor.

11 Ibid., 13 May 1831, pp. 68–73, and 2 and 19 September 1831, pp. 93–4.

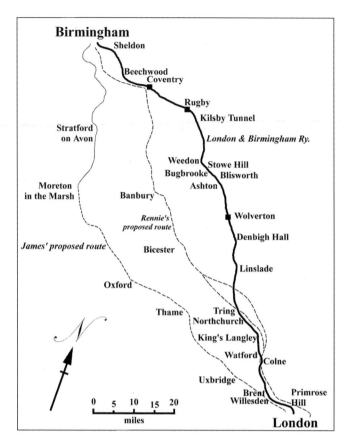

2.1 Stephenson's
London &
Birmingham
Railway route
compared with
proposed routes by
William James and
John Rennie

property ownership along the line.[12] Because of concerns about getting the 1833 bill through Parliament, Stephenson, Thomas Gooch and Edward Dixon (1809–1877) also surveyed an alternative route north of Tring via Banbury and Warwick.[13]

Project organization

The Act of Parliament gave rise to detailed surveying as a prelude to the purchase of land along the route, whilst capital had to be raised to finance the purchase and pay for the construction phase. Over the previous seventy-five years engineers had met similar challenges and developed established procedures for carrying out civil engineering works, but rarely on the same scale. With such major linear works, the greatest obstacle to completion had often been raising the necessary capital rather than the engineering challenges. This had stalled works on Smeaton's Forth–Clyde Canal, Brindley's Oxford Canal, Rennie's Kennet & Avon Canal, and Jessop's Grand

12 Minutes of Survey Committee, London & Birmingham Railway, **PRO**, RAIL 384/27. The surveyors were Owens, Simpson, Hewitson, Fairbank and Boultlea.
13 Thomas Gooch, Diary for 1833, **ICE**.

Junction Canal, as well as many lesser works. More recently the Liverpool &
Manchester Railway had sought an Exchequer loan.

The timing of the London & Birmingham Act was fortunate, as the
success of the Liverpool & Manchester Railway had emboldened investors,
the passage of the Reform Act promised political stability, and the economic
cycle was on an upturn. As work proceeded, circumstances began to change,
wages and costs rose, and in the late 1830s there was an economic recession,
by which time the London & Birmingham Railway had opened. The challenge for Stephenson, therefore, was to construct the railway as quickly as
possible to enable investors to see a return on their capital while they
remained confident.

As originally presented to Parliament in 1832, the proposed line was 111
miles long from Camden Town, London, to Curzon Street, Birmingham,
with gradients nowhere exceeding 16ft per mile (1:330), and involved 12
million cubic yards of excavation and nearly 11 million cubic yards of
embankments, as well as six viaducts, 300 bridges and three long tunnels. It
was on a scale rarely matched before or since.

In addition to his own experience, Stephenson could build on precedents
set by previous generations of engineers. In this the work of Smeaton was
particularly significant. In the early 1830s there was little available in the way
of engineering textbooks to draw upon, and Smeaton's published reports
provided practical illustrations of engineering.[14] Stephenson later acknowledged: 'Smeaton is the greatest philosopher in our profession this country has
yet produced.'[15]

For the Forth & Clyde Canal, Smeaton had elaborated a project management structure for linear works, with a 'consulting engineer', resident engi-
neer-in-charge, and assistant engineers in charge of more local works, and with
contracts divided into lots according to the likely financial resources of
tenderers.[16] The project organization of the London & Birmingham Railway
mirrored this model. The route was divided under assistant engineers, with
sub-assistant engineers and overseers responsible for the day-to-day supervision of shorter sections. Each division involved a number of contracts, based
on what were considered reasonable capital resources for a contractor.
Generally a balance of cuttings and embankments was sought in each contract
to minimize the need to haul over long distances.[17]

Separate contracts were drawn up for some major works and later works
such as station buildings (Plate 3 and Fig. 2.11, p. 61). Before contracts
could be issued, detailed calculations had to be undertaken so that estimates
could be prepared and tenders properly assessed, specifications and drawings

---

14 Skempton (1987). Also Smeaton.
15 Smiles (1861), p. 86.
16 Skempton (1991). Also 'A plan or model for carrying on the mechanical part of the works of the canal
    from Forth to Clyde', Smeaton, vol. 2, p. 122. Also *Letters between Redmond Morres … and John
    Smeaton*, Dublin, 1773.
17 Minutes of the London and Birmingham Committees, London & Birmingham Railway, 21 July
    1835, **PRO**, RAIL 384/32, p. 312.

prepared for inspection by contractors to enable them to price their work, and detailed land surveys carried out to enable land purchases to go ahead. All this required staff, and an engineering establishment, for which Stephenson brought in experienced and trusted individuals who would share his workload.

His experience in South America and with his early railway schemes enabled him to judge the qualities of staff that he would require for the execution of such a major project. There were few other engineers who were experienced in railway construction, and although many associates of George Stephenson & Son were tied up with other railways, the majority of his early appointments were of engineers and assistants known to him.

Although Stephenson must have been considering his subordinate staff requirements after May 1833, little could be done until his own appointment in September.[18] The following week he made his first recommendations to the directors who would make these full-time appointments. These were John Dixon and William Crosley (fl. 1802–1838) as assistant engineers, and John Birkinshaw, Edward Dixon, Charles Fox (1810–1874; Fig. 2.2) and S. S. Bennett as draughtsmen to work at the London end.[19] He then recommended Thomas Gooch as assistant engineer, with John Brunton, at the Birmingham end.[20] George Phipps (1807–1888), Francis Young (1814–1860) and B. L. Dickenson were engaged as draughtsmen soon afterwards.

John Dixon was at that time one of the Liverpool & Manchester Railway's resident engineers, and Stephenson's approach to him appeared to have been made without the knowledge of either of the railways' boards. The Liverpool directors may have been concerned at the loss of an experienced and competent engineer from that line, however, and Stephenson was instructed to look elsewhere.[21] The appointment of George Buck (1789–1854) and Frank Forster (1800–1852) as assistant engineers followed in the next three months.[22] Buck and Crosley, with whom Stephenson had not previously worked, had considerable construction experience, and Buck also had a reputation for the structural use of iron.[23] Fox's engineering experience was of a more mechanical nature, and he clearly had a commanding presence.[24]

By early 1834, Stephenson had four assistant engineers, several of whom had pupils – for example, Buck's pupil William Baker (1817–1878). He also had four sub-assistants, and at least eight office staff. Generally his

18 Gooch went on a continental holiday at this time. Thomas Gooch, Diaries and Autobiography, **ICE**.
19 Minutes of the London and Birmingham Committees, London & Birmingham Railway, 26 September 1833, **PRO**, RAIL 384/30. Also Skempton (2002), pp. 158–9.
20 Ibid., 27 September 1833.
21 Ibid., 10 October 1833. Also op. cit. (n. 2), 4 October 1833.
22 Op. cit. (n. 19), 26–7 September, 4, 10 and 11 October, 1 November, 18 and 20 December 1833. Gooch refers to 'quarreling about salary with the Directors'; Thomas Gooch Diary, 23 October 1833, **ICE**.
23 Skempton (2002), pp. 95–6. Reflecting their experience, Buck and Crosley received the highest salary (£600 per annum).
24 Conder, pp. 11–12.

2.2 Portrait of
Sir Charles Fox
in later life
(Courtesy of
Institution of
Civil Engineers)

management technique was to appoint young aspiring engineers to junior positions, entrusting them with more responsibility and independence as they proved themselves. He later wrote to Isambard K. Brunel, about George Phipps: ' ... I have always met that by reposing the utmost confidence in him taking care of course that my principles of conducting operations were adhered to ... .'[25]

Supplemented by the recruitment of Robert Dockray (1811–1871) as sub-Assistant Engineer in December 1835, this team of assistant engineers took charge of construction until March 1837, when Stephenson released Gooch to build the Manchester & Leeds Railway and promoted Phipps to resident engineer.[26] In 1837 the engineering staff on the line numbered 55.[27] This

25 Letter, Robert Stephenson to Isambard K. Brunel, 23 September 1838, **Brunel**, DM 1306/20.

26 Gooch began work for the Manchester & Leeds Railway in October 1835, preparing for its Bill; he gave evidence in the Spring of 1836, and in the autumn he prepared for staking out etc. He finally left the London & Birmingham works on 10 April 1837. Thomas Gooch, Autobiography, **ICE**.

27 'Dinner and Presentation of a Piece of Plate to Robert Stephenson Esq.', 23 December 1837, *CEAJ*, **I**, 1837/8, p. 76.

2.3 Eyres Hotel, St John's Wood, the initial engineering office for the London & Birmingham Railway (Courtesy of Institution of Civil Engineers)

figure is consistent with an engineering office staff of 20 people, although fewer were involved when work began.[28]

Surveying and levelling

Robert Stephenson and his team were initially based in Kilburn, but in May 1834 the office moved to the Eyres Hotel, St John's Wood (Fig. 2.3).[29] A subsidiary office was obtained at Coventry.[30] George Aitchison managed the accounting at St John's Wood,[31] while Peter Lecount (1794–1852) looked after the engineers' department.[32]

Stephenson's first task was to stake out the line of the railway, the Act allowing deviation within a band 100 yards wide.[33] The engineering team undertook the land surveys, thus gaining first-hand acquaintance with the

28 Jeaffreson, I, p. 192. Also Brunton, p. 36.
29 Robert Stephenson's Diary, 9 May 1834, **ScM**, 1947-135.
30 Thomas Gooch, Autobiography, **ICE**.
31 Record keeping and procedures for London Office, London & Birmingham Railway, 15 January 1834, **PRO**, RAIL 384/291.
32 Op. cit. (n. 2), 2 May 1834.
33 *An Act for making a railway between London and Birmingham*, 1833, **ICE**, MLG 84.

2.4
J. C. Bourne's
view of a
surveying team at
work during the
building of the
London &
Birmingham line
(J. C. Bourne,
1839)

route.[34] He himself had walked the line twelve times by May 1834.[35] Delays in early appointments meant that Paul Padley, William James' chief surveyor, with whom Stephenson had worked at the start of his career, was employed to begin staking out.[36] Land surveyors were required for valuation purposes.

The Act gave railway staff authority to enter property to fix the route. While some tenants and owners were treated summarily,[37] protracted negotiations were carried out with more influential interests, including peers, the Ordnance Depot at Weedon and the Grand Junction Canal Company. Stephenson spent twelve days in 1834 in discussion about the latter two.[38] Until the exact route was fixed, quantities could not be calculated, detailed estimates prepared, or agreements reached with contractors.

Levels were taken every chain (22 yards) along the line, enabling the preparation of accurate longitudinal and cross sections, and quantities determined (Fig. 2.4). Further trial shafts were sunk at several locations to obtain more complete strata information and samples for the contractors (see Chapter 8). Once the alignment was determined, drawings were made and specifications drawn up. The contracts were first let for the two ends of the line, where traffic was likely to be greatest and could generate income to offset against expenditure.[39] Thereafter, the most difficult contracts, at Tring and Kilsby Tunnel,

34 Op. cit. (n. 19), 26 September 1833.
35 Conder, p. 14.
36 Op. cit. (n. 19), 10 October 1833.
37 Conder, pp. 11–16 and 32–40.
38 Op. cit. (n. 29).
39 Op. cit. (n. 1).

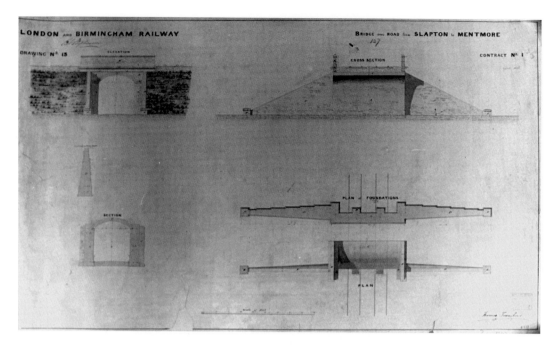

were prepared so that delays there would not hold up the opening of the whole line.

It took two man-days to prepare a drawing, and 2000 drawings were prepared for the line (Fig. 2.5).[40] At the northern end, Gooch and his assistants had fixed the route and determined where the structures should be by April 1834, after which preparation of detailed drawings began in the St John's Wood office.[41] There were 104 drawings for the first five contracts, each of which required a further three copies.[42] Stephenson himself spent at least three days supervising the preparation of three drawings for the Rea viaduct, and was also responsible for the specifications.[43] All the Birmingham drawings took 832 man-days, an average daily production of 15 drawings, with 30 staff. Brunton claimed to have worked twenty-hour shifts with only one night's sleep for a fortnight, personally delivering the drawings to Birmingham for inspection by the directors in July.[44] Drafts were ready that month,[45] and the contracts let in August.[46]

The preparation of the first contract drawings was a period of intense activity, and a number of staff began work in this period. Stephenson's team included Phipps, Brunton, Gooch, Birkinshaw, Dixon, Forster, Young and Dickenson, probably assisted by Lecount and Aitchison. Some, including Stephenson, Birkinshaw and Phipps, were also involved with the

2.5 Contract drawing for bridge over the road between Slapton and Mentmore signed by Stephenson and the contractor, Thomas Townshend (Courtesy of Institution of Civil Engineers)

40 Lecount (1839a), pp. 30–1.
41 Op. cit. (n. 29), 9 May 1834.
42 Engineers' reports, 19 August 1834, **PRO**, RAIL 384/101.
43 Op. cit. (n. 29), 24, 26 & 29 May 1834.
44 Brunton, p. 36.
45 Op. cit. (n. 42), 9 June 1834. Also, Minutes of the Birmingham Committee, London & Birmingham Railway, 13 June 1834, **PRO**, RAIL 384/66. Also, op. cit. (n.29).
46 Op. cit. (n. 2), 12 August 1834.

specifications.[47] Buck and Fox were largely tied up with the early contracts, and Forster with negotiations at Weedon. Crosley was making preparations for the contracts at Tring. Pupils were probably all drafted in to meet the deadline. Gooch took on two additional draughtsmen,[48] and encountered such demand for inspection that he had to prepare another room for the contractors.[49]

It was difficult to manage this process and, with these limited resources, Stephenson could not have prepared contracts for tender any more quickly. The number of engineers and draftsmen dictated how quickly contracts could be let and work commenced. The Birmingham directors expressed their disquiet at the delay in starting work at their end of the line.[50] Preparation of drawings was the equivalent of six man-years of work and, in addition, specifications had to be drawn up and estimates made. This situation was made more acute as work began on site requiring supervision, and preparations for the Camden to Euston extension Bill began.[51] George Bidder was brought in to assist,[52] but within eight months he had departed to help Stephenson survey the line to Brighton (see Chapter 3).[53]

Selecting the contractors

Once the specifications and contract drawings had been prepared, the contracts were put out to tender. Rastrick had recommended putting the contracts out in large lots. His idea was:[54]

Extensive contracts … become worth the attention of men of capital who should they unfortunately find that they have taken the work for too small an amount, or should the seasons become unfavourable for the execution thereof, so that they may run the risk of losing money by the contract they will still go on and complete the work sooner than suffer the least imputation on their character or respectability … whereas when work is let in little petty contracts they are generally taken by men of no capital whose security is good for nothing, and as soon as ever they discover or think that they have made an imprudent contract, begin immediately to have recourse to every expedient to get rid of it … I have always found that the work was much better done and that everything went on with more expedition and the Engineer's orders all were punctually attended to when the contractor had a fair and liberal compensation from his contract.

Palmer was of a similar mind, dividing the line into 16 contracts, excluding major structures.[55] Leading engineers discussed this approach in evidence presented to the House of Commons Committee on the London &

47 Letter, Robert Stephenson to Capt. Moorsom, 20 May, **PRO** RAIL 1008/91.
48 Op. cit. (n. 2), 6 June 1834, reporting letter from Thomas Gooch of 31 May. Eight staff were on the payroll at Coventry on 27 June 1834.
49 Ibid., 18 July 1834.
50 Ibid., 16 May 1834.
51 Act received royal assent, 3 July 1835 (5 *Will. IV, c. 56*).
52 Bidder appointed 17 September 1834, Minutes of the London & Birmingham Railway Board, 22 October 1834, **PRO**, RAIL 384/31.
53 Bidder departed 19 March 1835, op. cit. (n. 17), 28 April 1835.
54 Op. cit. (n. 1), p. 30.

Southampton Railway.[56] While Rastrick's theory may have been sound, there were practical problems – not least the availability of contractors with the financial resources to take on such lots. Although there were a number with many years of experience in civil engineering, only a handful had previously taken on contracts of more than £100,000 in value, and this may have cautioned a more circumspect approach.

In practice contracts were let in batches to suit project control, the office workload dictating the timetable, with lot size determined by convenience and the engineering challenges anticipated. Most were for four- to six-mile lengths, excluding special structures, and Robert Stephenson seems to have determined on a value of £30,000–£50,000.[57] In anticipation of the heavy work involved for the Tring contract, major contractors were selected to tender, but elsewhere selection was by open tender (Fig. 2.6).[58]

Stephenson and the Board were aware of the risks attached to accepting the lowest tenders from inexperienced or under-capitalized contractors, and they were therefore expected to provide sureties of 10%, and operate with 20% retention.[59] They were paid monthly for four-fifths of the work until the retention amounted to the 10% surety. Although the contract sizes were smaller than Rastrick and Palmer had advised, several contractors with experience and resources took several lots. However, eight of the thirty 'failed' during the project, and only few of them continued contracting into the 1840s. Some were possibly too old to meet the physical challenges involved, while their younger assistants, often their children, lacked the necessary experience.

Stephenson was generally on top of his job, and did well both for the contractors and the company. When the first contracts were let in 1834, he advised the Board directly on the wisdom of accepting some tenders.[60] Although William Mackenzie had been the lowest tenderer on three of the Birmingham contracts, Stephenson believed that his prices were too keen, advised that only two should be accepted, and noted in his diary that Mackenzie would fail in one of the contracts.[61] It was later evident that Mackenzie could not continue, and the contracts were re-let.[62] Time had thus been lost, but there was no suggestion that Mackenzie should not be paid for the work he had done.[63]

55 'Report of Henry Palmer to the London and Birmingham Railway Company', 13 May 1833, op. cit. (n. 42).
56 *Minutes of Evidence of the Select Committee on the London and Southampton Railway*, London, HMSO, 1833.
57 Op. cit. (n. 17), 12 November 1834. The first contracts were larger.
58 Letter, Robert Stephenson to R. Creed, 15 July 1834, in op. cit. (n. 52), 23 July 1834.
59 Conditions of contract signed by Townshend and Mackenzie in **ICE**, Townsend and Mackenzie collections. Also Crosley's estimates in J. S. Tucker, Specifications, vol. 1, **ICE**.
60 Op. cit. (n. 42), 12 August 1834. Also op. cit. (n. 52), 20 February 1835, and op. cit. (n. 17), 27 May 1835.
61 Op. cit. (n. 42), 12 August 1834 and 5 September 1834. Also op. cit. (n. 29), 12 August and 31 October 1834.
62 Initially to Richard Parr, 7 November 1834, then to Hugh Greenshields, 14 November 1834, op. cit. (n. 52), 7 and 24 November 1834.
63 Op. cit. (n. 42), 26 November 1834.

2.6 (This page and opposite) The first two pages of the contract document for the Tring contract signed by the contractor, Thomas Townshend (Courtesy of Institution of Civil Engineers)

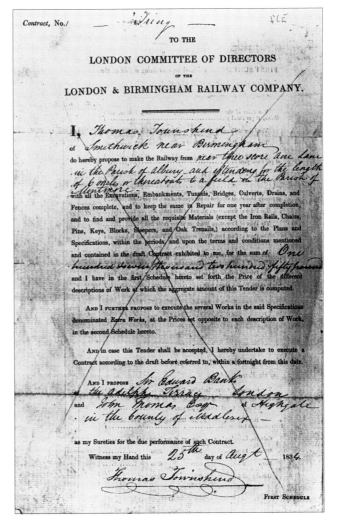

There were also problems at the Birmingham end. Shortly after Mackenzie's departure, Gooch wrote to Stephenson that Diggle had underestimated in his tender and was unable to afford the 20% retention: 'I hardly know what to do with him, but I have desired him to send in an amended schedule so as to make the account of his estimate.'[64] Within a week Stephenson had accepted Gooch's revisions to the schedules, although this did not remedy Diggle's poor progress.[65]

Stephenson was generally prepared to negotiate on prices, and showed understanding of the capital weaknesses of the contractors.[66] He regularly

64 Letter, Thomas Gooch to Robert Stephenson, 7 December 1834, Engineers Reports, op. cit. (n. 1).
65 Letter from Thomas Gooch, 11 December 1834. Also letter from Robert Stephenson to Capt. Moorsom, 12 December 1834, Engineers reports, in op. cit. (n. 42).
66 Early examples are 1 October 1834 (Soars, contract 2C), 28 November 1834 (Pritchard, contract 3G). Also letters Robert Stephenson to Capt. Moorsom, 12 December 1834 and 19 February 1835; Thomas Gooch to Capt. Moorsom, 5 March 1835; Frank Forster to Capt. Moorsom, 5 March, 31 July and 9 September 1835, op. cit. (n. 17 and 52).

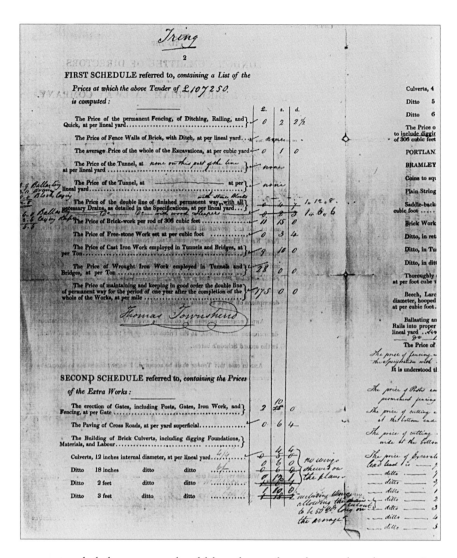

recommended that money should be advanced, and even that the retention money should be released.[67] He permitted advances to buy wagons and other equipment,[68] and recommended that the Board should purchase locomotives to make them available to the contractors to move material more effectively (see Chapter 6).[69]

He was less compromising on lack of progress, however.[70] In the case of Jackson's and Shildon's contract at Primrose Hill, where they made a promising start, problems were caused by friction between the partners, and Thomas Jackson's lack of capital resources meant that he could not continue

67 Robert Stephenson to Capt. Moorsom, Engineers Reports, London & Birmingham Railway, 10 and 19 March, 2 and 23 July 1835 and 8 June 1836, **PRO**, RAIL 384/102.

68 Op. cit. (n. 1), 8 January and 10 March 1835.

69 Op. cit. (n. 17), 25 & 30 November 1835. Also, Board Minutes of the London & Birmingham Railway, 11 and 25 October 1837, **PRO**, RAIL 384/33.

70 Op. cit. (n. 17 and 52), 8 January, 29 July, 16 September and 7 October 1835.

2.7 Construction
of Camden
winding engine
house
(J. C. Bourne,
1839)

alone.[71] Having already decided to supervise the contracts at the London end, Stephenson recommended that the Primrose Hill contract be taken into the Company's hands, relying on John Birkinshaw, who already had tunnelling experience.[72] Stephenson may have felt it problematic to find an experienced tunnelling contractor, and was prepared to employ Jackson on some later contracts.[73]

As work progressed (Fig. 2.7), Stephenson recommended that the Company should take over eight of the contracts, with a further four being taken over by other contractors. This was anticipated in a letter to Captain Constantine Moorsom, the Secretary to the Birmingham Committee, which encapsulates his attitude to the contractors:[74]

With contractors who understand the work and with adequate capital you will not have to do any more than urge them on and serve notices. With others the Company may need to enter the works and provide materials, as you have already had to in two cases.

At much the same time Forster was reporting:[75]

There seems a sort of fatality among our contractors. Nowell has been seriously ill and is still weak. Chapman is very ill of inflammation in the region of the heart, and

71 Op. cit. (n. 52), 7 and 24 November 1834.
72 Ibid., 5, 7, 12 and 19 November 1834.
73 Board Minutes, op. cit. (n. 69), 16 November and 28 December 1836 and 15 March 1837.
74 Robert Stephenson to Capt. Moorsom, op. cit. (n. 67), 30 November 1835.
75 Frank Forster to Robert Stephenson, ibid., 30 December 1835.

poor Hughes is lying in an almost helpless state at Northampton, of a paralysis of the limbs.

Stephenson was generally fair to the contractors, and paid them in full for their work.[76] However, contractors would not necessarily work to suit the railway,[77] and from the beginning assistant engineers and their sub-assistants recorded lack of progress and want of effort.[78] Stephenson accepted their failings but regularly had to recommend to the Board that notice should be served on them.[79] Having persevered with William Soars through all kinds of financial and engineering difficulties, he requested in May 1837 that the London Committee 'would authorize him to serve Mr Soars with notice of the termination of the contract, as the only resource which the Company had left ... .'[80] Furthermore, if he felt that he was being deliberately deceived he could display temper reminiscent of his father.[81]

Once work had begun in earnest, it was impossible for Stephenson to supervise all the works personally. He had to trust his sub-assistants, and concentrate his efforts where there were problems, most notably at Kilsby (see Chapter 8).[82] Generally this approach seems to have worked well, although the system broke down for the Blisworth contract, for which William Hughes was an experienced, but elderly contractor. Lecount later related:[83]

During the first year and a half the progress was extremely slow, owing to the want of proper energy on the part of the contractor, combined with general bad management … The time was frittered away without anything like a proper energy on the part of the contractor; and if this was evident at the commencements, where there were no particular difficulties to grapple with … At last, the Company were obliged to get rid of the contractor, by any means, and take the work into their own hands, with the knowledge, that in pulling up for the lost time the expenses would be considerably increased.

Although Lecount glossed over construction difficulties, warnings about lack of progress had been issued from early on, but Hughes was already ill and died in January 1836.[84] His son, also William Hughes, lacked experience to realize the scale of delays, and ultimately was unable to pay the workforce. Stephenson had probably looked to Hughes' experience and had not

---

76 For example, for Nowell's work at Kilsby, ibid., 2 June 1836.
77 Op. cit. (n. 55), pp. 7–15.
78 Later examples include op. cit. (n. 17), 25 and 30 November, 23 and 30 December 1835.
79 Examples recorded in op. cit. (n. 17), on 23 April and 30 December 1835 and 3 March 1836, and in op. cit. (n. 69), 1 March and 12 July 1837.
80 Op. cit. (n. 69), 17 May 1837.
81 Conder, pp. 23–4.
82 Examples in Engineers Reports, op. cit. (n. 67), 19 December 1835 and op. cit. (n. 17), 13 December 1835. Also descriptions of specific works and references listed below.
83 Lecount (1839a), pp. 41–4.
84 Forster first reported problems arising from the geology of the site on 13 June 1834 and recommended a deviation: Birmingham Committee Minutes, op. cit. (n. 42), 13 and 27 June 1834. The first hint of trouble was from Robert Stephenson, 30 November 1835; also reports, Frank Forster to Robert Stephenson, 30 December 1835 and 14 January 1836, op. cit. (n. 67). Also Skempton (2002), pp. 347–9.

identified the contract as one of likely difficulty, while Forster was fully occupied with the problems at Kilsby. Not until December 1836 did the Company take the contract over, and Stephenson was obliged to address the situation.[85]

Permanent way

Robert Stephenson's involvement with the design and development of the permanent way for the London & Birmingham Railway was a frustrating episode for him. Its selection was significant because of the quantities involved for the 112-mile railway, and the directors sought independent advice on the system to be adopted. The potential patent fees involved would have acted as a magnet for any inventor to urge their system upon the company. In his May 1833 report Rastrick had advised that the purchase of the material for the permanent way should be separated from the main construction contracts to help cost control.[86]

Some issues of permanent way design had been identified; namely the need for well-drained and compacted ballast to secure the sleepers; the need to secure the sleepers in position, and to fix the rails securely to these and each other; and the need to have sufficiently strong rails for the traffic. However, developments had been largely empirical, the only operating experience being that from the Liverpool & Manchester Railway. The permanent way comprised stone block sleepers set into sand and gravel ballast, with fish-bellied wrought iron rails. The stone block sleepers were laid continuously and squarely, with holes drilled to receive timber plugs into which treenails or equivalent could be driven to secure the rails to the sleepers by chairs or other means. Timber cross-sleepers were preferred on high embankments to facilitate adjustment. It was believed that track movement caused most problems, and improvements were to secure rigidity through the system adopted.

Although Stephenson spent four days in July 1834 compiling a report on the permanent way, and recommending fish-bellied rails and the use of his patent chairs, the directors would not entertain the idea of track that was dependent upon his patent.[87] This rejection anticipated the extraordinary battles over the type of locomotive to be employed on the line (see Chapter 6). The board therefore held a competition to stimulate innovation in new track design. A 100-guinea prize was offered 'for the most impressive construction of railway bars, chairs and pedestals, and of the best manner of affixing and connecting the rail, chairs and block to each'. John Rastrick and Nicholas Wood judged the entries, together with Peter Barlow (1776–1862) of the

85 Minutes of the Board of the London & Birmingham Railway, **PRO**, RAIL 384/67. Also Robert Stephenson, report on works on Birmingham Division, in Engineers Reports, London & Birmingham Railway, January and February 1837, **PRO**, RAIL 384/103.
86 Op. cit. (n. 1), p. 25.
87 Minutes of the Board of the London & Birmingham Railway, **PRO**, RAIL 384/2. Also Engineers' Reports, op. cit. (n. 1), pp. 85–6, and op. cit. (n. 29).

Royal Military Academy, the leading academic expert on the strength of materials. In December 1834 the judges reported, but felt unable to make a recommendation in the absence of experimental data.[88] No prize was given, although awards were offered to Robert Daglish (1777–1865) of £70 and Henry Swinburne of £35.[89]

Barlow carried out experimental investigations with various rail profiles, and produced a succession of reports in 1835.[90] He recommended a 50lb/yard parallel rather than fish-bellied rail. He was then asked to visit the Liverpool & Manchester Railway, accompanied by Robert Stephenson, Edward Dixon and Charles Vignoles, and some of the railway's directors.[91] They investigated the '60lb rail' (62lb/yard) recommended by Joseph Locke for the Grand Junction Railway, as its additional strength suggested a saving in blocks and chairs. The Liverpool & Manchester had been using such a rail at both 3ft 9in and 5ft bearings since May 1834.

In his report Barlow reaffirmed his recommendations regarding parallel rails, and recommended different cross sections according to the spacing of the sleepers. The directors, armed with Stephenson's reports, Barlow's investigations and Locke's report for the Grand Junction Company, decided on stone blocks, not less than 5 cubic feet in content, which were to be set diagonally and 'eased off each other'. As on the Liverpool & Manchester, blocks were adopted for cuttings, and timber cross-sleepers for embankments. The chairs and double-headed rail profile adopted by Locke for the Grand Junction were chosen. 64lb rails were ordered for use at 4ft bearings, and 75lb rails for use at 5ft bearings, with wooden wedges to secure to the chairs (Fig. 2.8). Rails were 15ft in length. A modified version of Stephenson's patent chair was endorsed.

Stephenson had been effectively ordered what to do,[92] and Peter Lecount infers bitterness amongst the associates over the way his advice was disregarded.[93] The original 50lb fish-bellied rails at 3ft bearings bore up to traffic better than the heavier rail at longer bearings, and there were problems keeping the parallel track in order. Additional blocks had to be added to provide intermediate support, with bearings reduced to 3ft 9in. Lecount claimed the closer bearing system was cheaper, although he himself acknowledged how little was still known about permanent way.

Stephenson continued to develop the permanent way for railways for which he was consulting engineer. The value of stone blocks and the obsession with a rigid roadway were laid to rest after experiments on the Manchester & Leeds Railway, where the rails, bolted to the rock in cuttings, had demonstrated the problems of a rigid track bed.[94] Although

88 Board Minutes, op. cit. (n. 87), Minute 153.
89 *MM*, **XXIII**, 1835, pp. 225–31.
90 Barlow (1835b and 1837). Board Minutes, op. cit. (n. 87), 12 and 18 February 1835.
91 Board Minutes, op cit. (n. 87), Minute 153, pp. 106–7. *MM*, **XXIII**, 1835, p. 380.
92 Board Minutes, op cit. (n. 87), Minute 152, p. 106.
93 Lecount (1836a, 1836b and 1839b).
94 William Adams, 'The Construction of the Permanent Way of Railways in Europe', *Proc. ICE*, **XI**, 1852, p. 244. Also contribution by Robert Stephenson, pp. 296–8.

2.8 '65lb' (i.e. 64lb) per yard parallel rail track and stone block sleepers (F. W. Simms, 1838)

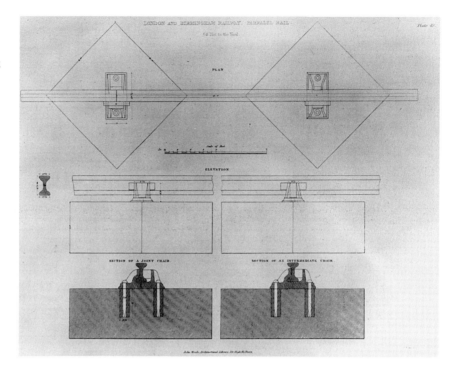

Stephenson resisted replacing 65lb rails in 1843,[95] because of concerns about the effects of a change on the consolidation of the ballast, he recognized the improved ride with timber sleepers, and by 1848 the London & North Western Railway was using 75lb or 82lb rails and timber transverse sleepers throughout (Fig. 2.9).[96]

Undulating railways

The 1830s were a decade of considerable experimentation on different railway and motive-power combinations. Railway boards, including the London & Birmingham, felt obliged to consider a range of proposals. If somebody got the ear of the board, Robert Stephenson would be asked to consider the ideas, however fanciful. In the midst of his preparations for letting the contracts in February 1834, he was called upon to report on 'the formation of railways by undulating planes'. This was in response to a request by Manchester share-holders and Drs Dalton and Lardner to lay an experimental length of 8–10 miles on this principle.[97]

The 'undulating' railway was to take advantage of momentum, acquired in the descent of an inclined plane, to overcome the resistance presented by ascending the next incline, to minimize the motion/traction force required,

95 Letter, Robert Stephenson to Richard Creed, 13 October 1843, **PRO**, RAIL 1008/90.
96 William Barlow, 'On the Construction of the Permanent Way of Railways', *Proc. ICE*, **IX**, 1849/50, p. 387. Also contribution by Joseph Locke, p. 406.
97 Op. cit. (n. 52). *MM*, **XX**, 1833/4, p. 367. Also Badnall papers, Salford University, mss 6.

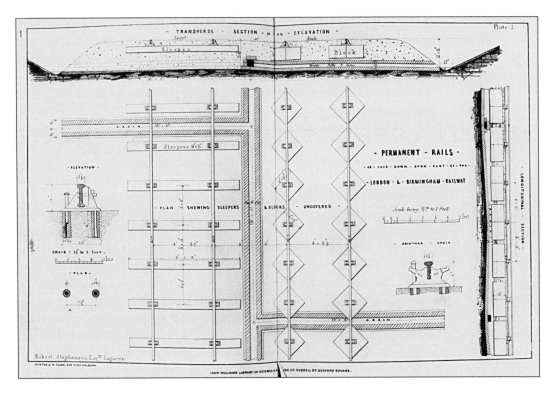

each such descent and ascent representing an undulation. One conclusion even suggested that it was faster to convey a carriage through an undulation than a horizontal plane.

Richard Badnall had initially proposed the advantages of such a system in 1832 when he drew up a patent. In 1833 experiments were carried out at the Adelaide Street Gallery of Practical Science, and on the Sutton incline of the Liverpool & Manchester Railway using the *Rocket* locomotive.[98] Stephenson's uncle, Robert Stephenson senior, among others, supported the idea, and even entered a partnership with Badnall to promote it. The merits of the system were discussed *in extenso* in the columns of *Mechanics Magazine*,[99] and, over two evenings at the Institution of Civil Engineers in 1834, John Farey drew up a version of Badnall's specification and 'compared it to perpetual motion'.[100]

The Liverpool & Manchester Railway's board had not been convinced of the benefits in 1833, and Stephenson was clearly frustrated at being asked to consider a departure from the agreed plans of construction: 'I need scarcely say that I have been so closely occupied that I found it impossible to reconsider carefully the opinions I had formed on the subject several months ago.'[101]

2.9 Plan, elevations and sections of the parallel rail track showing Stephenson's modified patent chairs (S. C. Brees, 1837)

98   Bailey and Glithero, p. 35.

99   *MM*, **XVIII–XXIII**, *passim*.

100 'On undulating railways', Minutes of Conversations, 28 January and 24 February 1834, **ICE**. Also Badnall papers, op. cit. (n. 97).

101 Op. cit. (n. 52), 5 May 1834, pp. 28–36; the report is reprinted in *MM*, **XXII**, pp. 388–92.

His May 1834 report considered the principles of undulating and horizontal railways, revealing his understanding of dynamic theory, and concluded 'that theoretically there is neither advantage nor disadvantage in the use of an undulated surface for a line of railway'. While accepting the probable capital savings of avoiding expensive earthworks to minimize gradients on a horizontal line, he enunciated a number of practical problems, namely the increased wear and tear on rolling stock induced by the great variations in velocity on an undulating line, the problems of designing the steam engine and boiler for optimum speed and efficiency, the effects of inflexible gradients on stopping places/stations, and the greater risk of accidents.

His greatest objection was the cost and waste of effort. Although the proponents had suggested an experiment would cost only £500, Stephenson estimated £800–£1000 a mile, for an experimental length built to appropriate gradients. He was persuaded by the 'considerable saving in the first cost of construction,' but, rather than an ill-conceived experiment on the London & Birmingham Railway 'I consider a trial upon some branch road may be made with advantage'. He concluded: 'I must, however, again repeat that no saving of power would be by any possibility effected.' His views were accepted and no experimental work was carried out on the Birmingham line.

While developments in locomotive design and railway construction soon consigned the discussion of 'undulating railways' to the history books, the notion of taking advantage of inclines and declines in the gradient to minimize traction effort and maximize acceleration was later a key aspect of Benjamin Baker's influential series of articles on 'Urban Railways'.[102] It was adopted for the design of London's Central Line tube route and Glasgow's underground system, where stations were built at the tops of inclines to aid braking on approach and acceleration on departure. As Stephenson had pointed out, however, any relocation of a station militates against flexibility.

Expenditure and cost control

In the wake of the extraordinary building effort (see Chapter 8), the cost of the London & Birmingham Railway, at £5.5 million, was twice that of the parliamentary estimates.[103] Robert Stephenson was criticized in the press for extravagance and the inaccuracy of his estimates, but the view of his contemporaries was generally one of respect for his achievement.[104]

Initial estimates, revised estimates and final costs were almost all grossly exceeded, but those within Stephenson's direct control, particularly the civil engineering work, were not disproportionately costly. The contractors' tenders came in within his estimates, and most other leading engineers

102 'Urban railways', *Engineering*, 1874. Benjamin Baker's copy, **ICE**, ML55a.
103 Various levels of expenditure have been quoted, for example Brees (1847) and Lecount (1839b).
104 'Engineers and their experience', *RM*, 1840, pp. 381–2.

broadly concurred with his figures. The initial idea was to let the London and Birmingham section contracts first, the early conclusion of which would bring in income, followed by those anticipated to take the longest. The delays in preparing the drawings and specifications, and the frailty of some contractors, exposed problems with this approach and put the construction timetable under pressure. The prospects of early revenue were thereby diminished.

As early as September 1835 Stephenson was under pressure to improve progress, and he made suggestions for speeding up work at Primrose Hill.[105] The crisis of confidence in his ability to contain the costs of construction reached its peak with the difficulties encountered over Kilsby tunnel. Captain Moorsom conferred with Stephenson, and was impressed enough to persuade the Board that it was not necessary to call on the services of another engineer.[106]

Following Stephenson's report on progress on the southern section in January 1836, there was concern about running out of finance and about contract targets not being met, and a special committee of directors was set up to inspect the works and report on the state of progress.[107] A further inspection was crushing in its condemnation of one contractor, and made it clear that, as things were, there was no prospect of opening the line on time.[108]

Stephenson came under increasing pressure to improve the position. By the end of 1836, the board's finance committee realized that the estimates would have to be revised, and reported accordingly to the shareholders. The problems were those posed by the difficult ground conditions on the Primrose Hill, Kilsby and Blisworth contracts, the increase in the volume of earthworks caused by modifications to the design slopes, all within Stephenson's sphere, together with unexpectedly high land prices and rising iron prices, and additional costs of stations. The prices of both land and iron, while attributable in part to the demand from the railway, were beyond its control. The increased costs of stations were attributed to the improving prospects for traffic, in part due to further connecting lines; this also led to the purchase of more locomotives and rolling stock. Stephenson had earlier made more realistic estimates regarding the stations.[109]

Directors' visits continued[110] and in April 1837 it was decided to assign individual directors to monitor each unfinished contract.[111] This could have undermined Stephenson's authority, although it may actually have enhanced it, as his engineering judgement, exposed to the utmost scrutiny, was being vindicated.

105 Board Minutes, op. cit. (n. 17), p. 392.
106 Jeaffreson, I, pp. 203–4. The story does not match with the railway's minutes.
107 Report of 26 January 1836, op. cit. (n. 17), 27 January 1836.
108 Op. cit. (n. 17), pp. 558–62, and Board Minutes, op. cit. (n. 69), p. 208, 1 February 1836, and p. 115, 26 May 1836.
109 Board Minutes, op. cit. (n. 17), pp. 392, 509, 558 & 562. Also report dated 26 January 1836, in Board Minutes, ibid., 27 January 1836. Also Board Minutes, op. cit. (n. 69) , 1 February 1836, p. 208, 26 May 1836, p. 115, 1-2 September, pp. 205–9, and 9 September 1836, pp. 212–16.
110 Board Minutes, op. cit. (n. 69), 30 September 1836 and 16–17 March 1837.
111 Minutes of the Board of the London & Birmingham Railway, 12 April 1837, **PRO**, RAIL 384/34.

2.10 Silver soup tureen presented to Stephenson as 'A tribute of respect and Esteem from the Members of the Engineering Department' (Courtesy of Birmingham Assay Office)

There were also concerns about him devoting too much time to other lines, particularly the London & Brighton (see Chapter 3).[112] He had promised a delayed opening at the end of 1836, but poor weather conditions caused him to withdraw all forecasts in December 1836.[113] In the end the effort involved was enormous, with regular night work endorsed by the directors in the pursuit of an opening of the railway.[114] The additional costs were met by additional borrowing and calls on shares permitted by supplementary Acts of Parliament.

The civil engineering industry has always had an unenviable reputation for cost overruns on major projects. These have typically occurred on prototype projects such as the Thames Tunnel, the Manchester Ship Canal and the more recent Channel Tunnel, particularly where ground problems have been experienced. The London & Birmingham shared many characteristics with these projects.

Conclusions

The successful completion of the London & Birmingham Railway in June 1838 consolidated Robert Stephenson's reputation among his contemporaries as the leading civil engineer of his generation. Although he could be criticized for his route selection requiring the Kilsby tunnel, close to an alignment that had already caused problems for canal builders, and for his initial recommendations regarding permanent way, the scale of his achievement was remarkable.

112 Board Minutes, op. cit. (n. 69), 18 February 1836, and 8 March 1837. Stephenson's attention was also directed towards the North Midland Railway and other lines (Chapter 3).
113 Board Minutes, op. cit. (n. 69), 7 December 1836.
114 Op cit. (n. 111), 9 August 1837.

Comparison between the London & Birmingham experience and other major projects of the time reveal where Stephenson may have been culpable. Although project cost and time both overran, much of this stemmed from changes to the original brief to accommodate more traffic. Although not evident from most other engineers' evidence, it is arguable that he should have recommended gentler slopes for the cuttings and embankments in his original estimates, and thus anticipated additional costs. Certainly past experience could have been used to justify this approach, but many engineers supported his recommendations, and it is noteworthy that many of the specifications had been altered before construction began, suggesting a flexible approach to engineering decisions.

2.11 Curzon Street station, Birmingham, shortly after the opening of the railway (J. C. Bourne, 1839)

Whilst it would seem that Stephenson's selection of contractors was poor, it was probably felt that they had been treated fairly, and that their tenders offered a prospect of profit. Stephenson's work and project control were generally exemplary, and it was the complexity of the project that determined the resources required.

Stephenson gained considerable respect from the building of the London & Birmingham line. Anticipating its conclusion, his engineering staff held a celebratory dinner in his honour at the *Dun Cow* tavern, Dunchurch, on 23 December 1837.[115] They presented their 'chief' with an elaborate silver soup tureen (Fig. 2.10). The *Railway Times* reported:[116]

115 *CEAJ*, **I**, 23 December 1837. Also Jeaffreson, I, pp. 211–12.
116 *RT*, 30 December 1837.

I think I never saw on any occasion a more fixed determination in the faces of all present to be completely happy … It would have done any man good to have heard the deafening applause which followed when the healths of the father and son [George and Robert Stephenson] were drunk; everyone felt they came warm from the heart and spoke of feelings that could not be uttered.

Although Stephenson may not have been universally admired, a further celebratory dinner organized for him by both civil engineering and material contractors at the Albion Hotel, London, in November 1839 was indicative of a man respected by all who worked with him.[117] He could have been in no stronger position to continue his career at the top of his profession. Stephenson continued to work as a consulting engineer for the London & Birmingham Railway and its London & North Western Railway successor until his death (see Chapters 3 to 5).

117 Broadsheet, Starbuck collection, **ICE**.

3

Chamber consultations

Michael Bailey

That he be in future allowed to act … as a Consulting Engineer in cases submitted to his opinion, provided such business be strictly confined to Chamber consultations …
London & Birmingham Railway Board, about Robert Stephenson, November 1835

By the beginning of 1839, when Robert Stephenson relinquished his position as engineer-in-chief of the London & Birmingham Railway, he had already gained a national reputation as a leading consulting engineer. This had been earned through a number of high-profile railway schemes with which he had become deeply involved, even whilst supervising the building of the Birmingham railway.

That he could become so involved in projects, quite unrelated to his London & Birmingham duties, was remarkable and prompts enquiry as to how he was able to establish his separate consulting activity, whilst fulfilling this main and ostensibly full-time role. The establishment of his consulting practice was dependent upon competent associates and confidence in delegation and good communication, as well as requisite engineering skills. Assessing this competence therefore includes an appreciation of the reliability, skill and tact of George Parker Bidder, Stephenson's senior associate and close confidant.

The breadth of Stephenson's client portfolio by the end of the decade suggested that he was pursuing a wider and more ambitious agenda towards becoming a leading authority on railway development, an aspiration that he clearly shared with his father. Indeed, the pioneering involvement of the two Stephensons since the 1820s had resulted in their expectation of a continuing and dominant role in the industry's growth, even though route multiplication would bring greater demands on organization and delegation.

Stephenson's developing role as a consulting engineer was dependent upon a growing circle of contacts in the business community, particularly in London and Liverpool. The respect that he had gained through his tenacious pursuit of the London & Birmingham scheme through Parliament would inevitably draw him to the attention of the wider business community. His increasing knowledge of railway building, together with a growing confidence and expertise in handling parliamentary procedures and enquiries, would clearly promote approaches for his representation of new schemes, particularly where contentious issues arose. None would be more contentious than the London to Brighton route, which presaged the events of the railway 'mania' a decade later.

3.1 George
Richmond
portrait of
Stephenson
(Courtesy of
Institution of
Mechanical
Engineers)

Stephenson's ambitions would, not least, be critically judged by his professional contemporaries. His membership of the Institution of Civil Engineers from 1830 was important to him in providing the venue to meet and exchange views with them. That he was acknowledged as one of the country's leading engineers by the end of the decade meant that he had earned their respect as a competent and innovative engineer. Earning this respect would, inevitably, attract both the admiration of other like-minded engineers of his new generation, such as Isambard K. Brunel (1806–1859), and the jealousy of others, such as Sir John Rennie (1794–1874), who had similar aspirations for a major involvement in railway projects.

Stephenson's success in achieving such a prominent role in railway affairs, which may be attributed to his extraordinarily heavy work programme, as well as his engineering and diplomatic skills, brought him significant financial reward. At the end of the decade, however, he suffered the indignity of near-bankruptcy arising from a naive misunderstanding of the consequences of a financial holding in the first of his client companies, the Stanhope & Tyne Railroad. His able handling of this personal and professional crisis would anticipate well the demands on him during the 'mania' years of the 1840s.

Initial consulting work

By the early 1830s, Robert Stephenson had gained experience in preparing parliamentary plans, sections and estimates, and in supervising the building of short rail routes, with responsibilities for contract negotiations and monitoring, and the delegation of supervisory work to resident engineers. As the railway network

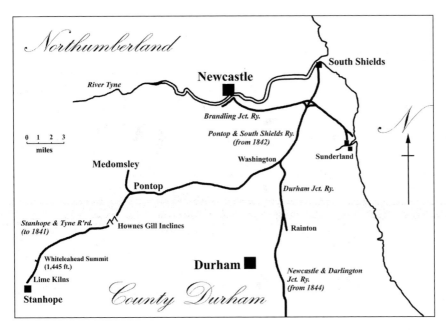

3.2 Stanhope & Tyne Railroad and the subsequent Pontop & South Shields Railway forming part of the through route to Newcastle

expanded, this experience would be called upon to advise new groups of proprietors on the most cost-effective way of pursuing their railway ambitions, including broad route and design considerations and parliamentary submissions. The demands on his time, however, would mean that detailed design and the supervision of the building work would have to be delegated to his associates.

Stephenson accepted his first assignment in September 1832, whilst still engaged on the intensive surveys and programme of parliamentary work for the London & Birmingham Railway. He informed his father:[1]

… I want to talk to you on several subjects particularly the Stanhope and Tyne Railway for which they have appointed me the Consulting Engineer at £300 per annum – There are several stationary Engines to be erected and there is one I want to have your opinion upon as the application of an Engine in the manner I propose is entirely new and I want you to see the situation –

In contrast to the London & Birmingham trunk route, the 37¾-mile Stanhope & Tyne line (including branches) was a mineral railway to convey limestone from Stanhope, and coal from the Pontop and Medomsley coalfields of County Durham, to the river Tyne for shipment. The Stanhope & Tyne Railroad Company had been formed by a group of north-east coal-owners and industrialists, led by the brothers William and John Harrison.[2] William Harrison's son, Thomas, who had been assisting Stephenson with the London & Birmingham survey, was appointed as engineer. It is likely that William Harrison approached Stephenson for assistance, because of his 24-year-old son's relative inexperience and good working relationship with him.

1   Letter, Robert Stephenson to George Stephenson, Tynemouth, 24 September 1832, **Stephenson**, Folder 18.
2   Tomlinson, pp. 212–3.

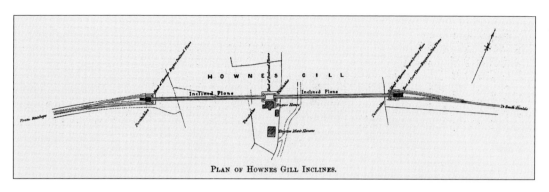

PLAN OF HOWNES GILL INCLINES.

3.3 Plan of the Hownes Gill inclines (W. W. Tomlinson, 1914)

Its route from the Stanhope limekilns, 800 feet above sea level, to the summit level of Whiteleahead (over 1400 feet), and down to the river Tyne at South Shields (Fig. 3.2), had severe gradients that required the steam (and self-acting) winding apparatus referred to by Stephenson in the letter to his father. The 'entirely new' arrangement was that for Hownes Gill, the 800-foot wide, 160-foot deep dry ravine to the west of Consett. It had been intended to carry the line over the gill by bridge, but Stephenson clearly felt that he and Harrison had insufficient experience for such a venture, the height of which would have been 2½ times that of the Sankey Viaduct on the Liverpool & Manchester line.

He arranged the installation of rail-mounted inclined planes (at gradients of 1 in 2½ and 1 in 3) traversed by platform trucks, from the tops of the west and east rims to the bottom of the gill (Fig. 3.3). The mineral wagons were each turned through 90° on turntables, and secured on the incline trucks. A 20-horsepower steam engine at the bottom of the gill wound the trucks up and down the inclines simultaneously, the weight of the descending loads assisting the engine. The wagons were exchanged at the foot of the inclines, by turntables and parallel tracks. It was claimed that twelve movements per hour could be maintained using the inclined planes.[3]

With Stephenson's encouragement and advice, Thomas Harrison undertook much of the design and installation work, including three large ship-loading coal drops at South Shields.[4] He no doubt communicated frequently with Stephenson as the line progressed, but the latter's time was limited as he oversaw the completion of the Leicester & Swannington Railway and attended to the second London & Birmingham Railway Bill, followed by the building of that line. Harrison completed the building of the Stanhope & Tyne line in September 1834, the achievement earning him considerable respect in the north-east, not least from Stephenson himself, with whom he was to enjoy a long association.

Stephenson's growing reputation extended into Europe, and in 1833 the directors of the newly formed Nürnberg [Nuremberg] and Fürth Railway in Bavaria approached him for assistance. He did not proceed with this assignment however, 'in consequence of his commands, which (although they would have been considered reasonable in England) owing to the great difference in the value of money in the two countries, seemed to the directors too high.'[5]

3 Ibid., pp. 212–18 and 241 8.
4 T. E. Harrison, 'Account of the Drops at South Shields', *Proc. ICE*, **I**, 1838, p. 11, and **II**, 1839, p. 9.
5 'Sketches of German Railways, No. III – Nuremburg and Furth line', *RC*, 11 October 1845.

Such approaches from aspiring railway groups, and the assistance that Stephenson gave to his father on other railway projects, concerned the directors of the London & Birmingham Railway, and, on his appointment as engineer-in-chief in September 1833, they required that 'his time and services should be devoted exclusively to the company'.[6] Although he applied himself so fully to supervising the building of the Birmingham line, he nevertheless interpreted this instruction loosely, and apparently felt entitled to pursue the interests of existing clients and to develop an involvement with new clients.

Stephenson also developed a good rapport with several of his contemporaries, early gaining their acknowledgement and respect. He first corresponded with Brunel in March 1834, a year after the latter's appointment as engineer of the Great Western Railway.[7] The two engineers, both with leadership and problem-solving abilities, in addition to their engineering expertise and propensity for hard work, were close colleagues throughout their careers. Their surviving correspondence confirms that, although they did not always agree on several significant issues, they were respectful of each other's talents and often consulted each other to obtain second opinions on a whole range of different issues.

George Stephenson gave evidence to the House of Commons Committee considering the Great Western Railway's first bill in 1834. Although the bill failed, Brunel developed his initial contacts with both Stephensons, who assisted him by giving evidence to the House of Lords Committee in July 1835. In spite of the limitations on his time away from the Birmingham line, Robert Stephenson gave evidence to the Committee over two days that month and argued in favour of Brunel's alignment.[8]

The London & Brighton project

The project that had the biggest call on Stephenson's extra-mural time during the building of the London & Birmingham line was the London and Brighton route. Three rail schemes incorporating a Brighton route had been proposed before 1831, but had all foundered.[9] Stephenson's association with the route began in 1831–1832, when George Stephenson & Son were retained to investigate a route through the North and South Downs. Although the scheme did not proceed, he gained a broad understanding of the route options.[10]

In 1833 a new group of proprietors pursued a London to Brighton scheme, for which a route was surveyed, under the direction of Sir John Rennie, by

6 Board Minutes, London & Birmingham Railway 1833–1837, 19 September 1833, **PRO**, RAIL 384/2, p. 17.
7 Letter, Robert Stephenson to I. K. Brunel, Kilburn Office, London, 15 March 1834, **Brunel**, DM 1306/1.
8 Robert Stephenson's evidence, House of Lords Select Committee enquiry, Great Western Railway Bill, 1835, Volume of Evidence L1, for Bill Code 14234. Act passed 31 August 1835 (5 & 6 Will. IV, c. 107).
9 Marshall (1936), pp. 255–6.
10 Robert Stephenson's evidence, House of Commons Select Committee on the Brighton lines, 16 March 1836. RM, NS **1**, June 1836, p. 144.

Francis Giles (c.1787–1847), who had just been removed as engineer of the Newcastle & Carlisle Railway because 'his errors seem to have arisen chiefly from the want of his personal presence in the North'.[11] Stephenson was consulted by Parliament on the Rennie/Giles plans, but this scheme was also abandoned.[12]

In 1834 two groups of investors pursued alternative schemes for the route. One group engaged Charles Vignoles (1793–1875), then engineer to the Dublin & Kingstown Railway; the other engaged Nicholas Cundy (1778–c.1837), who had come to notice through his survey of a ship canal route between London and Portsmouth. In December 1834, Stephenson's opinion was again requested by Parliament regarding the merits of the two routes. In strict interpretation of the terms of his engagement with the London & Birmingham Railway, he should have declined the invitation, but his accumulated knowledge of the route and his growing experience made him an important independent consultant. He agreed to undertake the review only after obtaining a ten-day leave of absence from the London & Birmingham directors. Although this was primarily to visit Newcastle concerning Robert Stephenson & Co, he also used the time to consider the London & Brighton scheme.[13]

Vignoles followed the shorter route, which required significant engineering works to cross the North and South Downs. Cundy's route, which passed by Dorking and followed the valleys of the rivers Mole and Adur, was nearly nine miles longer but required much less engineering work. The two groups of proprietors referred to these lines in their respective prospectuses as 'The Direct London and Brighton Railway' and 'The Dorking Line'.

Stephenson's report was issued in January 1835.[14] He considered that the Dorking route was preferable, but that Cundy's survey was 'perfectly erroneous' and could not be relied upon. Following the report, both groups of proprietors withdrew their schemes from Parliament, which led to 'a good deal of communication' between Stephenson and other engineers, and between the rival proprietors.[15]

Later in 1835, Stephenson was 'applied to' by another group of proprietors to become the engineer for their scheme adopting the route which he believed would be most appropriate for the railway. He was keen to follow up this approach, but was in a dilemma because of his commitments on the London & Birmingham line. No consideration seems to have been given to George Stephenson undertaking this work, presumably because of his heavy commitments elsewhere. He wrote that 'the Brighton Railway is carried on under Robert's guidance, he cannot attend to it more than examining the particulars laid before him'.[16]

11 Board Minutes, Newcastle & Carlisle Railway, 11 May 1833, **PRO**, RAIL 509/4.
12 Op. cit. (n. 10).
13 London Committee Minutes, London & Birmingham Railway, 1834–1835, Minute 306, 17 December 1834, **PRO**, RAIL 384/40, and Birmingham Committee, Minute 252, 16 December 1834, **PRO**, RAIL 384/66.
14 Published pamphlet, *The Direct London and Brighton Railway, … Reply to the Statement of Mr. Stevenson's* [sic] *Committee, in answer to their Prospectus*, n.d. but 1836, **ICE**, 625.1 (422.5), Tract 8.
15 Evidence, op. cit. (n. 10).
16 Letter, George Stephenson to Michael Longridge, Alton Grange, 5 June 1835, **IMechE**, IMS 131/6.

Robert Stephenson discussed his dilemma with the London & Birmingham directors, who, worried at the prospect of losing his services, raised his salary to a massive £2000 per annum and relaxed their exclusivity restriction:[17]

That he be in future allowed to act (with permission of the respective Committees in each case) as a Consulting Engineer in cases submitted to his opinion, provided such business be strictly confined to Chamber consultations, and in no instance demand his attention in the field;

Even before this motion had been passed, Stephenson began to make arrangements for a survey of his proposed Brighton route. He needed a diligent associate upon whom he could rely to supervise a survey and take levels and trial borings accurately, as he knew that parliamentary scrutiny would be intense. To undertake this task he was most fortunate in being able to recruit George Bidder, then an assistant engineer on the London & Birmingham line. Bidder's capability for independent initiative and high achievement quickly endeared him to Stephenson.[18] Bidder recorded in his diary in March 1835:[19]

Completing a copy of Mr. Stephensons reports on the London and Brighton Railway by Gibbs – Conversing with him on the subject of my quitting the London & Birmingham Railway to take in hand under him at a salary of one & a half guineas per diem the London and Brighton Railway and also the superintendence of his private business
   To receive all the profits if the produce falls short of £300 per annum

Bidder commenced his duties with Stephenson later that month, and was appointed by the London and Brighton Committee to begin the survey work in May 1835.[20] Stephenson had selected a route branching from the London & Southampton Railway near Wimbledon, by which means the Brighton traffic would have shared the Nine Elms terminus in south-west London. Joseph Locke, then engineer to the Southampton Company, clearly aided the planning for this option. From Wimbledon Common, the route followed the valleys of the rivers Mole and Adur to Hove, before dividing to serve two termini, to the north and west of Brighton town centre (Fig. 3.4). It thus generally followed the earlier 'Dorking' route proposed by Cundy, who claimed that Stephenson had 'pirated' it. Cundy's survey had been so discredited, however, that his protests were not taken seriously.[21]

With interest in railways spurred into another 'mini-mania' by the profits of early rail companies, the rival groups of proprietors anticipated the 1836 parliamentary session with a scramble for ascendancy, each employing engineers whom they hoped would argue the merits of their respective routes. To distinguish between the schemes, they were each identified by the name of their respective engineer. Thus, from 1836, Stephenson's name was thrust into prominent public debate, which may have caused him some

17 Op. cit. (n. 6), Minute 188, 6 November 1835, p. 122.
18 Clark (1983), *passim.*
19 Diary of George Bidder, 11 March 1835, **ScM**, GPB 1/1/6.
20 Ibid., 15 May 1835.
21 Jeaffreson, I, pp. 222–3.

3.4 London
to Brighton
rail schemes
1835–1837

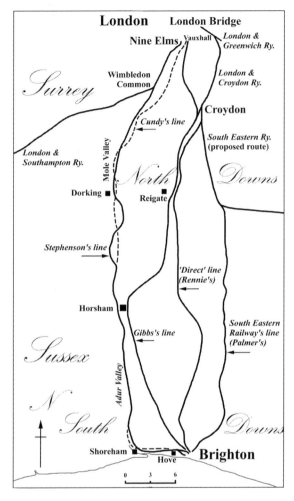

embarrassment with the London & Birmingham directors. John Herapath
wrote in April 1836:[22]

Probably no subject has so much occupied the attention of the rail-road public of late as
the rival lines to Brighton. Not less than six were some time since in the field at once –
one by Sir John Rennie, a second by Mr. Vignoles, a third by Mr. Cundy, a fourth by
Mr. Gibbs, a fifth by Mr. Stephenson, and a sixth by Mr. Palmer; to which might be
added the wild whims of some others that hardly arrived to a name before they died.

The Vignoles and Palmer projects (the latter on behalf of the South Eastern
Railway) were soon withdrawn, and the reference to Cundy's route harked
back to the earlier scheme which 'through sheer mismanagement, got hid
under a cloud'.[23] The more serious contender for the route was the group
acting in the interests of the London & Croydon Railway, represented by its
engineer, Joseph Gibbs (1798–1864). Its scheme was to extend the Croydon

22 *RM*, NS **I**, April 1836, p. 68.
23 Ibid.

line to Brighton and thus direct the Brighton traffic over its route and, via the London & Greenwich Railway, into London Bridge station.

With such large sums of money at stake, the Gibbs route proprietors made public an apparent contradiction in Stephenson's approach to the gradients of his route in comparison with theirs, and dredged up his House of Lords evidence concerning the previous year's Great Western Bill to support its assertions.[24] The Gibbs scheme was, however, not considered by Parliament 'owing to some irregularity or neglect'.[25] This prompted an early move by the 'Direct' line proprietors to re-recruit Sir John Rennie, and adopt an alternative route extending the Croydon line to Brighton.

Rennie was a prominent member of the engineering community who had regarded George and Robert Stephenson with some scepticism since the former's rapid rise to prominence in the 1820s. Having acted as joint Consulting Engineer, with his elder brother George (1791–1866), to the Liverpool & Manchester Railway in its parliamentary preparations in 1826, the Rennies declined the invitation to share responsibility for building the line with other engineers, notably including George Stephenson.[26] Whilst the Stephensons had become prominent in railway building, the Rennies' career had progressed in other branches of engineering. It is likely that Robert Stephenson regarded them as being amongst his 'enemies' to which he had referred on occasion.[27] Against this background, therefore, Stephenson found himself drawn in to an extraordinary series of exchanges between the two remaining groups of proprietors.

The 'Direct' line group prepared a prospectus for circulation amongst Members of Parliament, which brought a sharp riposte from the 'Stephenson' group:[28]

… Sir John Rennie has considered himself at liberty, even before any proceedings were commenced in Parliament, to deliver his Prospectus to Members of the House of Commons at the door and in the lobby of the House, containing comparisons between his line of Railway and that recommended by Messrs. Stephenson, resting on fallacious assertions, the Committee feel it to be done to the Public and to their Subscribers to circulate the following plain statement of facts …

A printed response set the tone of a vigorous campaign between the two groups in the 1836 parliamentary session.[29] In spite of intense efforts by the 'Direct' line sponsors, their line was rejected in June at the report stage in the House of Commons, whilst Stephenson's line was passed to the House of Lords.[30] This prompted a large number of petitions to that House by opponents

---

24 Pamphlet, *Remarks on Two Proposed Lines of Railway to Brighton*, n.d. but 1836, **ICE**, 625.1/2 Tract 26a.
25 Op. cit. (n. 22).
26 Board Minutes, Liverpool & Manchester Railway 1823–1830, 17 June 1826, **PRO**, RAIL 371/1.
27 For example: 'Means might have been taken to avoid the unpleasant triumph which our enemies will have', letter Robert Stephenson to George Stephenson, London, 15 November 1832, **Stephenson**, Folder 18.
28 Pamphlet, *London and Brighton Railway (The Line Surveyed by Messrs. Stephenson)*, n.d. but 1836, **ICE**, 625.1/2, Tract 18a.
29 Op. cit. (n. 14).
30 'Parliamentary Proceedings on Railways', *RM*, NS **I**, August 1836, p. 243.

and supporters of Stephenson's line, particularly regarding his choice of twin routes and termini in Brighton. The opponents petitioned more vigorously, however, and the bill was thrown out at the Committee stage. Thus, after no less than 80 days of parliamentary time, and considerable cost, Brighton still had no prospect of a rail link to London.[31]

After this time and financial waste, it might have been expected that the rival groups of proprietors would have sunk their differences and amalgamated to pursue a unified application to Parliament. Such were the reported profits of early rail schemes, however, that each group of entrepreneurs increased its resolve to succeed over its rivals. The 1837 Session saw five competing schemes bidding for the London to Brighton line, including the 'Stephenson' line proprietors.

To strengthen their case, and minimize any deleterious effect on the London & Birmingham project, Stephenson and his father became Joint Consulting Engineers, and appointed Bidder as 'Acting Engineer'.[32] They went to some lengths to ascertain what termini would be acceptable to the Brighton citizens. Alternative proposals were included in the new bill in the expectation that one or other would be acceptable, whilst the remainder of the route remained virtually the same as that previously submitted (Fig. 3.5). Stephenson communicated his approach in a letter circulated to committee members by the company's Secretary, Richard Till.[33] Till also noted with this communication that nine new Committee members had been appointed, including the Lord Mayor of London.

The most competitive group of proprietors was that pursuing the 'Direct' line from Croydon ('Rennie's Line'), whilst other groups pursued the earlier route extension from Croydon ('Gibbs's Line'), and Cundy's original 'Dorking' route, now represented by James Mills (fl. 1770–1842) who had been critical of George Stephenson's organization of the Liverpool & Manchester works.[34] The South Eastern Railway proposed a fifth scheme of its own, also starting at Croydon. It was estimated that the combined expense of these petitions was nearly £1000 per day.[35]

With three of the five groups arguing vigorously for an extension of the London & Croydon line, and in contrast to its views in the previous Session, the House of Commons Committee decided in April 1837 that Stephenson's route was 'circuitous and unfit for a direct railway communication to Brighton'.[36] There followed an extraordinary series of tactical manoeuvres in Parliament by Richard Till and his fellow proprietors in an effort to reverse the Committee's views.

31 'The Brighton Railways', *RM*, NS **I**, September 1836, p. 262.

32 Amplification on *Plan of a Proposed Railway.... To form a Communication Between London and Brighton*, 1836, **ICE**, 351.812 (422.3).

33 Letter, Robert Stephenson to the Directors of the Brighton Railway Company, London, 10 November 1836, printed and circulated to the proprietors by Richard Till, Secretary, Cornhill [London], 14 November 1836, **ICE**, 625.1/2, Tract 100a.

34 **ICE**, Telford Papers, T/LM 13.

35 *RM*, NS **II**, April 1837, p. 272.

36 *RM*, NS **II**, May 1837, p. 329.

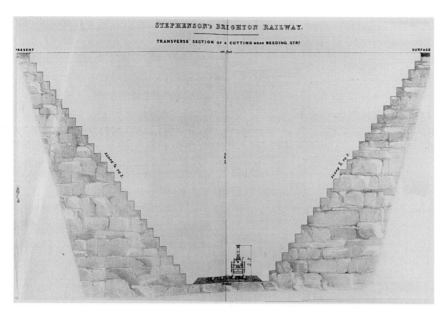

3.5 Cross-section of proposed cutting near Beeding Street, Shoreham, on Stephenson's London–Brighton line, showing angle of slopes (Starbuck collection, Courtesy of Institution of Civil Engineers)

At the end of May, the House of Commons was persuaded to refer the issue 'to some Military Engineer' to arbitrate on four of the five routes (excluding Mills' route) 'in an engineering point of view'.[37] Captain Robert Alderson, of the Royal Engineers, spent the month of June considering the merits of each route. In his report to the House he had 'no hesitation in stating, that the line proposed by Mr. Stephenson, considered in an engineering point of view alone, is preferable to either of the others'. However, because of its length and choice of termini in both London and Brighton, which were both regarded as being too distant from the town centres, Alderson concluded: 'I, therefore, adhere to the opinion already given in favour of the Direct line.'[38]

The 'Direct' line Bill made a swift passage through its remaining stages in Parliament and the Act was passed in July 1837.[39] The parliamentary contest was estimated to have cost the proprietors collectively £193 575.[40] Stephenson's involvement might have ended there, but the Act included provision for amalgamating the interests of the five groups of proprietors, with seven of the 20 directors being provided by the 'Stephenson' line proprietors. Before they invested in the 'Direct' line, however, Till wrote to Stephenson to seek his views on Alderson's report, and whether he had altered his opinion of the 'Direct' line.[41]

37 Exchange of correspondence between J. Russell (for House of Commons) and the Master General of the Board of Ordnance, reproduced in Report by Robert Stephenson to the 'original Shareholders of Stephenson's Brighton Railway', 24 October 1837, **ICE**, 625.1/2, Tract 99a.

38 'Report of the Military Engineer on the Brighton Railways' to the House of Commons, *RM*, NS **III**, August 1837, pp. 102–8.

39 *1 Vic., c. 119.*

40 Whishaw (1840), p. 269.

41 Letter, Richard Till to Robert Stephenson, Cornhill [London], 27 July 1837, reprinted in *Report from Mr. Stephenson to the Directors of the Western London and Brighton Railway Company*, 1837, **ICE**, 625.1/2, Tract 101a.

With so much of his attention needing to be focused on supervising the completion of the London & Birmingham line, Stephenson might have responded with a short pragmatic reply. He chose, however, to dismiss many of Alderson's arguments, and revealed a tenacious adherence to the route to which he had put his name, concluding his seven-page report:[42]

… At a period when I might fairly be considered to be unembarrassed by prejudice: I have now carefully reconsidered that opinion, and I am more than ever convinced that the Western is the only Line which, with safety to the Subscribers, can be adopted.

Not content to let matters rest there, however, he followed up this report with another, more detailed and very critical assessment of Alderson's report, which reveals that he believed the rejection of his recommended route undermined his hard-won professional standing. The strength of the language in this second report, and the tenacious adherence to what he so strongly believed to be right, were reminiscent of his father's character:[43]

… I cannot help feeling that Captain Alderson, in his report, has on the whole, made the worst possible selection of a line, as far as concerns the interests of the Public and the Shareholders …

I have a right to complain when I find facts perverted, omitted, and distorted in a way which will be seen …

When I see that all the errors, omissions, and perversions of fact to which I have alluded are invariably in favour of the Direct and against the western Line, I feel myself called upon to bring them in this way under your notice, and, I trust, that in adopting this course it will be considered that I am doing nothing more than is due to my professional character.

In spite of the time Stephenson spent on the reports, which were then printed and circulated amongst the proprietors of the 'Western' line, the directors of the 'Direct' line proceeded rapidly to set out the route and prepare working plans and estimates for tendering. John Rastrick was engaged as the line's engineer and Sir John Rennie as consulting engineer. There was no alternative for Stephenson than to accept the loss of the Brighton line and proceed with his growing portfolio of other projects, not least the completion of the London & Birmingham Railway.

The consulting practice

Robert Stephenson's consultancy commenced in the spring of 1835 when George Bidder began to superintend his 'private business', although he had been involved with Stephenson's work from the end of 1834, alongside his London & Birmingham duties.[44] The practice was at first based at Stephenson's London & Birmingham office in St John's Wood. From this modest beginning developed the great practice that was to play such a prominent part in the engineering development of mid-Victorian Britain and several overseas countries. The practice

42   Robert Stephenson's Report, 15 August 1837, attached to Richard Till's letter, op. cit. (n. 41).
43   Stephenson's Report, 24 October 1837, op. cit. (n. 37).
44   Clark (1983), pp. 32–4.

absorbed the interests of George Stephenson & Son, the shift of emphasis from the older to the younger generation meeting with the father's full and proud approval. Indeed, George Stephenson himself played a big part in the affairs of the practice, his growing responsibilities being shared with both his son and Bidder.

As engineer of the biggest railway project of the day, and with his ability to deal with the several planning and regulatory issues that arose with railway development, Stephenson's reputation grew widely. He received applications for assistance from proprietors of several railways in Britain and Europe, only some of which accorded with his agreement with the London & Birmingham directors. In May 1835, he accompanied his father to Belgium in response to a request from King Leopold, who was anxious to establish a national railway network to draw together the fragmented regions of that new kingdom.[45] Although Stephenson assisted his father during this and subsequent visits, his other commitments severely limited his time to assist the Belgian scheme.

Also in 1835, the Stephensons were approached by a group of promoters seeking to provide an urban railway between the City of London and the West India Docks, and to the Thames at Brunswick Wharf, adjacent to the East India Docks. Bidder surveyed a route for this 'Commercial Railway'. He had become familiar with the area from his time as resident engineer, both for the Commercial Road granite tramway in 1830, and for the construction of the Brunswick Wharf itself four years later.[46] Stephenson gave evidence in support of the bill in the House of Commons in 1836,[47] but a more southerly route, surveyed by William Cubitt (1785–1861), prevailed, and the Commercial Railway Act was passed later that year.[48]

Stephenson's growing portfolio of consulting work soon made the continued use of his London & Birmingham office untenable, and from early 1836 the practice leased premises at no. 16 Duke Street in Westminster,[49] close to Brunel's recently acquired property at no. 18.

In addition to the London & Brighton scheme, Stephenson assisted his father with the heavy programme of preparatory work for the parliamentary submissions for the Manchester & Leeds, North Midland, York & North Midland and Birmingham & Derby Junction railways. In April Stephenson even appealed to Brunel for assistance because of the heavy programme: ' ... I should certainly have made a point of being with you on the North Midland – I trust however you will be able to devote yourself to us a little – it is really of the greatest importance – therefore for heavens sake do strain a point – '[50]

45 Jeaffreson, I, pp. 220–1.
46 Clark (1983), pp. 27–8.
47 Robert Stephenson's evidence to the House of Commons Select Committee on the London & Blackwall Commercial Railway, 1836, Bill Code No. 62, Volumes of Evidence C15–17, days 24 and 25.
48 6 & 7 Will. IV, c. 123.
49 Evidence from two letters, George Stephenson to Nicholas Wood, February 3 and 12 1836, **NRO**, 602/7 and 602/9. Smiles (1862), p. 343, claims that the address was no. 9 Duke Street.
50 Letter, Robert Stephenson to I. K. Brunel, Sheffield, 9 April 1836, **Brunel**, DM 1758.

There is, however, no evidence that Brunel ever worked with the Stephensons, his own heavy programme keeping him quite independent of their interests.

Stephenson had developed a confident manner when giving evidence to parliamentary committees, and his demonstrable authority in dealing with detailed issues led to his being consulted as an independent witness for several railway schemes in the busy 1836 session. He gave evidence on four Bills to House of Commons committees and three in the House of Lords.[51]

The 'mini-mania' of 1836 led directly to a surge in railway building that engaged much of the Stephensons' attention for the next few years. From that summer, Robert Stephenson had only limited time for consulting work, being preoccupied with the completion of the London & Birmingham and Aylesbury Railways. He was, however, also appointed joint chief engineer, with his father, of the North Midland Railway, at a combined salary, including expenses, of £2000 a year.[52] George Stephenson had also been appointed as chief engineer of the Manchester & Leeds, York & North Midland and Birmingham & Derby Junction railways. This was in addition to the Preston & Wyre Railway, Harbour & Dock Company, to which he had been appointed the previous year. The London to Brighton route would have been yet a further responsibility had the 'Stephenson line' promoters been successful.

In accordance with the terms of his engagement with the London & Birmingham directors, Robert Stephenson was obliged to limit his involvement with the North Midland line, between Derby and Leeds, to opinion-forming, design work and contract negotiations. This was communicated through correspondence with his father and the young resident engineer, Frederick Swanwick (1810–1885). Swanwick, who had been engaged as a pupil in 1829, was appointed to the North Midland line following his completion of the building of the Whitby & Pickering line.

As their consulting and railway building work continued to grow, the Stephensons and Bidder required a larger London office, and in February 1837 they moved from Duke Street to larger premises at 35½ Great George Street, closer to Parliament Square.[53] The extra accommodation was required for the planning, design and documentation associated with route plans, levels and estimates for parliamentary applications.

In 1837 Stephenson accepted his first overseas assignment when he was consulted by the proprietors of the proposed Düsseldorf and Elberfeld railway in the German state of Westphalia. He undertook the work in the Westminster office, using maps of alternative route alignments sent by the railway's chief engineer, Bauconducteur Pickel. His assistant, Bauinspecteur Eduart

51 House of Commons: Birmingham & Gloucester Railway (Bill 33), Festiniog Railway (Bill 49), Glasgow & Falkirk Railway (Bill 51), and the London & Blackwall Railway (Bill 62). House of Lords: Oxford & Great Western Union Railway (Bill 14226), Cheltenham & Great Western Union Railway (Bill 14257), and the London & Brighton Railway (Bill 14264).

52 Board Minutes, North Midland Railway 1836–1842, 16 July 1836, **PRO**, RAIL 530/2.

53 Lease document for 35½ Great George Street, Westminster, 20 February 1837, **IMechE**, IMS/181.

Wiebe, had studied railways in Belgium and England in 1834–1835, and may have met Stephenson at that time. The ten-mile route from Düsseldorf, on the banks of the river Rhine, was to rise 350 feet to Elberfeld, now known as Wuppertal.

Significant gradients and earthworks would be required, but Stephenson recommended a line that could be worked by locomotives with the exception of a 1½-mile incline of 1 in 30 near Hochdahl.[54] Trains, with locomotives attached, would be coupled to a continuous rope operated by twin trackside winding engines, developed from the Camden incline operation (Chapter 6). In August 1837 Stephenson showed Pickel examples of rope-operated railways in operation, and arranged with Thomas Harrison for him to see the Stanhope & Tyne winding engines at work.[55] Although Stephenson's recommended route was built, the use of a five-kilometre tail-rope was rejected in favour of simple endless rope haulage from the Hochdahl engine-house. After only six months, however, Wiebe introduced a modified self-acting incline, with a locomotive and train going down the incline assisting a locomotive and train coming up, connected by a rope wound round the Hochdahl drum.

By the beginning of 1838, with the first lengths of the London & Birmingham line opened, and work on Kilsby tunnel well in hand, George Stephenson called upon his son for assistance with his own heavy railway-building programme. His biggest project was the Manchester & Leeds Railway, with Thomas Gooch the resident engineer. Stephenson deputized for his father with design work and contract negotiations for the building of the London & Blackwall, York & North Midland and Birmingham & Derby Junction Railways. The resident engineer for the York & North Midland Railway, between Normanton (for Leeds) and York, was Thomas Cabry, re-called from the Canterbury & Whitstable Railway.[56] The resident engineer for the Birmingham & Derby Junction line was John Birkinshaw, released early from his work on the London & Birmingham line.[57]

Responsibility for the construction of the London & Blackwall Railway had passed to the Great George Street practice in 1838, following the Stephensons' and Bidder's report recommending continuous rope haulage rather than locomotive power (Chapter 6). The railway's Board confirmed the Stephensons' recommendation, that Bidder should be appointed as resident engineer for the building programme.

54 Robert Stephenson, 'Bericht an die Directoren Düsseldorf–Elberfelder Eisenbahn', contained in a printed prospectus, *Denkschrift über die Anlage einer Eisenbahn zwischen Düsseldorf und Elberfeld*, Düsseldorf, 1837. The author is grateful to Wolfgang Flügel of Düsseldorf for bringing this document to his attention.

55 Letter, Robert Stephenson to T. E. Harrison, Newcastle, 24 August 1837, letter in private ownership.

56 The first reference to Stephenson's involvement with the Y. & N.M. line is in: Board Minutes 1835–1840, 1 March 1838, **PRO**, RAIL 770/1, p. 186.

57 Board Minutes, Birmingham & Derby Junction Railway, 1836–1844, 1 August 1838, **PRO**, RAIL 36/1, pp. 16–18.

Also in 1838, Stephenson was briefly engaged as consulting engineer to the newly formed Manchester & Birmingham Railway Company, with George Buck appointed as engineer.[58] Stephenson was so committed to other projects, however, that he was unable to provide sufficient time to the company, whose Board 'had an interview with Mr. Buck on the subject of the engineering arrangements' and 'afterwards saw Mr. Stephenson on the same matter'.[59] Stephenson was reappointed joint engineer with Buck, but this was itself a short-term arrangement as Buck was most capable in designing and building the railway's structures, and Stephenson's services may not have been called upon.

Stephenson's involvement with the railway apparently ended in the autumn of 1838. At the General Meeting in September, the Chairman stated that 'Mr. Robert Stephenson was the Company's Engineer, assisted by Mr. Buck'.[60] However, three weeks later Buck officiated at a stone-laying ceremony at which it was reported that 'Geo. Watson Buck, Esq. The engineer of the Company, officiated on the occasion'.[61] Buck continued his independent career thereafter, but remained a close colleague of Stephenson until his death in 1854.[62]

Stephenson frequently corresponded with Isambard K. Brunel, the two engineers often exchanging advice.[63] Their only significant difference of opinion was Brunel's choice of longitudinal timber and transom track and the seven-foot track gauge, contrasting with Stephenson's stone block sleepers and standard gauge. Their dialogue on the 'broad' gauge began with Brunel's proposal in September 1835, the month after the passing of the Great Western Railway's Act. Provision had been made for a junction with the London & Birmingham line near the location of the later Willesden Junction. Although mixed-gauge tracks could have been laid through to Euston, Stephenson was against the proposal, and the London & Birmingham directors were, in any event, not prepared to lease land for a separate terminus under acceptable terms. Accordingly, the Great Western directors obtained further powers from Parliament to deviate their line to their own terminus at Bishops Road, Paddington.

In August 1838, following several discussions between Brunel and the Great Western directors about the broad gauge, the railway's chairman, Charles Saunders, sought the independent views of James Walker (1781–1862), then President of the Institution of Civil Engineers, Robert Stephenson and his former mentor, Nicholas Wood. They were asked to consider not only the track gauge and method of construction, but also a comparative assessment of locomotive economy over the two gauges.[64] Walker and Stephenson both declined

58 Board Minutes, Manchester & Birmingham Railway 1837–1840, 12 March 1838, **PRO**, RAIL 454/1.

59 Ibid., 26 March 1838.

60 Manchester & Birmingham Railway General Meeting, *RT*, **1**, p. 510, 8 September 1838, quoting *Midland Counties Herald*.

61 Manchester & Birmingham Railway, *RT*, **1**, 29 September 1838, p. 558, quoting *Manchester Guardian*.

62 Memoir to George Watson Buck, *Proc. ICE*, **XIV**, 1854/5, pp. 128–30.

63 For example, letter, Robert Stephenson to I. K. Brunel, Haverstock Hill [London], n.d. but probably 1837, with advice on rope-hauled railways, **Brunel**, unreferenced.

64 MacDermot, I (Pt. I), pp. 64–87.

the invitation, and Stephenson felt obliged to communicate with Brunel his reasons, which provides an insight into their mutual respect:[65]

Dear Brunel

I find it quite out of my power to form a report on your permanent road – I have written to Sandars [sic] declining to do so. As my opinions of the system remain unchanged, you will I am sure readily see how unpleasant my position would be, if I expressed myself in an unequivocal manner in my report; and to do otherwise would be making myself rediculous [sic] since my opinions are pretty generally known – To report my opinions fully therefore would do harm instead of good to the cause in which you are interested and this I am sincerely desirous of avoiding.

I have carefully considered over what I saw with you the other day in our trip to Maidenhead and I am compelled to say that my former views as to the increased width of the Rails as well as the plan of laying them remain unchanged – I would put all my views to paper, but I am so pressed for time, now that our general meeting and opening throughout [of the London & Birmingham Railway] is approaching so near – You are however I think pretty well aware of my reasons which renders such a step less necessary on my part.

Yours very Truly

Rob Stephenson

Wood spent four months on an intensive investigation of the two rail gauges before reporting to the Board.[66] He recalled that Stephenson had 'in the most handsome manner' placed at his disposal the results of experiments he had recently conducted on the London & Birmingham line, for comparison with similar trials on the broad-gauge tracks.

Expansion of the practice

On 1 January 1839, Robert Stephenson stood down from his 'full-time' role as engineer-in-chief of the London & Birmingham Railway.[67] His priorities thereafter were twofold; firstly to maintain a part-time role as head of engineering affairs for that railway, and secondly to develop the Westminster practice through a greater involvement in the other railway programmes that it had embarked upon.

Stephenson spent 'a portion of my time' on the London & Birmingham Railway's affairs,[68] occasionally visiting the Camden engineering office to supervise both the resolution of outstanding issues and the occasional remedial works that arose because of material slippages (see Chapter 8).[69] He also

---

65 Letter, Robert Stephenson to I. K. Brunel, no address, 5 August 1838, **Brunel**, DM 1306/16.

66 Report, Nicholas Wood, 'To the Directors of the Great Western Railway', Killingworth, 10 December 1838.

67 Letter, Robert Stephenson to Capt. Moorsom, for the London & Birmingham Railway, 12 December 1838, **PRO**, RAIL 1008/90.

68 Ibid.

69 For example, letter, Robert Stephenson to Richard Creed, for the London & Birmingham Railway, Westminster, 27 March 1840, **PRO**, RAIL 1008/90.

oversaw the completion of the Aylesbury Railway. Robert Dockray, one of his able assistants on the line, was appointed as the railway's engineer in 1840. Stephenson maintained a close involvement, as consulting engineer, with the railway and its successor, the London & North Western Railway, until his death.[70] Through his close ties with Dockray, Stephenson was kept closely informed about the line's condition, and offered detailed advice on further remedial work that was required.[71]

The growing volume of work for other railways saw Stephenson supervising the resident engineers and negotiating with contractors, both for line construction and provision of equipment. He was directly answerable to the respective boards of directors for these responsibilities, and he regularly attended board meetings in London, Derby and York.

He required assistance with this growing volume of work and engaged, on Bidder's introduction, a personal assistant, James Berkley (1819–1862), to accompany him around the country and draft the many reports to his clients. He ensured that Berkley learned from the many engineering practices he became involved with, which thus formed the basis of his pupillage. Berkley became a competent engineer and loyal associate of the practice.[72] Stephenson also required a diligent and diplomatic assistant to organize the affairs of the Great George Street office, and deal with enquiries and correspondence on behalf of himself, his father and George Bidder. For this duty he engaged Berkley's younger brother, George (1821–1893), who also proved to be an able assistant, and, with a particular aptitude for mechanics, one who was equally anxious to pursue an engineering career.[73]

The Stephenson practice was neither a firm of employees with a hierarchical structure, nor a partnership. It was more akin to barristers' chambers, with each 'fee-earning' engineer being individually engaged by clients for a per diem fee or salary. Robert Stephenson was the 'senior' engineer of the practice, as his father was far less frequently in London, whilst Bidder and the resident engineers around the country were associates of the practice who benefited from being part of the Stephenson 'team'. The costs of the office were no doubt shared amongst the fee-earners. George and Robert Stephenson charged for their services at 7 guineas a day, whilst Bidder's rate had risen to 3 guineas, and later still 5 guineas a day.[74]

The work of the Great George Street office developed to meet the requirements of route planning, petitions to Parliament, and the development of bridge and other structure designs to meet ever more demanding route requirements. Stephenson encouraged design initiatives by Bidder and the

---

70 Stephenson's appointment as consulting engineer was effective from 31 March 1839. Board Minutes, London & Birmingham Railway 1837–1839, 4 April 1839, **PRO**, RAIL 384/3.

71 For example, letter, Robert Stephenson to Richard Creed, for the London & Birmingham Railway, Westminster, 10 October 1843, **PRO**, RAIL 1008/90.

72 Memoir for James John Berkley, *Proc. ICE*, **XXII**, 1862/3, pp. 618–24.

73 Obituary for Sir George Berkley KCMG, *Proc. ICE*, **CXV**, 1893/4, pp. 382–5.

74 Clark (1983), p. 342. Smiles (1862), p. 343, states that George Stephenson had been persuaded by Robert Stephenson to reduce his per diem fee from 10 to 7 guineas.

resident engineers, and bridge and structural design development was thus coordinated through the practice, with the benefits being passed to each of the 'Stephenson' lines. Hence, calculations and designs for iron bridges (see Chapter 10) and masonry structures (see Chapter 11) were developed for increasing length, height and span requirements, with large numbers being employed on lines around the country.

Plans, levels and structure drawings were contracted out to experienced draughtsmen, particularly Charles Cheffins (1807–1860), whom Stephenson had previously employed on the London & Birmingham line, and who thereafter set up his own cartographical and drawing business.[75] Detailed designs for bridges and other structures were undertaken at the respective site offices under the supervision of the resident engineers, with copy drawings forwarded, if required, to Stephenson for his consideration and approval, prior to being included with pre-tender documentation.

At the beginning of 1839 Stephenson was approached by the promoters of a proposed railway between Florence, Pisa and Leghorn (Livorno) in the Italian Grand Duchy of Tuscany. He accepted the post of Chief Engineer and travelled there to inspect the 60-mile route during April 1839.[76] The promoters of the line submitted their proposal, including Stephenson's report, to the Imperial Government a few weeks later, but not until the spring of 1841 did they receive the requisite legislation to proceed with the building of the line, to be named 'Strada Ferrata Leopolda (Leopold Railroad)' after the Grand Duke.[77]

Also in 1839, Stephenson took over from his father responsibility for the completion of the Preston & Wyre Railway, between Preston and the new port of Fleetwood, for which the resident engineer was James Routh. The railway was eventually completed and opened in July 1840 (see Chapter 9).

The Birmingham & Derby Junction Railway was opened in August 1839, but Stephenson was retained as consulting engineer, acting 'conjointly' with John Birkinshaw.[78] In the same month, he was approached by the Board of the Northern & Eastern Railway to take over the building of its line from Stratford, east London, to Cambridge and beyond to the north.[79] The building had been under the direction of James Walker and Alfred Burges (1797–1886), but a disagreement had arisen, although the reasons were not recorded. Stephenson was appointed engineer-in-chief, but with such a heavy workload elsewhere, the railway agreed to appoint Bidder as his deputy to supervise the line's building.[80] He also retained the resident engineer, Michael Borthwick (1810–1856), who became another of Stephenson's associates, being engaged as resident engineer on railway and water projects in many parts of East Anglia and, subsequently, overseas.[81]

---

75 Memoirs for Charles Frederick Cheffins, *Proc. ICE*, **XXI**, 1861/2, pp. 578–80.
76 *RT*, **II**, 29 June 1839, p. 502.
77 *RT*, **IV**, 8 May 1841, p. 517.
78 Birmingham & Derby Junction Railway Directors' Report, 27 February 1840, in op. cit. (n. 57), p. 32.
79 Board Minutes, Northern & Eastern Railway, 1836-1840, 30 July 1839, **PRO**, RAIL 541/3.
80 Ibid., 13 August 1839.
81 Memoir of Michael Andrews Borthwick, *Proc. ICE*, **XVI**, 1856/7, pp. 108–13.

The Stephenson practice thus benefited not only from his personal esteem following the completion of the London & Birmingham line, but also the respect that he and his associates earned from the several other projects they were taking on. Stephenson, himself, looked forward to a developing and influential career as a consulting engineer, quite unaware that one of the consequences of his first assignment, the Stanhope & Tyne Rail Road, was to cause him considerable distress into the early 1840s.

The Stanhope & Tyne affair

Although Robert Stephenson remained as consulting engineer to the Stanhope & Tyne company, there is no evidence of his direct involvement with the line following its opening in 1834. His fee for his three-year involvement during the building of the line was £1000, but money was short in the company's start-up phase and he agreed to accept £1000 worth of the company's shares in lieu. Although the railway was unincorporated, and the shareholders open to severe financial risks, the Board pursued an extraordinary policy in providing much of the capital through borrowed funds. The gearing was, in consequence, excessive by the standards of the time, and was made worse because the company had invested half its equity capital to promote the separate Durham Junction Railway.[82] This linked the Hartlepool Railway with the Tyne via a junction with the Stanhope & Tyne line near Washington (Fig. 3.2).

The company sustained operational losses through the 1830s, principally due to high way-leave charges and lack of demand for the Stanhope limestone. In spite of its poor financial state, the directors kept the railway operating until 1840. In April that year they consulted Stephenson about their fears for its continuation, but there is no evidence of any action taken.[83] In November, however, another firm, of which one of the railway's directors was a partner, was declared bankrupt, precipitating a loss of confidence. Cash rather than bills was sought by creditors, especially several north-east banks, which the company's high financial gearing could not sustain. The resulting cash 'implosion' led to the failure of the Stanhope & Tyne Company.

Stephenson apparently had no understanding that to hold £1000 of stock in an unincorporated company made him personally liable for a share of that company's adverse balance of £¼ million. He was much shaken by the realization, not only for his own financial position, but also for that of Robert Stephenson & Co., whose bankers were a creditor of the Stanhope & Tyne company. He wrote to his head clerk, Edward Cook (see Chapter 6):[84]

---

82 J. H. Baldwin, 'The Stanhope & Tyne Railway: A Study in Business Failure', in Guy and Rees, pp. 325–41.

83 Evidence of Charles Parker to Select Committee of House of Lords on the Stanhope & Tyne Rail Road Dissolution Bill, 26 April 1842, 5 & 6 Vic., c. 27, quoted in Baldwin, op. cit. (n. 82).

84 Letter, Robert Stephenson to Edward Cook, 2 December 1840, in Jeaffreson, I, p. 246.

I hope you will be able to make a dividend soon: I wish this for two reasons – firstly, because I want money, and secondly because I don't like your bankers. If they are not speculating beyond what is prudent I am deceived. And in that opinion I am borne out by several circumstances which have lately been brought before me in a way likely to affect myself very seriously. That prince of rogues has, I am sorry to say, involved all parties connected with the Stanhope and Tyne and almost all the banks of Newcastle and Sunderland. When I first became acquainted with the awful responsibilities which the Stanhope and Tyne had incurred, and the utter inability of the concern to meet them, I was perfectly stunned, and your bank has lent them on bills £51,000, which are at this moment floating.

Stephenson later reflected:[85]

The history of the Stanhope and Tyne is most instructive, and one miss of this kind ought to be, as it shall be, a lesson deeply stamped. If the matter get through, I promise you I shall never be similarly placed again. Ordinary rascality bears no relation to that which has been brought into play in this affair.

Stephenson's solicitor, Charles Parker, advised him to take the initiative and call an extraordinary general meeting of the shareholders. The meeting over two days in December 1840/January 1841, resolved to dissolve the Stanhope & Tyne company and form a new company, with a capital of £400 000, to absorb its assets and debts, and apply to Parliament for incorporation. It also confirmed that the shareholders, without limited liability protection, were personally liable for the company's debts. Stephenson already owed his father nearly £4000 at that time, and opted to sell half his shareholding in Robert Stephenson & Co, which he undertook with the agreement of his partners. His mood and financial straits were summed up in a further letter to Edward Cook:[86]

Your view as to my wishes respecting one half of my interest in the factory is exactly what I wish. The transaction is not intended to be otherwise than bona fide between my father and myself. The fact is, I owe him nearly £4,000, and I have not the means of paying him as I expected I should have a month or two ago. All my available means must now be applied to the Stanhope and Tyne. On the 15th[th] of this month I have £5,000 to pay into their coffers. The swamping of all my labours for years past does not now press heavily on my mind. It did so for a few days, but I feel now master of myself; and though I may become poor in purse, I shall still have a treasure of satisfaction amongst friends who have been friends in my prosperity.

Stephenson, together with 24 other Stanhope & Tyne shareholders, raised almost £340 000 towards discharging the company's debts prior to dissolution, he himself finding no less than £20 000.[87] His initial payment of £5000 in January 1841 was a deposit for 200 shares (£20 000) in the Stanhope & Tyne company.[88]

85 Letter, Robert Stephenson to Edward Cook, Westminster, 29 December 1840, in Jeaffreson, I, pp. 248–9.
86 Letter, Robert Stephenson to Edward Cook, Hampstead, 4 January 1841, in Jeaffreson, I, p. 249.
87 *Local Records of Gateshead*, 1842, p. 43; Jeaffreson, I, p. 249, and Tomlinson, pp. 442–4.
88 Robert Stephenson's Stanhope & Tyne Share Certificate, **ScM**, MS2033/14.

Stephenson, with Parker's aid, was motivated to lead the effort towards incorporation of the new London-based company, the Pontop & South Shields Railway. He recruited Richard Till as its Secretary, who had been so energetic as secretary of the 'Stephenson' London & Brighton project. In spite of some opposition in Parliament, Stephenson was not called to give evidence, and the new company's Act was passed in May 1842.[89]

The upper section of the Stanhope & Tyne line, which had made substantial losses, was given up and eventually taken over by the Derwent Iron Company. The Pontop & South Shields adopted the lower 24½-mile section from Pontop Colliery to the Tyne. In recognition of his substantial financial input, Stephenson became a director of the company, the only such appointment he held. Its first general meeting was held in February 1843, and by its second meeting the following August, Stephenson had been elected its chairman.[90]

The new company was more soundly based than its predecessor, and was profitable, not just because of the growing quantities of coal conveyed, but because of its inherited holding in the Durham Junction Railway. A month after the passing of the Pontop & South Shields Act, royal assent was given to the Newcastle & Darlington Junction Railway Act, the main line for which Stephenson had been appointed engineer-in-chief (see Chapter 4). The line linked Darlington with the Durham Junction Railway at Rainton near Durham, providing a through north–south route including the five-mile section of the Pontop & South Shields line. The last stretch to the Tyne was over the Brandling Junction Railway (Fig. 3.2).

The main line from London to the Tyne was opened in June 1844. This brought significant income to the Pontop & South Shields Railway, and after just three years under Stephenson's chairmanship, it had discharged the outstanding debts inherited from the Stanhope & Tyne company. It was sold on good terms to the Newcastle & Darlington Junction Railway in August 1846.

Although lacking direct experience of railway financing, Robert Stephenson had shown extraordinary resolve and tenacity in pursuing the resolution of the Stanhope & Tyne crisis. His experience of more than a decade in railway and parliamentary circles provided him with useful and willing contacts through whom he could devise and execute a strategy based on his foresight and involvement in the growing railway network. Although William and John Harrison had been largely responsible for the railway's failure, Stephenson had much respect for the abilities of Thomas Harrison, and appointed him to the important task of building the 22½-mile Darlington to Rainton line.

89 5 Vic., c. 27.
90 RT, **VI**, 4 March 1843, pp. 273–4, and 26 August 1843, pp. 929–30.

Diversification of the Stephenson practice

After the extraordinary boom in railway speculation in the mid-1830s, culminating in the authorization by Parliament of over 950 route-miles in 1836,[91] interest in further schemes had slowed, with investors cautiously holding back as a weakening economy became a recession in 1840.[92] In 1839 new mileage sanctioned had slumped to around 50.[93] The opportunity for railway consulting work was thus limited and, with much of the planning and design work completed for the current programmes, Stephenson diversified his interests from his mainstream railway consulting activities.

In 1840 he became engineer to the proposed London & Westminster Water Company, beginning an involvement with water engineering that he pursued throughout his career (see Chapter 12). In February 1840 he also agreed to act as consulting engineer for the Marquis of Bute regarding his 'Bute' docks in Cardiff, which was to be served by the Taff Vale Railway. This was the first of several dock schemes that Stephenson was consulted on during his career.

Since January 1839 he had been the North Midland Railway's locomotive superintendent, to oversee the provision of locomotives, and maintenance and operating depots (see Chapter 6). He took on further responsibilities, however, when just prior to its opening in the spring of 1840 he was appointed 'Chief Superintendent of the Line'.[94] This overcame a crisis following the 'lamented death' of Ashlin Bagster, the appointed superintendent, and formerly manager of the Leicester & Swannington Railway. With insufficient time to engage a successor, Stephenson stepped into the breach and ensured that staff were recruited and trained, and equipment was in place by the opening between Derby and Masborough in May, and between Masborough and Leeds in July 1840 (Plate 4).

Also that summer, Stephenson oversaw the completion of the York & North Midland Railway to its junction with the North Midland Railway at Normanton, near Leeds. He supervised the station's design for their joint use but, as the North Midland's Superintendent, it was necessary for him to reach satisfactory operating and financial arrangements with the York company. He was thus obliged to negotiate with George Hudson, the chairman of the York & North Midland Railway, who was, by then, a principal client (see Chapter 4).[95] This conflict of interest was the first of a number he faced as the railway network grew. The resulting arrangements were, however, found to be unworkable, and within two years they had to be renegotiated, again between Stephenson and Hudson.[96]

91 Lewin, p. 48.
92 Cottrell, pp. 11–16.
93 Lewin, p. 65.
94 Board Minutes, North Midland Railway, 1836–1842, 2 March 1840, **PRO**, RAIL 530/2.
95 Ibid., Record of a 'conference' between the York & North Midland and North Midland Railways, held at Wakefield on 12 November 1840. Also Board Minutes, York & North Midland Railway, 1835–1840, 26 November 1840, **PRO**, RAIL 770/1.
96 Board Minutes, York & North Midland Railway, 1841–1844, 7 September 1842, **PRO**, RAIL 770/2.

Stephenson continued as the North Midland Superintendent until the end of 1840, by which time: 'from his numerous other unavoidable engagements and from serious illness in his family it was impossible for him to devote sufficient time to the requisite personal inspection of the line.'[97] The reference to family illness is the earliest mention of his wife's cancer condition, which led to her death two years later (see Chapter 7). However, Stephenson retained his position as loco-motive superintendent until two months before she died.

Thus, by the end of the decade Stephenson's reputation as one of the country's leading railway engineers continued to grow as the several major schemes with which he was associated were completed. He had demonstrated technical innova-tion, as well as organizational and managerial skill. He had, furthermore, devel-oped a skill in handling parliamentary interrogations, in which he was demonstrably better than his father. He had the ability to brief himself on the engineering essentials of each scheme, recall those essentials under questioning and maintain an even temper. When called as an 'expert witness', his independent opinions were valued. Although his London & Brighton scheme had not been selected, such was the focus of attention on that debate that his name was frequently mentioned in both parliamentary circles and railway boardrooms.

The resulting high profile for both Stephensons inevitably provoked criti-cism as well as praise, particularly arising from the significant cost overruns of the London & Birmingham and other railway projects. A well-informed magazine correspondent reflected the views of many shareholders in criti-cizing these overruns.[98] The debate that this stimulated also included criticism of their dominance in railway engineering affairs, but one such critic nevethe-less summarized shareholders' mood at the end of the decade:[99]

It must be allowed, however, that the Stephensons have done a great deal of good; for as they possess much of the public confidence, and of their own too, they have prevailed upon capitalists to disburse, to carry out undertakings which otherwise must have dropped from want of means.

The Stephensons' prominence in railway development had inevitably led to some critical ill-feeling from established members of the profession, such as Sir John Rennie, although there is no evidence that Robert Stephenson ever let this ill-feeling influence his professional conduct. On the other hand, his rela-tionships with engineers of his own generation were remarkably good. These included Joseph Locke, whom he had known since 1824, and Isambard K. Brunel, with whom he had formed a strong bond since assisting him with evidence on the Great Western Bill in 1835.

Stephenson was much aware that his early advancement in the engineering profession had arisen from his father's rise to prominence, but he had built on this base to develop a reputation of his own. He had thus established himself as one of the country's senior consulting engineers by the beginning of the 1840s, which decade was to be such a turbulent one in the annals of railway history.

97 Op. cit. (n. 94), 11 December 1840.
98 Letter from 'An Unfortunate Speculator', RM, **II**, 30 May 1840, pp. 381–2.
99 Letter from 'An Old Subscriber', RM, **II**, 15 August 1840, p. 595.

4

Strategy, tactics and mania

Michael Bailey

… prepared by men whose time might be measured in minutes and valued by gold
Lord George Bentinck in 1847, about Robert Stephenson, George Hudson and
Samuel Laing

On 30 July 1850, Robert Stephenson was entertained to a public dinner in his honour in the new station at Newcastle-upon-Tyne (Fig. 4.1). Four hundred people attended under the chairmanship of the Hon. Henry Liddell, whose speech acclaimed Stephenson's achievements. He summarized all the railways with which Stephenson 'has been personally engaged', which he illustrated to the audience by red lines on a giant map of Britain.[1] According to Liddell's brief, these totalled 1800 miles, an extraordinary achievement which represented 30% of the country's total railway mileage, and was far greater than for any of his contemporaries.

In the decade just ended the country had experienced an extraordinary period of railway development, reflecting rapid social change, wild fluctuations in world and British economies, and a capital market that peaked in a 'mania' of unprecedented speculation, succeeding and preceding long periods of economic recession. That Stephenson had apparently been so influential in railway development during the decade is remarkable, but such generalized statistics offer an exaggerated explanation of his 'personal engagement'.

Stephenson had begun the 1840s as a leading railway builder, alongside his senior contemporaries, especially Isambard K. Brunel, Joseph Locke and George Stephenson. That he had, during the decade, apparently risen in the nation's estimation to become the premier railway engineer calls for explanation of how he developed his consulting practice to one of such influence, with an ability to deal with an extraordinary volume of work. That he succeeded to such an extent indicates his qualities as a remarkable leader as well as engineer, able to administer, motivate and reward his team of associates, who delivered reliable and professional services to their many clients.

By its very nature, the railway 'mania' was a controversial period, to which might well be applied Edward Heath's latter-day comment on 'the unacceptable face of capitalism'.[2] Stephenson's influence during the events of the mid-1840s

---

1 *ILN*, 10 August 1850, pp. 113–4.
2 Rt. Hon. Edward Heath MP, response to question in the House of Commons, 15 May 1973.

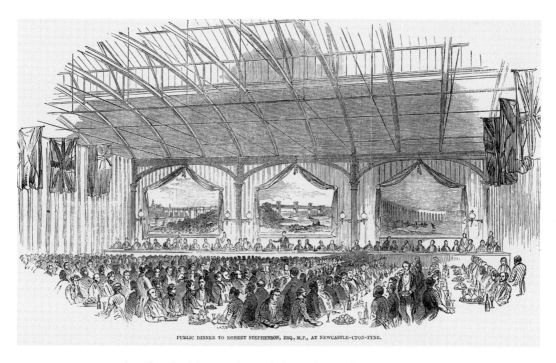

PUBLIC DINNER TO ROBERT STEPHENSON, ESQ., M.P., AT NEWCASTLE-UPON-TYNE.

4.1 Public
dinner to honour
Stephenson held
in Newcastle-
upon-Tyne
station
(*Illustrated
London News*)

therefore had been achieved through an ability to think strategically and act
tactically – qualities that went beyond the usual roles of civil engineering. Thus
Stephenson's role was far more than railway surveying and building, and the
development of novel solutions to more demanding structural problems. It was
a career that drew consulting engineering into national transport issues, in
which professionalism and capitalism were not always in accord.

The lack of any coherent national railway strategy, and the nation's
growing free-market system, resulted in a chaotic outcome in the mid-1840s,
with demonstrable harm to many private investors and the national economy.
Stephenson was steadfastly critical of this 'free-for-all', which saw uncoordinated schemes competing in Parliament. He was even more critical of the
parliamentary system that permitted the free-for-all, about which he expressed
strong views a decade later:[3]

The extraordinary features of the parliamentary legislation and practice consists in the
anomalies, incongruities, irreconcilabilities, and absurdities which pervade the entire
mass of legislation … Not only is the legislation irreconcilable, but throughout the
quarter of a century during which attention has been given to this branch of legislation, the Acts of Parliament have been wholly at variance with its own principles. To
illustrate this: several different select committees have, at various times, deliberately
reported against the possibility of maintaining competitions between railways, and to
this principle Parliament has as often assented. Yet the practical operation of the laws
which have received legislative sanction has been throughout, and at the same time,
directly to negative this principle, by almost invariably allowing competition to be
obtained, wherever it had been sought. Parliament has therefore been adding to the

3 Robert Stephenson, Presidential Address, *Proc. ICE*, **XV**, 1855/6, p. 136.

capital of railway companies, whilst it has been sanctioning measures to subdivide the traffic. The decline of dividends was an inevitable consequence.

Thus Stephenson's contribution to railway development in Britain was made against the background of growing dissatisfaction that the new transport mode that his father and he had done so much to bring into use was being exploited more for personal greed than for national benefit. His conduct during these years may thus be judged accordingly.

The railway 'mania'

British railway growth in the 1830s, achieved through unregulated opportunities for speculative joint-stock companies, had led to an unbalanced network, with many industrial areas still having no railways. With the exception of the trunk routes, there had been a proliferation of small companies pursuing relatively short routes. The motivation for their proprietors was the pursuit of local interests and short-term returns on investment, without anticipation of wider regional benefits, longer-term returns or economic stimulus. Although the Government had initiated an inquiry into 'Railway Communication between London, Dublin, Edinburgh, and Glasgow' in August 1839,[4] no moves were made towards a planned rail network.

There was a growing call for the substantial returns on railway investment to be partly redirected towards greater safety, and benefiting poorer citizens through lower fare opportunities. A parliamentary 'Select Committee on Railways' was appointed to take evidence and report on many issues, including a more equitable development of railways through regulatory procedures. Stephenson gave evidence on questions ranging from locomotive design to track layout.[5] One outcome of the Committee's recommendations was the establishment of the Railway Department of the Board of Trade in 1840.

Three regulation acts were passed between 1840 and 1844, each preceded by extensive debate, consideration in select committees and strong representations from railway companies.[6] The 1844 bill, steered through the House of Commons by William Gladstone (1809–1898), President of the Board of Trade, had received strong representations from the railways, and the resulting act had been considerably modified.[7] In marked contrast to the planned railway networks in some European countries, it did not address the issue of route regulation, leaving the capital market free to petition Parliament with its own routes, priorities and rates of investment.

---

4 Address of the House of Commons, 14 August 1839, 'that Her Majesty will be pleased to give directions that an engineer, or engineers, may be appointed to inquire and report upon the relative merits, and the preference which ought to be given to the respective already surveyed and projected railways between London and the cities of Edinburgh and Glasgow', etc.
5 *Second Report from the Select Committee on Railways, Together with the Minutes of Evidence and Appendix*, 9 August 1839, Minutes of Evidence, pp. 207–14 and 282.
6 *3 & 4 Vic., c. 97* of 1840, *5 & 6 Vic., c. 59* of 1842, and *7 & 8 Vic., c. 86* of 1844.
7 Professor Jack Simmons, 'Gladstone's Act', Simmons and Biddle, p. 177.

The country's leading engineers, including Stephenson, had been called upon to provide evidence in the pre-legislative fact-finding by the select committees, but had not been required to participate in the political infighting during the legislative process. Stephenson had, however, shown particular consideration for the less wealthy at the time of the debate over Gladstone's bill:[8]

Mr. Stephenson carried thoroughly with him the sympathy of all present when he said that railways had benefited the commercial man and the man of pleasure, but that they had yet fallen short of serving the poor man. The poor man had not yet got what he was entitled to – advance towards this was being made, but the true and full effect of railways would not take place until they were made so cheap in their fares that a poor man could not afford to walk.

Britain's recession in the early 1840s was accompanied by a decline in trade with her nearest European neighbours, and 'hostile tariffs' within the main Western trading world. There was a cutback in investment by the capital market, with dividends from continental securities returning to London rather than being reinvested in Europe. This gave rise to some £20 million to £25 million of inactive capital in the City of London alone, which was thus directly available for railway investment.[9] Interest in such investment began to grow from 1843, as existing railways declared good dividends, and this was further stimulated from 1844 with the removal of uncertainties over excessive regulation in Gladstone's act.

Railway investment accelerated in the following three years and, in October 1845, with investors scrambling to acquire shares in so many ill-considered schemes, the term 'mania' was coined by the Times, when it 'thundered':[10]

The mania for railway speculation has reached that height at which all follies, however absurd in themselves, cease to be ludicrous, and become, by reason of their universality, fit subjects for the politician to consider as well as the moralist. Whilst we contemplate with pity the enormous amount of individual misery which must inevitably, and at no distant period, fall upon thousands who have madly entered within the clutches of the iron Mammon, we must not lose sight of the fact that the character of the nation itself is at stake.

From 1844, the consequences of Parliament's regulatory changes, and the increasing investment and speculation in railways, were profound for the engineering profession as a whole, and for Stephenson in particular. Each new project, whether promoted as extensions to existing railways or by new groups of investors, required considerable input from engineers and surveyors in order to prepare plans, sections and estimates for parliamentary petitions, and to provide such evidence as was required by parliamentary committees.

---

8 Speech by Robert Stephenson on the occasion of a dinner and presentation of plate to George Bidder by the shareholders of the Northern & Eastern Railway, Blackwall, *RT*, **VII**, 1 June 1844, p. 622.
9 Jenks, p. 128.
10 *The Times*, 18 October 1845, p. 5.

Apart from the substantial capital requirements for railway building, each project required large sums of money to be raised in advance of its petition, to meet the engineering, legal and legislative costs. The circulation of prospectuses around the London and provincial capital markets became the focus of fund-raising; the more appealing the prospectus, the better the likelihood of attracting sufficient capital, and demonstrating competence and sincerity to the legislators. The names of the initial proprietors and senior officers and consultants thus became an important part of the capital-raising process; thus the more senior the engineer's name on the prospectus, the more attractive it would be to investors, and convincing to parliamentary committees.

Stephenson and his several senior contemporaries were approached by many aspiring groups of promoters to be named as their 'Principal', 'Chief' or 'Consulting' Engineer. The engineers required to be convinced of the efficacy of each group, and without assurances that some, at least, of the proprietors had experience of the legislative process, and could demonstrate a sound financial base, would decline the invitations. As the scramble for petitions reached a climax in 1845, large financial inducements were made to attract senior engineers to put their names to speculative schemes. Jeaffreson records that, in just one morning, Stephenson and Bidder received unsolicited cheques from various companies amounting to more than £1000 as inducements to representation.[11] They lost no time in returning them, and maintained a strictly professional stance in their representation of aspiring proprietors.

The consideration of so many bills during the chaotic parliamentary sessions made extraordinary demands on all participants. In the aftermath of the 1834 fire, which had destroyed so much of the parliamentary fabric, the committee rooms were temporary buildings located in front of the large Palace of Westminster building site (Fig. 4.2). With so many witnesses, lawyers, barristers and railway officers involved in the evidence, in addition to committee members and clerks, the rooms were uncomfortable and endured for days on end.[12] The lengthy and detailed questioning of witnesses was a strain on their tempers and a test of their powers of concentration.

During the four mania years alone, Stephenson gave evidence on more than a hundred occasions in the House of Commons committee rooms and on 37 occasions in the House of Lords.[13] The issues ranged from detailed descriptions of his clients' proposals and criticisms of competing schemes to the contentious debates on the atmospheric railway schemes and the 'gauge war'. From verbatim accounts of his evidence, is demonstrated his particular proficiency in responding to barristers' provocative questioning.[14] His skill in briefing himself ahead of each day's evidence was matched by his powers of concentration and recall of detail.

---

11 Jeaffreson, I, p. 287.
12 *RT*, **VIII**, 26 July 1845, p. 1131.
13 Analysis of database of witnesses to Opposed Private Bills, 1771–1917, House of Lords Library.
14 Ibid., volumes of evidence of railway bills.

4.2 North front
of Westminster
Hall in 1846,
showing the
temporary
committee rooms
erected after the
1834 fire, where
many of the
railway enquiries
were held
(Guildhall
Library)

The Westminster practice

Robert Stephenson's numerous engagements in the 1840s were principally for
the largest railways in England. Whilst most schemes were promoted directly
by these companies, others were for subordinate companies that, although
nominally independent, had the financial backing and encouragement of the
parent railways. He also represented other reputable groups of proprietors
seeking to establish new railway routes, several of which were for London-
based companies seeking to build railways in Ireland and overseas. The large
majority of the schemes were in Stephenson's name, which appeared on the
prospectuses.[15]

Stephenson worked extremely hard, over long hours, but he largely fulfilled
his commitments through delegation to his associates, leaving him to determine strategy and tactics and to oversee the development of novel engineering
practice. Whilst other leading engineers, such as Isambard K. Brunel and
Joseph Locke, ran practices or partnerships employing teams of engineers and
assistants, Stephenson was the head of the engineering 'chambers' in Great
George Street whose associates enjoyed independent professional status. The
Westminster practice was much respected, but its reputation depended upon
the abilities of the whole team. One of Stephenson's particular qualities was
therefore his ability to identify talented and reliable associates, the engagement of whom he could recommend to client railways.

George Bidder (Fig. 4.3) was the most senior associate, who, in addition to
his own growing portfolio of assignments, would frequently deputize for

15 Advertisements in *RT*, **VI** to **IX**, 1843–1846, *passim*.

4.3 1846 engraving of George Parker Bidder by John Lucas (Courtesy of E. F. Clark)

Stephenson, including much railway building supervision. George Stephenson was based at his Chesterfield residence, but often made use of the practice's facilities. The younger London-based associates, who quickly gained experience in the early 1840s, were James and George Berkley and, from 1843, Stephenson's cousin, George Robert Stephenson (1819–1905) and Henry Swinburne.

The large majority of railway planning and building projects was undertaken by Stephenson's other senior associates, who were engaged by railway companies in offices around the country. They included Robert Dockray in London, Thomas Harrison in Newcastle, Thomas Gooch in the Midlands and north, Frederick Swanwick in Derby, Thomas Cabry and John Birkinshaw in York, Michael Borthwick in East Anglia, and Alexander Ross (1805–1862), Hedworth Lee, Frank Forster and Edwin Clark (1814–1894) in North Wales. Other, subordinate engineers were engaged on projects around the country. These included William Baker, George Bruce (1821–1908), Charles Cawley (1812–1877), Edward Dixon, Thomas Dyson (1771–1852), John Forsyth (1815–1879), Charles Liddell (1812–1894), William Marshall (1816–1906), James Routh, and Francis Young.

The work programme for the Stephenson practice in the 'mania' years between 1844 and 1847 was greater than for other engineering practices. He accepted more than 160 assignments for over 60 different railway companies, a third of them being associates of his main client railways. The large majority of the projects proceeded beyond feasibility assessment, requiring plans, sections and estimates to accompany parliamentary petitions. In a period of such intense activity, the workload required extraordinary exertions by all the associates, together with complete reliance on delegation, whilst their technical capabilities had often to be backed up with diplomatic shrewdness.

In accordance with Stephenson's directions, and on behalf of their railway employers, the engineers supervised surveys, levelling, plans, sections and estimates for new routes. They also undertook design work and contract supervision, but consulted with the Westminster office on issues relating to the development of structures. They also attended public, general and board meetings, as well as giving parliamentary evidence. Survey work was usually contracted out to land agents with local knowledge and mapping and drawing facilities. Charles Cheffins usually undertook drawing work for Stephenson and Bidder.[16]

It was evident by 1843 that the Westminster premises were inadequate for the increasing workload, and Stephenson and Bidder opted to move the office up the road to 24 Great George Street. This was larger and, being near to Parliament Square, convenient for attendance in the parliamentary committee rooms. The new office, adjacent to the Institution of Civil Engineers' premises (Fig. 4.4), was occupied from June 1843.[17] Stephenson recruited his brother-in-law, John Sanderson, to be his office manager and personal assistant, which allowed George Berkley to become more involved with engineering matters.[18] Sanderson became a close aide to Stephenson, who much relied upon him during the frenetic years of the mania.

With the strength of a reliable team to undertake the more routine preparatory work, Stephenson was able to concentrate on the strategic and tactical requirements of the several lengthy parliamentary battles. He and Bidder also dealt with other issues, such as the contentious debates over track gauge and atmospheric propulsion. His high reputation also brought many approaches asking him to arbitrate over engineering disagreements and disputed financial awards. He was, in addition, consulted on a number of water-related engineering projects (see Chapter 12). Such was the level of his commitments from

16 Memoir of Charles Frederick Cheffins, *Proc. ICE*, **XXI**, 1861/2, pp. 578–80.
17 Letters relating to termination of Lease for 35½ Great George Street, June 1843, **IMechE**, IMS 182/1 and 2.
18 The earliest known correspondence in Sanderson's hand is dated 1 February 1844, (Robert Stephenson to Richard Creed), **PRO**, RAIL 1008/90.

4.4 Stephenson's office at 24 Great
George Street, Westminster, to the
right of the Institution of Civil
Engineers
(Courtesy of Institution of Civil
Engineers)

the mid-1840s, therefore, that his direct involvement in railway building was
limited to just a few projects, most particularly the Chester & Holyhead
Railway (see Chapter 9).

The adoption of the electric telegraph to aid railway operation and safety
also owed much to the keen pursuit of the associates, particularly Bidder.
Following initial trials and successful installation on the London & Blackwall
line, Bidder was instrumental in the establishment of the Electric Telegraph
Company in 1845, for which Stephenson was a major shareholder.[19]

Stephenson pursued an intensive work programme, working many hours
and writing several reports, letters and memoranda each day, and covering
many miles of travel each week. However, following the illness and death of
his wife Fanny, in October 1842, the escalating demands from the mania
schemes saw him apply himself totally to a level of work that few could sustain.
The long-term effects on his health became evident in the portraits of a prema-
turely ageing subject. The enquiry into how Stephenson was able to sustain
such a modus operandi is best told through assessment of each of the main
client groupings.

South Eastern Railway

Robert Stephenson's work on behalf of the South Eastern Railway was a particularly contentious episode. Although disapproving of combative and unregulated procedures for railway development, he demonstrated strategic and
tactical skills in route planning and parliamentary petitions. The extraordinary
battles were bruising experiences for him, reminiscent of the London &
Brighton contests of a decade earlier. His perseverance and tenacity, together

19 Kieve (1973). Also Clark (1983), pp. 262–78.

with that of George Bidder, were to win high praise from the railway's directors, but the events reinforced his negative views about the parliamentary system.

Stephenson was the railway's consulting engineer throughout the 'mania' years. He was engaged to develop the railway's network, whilst the company continued to rely on its chief engineer, William Cubitt (1785–1861), to oversee the building of the lines. The railway's ambition was to build a network of routes throughout Kent, and in northern France with routes to Paris and Brussels.

He was first consulted in January 1841, concerning the proposed branch from Ashford to Ramsgate. Cubitt, who was then building the main line between Redhill and Dover, and was himself a consulting engineer to other companies, including the London & Croydon Railway, was magnanimous during a debate about the route, saying that 'the Directors had very wisely and prudently consulted one of the highest railway authorities in the kingdom'.[20] Stephenson was also consulted about a proposed branch to Maidstone,[21] but, in the wake of the recession, further consideration was delayed.

In 1842, the South Eastern Railway pursued its ambitions for a route between Calais and Paris, to provide an integral rail and shipping service between the capitals. It sought to take advantage of new French legislation that ended considerable debate about railway planning and financing.[22] In contrast to British procedures, the new law introduced a planned rail network, the infrastructure for which would be built and paid for by the French Government, with concessionaires providing track and equipment and operating the services. Stephenson undertook a survey of route options, via Arras and Lille, which anticipated an extension to Brussels (Plate 5). It was reported: 'Every assistance has been rendered by the French Government.'[23]

Once he had determined the broad route options, Stephenson appointed the young James Berkley to prepare levels and sections and determine broad estimates of construction costs. Stephenson was under pressure to complete his report as soon as possible, but its compilation coincided with the serious illness and death of his wife. He completed and signed off the extensive report just four days after her death in October 1842, and three days before her funeral. His findings were published in full.[24] The railway's aspirations were not fulfilled, however, as the French Government offered the Paris to Lille concession to a French company.

In spite of the recession, the Maidstone branch, and a short branch to the new terminus at Bricklayers' Arms in south-east London, were promoted by the railway, for which Stephenson gave evidence before committees of both houses of Parliament.[25] Both acts were obtained in the summer of 1843.[26] With Cubitt

20 South Eastern Railway Special General Meeting, *RT*, **IV**, 23 January 1841, p. 75.
21 South Eastern Railway Half-Yearly Meeting, *RT*, **IV**, 29 May 1841, p. 576.
22 Brooke, p. 14.
23 *RT*, **V**, 30 July 1842, p. 790.
24 Robert Stephenson's Report on French Railways to the South Eastern Railway, *RT*, **V**, 12 November 1842, pp. 1160–1, 19 November 1842, pp. 1201–4, and 24 December 1842, pp. 1304–7.
25 House of Commons Private Bill 391, Volume of Evidence C15, 1843, Day 1, and House of Lords Private Bill 5148, Volume of Evidence L3, 1843, Days 2 and 3.
26 *6 & 7 Vic., c. 52* and *6 & 7 Vic., c. 62*.

preoccupied with the building of the Dover line, Stephenson was additionally asked to undertake the building of the Maidstone branch. With Bidder as principal engineer, this was the only line that Stephenson built for the South Eastern Railway (see Chapter 9), and included a bridge across the river Medway.

The first major extension was the 30-mile Ashford to Ramsgate line, for which Stephenson provided plans, sections and estimates, and evidence during the bill's committee stage in the 1844 session.[27] Cubitt was the engineer for the line, however, with his son Joseph Cubitt (1811–1872) the resident engineer.[28]

The availability of capital for network expansion from 1844 saw the South Eastern Railway embark on major schemes for route expansion. Stephenson's plans were for a north Kent main line to extend the London & Greenwich Railway to the Medway towns and Canterbury (Fig. 4.5)[29] Another route was to branch off beyond Greenwich to Tonbridge, to shorten the main line to Dover, whilst a further route, through Tunbridge Wells, was to serve Hastings.[30] Several branches were subsequently proposed to serve other towns.[31]

It was proposed to tunnel the north Kent line under Greenwich Park to avoid any problems with the Royal Observatory; this plan Stephenson discussed with Professor George Airy, the Astronomer Royal.[32] To satisfy Airy that there would be no vibration from the trains to upset the observatory's instrumentation, Stephenson arranged for a series of experiments to be carried out in the vicinity of Primrose Hill tunnel, Camden, on the London & Birmingham Railway. Robert Dockray carried them out and Airy attended on one of the days. At Stephenson's suggestion a special instrument was made, which he described thus:[33]

It consisted of a circular cup highly glazed with a flat bottom which was completely covered with Quicksilver this was kept free from oxidation by occasional filtering so that by observing a fixed reflection on its surface an infinitely slight movement could be detected.

The vessel was firmly bedded in the ground which was hard from the frost and therefore peculiarly adapted for communicating the vibration produced by the Train, and the Quicksilver was completely sheltered from the wind by the high side of the vessel.

The results showed that there was no risk of vibration affecting the Observatory. However, the Admiralty, to whom Airy was subject, refused to consider the experiments, and even before he had a chance to judge them for himself, he received a letter from the Secretary to the Admiralty:[34]

27 House of Commons Bill No. 475, Volume of Evidence C36, 1844, Day 1.
28 *7 & 8 Vic., c. 25*, royal assent 23 May 1844.
29 South Eastern Railway General Meeting, *RT*, **VII**, 14 September 1844, p. 1030.
30 South Eastern Railway Special Meeting, *RT*, **VII**, 9 November 1845, p. 1290.
31 'South-Eastern (Dover) Railway Company – Special Meeting', *RT*, **VIII**, 8 February 1845, p. 144.
32 **Airy**, RGO 6/47, folios 229–36.
33 Report, Robert Stephenson to the Directors of the South Eastern Railway Company, undated, but January 1845, **Airy**, RGO 6/47, folios 254–88.
34 **Airy**, RGO 6/47, folio 237.

4.5 South
Eastern Railway
routes, including
proposed lines

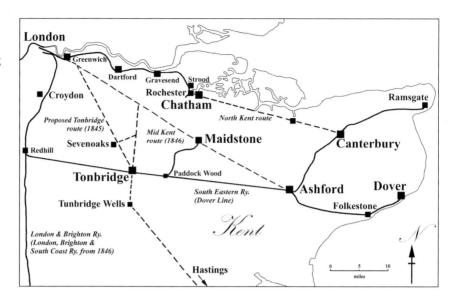

I am commanded by their Lordships to acquaint you that having already decided that
no Railway shall pass through Greenwich Park nor between the Royal Observatory
and the Thames … their Lordships will not give you the trouble of the experiments
which you propose.

The railway's petitions for new routes coincided with several competing
projects from other promoters. These included the 'North Kent Railway', for
which Charles Vignoles acted as engineer, and the London & Croydon
Railway, which promoted its 'Chatham and Gravesend' line as an atmospheric railway and was represented by its consulting engineer, William
Cubitt. From the resulting conflict of interest, Cubitt stood down as chief
engineer of the South Eastern Railway in September 1844 and was replaced by
Peter W. Barlow (1809–1885), the senior resident engineer during the
construction of the Dover line.

Once Stephenson and Bidder had agreed the route strategy for the north
Kent lines, Bidder supervised the levelling, whilst Stephenson liaised with the
directors on the tactics of promoting their routes. This included submissions
to an inquiry into the competing petitions by the Railway Department of the
Board of Trade. Stephenson accompanied the directors to see its Chairman,
Lord Dalhousie, following which the Department found largely in the South
Eastern Railway's favour.[35]

It was not however to be the case in Parliament itself, where Stephenson
was examined during scrutiny of the competing schemes in the summer of
1845.[36] The main-line bills were thrown out by the House of Commons, but
some of the shorter routes were given royal assent, as was the lease of the

---

35 RT, **VII**, 7 December 1844, p. 1442, and 'Report of the Railway Department of the Board of Trade on
the Kentish and South-Eastern Railway Schemes', 13 February 1845, RT, **VIII**, 22 February 1845, pp.
249–52.

36 House of Commons Private Bills Nos. 551 and 810, Volumes of Evidence C10 1845, Days 1 and 3,
and C89, 1845, Days 6 and 7.

London & Greenwich Railway in anticipation of its becoming a part of the north Kent route. The rejection of the main lines was as much a blow to Stephenson as to his client, but the competing lines also failed, and the South Eastern Railway lived to fight its corner in the next parliamentary session. In anticipation of this, and learning from all the arguments aired during the committee hearings, Stephenson was asked to reappraise the route strategy. The company was quick to put down a 'marker', as a warning to the other groups of promoters, when it published the following advertisement:[37]

SOUTH-EASTERN RAILWAY. – The Directors think it desirable to state, that they some time since instructed Mr. Stephenson to prepare for Parliament in the next session a complete system for supplying railway communication with the whole of Kent. It is proposed to provide direct lines to Tunbridge, Maidstone, Gravesend, Rochester, Chatham, Faversham, Canterbury, and Dover. The surveys have been for some weeks in progress, and the whole scheme will be very shortly in a complete state.

Stephenson, 'on whose talents the Directors have placed their faith', was instructed 'to prepare for Parliament the most perfect scheme which he could devise for completing, according to the present advanced ideas of the necessities of the country, an entire system of railway communication for the south-eastern district'.[38] His revisions were for a more direct route to Ashford to join the Dover line, together with branches to Tonbridge and Sevenoaks. The north Kent route was largely unchanged, however, and included Stephenson's plan for the railway to acquire the Thames & Medway Canal between Gravesend and Rochester, which had itself been granted railway status in the 1845 session. This ready-made 6½-mile route, the watercourse of which he proposed should be filled in to form the rail track bed, included over two miles of tunnel (Plate 6).

The debate included consideration of a Medway crossing at Rochester, which was to have been a combined rail and road bridge to replace the old river crossing. The 'Wardens' of the Rochester Bridge, who were to meet a large proportion of the cost, agreed to 'adopt' Stephenson's oblique three-arch masonry bridge design, rather than the alternative design by Vignoles, on behalf of the North Kent Railway.[39]

The 1846 parliamentary session was just as frustrating as the previous year. There were prolonged presentations and cross-examinations to the House of Commons committee, by Vignoles on behalf of the North Kent Railway, and Stephenson and Bidder for the South Eastern. Stephenson gave evidence on no less than nine days, and showed extraordinary tenacity under the intense interrogation.[40] Vignoles magnanimously noted that Stephenson had maintained a 'professional etiquette' by declining to adopt some of his own original route alignments.[41]

37   Advertisement, South Eastern Railway, 26 July 1845, *RT*, **VIII**, 2 August 1845, p. 1175.
38   'General Statement ... of the South Eastern Railway', *RT*, **IX**, 10 January 1846, pp. 40–5.
39   *RT*, **VIII**, 20 December 1845, p. 2403.
40   House of Commons Private Bills, Volumes of Evidence, C20–C23, Nos. 957–9, Days 7–9, 20–23, 25 and 32.
41   Evidence of Charles Vignoles, *RT*, **IX**, 21 March 1846, p. 443.

After a 'very severe contest' in committee, the South Eastern's bill for the north Kent line, although much truncated, was passed to the House of Lords, but not before the railway had agreed to 'purchase the plans of the North Kent Company' and thus remove further opposition.[42] The act was passed, but only allowing the South Eastern to open a through route between London Bridge and the west side of the Medway at Strood, including the London & Greenwich and Thames & Medway Canal alignments, together with new construction that avoided the Royal Observatory. With the mid-Kent line being thrown out by the House of Lords, only Stephenson's Hastings line and other, secondary lines received royal assent.

The tenacity of the railway's officers and of Stephenson was again called upon in the autumn of 1846 as further petitions for the Kent lines were prepared for the 1847 parliamentary session. Once more Stephenson arranged for the route between the Medway and Canterbury, and the mid-Kent Greenwich to Ashford route, to be resurveyed, and new plans, sections and estimates provided for the bill.[43] Other short routes, widenings and station enlargements were included in eight separate bills submitted to Parliament. In this session, however, the main opponent was the London Brighton & South Coast Railway (formed through amalgamation of the London & Brighton and London & Croydon Railways), for which William Cubitt was consulting engineer. The South Eastern Railway's Dover services operated over 21 miles of the Brighton route to Redhill, and thus its intent to build its own direct route to Dover was strongly resisted.

With several bills petitioned, and a protracted and expensive committee hearing in prospect, the two railway chairmen met but failed to reach a compromise, and the petitions proceeded.[44] Stephenson spent two days giving evidence and being cross-examined by the committee.[45] In spite of his efforts and those of the several other witnesses, the contested bills had a tortuous passage through Parliament, including reference to the Commissioners of Railways.[46] Such was the delay in getting them into the House of Lords, however, that following their second reading they were suspended by the Government's call for a general election. They were to have been reintroduced as 'privileged' bills in the new session, but in the wake of the recession by the end of that year, they were abandoned.

In September 1847, Stephenson resigned as consulting engineer to the South Eastern Railway.[47] He no doubt felt that after four arduous years his time could be better spent on other projects, which were less subject to unproductive battles for supremacy between rival railways. His experiences on behalf of the South Eastern Railway reinforced his critical views about the

42 South Eastern Railway Half-yearly General Meeting, *RT*, **IX**, 12 September 1846, p. 1290.
43 Ibid.
44 South Eastern Railway Special General Meeting, *RT*, **X**, 20 February 1847, pp. 244–7.
45 House of Commons Private Bills, Volumes of Evidence C1–C6, Nos. 1421–6, Days 10 and 11.
46 Captain H. D. Harness, Report of the Commissioners of Railways on the Proposed Railways for Kent, *RT*, **X**, 26 June 1847, pp. 858–60.
47 South Eastern Railway Half-Yearly General Meeting, *RT*, **X**, 18 September 1847, p. 1223.

unregulated procedures for private bills. After all his efforts, and those of Bidder, the only routes that had been achieved were the main line between Ashford and Ramsgate, and other, more secondary routes.

East Anglia

Robert Stephenson's experience in East Anglia was altogether different from the frustrations of Kent. Strengthened by his experiences in other parts of the country, he demonstrated a tactical ability for route development to overcome the predatory aspirations of competing promoters. This ability went beyond the normal remit of consulting engineering and, driven by his strong desire for harmony, his own actions soon influenced the developing network of railways in the region. His vision was clearer than seemed possible with disparate groups of promoters, the motivation for whom was as much driven by local agendas as by profit incentives. He was thus to diversify his ambitions from passive responses to unconnected railway promotions, to active encouragement of regional schemes.

Stephenson's first appointment in the region had been as engineer-in-chief of the Northern & Eastern Railway from 1839. Under his direction, George Bidder had supervised the building of the line through to Newport, south of Cambridge, for which Michael Borthwick was the resident engineer. The line was completed in the summer of 1845 (Fig. 4.6).

In early 1840 Stephenson was consulted by the directors of the Eastern Counties Railway, which had been authorized in 1836 to provide a line between London, Norwich and Yarmouth.[48] It was being built, with a 5ft track gauge, under the supervision of the company's engineer, John Braithwaite (1797–1870). The railway ran into severe financial difficulties, however, and was unable to proceed beyond Colchester. The directors were anxious for Stephenson's opinion about the estimates for completing this shortened route, but his report confirmed the 'perfect sufficiency' of the estimates,[49] and the line was opened in 1843.

In 1840, with no resolution to the Eastern Counties' financial problems, another group of promoters, largely from Norwich and Yarmouth, sought to pursue their own scheme for an alternative 'East Anglian Railway' route from London to the Norfolk towns. Surveyed by John Rastrick, it was to commence at Bishop's Stortford, and be routed via Cambridge to Norwich.[50] Stephenson was most concerned at the proposal, which would effectively prevent his further involvement with northward extensions of the Northern & Eastern Railway. He apparently discussed the implications with his father in early 1841, and both Stephensons thereon took the unprecedented step of taking the initiative to

48 *6 & 7 Will. IV, c. 106.*

49 Robert Stephenson report, 15 February 1840, in Board Minutes, Eastern Counties Railway, 1839–1843, 27 February 1840, **PRO**, RAIL 186/5.

50 *RT*, **III**, 2 January 1841, pp. 2–3.

4.6 East Anglian
rail routes
including
competing lines

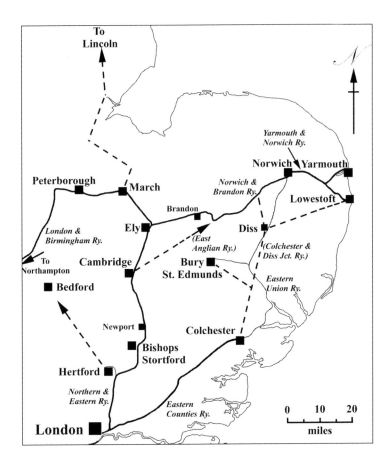

promote an alternative scheme to outflank the rival line.

Apparently meeting their own costs, they sought to promote their own route between Norwich and Yarmouth alone.[51] Their strategy was to achieve quick parliamentary approval for the route, which would challenge the viability of the 'East Anglian' scheme, particularly during a time of financial stringency. Stephenson used his connections with the Eastern Counties Railway Board to obtain agreement for the proposed line to supplant its originally authorized route, with the indication of longer-term cooperation between the two companies.

Stephenson selected a near-level 20-mile route that followed the winding river Yare, rather than Rastrick's 2½-mile-shorter route requiring more expensive earthworks and less favourable gradients. The speed of Stephenson's work, and of the group's parliamentary agent, meant that the bill was petitioned for the 1842 session and received royal assent that June.[52] He was appointed as engineer to the Yarmouth & Norwich Railway, but he delegated the task for supervising its construction to Bidder.[53] The resident

---

51 Advertisement, Great Yarmouth & Norwich Railway, *RT*, **IV**, 27 November 1841, p. 1246.
52 *5 & 6 Vic., c. 82.*
53 First meeting of the Yarmouth & Norwich Railway, *RT*, **V**, 2 July 1842, p. 694.

engineer was James Routh, who had recently completed the Preston & Wyre Railway. The costs of building and equipping the line were kept low by the use of single track and the installation of the electric telegraph. Stephenson was careful not to invest in the railway's shares to avoid any conflict of interest. George Stephenson, however, converted his backing into shares, and the railway's board appointed him chairman to the company, the only such appointment of his career.[54] The line was completed in two years.

The rival 'East Anglian' scheme was duly abandoned, and, following this success, Stephenson began to demonstrate a higher vision of regional and national railway development. To this end, he was now well connected with several City and professional persons, such as Richard Till, with whom he had first been associated on the London & Brighton scheme, and Messrs Parker and Hayes, solicitors, who represented him throughout most of his career.

With the building of the Yarmouth & Norwich Railway well in hand, Stephenson assisted groups of promoters by planning further links in the railway chain. These were southwards towards London, and westwards towards Peterborough to connect with the recently enacted Northampton line leading to the Midlands and north of England. Towards the end of 1843 the Norwich & Brandon Railway published its prospectus, which included these strategic indicators to potential investors:[55]

The project is brought forward with the full sanction and concurrence of the Eastern Counties and Northern and Eastern Railway Companies, who have publicly announced their intention of continuing the Line to London, either by way of Bury St. Edmund's and Colchester, or by Cambridge and Bishop's Stortford, as may be found most advantageous; and they have given the requisite notices to enable them to apply to Parliament in the next Session for powers to make either Line.

Notices have also been given by the Northern and Eastern Company for the continuance of the Line in a westwardly direction to Peterborough …

It was also significant that, with this shift of emphasis, and with Stephenson's services now in great demand throughout the country, his name was shown jointly with that of Bidder as engineers for the railway. This acknowledged Bidder's increasing responsibilities within the Westminster practice.

The Eastern Counties and Northern & Eastern Railways cooperated closely and, with increasing traffic levels on the Bishop Stortford and Colchester lines, their financial situation was improving.[56] It became clear that both companies should work towards a common policy. Outright merger would have been beneficial, but arguments over share exchanges were lengthy, and it was Bidder who brokered an agreement that allowed the Eastern Counties to lease its smaller neighbour from January 1844.[57] Stephenson was

54 Half-yearly meeting of the Yarmouth & Norwich Railway, *RT*, **VI**, 4 March 1843, pp. 293–4.
55 Prospectus for the Norwich & Brandon Railway, London, 6 December 1843, ICE, 625.1/2 Tract 29b.
56 Half-yearly meeting of Eastern Counties Railway, *RT*, **VI**, 26 August 1843, pp. 906–10.
57 The act (*6 & 7 Vic., c. 20*) confirming the lease was given royal assent on 23 May 1844. Bidder received a presentation of silver plate-ware from the Northern & Eastern Directors, *RT*, **VII**, 1 June 1844, pp. 621–2. Also Clark (1983), pp. 149 and 410–1.

appointed as consulting engineer to the enlarged Eastern Counties Railway from that date, with Braithwaite retained as engineer for the Colchester line.

Anticipating the wider network implications, Stephenson promptly recommended to the Board that its track gauge should be converted from 5ft. to standard. He arranged for George Berkley to supervise the work between September and October 1844.[58] With the Newport line well in hand, and encouraged by Stephenson's regional strategy, the Eastern Counties Railway petitioned Parliament for the route extensions between Newport and Brandon, through Cambridge (Fig. 4.7) and Ely, and from Ely to Peterborough.

The hiatus over the route extension beyond Colchester towards Norwich, however, had left a vacuum that was pursued by a rival group of promoters.[59] The rival lines threatened to compete with the Eastern Counties' Cambridge route. To counter this, both Stephensons and Richard Till encouraged the promotion of the Colchester & Diss Junction Railway, to link the Eastern Counties line with a branch from the Norwich & Brandon line.[60] Further lines to Bury St Edmunds and Lowestoft were included in their prospectus, in which Stephenson and Bidder were again shown as joint engineers.[61] The proposal was rejected by Parliament, however, which favoured the rival Eastern Union Railway scheme.[62]

The wider strategy for East Anglia included major regional routes to extend the Eastern Counties network northwards from March to Lincoln and westwards from Hertford to Bedford. Surveys for these routes were undertaken under Stephenson's direction in the spring of 1844, but were not proceeded with as the railway moved towards its new relationship with George Hudson, as shortly described. Stephenson extended his involvement with the region's railways, however, being confirmed as engineer-in-chief of the Norfolk Railway in 1845 just prior to the completion throughout of the Norwich to London line.[63] He was also appointed in a similar capacity for a branch off the Yarmouth line to Lowestoft.[64]

Thus, through his close involvement with railway development in East Anglia, Robert Stephenson had demonstrated a capacity for influencing events far beyond his professional calling. He was not directly involved in the supervision of railway building, having delegated the work to George Bidder and the resident engineers, Michael Borthwick and James Routh. Indeed, his main preoccupation was with route strategies and the preparation of material for parliamentary petitions. From the autumn of 1845, however, the Eastern

58 Obituary, Sir George Berkley, *Proc. ICE*, **CXV**, 1893/4, p. 383.

59 The Eastern Union Railway received its act for the Colchester to Ipswich route on 19 July 1844. Its associated Ipswich & Bury Railway threatened an extension to Norwich to compete with the Eastern Counties line.

60 Advertisement, *RT*, **VII**, 28 September 1844, p. 1119.

61 Advertisement for 'Diss and Colchester Junction Railway', *RT*, **VII**, 12 October 1844, p. 1184.

62 The Ipswich & Bury St. Edmunds Railway Act (8 & 9 Vic., c. 97) was obtained on 21 July 1845.

63 The Norfolk Railway was formed through amalgamation of the Yarmouth & Norwich Railway and the Norwich & Brandon Railway in June 1845 (8 & 9 Vic., c. 41).

64 The Lowestoft Railway & Harbour Co., which was leased to the Norfolk Railway in 1846, before its completion (9 & 10 Vic., c. 132).

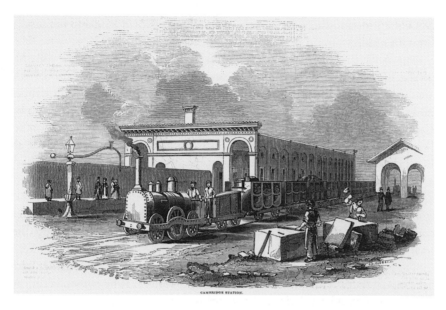

4.7 Cambridge
station of the
Eastern Counties
Railway
(*Illustrated
London News*)

Counties Railway moved into a new era with the appointment of George Hudson as its Chairman, prompting a new order of inter-regional route strategies, in which Stephenson was to become closely involved.

The 'Railway King'

Although the Government had initiated the 1839 enquiry for a trunk line strategy to link the nation's kingdoms, the country otherwise lacked a coherent railway strategy. The pursuit of uncoordinated schemes around the country prompted a need for proprietors with a much broader vision of railway evolution, who could provide leadership in railway boardrooms. There was therefore some affinity between Robert Stephenson and George Hudson (1800–1871, Fig. 4.8), the country's leading railway promoter (the 'Railway King'), who pursued such a broader vision.[65] Whilst Stephenson could identify and work towards a systematic regional and national network, and marshal professional engineering services to carry it forward, Hudson's motives were related to power, influence and profit.

Hudson's first railway promotion was the York & North Midland Railway, which, with the close collaboration of George Stephenson as engineer-in-chief, obtained its act in 1836.[66] Robert Stephenson may have met Hudson at that time, but his direct association with him began in 1838 when he assisted the company during the railway's construction.[67] The following year, Stephenson's several appointments, for the North Midland and Birmingham

65 Lambert (1934).
66 Board Minutes, York & North Midland Railway 1835–1840, 14 October 1835, **PRO**, RAIL 770/1, p. 4, and subsequent entries.
67 Ibid., 22 March 1838, p. 192.

& Derby Junction Railways as well as the York & North Midland line itself, brought him into frequent contact with Hudson.

The shock that Stephenson received in November 1840, with the collapse of the Stanhope & Tyne Railway, was followed a few weeks later by an approach from the Great North of England Railway. The Quaker fraternity, including Edward Pease, his partner with the Newcastle factory, funded the Great North railway, which was effectively an expansion of the Stockton & Darlington Railway. The first length of its York to Newcastle line, as far as Darlington, opened in early 1841, but several structures remained unfinished and some bridges were unstable. Thomas Storey, its engineer, resigned, and Stephenson was consulted regarding the best course of action to secure the bridges and complete the line. Following his report, he was appointed as the company's engineer-in-chief, and his prompt actions allowed the line to be opened for passenger traffic at the end of March.[68]

The opening of the line coincided with the publication of the long-awaited final report by the Government Commissioners into railway communication between England, Scotland and Ireland.[69] Their lengthy review of several route options concluded:

… that the advantages presented by the western route for the communication between Manchester and Edinburgh and Glasgow, as well as with the west of Scotland and the north of Ireland, more than balance the advantages which would belong to an eastern route from London, adopting even new line by Cambridge and Lincoln to York, as a portion of this great trunk railway.

Hudson was determined that York should be included on an England–Scotland route, with the York & North Midland Railway forming an integral part, but he knew that the Great North of England Railway, during the recession, would delay extending its line north of Darlington, making it difficult to argue against the west coast route. He therefore took an unprecedented step that was to influence the whole east coast route. At the end of April 1841, he called together the chairmen and directors of the several railways that, together with his York & North Midland Railway, represented the traffic interests for the route.[70]

Hudson proposed at the meeting that an alternative route should be pursued between Darlington and Newcastle, incorporating three existing short rail lines north of Durham, leaving just 20 miles of new route to be built (Fig. 4.9).[71] His audacious announcement that plans for this route had already

68 Board Minutes, Great North of England Railway 1841–1844, 19 January 1841, **PRO**, RAIL 232/3. Also Robert Stephenson's Report to Great North of England Railway, 3 March 1841, read to the General Meeting in Darlington, *RT*, **IV**, 13 March 1841, p. 315, and 20 March 1841, pp. 335–7.

69 Fourth Report of the Commissioners appointed by the Lords of the Treasury…. *Respecting Railway Communication between London, Dublin, Edinburgh, and Glasgow*, 15 March 1841, *RT*, **IV**, 1 May 1841, pp. 474–81.

70 These were the Great North of England, North Midland, Midland Counties, Birmingham & Derby Junction, Brandling Junction and Newcastle & Carlisle Railways. See article 'Extension of the Midland Line of Railway Communication Northward from Darlington to Newcastle, Carlisle and Edinburgh', *RT*, **IV**, 22 May 1841, p. 551, reprinted from *Leeds Mercury*.

71 The lines were those of the Durham Junction, Stanhope & Tyne (later Pontop & South Shields) and Brandling Junction Railways.

4.8 1847 published portrait of
George Hudson
(*Pictorial Times*)

been lodged confirms that Stephenson had been instrumental in planning the scheme with Hudson. He had undertaken the broad route survey and formulated a solution to the Stanhope & Tyne problem in the one scheme, as well as participating in a regional strategy that would contribute to the traffic prospects of his several client railways. At a time of financial constraint, Hudson's innovative plan for his Newcastle & Darlington Junction Railway was for all its shareholders to be drawn from the participating railway companies that would corporately guarantee the dividends.[72]

As the project's engineer, however, Stephenson placed himself in an awkward position with the Quaker community and the Great North of England Railway, which, unable to pursue its own Newcastle route, felt obliged to participate in the new scheme. In the autumn of 1841 Thomas Harrison undertook the detailed route survey under Stephenson's direction. The act was passed in June 1842,[73] and the line built under Stephenson's direction, with Harrison as engineer (see Chapter 9). It was opened in June 1844 and provided through rail communication between London and the Tyne. This was celebrated by the running of a special train from Euston to Gateshead in 9½ hours, attended by much publicity that strongly argued the case for the east coast main line.[74]

Towards the end of 1842, Hudson manoeuvred himself onto the board of the North Midland Railway and became its chairman.[75] Notably, Stephenson had relinquished his position as the railway's locomotive superintendent just a few weeks before, perhaps anticipating the ruthless cost-cutting measures that Hudson introduced on his appointment, and which affected many of the employees who had worked under Stephenson's direction. Indeed, with

72 Lambert, Chapter IV.
73 *5 & 6 Vic., c. 80.*
74 *RT*, **VII**, 22 June 1844, pp. 678–9.
75 Lambert, Chapter IV.

4.9 The Hudson
rail routes
1842–1844

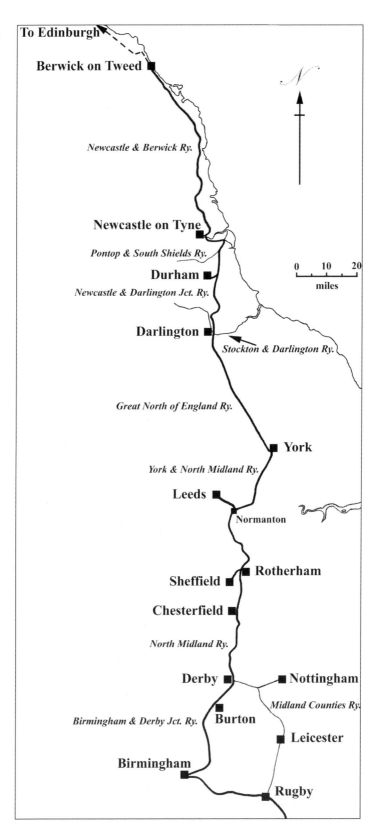

Hudson's reputation for harsh management policies, Stephenson was no doubt equivocal about his working relationship with his client.

Just a few days before the opening of the Newcastle route, Hudson pursued his ambition for greater control over the east coast route by bringing about the amalgamation of the small Midlands companies (North Midland, Birmingham & Derby Junction and Midland Counties Railways) to form the regionally-based Midland Railway, with himself as Chairman. He then controlled the route from Rugby to York and Darlington to Gateshead. In 1845, he sought to close the gap, and offered the shareholders of the Great North of England Railway an attractive share exchange offer with the Newcastle & Darlington Junction Railway. The offer was accepted, and the Great North line amalgamated with its northern neighbour to form the York & Newcastle Railway, for which Stephenson was engineer-in-chief.

In 1844, Hudson was keen to pursue the next stretch of the east coast route, from Newcastle to Berwick. George Stephenson had surveyed the route in 1836 and again in 1838 but, in the absence of a rail connection southwards to London, neither scheme had attracted sufficient interest. The two Stephensons shared Hudson's ambition of a through route to Scotland, and were keen to associate with his thrusting ambitions. In 1844, Hudson persuaded the proprietors of the Newcastle & Darlington Junction Railway to invest in a new Newcastle & Berwick Railway, which would apply to Parliament with a bill for the 1845 session.

George Stephenson recommended the route he had surveyed along the Northumbrian coast, in spite of opposition from Earl Grey, the landowner most affected. His son, Lord Howick, who led the protests against the coast route, visited the Stephensons' Westminster office to argue against it, but George Stephenson was unmoved.[76] With extraordinary tenacity, Lord Howick then took the exceptional step of promoting his own project for an inland 'Northumberland Railway', and persuaded Isambard K. Brunel to survey the route for 'atmospheric' operation. As chairman of one of the House of Lords committees, he had previously met Brunel, who had given evidence in favour of atmospheric operation.

Robert Stephenson partly amended his father's coastal route to try to meet the opposing views but, in October 1844, in the run-up to the parliamentary submissions, Lord Howick issued a lengthy statement addressed to other landowners appealing for their cooperation with the Northumberland Railway. His published statement was critical of Stephenson:[77]

I am bound to say that his opinion would have had more weight with us had we not thought that we discovered very strong symptoms of that bias of his mind in favour of the locomotive system, which, considering how much its brilliant success is owing to the exertions of himself and his father, was naturally to be expected to exist.

---

76 Smiles (1862), pp. 402–4.
77 'Northumberland Railway – Lord Howick's Circular', *RT*, **VII**, 2 November 1844, p. 1276.

The statement brought a sharp rebuff from Hudson, which was similarly addressed to the Northumberland landowners, and published. He dismissed Lord Howick's claims, argued in favour of the coast route and fully backed both Stephensons:[78]

As to his Lordship's attack upon Mr. Robert Stephenson, it is quite needless for me to say one word. The characters of the Messrs. Stephenson stand much too high in their native county to be affected by the observations of any individual who may attempt to lower them in public estimation. I would merely observe, that daily experience shows that Mr. Robert Stephenson's view of the Atmospheric system is correct.

The parliamentary contest between the two routes in the 1845 session was time-consuming and expensive. Stephenson gave evidence over two days in favour of Hudson's line, and spent a further two days arguing against the atmospheric system and Lord Howick's line.[79] Although both he and Brunel gave opposing evidence on their clients' behalf, they maintained, as always, their professional friendship. Brunel wrote a plea for the two engineers to mediate between their clients, to which Stephenson replied:[80]

Hudson has left town and I shall not see him until his return after Easter. I will do all I can, but I fear Lord Howick and he have so misunderstood each other that a reconciliation will be very difficult – Temper has in this instance like many others stepped in, and to all appearance is riding rough shod over reason – I fully participate in your views and will do my best

Lord Howick's petition was rejected, however, and Hudson's Newcastle & Berwick Railway Act was passed in July 1845.[81] Stephenson was appointed as engineer-in-chief to the company, and again delegated responsibility for building the line to Harrison (see Chapter 9). Under his direction, the line was built and opened in sections during 1847, with the exception of the High-level Bridge over the Tyne and the Royal Border Bridge over the Tweed. In both cases temporary timber viaducts were built to allow passage of trains from the autumn of 1848, whilst the permanent bridge and viaduct were completed and opened respectively in the summers of 1849 and 1850 (see Chapters 10 and 11).

In his 1844 statement to the Northumberland landowners, Hudson also revealed that he had invested in the North British Railway, thus signalling his intentions regarding the through route to Edinburgh:[82]

I may also add, that so anxious was I to procure a continuous eastern line of railway to Edinburgh, that when the North British Company was unable to go to Parliament for want of the requisite capital, the York and North Midland Railway company, on my suggestion, assisted them to obtain their Act and to proceed with the formation of their railway.

78 Statement 'To The Landowners of the County of Northumberland', *RT*, **VII**, 2 November 1844, p. 1256.
79 House of Commons Volumes of Evidence C77 and C79 for 1845, for Bill Nos. 765 and 778. Evidence given on 1–2 May and 16–17 May 1845 respectively.
80 Letter, Robert Stephenson to Isambard K. Brunel, Westminster, 21 March 1845, **Brunel**, D.M. 1306/24.
81 *8 & 9 Vic., c. 163.*
82 Op. cit. (n. 78).

With the completion of the North British Railway to Berwick in June 1846, Hudson made an offer to its shareholders to lease the line on attractive terms.[83] It was, however, rejected by the director,s who had no wish to become an extension of the Hudson 'Empire'. Stephenson may have expected an appointment as engineer-in-chief of this line, but the opportunity was lost and, throughout his railway career, he never represented a Scottish railway.

Hudson was anxious to minimize operating and administrative costs of his railways through economies of scale, and clearly anticipated the eventual amalgamation of the constituent railways on the England to Scotland route. With the completion of the Newcastle & Berwick line, bar the bridges, in July 1847, he brought about the amalgamation of the two companies north and south of the Tyne, to form the York, Newcastle & Berwick Railway, for which, again, Stephenson was engineer-in-chief. Through his several positions as consulting engineer and engineer-in-chief, Stephenson had thus become responsible for the entire London to Berwick main line. This confirmed his position as the country's leading railway engineer, contributing to his ambition towards a coordinated railway network.

As early as 1844, however, his aspirations, and Hudson's ambitions to control a large part of the England–Scotland traffic, were challenged by two rival schemes for a shorter route between London and York.[84] They were a threat to Hudson's east coast traffic, which he sought to counter by promoting an alternative route from the York & North Midland Railway, to a junction at Doncaster with a new line he proposed for the Midland Railway between Swinton and Lincoln (Fig. 4.10).[85] The Eastern Counties Railway was encouraged to re-address its original aspirations for a line to York, by promoting a continuation from Lincoln to March, via Spalding and Wisbech to provide a through route to London.[86] Stephenson conducted the surveys of the route in the spring of that year.

The challenge for the York route hardened in June 1844, when the two rival schemes merged, and requested Joseph Locke to be the Engineer.[87] His route from London was to be via Hitchin, Peterborough and Doncaster. Against this more focused threat Hudson believed that the Midland Railway would be better placed to raise the capital for the Lincoln route. He persuaded the Eastern Counties Railway to allow the Midland to build the entire 124-mile line from Swinton to March, to link in with the Eastern Counties route to London.[88] Stephenson probably liaised between the two Boards of Directors to bring about an accord for the route, as it was reported at the Eastern Counties General Meeting in August:[89]

83 Lambert, p. 203.
84 *RT*, **VII**, 27 April 1844, p. 487.
85 First General Meeting, Midland Railway, *RT*, **VII**, 20 July 1844, pp. 793–4.
86 Special General Meeting, Eastern Counties Railway, *RT*, **VII**, 4 May 1844, pp. 505–6.
87 General Meeting, London and York Railway, *RT*, **VII**, 8 June 1844, p. 637.
88 Op. cit. (n. 85).
89 Half-yearly General Meeting, Eastern Counties Railway, *RT*, **VII**, 10 August 1844, p. 878.

4.10 The
London–York
rail schemes
1845–1846

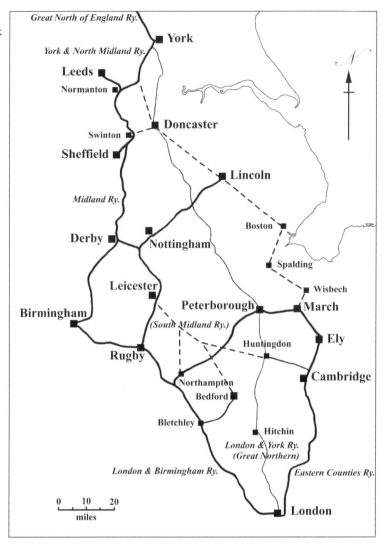

The Directors of the Great [*sic*] Midland Railway had agreed to make a line by way of Doncaster, Lincoln, Boston, and Spalding, to March, where, much to the advantage of the Eastern Counties proprietors, it would join the Ely and Peterborough line, thus bringing down a large portion of the traffic from Scotland and other places north of Doncaster, and feeding their trunk line with that traffic.

The announcement was greeted with cheers by the proprietors. Stephenson thus took the unusual step of diverting the plans and sections of the Lincoln to March route, carried out under his direction for the Eastern Counties Railway, to the Midland Railway.

A confrontation between Stephenson and Joseph Locke in a parliamentary debate over the York line was avoided by Locke's resignation following a dispute with the proprietors.[90] William Cubitt was appointed in his place. The rival schemes were scrutinized by the Railway Department of the Board of Trade, both being 'reported against', but by then they had been petitioned for the 1845 session.[91] Whilst the Midland Railway's bills for the Swinton to March lines failed at their second reading,[92] the London and York project was considered by committee in a contentious hearing that lasted for no less than 80 days, and only through Hudson's extraordinary manoeuvrings did the bill founder before consideration in the House of Lords.[93]

Hudson had bought a year's grace before the next parliamentary session, during which time he audaciously bought himself into the Eastern Counties Railway Company with a sufficient holding to dominate its board. He was appointed its chairman in October 1845 and, with Stephenson's full collaboration, prepared for new parliamentary petitions.[94] Once more, it was the Eastern Counties that proposed the March to Lincoln route, Stephenson again reassigning his original plans, whilst the Swinton to Lincoln route was repetitioned by the Midland Railway. The London & York also repetitioned for the 1846 session, and the stage was set for another confrontation.

With his vision of a national network, Stephenson was ever mindful of avoiding association with schemes that would divert traffic from existing rail routes. As consulting engineer to the London & Birmingham, Midland and Eastern Counties Railways, he was uniquely placed to influence their route development, avoiding conflicts of interest. He was a central figure in the debate over route expansion, and was much opposed to the London & York scheme. He was also influential in Hudson's plans for a southward extension from Leicester, which it was proposed to route to Northampton and Bedford, to feed traffic onto the London & Birmingham Railway, and to Huntingdon, to link with the Eastern Counties branch. This 'South Midland Railway' was, however, contested by a satellite company of the London & York Railway, whose ambition was to feed traffic onto it at Hitchin, for which Cubitt was again the engineer.

An extraordinary interview took place between Stephenson and the proprietors of the satellite company, who sought an alliance with the Midland Railway to head off the Hudson scheme. The 'hostile' interview, although reported by the latter, with subjective interpretation, indicated the strength of Stephenson's views:[95]

… between the London and York and the London and Birmingham Companies it was war perpetual, and war to the knife … that as the Engineer acting on behalf of the Midlands Company, it was impossible that he could enter into alliance or connection with any company who did not think fit to retain his services in preference to those of Mr. Cubitt.

91 Report, Railway Department of the Board of Trade, *RT*, **VIII**, 15 March 1845, pp. 391–2.
92 Half-yearly General Meeting Midland Railway, *RT*, **VIII**, 26 July 1845, pp. 1117–20.
93 Lambert, Chapter VII.
94 Special General Meeting, Eastern Counties Railway, *RT*, **VIII**, 1 November 1845, pp. 2141–3.
95 General Meeting, Leicester and Bedford Railway, *RT*, **IX**, 13 June 1846, pp. 825–6.

The outcome, however, was not to Stephenson's liking. The London & York Bill was passed in June 1846, whilst Hudson's alternative Lincoln route and the South Midland schemes were rejected.

Hudson's influence over the affairs of many miles of railway in England was profound. His pursuit of an 'east coast' route through York had resulted in an integrated system of railways that were harmonious in their relationships. Such harmony was fully endorsed by Stephenson, who strongly believed that such integration avoided wasteful duplication and competition. The strength of his opposition to the London & York scheme, renamed the Great Northern Railway, was further evidence of his influential planning role, well beyond a civil engineering remit.

Stephenson's association with Hudson was close and professional, although it is less clear how he regarded some of Hudson's more extreme tactics. Smiles recalls that Hudson, 'surrounded by an admiring group of followers', was a frequent visitor to Stephenson's office in Great George Street, suggesting that some, at least, of the strategy was determined in those chambers.[96] The association between the two men provided an alliance between the Midland and London & Birmingham Railways, during the latter's controversial arguments with the Great Western Railway. In marked contrast to the harmony between all the companies represented by Stephenson, the relationship between these two railways became a major preoccupation for him during the 1840s.

London & Birmingham/London & North Western Railway

The London & Birmingham Railway (and, from 1846, London & North Western Railway) was Robert Stephenson's leading client throughout his consulting career. His conservative, anti-free-market views on railway development were strongly reinforced by the extraordinary territorial battles which the railway conducted with the Great Western Railway during the mid-late 1840s. With both boards of directors intent on confrontation, not even his powers of persuasion and arbitration, even alongside Isambard K. Brunel, could resolve their differences. The issues were compounded by the two engineers' resolve on the use of broad- and standard-gauge track, which became battle symbols, the followers of which were unmoved by compromise.

With Robert Dockray as engineer to the London & Birmingham Railway, Stephenson was frequently consulted on matters of repairs, maintenance and improvements, as well as network expansion. Apart from the satellite Aylesbury line, the railway's first route expansions were between Coventry and Leamington, and between Blisworth and Peterborough.[97] George Bidder

---

96 Smiles (1862), pp. 376–7.
97 Coventry to Warwick/Leamington promoted by the Warwick & Leamington Union Railway (royal assent 18 June 1842, 5 & 6 Vic., c. 81). Powers transferred to London & Birmingham Railway (6 & 7 Vic., c. 3) on 3 April 1843. Line opened December 1844. Peterborough line promoted by London & Birmingham Railway (royal assent 4 July 1843, 6 & 7 Vic., c. 64). Line opened on 2 June 1845.

supervised the building of the 48-mile Peterborough line, whilst Stephenson maintained overall responsibility (see Chapter 9).

For its first five years of operation, the London & Birmingham Railway had been secure in its monopoly of the London to West Midlands traffic, and the company consolidated its financial position during the recession years without attempting expansion. In 1844, however, the building of the Oxford Railway, a broad-gauge line from London and satellite of the Great Western Railway, focused its attention on the risk to its monopoly that would arise from a north-ward extension of this line towards Birmingham.[98] Consideration was given to a new east–west route to Banbury to head off the perceived threat. Stephenson's views on the strategy were canvassed, and his report to the London & Birmingham directors illustrates both his wide remit as a consultant and his influence in the company's strategic affairs:[99]

… looking at the question as one of defence, and as a preventive to other Lines which might be projected through that country by other parties, it is clear that no object will be accomplished by a transverse line from Banbury to the London and Birmingham … for on the one hand, such a measure would not prevent the formation of a line southwards from Banbury to Oxford; nor, on the other hand, would it prevent a line from Oxford being carried on northward or westward from Banbury …

But it appears to me that the question of a through line … is one of the greatest importance to the existing interests of the London & Birmingham Company; & after much consideration I am strongly of opinion that, with the view of protecting those interests the line of the Coventry and Leamington Railway should be continued in the direction of Banbury. I think that, unless this is done, there is every probability of a line from Oxford to Banbury being extended, by other parties, northwards or west-wards (and perhaps in both directions) in a manner inconsistent with the interests of the London & Birmingham Company …

I need scarcely advert to the importance of carrying the narrow gauge as far as may be southwards thro' the country in question: it is manifest that the safety of the London and Birmingham Line, from inroads by other lines, depends greatly on this being done …

I feel it my duty to submit to your consideration the expediency of promoting a line in continuation of the Coventry and Leamington line, with the narrow guage, by way of Banbury to Oxford.

The Great Western Railway did indeed have plans for a northward exten-sion from Oxford, and selected a route to Rugby that would attract traffic from both the Midland and London & Birmingham lines (Fig. 4.11).[100] To counteract this, Stephenson's original scheme was expanded,[101] but before the details were completed, the London & Birmingham Board learned of plans for a second broad-gauge railway, to Worcester and Wolverhampton, which threatened their West Midlands traffic.[102] Accordingly, Stephenson arranged a

98 MacDermot, 1, Pt. 1, pp. 176–80.
99 Report, Robert Stephenson to Directors, London and Birmingham Railway, 11 April 1844, **PRO**, RAIL 1008/90.
100 MacDermot, 1, Pt. 1, p. 192.
101 The scheme was also for a line between Rugby and Oxford, with a branch to Leamington, together with an extension of the Aylesbury branch to Oxford. Advertisement, *RT*, **VII**, 13 April 1844, p. 443.
102 MacDermot, 1, Pt. 1, pp. 219–29.

survey of a route between Worcester and Weedon, south of Rugby, together with a line to Oxford.[103]

By autumn 1844 the railway's plans had developed further, and Stephenson's proposed route started from Wolverhampton and passed through Worcester, Stratford, Banbury, Bicester and Aylesbury, to the main line at Tring. The line, with branches from Rugby to Banbury and Bicester to Oxford, was surveyed by Dockray under Stephenson's direction, and was known as the London, Worcester & South Staffordshire Railway.[104] Plans for a southward branch from Oxford to Didcot, parallel to the broad-gauge line, to link with a proposed London & South Western Railway branch, were also prepared. With his disapproval of duplication, however, Stephenson may well have disliked the Didcot scheme.

As the deadline approached for deposit of plans and estimates for the competing schemes prior to their parliamentary petitions, an incident occurred which tested Stephenson and Brunel's relationship, as well as high-lighting their need for close supervision of subordinates and surveyors. Stephenson had learned that surveyors, acting on his instructions, had been chased off ground near Oxford, allegedly by Great Western supporters. He made no complaint to Brunel, but a few days later Brunel learned of the accu-sation and wrote promptly to assure him that the allegations were incorrect. His letter provides an insight into the prevailing mood between the two engi-neers representing their respective clients on such a contentious issue:[105]

I will not conceal from you that the GWR Co. consider the act of the Birm Co. in going to Parliament for a parallel line of 10 miles as one of the most unprovoked and unmitigated piece of hostility committed in all this bitter season of warfare – but in the midst of all this warfare we have all sought to avoid anything like personal hostility and depend upon it you are deceived in supposing that there has been any warning off our line at least to the knowledge or by the sanction of the principals therefore do not let us add bad feelings to what is already bad enough – we have made great efforts & successful ones to keep off Birmingham direct – and many other attempts to involve us in bitter hostility with the Birmingham and altho' we cannot but think the Oxford & Didcot a deadly stab in return – every individual in our Company is anxious to avoid offence.

Brunel even travelled to Oxford to interview the surveyors personally, in order to reassure Stephenson of the integrity of the Great Western team. Stephenson terminated the topic with an uncharacteristically terse response:[106]

I have made very particular enquiry and I am glad to find that the obstructions offered to our Surveyors were not persisted in and appear to have taken place without any instructions – I am perfectly satisfied

103 Worcester & London Railway, advertisement, *RT*, **VII**, 29 June 1844, p. 720.
104 Special General Meeting, London & Birmingham Railway, *RT*, **VII**, 30 November 1844, p. 1393.
105 Copy letter, Isambard K. Brunel to Robert Stephenson, Westminster, 6 December 1844, **Brunel**, Letter Book 3, p. 225.
106 Letter, Robert Stephenson to Isambard K. Brunel, Westminster, 10 December 1844, **Brunel**, D.M. 1306/23.

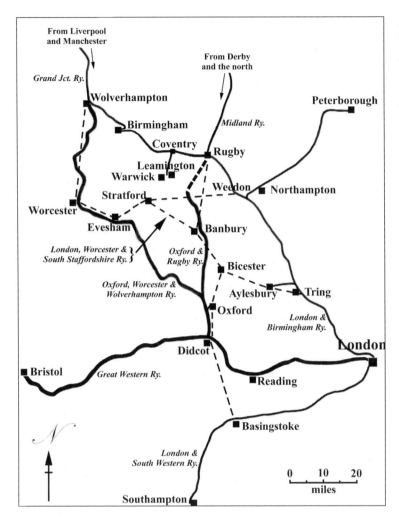

4.11 Competing
broad- and
standard-gauge
rail routes
1844–1845

The Railway Department of the Board of Trade considered the competing proposals, their report finding favour with the London & Birmingham scheme.[107] However, both schemes received second readings and proceeded to committee for a 19-day hearing, on two days of which Stephenson gave comprehensive evidence in favour of the London, Worcester & South Staffordshire line.[108] In spite of this and the Board of Trade's report, the bill was thrown out by the committee, which subsequently reported in favour of the bills for the broad-gauge lines.

The London & Birmingham Board set about an extraordinary campaign to oppose the committee's findings, their arguments centring on the gauge issue.[109] With wider implications for railway development, both the Midland

107 Railway Notice, Railway Department of the Board of Trade, Whitehall, London, 4 February 1845, *London Gazette*, same date.
108 Minutes of Evidence taken before the Select Committee of the House of Commons (Group F) in Parliamentary Papers, HC, Volume xi, pp. 246–92. Robert Stephenson's evidence on 19–20 May 1845. Also *RT*, **VIII**, 7 June 1845, pp. 817–8.
109 Debate on the Floor of the House of Commons, 20 June 1845, *RT*, **VIII**, 5 July 1845, p. 962.

4.12 Competing broad- and standard-gauge rail routes 1845–1846

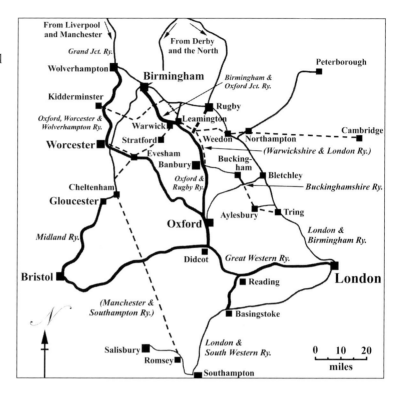

and Grand Junction Railways entered the debate, from which arose the setting up of the Gauge Commission by the House of Commons. Both broad-gauge lines, however, received royal assent in August 1845,[110] leaving the London & Birmingham Railway fearful for its long-term traffic prospects.

In the midst of this parliamentary battle during the spring of 1845 came a further attack on the London & Birmingham's monopoly of the London to West Midlands traffic, this time from the Grand Junction Railway. The two railways had been in dispute on several issues, but the Grand Junction's action in promoting, jointly with the Great Western Railway, a line from Birmingham to Oxford, was provocative.[111] Promoted as the Birmingham & Oxford Junction Railway, it was to be a broad-gauge line, with the indication of converting the Grand Junction to a mixed-gauge system (Fig, 4.12).[112] This extraordinary proposal brought Joseph Locke and Brunel together, pursuing the scheme on behalf of their respective clients, whilst maintaining a professional relationship with Stephenson, similarly engaged on behalf of the London & Birmingham.

Stephenson thus found himself participating in a series of counter-proposals to combat the new threat. The most innovative of these was for a resurrected Worcester to Weedon line, jointly promoted by the London & Birmingham and Midland Railways.[113] Following its formation in 1844, the

110 RT, **VIII**, 9 August 1845, p. 1232.
111 RT, **VIII**, 5 April 1845, pp. 475–6.
112 Circular from the Directors to the shareholders of the Grand Junction Railway, Liverpool, 11 June 1845, MacDermot, 1, Pt. 1, pp. 227–8.
113 The Warwickshire & London Railway.

Midland Railway, under Hudson's leadership, had ambitions for a major expansion. In July 1845, it leased the Birmingham & Gloucester Railway, and saw opportunity to provide a cross-country link to feed traffic through Gloucester to both London and eastern England.[114] As part of this grand scheme, the Midland and Eastern Counties Railways jointly petitioned for a railway between Weedon and Cambridge.[115] It is most likely that Stephenson was instrumental, not only in the three companies cooperating with petitions to Parliament for the 1846 session, but in planning this new network of lines.

A branch to Banbury was also petitioned, at which location a London & Birmingham satellite company, subsequently the Buckinghamshire Railway, was proposed to provide an alternative link via Buckingham and Aylesbury.[116] It was also proposed that this railway should build an intersecting line between Bletchley and Oxford, thus pursuing the parent company's effort to reach the city.

Stephenson also helped plan an even grander scheme for the 'Manchester & Southampton Railway', promoted by the Midland Railway to pursue a north-to-south standard-gauge network, to counter the broad-gauge Oxford & Rugby Railway. This was actually a new route between Cheltenham and Romsey, linking the Midland Railway's newly acquired route with the London & South Western Railway to reach Southampton. Both Stephenson's and Bidder's names appeared on the prospectus for this scheme.[117]

The relationship between the London & Birmingham and Grand Junction Railways became so fraught during the summer of 1845, owing to several strategic issues including the Birmingham & Oxford Junction scheme, that a dialogue was established to try to resolve the differences. After four days of intense negotiations, it was agreed to amalgamate the two companies. It was particularly notable that Stephenson accompanied the chairman and three directors of the London & Birmingham Company during these sessions.[118] This reflected not only his contribution to the debate about rail network development, but also his developing skills in arbitration.

The fusion of the two companies, together with the Manchester & Birmingham Railway, into the London & North Western Railway was confirmed by Act of Parliament in April 1846.[119] An inevitable outcome of the amalgamation was consideration of Stephenson's position as consulting engineer, together with that of Locke, who had been similarly engaged by the Grand Junction Railway. Given the seniority of both men and the prestigious positions they held, it might have strained relations between them, but there is no evidence of any dissent. They both continued their duties, as joint consulting engineers, with responsibility for the same geographical areas as

---

114 Advertisements, *RT*, **VIII**, 29 March 1845, p. 445, and subsequent editions. Also *RT*, **VIII**, 30 August 1845, p. 1412, and subsequent editions.
115 Joint Bill, No.1041, by the Midland and Eastern Counties Railways, House of Commons, Select Committee Volume of Evidence C51 for 1846.
116 Advertisement, *RT*, **VIII**, 30 August 1845, p. 1409, and subsequent editions.
117 Advertisement, *RT*, **VIII**, 9 August 1845, pp. 1202–3.
118 News report accompanying Editorial, *RT*, **VIII**, 1 November 1845, p. 2138.
119 *9 & 10 Vic., c. 204.*

hitherto. At the first general meeting of the new company George Glyn, the chairman, stated:[120]

Gentlemen, we owe a large debt of gratitude to our engineers. (Cheers.) We have the advantage of having for the amalgamated Company the services of both Mr. R. Stephenson and Mr. Locke – a combination of talent. These individuals, as you all know, have served the two Companies for a long time past; and, gentlemen, although the amount perhaps you cannot consider as anything at all, yet, if you pass the resolution, it will be received by those two individuals as a compliment unexpected by them. The testimonial we propose is 1,050*l* each to Mr. Stephenson and Mr. Locke. (Hear, hear.) … The resolution was carried by acclamation.

Following the amalgamation agreement, the Grand Junction Railway had withdrawn its involvement with the Birmingham & Oxford Junction scheme, but the Great Western Railway pursued it alone.[121] Bills for both this and Stephenson's Weedon scheme were again subject to intense argument during the Committee stage, his own evidence occupying three days in the House of Commons.[122] The argument in favour of competition for the West Midlands traffic convinced the legislators, however, and the Birmingham & Oxford Junction Railway Act was passed in August 1846, at the expense of Stephenson's route. The Buckinghamshire Railway Act was passed, however, creating an interface between the gauges at both Oxford and Banbury.

The arguments over gauge were to continue for several years, at the heart of which were the Oxford & Rugby and Birmingham & Oxford Junction Railways. The act for the former included provision for 'mixed'-gauge tracks, which the Board of Trade insisted should be adhered to. The Great Western Railway's directors felt further obliged to comply with the Board's directives, in the wake of the Gauge Act, to lay mixed-gauge tracks southwards from Oxford to Reading and Basingstoke. In an example of wider strategic thinking that lay behind so many of the mania's events, their complicity dissuaded the Midland Railway from proceeding with the Manchester & Southampton Railway, which was duly withdrawn.

Being consulting engineer to the London & Birmingham Railway had led Stephenson into a number of 'political' situations with which he was uncomfortable, but which, through a strong sense of responsibility to his client, he entered into tenaciously. In 1844, one of the several arguments between the London & Birmingham Railway and the Grand Junction Railway concerned an independent line promoted between Shrewsbury, Wolverhampton and Birmingham, for which Sir John Rennie and Captain W. S. Moorsom were the engineers (Fig. 4.13). With ambitions to expand northwards, the London & Birmingham arranged to lease the railway, for which purpose Stephenson approved Rennie's and Moorsom's line on its behalf.[123] Seeing the move as a threat to its traffic, the

---

120 First General Meeting, London & North Western Railway, *RT*, **IX**, 8 August 1846, p. 1094.
121 MacDermot, 1, Pt. 1, pp. 247–77.
122 House of Commons Volumes of Evidence, 1846, C55–C57, Bill Nos. 1058–1065.
123 Advertisement, Shrewsbury, Wolverhampton, Dudley and Birmingham Railway, *RT*, **VII**, 5 October 1844, pp. 1148–9.

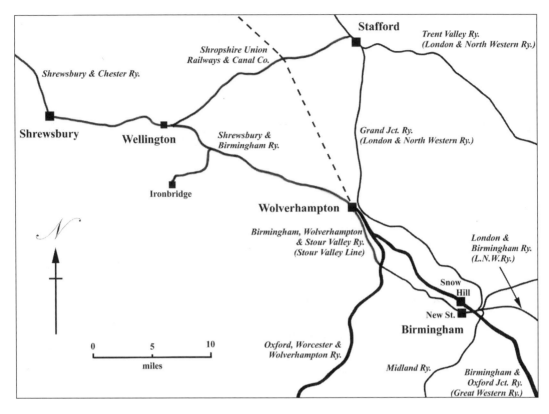

The map shows railway routes with the following labels: Stafford; Trent Valley Ry. (London & North Western Ry.); Shropshire Union Railways & Canal Co.; Shrewsbury & Chester Ry.; Shrewsbury; Wellington; Shrewsbury & Birmingham Ry.; Grand Jct. Ry. (London & North Western Ry.); Ironbridge; Wolverhampton; Birmingham, Wolverhampton & Stour Valley Ry. (Stour Valley Line); London & Birmingham Ry. (L.N.W.Ry.); Snow Hill; New St.; Birmingham; Oxford, Worcester & Wolverhampton Ry.; Midland Ry.; Birmingham & Oxford Jct. Ry. (Great Western Ry.); N; 0 5 10 miles

Grand Junction Railway alternatively proposed to lease the line, and 'that Mr. Locke, instead of Mr. Stephenson should be the Engineer to approve of the works.' The move was rejected, however, and the Grand Junction petitioned its own route to Parliament, but both schemes were thrown out in the 1845 session.

4.13 Shrewsbury–Wolverhampton–Birmingham rail routes

With the subsequent formation of the London & North Western Railway, the offer to lease the Shrewsbury & Birmingham Railway was replaced by an arrangement between the two companies to form a separate joint railway to build the expensive Wolverhampton to Birmingham section of route. Stephenson was appointed as chief engineer both to this railway (the Birmingham, Wolverhampton & Stour Valley Railway) and to the now inappropriately named Shrewsbury & Birmingham Railway. Both schemes were approved by Parliament in the 1846 session.

Also enacted in the session was a network of rail routes for Shropshire and surrounding counties formed by a union of three canal companies. Linking Chester, Stafford and Shrewsbury, mostly through canal conversion, the Shropshire Union Railway & Canal Company was promoted with interests from the Chester & Holyhead and Trent Valley Railways, which were themselves closely associated with the London & North Western Company. Stephenson was appointed as chief engineer, with William Baker appointed to build the line, as well as the Stour Valley and Shrewsbury & Birmingham lines.[124]

---

124 Plans and Sections of the Shrewsbury & Birmingham Railway, in the names of both Robert Stephenson and William Baker, **ScM**, 629.1 (42).

In 1847, the London & North Western Railway obtained acts to lease the Shropshire Union and Stour Valley Railways. The moves were again seen as defensive measures against the possibility of the Great Western Railway acquiring the routes and extending its network in competition. The Shrewsbury & Birmingham Railway, however, had its own agenda and maintained its independence by offering, with the adjacent Shrewsbury & Chester Railway, an attractive route northwards for the Great Western Company. It had the confidence to proceed independently because of a clause in the Stour Valley Act that permitted through running of its trains to Birmingham.

Relationships between the Shrewsbury & Birmingham and the London & North Western Railways deteriorated quickly. Stephenson and Baker therefore found themselves compromised between disputing clients. The building of the Birmingham to Wolverhampton line had been proceeding well,[125] but to prevent through running of Great Western trains to Shrewsbury and Chester, Stephenson was instructed by the London & North Western directors to delay and ultimately prevent its completion. This unprofessional and negative move placed him in a difficult situation, but he was obliged to abide by the instruction, not wishing to resign from the London & North Western Company over a relatively small dispute.

Whilst slowing the construction of one disputant railway, Stephenson and Baker proceeded with the building of the other.[126] The Shrewsbury & Birmingham Railway was opened in November 1849, which was the trigger for the dispute between the two companies to flare up into an extraordinary and protracted battle.[127] Having fulfilled their commitment to build the line, and assured themselves that the earthworks had properly consolidated, Stephenson and Baker resigned from the railway. At its General Meeting in March 1850, it was reported:[128]

The conflicting interests between this Company and the London and North-Western Company have caused Messrs. Stephenson and Baker to resign their office of engineers to your Company – an appointment which they could no longer hold with satisfaction to themselves.

The London & North Western Railway continued to prevaricate over the Stour Valley line, and only after expensive litigation in 1852 were Stephenson and Baker requested to complete the line to New Street station, Birmingham. Passage of Shrewsbury & Birmingham trains was then permitted, but the completion, in 1854, of a third Birmingham to Wolverhampton line, by the Great Western Railway, allowed through passage of trains between that system and Chester via Shrewsbury.[129]

125 Report, Robert Stephenson and William Baker, Birmingham, 25 August 1847, appended to Report of half-yearly meeting, Birmingham, Wolverhampton and Stour Valley Railway, RT, **X**, 28 August 1847, p. 1101.
126 Report, Stephenson and Baker, appended to Report of half-yearly meeting, Shrewsbury & Birmingham Railway, RT, **XI**, 26 February 1848, p. 228.
127 MacDermot, 1, Pt. 1, pp. 354–93.
128 RT, **XIII**, 23 March 1850, p. 290.
129 The Birmingham, Wolverhampton & Dudley Railway was acquired by the Great Western Railway in 1848, and the route was completed and opened for traffic in November 1854.

Thus, as the London & North Western Railway participated in the contentious territorial battles with its Great Western neighbour, Stephenson's aspirations for an orderly development of the railway network were contradicted. His loyalty to his client became stretched, but it made professional sense to retain his position with the Company. That he and Brunel failed to bring about any reconciliation between their respective clients was a measure of the mistrust and greed between the opposing companies, which further reinforced Stephenson's views against unregulated railway development. Central to this lack of agreement was the irreconcilability of the two track gauges, the consequences of which were to occupy Stephenson's attention for several years.

The gauge wars

Of all the confrontations that took up so much time and money of rival promoters and legislators alike, the most contentious was that over track gauge. George and Robert Stephenson's influence over many of the early lines had ensured that a 'standard' gauge had been adopted through their recommendation, rather than through legislation. It provided for inter-operation between adjacent companies, with ultimately the potential for their amalgamation. Robert Stephenson's firm views against the 'broad' gauge to Isambard K. Brunel in 1838 were based on the prevention of inter-operability and the consequent delays and costs at the interface between the two systems.

The Great Western Railway, and smaller adjacent railways, extended broad-gauge use throughout western England and South Wales. Its use was not only perceived to be technically better; it formed part of a wider business strategy for territorial consolidation and expansion. The Bristol & Gloucester Railway had been encouraged by the Great Western directors to adopt the broad gauge in 1843, not only to make through communication with its lines feasible, but also to provide a buffer at Gloucester to deter acquisition by standard-gauge railways. However, when the Great Western's negotiations to acquire the whole Bristol to Birmingham route failed in early 1845, the Midland Railway stepped in to secure the route.[130] As that railway's engineer-in-chief, Stephenson's role now extended to Bristol, although there was no immediate conversion of the Gloucester line to standard gauge.

Following the loss of the Birmingham route, the Great Western Railway resolved to expand its territory northwards from Oxford, and the 1845 battles over the route thrust the gauge issue into the centre of the mania stage. Whilst the Great Western Railway argued in favour of route competition, the London & Birmingham Railway argued for route monopoly, and this issue of principle was as much a part of the parliamentary debate as the merits of the two gauges. Stephenson's views against duplication of routes added weight to his strong advocacy for the standard gauge.

130 MacDermot, 1, Pt. 1, pp. 207–18.

Following the House of Commons' approval of the broad-gauge routes north of Oxford, the standard-gauge advocates obtained a resolution of the House:[131]

… to enquire whether in future private Acts for the construction of Railways, provision ought to be made for securing an uniform Gauge, and whether it would be expedient and practicable to take measures to bring the Railways already constructed or in progress of construction in Great Britain into uniformity of Gauge, and to enquire whether any other mode of obviating or mitigating the apprehended evil could be adopted, and to report the same to the House.

Three commissioners were appointed to undertake the enquiry, Lt. Col. Sir John Smith, the former Inspector-General of Railways, Professor Peter Barlow, from the Woolwich Military Academy, and Professor George Airy, the Astronomer Royal. They began taking evidence in August 1845, Stephenson being the first witness in a lengthy interrogation. He strongly advocated the standard gauge, and described the successful conversion of the Eastern Counties Railway gauge with minimal interruption to services. He also argued in favour of transverse sleeper track against Brunel's transom track.[132]

Concurrently a long statement was prepared for submission to the commissioners, apparently at Stephenson's instigation, and signed by over two dozen engineers and railway chairmen, which was endorsed:[133]

Statement signed by R. Stephenson dated 8 August 1845, professing to represent the views of the London & Birmingham and Midland Companies and other lines connected with them, representing on the whole upwards of 1000 miles of existing Railway in addition to extensions authorised in the present Season …

The statement raised five issues, each of which was expanded to emphasize the necessity for a standard gauge:

I   The want of uniformity of Gauge is an evil of the most serious description …
II   Transhipments of bodies of carriages & laying down additional rails are in many cases inapplicable & unsafe, and in all expensive & objectionable, and at best mere palliatives …
III   Evils are increased by every extension of the unusual Gauge, and will become very serious nationally …
IV   The adoption of 4 [feet] 8½ [inches] is the only thing practicable for uniformity & that it is sufficient for every thing …
V   There is now good opportunity … All lines of last session & future to be 4 [feet] 8½ [inches]

Brunel, equally strongly advocating the broad gauge, suggested in his evidence a series of experiments to compare the locomotive performances of the two gauges. These were held in December 1845 and January 1846 (see Chapter

131 Resolution of the House of Commons, 25 June 1845.
132 Manuscript notes by G. B. Airy of Robert Stephenson's evidence, 6 August 1845, **Airy**, RGO6/284, folios 331–5. Stephenson gave further evidence in January 1846, **Airy**, RGO6/310, folio 290.
133 Signed by Robert Stephenson, George Stephenson, Joseph Locke, George Hudson, James Nasmyth, Sir John MacNeill, Nicholas Wood, John Hawkshaw, James Rendel, James McConnell, Richard Roberts, and Chairmen and Directors of railway companies; **Airy**, RGO6/284, folio 322.

6). The commissioners laid their report before Parliament at the beginning of the 1846 session, finding in favour of the standard gauge and recommended:[134]

1st   That the Gauge of 4 feet 8½ inches be declared by the Legislature to be the Gauge to be used in all public Railways now under construction or hereafter to be constructed in Great Britain.

2nd That, unless by consent of the Legislature, it should not be permitted to the Directors of any Railway Company to alter the Gauge of such Railway.

3rd   That, in order to complete the general chain of Narrow Gauge communication from the North of England to the Southern Coast, any suitable measure should be promoted to form a Narrow Gauge link from Oxford to Reading, and thence to Basingstoke, or by any other route connecting the proposed Oxford and Rugby Line with the South Western Railway.

4th   That, as any junction to be formed with a Broad Gauge Line would involve a break of gauge, provided our first recommendation be adopted, great commercial convenience would be obtained by reducing the gauge of the present Broad Gauge Lines to the Narrow Gauge of 4 feet 8½ inches; and we therefore think it desirable that some equitable means should be found of producing such entire uniformity of gauge, or of adopting such other course as would admit of the Narrow Gauge carriages passing, without interruption or danger, along the Broad Gauge Lines.

Although Stephenson must have been satisfied with this outcome, the Great Western Railway quickly submitted a 50-page response, which both challenged evidence provided by its opponents, including Stephenson, and the conclusions drawn by the commissioners.[135] The Board of Trade was asked for its views on the commissioners' report, and in June 1846 it issued a more pragmatic Minute significantly modifying their conclusions. It argued that the existing Great Western main line and its feeder routes to the south should remain as broad-gauge, but that new lines in the remainder of the country should be built to the standard gauge. The exceptions, however, were the Oxford & Rugby and the Oxford, Worcester & Wolverhampton Railways, the respective acts for which already stipulated 'mixed' broad and standard gauges.

After intensive lobbying, however, Parliament further diluted the Commissioners' recommendations. The Gauge Act, passed in August 1846, stipulated the use of standard gauge for all new railways in Britain, but contained a sweeping exception for any 'present or future Act containing any special enactment defining the gauge or gauges' of railways.[136] This effectively left matters much as before, in the hands of the parliamentary Committees.

The Board of Trade's powers, passed to the newly formed Commissioners of Railways in November 1846, ensured that the Oxford & Rugby line was to be built to the mixed gauge, whilst the Birmingham & Oxford Junction line

---

134   *Report of the Gauge Commissioners*, 1846.

135   *Observations on the Report of the Gauge Commissioners*, published by James Bigg and Son, Westminster, 1846. With the subsequent publication of *Evidence and Appendix of Statistics to the Gauge Report*, 1846, the Great Western Railway further challenged its accuracy in *Additional Observations on the Report of the Gauge Commissioners*, James Bigg and Son, Westminster, 1846.

136   9 & 10 Vic., c. 57, 18 August 1846. The act included a stipulation for Irish railways to be built to a gauge of 5ft 3in.

was required under the Gauge Act to be built as a standard-gauge line. The building of both lines had been slowed, however, as ways were sought to adopt the broad gauge through to Birmingham. In January 1847, Brunel reported to the Great Western directors that he proposed to arrange the mixed gauge on the Oxford & Rugby line as a three-rail system, the outer rail for which would be common to both gauges.[137]

The Railway Commissioners received a copy of his report, and passed it to the London & North Western Railway for comment. Stephenson was requested to respond, but whilst preparing his report, the House of Lords ordered the Railway Commissioners to consider the adoption of a broad-gauge route to Birmingham. This sparked the second Gauge War, with Stephenson and Brunel at the very centre of the dispute, testing their close relationship.

Stephenson's report to the London & North Western directors pointed out that the commitment to a mixed gauge had already reached 90 miles for the Rugby to Basingstoke route and that, because of the Gauge Act, a further 150 miles of mixed-gauge route were planned. He set the tone of his critical report in his preface:[138]

Since, then, the notion of this untried system of Mixed Gauge, and the reliance upon it as a remedy for the evil of a Break of Gauge, and as a compromise between the conflicting systems of Gauge, seem to be spreading both in Parliament and with the public, I am desirous not to let pass the present opportunity of treating the subject as completely as our present experience permits.

His report, accompanied by several track layout drawings, was a systematic criticism of Brunel's proposals, focusing on the design of dual-gauge crossings and switches, which he argued could be unsafe as well as being costly to install. He also argued, unnecessarily provocatively, that mixing adjacent vehicles from the two gauges in the same sidings would not be possible, whereas Brunel had clearly indicated that complete trains of either gauge could be accommodated (Fig. 4.14).

Brunel was annoyed that the Commissioners had passed his report to the Great Western directors on to Stephenson, instead of their seeking an independent view. He indicated that Stephenson's view would be biased, and he denied nearly all of his assertions. The exchange was followed by an extraordinary series of claims and counterclaims to the Railway Commissioners by both railways, with the London & North Western protesting at the reopening of the gauge issue.

The Commissioners' report was published in May 1848 and, reflecting Stephenson's strong views against the mixed gauge, 'they cannot recommend

137 Copy of letter, Isambard K. Brunel to the Directors of the Great Western Railway, Westminster, 16 January 1847, forwarded to the Commissioners of Railways, who passed it to the Directors of the London & North Western Railway Company by letter, 15 April 1847, for their comments. Appended to Robert Stephenson's Report below.
138 Printed report, Robert Stephenson to the Directors of the London & North Western Railway, Westminster, 7 July 1847.

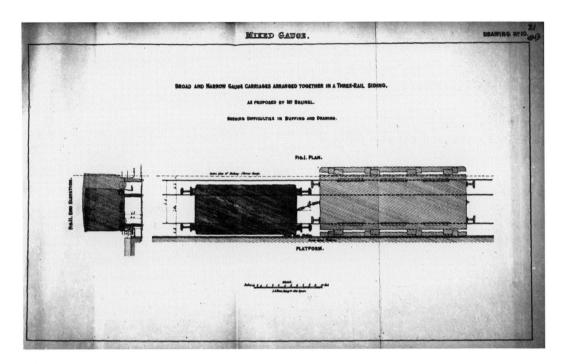

to the House of Lords that it should be at once sanctioned. Its success has not yet been proved."[139] However, the Great Western Railway tenaciously pursued its ambition to bring the broad gauge to Birmingham and obtained such powers under its act for acquiring the Birmingham & Oxford Junction Railway. In spite of extraordinary provisions and delays by the London & North Western Railway, Great Western trains began operating to Snow Hill station, Birmingham from October 1852.

Stephenson no doubt felt uncomfortable with the gauge war. In his anxiety to counter the growth of the broad-gauge network, he sought to present technical arguments against the mixed gauge that could not stand up to scrutiny. He would have been better standing back from the technical knockabout and left the competitive issues to the lawyers and parliamentary agents of the two companies. In spite of this confrontation with Brunel, the two engineers continued to enjoy a strong personal regard for each other. The second gauge war had occurred at a time of much difficulty for Stephenson following the failure of the Dee Bridge, Chester (see Chapter 10), and when Brunel was called upon to represent opposing interests over the affair he wrote:[140]

I have such a horror of the dog-eat-dog system of warfare which has grown up amongst professional men from parliamentary contests especially that I confess myself weak enough rather to stand by & see an injustice done to another than to involve myself in a contest in which I must attack the work of a professional brother – particularly of R. Stephenson for whom in spite of our very bitter contests I have a great

4.14 Stephenson's erroneous interpretation of Isambard K. Brunel's broad- and standard-gauge mixed trains (Report to the London & North Western Railway, 1847)

---

139 Report of the Railway Commissioners to the House of Lords, May 1848.
140 Copy letter, Isambard K.Brunel to H. Robertson (for the Shrewsbury & Chester Railway), 11 January 1848, **Brunel**, Letter Book 5, pp. 334–5.

regard – Indeed I sho[ul]d look upon the question of which company paid ... as very subordinate to the public reputation of one of our first engineers ...

Such words say as much about Brunel's character and judgement as they do about Stephenson's.

Independent railways

During the mania years, Robert Stephenson took on additional responsibilities for several independent railway companies, in Britain, Ireland, France and Belgium, in addition to the commitments for his major clients. His dilemma, because of his dislike of the whole speculative system, was whether to refuse the applications he received, or accept them and enter into the combative legislative process. Refusal would have allowed him to criticize the system, but acceptance of soundly based assignments had a threefold benefit. It ensured that he retained some influence in the rapid development of the nation's rail network, whilst providing good career progression for his associates and junior staff and ensuring an excellent income for his Westminster practice.

His most important clients were the Chester & Holyhead and Trent Valley Railways, both of which were independent, but which had strong connections with the London & Birmingham Company. The Chester & Holyhead line had been surveyed by George Stephenson in 1838–1839, but following the Treasury Commissioners' Report of 1841,[141] the recession had delayed implementation of the Irish route. In 1843, interest was renewed, and the Admiralty initiated surveys of Holyhead and Porth-dyn-llaen harbours, whilst James Walker undertook a comparative study of the several rail schemes that had been proposed.[142]

Holyhead was recommended for development, with Government financial assistance, and proprietors from the London & Birmingham Railway quickly formed the Chester & Holyhead Railway to promote the Euston rail route. With his father's assistance, Robert Stephenson reaffirmed the North Wales route, the plans and sections for which were quickly prepared by Alexander Ross and deposited before the end-November 1843 parliamentary deadline.[143] The railway received royal assent in July 1844 and Stephenson was appointed its engineer-in-chief.[144] The building of the 83-mile line and its pioneering bridges, and the events consequential to the failure of the Dee Bridge (see Chapters 9 and 10), formed a major part of Stephenson's professional life for the next seven years, which he undertook alongside his many other responsibilities (Plate 7).

141 Op. cit. (n. 69).
142 *RT*, **VI**, 28 October 1843. Also, Report by James Walker, *Railway Communication With Ireland*, to the Lords Commissioners of the Admiralty, Westminster, 6 October 1843, *RT*, **VI**, 4 November 1843, pp. 1186–7.
143 Board Minutes, Chester & Holyhead Railway, 1843–1848, 12 December 1843, **PRO**, RAIL 113/3.
144 Ibid., 8 July 1844, *7 & 8 Vic., c. 65.*

The 50-mile Trent Valley Railway, between Rugby and Stafford, was promoted by Manchester interests to reduce the journey time between that city and London. The project had failed with its first parliamentary attempts and, in seeking allegiance with the London & Birmingham Railway, it had added to the disputes between that company and the Grand Junction Railway.[145] The route survey was undertaken under Stephenson's and Bidder's superintendence, whilst Joseph Locke's views were also canvassed.[146] The act was passed in July 1845 and, although Stephenson was nominally engineer-in-chief, George Bidder largely filled this role, with Thomas Gooch as the line's engineer. The railway was merged into the London & North Western Railway during its building work, and the line opened in September 1847.

The North Staffordshire Railway was formed by promoters with interests in the Potteries and Manchester, together with the proprietors of the Trent Valley Railway. Its original ambition was for a route from the Mersey through the Potteries to the Trent Valley line, thus to compete with the Grand Junction Railway. Stephenson was appointed as consulting engineer in May 1845, but with his extensive workload, he again brought in Bidder and Gooch to oversee the preparation of plans, sections and estimates for parliamentary submission.[147]

Stephenson's appointment contradicted his views on route duplication, but he was apparently complicit in the wider tactical moves of the Trent Valley directors to persuade the Grand Junction Railway to work their railway from the outset, a manoeuvre that contributed to the formation of the London & North Western Railway in 1846. With the removal of the ambition for a Mersey route, the railway was reduced to a network of routes radiating from Stoke-on-Trent. Whilst Stephenson retained a watching brief over the line, Bidder became the principal engineer, again with Gooch as his resident engineer.

In addition to the many extensions for his principal clients, the intensity of Stephenson's involvement with other railway schemes made extraordinary demands on his time and attention. Other schemes included the Leeds & Bradford and Whitehaven & Furness Junction Railways. Many schemes foundered, however, because either the companies were unable to proceed or they failed at different stages of the parliamentary process. The more ambitious included the Liverpool, Manchester & Newcastle-upon-Tyne Railway, with 75 miles of new route, the 190-mile Welsh Midland Railway between Worcester/Shrewsbury and Swansea with a feeder line from Merthyr Tydfil, a 32-mile West Lancashire Railway between Liverpool and Preston, the London & Portsmouth Railway, and the Metropolitan Railways Junction Company that was to provide an 87-mile clockwise arc around London between Redhill and Tilbury, linking all the capital's radial routes.[148]

145 General Meeting, Trent Valley Railway, *RT*, **VIII**, 1 March 1845, pp. 266–8.
146 Advertisement, *RT*, **VII**, 13 April 1844, p. 445.
147 Advertisements, *RT*, **VIII**, 3 May 1845, p. 613, and 19 July 1845, p. 1057.
148 Advertisements, *RT*, 1844–1847, *passim*.

He was engaged by four London-based groups of promoters for railway projects in Ireland, reflecting the belief that railway development might go some way towards stimulating its economy and alleviating the recent tragic events following the potato famine.[149] Two of the projects, the 120-mile Limerick & Belfast Direct Union, and the 82-mile Dublin & Enniskillen were abandoned, but the 58-mile Londonderry & Enniskillen and 39-mile Londonderry & Coleraine Railways did proceed.

Stephenson's involvement with the Londonderry & Enniskillen line was unusual, as it had been surveyed and prepared for Parliament by Sir John MacNeill (c.1793–1880) at the request of the Irish Railway Commission. MacNeill declined to build the line when the act was passed in July 1845, and Stephenson agreed to take it on, delegating supervision to Alexander Ross. Following the latter's initial examination of the route, both engineers were placed in the uncomfortable position of having to criticize MacNeill's survey:[150]

We have inspected the entire line, and we have to report to you that much alteration is required to save expense, and to expedite the execution of the works very materially.

We are informed that the surveys were made in haste, and that Sir J. MacNeill, in the midst of his then pressing engagements, did not himself have time personally to go over the line.

Stephenson recommended that a further act should be sought, both to vary MacNeill's alignment and to extend the line to a more suitable terminus in Londonderry. Although the act was obtained and the first stretch of line to Strabane built, the extraordinary events that surrounded this contract (see Chapter 9) must have caused him to regret his association with the railway, and he withdrew from further involvement.[151]

Recession and end of the 'mania'

George Hudson had a major impact on Robert Stephenson's career during the mania years. Although he would not have identified with Hudson's aggressive tactics, Stephenson's senior consulting role with the Hudson companies gave him more influence in railway network development than engineering affairs alone would have required.

At the height of the mania, in July 1845, Hudson initiated a programme of public self-aggrandizement, through the promotion of testimonials, firstly for George Stephenson and then, through the agency of his senior associates, for himself.[152] Robert Stephenson must have considered, with a mixture of pride

149 *RT*, **VIII**, 9 August 1845, p. 1210, and 16 August 1845, pp. 1257–8.
150 Report, Robert Stephenson and A. M. Ross, London, 18 August 1845, with report of the first General Meeting of the Londonderry & Enniskillen Railway, *RT*, **VIII**, 30 August 1845, p. 1390.
151 Letter, Robert Stephenson to the Chairman and Directors of the Londonderry & Enniskillen Railway, Westminster, 11 January 1848, *RR*, **V**, 15 January 1848, pp. 56–7.
152 Proposed 'Testimonial of Respect' to George Stephenson Esq., Special General Meeting of the York & North Midland Railway, *RT*, **VIII**, 5 July 1845, p. 988. Also 'Testimonial to George Hudson', Half-yearly General meeting of the Midland Railway, *RT*, **VIII**, 26 July 1845, p. 1120.

and suspicion, the extraordinary way in which Hudson elevated his father's reputation, which was, perhaps, more to boost his ambitions than it was out of regard for George Stephenson himself. Hudson's election as Member of Parliament for Sunderland followed just over a fortnight later. Large donations were received for both testimonials, the names and contributions being published.[153] It is significant that Robert Stephenson's own reputation was not similarly subjected to Hudson's public relations endeavours.

Stephenson's own ambitions for a parliamentary career from the summer of 1847 (see Chapter 7), may well have been motivated by a desire to speak out against the free-market culture, which he believed brought about unregulated railway speculation. He was perhaps encouraged in this ambition by Hudson, who ascertained that the Whitby constituency could be obtained without opposition.

In the autumn of 1847, however, shortly after the election, Britain's economy again went into recession, the financial problems adding to the strain already imposed by the potato famine and partial failure of the American cotton crop, as well as sharp falls in corn prices following repeal of the 'Corn Laws'.[154] Well-established finance houses failed, including five Bank of England firms, and railway speculation ended abruptly. Petitions for new routes for the 1848 parliamentary session were largely re-submissions of proposals that had previously failed. Only 373 miles of new route were approved, compared to 1294 in the previous year.

The problems were compounded during 1848 by extraordinary political events, as riot and revolution took place in several European countries, whilst a resurgence of Chartism in Britain and unrest in Ireland all undermined confidence in the capital markets. As the events of 1848 unfolded, Stephenson reflected the mood of the time when writing to Michael Longridge:[155]

Railways are at a complete stand still; every body buttoning up their pockets except those who have empty ones. Railway shares and Radicals at a discount, the former unsaleable and the latter unbearable –
... the aspect of Europe is threatening – industry is becoming idle, commerce is paralysed, suspicion and apprehension are abroad, it is only the aid of powers higher than those of men that can put us right again, & I trust that they will be exercised.

Stephenson's response to this major downturn in railway work was to diversify to other activities, whilst retaining his appointments to his major clients. He and George Bidder were anxious to maintain a satisfactory level of work for their junior associates, who were encouraged to pursue the limited railway opportunities for themselves, rather than in a subordinate capacity to the practice. Thus Stephenson declined any further British railway work from this time, although his commitments, most particularly the building of the Chester & Holyhead Railway, were seen through to completion. In addition to his parliamentary duties, he pursued other branches of engineering, notably

153 Advertisement, *RT*, **VIII**, 20 September 1845, p. 1617 and subsequent editions.
154 Jenks, p. 153.
155 Letter, Robert Stephenson to Michael Longridge, London, 21 March 1848, letter in private ownership.

the development of overseas railways (see Chapter 5), and water-related engineering (see Chapter 12).

The year 1848 was a turning point in the affairs of the Great George Street practice. Although Stephenson was deeply affected by his father's death in August, he allowed himself only a brief period of mourning before returning to his heavy programme of work. Just a few days later he, too, almost died in a train accident but, with great good fortune, suffered no long-term effects.[156]

It was, however, the effects of the recession on Hudson's railway standing that had a major impact on Stephenson's consulting business. Between August 1848 and May 1849, without the resources to fulfil his inflated promises, Hudson's empire fell apart and he resigned all his chairmanships.[157] Although preoccupied with the building of the great bridges across the Tyne and Tweed and in North Wales, Stephenson would have been concerned that his reputation, and that of his practice, would be damaged by association with Hudson.

It was to his great credit that, in spite of all the revelations into Hudson's activities revealed by 'Committees of Investigation',[158] his reputation was unaffected. He had not profited through shareholdings and had retained his professional standing throughout. On the occasion of the 1850 Newcastle dinner in honour of Stephenson, George Leeman, Hudson's successor as Chairman of the York, Newcastle & Berwick Railway went out of his way to recall in his speech:[159]

… that throughout the financial annals of the affairs of that company, there had never been revealed an item or a figure but which redounded to Mr. Stephenson's professional honour (loud and long-continued cheers); and he might add, also, additional weight to his personal character. (Renewed cheers.)

Against the background of recession, however, the new chairmen of the former Hudson companies were less in need of Stephenson's advice on route development. Their own engineers, themselves Stephenson's associates, were quite competent to undertake improvements and network expansion. Thomas Harrison on the York, Newcastle & Berwick, Thomas Cabry and John Birkinshaw on the York & North Midland, William Barlow and Frederick Swanwick on the Midland Railway, and Michael Borthwick on the Eastern Counties Railway had all been in post for some years and had given good service.

Attention was later focused, however, on the settlement of Stephenson's claim for professional fees, dating back several years, from each of the Hudson companies. Why they had been allowed to accumulate to such an extent is not clear. The claims were an embarrassment to the directors that they were anxious to overcome with the minimum of external scrutiny.

156 *RR*, **V**, 9 September 1848, p. 888.
157 Lambert, pp. 230–74.
158 For example, Report of the Midland Railway Committee of Investigation, RT, **XII**, 25 August 1849, pp. 859–60.
159 Op. cit. (n. 1).

1 Canterbury & Whitstable Railway viewed from the top of Tyler Hill tunnel
(Elton collection, Ironbridge Gorge Museum Trust)

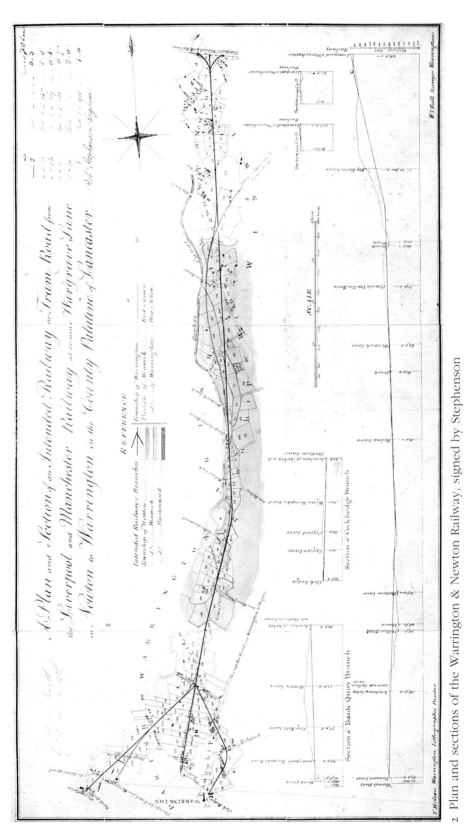

2 Plan and sections of the Warrington & Newton Railway, signed by Stephenson
(Courtesy of Institution of Civil Engineers)

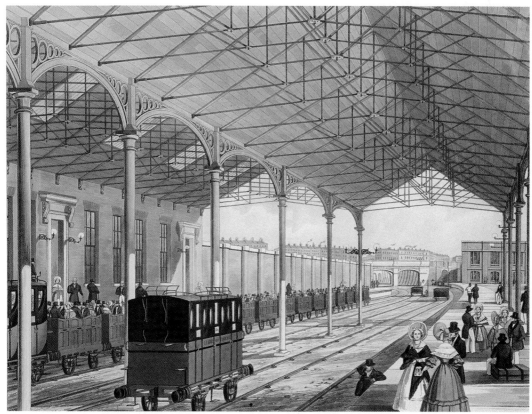

3 Euston station shortly after the opening of the London & Birmingham Railway
(T. T. Bury, *Six coloured views on the London and Birmingham Railway from drawings made on the line with the sanction of the Company*, 1837)

4 Belper cutting on the North Midland Railway (private collection)

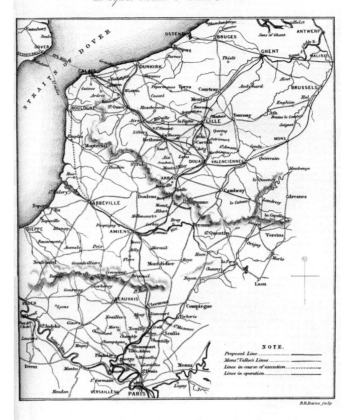

ROB^T STEPHENSON ESQ^{RS}
Report on the French Line.

NOTE.

Proposed Line _____
Monsr Vallée's Lines _____
Lines in course of execution ----------
Lines in operation _____

B.R.Davies sculp.

Pub. by John Weale, Architectural Library, 59 High Holborn.

5 Stephenson's
1842 proposal
for rail routes
in northern
France (Weale,
*Ensamples of
Railway
Making*, 1843)

6 The
converted
tunnel between
Gravesend and
Rochester on
the former
Thames &
Medway Canal
(Elton collection,
Ironbridge
Gorge Museum
Trust)

7 C. Picken's 1850 painting of Bangor station on the Chester & Holyhead Railway
(Elton collection, Ironbridge Gorge Museum Trust)

8 John Lucas's portrait of George and Robert Stephenson with a model of a 'long-boiler' locomotive
(Courtesy of Institution of Civil Engineers)

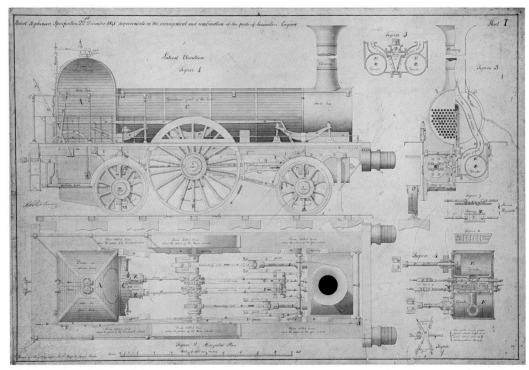

9 Drawing from Stephenson's 1841 patent of the 'long-boiler' locomotive type
(National Railway Museum/Science & Society Picture Library)

10 Early
electric
telegraph
signalling
apparatus
(Reynolds's
*Pictorial Atlas
of Arts,
Sciences,
Manufactures
& Machinery,*
1848)

11 The closing ceremony of the Great Exhibition
(Elton collection, Ironbridge Gorge Museum Trust)

12 Hampstead
cutting, London
& Birmingham
Railway
(T. T. Bury, *Six
coloured views
on the London
and
Birmingham
Railway from
drawings made
on the line with
the sanction of
the Company*,
1837)

Stephenson's claim from the Midland Railway was in excess of £40 000. Although £5000 was paid on account in both 1848 and 1849, special consideration of the balance was given by the chairman, deputy chairman and two senior directors.[160] In February 1850, agreement was reached with Stephenson for an immediate payment of £8000, a further £17 000 to be paid in interest-bearing debentures over three years, leaving the balance of over £8300 to be paid the following year.[161] Stephenson's long association with the Midland Railway and its predecessors ended from this time, although he was occasionally asked to assist the railway in matters of arbitration. The board even felt obliged to award him a free pass over its system, which had not hitherto been found necessary.[162]

The Committee of Investigation of the York & North Midland Railway considered Stephenson's claim for fees of nearly £9000, which were again paid through a combination of cheque and interest-bearing debentures over three years.[163] Stephenson's involvement with this railway after 1850 was limited to specific issues, notably the design and installation of the Brotherton Bridge (see Chapter 10).

He stood down as consulting engineer to the York, Newcastle & Berwick Railway in 1850, Thomas Harrison being appointed as chief engineer from that time. Until July 1852, however, Stephenson continued to undertake consulting work for the Eastern Counties Railway, the work on several medium and small projects being shared with George Bidder, George Robert Stephenson and George Berkley.[164] Thereafter, Stephenson stood down and Bidder assumed responsibility for this client.[165]

In the last eight years of his career, therefore, Stephenson's only major railway client in Britain was the London & North Western Railway, which position he continued to hold jointly with Joseph Locke. It was an acknowledgement of the seniority of both engineers that the railway's board felt unmoved to displace either man and were content to divide the responsibilities for their expanding territory between them. The matter was never a very satisfactory arrangement, however, and as late as 1852 it became necessary for the board minutes to record that 'both their names should in future appear in all matters in which either was employed to act for the Company.'[166] Thus was the situation with both men until their deaths, within a few weeks of each other, at the end of 1859.

160 Board Minutes, Midland Railway 1848–1850, 17 November 1848, 10 October 1849, and 7 November 1849, **PRO**, RAIL 491/15.
161 Ibid., 6 February 1850, 19 July 1850, 12 November 1850 and 7 May 1851.
162 Ibid., 5 May 1852.
163 Board Minutes, York & North Midland Railway, 27 July 1849 and 3 August 1849, **PRO**, RAIL 770/3.
164 Board Minutes, Eastern Counties Railway, 1851–1854, **PRO**, RAIL 186/10, *passim*.
165 Ibid., 29 July 1852.
166 Board Minutes, London & North Western Railway, 1849–1852, August 4 1852, **PRO**, RAIL 410/21.

Conclusion

The dinner in Newcastle Station in July 1850 was therefore a public demonstration of appreciation for Robert Stephenson's achievements during the previous turbulent decade. He was acknowledged for his extraordinary exertions towards the development of a railway network, whose impact on the nation's economic progress was profound. The contribution of the Westminster practice and of Stephenson himself, particularly during the mania years, had been greater than that of the other leading consulting engineers.

He had taken the engineering profession beyond surveying, designing and building of railway structures into active participation in the nation's network development. This contribution had carried with it the dangers of involvement with controversial disputes that a free-market system inevitably produced. That this involvement was so great, without any compromise of his professional standing, is a measure of the respect in which he was held.

His ardent belief in a regulated national railway network without wasteful duplication and competition was never fulfilled, but his contribution towards that aim was profound. That there were no territorial disputes between the Midland Railway and the London & North Western Railway, in marked contrast to the disputes with the Great Western Railway, may have resulted from his influence over the affairs of the respective boardrooms.

In the post-mania and -Hudson era, exhausted from his exertions, his planning role for Britain's railways was largely fulfilled. His future lay not only in his continued representation of the interests of the London & North Western Railway, but in his increasing contribution to the development of railways overseas, and to other branches of engineering, most notably water engineering. The national respect that he had earned, however, not least his ability to reconcile sharply opposing opinions in railway-related disputes, meant that his services as an arbitrator would continue to be called upon.

5

Wider horizons

Michael Bailey

… as soon as I can spare time you know you & I are to go and set the Railway out from the meditirranean to the Red Sea. & we shall send the young men to execute it after it is done we will take a trip to the east indes by that rute, and set them to work in that quarter …

George Stephenson, 1830[1]

At a time of rapid European railway development in the 1840s, Robert Stephenson's reputation for achievement as an engineer, strategist and tactician brought him to the attention of monarchs and governments, as well as capitalists. His reputation in the City of London and other financial centres, and amongst railway boardrooms, was equally high. He was well known to capitalists, such as Sir Joshua Walmsley and John Lewis Ricardo, and merchant banks such as Baring Brothers. He was seen as an achiever who had diplomatic skills to reconcile sharp differences between opposing factions, both within and between boards of directors. Although their early approaches were received during the 'mania' years, adding to the heavy workload of the Westminster practice, he was pleased to advise on foreign railway development, as well as undertaking specific route assessments and railway building.

The recession in the British economy from 1848 coincided with political turmoil in several European countries, leading to a sharp reduction in railway development. Stephenson and Bidder were aware of the need to diversify their activities, and considered the future of the practice. As the Chester & Holyhead and York, Newcastle & Berwick Railways moved towards completion, and with the immediate focus of Stephenson's attention being the great bridges at Conway, Menai, Newcastle and Berwick, it was necessary for the practice to develop other areas of engineering involvement. In addition, Stephenson had, from 1847, become a Member of Parliament and, from 1849, a Member of the Executive Committee planning the Great Exhibition (see Chapter 7), and he could have chosen this time to reduce his involvement with other projects.

He was, furthermore, mentally and physically tired after his intensive programme of work during the 1840s, and such a reduction would have

1 Letter, George Stephenson to Michael Longridge, Leverpool [*sic*] 8 February 1830, **IMechE**, IMS/131/1.

allowed him a slower lifestyle and, perhaps, a longer life. He witnessed the effects of intensive working on some of his associates whose health was suffering. Three who had kept up with his heavy programme of work were obliged to retire early. Thomas Gooch became ill through exhaustion in 1847 and, although he returned to work, his health declined and he retired in 1851.[2] Frederick Swanwick retired early from the Midland Railway in 1850,[3] whilst Robert Dockray also retired early through illness from the London & North Western Railway in 1852.[4]

Stephenson's partner Edward Pease put to him, in a letter, the prospect of early retirement on the completion of the Holyhead line, to which he responded:[5]

… I have pleasure in stating that the suggestion which it contains is quite in accordance with my own intentions & feelings respecting retirement, but I find it a very difficult matter to bring to a close so complicated a connection in business matters as that which has been established by 25 years of active & arduous professional duty –

Comparative retirement is however my intention and I trust that your prayer for the divine blessing to grant me happiness and quiet comfort will be fulfilled.

The outcome of this period of reflection was very different, however. Stephenson's hard-working lifestyle had been accentuated since 1842 to make up for the domestic vacuum since his wife's death and, in the wake of his father's death in 1848, he had no close family incentives for partial retirement. Furthermore, he would not easily wind down from such mental stimulation and, far from pursuing a more sedentary career, he substituted other involvements for the reducing number of British railway projects.

Whilst he continued as consulting engineer to the London & North Western Railway, the diversification of his other interests represents a further phase in his intensive career. He expanded his involvement with both overseas railway projects and water engineering schemes. In the more settled era of the 1850s, interest in railway development increased around the world, and Stephenson was approached both for strategic advice on national schemes and for his participation in individual projects.

In addition, he had become so well respected within British railway boardrooms that he was frequently called upon for advice. He earned particular recognition for his abilities as an arbitrator, to which tasks he brought strategic as well as tactical thinking to resolve disputes. Such involvements confirmed his long-held belief about the wastefulness of competition, and he sought to persuade competing boards to amalgamate into regional networks avoiding duplicated routes. In this endeavour, he was frustrated by the strong free-market beliefs of the day.

---

2 Obituary of Thomas Longridge Gooch, *Proc. ICE*, **LXXII**, 1882/3, pp. 300–8.
3 J. Frederick Smith, *Frederick Swanwick A Sketch*, printed for private circulation, 1888. The author is grateful to Mrs Brenda Tyler for sight of this sketch.
4 Memoir to Robert Benson Dockray, *Proc. ICE*, **XXXIII**, 1872/73, pp. 213–5.
5 Letter, Robert Stephenson to Edward Pease, London, 15 June 1850, **Pease–Stephenson**, D/PS/4/14.

Stephenson was always energetic in promoting the interests of his practice, and he encouraged the involvement of his associates, in their own capacity, in both railway and water engineering projects. The practice at 24 Great George Street remained busy throughout the remainder of his life and, indeed, for many years afterwards. Thus, in the last decade of his life, in spite of his sentiments in 1850 and increasing bouts of illness, he sustained a level of work that was far from 'comparative retirement'.

The associates

In the new era, some of Robert Stephenson's associates retired, and others moved on to other positions. Thomas Harrison pursued his independent career in Newcastle as engineer of the York, Newcastle & Berwick Railway. Through his efforts the east coast companies were amalgamated in 1854 into the North Eastern Railway, for which he served as engineer-in-chief for a further 34 years.[6] Thomas Cabry served under him as engineer of the railway's Southern Division until 1871,[7] whilst John Birkinshaw retired in 1849, but subsequently resumed as an independent consulting engineer.[8]

George Berkley set up on his own account in 1849, but remained a close colleague of Stephenson, for whom he was to undertake further work. Alexander Ross also acted independently and, on completion of the Chester & Holyhead Railway, embarked on other projects, notably as engineer of the Canadian Grand Trunk Railroad.

The associates who remained on Stephenson's projects around the country included Michael Borthwick, engaged on railway and water projects in East Anglia; James Berkley, resident engineer on the North Staffordshire Railway; and Edwin and Latimer Clark and Frank Forster, all engaged on the Chester & Holyhead line. On the completion of the Menai Bridge, the Clark brothers were appointed as engineers to the Electric Telegraph Company, whose directors included Stephenson and Bidder.[9] Forster spent a short time in the United States, before being appointed as chief engineer of the Metropolitan Commission of Sewers – again, no doubt, through Stephenson's influence.[10]

From 1850, therefore, the associates who were largely based at the Westminster office were George Bidder, George Robert Stephenson, George Phipps,[11] Henry Rouse, Henry Swinburne and William Lloyd. To them all, Stephenson was the 'Chief'. Lloyd later described the layout of the Stephenson office:[12]

6 Tomlinson, p. 515.
7 Lewis, pp. 45–65.
8 Memoir of John Cass Birkinshaw, *Proc. ICE*, **XXXI**, 1870/71, pp. 202–7.
9 Obituaries to Edwin and Latimer Clark, *Proc. ICE*, **CXX**, 1894/5, pp. 344–54, and **CXXXIV**, 1898/9, pp. 418–23.
10 Memoir to Frank Forster, *Proc. ICE*, **XII**, 1852/3, pp. 157–9.
11 Obituary to George Henry Phipps, *Proc. ICE*, **XCIV**, 1888/9, pp. 330–3.
12 Lloyd, pp. 37–8.

We occupied three floors of the house, the ground floor being that occupied by Mr. George Parker Bidder, C.E. ... He was associated with Mr. Stephenson in many things, and was invaluable in conducting Bills before Parliament, and, if somewhat rough in manner and address, showed me much kindness, when I least expected it. He seemed only to have an engineering secretary, and was always reading the *Times* and smoking a good cigar ...

The first floor of the house of three rooms were Mr. Stephenson's, one his secretary's, next the chief's private room, with consulting room adjoining; and on the second floor the nephew [*sic*] of Mr. Stephenson, George Robert, presided over myself and one or two others. This completed the staff, and I have often wondered at the work accomplished by so few of us.

Stephenson encouraged his associates to pursue further British railway schemes in their own name. Many were planned during the 1850s, principally by Bidder and George Robert Stephenson, and it is likely that Robert Stephenson was occasionally consulted about them.[13] The associates were also consulted on other engineering issues and appeared as expert witnesses in both Parliament and in law cases.[14]

The death, in October 1853, of his personal assistant and close friend, John Sanderson, was a serious blow that took Stephenson a long time to come to terms with.[15] He later recruited an engineering assistant, B. P. Stockman, who also undertook secretarial duties.[16] Stephenson was equally devastated in 1855 with the death of his agent and close friend, Edward Starbuck (see Chapter 6). With the importance of having a London representative for the locomotive factory, Stephenson called upon Charles Manby (1804–1884) to become the firm's London representative. For 17 years, Manby had been Secretary of the Institution of Civil Engineers, and, whilst remaining as the Institution's Honorary Secretary, he moved next door to the Stephenson office.[17]

European railway building

Robert Stephenson approved of the relatively ordered system of European countries that built their railway networks according to national and regional requirements in the 1840s. Concessions for each route were offered to capitalists for competitive tender, which he clearly regarded as a less wasteful form of free-market opportunity. The London capital market accepted the continental disciplines, and was particularly active in pursuing investment opportunities. Stephenson was keen to participate in such schemes and even acted, where necessary, as an intermediary in brokering deals with investment consortia.

13 For example the Boston, Sleaford and Midland Counties Railway, Advertisement, *RT*, **XV**, 30 October 1852, p. 1150.
14 For example, *South Yorkshire* v. *the Great Northern* at Liverpool Assizes, *RT*, **XVI**, 16 April 1853, p. 416.
15 Jeaffreson, II, p. 186.
16 For example, letter, B. P. Stockman to Professor Forbes, Westminster, 7 November 1855, **Forbes**, Msdep7, Incoming letters 1855, No.140.
17 Memoir to Charles Manby, *Proc. ICE*, **LXXXI**, 1884/5, pp. 327–34.

Released from his responsibilities on the London & Birmingham line, he spent three months in 1839 visiting France, Belgium, Italy and Switzerland.[18] He became acquainted with Paulin Talabot (1799–1885), the French engineer, who became a close colleague and regular correspondent.[19] Talabot became a prominent railway engineer and promoter in France, and later joined Stephenson in the survey of the Suez isthmus in Egypt (see Chapter 12).

Following his visit to Tuscany, Stephenson arranged the survey for the Leopold Railway between Florence, Pisa and Leghorn (Livorno), the legislation for which was passed in 1841.[20] At a time of limited rail work in Britain, he became the line's engineer-in-chief (see Chapter 9).[21] Whilst visiting the building works in 1845, he was consulted regarding extending the railway from Florence across the Apennine Mountains to Forli, but apparently concluded that it would be too costly.[22]

Following his 1842 study of routes between Calais/Lille and Paris for the South Eastern Railway, Stephenson was consulted on other French railway routes, including Boulogne to Amiens,[23] and two major schemes in 1845 for routes between Paris and Lyon and between Lyon and Avignon.[24] The latter would have joined the Marseille–Avignon Railway to provide a through route to the Mediterranean. There was intense competition between eighteen consortia seeking the route concessions from the French Government.[25] He was engineer to a Franco-British company, whose submissions were, however, rejected in favour of other groups of promoters. In 1851, he was involved with another London group seeking a concession for the 'Western Railway of France'.[26] This concession was also refused, and, in contrast to Joseph Locke, who undertook several projects in France, Stephenson was never involved with building railways in that country.

The state-owned Belgian railway system, about which George and Robert Stephenson had been consulted in 1835, was largely completed by 1845. A secondary network of over 850km was then planned, for which private companies tendered for nine concessions by the Belgian Government in 1845–1846.[27] The buoyant financial market produced a flurry of activity in the City of London, and several companies were formed to bid for the concessions, not all of which were soundly based.[28] The building of the lines was, however, severely

18 Jeaffreson, I, pp. 239–40.
19 Bertrand Gille, 'Paulin Talabot, recherche pour une biographie', *Revue d'Histoire des Mines et de la Métallurgie*, No. 1, 1967.
20 *RT*, **IV**, 24 April 1841, p. 464.
21 Giuntini, also Landi. The author is grateful to Dr. Stefano Maggi of Siena for information concerning the Leopold Railway.
22 *RT*, **VIII**, 8 November 1845, p. 2189, and 20 December 1845, p. 2412.
23 *RT*, **VII**, 16 November 1844, pp. 1354–5.
24 Advertisements, *RT*, **VIII**, 13 September 1845, p. 1557, 27 September 1845, p. 1669, and subsequent editions. The author is grateful to Mr Ian Cowburn of L'Argentière, France, for information about the Paris–Avignon schemes.
25 *RT*, **VIII**, 22 November 1845, p. 2285.
26 *RT*, **XIV**, 30 August 1851, p. 890.
27 Lamalle, p. 43.
28 Brooke, pp. 234–5.

affected by the 1848 recession and revolution in France. The resulting financial crises led to undercapitalization, and completion of the lines was largely dependent upon subvention from the Belgian Government.

In spite of the heavy demands on Stephenson's time and those of his associates during the 'mania' years, the Westminster practice acted as consulting engineers for four companies tendering for five of the routes, whose concessions totalled nearly 350km (Fig. 5.1). Stephenson sought his father's help and, although George Stephenson had retired from active involvement in railway work, he agreed to assist with two of the projects.

The first route was the 105-km Sambre–Meuse Railway, linking the river Sambre near Charleroi with Vireux on the river Meuse adjacent to the French border, together with branches serving coal-mining areas. The railway's consulting engineer had been William Cubitt, but following the award of the concession, the Stephensons replaced him, under circumstances that were not recorded.[29] George Stephenson visited Belgium escorted by Thomas Sopwith (1803–1879), a close friend of the Stephensons, who had carried out route surveys in relation to the coalfield geology.[30] Following his report, a Belgian engineer, de Grandvoir, supervised the building of the line, with Robert Stephenson as consulting engineer.[31] The company was undercapitalized by 1849, however, and the Belgian Government provided additional capital to complete the work.[32]

Robert Stephenson was approached about the 42-km Tournai–Jurbise line, linking the two main rail routes in the south-west of Belgium. This concession was curiously offered together with a 28-km line between Landen, on the main Brussels–Liège line, with Hasselt in the eastern province of Limburg.[33] A London-based company was awarded the combined concession in 1845, for which Bidder and Stephenson jointly acted as consulting engineers.[34] The Tournai–Jurbise line was the only concession line to be funded completely by the concessionaires, whilst the Landen–Hasselt line required a subsidy.

The largest of the concession lines was the 149-km West Flanders Railway, for which both Stephensons were consulting engineers. The railway was to be a network of routes linking several communities in western Belgium with both the national rail network and river quays.[35] The Stephensons also recommended linking it with Calais and Dunkirk to offer rapid communication with Britain, but this proposal did not proceed.[36]

29 RT, **VIII**, 24 May 1845, pp. 713–14.
30 RT, **VII**, 8 June 1844, p. 644, and advertisement, Sambre & Meuse Railway, 1 June 1844, p. 628. Also Memoir to Thomas Sopwith, Proc. ICE, **LIX**, 1879, pp. 345–58. Also Smiles (1862), pp. 435–8.
31 RT, **X**, 23 January 1847, pp. 109/110.
32 Half-yearly meeting, Sambre & Meuse Railway, RT, **XII**, 28 July 1849, pp. 743–4.
33 Lamalle, p. 44.
34 Brooke, pp. 234–5.
35 Printed and circulated report by George Stephenson to the Directors of the West Flanders Railways [sic] Company, Bruges, July 1845. Also Smiles (1862), p. 439.
36 Advertisement, Calais, Dunkirk and West Flanders Junction Railway, RT, **VIII**, 4 October 1845, p. 1799.

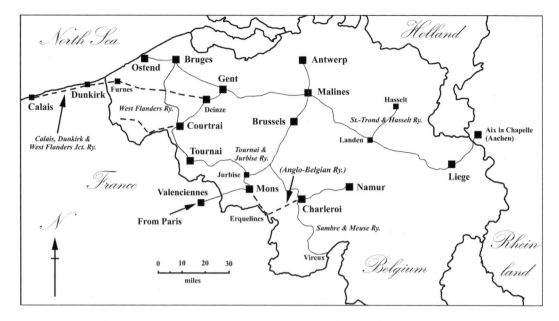

Robert Stephenson acted alone as consulting engineer during the building of the West Flanders line, but from 1848 the railway became undercapitalized, and only the main route between Bruges and Courtrai was built. At the company's half-yearly meeting in London in November that year, Stephenson attended to make a statement about his father's involvement with the railway.[37] It seems that George Stephenson had invoiced the company for his services, some items of which were disputed, and he had commenced legal proceedings against the Board just prior to his death in August.

Robert Stephenson was therefore placed in a difficult position when, as executor and principal beneficiary of his father's estate, he became aware not only of the proceedings, but that the West Flanders Company, now his client, was taking counter-proceedings against the estate through the Court of Chancery. Stephenson boldly announced to the shareholders that he had discontinued his father's proceedings and that:[38]

They were instituted without his knowledge; for had he been acquainted with the particulars, he was quite sure he should have been enabled to have explained the error of those proceedings. He was now, however, in a position to state that the bill contained charges which he had no hesitation in saying were wholly unfounded.

In speaking of the benefits of submitting 'differences to the arbitration of independent parties … in place of the tedious, expensive, and obscure proceedings of the Court of Chancery … ', he reflected his strong belief in arbitration to resolve disputes, and his own growing involvement in this discipline. That his father had ended his career in litigation with an important client must have been both a sorrow and an embarrassment for Stephenson, who nevertheless dealt decisively with the issue.

5.1 Belgian rail routes, including the 1840s concession lines

37 Half-Yearly Meeting, West Flanders Railway, *RR*, **V**, 18 November 1848, pp. 1115–6.
38 Ibid.

Robert Stephenson and George Bidder also acted as consulting engineers to the Anglo-Belgian Railway Company, a joint venture between capitalists in Brussels and London.[39] The company proposed a 24-km route from the main line near Charleroi to Erquelines on the French border, together with a 24-km canal from Erquelines to Mons, offering significant improvements to through traffic between Paris, Antwerp, Holland and north Germany. Stephenson and Bidder ordered surveys, but the scheme was abandoned in 1848 in the wake of the political changes in France and Germany.

Interest in railway development in Spain followed a decree seeking concessions in 1844.[40] One of several schemes during 1845 was the 270-mile route from the north coast port of Avilés, which passed through the Asturian coalfield and León down to Madrid. This joint venture between Spanish and British capitalists received the 'especial protection' of the Spanish Queen as the 'Royal North of Spain Railway'.[41] Whilst Robert Stephenson was consulting engineer to the company, the survey was arranged by James Rendel (1799–1856), whom he knew well (see Chapter 12).[42]

Although the Spanish Government promised incentives, the Royal North scheme was ill-founded, leading to allegations of share allocation malpractice.[43] Some directors, notably Sir Joshua Walmsley, also expressed doubts that viability could be assured without a more thorough assessment of the route and better financial incentives. Robert Stephenson asked his father to undertake a further route survey, which was a long and difficult assignment for George Stephenson. On arrival in Madrid he had formed 'an unfavourable opinion' of it, and persuaded Walmsley not to make a deposit with the Spanish Government for the concession.[44] The other directors subsequently endorsed their decision, and the project was abandoned.

With the practice overstretched with British work in 1845, it had been reassuring to Stephenson that his father could assist with some of the broad survey and feasibility work. This opportunity ended with George Stephenson's serious illness on his return from Spain, however, and although he recovered to spend a further three years in active retirement, he did not undertake any further fieldwork.

Robert Stephenson visited Norway with George Bidder in 1846 to consider a request, from its King and Government, regarding the country's first rail line. The 40-mile Norwegian Trunk Railway (Fig. 5.2) was to run northwards from Christiania (now Oslo) to Eidsvold (Eidsvoll) at the southern tip of Lake Myosen (Mjøsa). The lake was an important artery for timber and other traffic, and the railway would extend this movement to the capital for export.[45] Norway was a young country with inadequate capital, and it was necessary to

39 Advertisement, Anglo-Belgian Railway Company, RT, **VIII**, 9 August 1845, pp. 1196–7.
40 Chrimes et al., pp. 46–50.
41 RT, **VIII**, 15 March 1845, p. 369.
42 Memoir for James Meadows Rendel, *Proc. ICE*, **XVI**, 1856, pp. 133–42.
43 RT, **VIII**, *passim*.
44 Smiles (1862), pp. 439–44.
45 Clark (1983), pp. 230–51.

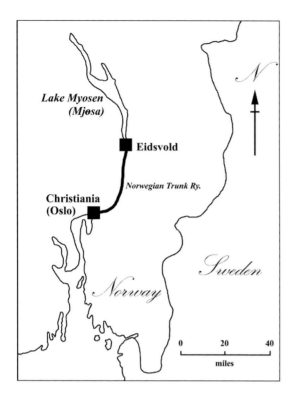

5.2 Norwegian Trunk Railway between Christiania and Eidsvold

plan an inexpensive line. Stephenson subsequently recalled the efforts to which he and Bidder had gone to keep the cost low:[46]

> The best engineer is the man who most appropriately applies the materials which are available in every country to his purposes; and his ability and talents ought to be measured in accordance with those applications. Mr. Bidder and I, originally, in designing this Norwegian line, devoted our best energies to the conception of a construction such as would come within reach of the Norwegian government ... this is the cheapest line of Railway that was ever made over a rough country ...

With the cost estimated at below £½ million, the £800 cost of the subsequent survey and preparation of plans, sections and estimates was met by Stephenson himself, remaining as a loan in his Norwegian account.[47] Although the work was completed by early 1847, Stephenson did not approve them until the end of the year, by which time it was difficult to raise the capital because of the recession. Further attempts over three years were unsuccessful until, in 1850, Stephenson himself brokered an agreement between the Norwegian Government and a consortium of British contractors:[48]

> ... I was the means of bringing this contract into Norway ... I have the responsibility of having begun it, – of adopting every means that brought the execution of the railway to a completion, – the Norwegian government would never have had a

---

46 Arbitration evidence 'Re The Norwegian Trunk Railway Before Robert Stephenson Esq. M.P.', London, September 1856, **ScM**, GPB1/3/3f, p. 21.
47 Jeaffreson, II, pp. 130–1.
48 Op. cit. (n. 46), p. 18.

Railway if it had not been for Mr. Crowe [British Consul General in Christiania] and myself ... to deal with people who have come forward with money, with English capital ...

The three major contractors Thomas Brassey, Samuel Peto and Edward Betts formed the consortium, together with the financier John Lewis Ricardo. Bidder was both the engineer for the line and 'agent' for the consortium. Whilst sufficient capital was found to launch the project, the balance was obtained by a flotation once building had begun.[49]

Stephenson was the consulting engineer, and made a speech at the ceremonial 'cutting of the first sod' in August 1851.[50] He visited the line twice, with Bidder, to monitor progress, and attended the opening festivities in September 1854 (Fig. 5.3).[51] It is likely that he was awarded the Grand Cross of St Olaf on this occasion, although his obituary suggests that he received this in 1848.[52]

The agreement that Stephenson had brokered specified that the contractors should operate and maintain the line for five years and that, in the event of any disagreement with the Norwegian authorities, the matter would be referred to him for arbitration. He was obliged to officiate over a dispute during this period as the railway's representatives claimed that the line was substandard (see Chapter 9). The matter was satisfactorily resolved and, to celebrate the handing over of the railway to the Norwegian authorities in 1859, a dinner was held in Stephenson's honour. During his speech, which was marred by illness, he emphasized that it was 'to Mr. Bidder that the chief honour belongs for establishing this railway, which is now completed with English skill, aided by no inconsiderable Norwegian capital and liberality.'[53]

Strategic railway planning

In contrast to the British system of competitive route developments and combative legislative appraisal, Robert Stephenson was impressed by invitations he received from some European countries for advice on transport network planning. Since the mid-1830s, when he helped his father plan the Belgian national rail network, he had favoured strategic route planning according to the population and economic activity of each region, and using the most suitable transport modes. Consideration for each route required appraisal of its topography and geology, leading to recommendations on ruling gradients, structural and material requirements and the motive-power implications. His opportunities to pursue this form of strategic planning came in the 1850s from Switzerland, Denmark and Sweden.

49 *RT*, **XV**, 16 October 1852, p. 1093.
50 *ILN*, 13 September 1851, p. 324.
51 *ILN*, 7 October 1854, pp. 336–8.
52 Memoir to Robert Stephenson, *Proc. ICE*, **XIX**, 1859/60, p. 179.
53 Jeaffreson, II, p. 256.

5.3 Eidsvold
station at the
opening of the
Norwegian
Trunk Railway
on 1 September
1854
(*Illustrated
London News*)

Switzerland became a confederation of cantons in 1848, following the
Sonderbund War. Feelings between the cantons continued to run high,
however, and jealousies threatened to undermine the country's progress. The
government was thus anxious to draw together the diverse economies and
political aspirations of the cantons through a unifying development plan, for
which railways were seen as a primary constituent.

An independent professional assessment was called for, and in 1849 the
Federal Assembly set up a feasibility study for transport development, largely
based on railways.[54] The Swiss Consul-General in London approached
Stephenson and asked him to undertake both an assessment of traffic opportunities between main centres of population and broad route surveys with which
to assess route priorities, capacity requirements and the most economic transport modes.[55] The approved rail routes were to be offered to concessionaires.

In the summer of 1850, Stephenson considered sending Thomas Gooch to
undertake the first fact-finding tasks and initial route surveys, but his health
remained poor, and Stephenson called upon Henry Swinburne to undertake
the work. He was to consider a route network linking the French railway
system in Basel (Basle), the railways of the German states of Baden,
Württemberg and Bavaria, adjacent to Lake Constance (Bodensee), and
across the Alps to Lugano on the Italian border (Fig. 5.4). Having received his
first two reports, Stephenson was impressed with Swinburne's initial work
and wrote that he was 'agreeably surprised at your rapid progress'.[56]

In a subsequent letter to Swinburne, however, Stephenson showed a gratu-
itous arrogance in relation to his engineering expertise, when he wrote:[57]

54 Clark (1983), pp. 366–8.
55 Elsasser, pp. 25–6.
56 Letter, Robert Stephenson to Henry Swinburne, London, 3 July 1850, **NRO**, ZSW 539/32.
57 Letter, Robert Stephenson to Henry Swinburne, London, 14 July 1850, **NRO**, ZSW 539/32.

5.4 Stephenson's transport schemes for Switzerland proposed in his 1850 report to the Swiss Government

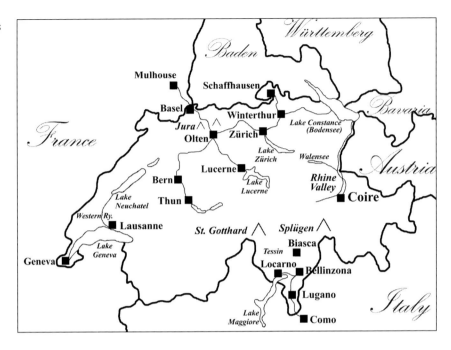

It will really be delightful if you have discovered a better line than any of the local Engineers I think it is not at all improbable for I have often been astonished at the ignorance of some of the Continental Engineers in appreciating the features of a country. They seem to have no feeling for the subject, what sometimes appeared to me so simple and obvious as to be axiomatic appeared to them difficult and requiring a lengthened demonstration.

Swinburne first surveyed a northern network serving Basel, Lucerne, Olten, Bern (Berne), Thun, Zürich, Winterthur, Schaffhausen, and Lake Constance.[58] With the more difficult trans-Alpine routes still to be considered, Stephenson and Bidder met up with Swinburne and surveyed a route southwards along the Rhine valley to Coire (Chur).[59] Stephenson and Swinburne alone then sought a route across the Alps, between the Splügen and St Gotthard mountains, to Biasca on the Italian side of the range. They returned to Lucerne and Bern, where Stephenson arranged to meet Swiss Government Ministers, 'after which piece of etiquette' he wrote up his report.[60]

Stephenson's comprehensive report recommended a mixed transport system of locomotive railways, rope-worked incline railways, lake steamboat services and road improvements. He did not recommend a trans-Alpine railway, suggesting no doubt that railway technology had yet to achieve an economic capability for the extensive tunnelling that would be required.[61] The route between Basle and Olten crossed the 1000-metre high Jura range, for

58 Bärtschi, p. 128. The author is grateful to Mr A. Heer-Schönenberger of Flawil, St Gallen for his assistance.
59 Clark (1983), pp. 78–9.
60 Letter, Robert Stephenson to Edward Starbuck, Zürich, 15 September 1850, **Stephenson**, Folder 18.
61 Elsasser, p. 26.

which he recommended inclines worked by rope-haulage and stationery engines, similar to that in operation on the Düsseldorf to Elberfeld line.

In addition to a northern rail network between Thun and Lake Constance, he recommended a rail route in the southern canton of Tessin, and he confirmed the choice of route, previously surveyed by a Swiss engineer, between Lake Geneva and Lake Neuchâtel (Neufchatel). Paddle steamers were recommended for Lakes Geneva, Neuchâtel, Lucerne, Zürich, Walensee and Constance, with road improvements for the trans-Alpine routes.

His report caused arguments between the cantonal and national governments, with some cantons feeling disadvantaged.[62] The Federal Council drew up a 'decree' for Stephenson's proposed railway network, which totalled over 400 miles at a cost exceeding 100 million francs,[63] but some changes were insisted upon by the cantons. The first line to proceed was between Lakes Geneva and Neuchâtel, for which the 'Western Railway of Switzerland' was granted a concession in the autumn of 1852.[64] George Phipps was appointed as engineer-in-chief for building this railway.[65]

The building of the Semmering line in Austria as the first mountain railway, however, demonstrated to the Swiss authorities that Stephenson's recommendations had not taken into account the advanced possibilities that such alignments might allow in the Alpine regions. The Semmering line was a more ambitious main line for locomotive haulage than Stephenson contemplated, being built to a more demanding ruling gradient, and accepting the challenges of viaduct and tunnel construction beyond previous experience. There is no evidence to indicate Stephenson's views about the progress being made in Austria, and he was not subsequently asked for a reassessment of the Swiss network taking such specifications into account. Neither the Stephenson factory nor any other British manufacturer put forward locomotives to take part in the Semmering Trials of 1851, although three or four had contemplated it.[66]

The building of the Norwegian Trunk Railway encouraged renewed interest in railway development in Denmark in 1851. The interest was prompted by 'British speculators', stimulated by Samuel Peto, whose business interests were much wider than his contracting activities.[67] He had acquired and modernized the port of Lowestoft, and encouraged the introduction of a steam packet service between the port and the Danish west coast, to ship livestock and other agricultural produce.[68]

The Danish Government was keen to take advantage of this interest, with its prospect of attracting significant amounts of capital, and sought to

62 *RT*, **XV**, 30 October 1852, pp. 1127–8.
63 *RT*, **XIV**, 12 July 1851, p. 682.
64 *RT*, **XV**, 10 July 1852, pp. 683–4, and 6 November 1852, p. 1183.
65 Obituary of George Henry Phipps, *Proc. ICE*, **LXXXIX**, 1888/9, pp. 330–3.
66 F. J. G. Haut, 'The Centenary of the Semmering Railway and its Locomotives', *TNS*, **XXVII**, 1949/ 51, pp. 19–29.
67 *RT*, **XIV**, 30 August 1851, p. 890.
68 Brooks, pp. 140–9.

promote a nationwide review of the country's railway potential. In 1851, Stephenson and Bidder visited Copenhagen with Peto to discuss railway development.[69] Whilst representing Peto's interests, in partnership with Thomas Brassey, Edward Betts and John Ricardo, Stephenson discussed with the Danish Government an extension of the existing Copenhagen to Roskilde line to Corsor (Korsør), on the west coast of Zealand, together with routes in Jutland and Schleswig-Holstein (Fig. 5.5). The Danish King was 'very favourable to Mr. Stephenson's plans.'[70]

A railway had been proposed in 1847 between Tönning, on the west coast of Schleswig-Holstein, and Flensburg on the Baltic coast, but this had failed due to the recession and the 1848 political turmoil affecting both Denmark and her neighbours.[71] The priority was therefore to reaffirm interest with this route, together with a branch to Rendsburg.[72] The British consortium was granted a concession in 1852, the railway being known as 'King Frederick VII's South Slesvig Railway', shortened in its British prospectus to 'Royal Danish Railway'.[73] Stephenson limited his involvement to the wider planning remit, however, with Bidder being appointed as the railway's engineer-in-chief.

In 1853, Stephenson and Bidder were asked to consider the development of a railway network in Sweden by a 'powerful combination of capitalists.'[74] They despatched William Lloyd to that country to carry out broad route surveys for some 700 miles of railway. The routes were to serve Malmö, Kristianstad, Gothenburg, Stockholm, Uppsala, Gävle and Falun (Fig. 5.5). Lloyd spent five arduous months on the work, assisted by thirty Swedish military engineers. The Swedish Government compensated the 'English syndicate' for the costs of Lloyd's survey, and undertook to build the railways engaging Swedish engineers. The first main line of the Royal Swedish Railways was opened in 1856.

Whilst Stephenson had grasped the opportunities to investigate and report on the extended transport requirements of the three countries, it would have been apparent to him that the aspirations and priorities of governments and capitalists were not necessarily in accord with his recommendations. Railway development that took place was a compromise that did not necessarily follow planning logic. His reports did not always lead to further work for the Westminster practice, although the close association with Peto, Brassey and Betts had led to their engaging Bidder and George Robert Stephenson for the Royal Danish Railway.

Stephenson's arrogance regarding the 'ignorance of some of the Continental Engineers' was wholly misplaced, as amply demonstrated by the building of the Semmering line and subsequent routes. Although several British consulting engineers were engaged on railway schemes on the

---

69 Thestrup, p. 77.
70 *RT*, **XIV**, 30 August 1851, p. 890.
71 Thestrup, pp. 9–73.
72 Clark (1983), pp. 252–8.
73 *RT*, **XVI**, 9 April 1853, p. 395.
74 Lloyd, pp. 40–8.

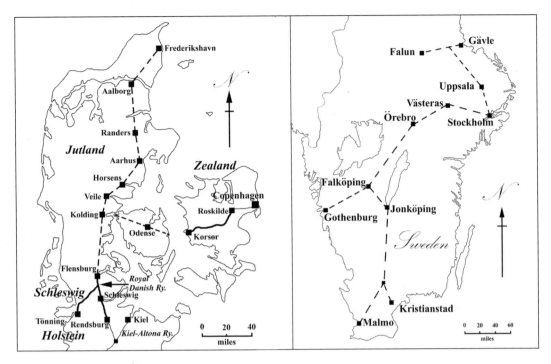

5.5 Stephenson's Danish and Swedish rail route proposals

Continent, engineering expertise developed quickly in each country, and those engineers made notable contributions to railway building in their home countries. Stephenson undertook no further work in European railway planning, however, his attention being drawn to the several schemes being considered for Egypt, India and other distant countries.

'Intercourse with India'

Robert Stephenson's most ambitious strategic scheme was that for improving communication between Britain and India, which echoed his father's predictions of twenty years earlier (p. 135). The East India Company and the British Government were attracted by the potential for improved communications, and the savings in time and money that would be achieved by a rail connection across Egypt, and by rail routes between the Indian port cities and the interior of the 'peninsula'. Putting aside thoughts about partial retirement, his enthusiasm was carried forward into participation as consulting engineer for these schemes. Such work formed an important part of the diversification of the Westminster practice in the wake of the slowdown in British railway development.

Stephenson first visited Egypt in 1848–1849, following the completion of the Conway Bridge, and preceding the erection of the Britannia Bridge.[75] He was accompanied by other engineers, including Paulin Talabot and the

---

75 Stephenson was subsequently mistaken about the date of his first visit, claiming it to have taken place in 1847. House of Commons debate, 17 July 1857, on proposed Suez Canal, Jeaffreson, II, pp. 148–50.

Austrian, Alois de Negrelli (1799–1858), to consider the possibility of a canal between the Red Sea and the Mediterranean (see Chapter 12).

During a second visit to Egypt in 1850, the Viceroy, Abbas Pasha, approached him for assistance in planning a railway between Alexandria and Cairo.[76] Stephenson was enthused by the project ('I have become much pleased with this subject and the Pacha is very anxious to have my views'), and agreed to carry out a route survey.[77] He also thought that an alternative scheme for a canal, considered by Talabot, was 'quite out of the question'. He considered the route, availability and price of materials, availability and cost of workmen, and procedures for contracting out the building work.[78]

On his return to London, Stephenson received a letter from the British Consul-General in Cairo, to which he replied:[79]

I fully value the high trust His Highness the Pacha has been pleased to place in me and in accepting his appointment it will be my duty to carry out his views about a Railway from Cairo to Alexandria in as effective and economical a manner as possible. –

The involvement of the Consul-General meant that the British Government was alerted to the wider strategic possibilities that a railway across Egypt would present. The route between Alexandria and Cairo could be extended to Suez and provide a major improvement in communication with India. Stephenson was keen to pursue a project of such strategic importance, and wrote in glowing terms:[80]

The journey has been full of interest in many respects; in the first place the country and people offered an entirely new aspect of human society to me, in the second the natural scenery was totally different from any thing I have yet seen in my extensive wanderings over the face of the globe, and in the third it is a district in which Engineering works are likely to form a conspicuous and important feature, in connection with our intercourse with India.

The Viceroy has intimated his wish that I would undertake the construction of a Railway from Alexandria to Cairo, which I regard as an important instalment of the entire communication between the Mediterranean and Red Seas -

He despatched Michael Borthwick to Egypt in the summer of 1851 to undertake a detailed route survey and to prepare plans, levels and estimates. The route was to have been a direct link between the two cities, to the west of the Nile delta, but whilst such a strategy fulfilled the wider British remit, the Viceroy had local and regional aspirations for the railway, and disagreed with the route (Fig. 5.6). He also insisted on the widest opportunities for local artisans and materials.[81]

76 Jeaffreson, II, pp. 173–4.

77 Letter, Robert Stephenson to Edward Starbuck, Suez, 1 January 1851, **Stephenson**, Folder 18.

78 Letter, Robert Stephenson to Hon. Chas. A. Murray, Westminster, 5 April 1851, **PRO**, FO/141/19/ Part 2.

79 Letter, Robert Stephenson to The Honble. Charles A. Murray, Westminster, 24 March 1851, **PRO**, FO/141/19/Part 2.

80 Letter, Robert Stephenson to Edward Pease, Westminster, 3 April 1851, **Pease–Stephenson**, D/PS/4/16.

81 Letter, Robert Stephenson to he Honble. Charles A. Murray, Westminster, 24 May 1851, **PRO**, FO/ 141/19/Part 2.

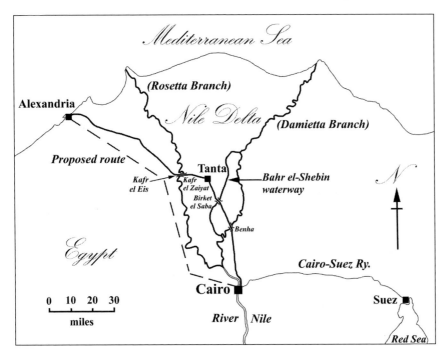

5.6 Alexandria–Cairo rail route and Suez extension

The Viceroy insisted that the line should serve the town of Tanta in the heart of the delta region, taking the route across its low-lying terrain and many watercourses, particularly the Rosetta and Damietta branches of the Nile, and the Bahr el-Shebin navigable waterway. The requirement for large bridges became crucial to the route alignment and the character of the railway itself. Stephenson was obliged to accept this revision as he recorded in a letter to the Consul General:[82]

Although I have a predilection in favor of the line which I have already suggested I am quite prepared on my next visit to Egypt to go dispassionately into the whole subject – Crossing the Nile twice invokes grave questions not merely on the regional construction, but on the future working of the line – His Highness may rest assured that the whole subject shall have my serious attention immediately on my arrival …

Borthwick and Stephenson returned to Egypt and, after lengthy negotiations, the revised route and methods of construction were agreed, leaving the design of the large Nile bridges to be determined on their return to England. They were to be wrought iron tubular bridges across the Nile branches, and a smaller tubular swing-bridge across the Bahr el-Shebin waterway (see Chapter 10). The line was to be largely on embankments, with some stretches crossing soft alluvial deposits that were periodically inundated by the Nile floods.[83]

The first stretch, between Alexandria and Kafr el-Eis, on the banks of the Rosetta Branch, opened in 1853, but suffered from inundations of the Nile in

82 Letter, Robert Stephenson to The Honble. C. A. Murray, London, 19 September 1851, **PRO**, FO/141/19/Part 2.

83 *RT*, **XVI**, 8 January 1853, p. 29.

its early months of operation.[84] The remainder of the line, with the exception of the Rosetta Branch crossing, was opened in 1856 (Fig. 5.7), by which time Abbas Pasha had died. Stephenson postponed the design and construction of this bridge owing to uncertainties over the river's behaviour in flood conditions and its effect on the river-bed.[85] To allow through train operation, therefore, a large chain ferry was designed and built at the Stephenson factory in Newcastle to convey carriages across the Nile (see Chapter 6).[86]

The three waterway crossings greatly increased the cost of the railway, and Stephenson visited Egypt in 1856 to negotiate a financial settlement between the Egyptian authorities and the contractor, Edward Price, which was considerably more than the original estimates (see Chapter 9).[87] He also reached agreement to proceed with the design and construction of the Rosetta Branch tubular bridge at Kafr el-Zaiyat.

It is also likely that he discussed the continuation of the railway from Cairo to Suez with the new Viceroy, Saïd Pasha. Although he had previously travelled to Suez and had a broad route plan in mind, the new Viceroy apparently had other ideas. They disagreed and the Viceroy commissioned another engineer, M. Mouchelet, to undertake the work.

In 1858 Stephenson made his last visit to Egypt, to check on the progress of the Kafr el-Zaiyat bridge and settle other matters associated with the railway. He also travelled along the Suez line, the building of which was then concluding. He was uncompromising in his criticism of the line:[88]

It is very much what I had expected it would be, a huge Engineering blunder – ... The Engineer Mouchelet met me at Suez evidently for the express purpose of getting my opinion upon the line, indeed I have good reason to believe that this arrangement was preconcocted – I told him that I congratulated him in having overcome the difficulties of the country so well but that I deeply regretted so much ability had been spent upon so disgraceful an example of R.way Engineering, alluding of course to the designing of the line which I knew was the Viceroy's – These observations with many others, I am informed made their way to his highness in a few hours. He has got an attack of boils since, & I have not been able to see him ...

In May 1859 the Kafr el-Zaiyat bridge was completed and the chain ferry withdrawn. Through rail services between Alexandria and Suez began later that year, opening up faster communication between Britain and India, the urgency for which had been emphasized by the 'mutiny' in the Subcontinent two years earlier.

84 The author is grateful to Dr Ishida Susumu of the International University of Japan and Mr Alan Clothier of Whitley Bay for advice on the Egyptian Railway.

85 Letter, Robert Stephenson to The Honble. Frederick Bruce, Alexandria, 5 January 1857, **PRO**, FO/ 141/33.

86 Thomas Sopwith, 'Account of the Steam-ferry over the River Nile, at Kaffre Azzayat' [sic], *Proc. ICE*, **XVII**, 1857/58, pp. 53–67.

87 Letter, Robert Stephenson to The Honble. Frederick Bruce, Alexandria, 5 January 1857, **PRO**, FO/ 141/33.

88 Letter, Robert Stephenson to G. P. Bidder, Alexandria, n.d. but mid-December 1858, contained in *Lizzy, The Story of George Stephenson's Goddaughter, Elizabeth Harby Stanton (née Bidder)*, Edited and Introduced by E. F. Clark, 1986, **ScM**, GPB5/9/1.

THE CAIRO RAILWAY STATION.

The first consideration for a railway in India had been in 1845. The Great Indian Peninsula Railway Company was formed in London during the height of the mania, with ambitions to build a 1300-mile network, for which a capital of £6 million was estimated.[89] The railway was to link the 'Peninsula' with the port of Bombay (Mumbai) and 'the best port on the east coast'. The Madras Railway was also formed during 1845, but with a less ambitious proposal for an initial 70-mile line between Madras and the military base at Arcot.[90] Stephenson agreed to act as consulting engineer for the two railways, both of which had the backing of the 'Honourable East India Company'.

Stephenson reported on the preliminary survey findings to the directors in early 1847, although he cannot have been in a position to provide more than general advice and a review of the material gathered by the surveys. This concluded that the best method for trains to climb 1800 feet over the Ghat mountains in just 15 miles was to use locomotives assisted by ropes worked by stationary engine.[91]

The subsequent recession removed the financial incentive for railways in India, and the Madras scheme was dissolved the following year.[92] The Great Indian Peninsula scheme continued, but only through the involvement of the East India Company, which undertook to guarantee a minimum 5 per cent

5.7 Cairo station opened in 1856 (*Illustrated London News*)

89 *RT*, **VIII**, 21 June 1845, pp. 862–3, and subsequent editions.
90 *RT*, **VIII**, 5 July 1845, p. 956, and subsequent editions.
91 *RT*, **X**, 6 February 1847, pp. 165–6.
92 Response to Parliamentary Question by Sir J. C. Hobhouse, President of the Board of Control, in the House of Commons, 26 June 1848, *RT*, **XI**, 1 July 1848, p. 715.

5.8 Great Indian
Peninsula
Railway routes
from Bombay

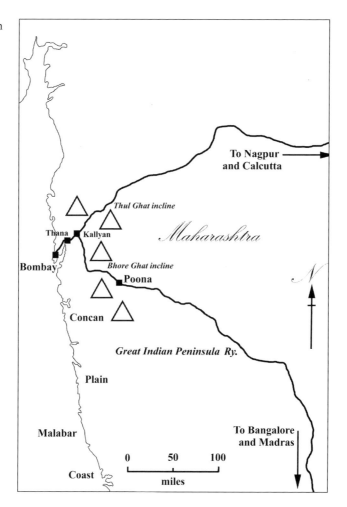

dividend to encourage capital from the London market.[93] The company insisted that only a 35-mile route between Bombay and Kallyan (Kalyan) should be built in the first instance, with subsequent consideration being given to route extensions (Fig. 5.8).

Stephenson provided the directors with cost estimates, and tenders were invited from English contractors.[94] As Stephenson had 'strongly recommended', James Berkley was 'unhesitatingly appointed' by the directors as chief engineer to supervise the building of the line and its subsequent extensions. He left for Bombay in 1850, accompanied by two assistants (see Chapter 9).[95]

Although Stephenson was retained as consulting engineer until his death in 1859, his health and other commitments led him to appoint George Berkley, now an independent consulting engineer, as his representative in dealing with the

93 RR, **V**, 3 June 1848, p. 545, 29 July 1848, p. 748, and subsequent editions.
94 RR, **V**, 9 September 1848, p. 858.
95 Memoir to James John Berkley, *Proc. ICE*, **XXII**, 1862/3, p. 619. RT, **XIII**, 4 May 1850, p. 437.

company's affairs.[96] Thus James Berkley liaised with his brother on certain issues, including negotiations with British manufacturers. The first stretch was opened in 1853,[97] and the whole line to Kallyan the following year (Fig. 5.9).[98]

Berkley arranged new surveys for two alignments across the Ghats; the south-eastern route to Poona, and onwards towards Bangalore and Madras, and the north-eastern route to Nagpur and onwards towards Calcutta, their total length exceeding 1200 miles.[99] Stephenson was consulted about Berkley's proposals for these difficult inclines and, in a speech honouring him in 1856, he said:[100]

The question of the ascent of the Ghâts, is one of considerable difficulty, and demanding much knowledge, skill, and consideration. Excellent designs of them have, however, been prepared by Mr. Berkley, and the explanations he has afforded me are so minute and interesting, that I assure you I should feel proud of being the author of the plans he has proposed.

The inclines took several years to build – their strategic significance, in the aftermath of the 'mutiny', adding urgency to their conclusion.[101] George Berkley was appointed as consulting engineer on Stephenson's death in 1859,[102] but his brother was obliged to return from India through ill-health in 1861, just prior to completion of the inclines.

Stephenson was involved in a number of other schemes in India. He was approached to represent the 'Upper India Railway Company' in 1852, to pursue a 400-mile route between Delhi and Allahabad. He passed this to George Bidder, who represented the railway company jointly with Michael Borthwick, but the scheme did not proceed.[103]

In 1851, the East Indian Railway commenced from Calcutta, with George Bruce (1821–1908) assisting James Rendel. Bruce had served his apprentice-ship at Stephenson's factory in Newcastle, and worked under Thomas Harrison on the Newcastle & Berwick Railway. In 1853 he was 'transferred to the appointment of Chief Engineer of the Madras Railway', which had also been under Rendel's direction.[104] This railway had taken over from the earlier failed scheme, and Stephenson influenced Bruce's appointment. He returned from India in 1856 and set up his own consulting practice in Westminster, remaining on close terms with his mentor.[105]

Stephenson was also consulted by the Scinde Railway of north-west India, and regarding a railway for Ceylon (Sri Lanka).[106] John Brunton was appointed

96   Obituary to Sir George Berkley KCMG, *Proc. ICE*, **CXV**, 1893/4, p. 384.
97   The line was described in *RT*, **XVI**, 1 January 1853, p. 3.
98   *ILN*, 8 July 1854, pp. 3–4.
99   Op. cit. (n. 95).
100 Ibid.
101 J. J. Berkley, 'The Great Indian Peninsula Railway', in Medley, Paper No. CV.
102 Op. cit. (n. 96).
103 *RT*, **XV**, 25 December 1852, p. 1369.
104 Obituary for Sir George Barclay Bruce, *Proc. ICE*, **CLXXIV**, 1907/8, pp. 369–373.
105 Ibid.
106 Representatives of both railways, for which 'the deceased had been connected', were present at Stephenson's funeral in 1859, *RT*, **XXII**, 22 October 1859, p. 1178.

5.9 The Great
Indian Peninsula
Railway crossing
the Concan Plain
(*Illustrated
London News*)

THE   GREAT   INDIAN   PENINSULA   RAILWAY.

VIEW FROM SION HILL.—THE RAILWAY CROSSING THE MARSH.

as chief engineer of the Scinde Railway in 1857, probably through Stephenson's recommendation.[107] Following Stephenson's death in 1859, George Bidder was appointed as the railway's consulting engineer.[108] W. T. Doyne was appointed to survey the first rail route in Ceylon, between Kandy and Colombo. The route involved a steep climb from the coast to the capital at a height of over 2000 feet, and Doyne approached Stephenson and Brunel for advice.[109]

The railway world

In the 1850s there was an increasing interest in railways from several more distant countries, many of which looked to London for both capital and engineering expertise. Colonial and other national governments sought to promote their underdeveloped countries, whilst capitalists pursued good returns on investments. Stephenson was approached for assistance or guidance on several schemes, and although he did not seek further work, he was anxious to recommend his associates, and encourage business for the Westminster practice.

The exception was an approach from Canada in 1852, by which year several companies were developing railways radiating from Montreal, to Portland (Maine), Quebec and Lake Huron. The unification of these companies into the Grand Trunk Railroad was accompanied with a determination to link the routes by a bridge across the St Lawrence River, to be known as the Victoria Bridge.

107 Brunton (1930) does not confirm this in his small posthumous autobiography.
108 Clark (1983), p. 106.
109 Copy letter, W. Barber, for I. K. Brunel, to Robert Stephenson, London, 5 November 1857, **Brunel**, Letter Book 10, p. 356.

Alexander Ross was appointed engineer-in-chief to the railroad, whilst George Bidder's brother Samuel (1811–1872) was appointed its general manager.[110]

Ross considered the surveys and the design options for the bridge and returned to England to discuss them with Stephenson, who was retained as consulting engineer for the project.[111] Stephenson also agreed to act as arbiter between the London-based Great Western Railway of Canada and the Grand Trunk Railroad, as the two companies sought to develop competing routes through Ontario, with potential for disputes.[112]

Stephenson largely supported Ross's designs, and they presented a joint report on their proposals for the bridge design to the Board of Railway Commissioners.[113] Stephenson followed this up by a visit to Montreal in August 1853. He was well received by the city fathers, who put on a banquet in his honour at which he made a speech, described by Jeaffreson as 'the best he had ever made in public'.[114] He included an appeal to the Canadians to appoint a 'disinterested Board of Commissioners' to determine route allocation and avoid disputes such as those the Great Western and Grand Trunk companies were then facing.[115]

The bridge, the largest in the world at the time of its construction, was confirmed to be of tubular form, developed from the Britannia Bridge (see Chapter 10), and supported on masonry piers designed to withstand the strong flows of ice in spring (see Chapter 11).[116] Stephenson died just before the completion of the bridge, which was opened by the young Prince of Wales in August 1860.

There were few parts of the world for which Stephenson did not receive requests for assistance. As early as 1848, the 'Barbadoes General Railway Company' engaged Thomas Statham as its engineer, 'a gentleman recommended by Mr. Robert Stephenson as fully competent for the duties to be entrusted to him.'[117]

In 1852 the Sydney Railway, the first in Australia, applied to consulting engineers for assistance in appointing an engineer to complete the building of its 13-mile line to Parramatta. It had been commenced under the direction of Francis Sheilds, who had resigned after a disagreement.[118] The successful applicant was James Wallace, who received testimonials from both Stephenson and Borthwick.[119] Wallace, who had worked under Borthwick in both East Anglia

110 Clark (1983), pp. 96 and 379.
111 *RT*, **XVI**, 7 May 1853, p. 483.
112 *RT*, **XVI**, 14 May 1853, pp. 496–7.
113 Passfield.
114 Jeaffreson, II, p. 181.
115 *RT*, **XVI**, 12 November 1853, pp. 1174–5.
116 Hodges.
117 *RR*, **V**, 1 January 1848, p. 4.
118 D. D. Hagarty, 'Engineers of the Sydney Railway Company – 6, Francis W. Sheilds', *Bulletin of the Australian Railway Historical Society*, **50**, October 1999, pp. 367–84, and November 1999, pp. 407–25.
119 Little is known about Wallace, other than that he was involved in railway building in Scotland before being 'attached principally to Mr. Stephenson's staff in England'. The author is grateful to Mr Dan Hagarty of New South Wales, regarding Wallace's career.

and Egypt, spent four years in the colony, returning to England in 1856 on the completion of the railway.

In 1853, an approach was received for assistance with a scheme for a railway between Recife and the river São Francisco in Brazil's Pernambuco State. Michael Borthwick was appointed as engineer-in-chief of the Recife and São Francisco Railway, but Stephenson was saddened to learn that during his second visit to Brazil in 1856, Borthwick had contracted cholera and died.[120]

In 1854 an approach was received from the Government of Chile for engineering services towards the establishment of a railway system in that country. Funding was arranged through Baring Brothers, the London merchant bank. Stephenson recommended the appointment of William Lloyd, who had recently completed his report on the Swedish railways. Lloyd spent the next ten years surveying and building railways in Chile and Peru.[121]

In 1858 an approach was received from the Transport Commissioners of Christchurch in New Zealand, requesting advice on the development of a railway to Lyttelton Harbour. Stephenson passed this enquiry to George Robert Stephenson, who later travelled there to supervise the survey and the arrangements for building the line, partly in tunnel, through Mount Pleasant. He enjoyed a long association with the country, for which he designed several other works during the mid-nineteenth century.[122]

Arbitration

Robert Stephenson's reputation as a leading figure in railway development was earned as much for his diplomatic and negotiating skills as for his engineering expertise. With such large sums of money involved in railway building, and with the operation of services in a competitive environment, disputes arose both between railway companies and with their contractors. Stephenson abhorred litigation to resolve disputes, considering it unnecessarily protracted and expensive. He firmly believed that parties should refer the facts of a dispute to a referee who was respected and knowledgeable about the principles involved. Such respect would ensure that disputants accepted the referee's ruling.

Stephenson himself earned just such a wide reputation, and was frequently consulted to arbitrate on disputes, or to provide an independent interpretation of an agreement or valuation of assets. Disputes were often more financial than technical, and could range from claims for extra payments by contractors to interpretation of contentious agreements between railway companies. Although occasionally he was a consultant to one of the parties, the respect in which he was held usually led to acceptance of his adjudications.

In some cases, Stephenson was one of a panel of arbitrators, each of whom brought expertise to complex issues. In 1846, for example, Stephenson acted

120 Memoir of Michael Andrews Borthwick, *Proc. ICE*, **XVI**, 1856/7, pp. 108–13.
121 Lloyd, pp. 48–68.
122 For example *Engineering*, 25 September 1874, pp. 235–7.

alongside George Glyn, Chairman of the London & North Western Railway, and George Hudson to adjudicate on the entitlements of shareholders to the proposed Knightsbridge extension of the West London Railway. He had been the railway's consulting engineer, and remained concerned with its affairs following its joint lease by the London & North Western and Great Western Railways. The abandonment of the Knightsbridge project led to difficult issues of shareholder entitlement, and the panel made their award after an assessment of the legal and financial matters that had arisen.[123]

A contentious issue for the much-disputed London & York Railway in 1847 had been a proposed westwards branch by a subsidiary company through the East Midlands into Staffordshire. The scheme was vigorously opposed by the Midland, Trent Valley and North Staffordshire railways, and the matter concluded with its acquisition by the latter company for £13 000, thereby suppressing further territorial ambitions. As consulting engineer to all three companies, Stephenson was in a special position to award an equitable division of this sum between them.[124]

The combined expenses of the London & North Western, Midland and Eastern Counties railways in opposing the Great Northern Railway's Bill of 1847 were the subject of disagreement over the proportion to be met by each company. The matter dragged on until 1851, when Stephenson was called in to arbitrate, which the respective boards promptly accepted.[125] He also adjudicated on behalf of the Midland and Eastern Counties Railways, regarding financial arrangements for the use of the Eastern Counties station in Peterborough. The issue dated back to the opening of the Stamford and Peterborough line in 1846, and by 1851 there was some urgency to reach agreement on both the historic and future charges. Both boards promptly accepted Stephenson's award.[126]

In 1852, the most far-reaching issue on which Stephenson arbitrated related to a serious dispute between the London & North Western and North Staffordshire Railways. He was accompanied on the lengthy enquiry by James Hope Scott QC.[127] The core of the dispute was through-running rights for the former company's trains over the North Staffordshire system, and other traffic arrangements. Stephenson's long-held view, that squabbles between railway companies were wasteful of management time and money, was reinforced by this dispute. He saw opportunity to pursue a closer cooperation between the companies and, if possible, effect their amalgamation.

The recommendation by Stephenson and Scott went far beyond the issues relating to the core dispute. They proposed that the London & North Western Railway should acquire all the assets of the North Staffordshire Railway, and provide guaranteed dividends in future years on its ordinary

123 *RT*, **IX**, 19 September 1846, pp. 1345–7.
124 Letter, Robert Stephenson to G. Carr Glyn for the London & North Western Railway, Westminster, 14 April 1847, **PRO**, RAIL 1008/91.
125 Board Minutes, Eastern Counties Railway, 1851–1854, 20 May 1852, **PRO**, RAIL186/10.
126 Ibid., 25 September 1851.
127 *RT*, **XV**, 8 May 1852, p. 472.

share capital.[128] The integration of their services would immediately resolve all disputes. The recommendation was quickly accepted by the boards of both companies and approved by the shareholders, by which time a bill had already been petitioned to Parliament to put the amalgamation into effect.

A more far-reaching amalgamation had also been negotiated in 1852, between the London & North Western and Midland Railways. Although Stephenson no longer had any formal connection with the latter railway, it is quite possible that his views on railway integration, well known in both boardrooms, played a part. A bill for the amalgamation of these two large companies was also deposited in Parliament for the 1853 session, as were amalgamation bills for other railways.[129]

The bills triggered a response against amalgamation by Members of Parliament, who saw them as contrary to free-market enterprise. They were particularly opposed by the Great Western Railway, for which the amalgamations threatened its northward territorial ambitions. The House of Commons appointed a committee chaired by Edward Cardwell, President of the Board of Trade, to consider all the issues raised by amalgamations, and suspended the bills for the 1853 session.[130] Evidence was taken over two months, including from Stephenson speaking as a consulting engineer of the London & North Western Railway. His pro-amalgamation and anti-competition opinions made him unpopular with some capitalists, and it was subsequently noted that: 'It was a dictum of Mr. Stephenson, that where combination was possible, competition was impossible.'[131]

The free-market opinion prevailed in the Cardwell Committee's report, which determined that Parliament would need to be satisfied of certain criteria before it would accept further amalgamation petitions.[132] The opposition had been largely directed against the London & North Western Railway. Notably, in the following session, the North Eastern Railway was formed, through amalgamation, without parliamentary opposition.

Stephenson's opinion of the committee's findings is not recorded. His influence over the affairs of the London & North Western and Midland Railways continued, however, when, in the absence of amalgamation, the companies agreed to extend their long-standing traffic arrangements, with Stephenson a joint referee with both Scott and Samuel Laing.[133] A further attempt at amalgamating the North Staffordshire Railway with the London & North Western Railway occurred in 1855, again without success, requiring a further renegotiation of their traffic agreement by Stephenson and Scott.[134]

128 *RT*, **XVI**, 5 February 1853, pp. 118–19.
129 *RT*, **XVI**, 8 January 1853, pp. 22–4.
130 *RT*, **XVI**, 19 February 1853, p. 195.
131 Evidence of Captain Huish of the London & North Western Railway to 'Directorial Debate' on the 'Cardwell Clauses' for the 1854 'Cardwell Act', *RT*, **XVII**, p. 373.
132 *RT*, **XVI**, 16 April 1853, pp. 398–9, 403–4, 411.
133 Communication from the London & North Western Railway, *RT*, **XVII**, 9 December 1854, p. 1316.
134 *RT*, **XVIII**, 19 May 1855, p. 516.

Conclusion

The last years of Stephenson's life were devoted to a volume of work that few men of lesser constitution could have withstood. In spite of deteriorating health and his duties as a Member of Parliament, he was involved with many topics, ranging from railway and water engineering to the resolution of disputes between squabbling companies. He also presided over the maintenance of good practice by his Westminster associates, and no doubt offered opinions to them about their designs for bridges and other structures, and the strategies for further railway development.

Stephenson's overseas railway exploits were extensive. Although he was responsible for building the Leopold Railway, his later British and international commitments left him no time to supervise later railway construction, which was delegated to his associates (see Chapter 9). He made an important contribution to the improvement of railway communication with India. In Egypt, however, he had first pursued a route strategy through a British perspective, with insufficient account of the country's parochial needs. As he had attained a widespread reputation, the blunt rejections of some of his recommendations may have been difficult for him to accept. His dismissal from the Cairo–Suez line clearly upset him, and prevented his aspiration to link the Mediterranean with the Red Sea.

Although the extensive railway-building programme in India, which he never visited, came late in Stephenson's life, he helped lay the foundations of its railway system. Through his recommendation, engineers such as the Berkley brothers and John Brunton were the precursors of the many British consulting and resident engineers who, during the nineteenth century, met the formidable challenges of railway building in the Subcontinent.

Respect for Stephenson was universal. His opinions were sought by monarchs and governments, anxious to pursue railway networks to aid the development of their nations, and by capitalists, anxious to obtain high returns on their investments. He resolved disputes and obtained agreement amongst parties who might otherwise have resorted to lengthy and expensive legal intervention. He was clearly persuaded that, health permitting, he should play a continuing role as both a transport and engineering consultant, in spite of anticipating 'comparative retirement' as early as 1850. Stephenson liked to be consulted, as it provided him with contacts and influence with which to maintain his professional life, against a domestic life that lacked so much.

His professional standing was unchallenged in his last years. His election as president of the Institution of Civil Engineers for 1856–1857 followed his appointment as president of the Birmingham-based Institution of Mechanical Engineers eight years earlier (see Chapter 6). Such appointments were the pinnacles of his long service to the engineering profession, and he was clearly proud to hold such high office with both institutions. The proximity of the 'Civils' to his offices allowed him to attend its meetings regularly, and contribute frequently to the many subjects that the Institution addressed. He also used his presidential position to criticize openly the defects that he perceived in the parliamentary system.

Stephenson's attendance at the Institution allowed him to maintain his standing with his professional colleagues, many of whom had themselves developed strong international reputations in railway, bridge and water engineering. He liaised closely with Isambard K. Brunel and Joseph Locke, the three engineers consulting each other on a range of professional issues, as a senior 'triumvirate'. When the Bridge Commissioners sought to direct future iron bridge design in 1848 (see Chapter 10) they campaigned together against 'the mischievous effects of such attempt at dictation'.[135] They also campaigned together in 1853 in favour of completing the nationwide mapping at one inch to the mile by the Board of Ordnance.[136]

Brunel and Locke attended the launch of the tubular bridges in north Wales to offer advice on the difficult launching and raising procedures. Stephenson was keen to reciprocate when Brunel was faced with the challenges of launching his *Great Eastern* steamship in 1857–1858. He visited Milwall on several occasions and offered Brunel encouragement whenever he could, particularly when others were critical:[137]

For heaven's sake don't let what [John Scott] Russell said, give you the least annoyance nor the Globe [newspaper] either They are both perfectly indifferent to me
   Would Saturday suit you for me to come down to Milwall as well as to morrow …
   Never mind Russell in the papers. I shall always be at hand happen what may, to aid & do every thing in my power & without shrinking any responsibility if need be –

A year later, Brunel's visit to Egypt coincided with Stephenson's last visit to the country. Jeaffreson immortalized their dinner on Christmas Day 1858, in the Hotel d'Orient in Cairo, and George Bidder's daughter, 'Lizzie', who accompanied Stephenson, described the event as being 'a rather elegant dinner and a tolerably slow evening'.[138]

Stephenson's declining health in the late 1850s slowed rather than ended his demanding workload. He continued to work up to his visit to Norway in September 1859. His attendance at the event to mark the conclusion of the contractors' five-year term demonstrated remarkable loyalty to his associate and close friend, George Bidder. Stephenson died the following month, a respected consultant with a worldwide professional reputation.

135 Copy letter, I. K. Brunel to R. Stephenson and J. Locke, 15 March 1848, **Brunel**, Letter Book 5, p. 359.
136 Copy letter, I. K. Brunel, Robt. Stephenson and Joseph Locke to Sir C. C. Trevelyan, for the Lords Commissioners of Her Majesty's Treasury, London, 3 May 1853, **Brunel**, Letter Book 2, pp. 337–9.
137 Letter, Robert Stephenson to Isambard K. Brunel , London, December 1857, **Brunel**, D.M. 1306.
138 Jeaffreson, II, p. 249. Also op. cit. (n. 88), 25 December 1858.

6

The mechanical business

Michael Bailey

Robert Stephenson's ... business as an engine-builder and engineer is of an extent that is literally incredible, and it still seems a progressive one.[1]

Robert Stephenson's reputation was as much earned through his mechanical engineering talents, and his management of the manufacturing firm that bore his name, as for his railway, bridge and other engineering pursuits. Mechanical engineering was first considered an integral part of civil engineering, and he saw his involvement with locomotives and other machinery as being an important adjunct to the consulting service provided to his clients. Only in 1847 did mechanical engineering begin its path to separate professional status with the foundation of the Institution of Mechanical Engineers. Stephenson was its second president, following the death of his father in 1848.

As a leading consulting engineer he maintained a close understanding of engineering progress. Innovation required demonstrable economic advantage and operational reliability as well as commercial acceptance. Recommending mechanical innovation to his clients was a measure of both his own pursuit of improvements and his ability to keep abreast of the work of his contemporaries.

Stephenson was closely involved with advances in mechanical and material knowledge, which he pursued throughout his career. The very nature of the mechanical progress, and particularly the work undertaken at the Newcastle factory, demonstrated his comprehensive understanding of mechanical principles and material limitations, even as he directed development work *in absentia*. A more limited understanding of these issues would have restricted his involvement to that of decision-making alone.

Robert Stephenson & Co. had been established in 1823 to manufacture steam engines and other equipment to meet the requirements of the developing railway industry. It was a perceptive entrepreneurial decision, reflecting the prediction of its five partners that the industry would grow extensively. The introduction of main-line railways in 1830 resulted from the work of the Stephensons and their team in developing the locomotive to meet the requirements of inter-city goods and passenger movement. They believed that their involvement with railway building should include the provision of mechanical equipment, especially locomotives. This naive view would soon be challenged,

---

1 *RR*, 19 August 1848, p. 808.

however. The subsequent growth of railway routes, and investors' demands for high returns on capital, quickly encouraged competition from other manufacturers diversifying into railway equipment, particularly locomotives.

Stephenson's involvement in manufacturing, with the opportunity of influencing the winning of orders to the Newcastle factory, thus brought about a conflict of interest and a risk both to his reputation as an independent consultant, and opportunities for expanding the locomotive business. His response to the commercial realities of competitive manufacturing, and the evolution of tendering and contracting procedures, was therefore a measure of his integrity, business aptitude and commercial judgement.

Robert Stephenson & Co.'s rapid development in the 1830s was later curtailed, both by competition from other manufacturers and by extraordinary fluctuations in demand that accompanied the cyclical fortunes of national and international economies. Stephenson and his partners were instrumental in developing the firm's investment strategies. As managing partner, he also had responsibility to oversee and direct the firm's product and employment policies and maintain its profitability within the unpredictable market. These included innovative designs whilst implementing product diversification to combat market fluctuations.

The responsibilities that Stephenson placed upon himself by his pursuit of both mechanical and thermodynamic progress, and by the management of a progressive manufacturing concern, whilst coping with the heavy demands on his time as a consulting engineer, became the central feature of his professional life. The demands on his time meant that his visits to the Newcastle factory were infrequent and of short duration. He was alone amongst his contemporaries in the pursuit of such ambitious goals. For most engineers, manufacturing administration and management would not have sat comfortably with their primary discipline.

This aspect of Stephenson's career therefore focuses as much on the development of his managerial skills as on his understanding of mechanical engineering. The extent to which Stephenson succeeded with his senior appointments and, from a distance, in directing, delegating, motivating and maintaining the respect of his subordinates, was a measure of his managerial aptitude and ultimately the firm's progress and profitability.

Early mechanical skills

Robert Stephenson had gained basic metalworking and machinery skills from his father, and his apprenticeship under Nicholas Wood had taught him more of machinery and material capabilities and limitations.[2] In the absence of manufacturing experience, however, he was dependent upon his father and Michael Longridge in selecting personnel and machine tools for the new factory.[3]

---

2 Bailey (1989), pp. 6–12 and 51–66.
3 Bailey (1978/9), pp. 109–38.

Orders were taken for a wide range of products to sustain sufficient work for men and machines.[4] Thomas Richardson's introduction to potential customers helped develop a customer base not wholly dependent upon the north-east coal industry. Through these introductions, Stephenson and his father undertook visits to Ireland and London. They gained orders for steam-heated paper-drying machines for several mills making banknote and other high-quality paper, in County Cork and the English home counties, owned by the influential Magnay family from the City of London.

Stephenson designed the machines, basing his ideas on paper-handling machinery he witnessed on a visit to London:[5]

The Magnays got me an introduction to the Times printing office, where I was almost as much delighted as I was in the Mint. The facility with which they print is truly wonderful. They were working papers at the rate of 2,000 per hour, which they can hold for any length of time. The mode they have of conveying the sheet of paper from one part of the machine to the other, is, I think, precisely what is wanted in the drying machine.

The earliest paper-drying machines had been introduced about 1817, but in 1820 Thomas Crompton patented the use of felt loops to conduct paper over drying cylinders to prevent 'cockling'.[6] Stephenson appears to have initiated the use of continuous felt to carry paper over three drying cylinders, thus overcoming the differential drying rates that Crompton experienced. The Stephenson Company's second drying machine, installed at Albury Mill, Surrey, had three cylinders in a 'reel up' formation. The first cylinder was apparently heated to 80°F, the second to 100°F and the third to 120°F (Fig. 6.1).[7] The use of continuous felt to resolve one of the fundamental problems of continuous paper production was the first example of Stephenson's originality in overcoming mechanical problems. However, he left for Colombia before completing development work on the machines, leaving it to his father and the factory foremen to install them.

During his absence in Colombia, the firm was left under Longridge's direction.[8] His responsibilities at the Bedlington Iron Works, however, meant that he could give only part of his time to its affairs. He was upset that he had been left to maintain direction, and asked Richardson for another manager to be appointed:[9]

Circumstances, over which I had no control, have unfortunately for me thrown the responsibility [for managing the factory] upon my Shoulders for the present: but I do hope that Robert's early return to England will soon relieve me: and in the meantime, if you or Mr. Pease can appoint a more suitable Person, it will much oblige

4 Accounting ledger, 1823–1831, **Stephenson**.
5 Letter, Robert Stephenson to George Stephenson, London, n.d. but late April/early May 1824, Jeaffreson, I, pp. 71–2.
6 Hills, pp. 115–17.
7 *PM*, **2**, Supplement to issue 96, 28 September 1833, pp. 379–84.
8 Bailey (1984), pp. 45–50.
9 Letter, Michael Longridge to Thomas Richardson, Bedlington Iron Works, 7 March 1825, **Pease–Stephenson**, U415J, vol. III, Item 7.

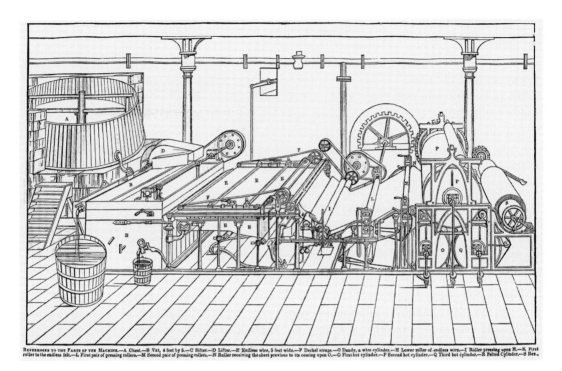

REFERENCES TO THE PARTS OF THE MACHINE.—A Chest.—B Vat, 4 feet by 5.—C Sifter.—D Lifter.—E Endless wire, 5 feet wide.—F Deckel straps.—G Dandy, a wire cylinder.—H Lower roller of endless wire.—I Roller pressing upon H.—K First roller to the endless felt.—L First pair of pressing rollers.—M Second pair of pressing rollers.—N Roller receiving the sheet previous to its coming upon O.—O First hot cylinder.—P Second hot cylinder.—Q Third hot cylinder.—R Felted Cylinder.—S Rec.,

6.1 Paper-
making
machinery
at Albury Mill,
Surrey, showing
Stephenson's
paper-drying
rollers
(*Penny Magazine*)

In spite of this plea, Longridge continued to provide part-time direction over the factory's affairs until Stephenson's return. Following the failure of the first Liverpool & Manchester Railroad Bill in 1825, however, George Stephenson returned to direct the firm's manufacturing affairs. He recruited senior foremen to develop and manufacture machinery, particularly steam engines. An order for two tugboat engines prompted him to engage James Kennedy (1797–1886), a Scottish engine-wright with marine engine experience.[10] He remained at Newcastle for eighteen months, overseeing the manufacture of the tugboat engines, the company's first locomotives, and several stationary engines for mining and railway customers.

George Stephenson also recruited Timothy Hackworth (1786–1850), then foreman-smith at Walbottle Colliery.[11] His engagement was short, however, and he was subsequently appointed as engine superintendent for the Stockton & Darlington Railway.[12] Hackworth and Kennedy's short time at Forth Street emphasized the need for continuity of superintendence. This was recognized by the partners when William Hutchinson (1792–1853), who had worked for the Stephensons since 1821, was appointed head foreman in overall charge of manufacturing, a role he fulfilled until his death.[13]

George Stephenson's appointment as engineer of the Liverpool & Manchester Railway in July 1826 meant that, once again, the absence of both

10 Memoir to James Kennedy, *Proc. IMechE*, **37**, 1896, p. 532.
11 Young, p. 77.
12 Letter, Thomas Nicholson, for R. Stephenson & Co., Newcastle, 3 February 1825, **PRO**, RAIL 667/1158.
13 Articles, *Newcastle Chronicle*, 13 and 19 August 1853.

Stephensons would leave Longridge solely responsible for the factory. His partners therefore agreed to recruit a deputy manager, and Harris Dickinson, 'a very pushing young man', was appointed.[14] He saw himself as having more authority than was intended, and his actions sometimes caused embarrassment. By 1827, the partners were irritated by the absence of both Stephensons, as Edward Pease indicated in a letter to Robert Stephenson:[15]

I can assure thee that your business at Newcastle, as well as thy father's engineering, have suffered very much from thy absence and unless thou soon return, the former will be given up as Mr. Longridge is not able to give it that attention it requires and what is done is not done with credit to the house.

Pease considered closing the factory, as Longridge reported to Stephenson in 1827 that he was 'vastly out of humour about it but I will endeavour to pacify him until you get back, when we must come to some arrangement respecting this place'.[16] No dividend was paid for the first five years of the firm's existence. In addition, the partners were required to provide large loans as working capital, to overcome cash-flow difficulties due to the poor financial performance of several customers.[17] Thus on Stephenson's return from Colombia, and his resumption as managing partner, he was required to establish both new direction for the firm's product development and a new business strategy.

Origins of the main-line locomotive

In taking over the factory from the beginning of 1828, the 24-year-old Robert Stephenson inherited the parallel objectives of making the business financially sound, and developing the technology of locomotive design to meet the anticipated requirements of main-line operation. An upturn in orders, particularly for steam engines, gave him the opportunity to direct a major development effort for the locomotive. His endeavours and those of his subordinates represented a major advancement in design, material development and manufacturing technique, as he sought to fulfil the requirements and expectations that his father had undertaken to provide for the Liverpool & Manchester Railway. Stephenson was to show ingenuity and technical competence as well as resolve and leadership during this time.

As chief engineer of the Liverpool & Manchester Railway, George Stephenson was a strong advocate for locomotives.[18] The railway's act included provision for their use, and from the outset its directors:[19]

---

14 Letter, Joseph Locke to Robert Stephenson, Liverpool, 28 February 1827, **IMechE**, IMS/165/2.
15 Letter, Edward Pease to Robert Stephenson, 9 April 1827, Smiles (1862), p. 250.
16 Letter, Michael Longridge to Robert Stephenson, London, 2 February 1827, **IMechE**, IMS/164/2.
17 Bailey (1984), pp. 93–101.
18 Bailey (1980/1).
19 Printed report of the Railway Committee to the First Meeting of the Liverpool & Manchester Railway Proprietors, 29 May 1826.

looked forward to the locomotive engine as the power advantageous to the company and the public. They have never doubted that the ingenuity of the country would be exerted to construct an efficient and unobjectionable machine for this purpose.

This acknowledged that significant improvements were required to develop the cumbersome 'colliery' type employed on the Stockton & Darlington and other early railways to a form that was both suitable and reliable for main-line service. Whilst assuring the directors of the potential for improvement, George Stephenson's responsibilities in directing the building of the line left him little time to pursue them. He therefore passed that role to Robert Stephenson, who wrote to Michael Longridge at the beginning of 1828:[20]

Since I came down from London, I have been talking a great deal to my father about endeavouring to reduce the size and ugliness of our travelling-engines, by applying the engine either on the side of the boiler or beneath it entirely, somewhat similarly to Gurney's steam-coach. He has agreed to an alteration which I think will considerably reduce the quantity of machinery as well as the liability to mismanagement.

Stephenson thus began a systematic development programme to improve the dynamic and thermodynamic characteristics of locomotive design. Whereas his father had achieved incremental and empirical improvements, Stephenson sought to consider each component separately, to understand its function fully and make improvements through better arrangements and materials.

He pursued four development programmes: boiler design, to increase steam generation; thermal efficiency, to reduce heat loss between boiler and cylinder; transmission design, to simplify conversion of reciprocating piston action into vehicular movement; and suspension design, to reduce dynamic forces between locomotive and track. Stephenson was assisted by William Hutchinson, whose respect he quickly gained, and whose manufacturing experience ensured that notions could be carried through into production. He also recruited George Phipps as a draughtsman to prepare arrangement drawings, acknowledging the need to reconcile component requirements with weight and space limitations.[21]

Whilst exchanging ideas with his father by correspondence, Stephenson directed his team to arrange and manufacture a series of prototype locomotives, whilst he was largely absent from Newcastle pursuing railway surveying and building. His reliance on his subordinates was well rewarded, as each prototype built for service in Britain and overseas made a contribution towards the goal of the main-line locomotive.[22]

With the programme only a few months in hand, however, came the first indication that the Liverpool & Manchester directors had doubts about locomotives. Stephenson wrote to Hackworth following reliability problems with the Stockton & Darlington fleet:[23]

---

20 Letter, Robert Stephenson to Michael Longridge, Liverpool, 1 January 1828, in Jeaffreson, I, pp. 114–5.
21 Bailey (1978/9), p. 125.
22 Bailey and Glithero (2000), pp. 5–9.
23 Letter, Robert Stephenson to Timothy Hackworth, Liverpool, 7 July 1828, **ScM**, MS1570.

The Directors having heard by some channel or other not favourable to the Locomotive Engs ... that the horses were beating the engines off ... I cannot wonder at the travelling engines having so much to contend [with] when I come in contact with enemies to them every hour, and they prove to be enemies without reason, they oppose the engines merely because certain things have been said against them.

The 'enemies' included a number of the Liverpool & Manchester directors, particularly Dr Brandreth, a barrister and would-be inventor, and James Cropper, a wealthy Quaker merchant.[24] An extraordinary debate over fifteen months about the merits of locomotives, rope-haulage and horse power culminated in the Rainhill Trials of October 1829. George Stephenson argued tenaciously for the adoption of locomotives, but he also argued that the Newcastle factory was the best site to make them. The debate focused on the contrasting perceptions, of conflict of interest seen by directors such as Brandreth and Cropper, and the provision of best equipment for his client, seen by George Stephenson. The Rainhill Trials were the forum for the Stephensons to demonstrate conclusively that their locomotives really were the best main-line motive power available.

Robert Stephenson's programme produced remarkable improvements in 1828–1829, culminating in the *Rocket*, the design of which he had overseen, as Phipps later recalled:[25]

Having made the original drawings under Mr. Robert Stephenson, I can bear witness to the care and judgment bestowed by him upon every detail. The arrangement of the tubes with the method of securing their extremities, the detached fire-box, and many other matters of detail, all requiring much consideration. Mr. Stephenson was well aided in all the mechanical details by the late Mr. William Hutchinson.

Although Henry Booth (1789–1869), the Secretary of the Liverpool & Manchester Railway, originated the notion of a multi-tubular boiler, first fitted to *Rocket*,[26] it was the Stephensons who undertook the design and construction of a workable and reliable boiler with a separate firebox (Fig. 6.2). Booth joined George Stephenson to enter *Rocket* for the trials, but Robert Stephenson felt that his role also warranted participation in the partnership. Booth later wrote:[27]

The important day of the competition was the 8th October 1829, but some time previous to that date Mr. Stephenson told me that his son Robert (who was building the engine at Newcastle) was very desirous to become a partner with his father and me in the venture for the prize. I had no wish to dilute my interest in the little speculation I had entered upon, but as father and son seemed bent on it, made no objection, and it was settled that we should share the profit or loss in the speculation proportionately, that is in thirds.

24 Bailey (1984), pp. 174–8.
25 Letter, G. Phipps to *The Engineer*, published within the article 'Links in the History of the Locomotive No. IX', 17 September 1880, p. 217.
26 Booth, p. 74.
27 Account by Henry Booth, reproduced in Whitting, pp. 21–2.

6.2 *Rocket*
locomotive as
built by Robert
Stephenson &
Co. in 1829
(Courtesy of
John P. Glithero)

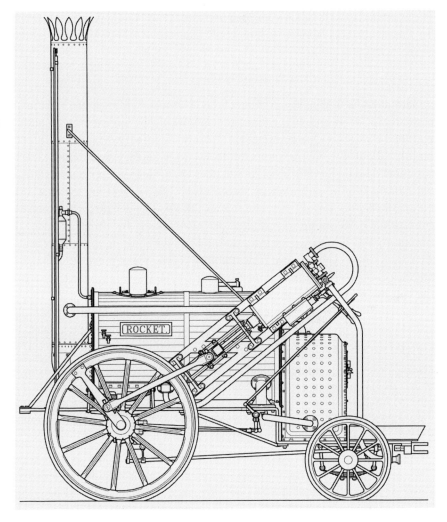

Rocket's outstanding performance at the Rainhill Trials eclipsed the
endeavours of Hackworth's *Sans Pareil*, and the *Novelty* of John Braithwaite
and John Ericsson (1803–1889).[28] At the conclusion of the trials[29]

to show that it [*Rocket*] had been working quite within its powers, Mr. Stephenson
ordered it to be brought on the ground and detached from all incumbrance, and in
making two trips it moved at the astonishing rate of 35 miles an hour.

Booth and the Stephensons were awarded the £500 'Premium'. To reinforce the significance of *Rocket*'s performance, and the superiority of locomotive haulage over alternative forms of motive power, Stephenson found time
to write, in conjunction with Joseph Locke, a book setting out the arguments
his father had been advocating, and recording the Rainhill events.[30]

28 Bailey and Glithero, pp. 21–27 and 183–4.
29 Stephenson and Locke, p. 79.
30 Ibid.

From the experience with *Rocket* during and after the trials, Stephenson's development programme continued apace. He used the lengthening Liverpool & Manchester route as a test track, and was assisted by Locke, William Allcard and John Dixon, in addition to the work of Phipps and Hutchinson in Newcastle. Phipps later recalled Stephenson's direction over locomotive development, which culminated with the *Planet* class locomotives:[31]

With regard to the position of the cylinders, repeated conversations were held between Mr. Stephenson, the late Mr. Hutchinson, and himself, with respect to the saving of fuel that would be effected by placing the cylinders within the smokebox; they also had a great desire to fix the cylinders in a horizontal position, as it was found necessary when an engine travelled at a quick speed, that the vertical motion of the springs should be eliminated from the cylinders, and this naturally led to the horizontal arrangement.

On 3 September 1830, twelve days before the opening of the Liverpool & Manchester line, the first *Planet* locomotive was completed in Newcastle and despatched by sea to Liverpool. It was the first locomotive class incorporating the design characteristics that were adopted by the world's railways for the following century and a half (Fig. 6.3). Stephenson's programme to improve the locomotive from the mineral railway 'travelling engine' to the faster, more economic and more powerful *Planet* type had thus been achieved in just 33 months. It was a remarkable achievement that ranks amongst the foremost of technological advancements.

The rapid rise in passenger and goods traffic experienced on early main-line railways called for a high level of locomotive reliability. Such had been the speed of design innovation, however, that material reliability remained poor, particularly for wheels, axles, fireboxes and boiler tubes, and failures were frequent. Between 1830 and 1834, particular attention was required by the Stephenson team to introduce new materials, especially copper plate for fireboxes and brass for boiler tubes.[32]

Stephenson and his father were too preoccupied during the development period to take out patents for any of the novel features, or to instruct agents to prepare submissions for them. There is no doubt that Edward Pease and Thomas Richardson would have been upset at the omission and the loss of revenue that resulted. As early as 1824 they had anticipated that George Stephenson's 1815 joint patent with Ralph Dodds for locomotive crank pins[33] was coming towards the end of its validity, as Pease pointed out to Richardson:[34]

… we must keep our eye on this last article [locomotives] the patent expires in 4 years, it will be that length of time before either the Liverpool, Birm. or any Rail way can want such Engines, if it be possible we must have GS to adopt some improvements for these Engines & get a new patent, I mean to write him in a day or two to enter a caveat

---

31 George Phipps, discussion on paper by Daniel Kinnear Clark, 'On the Improvement of Railway Locomotive Stock, and the Reduction of the Working Expenses', *Proc. ICE*, **16**, 1856/57, p. 25.
32 Bailey (1984), pp. 293–310.
33 Patent No. 3887, 28 February 1815.
34 Letter, Edward Pease to Thomas Richardson, Darlington, 10M 23 (October): 1824, **Pease–Stephenson**, D/HO/C 63/5.

6.3 Prototype *Planet* locomotive built by Robert Stephenson & Co. in 1830 (I. Shaw, *Views of the Most Interesting Scenery on the Line of the Liverpool and Manchester Railway*, 1831)

PLANET ENGINE.

Published, March 1st 1831 by I. Shaw, Post Office Place, Liverpool.

in the patent office, for improvements, for I cannot doubt such is the enquiry about Railway & any but these engines will be a most important thing & <u>ought to leave us no small sum</u> for either making or Licenses

The Stephensons were to regret the omission, as the growth of main-line railways soon attracted competing manufacturers, including and especially Edward Bury (1794–1858), the proprietor of the Clarence Foundry in Liverpool. The competitors tendered to supply locomotives incorporating the novel features, and it was apparent that Robert Stephenson & Co. had been disadvantaged by the omission.

In spite of his intensive work programme, particularly on the London & Birmingham Railway survey, Stephenson continued to produce new ideas. In 1830 he proposed a novel wagon axle arrangement, which he believed would overcome lubrication problems. The wheels were fitted to a tube that revolved around a static axle, the outer ends of which supported the wagon body (Fig. 6.4). He wrote to his father:[35]

On thinking its advantages carefully over they are of such a nature as to warrant a patent and the specification may be drawn up so as to avoid infringement … I hope you will think it well over, but as it is new and likely to answer, let us take a patent for it, the patent cannot cost much and if [it] does get introduced upon Railways a very small additional price on each carriage would produce a great deal of money –

35 Letter, Robert Stephenson to George Stephenson, Stone Bridge, 8 November 1830, **Stephenson**, Folder 18.

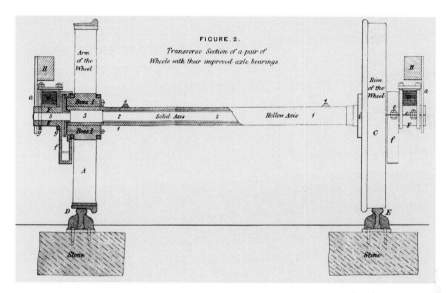

FIGURE. 2.

Transverse Section of a pair of
Wheels with their improved axle bearings

6.4 Drawing from Stephenson's first patent of 1831, showing a hollow external wagon axle to revolve around a static supporting axle

Stephenson took out the patent – his first – in July 1831,[36] but the additional cost of his arrangement was unacceptable, and simple wheel-sets revolving under half-bearings continued to be used for many years. In 1833, however, he took out a comprehensive patent for the next generation of locomotives. The extraordinary rise in traffic on the Liverpool & Manchester line needed larger and more powerful locomotives and, with the continuing axle-load limitation due to light rails, the *Planet* design was extended to incorporate a third axle.[37]

The first locomotive incorporating the improvements was named *Patentee*, this being Stephenson's statement to an increasingly competitive market that he was seeking to reassert the dominance that had slipped since the development period.[38] Whilst the use of a third axle was not novel, he patented the use of a flangeless middle wheel-set, which allowed a longer wheelbase to be used on tight curves (Fig. 6.5). A second invention in the patent, a steam-activated braking system, showed remarkable foresight, but the system was not adopted, being some 40 years ahead of its time. The *Patentee* type was employed for locomotive fleets throughout the decade, being adopted by competing factories under licence as well as by the Newcastle factory.

The development era from 1828 and the improvements of the 1830s produced a major advance in technical knowledge and engineering execution. The extraordinary progress in dynamic and thermodynamic capabilities and efficiency was the driving force, figuratively as well as practically, that powered the rapid growth of main-line railways. It was achieved through the joint efforts and ingenuity of the whole Newcastle team, under Stephenson's leadership. That he achieved this success at a time when he was so preoccupied with railway surveying and building demonstrated both talent and leadership.

---

36 Patent Specification No. 6092, inrolled 11 July 1831.
37 Patent Specifications Nos. 6372, inrolled 26 January 1833, and 6484, inrolled 3 December 1833.
38 Works No. 37, 2–2–2 locomotive completed at Newcastle, 25 September 1833.

6.5 Drawing from Stephenson's 1833 patent for the *Patentee* locomotive

Stephenson, however, later played down his role in locomotive development, loyally promoting his father's contribution:[39]

It was in conjunction with Mr. Booth that my father constructed the 'Rocket' engine which obtained the prize at the celebrated competition which took place a little prior to the opening of the Liverpool and Manchester Railway …

From the date of running the 'Rocket' on the Liverpool and Manchester Railway, the locomotive engine has received many minor improvements in detail and especially in accuracy of workmanship, but in no essential particular does the existing engine differ from that which obtained the prize at the celebrated competition at Rainhill.

Specification, tendering and contracting

For the Newcastle factory to become a leading and profitable concern, Robert Stephenson needed aptitude for business as well as mechanical engineering. In the early 1830s, however, he faced the harsh realties of the commercial world, in which he was inexperienced and reliant on the advice of Pease, Richardson and Longridge. This testing time focused on the evolution of tendering and contracting for locomotives, and the conflict of interest that would arise from his dual roles.

39 'Robert Stephenson's Narrative of his Father's Inventions', &c., contained in Smiles (1862), p. 496.

The Stephensons believed that their responsibilities as railway engineers included the specification of locomotive requirements. As the specifications inevitably represented the latest design and material characteristics of their Newcastle products, they sought to influence orders to the factory without tendering, the resulting conflict of interest causing argument with the directors of their client railway companies.

The rapid expansion of rail use in the early 1830s resulted in an unexpected demand for locomotives. In spite of William Hutchinson's best endeavours, the Newcastle factory took time to step up production to meet this demand. Lancashire manufacturers, particularly Edward Bury, saw opportunities to diversify into locomotive production, and several prototypes were offered to the new railways.

Stephenson was thus faced with his first major business strategy decision. He believed that to maintain a near-monopoly of locomotive supply, it was necessary to establish a second factory, in the north-west, probably in Liverpool. He anticipated that his partners would not invest in a second factory, which would at first draw orders away from Forth Street, when they had yet to see a return on their investment. He and his father therefore discussed a new partnership with Charles Tayleur (1775–1854), a director of the Liverpool & Manchester Railway, and his son, also Charles Tayleur (d. 1859), who had spent some months working at Forth Street. With these discussions at an early stage in December 1830, Stephenson broached the subject with Michael Longridge, who reacted with considerable concern to the proposal:[40]

… you should consider maturely the effect of the proposal you intend making to Mr. Pease. The establishment you contemplate at Liverpool appears to me fraught with injury to Forth Street: the chief employment of which will be transferred to your new establishment. How then are you ever to pay the Dividends and redeem the Capital?

The great demand for engines for a few years will be in Lancashire & Yorkshire – and if you and your Father give your Time and Influence to the New Works – down goes Newcastle.

My own individual Interest is so very small, that it cannot be put into competition with yours, and I therefore only mention it that you may clearly understand that whatever Mr. Pease & Mr. Richardson determine upon, I shall be guided by.'

Stephenson visited Longridge and persuaded him, and through him also Pease and Richardson, not to prevent the new venture from proceeding. Longridge obliged Stephenson to sign an understanding in March 1831, briefly setting out the terms:[41]

Should I become connected with another Manufactory for building Engines in Lancashire or elsewhere I have no objections to bind myself to devote an equal share of my time and attention to the existing establishment at Newcastle. I will also pledge

---

40 Letter, Michael Longridge to Robert Stephenson, Bedlington Iron Works, 13 December 1830. Copy appended to letter, Michael Longridge to Edward Pease, Newcastle, 22 December 1830. **Pease–Stephenson**, D/PS/2/34.

41 Included within letter, Michael Longridge to Thomas Richardson, Bedlington Iron Works, 24 March 1831, **Pease–Stephenson**, D/PS/2/62.

myself <u>not to hold a larger interest in any other factory</u>, than I have in Forth Street and <u>to divide the Locomotive Engine Orders equally</u>.

When Pease and Richardson became aware of the understanding, however, they insisted on two further conditions, namely[42]

That the firm at Liverpool shall be Charles Tayleur, Junr. & Co. or any other Firm not embracing the name of 'Stephenson' so as to distinguish it entirely from the Newcastle House. That during the continuance of the copartnership, neither the said Robert Stephenson nor his father shall withdraw any part of their money which is now employed in the Newcastle Factory, either as 'Capital' or 'lent at interest' without the consent of the other partners.

The project was, however, postponed during a period of intense debate between George Stephenson and the directors of the Liverpool & Manchester Railway, during which he argued that he alone should determine the locomotive type for the line. Some directors, notably James Cropper, criticized the conflict of interest with his position as Chief Engineer. Stephenson made determined efforts to prevent Bury supplying locomotives to the railway, and rejected his frame and firebox designs as not meeting his *Planet*-type specification.[43] The issue was publicized when Dr Dionysius Lardner criticized the Stephensons in the *Edinburgh Review*.[44] A war of words passed between Lardner and Hardman Earle (1792–1877), a pro-Stephenson director. Earle sought to prevent publication by writing to Lardner:[45]

… Are we, for the chance of their services [of other manufacturers], to relinquish the services of, beyond dispute, the soundest railway engineer in the kingdom, or to cease to employ the most successful engine-builder, because to retain both is a violation of a mere theory? Railways, it is true, have long been in use, but it is to the genius and perseverance of Mr. Stephenson and his son that we are indebted for the present compact form of the Planet class …

Following publication of Lardner's article, the directors published a vigorous response to his criticisms, pointing out:[46]

It is true that the son of the engineer is [a] partner in a manufactory at Newcastle-on-Tyne, where many of the best engines on the road have been made, and on the model of which (with progressive improvements) all the most successful machines, from whatever quarter they may have come, have been built.

The directors had given the Stephensons a strong endorsement and, after an independent assessment in January 1833 also found in favour of the Stephenson design, an aggrieved Bury gave up his endeavours to sell locomotives to the line, and Cropper left the board shortly afterwards.[47] Although

---

42 Partners' Minute Book, Robert Stephenson & Co., 27 June 1831, **ScM**, Inv. 1947-134.
43 Bailey (1984), pp. 186–200.
44 'Inland Transport', *Edinburgh Review*, LVI, October 1832; written anonymously, but subsequently revealed as being by Dr Lardner.
45 Letter, Hardman Earle to Dr Dionysius Lardner, 16 July 1832, in Warren, pp. 83–4.
46 Pamphlet, *Liverpool and Manchester Railway, Answer of the Directors to an Article in the Edinburgh Review for October 1832*, Liverpool, November 1832.
47 Board Minutes of the Liverpool & Manchester Railway, 21 and 28 January 1833, **PRO**, RAIL 371/2.

George Stephenson's work on the Liverpool & Manchester line was largely finished anyway, the debate about the conflict of interest contributed to his decision, in May 1833, to stand down as chief engineer.[48]

Against this background, the Stephensons and the Tayleurs moved to establish the firm of Charles Tayleur & Co., with the younger Tayleur as managing partner. In the second half of 1832 they chose a site at Newton-le-Willows, adjacent to the newly opened Warrington & Newton Railway, near its junction with the Liverpool & Manchester line. The 'Vulcan Foundry' was erected during 1833 and began manufacturing at the beginning of 1834.

They engaged the services of Matthew Loam (1794–1875) as head foreman in 1833.[49] Although Loam was an experienced engineer, Stephenson was at first reluctant to engage him, explaining to his father:[50]

I have considered once [again] the matter concerning Loam and altho I concede him a clever man I am unwilling to introduce him into our factory because it is only teaching another man to manage the details of Locomotive Engines – If [James] Kennedy had not obtained a great deal of information from us here, we should have stood much higher as Locomotive Engine makers than we do now –

Kennedy had joined Edward Bury after leaving Forth Street, and Stephenson clearly felt that Bury's ability to enter the locomotive market was due to him. He was anxious to avoid a repetition, but was persuaded to engage Loam, who remained at the Vulcan Foundry until 1841.

In October 1833 Charles Tayleur & Co. proposed to the Liverpool & Manchester Railway to take over the operation and maintenance of its locomotives.[51] The basis of the proposal was, almost certainly, that it would undertake design specification and construction or licensing of locomotives as well as operation and maintenance. By this means orders would have been obtained for the Vulcan Foundry, with consequent benefits for the Newcastle factory under the sharing arrangement. Although the Board briefly considered the proposal, it introduced open tendering procedures from the beginning of 1834.

Robert Stephenson's conduct as engineer-in-chief of the London & Birmingham Railway was monitored by Edward Cropper, Theodore Rathbone and Philip Garnett, who represented the interests of the Liverpool investors. Their strong free-market beliefs were to require complete transparency with the railway's specification and tendering procedures.

In December 1834, with construction work on the line already in hand, locomotives were required to assist the contractors in the London Division. Stephenson specified two four-coupled *Planet*-type locomotives, and the London Committee ordered one from the Vulcan Foundry, the other from Forth Street.[52] When Cropper and Rathbone read the Committee's minutes

48 Board Minutes of the Liverpool & Manchester Railway, 6 and 13 May 1833, **PRO**, RAIL 371/3.
49 Allen, pp. 21–2.
50 Letter, Robert Stephenson to George Stephenson, Newcastle-upon-Tyne, 18 December 1832, **Stephenson**, Folder 18.
51 Op. cit. (n. 48), 14 October 1833.
52 London Committee Minutes of the London & Birmingham Railway, 10 and 24 December 1834, **PRO**, RAIL 384/40.

they reacted strongly to what they saw as a repeat of the Liverpool & Manchester monopoly. They spoke out against Stephenson, who was upset by their personal attack, as he wrote to Michael Longridge:[53]

Our enemies viz Rathbone & Cropper are raising a hue and cry about our having an Engine to build at Newcastle – they say another article will be brought out by Lardner on the subject – They half intimate that I shall withdraw either from the Railway or the Engine Building – The revenge of these people is quite insatiable – This distresses me very much Can I withdraw temporarely [sic] from the Engine building – I wish you would think this over – for the above named parties are annoying me all they can by advancing Vignoles and his opposite opinions – The [other] Directors support me, but it makes it sad uphill work.

Longridge understood Stephenson's dilemma and encouraged a compromise:[54]

I have maturely considered what you say concerning disposing *pro:tempore* of your shares in the Engine Building concern – this can easily be accomplished by your Father taking them on his own account with an understanding that he is to transfer them again to you upon your having finished your Agreement with the Directors of the London & Birmingham Rail way.

I feel very solicitous that you should devote the whole of your faculties undividedly to this magnificent Undertaking: this being once well accomplished, your name and future are built upon a Rock, and you may afterwards smile at the Malice of your enemies. The only reason which induces me to approve of these arrangements is that it will leave your mind quite at ease. Were you as case hardened in these matters as myself, I would set Messrs. Cropper, Rathbone, Dr Lardner and all such envious curs at defiance – but you have not yet attained sufficient philosophy to say 'None of these things move me' – When you arrive at the safe age of Fifty you will bear these Rules better.

For Stephenson to dispose of his shares in the Newcastle factory, and relinquish his position as managing partner, required a meeting of his partners, but Rathbone and Cropper gave him no respite, as he wrote in his reply to Longridge:[55]

The subject of disposing of my Engine Building shares *pro tempore* must stand over untill I meet you in London – my Liverpool friends are annoying me more than I anticipated even when I wrote you last. They have passed a resolution in the shape of a recommendation, to our Directors, that no Director or Engineer shall have any connexion directly or indirectly with any Contract with the Company, more particularly for Locomotive Engines. –

The Liverpool people do not disguise that this recommendation to our Directors is aimed especially at me – the Directors will be compelled to act upon it – This has all sprung from the Quakers and Bury our Liverpool Rival.

Stephenson's reference to Edward Bury was the first indication that he had aspirations towards supplying locomotives to the London & Birmingham line. Following his failure to break into the Liverpool & Manchester market, Bury would have been pleased to retain the confidence

53 Letter, Robert Stephenson to Michael Longridge, London, 26th January 1835, **Pease–Stephenson**, D/PS/2/67.
54 Ibid., letter, Michael Longridge to Robert Stephenson, Bedlington Iron Works, 4 February 1835.
55 Ibid., letter, Robert Stephenson to Michael Longridge, London, 21 February 1835.

of Cropper and Rathbone. Longridge was prompt in his reply to Stephenson:[56]

... If as you suppose – 'the Directors will be compelled to pass a Resolution' that no Director or Engineer shall have any connection directly or indirectly with any Contract with the Company – you must decide whether you will resign your situation of Engineer – or dispose of your shares in the Engine Building Factories. If you determine upon the former, you will suffer in your Future – and still more in your Fame and your Enemies will mightily triumph over you. If you absolutely sell your shares bone fide to your Father, you will not eventually suffer in your Fortune, and your mind will be set at ease, so that you can devote the whole of your Time and Talents to the great Undertaking in which you are engaged. This is the substance of what may be urged as far as your individual Interest is concerned. And as to Messrs: Pease Richardson and myself, if your Father will take your shares & Responsibility, I do not foresee any reasonable objections on our side ...

The railway's main board approved Rathbone's and Cropper's resolution in February 1835. It was minuted:[57]

That in all notices for contracts for the supply of rails, chairs, sleepers or locomotive engines it be publicly made known that no Director, Secretary, Engineer, Sub-Engineer or servant to the Company can be a Contractor and that no tender be received from any party without a declaration that they are not directly or indirectly connected in business or in that tender with any of the afore-named persons or servants of the Company.'

Stephenson was therefore forced to the conclusion that 'I must sell my shares or suffer the Newcastle House to withdraw from competition on this line of road ... '[58] There is, however, no evidence that he stood down as managing partner of Robert Stephenson & Co.

It was the autumn of 1835 before the railway's operating fleet was considered, by which time Stephenson was confident that he could specify the six-wheel *Patentee* type. Protected by his own patent, a royalty would have been due whichever manufacturer was awarded the contracts. He recommended to the London Committee that ten locomotives should be acquired to operate the first stretch of line from Camden to Watford. The Committee resolved to invite tenders according to his *Patentee* specification, but the implied requirement for manufacturers to include a royalty to Stephenson in their quotations clearly met the disapproval of the Liverpool directors.[59]

Stephenson therefore proposed to the Committee an all-embracing motive power contract, similar to that made to the Liverpool & Manchester Railway two years earlier. The proposal, again prepared by Charles Tayleur & Co., was for the Vulcan Foundry to be wholly responsible for the London & Birmingham locomotive fleet, based on a calculation of conveying 1000 passengers a day a distance of thirty miles.[60] It would have ensured the use of

56 Ibid., letter, Michael Longridge to Robert Stephenson, Bedlington Iron Works, 26 February 1835.
57 Board Minutes of the London & Birmingham Railway, 13 February 1835, **PRO**, RAIL 384/2.
58 Letter, Robert Stephenson to Michael Longridge, London, 9 March 1835, in op. cit. (n. 53).
59 London Committee Minutes of the London & Birmingham Railway, 9 September 1835, **PRO**, RAIL 384/41.
60 Ibid., 14 October 1835.

Patentees, manufactured at both Newcastle and Newton-le-Willows. The Liverpool directors rejected the proposal, no doubt on the grounds that Stephenson's partnership in the Tayleur Company infringed the directors' February resolution.

The failure of this proposal apparently precipitated the Stephensons' separation from the Tayleur partnership in October/November 1835 after less than two years. The reasons are not recorded, but the issues appear related to the London & Birmingham dispute and similar events with George Stephenson on the Grand Junction Railway.

In November the London & Birmingham directors, who had just raised Stephenson's salary to £2000 a year, urged him to complete the 'Contract for Locomotive Power' specification for tender applications, which he did shortly afterwards.[61] It was for the *Patentee* type, which prompted Cropper and Rathbone to add an extraordinary and carefully worded addendum to their engineer's specification:[62]

N.B. The Directors will receive tenders for the supply of Locomotive Engines which may not be conformable to the foregoing specification provided the construction of such engines shall be considered by the Directors better adapted for the intended work.

The Liverpool directors also persuaded their fellow directors that they should form a locomotive subcommittee to evaluate the tenders.[63] Seven tenders were referred to it, including those from Edward Bury, Charles Tayleur & Co. and Robert Stephenson & Co. itself.[64]

In December 1835, however, Edward Bury proposed an exclusive motive power contract to the directors, very similar to that which the Stephensons and Tayleurs had proposed a few weeks earlier. It caused a flurry of activity among the directors, some of whom were concerned that consideration of Bury's proposal would delay the opening of the line to Watford. One of the Liverpool directors, urged 'that measures should be taken without delay for securing a supply of engines as there is great risk that the company may not obtain a sufficient number in time for the partial opening of the Line …'.[65] Stephenson acted quickly to take advantage of this mood, before Bury's proposal had gained credence. William Cubitt, the contractor for the Berkhamsted contract, agreed to use a *Patentee* locomotive as a works engine, which could be demonstrated to the directors. Stephenson instructed the Newcastle factory to divert to Berkhamsted the first available newly completed locomotive.[66]

In contrast to the *Patentee* type, Bury's proposal specified his own two-axle design with bar frames, round firebox and inside bearings. A confrontation

61 Op. cit. (n. 57), 5 and 6 November 1835.
62 Op. cit. (n. 59), 18 November 1835.
63 Op. cit. (n. 57), 6 November 1835.
64 Op. cit. (n. 59), 2 and 9 December 1835.
65 London Committee Minutes of the London & Birmingham Railway, 23 December 1835, **PRO**, RAIL 384/42.
66 Works No. 123, destined for the Belgian State Railways, named *Harvey Combe*.

was inevitable, and Stephenson wrote to the directors: 'with reference to the specification of Mr. Bury's engines, his own decided preference of engines supported on six wheels with his reasons for such preference.'[67] His letter found no accord with the subcommittee. Bury's proposal was accepted, and he responded to Stephenson's criticisms with a strong reiteration of his preferences for four-wheeled locomotives.[68]

This confrontation between Stephenson and Bury was an embarrassment to the directors, and the London Committee resolved to put the dispute to arbitration by an independent trio of engineers, Sir Marc Brunel (1769–1849), John Farey (1791–1851) and a Mr Roberts.[69] This was apparently a means of assuaging Stephenson's annoyance, as there was no corresponding delay in drawing up Bury's contract.

Stephenson's room for manoeuvre was limited. He could not risk waiting for the views of the mediators (which went unrecorded), but was determined to demonstrate a *Patentee* on passenger duties as the best means of disproving Bury's allegations. He seized his opportunity in January 1836 following a report by Theodore Rathbone that Bury's Clarence Foundry would not be able, because of a full order book, 'to execute a single engine for the opening of the line'.[70] Stephenson advised the directors that the opening would be delayed unless twelve locomotives were ordered promptly. In the absence of the Liverpool directors, the London Committee agreed to order the *Patentee* locomotives, adopting three of the tenders submitted the previous month. The orders included two with Robert Stephenson & Co., which contradicted the directors' ruling of eleven months previously.

The ordering of the twelve *Patentees* in London was followed two days later by a meeting of the Birmingham Committee, attended by the Liverpool directors, whose reaction was swift and very direct:[71]

Resolved unanimously,

That the Committee now consider themselves called upon by their responsibility as an integral part of the direction of the company and by the strong opinion they entertain that the arrangements proposed by Mr. Bury are of vital consequence to the interests of the Proprietors, to represent to the London Committee, That no time should be lost in concluding the agreement with Mr. Bury and no arrangement entered into which might interfere with it.

That although the agreement would only come into operation on the opening of the whole line, yet as Mr. Bury has offered to undertake the working of the portions which may be first opened on terms which appear to this Committee so very advantageous, the arrangement for these portions should be made conformable to the provisions of the agreement;

67 Letter, Robert Stephenson to the London & Birmingham Railway, 29 December 1835, London Committee Minutes, op. cit. (n. 65), 30 December 1835.
68 Letter, Edward Bury to the London & Birmingham Railway, Liverpool, 14 January 1836, **PRO**, RAIL 384/132.
69 Op. cit. (n. 65), 7 January 1836.
70 Ibid., 13 January 1836.
71 Minutes of the Birmingham Committee of the London & Birmingham Railway, 15 January 1836, **PRO**, RAIL 384/67.

That consequently the Locomotive Engines now ordered should be of Mr. Bury's Specification as he may finally arrange it, particularly as Mr. Bury states that it is essential to the success of his Plan that all the Engines should be exact fac similes of each other –

After considerable debate the London directors reversed their decision and compromised with their Birmingham and Liverpool colleagues, to whom the specification would be left. Failing agreement, the 'non-resident' directors would have 'to take such measures as may be necessary to induce the Engine makers in possession of the orders of this Committee to resign the Contracts in question altogether'.[72] Messrs Cropper and Rathbone refused to sanction the *Patentee* design.

Several London directors who were sympathetic to Stephenson attempted to reduce the influence of the Liverpool directors through an extraordinary boardroom 'coup' attempt in February 1836.[73] They introduced a motion to elect six new directors to represent the Lancashire proprietors. The nominees included several Liverpool & Manchester Railway directors, who were favourably disposed to the Stephensons. Rathbone and Cropper expressed 'unqualified surprise' at this attempt to oust them from the board, which they succeeded in avoiding.

The locomotive contract with Bury was duly signed in May 1836.[74] However, with Bury and the Liverpool directors employing similar tactics to the Stephensons and the Tayleurs, the principle of transparent competitive tendering remained absent. Bury's specification was passed to six other manufacturers, in addition to the Clarence Foundry. It was notable that all their tenders were identically worded, with the same quotation per locomotive. Only the delivery dates varied in what was clearly a cartel arrangement.[75]

The strained relationship between Stephenson and Bury continued for many years. They had to tolerate a working association until Stephenson stood down as engineer-in-chief from the beginning of 1839. The wide acclamation that he enjoyed from the completion of the line was, for him, diluted by the use of Bury's locomotives operating the railway's services.

The national locomotive market was thus divided between the Stephenson three-axle type and the Bury two-axle type. Bury sought every opportunity to promote his type as being safer and more economic, and he perpetuated his four-wheeled designs well into the 1840s. Stephenson, in turn, undertook a vigorous campaign to promote the *Patentee* type. The publication of its design details in 1838 was to persuade customers, and was the first example of a promotional publication by a manufacturer.[76] Bourne's view of Primrose Hill Tunnel provocatively shows a *Patentee* locomotive (Plate 21). This was followed by a public 'war of words', including a

72 Op. cit. (n. 65), 27 January 1836.
73 Op. cit. (n. 57), 22 February 1836.
74 Ibid., 11 May 1836.
75 Specification and Tenders for locomotive engines, **PRO**, RAIL 384/265–9.
76 Marshall (1838).

paper to the Institution of Civil Engineers,[77] evidence to the 1839 Select Committee on railways,[78] and several 'fiercely debated' letters and articles published up to 1843.[79]

When Stephenson began to supervise work for other railways, he was anxious to prevent Bury promoting his locomotives. On 1 January 1839, when he stood down from his full-time involvement with the London & Birmingham line, he signed an agreement with the North Midland Railway, in an extraordinary diversification from his engineering career.[80] He was appointed as the company's locomotive superintendent, with responsibility for supplying locomotives and their operational and maintenance facilities, and recruiting and training the footplate crews and their supervisors. It thus placed him in a position of authority, allowing him to specify his designs and avoid further incursion of the Bury type.

The agreement was similar to that awarded to Bury by the London & Birmingham Railway. However, unlike Bury, who moved to that railway's Wolverton depot to supervise directly the operation and maintenance of the fleet, Stephenson selected competent foremen and implemented his policies through delegation of responsibilities. The railway's board ratified his appointment in February 1839 – an acceptance of his impartiality in ordering the locomotive fleet, even whilst remaining the managing partner of the largest manufacturer.[81] He oversaw the introduction of the railway's passenger and goods services between May and July 1840, and by the conclusion of his term in August 1842,[82] 44 locomotives had been introduced from nine different manufacturers, all to his specification.[83]

Robert Stephenson 'came of age' during the long struggle with Bury and the Liverpool financiers. His initial immaturity in business issues reflected his preoccupation with engineering matters. He needed to understand more fully the consequences of the conflict of interest in which he had placed himself and, to his credit, he hardened his response to the pressures put upon him. Although he lost the London & Birmingham battle with Bury, he had gained maturity in business negotiation. The promotion of the *Patentee* type had the underlying prospect of royalty payments but, ironically, the track improvements of the 1830s largely removed the necessity for flangeless driving wheels.

The establishment of the Vulcan Foundry reflected Stephenson's immature business judgement, which annoyed his Newcastle partners. The two

---

77 Edward Woods, 'On the Relative Merits and Disadvantages of Four and Six Wheels for Locomotives', Paper to the ICE, 30 January 1838, in *CEAJ*, **I**, 1837/8, p. 139.

78 Evidence to the Select Committee on Railways, *Second Report, Together with Minutes of Evidence and Appendix*, including Robert Stephenson, evidence of 2 July 1839, pp. 207–14, and Edward Bury, evidence of 9 July 1839, pp. 230–9.

79 'Art. IX. – Bury's Locomotives', *Art*, I, February 1843, pp. 44–5, and March 1843, p. 71.

80 *An Agreement made and entered into the first day of January One thousand eight hundred and thirty nine Between The North Midland Railway Company…. And Robert Stephenson*, **IMechE**, IMS/174.

81 Minutes of the Board of Directors of the North Midland Railway, 7 February 1839, **PRO**, RAIL 530/2.

82 Minutes of the Board of Directors of the North Midland Railway, 2 and 24 August 1842, **PRO**, RAIL 530/3.

83 Op. cit. (n. 81 and 82), and London and Leeds Committees Minutes, **PRO**, RAIL 530/41, *passim*.

years of cooperation had been of more long-term benefit to Charles Tayleur & Co. than to Robert Stephenson & Co. Without safeguards, he had inadvertently introduced another formidable competitor into locomotive manufacture, providing it with the benefits of Forth Street's extensive development work and contacts with railway customers. Although, in accordance with his undertaking, locomotive orders had been shared between the two factories, the effects were mitigated by the rapid growth of the locomotive market in the mid- to late 1830s, which provided Forth Street with a growing order book and healthy profits for the partners.[84]

Management and development

In spite of his heavy work programme, Robert Stephenson maintained a close involvement in the affairs of the Newcastle factory through regular correspondence and infrequent visits. Harris Dickinson, the resident manager, had died of cholera in 1832, but Stephenson decided not to replace him.[85] He preferred to manage the firm's affairs directly, through his 'head clerk', 'head foreman' and 'head draughtsman'. With the prolonged absence of both Stephensons, however, Michael Longridge was still obliged to attend the factory to deal with accounting and personnel matters.

In spite of his warm encouragement to Stephenson during his London & Birmingham dispute, Longridge became disillusioned with the direction of the factory and the Stephensons' involvement with the Vulcan Foundry. He informed his partners in the autumn of 1835 of his intention to withdraw from his executive role and to establish his own locomotive factory at Bedlington. He was initially dissuaded, but when Stephenson visited Forth Street in April 1836, his first visit in sixteen months, he found Longridge proceeding with his plans for the Bedlington factory. He wrote to Joseph Pease:[86]

I had considered from previous communication with Longridge & Starbuck that Mr. L. had given up the intention of building Engines at Bedlington. On my arrival here however I was surprised to learn that he had resumed the intention – and from what I can hear it is more than probable that he will carry this intention into effect … If however he has made up his mind I have little hopes of changing his views …

The concern is now I believe doing tolerably well, but the high prices which we are getting is bringing others daily into the field, and though I do not doubt that we may keep some little ascendency over others for a few years I am not so sanguine as to expect any thing like extraordinary profits and rather than allow Mr. Longridge to proceed in raising a similar Establishment for the Bedlington Iron Co I think it is worth considering whether Forth Street may not be offered to the Bedlington Co –

84 Bailey (1984), pp. 150–9.
85 Letter, Robert Stephenson to George Stephenson, Newcastle-upon-Tyne, 12 September 1832, **Stephenson**, Folder 18.
86 Letter, Robert Stephenson to Joseph Pease, Newcastle-upon-Tyne, 12 April 1836, **Pease–Stephenson**, D/PS/2/54.

It is doubtful if Stephenson's last comment was made seriously, but it reflected the partners' frustration with Longridge and, although they sought to dissuade him, he proceeded with his plans. Stephenson hoped 'that the change at Forth St may be arranged without causing an actual rupture with Longridge'.[87] Although Longridge remained a partner of the Stephenson Company, his withdrawal from an executive role prompted consideration of appointing a resident manager. Stephenson remained unequivocal in his dislike of such an appointment in his letter to Joseph Pease:[88]

… Neither do I believe that the management will be much impressed by employing a manager of the description named in your letter – Dickinson was precisely the kind of man you allude to – he was active, intelligent and what is usually termed a man of business – but the Est.[ablishment] would have been ruined by this time had that kind of management not been entirely altered … If any manager is brought to Forth Street, he ought to have a share – and ought to confine his attention to the financial department, as any interference with the mechanical will I fear throw all wrong –

Stephenson allowed the subject to drift without decision at a time of intense activity on the London & Birmingham line, particularly with his problems at Kilsby tunnel. He next wrote to Joseph Pease on the subject in September 1836:[89]

I have been so closely engaged since the receipt of your letter at one of our difficult Tunnels in this neighbourhood that I have not been able to turn my attention to Forth St. concerns – I had a letter from Mr. Longridge the other day, in which he asks if I have found any one to take his situation. I informed him in reply that I expected to do so very shortly – What we want is an experienced responsible clerk – one who knows nothing of mechanics – for if he does Hutchinson and he would soon quarrel, in which case we should be worse of [sic] than without a manager at all. I have a person of this kind in view … With respect to the kind of ability which I think necessary for a person to possess in such a situation I trust in consideration you will agree with me – This point once settled, the question is all but solved –

The position was taken by Edward Cook, who had formerly been engaged by Stephenson's father-in-law: 'I have known him myself for nine years very intimately.'[90] Cook took up his post in November 1836, from which time Longridge had no further executive role.

From the late 1830s, Stephenson's growing experience of man-management led him to be a confident, assertive and respected employer and leader, which characterized the remainder of his career. In Edward Cook and William Hutchinson, Stephenson had two reliable employees who had the encouragement to take initiatives where tactical decision making was required, whilst looking to him for direction with strategic issues. The factory's order book was then full and prospects for future profitability very encouraging. After the difficult

87 Ibid.
88 Ibid.
89 Letter, Robert Stephenson to Joseph Pease, Weedon, 7 September 1836, **Pease–Stephenson**, D/PS/2/55.
90 Letter, Robert Stephenson to Edward Pease, London, 27 October 1836, **Pease–Stephenson**, D/PS/2/65.

relations that had prevailed in 1835–1836, the partners were now in a more confident mood and, dismissing any further thoughts of closure, recorded that 'every thing wears a business like and cheerful aspect'. [91]

Locomotive development

In the late 1830s, Robert Stephenson remained involved with locomotive design and material development, and directed improvements towards maintaining market initiative. With the market strong and prices high, other manufacturers were attracted to diversify into locomotive production. Although the Stephenson Company remained the largest manufacturer, it was competing against 33 other firms by 1840. [92] William Hutchinson had continued to improve component designs and materials within the *Patentee* arrangement, but it was evident that a more radical improvement was required. Railways were seeking locomotives with more power, and greater economy and reliability in operation and maintenance.

Stephenson took the initiative towards the development of a new locomotive type, the design for which was supervised by Hutchinson. A longer boiler was introduced to increase heating surface, whilst minimizing 'the escape of a large quantity of waste heat up the chimney.'[93] He understood the combustion characteristics of coke, as he revealed in two contributions to later debates at the Institution of Civil Engineers. He first noted that[94]

… in a locomotive boiler, where the combustion was very rapid, the quantity of unconsumed carbonic oxide [carbon monoxide] was very small. Still it had only been practicable to evaporate from 8 lbs. to 10 lbs. of water with 1 lb. of fuel, even by lengthening the locomotive boilers to such an extent that the temperature in the chimney was only about 410 ° Fahr. whilst that of the steam was 300 ° Fahr.'

The long boilers, with larger fireboxes placed behind the rear axle, provided economies in ton-mile operating costs. Stephenson later observed that[95]

At a white heat it was found that nearly pure carbonic acid was generated … If it were true that the quantity of heat developed in consuming carbon was in proportion to the oxygen brought in contact with it, then the admission of oxygen, within certain limits, should cause economy. He had never known more than 5 or 6 per cent. to be saved by smoke-preventing apparatus. He argued, therefore, that there was very little imperfect

---

91 Letter, Edward Pease to Robert Stephenson, Darlington, 10 m. 6 [6 October] 1836, **Pease–Stephenson**, D/PS/2/65.

92 Bailey (1999), p. 57.

93 Printed Report, 'Mr. Stephenson's Report to the Directors of the Norfolk Railway', Westminster, 21 January 1846, **ICE**, Ref. 04.

94 Discussion following Papers No. 871 by Admiral The Earl of Dundonald, 'On the Results of the Use of Tubular Boilers' &c., No. 873 by John Scott Russell, 'On Certain Points in the Construction of Marine Boilers', and No. 874 by Pierre H. Boutigny, 'Description of a Diaphragm Steam Boiler', *Proc. ICE*, **XI**, 1851/2, p. 401.

95 Discussion following papers Nos. 887 by Daniel K. Clark, 'Experimental Investigation of the Principles of the Boilers of Locomotive Engines', and 891 by John Sewell, 'On Locomotive Boilers and on Fuels', *Proc. ICE*, **XII**, 1852/53, pp. 415–16.

combustion. Unless the oxygen entered through the fire, in his opinion it did little good. He had tried the admission of air at various heights in the fire-box, without producing any good effect …

In comparing the long with the short boiler experiments, it was important to know the rate of evaporation. For moderate speeds moderate firing might be practiced, and short boilers might then be usefully employed. Long boilers might be better with heavy loads, and short boilers with light loads.

Inside iron plate frames were introduced, and a common steam-chest fitted between the inside cylinders serving near-vertical slide valves. Boiler feed-pumps were activated by the valve eccentrics, instead of cross-heads as hitherto. The 'long-boiler' type was patented at the end of 1841 (Plates 8 and 9).[96] Stephenson's personal input to the design effort is recorded in a letter from him, probably sent to Edward Cook:[97]

… I must just leave it in Hutchinson's hands to put a new Engine in hand as soon as possible and to push it in every way he can with prudence for I consider it of the [utmost] importance to have one of these Engines tried upon the N Midland Line with the least possible delay.

I send also a drawing of a slide valve and parts such as I wish put on to the new class of Engine – The overlap shown inside of the valve is merely for the purpose of experiment as I expect we shall have to take it off and thus we can do without making a new valve –

I have put a drawing in hand shewing precisely what I mean respecting the working gear which will be sent to you, but as I expect Hutchinson will easily understand my description you need not delay proceeding with the drawings in hand.

Stephenson retained an intuitive and experienced understanding of materials and manufacturing practice, as indicated in a rather tetchy letter written to Cook:[98]

Tell Hutchinson that calculations must either be right or wrong. – if subscribed to, it is to be assumed that they are right and worthy of being acted upon – on the other hand if not worthy of being acted upon, dont subscribe to them. If my calculations be right and I am confident they are, a tire which is shrunk 3/8 of an inch should be on the point of breaking which the fact derived from experience seems to bear out.

Taking the area of the tire at 8 inches then the present shrinkage will certainly throw a strain of 80 Tons upon it, now I submit that the tire of one of our Engine wheels would be perfectly secure against the casualty. Hutchinson speaks of 40 Tons of tension would be applied instead of 80.

'Long-boiler' locomotives were a satisfactory response to railway requirements, both in Britain and the growing European networks, for greater efficiency and economy, whilst constrained by the many small turntables that limited their wheelbase.[99] Many were built, both at Forth Street and by other British and European manufacturers under licence.

From the mid-1840s, however, growing competition between Britain's trunk railways led to higher-speed services. With their short wheelbase, the

---

96 Patent No. 8998, inrolled 22 December 1841.
97 Part letter, Robert Stephenson, probably to Edward Cook, June 1841, **IMechE**, IMS 168/4.
98 Letter, Robert Stephenson to Edward Cook, Cardiff, 21 February 1840, **IMechE**, IMS 168/3.
99 Discussion following Paper No.794, by Thomas R. Crampton, 'On the Construction of Locomotive Engines' &c., *Proc. ICE*, **VIII**, 1849, p. 241.

locomotives were not well set up for speeds above 40 miles per hour, which resulted in a 'yawing' motion. The type was more widely adopted on the slower-speed European railways, particularly in France and the German states.

In 1842, an important design initiative was taken by two of the Forth Street employees, William Williams, a premium apprentice engaged in the drawing office, and William Howe, a patternmaker. They developed the 'link' motion, providing a variable steam cut-off for the valves, with which to reduce steam consumption and significantly improve operating economy. Howe made a wooden model, with improvements on Williams' original sketch, which was sent to Stephenson in London for his views. He wrote to Cook:[100]

I have just received the model and like the idea exceedingly, but I fear the truth of the motion is rather questionable, although it may not perhaps be to such an extent as to render it useful. I shall have the accuracy of it tested before I reach NCastle – On the first blush it is very satisfactory and I sincerely hope a more mature investigation will prove equally so. –

My impression is that at certain parts of the stroke the motion of the slide valve will be backwards instead of forwards and vice versa. – I think it can hardly be otherwise and the working of the model rather supports this opinion, but it is so small that no decided conclusion can be drawn from it – I should wish a full sized model to be made for that alone can decide the point – If it answers it will be worth a jew's eye and the contriver of it should be rewarded.

The development work on the 'Stephenson link' motion led to the first locomotive application just three months later, the economy it offered encouraging a rapid introduction into general use. Although it was an important technological step, Stephenson did not apply for a patent. Giving evidence to a patent tribunal in 1851, Howe stated: 'I do not think there was ever one [patent] applied for. There seemed to be a doubt whether it would act effectively or not at the time.'[101] The tribunal, which enquired into precedence of expansion valve gear, arose out of action by John Gray (1810–1854), patentee of the 'horse-leg' valve gear of 1839, against the London & North Western Railway for its use of the Stephenson link motion. Gray's gear may have influenced Stephenson's decision not to patent the link motion, although its form was sufficiently novel.

The gauge wars of 1845–1846 stimulated locomotive innovation and trial. The gauge debate broadened into the benefits and disadvantages of locomotive power for the standard gauge against the broad gauge adopted by Isambard K. Brunel for the Great Western Railway and adjacent companies. During the debate Stephenson was pitched into a sharp public disagreement with Maj.-Gen. C. W. Pasley, the Government's Inspector of Railways, which threatened the reputation of both men.

Gen. Pasley had ridden on several locomotives around the country without incident, with the exception of a 'long-boiler', the *White Horse of Kent*, on the

100 Letter, Robert Stephenson to Edward Cook, Westminster, 31 August 1842, **IMechE**, IMS 168/6.
101 R. T. Smith, 'John Gray and His Expansion Valve Gear', *TNS*, **50**, 1979/80, pp. 139–54. Also Warren, pp. 359–70. Also correspondence in *The Engineer*, **XXIX**, January–June 1870, *passim*.

South Eastern Railway. He declared that this run was particularly unsteady and unsafe above 45 miles an hour, although without generalizing that all 'long-boilers' were unsafe.[102] Stephenson subsequently reported that the South Eastern engine had not been adequately maintained, leading to its instability,[103] but the champions of the broad gauge took Pasley's view as an indication of the limitations of the standard gauge.

With both factions arguing the merits of their case, the Gauge Commission was set up to consider the desirability for 'a uniform gauge'. The three Commissioners were Lt. Col. J. M. F. Smith, Professor P. Barlow, and Professor G. B. Airy. Stephenson was the first witness to give evidence, in August 1845. It was largely related to locomotive arrangement and performance, in which he sought to argue that gauge was not an issue in relation to power or speed:[104]

At present I believe that there are more powerful engines working upon the narrow gauge than there are upon the broad gauge lines. There are engines capable of taking 400 tons at 15 and 16 miles an hour, or more; and I do not know of any engines upon the Great Western that are equal to that task … I believe we have now as great a weight upon six wheels upon the narrow gauge as ought to be put on six wheels; and that will be, in my opinion, hereafter the limit of power, not the width of the gauge …

Every day we [sic] are running upwards of 50 miles an hour with our passenger trains … On the North Midland I tried some [locomotives with driving wheels] of 6 feet diameter, and they are there constantly running 50 miles an hour. There is no difficulty whatever in making an engine upon the narrow gauge to take 40 tons at 60 miles an hour; or even more than that.

Stephenson was challenged about the reasons for the 'yawing' tendency of the outside cylinder 'long-boiler' locomotives. Although it was an issue that he and other engineers were still considering, and just prior to the publication of a learned study of the subject,[105] his response was perceptive in its appreciation of out-of-balance forces:

I cannot make up my mind about it. If you consider the action of the cylinder, it is perfectly rigid metal – engine and cylinder together. Now, when the steam presses upon the piston, it is at the same time pressing against the lid of the cylinder; the action and the reaction must be equal. Therefore, I do not believe that it is the steam that causes the irregular action, but I believe it to be the mere weight of the pistons themselves, and therefore if we could contrive to balance the pistons by the weight upon the wheel, we should get rid of that very much; but in the most recent designs of engines of that kind, I have brought the cylinder much nearer to the driving wheel and nearer to the centre of the engine; at present they hang over the wheels a good deal; now I have brought them within the wheels.

102 Discussion following paper 'On the Construction of Locomotive Engines' &c., by Thomas Crampton, *Proc. ICE*, **VIII**, p. 255.
103 *Mr. Stephenson's Report to The Directors of the Norfolk Railway*, Westminster, 21 January 1846. Printed and circulated, also published *RT*, **IX**, 31 January 1846, pp. 157–8.
104 *Report of the Gauge Commissioners*, with Minutes of Evidence, 1846, pp. 1–18.
105 Le Chatelier.

Other evidence submitted to the Commissioners perpetuated the argument about power, speed and economy of broad- and standard-gauge locomotives. This included evidence by George Bidder, who strongly backed Stephenson's thesis that gauge was irrelevant in comparing locomotive designs, and Daniel Gooch (1816–1889), the Great Western Railway's locomotive superintendent, who argued the reverse. On Brunel's initiative, however, comparative trials were conducted in December 1845/January 1846, adopting the best examples from the two gauges.

The standard gauge 'long-boiler' locomotive (the 'A' engine), which Stephenson adopted for the trial on the Great North of England Railway between Darlington and York, was a new design, incorporating the improvements referred to in his evidence. Its driving axle was just in advance of the firebox and its cylinders towards the centre of the boiler (Fig. 6.6). Disagreements marred the trials, with Gooch describing it as 'exceedingly unsteady'.[106] The track was not laid to a 'high-speed' standard, and Stephenson should have been alert to the implications. A further trial using an inside cylinder 'long-boiler', with Professor Airy on the foot-plate, ended when it 'jumped the rails, falling on her side' at about 45 miles an hour. The Commissioners reported that:

The engine was less steady than that of the Great Western Railway; but the unsteadiness was unimportant. It was related to the strokes of the piston but seemed rather to be produced by faults in the road.

A more serious accident occurred on Christmas Eve 1845 on the Norfolk Railway with a 'long-boiler' locomotive on a service train, resulting in the death of both driver and fireman.[107] At the subsequent inquest Gen. Pasley, following only a short enquiry, made extraordinary allegations about the instability of the 'long-boiler' type.[108] The inquest verdict determined 'excessive speed' as the cause of the accident. However, as Stephenson's reputation had been challenged by the Government's Railway Inspector, he responded with a three-page printed report to his clients, the directors of the Norfolk Railway, which was circulated to the press. It was a vigorous refutation of Pasley's allegations:[109]

… I must observe, that I have experienced considerable difficulty in dealing with them, in consequence of their being merely expressions of opinion, without adducing arguments or specific facts to support them … the subject from the tone assumed, is made not merely a scientific one, but one involving professional character. I shall, however, confine my remarks to the former.

After emphasizing the importance of locomotive maintenance and the potential for accident if their condition was poor, Stephenson noted that:

I have reason to know that the White Horse of Kent, the only engine which General Pasley quotes as having oscillated excessively, although he has tried several others, was

106 Op. cit. (n. 104), Appendix, p. 681.
107 *The Times*, 26 December 1845, p. 5.
108 *The Times*, 14 January 1846, p. 5.
109 Op. cit. (n. 103).

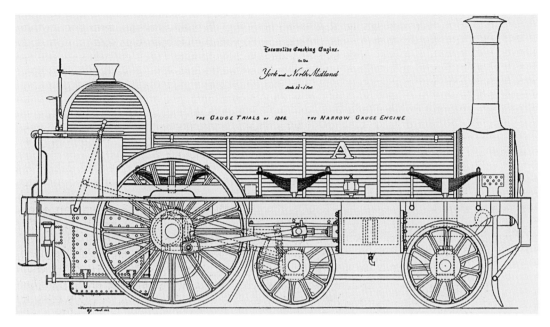

Locomotive Coaching Engine.
On the
York and North Midland

THE GAUGE TRIALS of 1846   THE NARROW GAUGE ENGINE

A

not in the best working condition at the time he made the experiment, no opinion, with reference to its motion, could therefore with propriety be drawn, without taking into account the condition in which the bearings were at the time, together with the disposition of weight upon the wheels …

In bad weather, when the rails are slippery, the temptation to the engineman to increase the weight upon the driving wheels, is very great; and I have frequently known it carried to an improper extent. How far this may have operated in the Norfolk Railway accident, cannot now be ascertained; but referring to that which took place during the progress of the experiments on the Great North of England Railway, under the Gauge Commission, I have ascertained that this improper distribution of weight was one of the chief causes of the engine leaving the rails.

6.6 Drawing by David Joy of Stephenson's 'A' locomotive (Courtesy of Institution of Mechanical Engineers)

Stephenson undertook a dramatic demonstration, using the 'A' locomotive between Darlington and York, to illustrate the safety of a well-balanced and maintained 'long-boiler' locomotive. With himself, Thomas Harrison, and Edward Fletcher (1807–1899), the Locomotive Superintendent, on the footplate, the run, made in 'a boisterous side wind', exceeded 50 miles an hour for several miles, and for some stretches the 'A' achieved 60 miles an hour. Stephenson was 'enabled to declare most positively, that this engine was not only entirely free from any dangerous oscillation, but as steady as any engine I ever rode upon.'

Both Stephenson and Pasley returned to their disagreement more than three years later. In a debate at the Institution of Civil Engineers, Pasley again stated that 'he thought Mr. Stephenson's original plan, of placing the axles of the wheels so close together was erroneous' but that 'he had never made any sweeping condemnation of the long-boiler engines, but on the contrary, he was inclined to think well of them.'[110] Stephenson was clearly annoyed when he responded

110 Op. cit (102), pp. 255–6.

that although he deprecated rendering the Institution an arena for anything approaching to personal discussion, the gauntlet had been so pointedly thrown down with respect to the long-boiler engines, that he must notice it … when the question was purely mechanical, Mr. Stephenson must be permitted to retain his own opinion, however widely it might differ from that of the General, and he believed the Institution would so far coincide with him.

To meet the trunk railways' higher speed aspirations during the late 1840s, and to counter the concerns about the original 'long-boiler' designs, Stephenson pursued development of 'high-speed' variants of the type. With the driving axle located immediately in front of the firebox, the 4–2–0 design with outside cylinders achieved some remarkable performances on the London to Birmingham route, including average speeds of 60 mph or more.[111]

Although free-steaming and free-running, these outside-cylinder locomotives continued to 'yaw' and pitch in an era preceding the general introduction of wheel balance-weights. The breaking of cranked axles had been the main reason for changing to outside cylinders, an important matter for European railways that had difficulty in replacing them. Stephenson concluded that he 'had been one of the first innovators, in using outside cylinders, but after years of experience, he was inclined to regret the change'.[112]

In efforts to reduce yawing and pitching, the Stephenson Company manufactured a pair of experimental three-cylinder locomotives, adopting an 1846 patent taken out jointly by George Stephenson and William Howe.[113] One of these locomotives achieved a maximum speed of 64 mph, 'the motion at the highest velocities … being perfectly steady'.[114] The three-cylinder arrangement was, however, well ahead of its time, its maintenance costs being high. Further efforts were made to increase the steam-raising capability and economy of the long-boiler design by a further increase in grate area and heating surface. The increase in weight led to an extended 4–2–2 type with the rear carrying wheels behind the firebox, the company thereby moving away from the 'long-boiler' arrangement.

With the 1840s the busiest decade in Stephenson's career, it was remarkable that major design progress was made under his direction, the programme requiring both his understanding of dynamics and thermodynamics and his ability to direct it through correspondence. This undoubtedly helped the Stephenson Company remain competitive against the progressive designs of its contemporaries. The depth of Stephenson's mechanical knowledge and convictions had been well demonstrated during the gauge dispute. That depth was also evident during the parallel, equally public debate on the atmospheric railway system.

---

111 *Morning Chronicle*, 29 April 1847, in *RT*, **X**, p. 615, 1 May 1847.
112 Op. cit. (n. 102), pp. 241–2.
113 Patent No. 11,086 of 1846.
114 Op. cit. (n. 111).

Alternative motive power

Although the 'Stephenson' main-line railway system was synonymous with steam locomotives, alternative forms of motive power continued to be considered, both for better economy and to meet different operating requirements. The debate considered the merits of locomotive power against trackside power using different forms of transmission, the broad issues being comparable with today's diesel and electric traction options.

From the outset, both George and Robert Stephenson had adopted trackside steam engines and rope-haulage, and gravity-worked 'self-acting' inclines, where dictated by gradient or operating requirements. The ropes, hooked onto the vehicles and paid out over track-sheaves, were usually one-way 'tail-ropes' wound onto large winding drums with gravity return, or endless ropes around large driving wheels for bi-directional working. In 1829–1830 Robert Stephenson had overseen the installation of the winding engines for tail-rope operation on the Canterbury & Whitstable Railway (Plate 1). He had also advised Thomas Harrison on the use of both self-acting and steam winding gear installed on the Stanhope & Tyne Railroad.

In 1837 Stephenson supervised the installation of an endless rope system down the 1 in 77 bank between Camden and Euston Square on the London & Birmingham line (Fig. 2.7, p. 52). This arose from the insistence of residents living adjacent to the line that they should not be disturbed by the noise of locomotives, and was a concession to achieve the passage of the Euston extension act.[115] The haulage method was an enlarged version of that installed at Edge Hill on the Liverpool & Manchester line. The 7-inch circumference rope, just over 4000 yards long, was hauled by a 20-foot-diameter driving wheel driven by two 60hp engines, installed in a sub-ground-level engine-house. The rope passed around a tightening sheave, to take up slack, and was fitted to a counterweight in an 82-foot well.[116]

The rope haulage system required good communication between Euston and the Camden engine-house, and its installation coincided with an approach to Stephenson by Professor Charles Wheatstone (1802–1875) and William Cook (1806–1879), who had recently taken out a patent for the 'electric telegraph'.[117] Cook had successfully tried the system on the Liverpool & Manchester Railway, and Stephenson recommended its trial between Euston and Camden. It was installed, using 16 miles of wire to serve the independent 'five-needle' system, but it was considered crude and expensive and soon discontinued.[118]

Stephenson replaced it by a 'pneumatic telegraph' using compressed air forced along an underground tube and through an organ-pipe or whistle when trains were ready to depart.[119] At Euston the air was compressed, in a water-filled gasometer-like cylinder, by the release of a weighted inner cylinder. The

115 *1 Vic., c. 64.* Bourne, p. 16.
116 Whishaw (1840), pp. 229–31.
117 Kieve.
118 Clark (1983), p. 264.
119 Roscoe and Lecount, p. 44.

6.7 Minories station, London & Blackwall Railway, showing winding drums and electric telegraph instrument (Science & Society Picture Library)

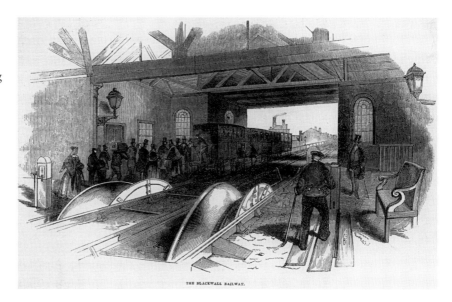

THE BLACKWALL RAILWAY.

compressed air took less than four seconds to reach Camden.[120]

Developing his experience with the Camden rope system, Stephenson then designed a novel form of endless-rope haulage system for the London & Blackwall 'Commercial' Railway.[121] In a report to the directors, George Stephenson and George Bidder recommended a two-track rope haulage system for the 3¾-mile line, in preference to a four-track locomotive line proposed by William Cubitt, the company's first engineer.[122] This was to meet the high passenger demand of the densely populated route between Fenchurch Street and the West and East India Docks. Less property acquisition, and the construction of a narrower viaduct with steeper gradients of up to 1 in 100, reduced the cost estimates and induced the directors to accept the Stephensons' proposal. Noise reduction and removal of fire risk were further benefits that favoured the rope system.

Robert Stephenson's design was for endless ropes, serving both tracks, wound round large drums at both ends of the line (Fig. 6.7). In contrast to the Camden system of hooking the rope ends onto the carriages, the novel arrangement was for the continuous rope to pass under the carriages, to which they could be gripped for motion, and released when approaching their destination. Gripping was achieved by a simple hook, clamp and locking/releasing device, designed by Bidder (Fig. 6.8). Powerful twin marine-type condensing engines drove the large drums.[123]

The railway, which operated a 15-minute service in busy periods, had seven intermediate stations, each served by individual carriages. With the rope

120 Britton, in Bourne, p. 15.
121 Robert Stephenson evidence, House of Lords Committee on Croydon and Epsom Railway Bill, *RC*, **I**, 5 October 1844, p. 629.
122 Report George Stephenson and G. P. Bidder to the London & Blackwall Commercial Railway, *RT*, NS **I**, 13 January 1838, pp. 1–2.
123 Whishaw (1840), pp. 255–69. Also Stephenson (1844), Appendix, p. 41.

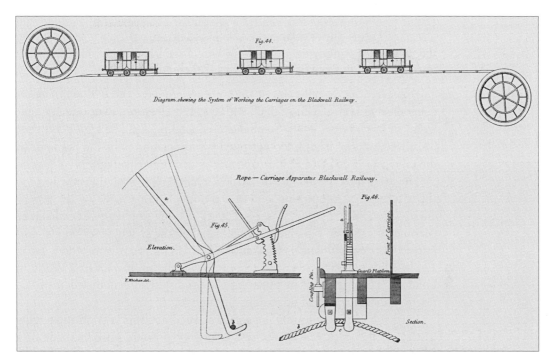

running continuously for 12 minutes, trains leaving Fenchurch Street released carriages from the rear at each station in turn, the last two running through to Blackwall. After being released from the rope, the carriages, running under their own momentum, were brought to a halt at their respective destination stations by braking. The carriages were re-gripped to the stationary rope prior to the return journey, and released from the moving rope on the approach to Fenchurch Street, free-running into the platform and re-forming as a train for the next outbound service.[124]

The use of the rope haulage system for such an intensive service required good communication between the engine-men and train staff. To provide this, Stephenson and Bidder again turned to the electric telegraph, having been impressed by improvements made by Cook and Wheatstone, during recent experiments on the Great Western Railway.[125] The Blackwall Railway was the first to rely on the telegraph for its operations, using it from its opening in July 1840 (Plate 10).[126]

The railway operated until the autumn of 1849, when locomotive power was substituted. Although achieving some 2.5 million passenger-journeys annually, the directors had been concerned about the costs of Stephenson's system, in particular the heavy cost of repairing and replacing the rope. In 1844, he had argued strongly against the use of locomotives as:[127]

6.8 London & Blackwall Railway rope and carriage apparatus and George Bidder's hook, clamp and locking/releasing device (F. Whishaw, 1840)

124 Whishaw, op. cit. (n. 123).
125 Kieve.
126 Whishaw (1840), p. 269.
127 Stephenson (1844), Appendix, p. 41.

Unless … some expedient with which I at present am unacquainted can be devised for obviating the necessity of stopping at each intermediate station, it would appear that the [locomotive-hauled] trains could not be run more frequently than at ½-hour intervals … and this too without any saving in the working expenses.

However, the overall costs of the rope system were twice as expensive as using more powerful locomotives, with good acceleration, that were available from the late 1840s.[128] With Stephenson's operating and cost arguments then disproved, and he having discontinued his association with the railway, the directors proceeded with the conversion to locomotive haulage.

The more novel form of trackside power and track-length transmission was the 'atmospheric' propulsion system, developed and patented by the experienced gas engineer Samuel Clegg (1781–1861). Developing his knowledge of pressurized cast iron pipe-work, Clegg patented the system in 1839. He then pursued its development in association with two industrialist brothers, Jacob and Joseph Samuda (d.1844 and 1813–1885) at the Southwark Iron Works in London. Their tenacity in pursuing the atmospheric system led to a far-reaching debate and trial operations throughout the 1840s.[129]

Trackside steam pumping engines evacuated air from a continuous pipe laid along the track centre, the differential air pressure on either side of a piston, within the pipe and attached to the underside of a train, providing the motive force (Fig. 6.9). A robust arm, connecting the piston to the train, passed along a slot in the upper part of the pipe, which was sealed to maintain the vacuum by leather flaps that allowed the passage of the arm. The efficiency of the system depended upon its ability to maintain the vacuum, and as the trials progressed it was evident that leakage was always going to be a problem.

The first trial took place at Wormwood Scrubs on the Birmingham, Bristol & Thames Junction Railway in June 1840.[130] Stephenson attended the trial, together with other engineers, including Brunel. The trial and subsequent efforts by the Samuda brothers to interest railway companies in its application led to a Board of Trade enquiry which reported in 1842.[131] The system was adopted by the Dublin & Kingstown Railway, for its extension to Dalkey, which commenced its atmospheric service in March 1844 and became the focus of investigation by visiting engineers.[132]

In early 1844, Stephenson was invited by the Chester & Holyhead Railway directors to report on the possible application of the atmospheric system to that line. He visited the Dublin & Kingstown line and carried out a small series of trials to understand its operating characteristics, efficiency and cost-effectiveness. His results had too many anomalies, however, and he instructed George Berkley and William Marshall to undertake a further series of 86 trials.

128 *RT*, **XII**, 13 October 1849, p. 1047.
129 Hadfield.
130 'Atmospheric Railway Experiment', *RM*, NS **II**, 13 June 1840, p. 428.
131 *Report of Lieut.-Colonel Sir Frederic Smith, Royal Engineers, and Professor Barlow, To The Right Honourable The Earl of Ripon, President of the Board of Trade, on the Atmospheric Railway*, presented to both houses of Parliament, London, 1842.
132 Murray, pp. 45–62.

6.9 Atmospheric railway driving vehicle and vacuum tube (*Illustrated London News*)

His findings were reported to the Chester & Holyhead directors and subsequently published.[133]

Stephenson's report was a thorough consideration of the system based on the trials. He described the atmospheric railway as 'a singularly ingenious and highly meritorious invention'. However, he recommended that the system should not to be adopted for a long-distance main line such as the Chester & Holyhead, giving seven reasons for his conclusion:

1st   That the atmospheric system is not an economical mode of transmitting power …
2nd That it is not calculated practically to acquire and maintain higher velocities than … locomotive engines.
3rd   That it would not … produce economy in the original construction of railways …
4th   That on some short railways, where the traffic is large … requiring high velocities and frequent departures, and where the face of the country is such as to preclude the use of gradients suitable for locomotive engines, the atmospheric system would prove the most eligible.
5th   That on short lines of railway … in the vicinity of large towns, where frequent and rapid communication is required between the termini alone, the atmospheric system might be advantageously applied.

133 Stephenson (1844).

6th That on short lines, such as the Blackwall Railway, where the traffic is chiefly derived from intermediate points, requiring frequent stoppages between the termini, the atmospheric system is inapplicable; being much inferior to the plan of disconnecting the carriages from a rope …

7th That on long lines of railway, the requisites of a large traffic cannot be attained by so inflexible a system as the atmospheric, in which the efficient operation of the whole depends so completely upon the perfect performance of each individual section of the machinery.

Stephenson's report preceded by four months Brunel's report to the directors of the South Devon Railway, recommending the adoption of the atmospheric system for that line. With its gradients of up to 1 in 41 through the south Devon hills, Brunel's recommendation appears not to have conflicted with Stephenson's fourth conclusion. It is likely that the two engineers conferred on the issue. As early as November 1841, Stephenson had made available to Brunel drawings of the large Blackwall Railway winding drums, suggesting that he may also have considered rope haulage for the south Devon banks.[134]

Following Jacob Samuda's accidental death in November 1844, the debate became more intensive, and other railways proposed to use the atmospheric system. In response to the debate, a Select Committee of the House of Commons sought evidence to establish the system's true merits. Stephenson was interviewed at length and provided a succinct comparison between locomotive, rope and atmospheric systems:[135]

I believe … the cost of producing a certain amount of available power … is very much the same …

The proportion of the gross power developed by the [locomotive] engine bears very nearly the same proportion to the gross power that the friction of the rope does to the [stationary] engine; it is very approximate …

… with respect to the atmospheric [system] you have no friction at all except the friction of the engine itself, which of course is just the same as in the case of the common stationary engine; therefore the comparison between the atmospheric and the stationary engine is simply a comparison of the friction of the rope and the leakage …

the effect of the leakage is varying at every different pressure … as you increase the necessity of working with a higher vacuum, you make the atmospheric worse than the rope … It appears that a mile of double rope is equal to about a mile and a half of atmospheric pipe …

A very large proportion of the leakage … takes place, not in the connecting pipe, but in the pump itself … it is a place … where a good deal of derangement or wear and tear goes on …

After delays with the building of the South Devon line, atmospheric train operations began in September 1847, but experience quickly showed that problems of component and material reliability led to frequent breakdowns. Heavy leakage in both the pumps and the continuous leather pipe-valve led to

134 Letters I. K. Brunel to R. Stephenson, London, 1 and 8 November 1841, **Brunel**, Letter Book 2b, pp. 225–6.

135 *Report from the Select Committee on Atmospheric Railways; Together with Minutes of Evidence &c,* Communicated by the House of Commons to the House of Lords, May 1845, Evidence of Robert Stephenson, 9 April 1845, Questions 1196–1219.

excessive fuel costs, whilst breakdowns made the service unreliable. The atmospheric equipment was withdrawn after just twelve months, and services operated by locomotives.

Stephenson's development of rope haulage systems and his assessment of the atmospheric system demonstrated a close understanding of the engineering and operating issues affecting their implementation. Although he was largely perceived, like his father, as the champion of locomotive haulage, he was experienced with rope haulage systems and demonstrated that their successful adoption depended upon the gradient and traffic characteristics of each railway. Although it was ironic that his Blackwall Railway rope system had been supplanted by improved locomotive technology, he maintained his views on rope haulage for unavoidable inclines. In a discussion at the Institution of Civil Engineers, however, he sought to 'impress upon the Members, that such inclines should not be introduced with impunity, but only when imperatively called for, or where no other course was practicable'.[136]

With the assistance of his close colleagues and subordinates, particularly Bidder, Berkley and Marshall, he had developed a full grasp of the alternative technologies, and their economic implications, through systematic trial and recording. His independent views, based on trials and growing experience, commanded considerable attention in parliamentary enquiries and in the wider debates over controversial issues such as the atmospheric system.

Expansion and mania

Robert Stephenson strongly believed that locomotive orders should be obtained through the initiative of manufacturing concerns pursuing design improvements, and offered to railway companies at a competitive charge. He did not like the growing practice of railways specifying their own requirements and offering these to a range of manufacturers for competitive tenders. Stephenson's naive view further arose from his position as both a railway engineer and locomotive manufacturer.

Tendering and contracting procedures continued to develop, as his contemporaries had no such conflict of interest and no inhibitions in seeking competitive prices from manufacturers for their clients. The practice led to railways receiving locomotives of nominally the same design from several manufacturers with components that were far from interchangeable. The resulting maintenance difficulties prompted the larger railways to specify not only designs, but also component standardization, a prelude to their entry into locomotive design and manufacture.

Stephenson sought to get round his conflict of interest by engaging a reliable agent and distancing himself from the process of tendering and contracting, whilst still specifying his own broad design requirements to his clients. With

---

136 Discussion following Paper No. 846, by Captain John Milligan Laws, RN, 'Description of the Mode of Working an Incline … on the Oldham Branch.', *Proc. ICE*, **X**, 1850/51, p. 256.

competing manufacturers developing important new designs, the continuing success of Robert Stephenson & Co. in the 1840s was due not only to its design innovations, but also to its London-based agent, Edward Starbuck. He represented the company for all its products, particularly locomotives, and negotiated many Continental contracts and some British ones.[137] He also represented Stephenson personally on matters relating to patent royalty payments.

Starbuck had been the agent for Michael Longridge and his son, Robert, when they established the Bedlington locomotive works in 1837, and obtained some notable European orders. In 1840, however, Stephenson reported to Joseph Pease:[138]

You have probably heard that Longridge and Starbuck no longer carry on business together, the latter intends commencing a commission business in his own account and has applied to me to allow him to act for R S & Co more particularly on the Continent where he has already been very instrumental in establishing a connection for Longridge & Co in the Locomotive department.

Stephenson highly regarded Starbuck, who vigorously represented the company's interests. From his London office, he frequently travelled to the Continent pursuing orders and gathering intelligence about railway development and competing manufacturers.[139] Keeping track of licensees' output, and of manufacturers who infringed the 'long-boiler' patent, was another time-consuming activity for Starbuck. His commission accounts show that Stephenson earned several thousand pounds in royalties between 1844 and 1847, which contributed to his increasing wealth during the decade.[140]

As early as 1842, Stephenson had proposed that Starbuck should become a partner in Robert Stephenson & Co. to replace Michael Longridge. Edward and Joseph Pease and Thomas Richardson would not agree however, leaving Stephenson unusually wrong-footed with his partners. Stephenson wrote a 'strictly private' letter to Starbuck:[141]

I wish I could have made this letter more satisfactory but I am sure you will do me the justice to believe that my best exertions have been made. To have done more than I did would only have led to some chance of misunderstanding which it is of interest to avoid at this juncture when our interests are exactly balanced which has not hitherto been the case. I hope I have arranged the terms upon which Longridge retires.

The market for locomotives was always difficult to predict. Demand rose and fell according to varying rates of railway route expansion and traffic carried, reflecting the economic health of Britain and other countries with developing railway systems. It was necessary for the Stephenson Company, as with other manufacturers, to maintain a capability for manufacturing other types of engines and machinery to provide work for men and machines when

137 **Starbuck**.
138 Letter, Robert Stephenson to Joseph Pease, London, 24 October 1840, **Pease–Stephenson**, D/PS/ 2/56.
139 Starbuck's scrapbook, **ICE**, Ref. 625.1/2.
140 **Starbuck**, 131/53.
141 Letter, Robert Stephenson to Edward Starbuck, York, 25 October 1842, **IMechE**, IMS 189/1.

locomotive demand was low. The strategic decisions for Stephenson and his partners were, therefore, the timing and extent of reinvestment and expansion of the factory to meet a sustained growth in locomotive demand.

The mid-1840s 'mania' resulted in an extraordinary rise in demand for locomotives.[142] From the experience of the previous demand surge of the late 1830s, which had been followed by a substantial drop in the early 1840s, Stephenson prudently avoided major investment at the cramped Forth Street site. To meet the demand, the firm leased premises, the 'West' factory, about half a mile from Forth Street. Even this was insufficient to keep pace with demand, and several orders were subcontracted, the company forming alliances with other manufacturers, such as Nasmyth Gaskell & Co. of Patricroft and Jones & Potts of Newton-le-Willows, whose reputation was acceptable to railway customers, but whose longer-term interests would not conflict with its own.

Stephenson's heavy commitments during the 'mania' led him to place full executive responsibility for the firm's affairs with William Hutchinson and Edward Cook. Cook died in 1845, however, and Stephenson appointed W. H. Budden to replace him as head clerk.[143] Through Hutchinson's endeavours during this period, the factory maintained a high level of output, and he wrote to Stephenson in May 1845 requesting that consideration be given to his becoming a partner.[144] With Stephenson's full backing, he was appointed as managing partner shortly afterwards.[145] To maintain design progress, one of the firm's draughtsmen, William Weallens (1823–1862), was promoted to 'Head Draughtsman' from February 1846.

Stephenson continued to direct the firm's strategy through correspondence with Hutchinson, Budden and Weallens. He was well respected by the firm's 850 employees, who were rewarded in September 1845 when they processed through Newcastle and dispersed to various inns, 'to celebrate the passing of the Newcastle and Berwick Railway Act'.[146]

Established railways had difficulties in obtaining locomotives during the 'mania', being in a common queue with new companies. They sought priority, giving rise to an extraordinary postscript to Stephenson's battles with the Liverpool directors and Edward Bury nine years earlier. In October 1845, Richard Creed, the secretary of the London & Birmingham Railway, wrote to Robert Stephenson & Co., the irony of which would have been well noted:[147]

I am desired to say, that our Company are prepared to deal with you for a supply of Engines to an extent that would probably make it worth your while to devote your

---

142 Bailey (1999), p. 57 and Appendix.

143 Letter, Wm. Pearson, probably to Edward Pease, Newcastle, 28 February 1845, **Pease–Stephenson**, D/PS/2/53.

144 Letter, William Hutchinson to Robert Stephenson, Newcastle, 2 May 1845, Warren, pp. 97–8.

145 Pease, p. 213, 21 August 1845.

146 'Public procession of and Dinner to the Workmen in the Employ of Messrs. R. Stephenson & Co., *Newcastle Chronicle*, 6 September 1845.

147 Letter, R. Creed, for the London & Birmingham Railway, to R. Stephenson & Co., via E. F. Starbuck, Euston Station, 30 October 1845, **Pease–Stephenson**, D/PS/2/64.

Establishment to the execution of our orders exclusively & with a view to a more prompt delivery of them than might under other circumstances be thought convenient …

The offer was declined, however, the firm's interests being far better served by large orders from many railways. At the height of the 'mania', orders were taken for delivery up to three years later, a lead-time that persuaded some of the larger railways to embark on their own locomotive-manufacturing programmes. Investment in workshops, such as Crewe, enabled repair facilities to be adapted to locomotive construction. Stephenson was against this movement, which further promoted the development of railway-based designs and threatened the independent locomotive industry. This trend, he perceived, would reduce the industry's opportunity for innovation.

In 1852, in a lengthy debate at the Institution of Civil Engineers on the proposed rolling of rails by railway companies, Stephenson broadened the discussion to argue against 'the evil effects of competition' in relation to the tendering/ contract system of procurement.[148] He believed that 'a single good house' should be applied to, and agents appointed to superintend manufacture and testing, repeating 'his conviction, that it was only by private negotiation, that good quality could be insured'. Broadening the debate, Stephenson set out his reasoning:

Now with respect to locomotives … The first [locomotive made by a railway company – the Liverpool & Manchester] was said to have cost £400 less than they had been charged for similar engines, but on going into the particulars, it was found that the cost of the different items of materials, tools, coals, engine-power, capital rent of workshop, and rates and taxes, had not been carried into the account, and that when these were added, the actual cost of this engine, (which after all, was not very successful,) greatly exceeded the amount they had previously paid. So it must always be with every large company who undertook to make small articles; they lost the advantage of improvements, and of the division of labour. It would no more repay an Engineer to manufacture all that he required, than it would a watchmaker …

The debate on the role of railway workshops was a precursor to a topic that would be prevalent in British railway circles until the late twentieth century. Stephenson's fears were realized as, in contrast to most other industrial countries, locomotive manufacture in railway workshops became a significant part of railway life. Sixteen workshops were in production by the end of the 1850s, with several, such as Crewe and Swindon, becoming major manufacturing centres, each employing its own chief mechanical engineer and design team. Private firms became more dependent on overseas orders, and, although many British orders continued to be placed with them, their designs were increasingly to the individual requirements of railway engineers rather than those of the manufacturers.

148 Discussion following paper No. 875 by Braithwaite Poole, 'The Economy of Railways as a Means of Transit' &c., *Proc. ICE*, **XI**, 1851/2, pp. 462–4.

Diversification

Following his father's death in 1848, Robert Stephenson inherited his holding in the Stephenson Company to become the largest investor. This was, however, an inauspicious time as the country's recession from the end of 1847, and the turbulent political events in Europe in 1848, sharply reduced railway growth and demand for locomotives. The company's large backlog of orders kept Forth Street busy until 1849, but from 1850 orders were hard to come by and prices low. Stephenson felt obliged to defend Edward Starbuck's commission on one locomotive order, even though his commission was greater than the profit:[149]

If he [Starbuck] had not gained access to the Chairman [of the South Eastern Railway] after a very great deal of trouble, we should have been shut out from tendering, and that at a time when we were almost standing still for want of an order.

Important decisions were therefore needed concerning the factory's future. Not only was its market reducing; its cramped site raised questions regarding its suitability for locomotive manufacturing in the longer term, and hence the company's competitiveness against other, better-sited and -equipped manufacturers. As senior partner, with the best understanding of railway development and locomotive demand, and with Pease and Richardson both now elderly, Stephenson's role in strategic decision making was paramount.

In 1850 he perceived that over-dependence on the locomotive market would place the Forth Street business at risk. The lease on the 'West Factory' was not renewed, and it is unlikely that consideration was given to a new site that would have been required to prepare for an upturn in the locomotive market. Stephenson would have known of the difficulties faced by E. B. Wilson & Co. of Leeds, who in December 1847 had completed a large and well-equipped locomotive workshop, just as the recession was commencing and orders were reducing. Whilst all manufacturers had large order books to carry them through the beginning of the recession, the subsequent lack of orders meant that by 1851 several long-established companies, especially Edward Bury's Clarence Foundry, went out of business.

It was against the background of recession in the locomotive market that an extraordinary 'open' letter to Stephenson was published in railway journals.[150] It was written by John Hackworth (1820–1891), Timothy Hackworth's son, who had assisted his father to develop and build a main-line locomotive. This contrasted with the mineral-type locomotives that they had previously specialized in at their Soho Works in Shildon. In challenging Stephenson to a contest with one of the recent Forth Street products, Hackworth wrote: 'I come forward and tell you publicly that I am prepared to contest with you, and prove to whom the superiority in the construction and manufacture of locomotive engines now belongs'.[151]

149 Letter, Robert Stephenson to W. H. Budden, Westminster, 18 September 1851, **Starbuck**, 131/45.
150 *RT*, **XII**, 27 October 1849, p. 1081.
151 A transcription of the letter was published in Young, p. 328.

6.10 The 527 gross ton *Cagliari* steamboat built by C. Mitchell & Co. of Low Walker yard, Newcastle, in 1853. The screw-driven vessel was fitted with a 70 nhp vertical direct steam engine (no. 14) and boiler, built by Robert Stephenson & Co. at the Forth Street works (Tyne & Wear Archives Service)

There is no evidence of any response to this outburst, which would have been seen as a last desperate effort to gain orders for the Soho Works. Stephenson's attention at the time was focused on the North Wales tubular bridges and he would have had little opportunity to respond. The struggle to keep the Soho Works in business may have contributed to Timothy Hackworth's ill-health and death in July 1850, following which the works were closed.

After nearly 30 years of production, Forth Street had grown, piecemeal, far beyond original expectations, and the cramped site was unsuitable for economies of scale from large orders. However, Stephenson anticipated that the locomotive market, whilst remaining subject to cyclical demand, would offer scope for the company's continued involvement in small batch production dependent upon the craft skills of each workshop. To provide continuity of employment for its men and equipment, however, it was decided to diversify back into other products that could similarly employ the firm's craft-based skills. This decision committed the partners to a long-term presence at Forth Street, and, although further extensions and improvements were made, the partners avoided the major capital expenditure of a new site.

William Hutchinson implemented the diversification policy, and from 1850 the company competed in marine engine manufacture for the growing Tyneside shipbuilding industry, in addition to locomotives. It was a bold decision that succeeded well, and production of large, mostly oscillating and 'vertical direct' marine engines of between 40 and 200hp reached an average of one engine per month from 1854 (Fig. 6.10). They were supplied to several large and medium-sized shipyards building vessels for international customers.[152] The largest was a 400hp horizontal engine fitted to a warship for the kingdom of Sardinia. The diversification policy sustained the

---

152 The shipyards included those of Palmer Bros., Thomas Toward, C. Mitchell & Co. and A. Leslie & Co., building vessels for Egypt, China, Hong Kong, Norway and other overseas customers, as well as British shipowners.

partnership's profitability, as Edward Pease noted in his diary, albeit not without reservations determined by his Quaker principles:[153]

The accounts of the Forth Street works were received and made it appear that I may be benefited by the last year's work £2,000, after giving to R. Stephenson and W. Hutchinson the profit which I cannot touch as a profit resulting from making some war steamers' engines [sic] for the King of Sardinia. The profit in 1852 appears to be £17,000.

The firm's continuing achievements and profitability vindicated Stephenson's policy of delegation and reliance on his senior personnel. At a time when most manufacturing firms relied on executive partners, the company continued to depend on strategic direction by non-executive directors, especially Stephenson himself, whilst tactical direction was left in Hutchinson's capable hands. Hutchinson's death, in August 1853, was therefore a big blow for the partnership, as well as the 800-strong workforce who attended his funeral.[154]

Stephenson promoted William Weallens to General Manager, in which capacity he demonstrated competence and authority, both to run the factory effectively and profitably, and pursue the diversification strategy. Stephenson strongly believed in the incentive of financial participation, however, and two years later the partners appointed Weallens as managing partner. The position of head foreman was given to George Crow (1819–1887), who was to serve in that capacity, with a high reputation, until his death.[155] The new chief draughtsman was Edward Snowball (1830–1911), an outstanding draughtsman who had begun his apprenticeship at the factory in 1846.[156]

Thomas Richardson also died in 1853. Stephenson agreed to his shareholding in Robert Stephenson & Co. being passed to Joseph Pease.[157] At the same time, Edward Pease, then 86, made over his holding in the company to his son, to hold in joint account.[158] Although Joseph Pease had long taken an interest in the company's affairs, he was now to play an important part in its strategic direction.

Although Stephenson reduced his involvement in engineering detail in the 1850s, he continued to offer opinions and support to his subordinates wherever he thought helpful. He wrote to Crow about a new marine engine design that was both perceptive and encouraging:[159]

Mr. Weallens has shewn to me your modified arrangement of your plan of marine Engine – I like it very much, and think it much superior to the original one with the long crank pin which I am sure would be liable to heat and get out of order – In such large Engines it is absolutely necessary to keep the main strains acting in simple direct

153 Pease, p. 303, 9 March 1853.
154 Newcastle Chronicle, 19 August 1853.
155 Robert Weatherburn, 'Leaves from the Log of a Locomotive Engineer', XIX, The Railway Magazine, 34, 1914, pp. 294–300.
156 Edward Snowball obituary, The Engineer, 30 June 1911.
157 Pease, p. 304.
158 Robert Stephenson & Co. Balance Sheet, 31 December 1855, Pease–Stephenson, D/PS/2/30.
159 Letter, Robert Stephenson to George Crow, Westminster, 30 March 1855, IMechE, IMS/170/2.

lines, & in this respect I have a slight objection to your split connecting rod – It is extremely difficult if not almost impossible to keep an equal strain upon both sides, but your practical experience must have suggested this to you in considering the subject.

I have no doubt that a good Engine may be constructed in this way with care, but the best workmanship is absolutely required and a watchful Engineman.

I am very glad that you have registered it and I shall be glad to have an opportunity of aiding you in bringing it into use.

Stephenson sought to ensure that the contributions of his subordinates were acknowledged. When the company exhibited one of its latest locomotives at the Paris Universal Exhibition of 1855,[160] the international jury identified three of the senior Newcastle staff for 'distinction', namely George Crow, Lawrence Kirkup and Edward Snowball.[161]

From the success of its marine engine business, the firm was encouraged to pursue other markets. Stephenson's wide circle of contacts undoubtedly promoted invitations to quote for a range of structures, engines and other machinery. Although he advised potential customers, who often had insufficient knowledge regarding the provision of such equipment, there is no evidence of undue influence in the awarding of contracts to Forth Street. Stephenson would leave negotiations over manufacturing terms to Edward Starbuck, thus preserving a distance between himself and his clients.

Starbuck's death in 1855 or 1856 was a great loss to Stephenson, both as a business associate and a close colleague. The loss of such an enterprising agent was hard to overcome, but rather than seek a replacement, Stephenson turned to Charles Manby, the Secretary of the Institution of Civil Engineers, whom he had known for many years. Manby became the London representative of Robert Stephenson & Co., for which position he was well suited through his good European contacts.[162]

Bridges and bridge girders were fabricated at Forth Street from 1853, although these were restricted in size by limited space and handling equipment.[163] The largest bridge-type structure to be made was the 80 feet long by 60 feet wide pontoon ferry-bridge to carry the Alexandria to Cairo railway vehicles across the Nile at Kafr el-Zaiyat (Fig. 6.11).[164] The pontoon, designed by George Robert Stephenson, incorporated a lifting platform to accommodate the variable height of the river, and allow rail vehicle access on and off the river piers.

From 1856, the company returned to building large stationary engines for use in collieries and manufacturing sites. Its first quotation was for a pair of 70hp horizontal compound engines for the Priestgate woollen mills in Darlington of Henry Pease & Co. At a 'conference' to consider the

160 Works No. 945, a 2-2-2 named *Emperor* for the Chemins de Fer Lyon–Méditerranée.
161 Letter, G. F. Duncombe, for the Board of Trade (Department of Science and Art) British Section of the Paris Universal Exhibition of 1855 to Messrs Stephenson & Co., Marlborough House, London, 5 April 1856, **NRO**, 793/4.
162 Chaloner and Henderson, pp. 63–75.
163 Engines Finished Book, pp. 137–9, **Stephenson**.
164 Thomas Sopwith, 'Account of the Steam-Ferry over the River Nile, at Kaffre Azzayat', Paper No. 975, *Proc. ICE*, **XVII**, 1857/58, pp. 53–67. Also, Jeaffreson, II, pp. 174–6.

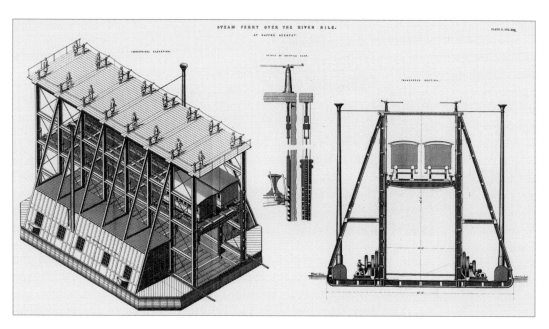

requirements, Stephenson used his influence with the Pease family to provide the opportunity to quote for the engines, but:[165]

> RS stated that it was impossible for them [the Stephenson Company], never having made engines of the same kind, to state the exact cost, but that if H[enry] P[ease] & Co. gave them the order, they should not mind incurring a loss on this particular order in the hopes of gaining fresh experience and a character as makers of first class factory engines.

The engines were built in 1856–1857, and were followed by further orders for new and rebuilt engines.

The company also diversified into agricultural engineering through the initiative of John Fowler (1826–1864), who later established the Steam Plough Works in Leeds. He married Joseph Pease's daughter, and was introduced to the Forth Street factory and to Stephenson. On hearing Fowler's views, Stephenson was said to have 'taken completely to the idea of steam ploughing'.[166] A windlass and anchor carriage were developed to meet Fowler's evolving techniques,[167] and a twin-drum grooved windlass was mounted under the boiler and smokebox of a portable engine, supplied by Ransomes and May of Ipswich.[168] The arrangement was demonstrated at the Royal Agricultural Society of England's show in Chester in 1858, the arrangement earning Fowler a £500 prize (Fig. 6.12). Forth Street went on to manufacture sets of ploughing and self-moving gear to fit any make of portable engine.[169]

6.11 Ferry-bridge manufactured by Robert Stephenson & Co. and operated across the river Nile at Kafr el-Zaiyat (*Minutes of Proceedings of Institution of Civil Engineers*)

---

165 Statement about the Darlington Mills engines, n.d., but *circa* March 1856, **Pease–Stephenson**, D/PS/2/72.
166 Lane, p. 40.
167 Ibid., p. 19.
168 Ibid., p. 30.
169 Ibid., p. 33.

6.12
Demonstration
of John Fowler's
steam ploughing
techniques at
the Royal
Agricultural
Society of
England's show
in Chester in
1858
(John Fowler
illustrated
catalogue,
October 1858)

For all the success of the diversification policy, the majority of the factory's work remained the manufacture of locomotives. The economic recovery in Britain and Europe from 1851 saw locomotive demand rise, and by 1857 manufacturing levels had returned to those of the mid-1840s. Although Stephenson no longer involved himself in design improvements, some notable advances were made during the 1850s. There was, however, a shift in the company's standing in relation to its competitors, as major investment in both existing and new sites in Manchester, Leeds and Glasgow saw other manufacturers providing economies of scale that the cramped Forth Street site could not provide. Although in 1857 the company secured the largest order that had thus far been placed,[170] the underlying trend saw the company become less competitive for larger orders, and by the end of the decade the company had dropped to fourth largest in terms of locomotive production.

Mechanical engineer and businessman

Stephenson's developing career was focused on mechanical, thermodynamic and material progression, as well as railway-building and other consultancy work. His twin roles, as a leading consulting engineer and managing partner of the Stephenson Company had given him a breadth of knowledge and experience that placed him in a unique position compared to his contemporaries.

From the start-up of the Forth Street factory, Stephenson had demonstrated considerable aptitude in mechanical design. His early development of the main-line locomotive was one of the outstanding advances in technological progress that did much to accelerate railway development. As his consulting career developed, however, his time for mechanical pursuits was limited, but his interest and perception of locomotive design and performance was undiminished. His comprehension of the opportunities and limitations

170 Fifty locomotives for the Lombardo Venetian Railway in 1857. **Stephenson**, Works Books.

of rope-hauled and atmospheric systems emphasized his abilities both as a mechanical engineer and as a consultant responsible for the total railway.

Stephenson maintained a close understanding of material technology. In 1849, for example, he was the principal witness regarding an application by Messrs Hardy, Geach and Walker for an extension to their patent right for railway axles. He noted that in 1841 'he had subjected a great many axles, of various manufactures, to some very severe trials, the patent axles among others, by twisting them and letting heavy weights fall upon them … and was satisfied by them of the great superiority of the patent axles'.[171] His evidence was largely responsible for the applicants obtaining a five-year extension of their patent rights.

The conflicts of interest that his position as managing partner of Robert Stephenson & Co. brought to his civil engineering career were profound, and he was naive to have thought otherwise. He learned a painful lesson that might have cost him his position as engineer-in-chief of the London & Birmingham Railway, and with it the reputation that led him to such a premier position in engineering circles.

Remarkably, Stephenson established a modus operandi that largely avoided further conflict of interest, and left matters related to locomotive promotion to Edward Starbuck and the Forth Street managers. He and his subordinate engineers continued to influence the provision of locomotives, however, by specifying the Forth Street designs for many of their railway clients. Even where examples of the patent designs were manufactured elsewhere, royalties were returned to Stephenson.

Following his father's death, Stephenson was pleased to accept the appointment as President of the Birmingham-based Institution of Mechanical Engineers:[172]

I am highly honored by the Council of the Institution of Mechanical Engineers having unanimously expressed a wish that I should accept an office held by my revered parent.

I am prompted to a compliance with this wish, not only from a deep sense of the compliment which is thus paid me, but by something like an intuitive impulse that I am performing a duty towards the memory of my dear Father.

… I shall endeavour to watch over the interests of the Institution in such a manner as will give satisfaction to its Members and prove my affection and adoration for the departed.

Stephenson's appointment was important to the new Institution, as his high profile attracted the attention of engineers, and thus ensured a growth in membership. His major contribution during his term of office was to arrange for a dinner in June 1851, at the Society of Arts, for 'Foreign Engineers, Mechanical Jurors and other guests … in celebration of the Great Exhibition of Industry of all Nations'.[173] Stephenson, who was made a life

171 'Patent Railway Axles', *RT*, **XII**, 24 February 1849, pp. 195–6.
172 Letter, Robert Stephenson to B. Fothergill, London, 18 September 1848, IMechE Council Minute Book, **IMechE**.
173 Minutes of Council Meeting of the IMechE, London, 28 June 1851, **IMechE**.

member in April 1850,[174] served as president for over four years, but he thought that this was too long and that future terms should be curtailed to one or two years.[175]

Although he had no knowledge of business affairs when he began as managing partner of the Stephenson Company, he learned well from his partners the requisite judgement for investment, employment and profitability. He also developed a good sense of strategic planning, which had been essential for survival in a turbulent and unpredictable market for locomotives.

Whilst the ageing Stephenson partnership had pursued a diversification policy from 1850, a younger partnership might have decided to invest elsewhere in a new purpose-built factory for series locomotive production. Once the decision had been taken to develop the Forth Street site with piecemeal workshop rebuilding and acquisition of adjacent premises, the company was committed to continuing as a craft-based manufacturer. From the mid-1850s, however, the growth of overseas locomotive markets saw competing firms, such as Beyer Peacock & Co., developing new sites whose economies of scale reduced the unit cost of manufacture.

Robert Stephenson & Co. continued in production for the remainder of the century under George Robert Stephenson, but the site became increasingly uncompetitive. It suffered substantial losses from the 1870s and went into liquidation in 1899.[176] Its name lived on, however, when a new public limited company was established, building a purpose-built factory in Darlington, opened in 1902.

Stephenson maintained a firm direction over the work of the Forth Street factory, and was an outstanding employer of its large workforce. He achieved this through his ability to select competent senior personnel to whom he could delegate full executive responsibilities. Through them he maintained the respect and motivation of his employees, to whom he could demonstrate an experienced and practical understanding of mechanical skills, as well as the necessity for innovation and diversification to meet market changes. Even though he was only able, through force of circumstances, to visit Newcastle infrequently, his concerns for the well-being of the workforce and his interest and constructive criticism of their work, earned him considerable respect as the 'Chief'.

174 Minutes of Council Meeting of the IMechE, Birmingham, 4 April 1850, **IMechE**.
175 Minutes of the Annual General Meeting of the IMechE, 26 January 1853, **IMechE**.
176 Kirby, p. 79.

7

Robert Stephenson in society

Julia Elton

A man in whom all parties would have confidence

Stafford Northcote[1]

Robert Stephenson was regarded as the greatest engineer of his time and as a public figure of unimpeachable integrity and sound judgement. However, many of his contemporaries achieved as much without attracting the accolades and admiration of a wider world. His early death, when he was only 56, caused widespread grief amongst the engineering fraternity – far more so than that of his contemporary, I. K. Brunel, by whom in modern times he has been eclipsed. To discover why Stephenson was so loved and admired across the whole spectrum of nineteenth-century society, it is necessary to look beyond the railways and the spectacular bridges to his other activities and to his relationships with his friends and family, and see what these might reveal of the character of a remarkable man.

He was a loving and dutiful son to his father and stepmother, kept in touch with his numerous relatives, and had a small and close-knit group of friends, mostly drawn from his family circle and his engineering associates. What personal letters remain give an impression of a loyal and generous man. This impression is reinforced by the numerous bequests in his will to friends, family, engineering staff and old retainers as well as to public bodies.[2]

He served on innumerable parliamentary committees and at the height of his career, particularly during the crowded years of the 1840s, he was deeply involved with what became the Great Exhibition of 1851 and was concerned with a string of businesses, some of which he was active in running. The year 1847 saw the collapse of his Chester Dee Bridge, the worst engineering disaster of his career, which he nevertheless managed to weather, becoming MP for Whitby that same year and going on into the calmer 1850s as a respected establishment figure, whose advice was sought on a wide variety of technical matters. He pursued the interests of a rich and successful man – in his case, art collecting and yachting – but understandably his pictures were largely of engineering subjects and his two yachts, made of iron, were designed

---

1 Letter, Stafford Northcote to Colonel Grey, 2 February 1850, Royal Archives at Windsor, on permanent loan to the Royal Commission for the Exhibition of 1851.
2 **ScM**, GBP 5/12/1.

along the latest design principles by no less a naval architect than his friend and associate, John Scott Russell.

According to Jeaffreson, it was his stint in South America with the Colombian Mining Association which began his transformation into a sophisticated establishment figure. He managed to shed his Northumberland accent and also to learn Spanish, as well as continuing to educate himself in mathematics and natural sciences.[3] When he left England in June 1824, it was at a particularly inconvenient moment for his father and for his partners in the newly founded firm of Robert Stephenson & Co., but he was young and adventurous and perhaps was also asserting his independence from his father. His time in South America turned out to be a frustrating experience, and Stephenson must have regretted his youthful impetuosity, but the existing correspondence from this period gives an invaluable insight into his relationships with his family and friends.

Judging by the tone of his letters to her, Stephenson was on close and affectionate terms with his stepmother, Elizabeth Hindmarsh, whom his father had married in 1820. On the eve of sailing to South America he writes to her (a shade guiltily since his father and associates were then unaware of the proposed length of his stay):[4]

I seized hold of my pen as soon as opportunity would permit me after the arrival of my dear father to let you know all is well and safe and we are as happy as can be expected, considering that I have to part with him on Thursday morning. When I think of this early parting I almost regret that I had seen him, but still I reconcile myself by saying that all is meant right. I scarcely dare think of my father's engagements. Indeed if I was it would only render me unfit for the undertaking in which I have engaged myself. Many will say that I am wrong but I will never say that; I know the experience which I shall gain is worth all the trouble. Indeed I have already improved myself materially in scientific enquiry.

He goes on jokingly to ask her to pick out a bride for him while he is away.

His homesickness and his unhappiness at being kept away from the developments in the railway world, of which he was kept abreast by a variety of correspondents, including Longridge, the Peases and the young Joseph Locke, who remained a lifelong friend, are also clear from the correspondence. Locke wrote to him in 1825:[5]

My dear friend. I was favoured with your kind letter which gave me great pleasure to hear of your enjoying good health. At the same time was sorry that you was not so comfortably situate as you could wish. I should have thought that the extent of country which you must ere this have travel'd over would have produced some object of great pleasure and dissipate the blow of melancholy which seems to settle over you; if not, then business is the only resource which unsettled minds in such circumstances can seek.

Stephenson himself wrote wistfully to his stepmother a year later, about the opening of the Stockton & Darlington Railway:[6]

3 Jeaffreson, I, p. 92.
4 Letter, Robert Stephenson to Elizabeth Stephenson, Liverpool [June 1824], **ScM**, MSL 8/2.
5 Letter, Joseph Locke to Robert Stephenson, Newcastle-upon-Tyne, 24 November 1825, **IMechE**, IMS 165/1.
6 Letter, Robert Stephenson to Elizabeth Stephenson, Santa Ana, 20 June 1826, **ScM**, MSL 8/8.

I need not tell you how delightful it would have been to have witnessed the performance of the Brusselton engine with the long patent rope which they talk about in the newspaper. I have wondered what the patent rope was. I suppose it is something new since I left. Indeed the accounts which I have been able to catch in this country about the grand inventions which have lately come to light in England, quite puts me in bad spirits. I sometimes think that I shall not be able to make up the ground which I have lost and my father in one of his letters tells me I shall be a long way in the background when I return, but we will see.

The same letter reveals something of the love he felt for his father:

My dear father's letter ... was an affectionate one, and when he spoke of his head getting grey, and finding himself descending the hill of life I could not refrain from giving way to feelings which overpowered me.

The only shadow on their relationship seems to have occurred when, shortly before he died, George Stephenson married his third wife, Ellen Gregory (Elizabeth Hindmarsh had died in 1845). However, this was over-come thanks to the intervention of Sir Joshua Walmsley, a close friend and business associate of both the Stephensons:[7]

In January 1848, Mr. Stephenson married for the third time. The marriage was contracted without Mr. Robert Stephenson's knowledge, and it caused some ill feeling between him and his father. Sir Joshua Walmsley became the mediator between the two. Letters before us, of a nature too delicate and private for publication, show the tact and zeal with which he pursued his self-imposed task. No one under-stood better than he the strong affection that bound the father and son. Mr. Robert Stephenson has said that he never had but two loves in his life, his wife and his father; and this only son was the chief pride of the old man's heart. Suddenly, on 10th August of this same year, Stephenson died ... His son was with him – his faithful and tender nurse to the last during this illness ...

Robert Stephenson finally returned from South America in November 1827 via New York and a brief flirtation with Freemasonry, when he was received into St Andrew's Lodge No. 7 in New York State on 21 September 1827.[8] However, there is nothing to show that he had further connection with the Masons, for there is no trace of him having joined an English lodge, nor was there any Masonic presence at his funeral.[9]

When Stephenson arrived home, he flung himself into locomotive devel-opment and railway surveying. He also re-established his acquaintance with Fanny Sanderson, daughter of a London merchant. After their marriage in June 1829 they first lived in No. 5 Greenfield Place, Newcastle, but in 1833, when Stephenson took up his appointment as engineer-in-chief to the London & Birmingham Railway, they moved to London, living for a few months in St Mary's Cottage, Downshire Hill, in Hampstead.[10] By May 1834 they were ensconced in their marital home on Haverstock Hill.[11]

7   Walmsley, pp. 157–8.
8   **IMechE**, IMS/175.
9   Private letter from J. M. Hamill, Librarian and Curator of the United Grand Lodge of England.
10 *MM*, **XX**, 28 December 1833, p. 224
11 Robert Stephenson diary, 1834, **ScM**, MS 603, records 'A party at Haverstock Hill in the evening' on 30 May.

Because so much of Stephenson's time was taken up by his professional and business engagements and the travelling this entailed, and because Fanny died so young, it is hard to gain much of a first-hand impression of his private life as a married man. Jeaffreson[12] notes that they were happy – borne out by the Walmsley quote above – and that Fanny, much liked by all, 'ruled her husband without ever seeming to rule him', though they regretted that they had no children. Perhaps a further indication of the success of the marriage is that Stephenson was on close terms with Fanny's brother, John Sanderson and his wife Mary. The couple joined him on some of his European travels and after Sanderson's death in 1853 his wife travelled to Nice 'with dear Mr. Stephenson's old courier whom he kindly lends to me for the journey'.[13]

A rare surviving personal letter, written to Edward J. Cook, chief clerk at Robert Stephenson & Co., and another member of Fanny's family,[14] gives a glimpse into Stephenson's relationship with his wife:[15]

Dear Edward. I bought when last in Newcastle two plaids which have been intensely admired and this compels me to venture in troubling you to purchase two more of the same pattern. The ladies [Fanny Stephenson and a relation] have determined upon sporting plaids of this character in the precincts of the Metropolis and in a season or two they expect to be designated scotch lassies. The above sketch is made with the view of guiding you in selecting the same pattern, by which you will perceive that the ground is green with stripes of red and what I call black, but what I call the black stripe seems to partake of the qualities of the chamelion, for Fanny declares it to be Lavender … I purchased these said admired plaids at Robson & Henderson and they may perhaps recollect a strange outlandish looking gent purchasing two plaids and requesting them to be forwarded to the Queen's Head … Fanny I think is going on well although she is still grazing on macaroni and occasionally a little marine flesh, vulgarly called fish. She desires to be kindly remembered to all …

The letter was written in 1840, and Fanny was clearly already ailing.

As noted in Stephenson's engagement diary for 1834,[16] on those Sundays when he was at home in London the couple attended Hampstead parish church, St John's in Church Row, and Well Walk Chapel in the middle of the year while St. John's was being altered. On 16 November, the first Sunday St John's opened after the rebuilding was finished, they went to hear the Bishop of London preach there.

By 1838 his success was assured and he was beginning to make a great deal of money. He therefore acceded to his wife's desire for a coat of arms, which he was granted by the College of Heralds on 21 November 1838.[17] His motto was *Fidus in Arcanis*, which, translated literally, means 'Faithful in secret things', but which could be read to mean 'a man you can trust with your deepest secrets'. Fanny died on 4 October 1842 and was buried in the churchyard of St

12 Jeaffreson, I, p. 232.
13 Letter, Mary Sanderson to Mrs. Bidder, **ScM**, GPB 5/12/6a.
14 Jeaffreson, I, p. 233.
15 Letter, Robert Stephenson to Edward Cook, 7 February 1840, **IMechE**, IMS 168/2.
16 Diary, op. cit. (n. 11), *passim*.
17 Jeaffreson, I, p. 237.

John's, Hampstead. Shortly thereafter, in 1843, Stephenson moved from Haverstock Hill to a more centrally located house at 15 Cambridge Square, just north of Bayswater Road.

Stephenson's closest personal friend was undoubtedly George Parker Bidder, who also became his associate in the Great George Street office. Something of what Robert Stephenson must have been like as a man, rather than as an engineer, emerges from the correspondence between Bidder and his wife, and between Stephenson and the Bidder family as a whole. For instance, there is a charming letter from Stephenson to the Bidders' ten-year-old daughter, Bertha:[18]

I have received with much pleasure, the beautiful little short purse you have been so very kind as to knit for me. It is exactly the kind of purse I wanted, for several young ladies have made me a similar present, but they are generally so long and covered with such heavy metallic ornaments that I found it very inconvenient to wear them. The consequence is that they were laid aside and I have now got nearly a drawer full of them. Yours however is so neat, elegant, & compact that you may rest assured it will not share the same fate, but be worn in remembrance of your romping with me.

When Bidder bought an estate in Norway in 1852, he reported back to his wife that 'Robert, who is in high glee and health will persist in calling [it] Mitcham stadt'.[19] (The Bidders had bought Mitcham Hall in 1846.)

The friendship between Bidder and Stephenson, and their relationship with the Sandersons, comes over clearly in a letter Stephenson wrote in 1852 to invite the Bidders to his birthday party at his home:[20]

My dear Bidder, I have not for years past been in my native land on my birthday, next Tuesday Mr. & Mrs. Sanderson intend to commemorate it by a quiet party at 34 [Gloucester Square] – If you and Mrs. Bidder will join the party I need hardly say, that it will afford me great pleasure as I shall regard it as a testimony of a long & satisfactory private as well as professional friendship between two who were at Edinburgh together and who were afterwards thrown together by accident in a course of Engineering which can scarcely be said to have had a parallel.

When George Stephenson died in 1848 at his home in Tapton House, Bidder was there, and an indication of Robert Stephenson's distress comes through in a letter he wrote to his wife:[21]

Robert I am sorry to say is not so well this morning. He can get very little sleep and this day old recollections come over him and depress him very much … He relies much upon me for keeping his mind occupied & relieved and I hardly expect to get away until after the funeral on Thursday.

A further indication of the close links between Stephenson and Bidder can be seen by the amount of capital Stephenson had tied up in some of Bidder's overseas engineering and other business enterprises at his death.[22] For instance, he held 250 shares, worth £3750, in the Royal Danish Railway and 750 shares,

18 Letter, Robert Stephenson to Bertha Bidder, London, 6 November 1856, **ScM**, GPB 5/12/8.
19 Letter, George Bidder to Georgina Bidder, 31 August 1852, **ScM**, GPB 5/2/1.
20 Letter, Robert Stephenson to George Bidder, London, 14 November 1852, **ScM**, GPB 5/12/4.
21 Letter, George Bidder to Georgina Bidder, Tapton House, 14 August 1848, **ScM**, GPB 4/5/41.
22 List of stocks and shares dated 27 March 1862, **ScM**, MS 2033/11–16.

worth £7500, in the Danish Gas Co. along with just over £1000 worth of shares in the Netherlands Land Enclosure Co., the enterprise for draining a large amount of land in the Eastern Scheldt. He also held over £6000 in Bidder's company set up to build the Thames (later Victoria) Graving Dock, a scheme in which Edwin Clark was also involved. Stephenson also had shares in the Electric Telegraph Company, set up in 1845 by Bidder, who had been interested in this pioneering method of telecommunication since the earliest British experiments made in 1837 on the London & Birmingham Railway. Stephenson was briefly chairman of the company in the mid-1850s.

Stephenson must have learned much about the basics of investment, accounting and other financial disciplines from his partners in Robert Stephenson & Co., all more sophisticated businessmen than he and his father, which bore fruit when the two of them began to acquire business interests outside their railway concerns. Associated with them in these ventures were a small group of men whom they trusted, particularly George Hudson, and two powerful Liverpool businessmen, Joseph Sandars and Sir Joshua Walmsley. The earliest and perhaps the most successful of their business enterprises was Snibston Colliery in Leicestershire. According to Walmsley, it was Robert Stephenson who initiated it in 1831:[23]

When Robert Stephenson was superintending the construction of the Leicester & Swannington railway, he came to the conclusion that coal was to be found in the Snibstone Estate, near Ashby, which was then in the market ... [George] Stephenson bought the estate, and then invited Mr. Sanders and me to take shares in the undertaking. We relied so implicitly on his judgment that we at once complied.

In order to develop Snibston Colliery, George Stephenson went into partnership with Sandars and Walmsley, both of whom had been instrumental in launching the Liverpool & Manchester Railway.

Although George Stephenson was primarily responsible for developing the mines, Robert Stephenson also played a role, particularly in the construction between 1833 and 1836 of a rail link to the Leicester & Swannington Railway. His engagement diary for 1834 notes that he went up to Snibston three times, despite his almost full-time preoccupation with the London & Birmingham Railway.[24] Despite some difficulties in the early stages of the enterprise, it turned out to be extremely profitable, producing coal continuously until 1983. When George Stephenson died in 1848 he left his son his third share of it and when Robert Stephenson himself died, his holdings were valued at £41 800.[25]

A less successful business, though one which serves to show Stephenson's enduring and loyal relationship to George Hudson, was the glass-making firm of R. W. Swinburne & Co.[26] On 28 December 1847, Robert Stephenson went into partnership with George Hudson, Nicholas Wood, Robert Walter

23 Walmsley, p. 73.
24 Diary, op. cit. (n. 11), *passim.*
25 Robert Stephenson probate document, **ScM**, MS 2033/95.
26 Indenture, 5 July 1860, between the executors of Stephenson's estate and Nicholas Wood and others, **ScM**, MS 2033/105.

Swinburne, William Alfred Swinburne, Thomas James Swinburne and George Cockburn Warden.[27] Hudson was the principal shareholder and apparently he used the firm to supply glass for the roofs of the stations on his railways.[28] The firm's major site was at South Shields, but there was also a plate glass works in Newcastle-upon-Tyne and substantial London premises.[29]

The capital was divided into 8½ parts, of which Hudson had four parts and Stephenson and Wood one part each. On 23 June 1853, Hudson, by then in disgrace and in the throes of Chancery suits and selling up his house, Newby Park, mortgaged some of his shares to secure '£20,000 and interest upon certain trusts for his wife and children.'[30] However, the business was already heavily encumbered with mortgages of £60 000 plus interest, for which Hudson remained liable. At some point after this, Robert Stephenson, who had never taken part in the management of the company, effectively bailed Hudson out, advancing what seems to have been a substantial sum of money to the partnership.

In about August 1858 Stephenson realized that the Swinburne Company was insolvent and demanded that its books and affairs be investigated by Barwis, an accountant, who seems also to have been involved with Robert Stephenson & Co. Barwis found that not only was the concern heavily indebted to Stephenson himself, but was also 'involved in very large and pressing liabilities to strangers'.[31] In the following September, Stephenson lent the firm £25 918 6s 4d, though understandably with very tight conditions. In April 1859, Nicholas Wood was appointed as one of three liquidators, empowered to continue the business though with a view to closing it as soon as practically possible. Wood eventually bought out the debts of the other partners in July 1860 after Stephenson's death. When Wood died in 1865, that part of the business comprising the glass works at Skinner Burn, Newcastle-upon-Tyne, was sold to the North Eastern Railway Co., and in 1868 Stephenson's estate received £20 000, presumably in part payment of the monies advanced by him in 1858.

Stephenson's role as a director or proprietor of a company emerges most clearly from the minutes of the Clay Cross Company dating from 15 November 1848, just after the death of his father.[32] During the driving of the North Midland Railway's Clay Cross tunnel from 1837 onwards, coal seams and later ironstone were discovered. George Stephenson began to buy up parcels of land and mineral rights in the area from early 1838, and in 1840 set up a company, George Stephenson & Co., to establish collieries at Clay Cross together with lime works at nearby Crich.[33] His first partners were Robert Stephenson and again his two Liverpool associates, Walmsley and Sandars, together with George Carr Glyn, banker and chairman of the London & Birmingham Railway, and

27 Ibid.
28 Lambert, p. 21.
29 List or schedule of deeds and writings relating to freehold hereditaments [etc.], **ScM**, MS 2033/106.
30 Ibid.
31 Schedule 10, **ScM**, MS 2033/95.
32 Minute Book, Clay Cross Co., **DRO**, D5375/23/1.
33 Indenture, 1 May 1852, **DRO**, D4111/1/2.

George Hudson. They were later joined by the contractor, Samuel Morton Peto, William Jackson MP and William Claxton. George Stephenson initially invested £2626 4s 3d in the Company, while the others, including Robert Stephenson, each put in £2500. By the end of December 1841 the six original proprietors had invested £90 000 in total, of which Robert Stephenson's portion was £13 331 5s 11d.[34] In this year, too, the Company built limekilns on land which they leased from Lord Thanet at Crich.[35]

Throughout the early 1840s, George Stephenson, sometimes in association with his partners and sometimes independently, continued to buy parcels of land. Initially, he was interested only in the underlying coal seams, but in 1847 he began to buy up the ironstone rights as well.[36] In all, George Stephenson leased or bought nearly 60 separate parcels of land and mineral rights. On 15 November 1848, at the first meeting of the proprietors after his death, the drawing-up of the necessary new deed of partnership was put in hand. At this meeting Robert Stephenson, who was now the biggest shareholder, having inherited his father's shares, was 'requested to accept the same position in reference to Clay Cross Collieries and Iron Works which his late father occupied [Company chairman], and that £500 per annum be placed to his credit for such general and professional services'.[37]

Between November 1848 and September 1851, there were twenty-three meetings of the proprietors, often at monthly intervals, of which Stephenson himself chaired ten, mostly in 1849 and 1850, despite his consuming work on other commitments, notably the tubular bridges. There are also frequent references to him throughout the minutes and he clearly kept a close eye on things. Virtually all the meetings were held at 24 Great George Street, and despite resolutions to hold at least half-year meetings at Clay Cross itself, this seems almost never to have happened.

On 4 July 1849 Stephenson chaired a meeting at which the subject of the tolls charged by the railway companies for carrying coals was discussed. He was asked to confer with his old friend John Ellis, chairman of the Midland Railway, concerning lower charges enjoyed by the Erewash Valley collieries, which gave them an advantage over the Clay Cross coals. At that meeting, Peto offered to supply the Clay Cross Company with wagons, charging it only the interest on the capital cost of these, with the sum to be decided by Robert Stephenson. In doing this, Peto was effectively subsidizing the company, in which he had shares, from his contracting business.

Later that year, Charles Binns, the Company's general manager, 'reported that without any further outlay of capital he could send 60,000 tons of coal annually to London by withdrawing from other markets'.[38] This was the tonnage that the Midland Railway had offered to carry for them, but Binns stated that, 'with an outlay of £10,000 for [miners'] cottages and the sinking of one pit he could send 100,000 tons.'[39] In the light of this, it was resolved

34 Balance Sheet, Clay Cross Co., **IMechE**, IMS/152.
35 **ScM**, MS 2033/69.
36 Schedule of Indentures, **DRO**, D4111/1/1.
37 Op. cit. (n. 32).
38 Ibid.

that better terms should be negotiated with the Midland and London &
North Western Railway companies. Stephenson himself was to make
arrangements for a coal depot at Camden Town station (on the London &
Birmingham Railway) and be authorized to purchase land, which the
company would then rent from him, for a wharf on the West India Docks
Railway.

By the October 1849 meeting, it was resolved 'That a central office in
London be established & that all papers and general business of the [Clay
Cross] Company be transacted there!' In March 1850, at a meeting chaired by
William Jackson, it was decided that he 'be requested to consult with Robert
Stephenson on establishing a London central office'. The company did not
start to make a profit until 1854, though it seems to have been breaking even,
and on 17 October 1851 Stephenson, Sandars, Hudson and Claxton sold
their shares to Peto, Walmsley and Jackson.[40] Their reasons for selling may
have had something to do with the unstable financial climate of the early
1850s, though F. S. Williams states that Stephenson refused to sanction the
carriage of 60 000 tons of coal via the London & North Western Railway at so
low a rate as a halfpenny per ton per mile[41]

on the ground that such a rate of carriage would be injurious to the railway
company; and he would not, he said, consent to sacrifice the interests of the
company, of which he was the consulting engineer ... for his private interest as a
Clay Cross proprietor.

Stephenson and Peto, who were friends as well as business partners and
engineering associates, also came together on the Great Exhibition, for it was
Peto's offer to guarantee £50 000 to the Royal Commissioners that ensured
that the event would take place, while Stephenson was involved from the
outset, first as a member of the Society of Arts and later as a Royal
Commissioner.

Stephenson was elected a member of the Society of Arts (now the Royal
Society of Arts) on 20 April 1842. On 7 April 1847 he was elected onto the Soci-
ety's Committee of Mechanics under the chairmanship of the engineers, John
Farey and Joseph Woods and on 5 April 1848 became a vice-president of the
Society, remaining so until his death. As vice-president, Stephenson found time to
chair four of the ordinary meetings, including a paper on 15 May 1850 given by
C. W. Siemens on his regenerative condenser, at which he took a leading role in
the discussion, and one on 19 May 1852 given by the geologist, D. T. Ansted.

Ansted's paper, on the non-metallic mineral manufactures shown at the
Great Exhibition, concluded with the statement that, 'his general impression
of the whole of this department at the Exhibition ... was that the English as a
nation are wanting in the good taste to select the right material for any
required purpose of decoration'. This stung Stephenson into the revealing
reply that, 'he thought we ought to be proud to stand pre-eminent as doers;

39 Ibid.
40 Memorandum, 17 October 1851, **IMechE**, IMS/184.
41 Williams, pp. 439–40.

and it was at least a question whether the ability for making railroads and steam engines was not of equal value with that for appreciating the curves of a vase or the tints of a shawl'.

The Great Exhibition of 1851 owed its existence to the Society of Arts, for it grew out of a modest exhibition held in the Society's rooms in 1844 by Francis Whishaw. Whishaw, secretary of the Society, was a well-known railway engineer, who had worked under George Stephenson on the Manchester & Leeds Railway. Robert Stephenson's connection with the Society and his close relationship with some of its most prominent members, many of whom were engineers associated with him professionally, led inevitably to his close involvement with this extraordinary event. His role in its success has been greatly underestimated.

A special committee of the Society of Arts was convened in 1845 with the object of holding a larger exhibition. At its first meeting, Stephenson offered a generous loan of £1000 towards the project, but sufficient other funds were not forthcoming, so a series of small exhibitions was held instead.[42] In 1849, however, the Society committed itself to a national exhibition on a large scale and on 23 August appointed an Executive Committee to run it. This included Henry Cole, Francis Fuller and two mechanical engineers, John Farey and Joseph Woods, both old friends of Stephenson. When Woods died shortly thereafter, he was replaced by Wyndham Harding, a railway engineer who, like Whishaw, had worked under George Stephenson on the Manchester & Leeds Railway. On the same day as the Executive Committee was formed, a preliminary agreement was signed with the contracting firm of James and George Munday, who, because the Society did not itself have the money, undertook to finance the project. However, shortly thereafter trouble began.

It was reported in the Society of Arts Council's minutes on 7 November 1849 that some members of the Executive Committee felt that 'as at present constituted, [it] could not act with that unity of object, design and feeling which was essential to the success of the Great Exhibition', and Harding and Farey were replaced by Robert Stephenson and C. W. Dilke (who remembered Stephenson years later as a man 'to whom I wanted to be bound apprentice'[43]). This did not take place without considerable activity behind the scenes, mostly involving Stephenson.

The trouble seems to have been caused by John Farey. An unsigned manuscript report, almost certainly written by Whishaw, indicates what happened. 'Mr. Stephenson elected on the Executive Committee in place of Mr. Farey who did not approve of some clauses in the contract [with the Mundays].'[44] A week earlier, on 29 October 1849, Henry Cole noted in his diary: 'Up by rail, met Harding in train. Farey had been to him … Executive Committee met at Society of Arts. Robert Stephenson came as Farey's representative. Said he had

---

42 *Statement of Proceedings Preliminary to the Great Exhibition of the Industry of All Nations*, London, 30 December 1849.

43 **BL**, Dilke Papers 43930,84.

44 **RSA**, Scott Russell papers, II, p. 670.

poured oil on the waters.'[45] On 7 November he noted, 'Council meeting. Superseded old Farey, & Robert Stephenson appointed in his place', but two days later Digby Wyatt, 'came to say that Stephenson would not act. At Ex.C. [Scott] Russell explained that Stephenson sd he wd act <u>with</u> Farey but not take his place'. On 11 November Stephenson 'said he wd reconsider the point'. Finally, on 5 January 1850, Stephenson consented to serve and on 8 January he took the chair for the first time.

On 3 January 1850, the responsibility for the Great Exhibition passed from the Society of Arts to a Royal Commission and immediately there were tensions, concerning both the role of the Society's Executive Committee in the new set-up and the attendance of its members at Commissioners' meetings. In his auto-biography, Cole notes that he and Dilke 'were not summoned to attend the early meetings of the Commission, and this we felt much impeded our work'.[46] That Stephenson was also upset over this state of affairs is clear from Cole's diary, where he records after a meeting of the Executive Committee on 25 January that 'Stephenson indignant at our present position: thought we ought to resign but not hastily'. In the middle of all this, Stafford Northcote, one of the secretaries to the Royal Commission, was writing to General Charles Grey, Prince Albert's secretary, about the make-up of the Executive Committee. This letter makes clear the enormous respect commanded by Stephenson, 'a man in whom all parties would have confidence'.[47]

Northcote's solution was[48]

to transfer Mr. Stephenson from the Executive Committee to the Commission, and to appoint some man of equally high standing, and who will give his time and attention to the work, to take the Chair of the Executive Committee, <u>with very great powers</u> … It is pretty clear that the Commission is unfit for executive functions. It is clear also that the executive functions must be assigned to some one or more persons possessing the public confidence; and it is pretty evident that the present men of the Executive Committee (Stephenson being set aside) are not men of a <u>calibre</u> to command that confidence, though they have great merits …

It was thus decided to replace Stephenson as chairman with Lt. Col. William Reid.

Alas, before these excellent intentions could be carried out, a serious mis-understanding took place, whereby Stephenson felt himself to be personally insulted. As Cole records in his diary on 7 February:[49]

the Ex.Com was sent for [by the Commissioners]: & told Col. Reid was to be Chairman, Labouchere saying it was agreeable to Stephenson … Saw Stephenson, he wd never consider any one his friend who did not resent the indignity put upon him. Agreed to resign.

45 Henry Cole diary, **V&A**, National Art Library.
46 Cole, 1, p. 161.
47 Op. cit. (n. 1).
48 Ibid.
49 Op. cit. (n. 46).

Next morning, 8 February, Cole breakfasted with Dilke and Stephenson and they all signed a letter of resignation which Dilke immediately showed to the Finance Committee. Lord Granville, Chairman of the Finance Committee, and Labouchere, President of the Board of Trade, were clearly concerned above all to pacify Stephenson, as described in a letter written on the same day by Northcote to Grey:[50]

We have been in the hottest of water since yesterday, but I think it is beginning to cool a little … I am sorry to say there has been a little misunderstanding with [Mr. Stephenson], and that he has felt somewhat annoyed at the appointment of Col. Reid without any previous communication with himself. Most unfortunately the matter was first broken to him by Mr. Cole and Mr. Dilke, who were themselves annoyed, and who perhaps did not put the case in the best way. The result was that Mr. Stephenson, Mr. Cole and Mr. Dilke drew up a paper and signed it, to the effect that they could no longer attend the Executive Committee. However, Mr. Labouchere and Lord Granville saw Mr. Stephenson this morning and explained matters, as they think, to his entire satisfaction, and he will not send the paper in question, but will, I believe, ask to be allowed to resign. I find at the Home Office that the warrant appointing Col Reid may run in such a form as to show that Mr. Stephenson was not superseded but had resigned, and we think that will be the best course … If H.R.H. saw no objection to adding Mr. Stephenson to the Commission a week or two hence I think it would gratify him, and would then lead to no confusion. It might confuse the arrangement to add him now, but he might be told he would be added in a little while.

The following day, Stephenson himself sent a graceful letter to Lord Granville:[51]

My Lord. I have just seen Mr. Scott Russell with whom I have hitherto chiefly conferred on the subject of the affairs of the Commission & Executive Com. & he has so fully explained to me the facts of the case & the views of his Royal Highness & the Commissioners with reference to the Executive Committee that I have thought it right on the whole to express my willingness for the present to continue to act but understanding from your Lordship & Mr. Labouchere that it is deemed expedient by the Commission that the Chairman should be a paid officer devoting the whole of his time to the service of the Commission & this being quite incompatible with both my occupation & wishes I will only add that I shall be glad to forward in every other way in my power the wishes of the Prince & the views of the Commissioners.

On 12 February Stephenson was promoted onto the Royal Commission, and the Executive Committee was reconstituted under it. He attended his first meeting on 7 March 1850 and continued to attend regularly until mid-July of that year and again from March 1851 through to 13 October, two days after the Exhibition closed. He was also present at the banquet held at the Mansion House in honour of the exhibition on 21 March 1850.

Because of his reputation for objectivity and the respect accorded him for his all-embracing engineering experience, he was able to play a crucial role in

---

50 Letter, Stafford Northcote to Colonel Grey, 8 February 1850, Royal Archives at Windsor, on permanent loan to the Royal Commission for the Exhibition of 1851.

51 Letter, Robert Stephenson to Lord Granville, 9 February 1850, Royal Archives at Windsor, on permanent loan to the Royal Commission for the Exhibition of 1851.

resolving two issues that threatened the success of the whole exhibition. The first of these was the issue of the Mundays' contract. The Mundays had agreed to erect a building, to pay all advertising, printing and other costs, and to provide £20 000 in prize money, receiving in return a percentage of profits on the exhibition. When the Royal Commission was formed in January 1850, its first task was to terminate this contract, because by now it was felt that allowing a national exhibition to become a source of profit for a private investor was inappropriate. The Mundays naturally made a great many difficulties and the first attempt to agree financial compensation, involving the engineer James Meadows Rendel as arbitrator, failed.

In May 1850, another arbitrator was proposed to the Mundays but although they immediately refused him, they suggested a list of five people, including Peto and Stephenson, any one of whom they were prepared to accept as a referee.[52] In the ensuing correspondence, the relief of the Commissioners in finding that Robert Stephenson's name was on the Mundays' list is palpable. Grey wrote to Labouchere that[53]

as [the Mundays] name Robt. Stephenson among those to whom they would be satisfied to refer the decision of their claims, they may possibly still mean fairly. At all events H.R.H. thinks … that Mr. Stephenson should be at once accepted as sole referee. I hope there is no danger of his declining the office.

On 21 July 1851, Stephenson decided that the Royal Commission should pay £5120 in compensation and that the Society of Arts should pay costs of a further £587. Just before Stephenson made his award, an article in the *Railway Times* remarked that[54]

we feel that the arbitrator has undertaken a most difficult task – difficult because of the influence, secretly and openly, which can be made to act in a case in which rank and power are all on one side, and scarcely half a dozen men in the kingdom could be found who would have been able to have resisted such influence. The contractors [the Mundays] must have felt assured that Mr. Stephenson's fame and high standing placed him far above all this influence, and they were right.

Francis Fuller, a member of the Executive Committee, adds an interesting footnote to Stephenson's part in this story. It seemed that the Mundays were also expected to pay the salaries of the committee, and Fuller was intending to write to them to this effect. However, his letter was never sent, 'in consequence of Mr. Stephenson having determined not to receive money for his services'.[55] Getting rid of the Mundays meant that the Commissioners had to find other ways of financing the exhibition, and they began by attempting to get the public to subscribe. Once it became clear how much a purpose-built exhibition hall would cost, it was obvious that other sources of finance had to

52 Letter, the Mundays to Henry Labouchere, 18 May 1850, Royal Archives at Windsor, on permanent loan to the Royal Commission for the Exhibition of 1851.
53 Letter, Colonel Grey to Henry Labouchere, 20 May 1850, Royal Archives at Windsor, on permanent loan to the Royal Commission for the Exhibition of 1851.
54 *RT*, **XIV**, 28 June 1851.
55 Fuller, p. 125.

be found, and in July 1850 a guarantee fund was set up, to which Stephenson contributed £3000.

Stephenson, a member of the Building Committee since its inception in January 1850, also played what was clearly an indispensable part in the last-minute replacement of its heavy-handed design for an exhibition hall (Fig. 7.1) by Paxton's Crystal Palace. Paxton was a close friend of both the Stephensons, so perhaps it is not surprising that his revolutionary design and the speed with which it was executed and accepted revolved around Robert Stephenson and his friends and associates on the Midland Railway, of which Paxton had been a director since September 1848. The story begins on 7 June 1850, when Paxton went to the House of Commons to see John Ellis MP, all-powerful chairman of the Midland Railway, on railway business. Paxton intimated that he had an idea for an exhibition building, and despite the fact that it seemed as if no further designs could be accepted, Ellis immediately took him to the Board of Trade, where he saw Henry Cole and 'heard that the specifications would contain a clause by which those who tendered might also tender for designs differing from the plan of the Building Committee. From this moment I decided that I would prepare plans for a glass structure.'[56] Paxton then immediately left for Bangor to witness the floating of the third tube of Stephenson's Britannia Bridge on 10 June. On 11 June Paxton went to Derby to chair a meeting of the Midland Railway, during which he drew the famous blotting-paper sketch. He then had his assistants at Chatsworth estate office prepare a set of working drawings, and W. H. Barlow, resident engineer of the Midland Railway, calculated the strength of the columns and girders.[57] On either 20 or 21 June, Paxton met Stephenson by chance at Derby station and showed him the drawings on the train as they travelled back to London together. What then ensued was described by Paxton to Charles Dickens in a graphic account published in *Household Words*:[58]

Accordingly the plans were unrolled. 'There they are,' said the impromptu architect [Paxton, to Stephenson]; 'look them over, and see if they will do for the great Building for eighteen hundred and fifty-one!'. 'For what?' asked the engineer, looking at his friend with the serio-comic surprise of incredulity. 'I am serious.' 'But you are too late; the whole thing is settled and decided.' 'Well, just see what you think of them. I am very hungry, and if you will run them over while I eat my dinner, I'll not speak a word.' 'Neither will I disturb *you*, for I *must* light a cigar;' and in spite of every regulation in that case made and provided, the engineer began to smoke.

There was a dead taciturnity; the Royal Commissioner went over the plans slowly and carefully; their originator narrowly watching their effect on his mind. It was an anxious moment for the one; for upon the opinion of the other no little depended. At first there was not much to augur from. The drawings were scanned with no more than a business-like attention. No word of commendation was uttered; no sign of pleasure or surprise appeared. The smoke rose in regular wreaths; but, presently, they grew fainter and more intermittent, and by-and-by the cigar went out; yet the suction

56 *The Times*, 7 August 1851, reporting Paxton's speech to a dinner at Derby.
57 Ibid.
58 'The Private History of the Palace of Glass', *Household Words*, 18 January 1851.

7.1 Original scheme for the Great Exhibition building (private collection)

was continued as vigorously as ever. The projector's hopes rose; his friend's attention was evidently drawing into a vortex, for he went on during twenty minutes, puffing away at the effete weed, quite unconscious that it was extinguished! At length, gathering the unrolled papers up in a bundle, he threw them into the opposite seat, exclaiming – 'Wonderful! – worthy of the magnificence of Chatsworth! – a thousand times better than anything that has been brought before us! What a pity they were not prepared earlier!' 'Will you lay them before the Royal Commission?' 'I will.'

As it turned out, Stephenson was unable to present the plans on 29 June to his colleagues on the Commission and the Building Committee turned the design down, whereupon Paxton, whose confidence in the design was surely enormously strengthened by Stephenson's approbation, had it published in the *Illustrated London News* on 6 July and the building was finally accepted (Fig. 7.2).

Interestingly, when Peto wrote on 12 July to Colonel Grey offering the £50 000 guarantee, he added a postscript to his letter:[59]

Perhaps I might take the liberty of saying that I consider the success of the Exhibition would be considerably increased by the adoption of Mr. Paxton's plan.

Given their close professional and personal relationship, it is tempting to speculate that Peto and Stephenson had discussed Paxton's design.

Stephenson had been MP for Whitby since 1847 and as such was also able to speak effectively in the Commons debate on 4 July 1850, following the motion brought against the Exhibition by Colonel Sibthorp, much of which revolved round the proposed use of Hyde Park. Stephenson confidently

59 Peto, p. 89.

refuted many of the concerns of the opposition about increased traffic, street congestion and damage to trees, as recorded in *Hansard*:[60]

The figures … with regard to the inconvenience of the cartage of 40,000 tons of material into Hyde Park, were at first sight almost overpowering. But it was not so great as was imagined. From the Camden Town station, 8000 tons were weekly carted through two openings into that station, independently of coals and cattle; and no inconvenience had been felt … It was not the intention of the Building Committee to encroach upon the trees beyond what had been already done. He must, therefore, ask the House to look upon the whole question as practical men.

Sibthorp's motion was defeated by a majority of 120.

Stephenson had consented to stand as Whitby's candidate on 14 June 1847 in the general election called that year as a result of the corn-law crisis of 1846, which split Peel's Conservative party in two, pitting protectionists against free-traders. One has to wonder why Stephenson was prepared to do this, particularly in a year which must have been one of the busiest and most difficult of his life. He was deeply absorbed in the design and construction of the tubular bridges, and the catastrophic collapse of his Chester Dee Bridge happened only three weeks before his nomination. Furthermore, although Stephenson was a Conservative and Whitby a traditional Conservative stronghold, it seems strange that a famous railway engineer should be chosen to represent a town whose interests lay wholly in shipping and the coasting trade. Indeed, there is a strong implication in *The Yorkshireman* that Stephenson was shoe-horned in over another, possibly more suitable candidate, by 'the inconsistent gentry' (inconsistent because they were all in shipping) of his election committee.[61] In the event, Stephenson's subsequent performance as an MP on local issues and the circumstances surrounding both the 1847 and 1852 elections reflect little credit on him.

Stephenson was the nominee of his friend, George Hudson, Conservative MP for Sunderland.[62] Hudson was fiercely protectionist, as was Stephenson, and was in the middle of manipulating the election in York to ensure the success of his protectionist candidate there.[63] He was also promoting Whitby (now linked to the outside world by a Stephenson railway) as a seaside resort, developing his property holdings there.

Stephenson, accompanied by his father, made his first appearance as candidate on 27 July, three days before the election. He was introduced by the chairman of his election committee, Thomas Fishburn, whose family had been building ships in Whitby since at least the middle of the eighteenth century. In his own speech, Stephenson did his best to reassure potential electors of his dedication to maritime causes:[64]

60 *Hansard*, 4 July 1850.
61 *The Yorkshireman*, 31 July 1847.
62 *The Yorkshireman*, 19 June 1847.
63 Op. cit. (n. 61).
64 Ibid.

7.2 The Crystal Palace in Hyde Park (Royal Commission for the Exhibition of the Works of Industry of all Nations, *Reports by the Juries on the Subjects in the Thirty Classes into which the Exhibition was divided*, 1852, special limited edition containing a series of calotype photographs by Fox Talbot. Elton collection, Ironbridge Gorge Museum Trust)

I confess I am ignorant of maritime affairs. I have read, however, the evidence given before the committee on the navigation laws, and I cannot, in any way whatever conceive it possible for the maritime interests of this great country to prosper, were those laws abrogated. Let anyone look at the history of the past century and ask himself, what has been effected under their existence. The 'Wooden Walls' of England were reared and manned by brave British sailors (cheers) – commerce flourished, and her flag was seen floating over every sea which could not have been the case without protection.

During these three days, Stephenson also wrote a letter about his campaign to John Sanderson, which gives an indication of the pressure he was under in his professional life:[65]

Yesterday was chiefly spent in visiting the principal members of my Com[mitte]e but in the course of the afternoon I canvassed 80 votes. They were very civil and to a man offered me support although we might differ a little in politics. Today I expect to complete the canvass in the town – on Friday the election will take place and on Saturday morning & Tuesday, the Com[mitte]e say I must spend in calling upon the outlying voters who are scattered about in all distances at some distance in the country varying from 5 to 10 miles, it is clearly therefore impossible for me to get to London in time to write my Holyhead report as suggested by Clark.

On Friday 30 July 1847 Stephenson was elected unopposed, taking his seat on the opposition benches to Lord John Russell's Liberal government.

By the next election, in 1852, there was such dissatisfaction with Stephenson's performance that, in a revolutionary step for Conservative Whitby, a Liberal candidate, the Hon. Edmund Phipps, member of a famous

---

65 Undated letter (endorsed 30 July), Robert Stephenson to John Sanderson, **ICE**, Stephenson–Clark correspondence.

local Liberal family, was put forward to oppose him. Significantly, the chairman of Phipps's election committee was Christopher Richardson, who had been a member of Stephenson's committee at the 1847 election.

Phipps's supporters circulated posters complaining that Stephenson had neglected his duties as Whitby's MP by attending only one in twenty divisions 'on an average, (nay I beleive [*sic*] it much less)' and itemizing some instances of this dereliction of duty, such as not being in the House to vote against the Liberal Party's proposed abolition of the duty on all timber for shipbuilding purposes. Another poster avers that Stephenson was neglecting the interests of the coasting trade in favour of the railway interest, and calls upon British shipowners to vote against him.[66]

Stephenson's party fought back openly but also, as reported at length in *The Yorkshireman*, in a variety of underhand ways. Although such tricks were permissible at that time before the second great reform bill of 1867 and the 1870 introduction of the secret ballot, and even allowing for the newspaper's liberal, pro-free-trade and anti-Hudson bias, a discreditable tale nevertheless emerges.

When Phipps arrived in the town he was forced to address voters in the open air, because every large room in the town had been booked by Stephenson's party to prevent his using them.[67] A cheese merchant from Fylingdales wrote a letter to *The Yorkshireman* to say that, 'One of my Whitby tradesmen tells me he has been *marked*, and has had the monthly account of one of his (Tory) customers taken away after not promising for Stephenson,'[68] while Conservative agents, acting on behalf of his election committee, 'went to the tenant farmers, and told them if they did not vote for Stephenson they would lose their farms; and also to the tradesmen, and talked of loss of custom and ruin'.[69]

Nomination day was on 8 July 1852, when, after a show of hands, the returning officer declared in favour of Phipps. Stephenson's party immediately demanded a poll. That evening there was a riot when, 'blood streamed from faces into gutters – one man was picked up for dead and then another – women shrieked – children yelled'.[70] This was incited by a mob of thugs hired by the Conservative party. Each man had his travelling expenses paid and was provided with dinner, drink and 5s as wages. When it was all over the thugs were removed from Whitby 'by special train forwarded by the York and North Midland Railway Co.'.

The following day a poll was taken, resulting in a majority of 109 votes in Stephenson's favour. An anonymous writer, 'Oculus', reporting all this to correct an earlier account by *The Yorkshireman*'s conservative reporter, remarked that:[71]

Your readers will form some idea how this majority was gained, when I state that one man said in the morning, he would lose his arms rather than vote for Stephenson; but long before the polling closed, he entered one of the polling halls, and with the cold perspiration on his forehead, tendered his vote for Stephenson. Oh Mammon!

66 Posters in Whitby Lit. & Phil. Society Library.
67 *The Yorkshireman*, 17 July 1852.
68 *The Yorkshireman*, 3 July 1852.
69 Anonymous letter from 'Oculus', *The Yorkshireman*, 17 July 1852.
70 *The Yorkshireman*, 17 July 1852.
71 Op. cit. (n. 69).

Perhaps the last word on this rather unsavoury affair is best left to the defeated Phipps, who remarked in his final speech that Stephenson[72]

told you yesterday that he has withdrawn from his professional engagements; but we all know when they talk of building bridges, boring tunnels and making embankments in Egypt, that all these are the work of time; and these duties are incompatible with those of a Member of Parliament. He said he was not gradually withdrawing, but he had withdrawn from his professional engagements. I pity him when he says he has withdrawn from pursuits in which he should, and in which he has earned a name which posterity will look back upon with delight when they gaze upon the noble works which he has achieved. I pity him, when he leaves these to go into Parliament with the views that he professes to hold. Surely with such views, he will have to sit in a corner, and see the age steam past him while he is asleep with protection in his arms.

He goes on to say, referring back to Stephenson's speech of 1847,

… if we ask who has done most harm to shipping the answer is 'Stephenson and Co.' for they have actually been carrying coals to London at a loss. This may be play to a wealthy railway company, but the small shipowner cannot live by his losses. As Mr. Stephenson has now done with his professional duties, he will have ample time to attend to the shipping interest. I would therefore suggest that as soon as he gets into Parliament he makes a speech about the Wooden Walls of old England and the honest Jack Tar, and then introduce a bill for the special protection of shipping against railways.

This time, Stephenson served as a majority party MP, remaining an old-fashioned protectionist Tory to the end. Even if the methods by which he was elected were not unusual for the time and although his reputation was apparently unaffected by them, it nevertheless seems extraordinary that a man of his acknowledged integrity would allow himself to be manoeuvred in this way. However, inadequate as he may have been on behalf of Whitby's maritime interests, he was extremely effective on subjects of wider national interest where he was knowledgeable.

Hansard at this period was selective in what debates it reported and Stephenson is therefore recorded as speaking in only eight, all on issues in which he had some involvement. One of these concerned the Ordnance Survey, on which he spoke on 19 June 1856.[73] Although a uniform one inch to the mile map of the United Kingdom had originally been intended, the Ordnance kept changing its mind, particularly after 1842, when it decided to adopt Ireland's six-inch scale. As early as 1853, Stephenson, with Brunel and Locke had formed a powerful triumvirate to campaign for the completion of the national one-inch map. They also appealed for urban plans to be prepared using a 20-inch scale to aid future engineering work and simplify transfer of property.[74]

The debate was provoked when £50 000 was granted to the Ordnance to make a 25-inch map of Scotland. Stephenson, who was a member of the Select

---

72 Final speech of Edmund Phipps, *The Yorkshireman*, 17 July 1852.
73 *Hansard*, 19 June 1856, Debate on 'Supply – Army Estimates'.
74 Copy letter, I. K. Brunel, Robt. Stephenson and Joseph Locke to Sir C. C. Trevelyan, for the Lords Commissioners of Her Majesty's Treasury, London, 3 May 1853, **Brunel**, Letter Book 2, pp. 337–9.

Committee on the Ordnance Survey of Scotland, dissociated himself from its report that recommended the scale:[75]

He [Stephenson] disapproved every paragraph of it from the first to the last, and, suffering under a malady which rendered it undesirable that he should expose himself to excitement, he stayed away from the Committee for fear he might express himself too strongly on the subject.

Drawing on all his engineering authority, he spoke strongly on this subject during the same debate, saying:[76]

each scale had its peculiar advantages, yet ... for practical references the one-inch map was the best of all ... He had frequently consulted the six-inch maps in [Ireland], but invariably found them worse than useless for engineering purposes. It gave him nearly as much trouble to gather information from them as to realize it on the ground. What the engineers engaged in various parts of the United Kingdom had for years been endeavouring to obtain from Parliament was an assurance that the one-inch map would be completed before any other piece of surveying was taken in hand ... Over and over again the engineers of Great Britain had given the government to understand that maps on the six, the twelve, or the twenty-five inch scale were alike useless to them, but the Ordnance turned a deaf ear to all their protestations, and went on constructing maps which the engineers did not want and would never consult.

The one-inch map was finally completed in 1890.

Long before he became an MP Stephenson had been familiar with the workings of Parliament through appearing before numerous committees. Something of the respect in which he was so widely held can be extrapolated from the mass of evidence contained in the Parliamentary Blue Books, for once the inner ear has rounded out the flat phrases of verbatim reporting it is possible to hear Stephenson at work. During the 1850s, he was often called in to give advice or to provide guidance to committee members. Such an example is the 1855 River Tyne Commission in 1855, whose chairman, Vice-Admiral William Bowles, said, 'We have thought it right to call you more particularly for our own information and guidance ... We wished to have your opinion upon the subject before us'.[77]

His integrity and fairness when asked to judge some engineering matter in committee seems to have been virtually absolute. In 1856 he was the key witness at the enquiry into Thomas Page's new Westminster Bridge, which took place when the ironwork contractor, C. J. Mare & Co., went bankrupt. The enquiry hinged on the foundations for the piers and Stephenson, despite having, 'never, either professionally or otherwise, examined in detail the plans of the New Westminster Bridge now in progress',[78] cast serious doubts on Page's elaborate scheme, particularly his 'novel' use of cast-iron sheet piling.

---

75 Ibid. Also op. cit. (n. 73).
76 Op. cit. (n. 73).
77 *Report of the Commissioners appointed to inquire into the present state of the River Tyne*, May 1844, para. 4090.
78 *Report from the Select Committee on New Westminster Bridge*, London, House of Commons, 23 July 1856, p. 26.

However, three days later, having been over the works with Page, Hawkshaw and Fowler, Stephenson retracted his views completely:[79]

With regard to the character of the works which have already been done, I feel it quite necessary, after what I said the last time, to say that they have been done in a very masterly way. There are differences of opinion between Mr. Page and myself, but they are of minor importance.

The bridge was successfully completed to Page's original designs in 1862.

Almost inevitably, Stephenson became embroiled in some of the rows that dogged the rebuilding of the Houses of Parliament, particularly the ventilation of the House of Commons, carried out by D. B. Reid. In 1852, when the building was at last occupied, there were immediate complaints about the extreme discomforts of the chamber, a situation exacerbated by the heat generated by Barry's large Gothic gasoliers. A select committee to investigate the problems was convened on 19 March 1852 and four days later, on 23 March, Stephenson and Locke were added to its members in order to supervise the alterations proposed by Reid.[80] They were also asked to look into the problems of the lights. The committee met twenty-three times between 23 March and 21 May 1852 and Stephenson attended sixteen of these meetings, clearly finding the whole situation somewhat onerous as he wrote ruefully to Brunel:[81]

The ventilation [problems] have saddled Locke and myself with the management of Barry & Reid during the Easter recess and to superintend the alterations proposed to be made in the H.C. [House of Commons] to improve if possible the present insufferable state. I feel as Serjt. Murphy says 'like a cat in hell without claws' but as we have undertaken it I am determined to stick to it.

One does not normally associate Stephenson with expertise in lighting, but his lucid evidence on the subject to the select committee is an impressive demonstration of the wide range of his technical capabilities.[82]

By 1847, the year he became an MP, Stephenson was a wealthy man, and around November of that year he moved a short distance from the Cambridge Square house to an infinitely grander establishment at 34 Gloucester Square, where he began to entertain lavishly and to buy or commission works of art.[83]

Of course, he already had a number of prints and drawings in Great George Street, rather in the manner that engineers today hang photographs of their achievements in their offices, and sketchy details of these were listed on an inventory made when the building was sold in 1876.[84] These included '2 large sepia pictures (Menai [Britannia] Bridge)' (probably the Hawkins or Russell lithographs published by Day & Son in 1849 or 1850), a sepia drawing and

79 Ibid., para 675.
80 *First report from the Select Committee on ventilation and lighting of the House*, House of Commons, 6 April, 1852.
81 Letter, Robert Stephenson to I. K. Brunel, 7 April 1852, **Brunel**.
82 *Second report from the Select Committee on ventilation and lighting of the House*, London, House of Commons, 24 May 1852, paras. 3906–45.
83 Jeaffreson, II, p. 159.
84 **ScM**, GPB 5/12/2.

print of the Victoria Bridge, a print of the Royal Border Bridge and '1 large oil painting (High Level Bridge)'. Also listed are a portrait in oils of James Watt and a proof print of a portrait of Richard Creed, secretary of the London & Birmingham Railway (presumably the mezzotint portrait of 1848 by Edward McInnes after H. W. Phillips), as well as the small statuette in bronze of George Stephenson by E. H. Baily.

Equally, many of the pictures that hung in Gloucester Square reflected Stephenson's life, and his preferred painter was John Lucas, the portrait painter. The two men met some time in 1845, when a committee of shareholders of the London & North Western Railway commissioned Lucas to paint Stephenson's portrait. This shows him seated with his hand resting on a drawing of the long-boiler locomotive, taken directly from the patent specification of 1841.[85] Stephenson himself then commissioned Lucas to paint the full-length portrait of his father standing on Chat Moss. (T. L. Atkinson's engraving of it hung in the front room in the 24 Great George Street office.) The pair to this painting, a full-length portrait of Stephenson himself standing in front of the Britannia bridge (Frontispiece), was executed in 1850 in 'nine sittings having been received in unusually quick succession'.[86] He also commissioned two further pictures from Lucas, *Killingworth Colliery* and *Crossing the Brook*. This last one shows a child being carried over a stream with the Britannia Bridge in the background, and apparently filled a panel in the drawing room of 34 Gloucester Square.

The most famous of Lucas's engineering pictures – of which an engraving also hung in the office – was *Conference of Engineers at the Menai Straits prior to floating a tube of the Britannia bridge* (Plate 19). The idea for the picture came from a group of friends and colleagues, notably Peto, who undertook to organize the finance from those interested in the project. Although the painting did not represent an actual conference, such meetings had occasionally taken place, 'when some of the greater difficulties presented themselves in the execution of the scheme', engendering much camaraderie, which the painting was intended to commemorate. The painter took enormous pains over the picture, going to Bangor and spending some days, 'acquainting himself thoroughly with the personalities of the very interesting group of men acting as Stephenson's lieutenants in this great undertaking'.[87] According to Lucas, Stephenson had too much sense of honour to be able to accept the picture as a gift but it is nevertheless recorded by Jeaffreson as hanging in 34 Gloucester Square.[88] Peto also commissioned the portrait group of Robert Stephenson and his father, painted in 1851 after George Stephenson's death.

However, not all of the Gloucester Square art works were of engineering subjects. After the Great Exhibition closed (Plate 11), Stephenson bought Hiram Powers' sculpture *The Fisher Boy*, companion piece to the more

---

85 Lucas, p. 52.
86 Lucas, Catalogue of Paintings, p. 113.
87 Lucas, pp. 65–6.
88 Jeaffreson, II, p. 160.

famous *Greek Slave*, and he owned at least three fine paintings by well-known or fashionable artists: Francis Danby's *The Evening Gun – a calm on the shore of England*, *The Twins* by Landseer and Clarkson Stanfield's *Tilbury Fort – Wind against Tide*.

The Danby picture, now lost, was bought by Stephenson in 1855. It was shown that year in Paris, when David Roberts said about it that it 'was the picture ... all the painters were talking about it',[89] and Stephenson must have bought it while visiting the Paris Exposition. He lent it to the exhibition of art treasures in Manchester in 1857. Landseer's *The Twins* was presented to Stephenson by the London & North Western Railway Company. He 'had been offered a present of plate but ... elected to have a picture by Landseer, Sir Edwin remarking it was the first time he had ever heard of a man choosing to have a picture in place of a service of plate, and he added: 'He shall have a good one.'[90] The picture, showing a pair of sheepdogs watching over a ewe and lambs, was painted in 1853 and exhibited in the Royal Academy that year. Perhaps Stephenson was influenced in his choice of a Landseer painting by the fact that both I. K. Brunel and the railway contractor E. L. Betts commissioned or owned pictures by this artist.

Clarkson Stanfield's *Wind against Tide – Tilbury Fort*, painted for Stephenson in 1849,[91] was also presented to him by the London & North Western Railway. Like the Danby, the Stanfield painting was exhibited in Paris in 1855, presumably lent by Stephenson. It shows the rough sea produced by wind blowing against the run of the tide, a condition with which a yachtsman would be only too familiar.

The Stanfield painting reflects Stephenson's passion for sailing, which seems to have been sparked off when he and Bidder hired a yacht for a week at the end of September 1848, just after George Stephenson's death. They sailed her from the south coast to Holyhead from whence Stephenson went to Conway for the floating of the second tube of the bridge. Following this trip he commissioned his friend, the great naval architect, John Scott Russell, to design and build him a yacht to be named *Titania*, a schooner.

Titania was the first iron yacht to use Scott Russell's revolutionary waveline form, apparently at Stephenson's own behest.[92] However, at that time racing yachts were rated according to yacht club rules which did not measure true tonnage, but exaggerated the tonnage of broad-beamed boats. This meant that a vessel of a given displacement would, if of a sensible beam, be classed with, and thus compelled to compete against, vessels of much larger tonnage. Scott Russell was therefore forced to modify the design of *Titania* to conform to these regulations by cutting[93]

89 Francis Greenacre, *Francis Danby 1793-1861*, Bristol City Art Gallery, 1988, p. 119.
90 Algernon Graves, *Catalogue of the Works of the late Sir Edwin Landseer RA*, London, [1874].
91 James Dafforne, *Pictures of Clarkson Stanfield, R.A.*, London, n.d., p. 6.
92 Russsell, pp. 612–3.
93 Ibid.

two large slices off her, on each side, at the loadwater-line, to make her extreme breadth come within the law for tonnage. He had to cut off the water-lines where they should have had a gentle swell in the middle and make them flat and straight, and he had to cut off from the heel a large amount of the area of longitudinal section, which was absolutely necessary to make the vessel windwardly.

The ship was launched in early 1850 and by the beginning of May Stephenson had had some trial trips in the vessel, as he wrote to Thomas Brodrich:[94]

I have had a sail or two in the Titania in very rough weather … She behaved very well, beating any thing we could find to run south. She is certainly very fast say 11 knots or 12½ miles an hour and as a necessary consequence rather wet. I suppose it is in navigation as in mechanics, you cannot have both power & speed at the same time. We must therefore not expect velocity & dryness in a vessel in a boistrous sea & beating to windward.

By September of that year, Stephenson was writing to Russell himself, that:[95]

[I] shall in a week or ten days proceed towards Genoa when I hope to meet the Titania to set sail for the [illegible] in the Mediterranean. I have no doubt of her conducting herself creditably.

He was clearly pleased enough with his new possession to have her added to the engraving of Lucas's portrait of him, commissioned in 1850, this same year (Fig. 7.3).

With the launch of *Titania*, Stephenson applied to join the famous Royal Yacht Squadron at Cowes, but he was blackballed by its aristocratic members. Almost immediately a proposition from William Herbert Saunders appeared in the Squadron's Notice Book:

I propose that R. Stephenson Esq, the author of the most Stupendous Monument of Mechanical Science [the Britannia Bridge] hitherto known to the civilized world – be admitted by Acclamation as a Member of the R.Y.S. at the next General Meeting for ballot.

This is all the more remarkable because election by acclamation was usually reserved for members of royalty. Stephenson was successfully elected this second time round. His proposer was the Commodore, Lord Wilton, but the page in the Candidate's Book contains many more signatures in support than the usual two. Stephenson remained a member of the RYS until his death in 1859, and on the day of his funeral his yacht, which was at Cowes, fired 56 minute guns and hoisted her colours until sunset.[96]

In 1851 *Titania* earned enduring fame and influence when she was the only English boat to accept a challenge posted in the Clubhouse of the Royal Yacht Squadron to compete against the American engineer John Stevens's famous racing yacht, *America*, 'a pure wave-line vessel built without the trammels of

94 Letter, Robert Stephenson to Thomas Brodrich, 6 May 1850, **IMechE**, IMS/190.
95 Letter, Robert Stephenson to John Scott Russell, Lucerne, 23 Sept 1850, **RSA**, Scott Russell Papers.
96 Diana Harding, Archivist, Royal Yacht Squadron, leaflet.

7.3 Lucas engraving of Stephenson and the Britannia Bridge showing his schooner-rigged yacht omitted from the painting (compare with book cover and frontispiece)

measurement tonnage'.[97] Scott Russell reports that although *Titania* had no hope of winning, 'for she was outmatched in … every element of racing', Stephenson 'was chivalrously unwilling that the American engineer should leave Cowes without the courtesies of tournament'. Stephenson's citation of Stevens in the Iron Commissioners' report ('Mr. Stevens, of New York … says they have given up the lattice bridges entirely') makes it clear that they knew each other.[98]

Stephenson's gesture of goodwill revealed to British yacht designers the folly of a tonnage regulation which forced vessels to be so narrow that they would always be at a disadvantage compared with broader vessels such as *America*. As a result of the race the yacht clubs 'instantly swept from their books those legislative enactments which compelled their yacht-builders to

97 Op. cit. (n. 94).
98 *Royal Commission on the Application of Iron to Railway Structures*, House of Commons, 1849, para. 938.

dance in fetters'.[99] This race between the two vessels was the first of the world-famous 'America's Cup' races.

In 1852, Stephenson lent *Titania* to his cousin and heir, George Robert Stephenson, who accidentally burned her out. Stephenson, who needed the boat as much for escape as for relaxation, immediately commissioned a new vessel, writing to Admiral Moorsom at this time: 'I find I can get no peace on land. I am therefore preparing another sea lodging house.'[100] This second vessel, launched in June 1853, was built to Scott Russell's ideal wave-line form. At 90 feet long and of 184 tons displacement, she was bigger and longer than her predecessor. Her exceptionally large saloon was 16 feet by 15 feet and 8 feet high and it and the cabins were luxuriously fitted out. There was also a library and she was manned by a crew of sixteen. Stephenson wished to retain the name *Titania*, and so when the first yacht was rebuilt, she was re-christened *Themis*.

Stephenson used his yacht frequently and was therefore a member of several other yacht clubs, notably the Royal Thames, the Royal London, the Royal Welsh and the Royal Yorkshire. This last had been founded in Whitby in 1847, the year of his election as the town's MP, by several members of his election committee with support from George Hudson.[101] Stephenson would sometimes race *Titania* against Bidder's yacht, *May Fly*, for their mutual love of sailing brought the two men even closer together,[102] and in October 1858, Stephenson left Britain in *Titania* to cruise to Egypt. He was accompanied by a group of friends, including the 19-year-old Lizzy, Bidder's eldest daughter, stopping off to sightsee in Gibraltar, Granada, Tangier and Malta on their way to Alexandria. Lizzy kept a diary on the voyage, describing Stephenson 'gravely ordering groceries' or 'delicately manipulating a pomegranate' in Gibraltar.[103] She also records his failing health, and indeed it was when he was cruising on *Titania* in Norway during August 1859 that his final illness overtook him. He died on 12 October, shortly after arriving home.

Robert Stephenson's death was mourned throughout the country. In Newcastle[104]

Funeral chimes have pealed from the belfries of the parish churches, and with scarcely an exception all the vessels in the Tyne and Wear and in the Northumberland and Tyne Docks, and in the Sunderland South Dock and Monkwearmouth Dock, have their flags half-mast high. At noon the shops, merchants' offices, banks, and other places of business closed, and trade ceased in all the busy thoroughfares of Newcastle.

In London thousands packed Westminster Abbey and thronged the streets along the route of the cortège. His funeral was attended by every major engineer of the day – everyone, that is, except William Fairbairn, with whom he

99 Op. cit. (n. 92).
100 Letter, Robert Stephenson to Admiral Moorsom, 25 May 1852, in Jeaffreson, II, p. 171.
101 *The Yorkshireman*, 17 April 1847.
102 Clark (1983), pp. 189–90.
103 Diary of Lizzy Bidder, **ScM**, GPB/5/9/1.
104 Unattributed clipping, presumably *Newcastle Courier*, in album, **IMechE**, IMS/173.

had quarrelled so catastrophically over the Britannia Bridge. Even Fairbairn's brother Sir Peter Fairbairn, Mayor of Manchester, attended. It is understandable that Newcastle and the engineering profession might react to his death in such a manner, but that London and the Establishment did is perhaps less obvious to us now. Stephenson had, of course, achieved widespread fame with the dramatic design and construction of the Britannia Bridge, which brought many honours in its wake. He was elected a Fellow of the Royal Society in June 1849 (late compared with I. K. Brunel, elected at a much younger age in 1830) and in 1850 received an honorary degree from Durham University specifically for the bridge.[105] The bridge also earned him the Great Gold Medal of Honour at the 1855 French Exposition and he received an honorary Doctorate of Civil Law from Oxford University in 1857.

But as the Britannia Bridge was nearing completion, Stephenson must have been thinking about moving away from engineering and towards a second career as an MP and public figure. Did he consent to become an MP in 1847, when a vacancy, which George Hudson could control, presented itself so opportunely, because he saw it as a potential escape route from the terrifying responsibilities resting upon him? Or was it that he saw the possibility of being able to influence a move away from the free-market system he had come to dislike from dealing with the effects of the railway 'mania'?[106] Either interpretation is possible. His performance during his first four years of office may have been lamentable from the point of view of his constituents, but during this period he was still absorbed with the tubular bridges. However, during that surprisingly dubious election campaign of 1852, he stated his willingness to relinquish his engineering career[107] and certainly by 1856 he thought of himself as having largely retired.[108] In fact, he never did quite retire, though he may not have given his professional commitments the detailed concentration of earlier years. Nevertheless, to have inspired such an astonishing outpouring of admiration he must have managed to combine his life as a consulting engineer and a dedicated public servant with considerable success.

---

105 *Durham County Advertiser*, 21 June 1850.
106 Presidential address in *Proc. ICE*, **XV**, 1855/6, p. 136.
107 Op. cit. (n. 72).
108 Op. cit. (n. 106), p. 154.

Part II

Innovation and technique

Stephenson
photographed
in 1851
(Courtesy of
National Portrait
Gallery, London)

Building the London & Birmingham Railway

Mike Chrimes

The London & Birmingham Rail Way ... being once well accomplished, your Fame
and Future are built upon a Rock

Michael Longridge to Robert Stephenson, 1835[1]

Introduction

The London & Birmingham Railway was the largest civil engineering project yet
attempted in the country. It was also the great exemplar of geotechnical engineering
in the new railway age. Its long tunnels and deep cuttings and embankments crossed
practically every geological stratum from London clay to carboniferous sandstone,
including glacial deposits. Knowledge of the characteristics and behaviour of many
of the materials, initially limited, was learned as work proceeded.

The task for Robert Stephenson and his assistants was to identify the characteristics as soon as possible, both by preliminary investigation and by observation of the materials as handled by the contractors. To Stephenson fell the
responsibility of deciding the angles of slope for cuttings and embankments,
and courses of action to deal with the behaviour of each material as experience
was gained. He developed innovative techniques, including some arising from
remedial work following slippages. He shared the experiences with his
contemporaries through the Institution of Civil Engineers, and formed the
basis of much of the construction technology of the railway age.

By a concentrated effort, probably without parallel in the history of civil engi-
neering, and not surpassed for a long time afterwards, the 32 miles from Euston to
Tring were opened in October 1837, the 29-mile stretch from Birmingham to
Rugby in April 1838, and the line was opened throughout in September 1838.[2]

Earthwork and structural design

Robert Stephenson's railway experience had made him alert to the importance
of thorough site investigation prior to the submission of plans and levels to

---

1 Letter, Michael Longridge to Robert Stephenson, Bedlington Iron Works, 4 February 1835, **Pease–
  Stephenson**, D/PS/2/67.
2 Trains were running through from London to Birmingham before this date, but not as part of a full service.

Parliament. The vast quantities of earthwork made it necessary to use exceptional care in deciding on the slopes to be adopted in cuttings, for which purpose the stratification at key localities had to be known. Under his direction, the resident and sub-engineers supervised trial borings, made with shell, auger and chisel operated by hand-winch.[3] There were about 45 borings, mostly from 30 to 60ft deep. Well records were also examined, and observations made in adjacent quarries and road or canal cuttings.

Results of the site investigations were submitted to the House of Lords Committee in July 1832, during which Stephenson summarized his geotechnical decisions.[4] All embankments were to have 2:1 slopes even if the material had a steeper angle of repose. Heavy cuttings in London clay were to be at 2:1, though cuttings of less than 25ft and cuttings in other clays, such as plastic clay and the lias, could be 1½:1. Cuttings in red Keuper marl in the Birmingham district were first planned at 1:1 but he later modified this to 1½:1. Cuttings in chalk were to be ¾:1, though the deep lower chalk cutting at Tring would be 1:1. This was a last-minute decision he made after a visit with Thomas Gooch, during the committee proceedings, to examine a cutting on the Holyhead Road at Dunstable.[5] Cuttings in limestone at Blisworth, and in hard sandstone at Coventry, were to be dressed off at ¼:1.

Tunnels were to have an arched lining 'two bricks' thick with an invert, and the lining was to be reinforced for a length of 100ft from the portals at each end by iron tie-rods bolted to cast-iron plates in the arch. Stephenson noted that this lining thickness had proved sufficient for the Liverpool & Manchester Railway tunnel through shale and clay as well as sandstone.

John Rastrick went over the whole line and checked Stephenson's plans.[6] In evidence to the Committee, he agreed with most of the cutting slopes, but felt they should be made flatter in some instances, and especially in London clay, which he ventured might be 2½:1. To allow for the 'increased slopes', he increased estimated costs by eight per cent, but in other matters he considered Stephenson's estimates to be so generous that no addition would be needed. Henry Palmer also agreed unreservedly with the proposals, but stating that 2:1 slopes would be sufficient for London clay.[7] Joseph Locke gave evidence on the Liverpool tunnel, for which he had been resident engineer and, having carefully checked Stephenson's tunnel designs, agreed almost exactly with the estimates.[8]

Stephenson's specifications were generous in comparison with those he adopted later on less heavy works.[9] A typical embankment specification stated:[10]

3 Haskoll.
4 Minutes of Evidence, Lords Committees … Railway from London to Birmingham, 1832 [HL 181], pp. 109–10, 112–15, 121–7, 134–42, 180–4.
5 Jeaffreson, I, pp. 177–8; op. cit. (n. 4), pp. 180–4.
6 Op. cit. (n. 4), pp. 147–55.
7 Op. cit. (n. 4), pp. 148.
8 Ibid.
9 Brees (1837).
10 For example: specification for Saltley contract, 19 August 1834, **ICE**, Townshend collection, or Blisworth, 1F, February 1835, in Brees (1837), pp. 50–82.

All embankments in the contract shall have slopes of 2:1 and they shall be 33ft wide at formation level. Each embankment shall be uniformly carried forward, as nearly at the finished height as due allowance for shrinking of the materials will admit. The surface of the embankments shall be kept in such form as will always prevent the formation of pools of water upon them, and ensure the banks being kept as dry as possible. Material teamed over the end of the embankment shall be trimmed to its proper slope, and this operation must proceed at the same time with the end of the embankment. When the materials brought to the embankments consist of large lumps they shall be broken into pieces not less than 6 inches in diameter, unless they consist of rock. As the embankments advance and become consolidated the slopes shall be covered with turfs or with soil uniformly laid on and sown with rye-grass and clover-seeds at the proper season, the turf or soil to be removed from the base of the embankment before construction.

Stephenson was closely involved in the detail of the drawings and specifications. He discussed his ideas with his assistants, for example the details of skew bridges with George Buck.[11] Such discussions were not confined to senior colleagues, as he readily accepted Charles Fox's contributions to the design of the iron station roofs (Plate 3) and bowstring bridges. Despite the attention paid to specifications, he was prepared to modify designs, and recommended increasing costs where necessary, as with his early decision to substitute roman cement for lime mortar in the bridges, influenced no doubt by the work at Primrose Hill tunnel (see Chapter 11).[12]

Stephenson provided general plans and instructions on what he expected for station designs, and offered guidance to ensure that stations could accommodate anticipated traffic.[13] Architects designed the station buildings, excluding the platforms and train-shed roofs. Philip Hardwick was responsible for the main station buildings, including the Euston portico,[14] whilst George Aitchison designed the intermediate stations and measured up the work.[15] Details of station layouts were organized by Daniel Bagster.[16] From December 1838, Francis Thompson provided additional support, and assisted with the design of the unfinished stations including the goods stations at Birmingham and Camden Town.[17]

Construction

After eight months of surveys, design work and contract preparation, the first three contracts were let in May 1834, covering 20 miles from Camden to King's Langley. Another eight followed by November, and by February 1835 work was

11   Robert Stephenson's Diary for 1834, entries for February, **ScM**, 1947-135.
12   Engineers Reports, London & Birmingham Railway, 28 May 1835, **PRO**, RAIL 384/102.
13   For example: Board Minutes of the London & Birmingham Railway, 27 July and 16 November 1836, **PRO**, RAIL 384/33.
14   Ibid., 27 July, 14 September, 12 October, 16 and 23 November 1836. Also signed contract drawings for Birmingham Station, **NRM**, DS1/106.
15   Letter, Robert Stephenson to Capt. Moorsom, 3 April 1838, **PRO**, RAIL 1008/90.
16   Board Minutes of the London & Birmingham Railway, 10 February 1836, **PRO**, RAIL 384/32.
17   Letters, Robert Stephenson to Capt. Moorsom, 12 December 1838, **PRO**, RAIL 1008/90.

8.1 Building the London & Birmingham Railway (Study for J. C. Bourne, 1839, private collection)

proceeding on more than half the line.[18] By June 1835 work was in progress on twenty contracts with upwards of 4000 men employed. All contracts had been let by November 1835 and, the following month, work started on the extension from Camden to Euston. During the following two years, along the whole 112-mile length, up to 12 000 men were employed (Fig. 8.1).[19]

Some insight into the scale of the navvies' task was later noted by Robert Rawlinson, a sub-contractor with 'from 500 to 700 in my own pay … I employed foremen to superintend the different gangs; I sub-let some small portion of the excavation, but always kept it immediately in contact with myself.'[20] Because of the urgency to complete the line, night work was carried out 'for 15 or 16 months'. With the company driving on the contractors, they took many risks with the safety of their workforce: 'There was a considerable loss of life, and very many accidents upon the work … these gangers, many of them, are reckless and disregardless of anything but the present moment.' For the navvy there was the attraction of high wages, but safety was down to the judgement of the contractors, and the commonsense of workers.

As construction proceeded and experience was gained, the slopes at many cuttings and embankments were given less inclination. Clearly Stephenson had given much further thought to the clay slopes,[21] prompted by Rastrick's evidence and probably influenced by Henry Parnell's *Treatise on Roads*

18 Engineers' Reports, London & Birmingham Railway, **PRO**, RAIL 384/101–103.
19 Lecount (1839a).
20 Select Committee … into the Condition of the Labourers Employed in the Construction of Railways …, London, 1846, pp. 46–56.
21 Thomas Gooch, manuscripts, **ICE**.

published in 1833.[22] London clay slopes in cuttings more than 30ft deep became 3:1 instead of 2:1, and in shallow cuttings of less than 30ft they were 2:1 instead of 1½:1. These changes were made before May 1834, as were all embankments of London clay fill, even of modest heights, which became 3:1 instead of 2:1. Other clay slopes became 2:1 instead of 1½:1. The effect was to increase the total volume of excavation to more than 12½ million cubic yards, with perhaps about 11½ million in the embankments, with consequent increase in costs. Ultimately perhaps 14 million cubic yards were excavated.

Practical experience of construction dictated further changes, as at Wolverton embankment, in response to problems of stability. While many modifications had been introduced before the contracts were let, some were done shortly afterwards, perhaps in response to better knowledge of the ground. In March 1835 Stephenson recommended modifying the slopes of one rock excavation from 2:1 to 1.5:1, and in a clayey marl excavation from 1.5:1 to 2:1.[23]

The piers and abutments of bridges and viaducts were built on spread footings, usually on a concrete base, taken to a minimum depth of 4ft, and sometimes to much greater depths; for example, 17ft at Watford viaduct to found in chalk beneath alluvial clay and gravel.[24] Stephenson's site visits were arranged to enable him to inspect the foundations of major structures, and there is no record of settlement problems or foundation failures.

Cuttings

Cuttings were generally executed at the design slopes without any slips of consequence, except for rock falls in the 60ft-deep approach cutting to Watford tunnel. These were due to the 'jointy nature of the chalk' and gravel-filled fissures,[25] and the upper 20 feet were cut back at 1½:1. In March 1836 Robert Stephenson remarked on the danger 'from the uncertainty of chalk' and said he would rather work in clay, even London clay, an opinion he would not have given eight or nine months earlier.[26]

Tring cutting was one of the heaviest contracts on the line but the contractor, Thomas Townshend, was experienced in heavy earthworks, having undertaken the deep excavations of the Birmingham Canal improvements in the late 1820s.[27] 1.34 million cubic yards of mostly chalk were excavated for the 2½-mile contract, almost 100 000 more than originally estimated. In March–April 1837 thirty-one gangs, probably of eight men, were excavating 10 000 cubic yards a fortnight using horse runs, although more gangs would have been employed at different times during the 3¼-year

22 Parnell. Thomas Telford had spent several days in 1833 revising Parnell's book, which reflected his practice, particularly on the Holyhead Road.
23 Op. cit. (n. 12), 5 March 1835.
24 Conder, pp. 12–13.
25 Lecount (1839a).
26 Op. cit. (n. 12).
27 Skempton (2002), pp. 712–14.

8.2 Tring
cutting
(J. C. Bourne,
1839)

contract.[28] Bourne's lithograph of June 1837 suggests there were 60 barrow runs in a half-mile length, for which the workforce may have risen to 2500 (Fig. 8.2). When Townshend got into financial difficulties, the company took over the works, using some of his staff to control the workforce.[29] Despite the difficulties, the work was completed by the end of 1837.

The large Blisworth cutting was an outstanding example of the complexity of the earthwork challenges (Fig. 8.3). The stratum was Blisworth clay with a capping of boulder clay, overlying great oolite limestone, in turn overlying soft mudstone of the upper estuarine series. Work began about March 1835, but by December 1836, with the contractor seriously behind schedule, the company took over the work under the resident engineer, George Phipps. In the following year 700 to 800 men were employed, with locomotives hauling wagons of spoil to the nearby Ashton and Blisworth embankments, and a steam pumping engine to cope with substantial inflows of groundwater.

The clays were cut at 2:1 with a 9ft-wide bench left on top of the limestone. The limestone rock had to be removed by blasting, requiring as many as twenty-five 100lb barrels of gunpowder per week. The powder was placed in 1-inch holes drilled vertically to a depth determined by the thickness of the beds. It was estimated 870 000 cubic yards of clay, rock and shale had to be excavated. The cutting reached completion in May 1838, but because of the different strata, with rock underlain by softer ground, it was necessary to employ undersetting, with the rock underpinned by masonry walls and inverts, where required, using excavated

28 Townshend papers, **ICE**.
29 Memoir, Richard Townshend, *Proc. ICE*, **XCIII**, 1888, pp. 492–5.

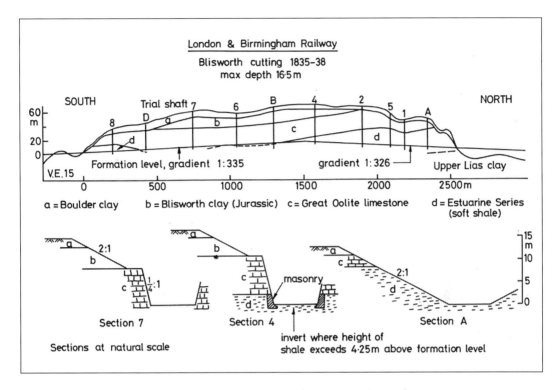

8.3 Section and details of Blisworth cutting (Prof. A. W. Skempton)

material for the stonework (Fig. 8.3, Section 4, see also Fig. 11.2). Stephenson correctly anticipated that this operation and the laying of permanent way would be finished by the end of August, and the line opened the following month. In the event, over 1 million cubic yards of material were removed.[30]

A few months later, several slips occurred in the clay slopes, and these were repaired by the installation of rubble-stone counterforts with a small retaining wall at the toe. Stephenson had first employed the technique at Denbigh Hall cutting, probably in early 1839, and adopted it for Blisworth in March 1840.[31] These delayed failures occurred in the winter rains following a relatively dry period in the later stages of construction. It was surprising that the failure at Blisworth occurred so soon in 2:1 slopes only 23 ft deep in clay. So far as is known, Stephenson's adoption of 'gravel counterforts' was the earliest in England and perhaps in any clay cutting.[32] Reviewing their use in October 1843, he remarked:[33]

though it had been originally expensive it would ultimately be by far the most economical: and not merely so – for I am persuaded no other scheme less expensive would have answered the desired purpose – and from the magnitude of these slips it is more than probable that movements equally rapid and more expensive would have taken place during last winter in [Denbigh Hall] cutting than those which fell so suddenly in the Bugbrook cutting … When a slip takes place the most usual

30 Robert Stephenson, Progress Report, 17 February 1838, Lecount (1839a), pp. 62–71. Also Specification for Blisworth cutting in Simms, pp. 41–3.
31 Letter, Robert Stephenson to Richard Creed, 27 March 1840, PRO, RAIL 1008/90.
32 Discussion following 'Railway cuttings and embankments; with an account of some slips in the London clay, on the line of the London and Croydon Railway', Proc. ICE, III, 1844, pp. 145–73.
33 Letter, Robert Stephenson to Richard Creed, 10 October 1843, PRO, RAIL 1008/90.

proceeding is to remove a portion of it by way of reducing its weight from an impression that its tendency to descend will be lessened. Now this expedient can only to a small extent diminish the descending force ... daily experience proves that this would be futile ... The examination of all the slips which I have just made ... induces me to recommend that all the slopes should be dressed off to the original slopes as far as practicable ... that they should be cut at right angles to the line of railway with channels deep enough to reach the base of the slip – that these channels should be completely filled with gravel and sand or a mixture of them – that the slope at the back of the slips be reconstructed – that additional land where necessary be at once purchased – and finally that the whole should be carefully soiled and sown with seed in accordance with the specifications under which the works were originally executed

The counterforts were made by excavating trenches 5ft wide at 20ft centres through the slip into solid clay below and filling them with gravel, rubble stone or hard chalk, well rammed down to form an immovable mass. Robert Dockray explained that, according to Stephenson's initial concept, 'the slip was thus divided into a number of isolated portions, of comparatively small dimensions, each side of which comes into contact with the side of a counterfort, and the friction between the masses ... [is] sufficient to retain the slip from further movement'.[34] The particular merit of gravel counterforts was that they provided support, while also draining the slip mass. They became the preferred remedial measure for slips in clay cuttings for at least a century.

Bugbrooke cutting provided another example of Stephenson's innovative recommendations. Delayed failures in clay cuttings became notorious after the New Cross slips in 1841–1842, but the clearest instance of this phenomenon was at Bugbrooke, near Northampton, where a large slip occurred in September 1842, more than four years after excavation. The cutting was excavated entirely in upper lias clay with a maximum depth of 45ft and 2:1 slopes (Fig. 8.4). The Railway Inspector's report stated:[35]

The whole extent of this slip was about 250ft in length. They assured me that in the central part of it, it had covered the down line of rails to the depth of about 15ft, and the up line 4ft or 5ft. ... it had been necessary to reform part of the permanent roadway, and to lay new lines of rails, because the original road had been partially raised about a foot above its former level by an upheaving of earth from below, and the old rails had been violently displaced and bent ... Mr Dockray has since written to me to explain the measure proposed by Mr Robert Stephenson, for giving a new profile to this side of the cutting, as well as for draining it more effectually, in order to secure its stability for the future, which I consider very judicious.

The Inspector outlined the generally held view that continued rains saturating the clay after being cracked by previous hot and dry weather caused slips, yet water under ground was an important factor. This was a step towards recognition of deep-seated progressive softening in fissured clays, later

---

34 Op. cit. (n. 32).

35 C. W. Pasley, 'Report on the slip of earth at the Bugbrooke cutting ... with observations on embankments and cuttings', 20 September 1842, *Reports ... of the Railway Department*, 1843, pp. 225–6.

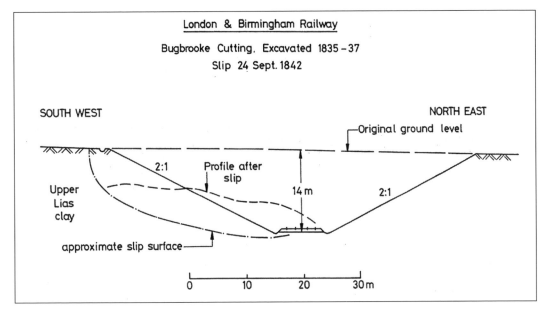

London & Birmingham Railway

Bugbrooke Cutting. Excavated 1835–37

Slip 24 Sept. 1842

SOUTH WEST

NORTH EAST

Original ground level

2:1   Profile after
        slip

Upper
Lias
clay

14 m

2:1

approximate slip surface

0   10   20   30 m

propounded by Charles Gregory.[36] Stephenson's diagnosis had previously appeared in a letter to Richard Creed, the Company Secretary:[37]

The embankments … which were originally the chief source of anxiety and expence [sic] may now be considered as nearly completely consolidated but the time and alterations which have accomplished this for the embankments has been producing directly the reverse effect in the clay cuttings.

Fissures exist in all clay which admit of water descending into them producing a slippery surface upon which the superincumbent mass of clay or earth slides down. Whatever may be the source of these fissures – whether existing in the clay previous to the cutting being made – or whether they are a consequence of the cutting, is quite immaterial. The fact is sufficiently general to be regarded as the immediate cause of all slips.

Delayed failures could take several decades to develop.[38] Winter rain was the trigger rather than the cause of these delayed slips, as Bugbrooke cutting survived previous heavy rains before failing in only moderate rainfall. Comparison of the cutting with others in the upper lias indicates that the stratum appears to be characteristic of this stiff fissured clay; typically oxidized to a depth of 20ft, and physically weathered to more than twice that depth. Even without knowledge of water content, liquid and plastic limits and clay friction, Stephenson was able to provide a solution to an unexpected problem that aroused the admiration of his contemporaries.

8.4 Cross-section of Bugbrooke cutting (Prof. A. W. Skempton)

36 C. H. Gregory, 'Railway cuttings and embankments; with an account of some slips in the London clay, on the line of the London and Croydon Railway', *Proc. ICE*, **III**, 1844.

37 Op. cit. (n. 33).

38 R. J. Chandler and A. W. Skempton, 'The design of permanent cutting slopes in stiff fissured clays', *Geotechnique*, **24**, 1974, pp. 457–66. This includes references to earlier papers on the weathering and fabric of upper lias clay.

Embankments

Construction of embankments was generally carried out at full height, by tipping material at the end until the final height was reached, rather than tipping at several levels simultaneously. The latter method had some attractions as work could take place in several places simultaneously with less likelihood of subsidence, but in practice it proved difficult to manage such operations safely. Typical annual rates of progress were c.190 000 cubic yards on the Watford embankment, and c.160 000 cubic yards for the Willesden embankment. More material could be removed if it was being excavated to spoil, and at Tring the average rate was 400 000 cubic yards a year. Overall about 3.1 million cubic yards of material were excavated per year, a scale not repeated elsewhere in the country until some 60 years later.[39]

Most embankment slips were remedied by adding material at the top until the resulting displacement at the foot reduced the overall slope to a stable angle, corresponding roughly to the residual angle of shearing resistance of the clay, such as 4:1 at Bugbrooke and 5:1 at Brent embankment. In February 1838, Robert Stephenson reported on the line between London and Tring, which had opened to traffic:[40]

the permanent road is in tolerably good order, except on the Brent Embankment, near London, and on the Colne Embankment, near Watford. Both these works have continued to subside, with scarcely any intermission, more or less rapidly since their formation; the former forms the slippery nature of the material, which composes it, the latter from the unsoundness of its sub-stratum in the valley of the Colne. The gradual subsidence of embankments left no other remedy than maintaining the level of the railway by the constant supply of new sound material adopted for ballasting.

The 40ft-high Brent embankment, with 3:1 slopes, exemplified the lack of stability of poorly compacted London clay fill. The lumps were strong enough initially to sustain relatively large pore spaces into which rainwater could penetrate and cause the lumps to soften. Slips of this type also occurred in the 33ft-high Bugbrooke embankment and 40ft-high Ashton embankment, both with 2:1 slopes, of upper lias and Blisworth clay respectively.[41]

By contrast no problems were experienced with embankments built of keuper marl, the highest being the 42ft Sheldon embankment with 2:1 slopes. The Blisworth embankment was built without serious engineering problems to a maximum height of 45ft, chiefly using soft mudstone, equivalent to hard clay. Little softening could take place in chalk fill, and none at all in gravel. Embankments in these materials were therefore perfectly stable with 2:1 slopes, with the exception of Watford, where a failure occurred in the underlying stratum, the alluvial clay of the Colne valley.

On the south side of Wolverton viaduct months were spent trying to build and consolidate the 45ft-high embankment with Oxford clay. As Lecount later recorded: 'As fast as it was tipped in at the top it kept bulging out at the bottom,

39 A. W. Skempton, 'Embankments and Cuttings on Early Railways', *Construction History*, **11**, 1996, pp. 33–50.
40 Op. cit. (n. 35).
41 Progress report, op. cit. (n. 30).

8.5 Wolverton embankment (J. C. Bourne, 1839)

till it had run out 160 to 170ft from the top of the embankment (a slope of about 4½:1).'[42] A temporary timber bridge was built from which to tip material, but slippages continued to occur (Fig. 8.5).[43] 'It was months before it was conquered, and this was done at last by barrowing as much earth to the wider part of the slip, as would balance the weight on top.' In February 1838 Stephenson reported that work had been proceeding satisfactorily, and the bank was completed in May.[44]

Whilst slips in clay embankments during construction were not uncommon, it was surprising that the Blisworth embankment failed over two years after completion. It was the first recorded example of a delayed embankment failure. More than a mile in length, it contained soft mudstone from Blisworth cutting, but no slips occurred during or immediately after construction. In January 1840 it was reported that:[45]

On Saturday evening a considerable subsidence took place at the Blisworth embankment, half way between the station and the bridge over the [Grand Junction] canal. The earth having become thoroughly saturated by the late rains, gave way at the bottom and the surface in consequence gradually sank, at one point several feet. Since then it has continued to subside at the rate of about a foot an hour, and on one occasion between two and six in the morning ... it sank eight feet. A large force of men were collected the moment the slip was discovered, and employed day and night replacing the soil that had given way with ballast ...

The slip location corresponded closely to the section of maximum height; and although it was probably approaching an unstable state beforehand, the

42 Lecount (1839a), pp. 37–8.
43 Bourne.
44 Progress report, op. cit. (n. 30).
45 *Northants Mercury.*

8.6 Tunnel excavation on the London & Birmingham Railway (Detail from J. C. Bourne study, 1839)

failure was triggered by heavy rain in the preceding two months. This offered evidence that, while clay fills of high plasticity, such as upper lias and London clay, can soften quite quickly to the strength at which failure occurs, harder clays and fill placed in dry weather require a longer time. Sandy clays and clays or mudstones, such as the keuper marl, in which the particles are aggregated into silt-size clusters, may never soften sufficiently for a slip to occur, and the 40ft. high Sheldon embankment remains in good condition.

Tunnels

Canal construction and the more recent Thames Tunnel had illustrated how difficult tunnelling could be. Robert Stephenson had himself encountered difficulties at Glenfield tunnel on the Leicester & Swannington line. In the canal era, specialist contractors had emerged, some of whom were engaged on the London & Birmingham line, with its major tunnels at Primrose Hill, Watford, North Church, Linslade, Kilsby and Stowe Hill (Fig. 8.6). Stephenson gave particular attention to the tunnel contracts, both in preparing specifications for the contractors and through the close supervision of his staff. Several tunnels presented unforeseen problems in construction.

The 1100-yard Primrose Hill tunnel presented a major problem. In blue London clay, it formed part of a 6-mile contract that included Brent viaduct and a shallow tunnel at Kensal Green. Following initial difficulties, the company took over the contract in November 1834. Apart from 21 yards at each end, built in 'cut and cover', the tunnel was excavated from four 8ft-diameter shafts, the working face not being allowed to advance more than 6½ft ahead of the brickwork lining (Fig. 8.7).[46]

46 Simms, p. 23. Also Lecount (1839a), pp. 182–3. Also op. cit. (n. 47).

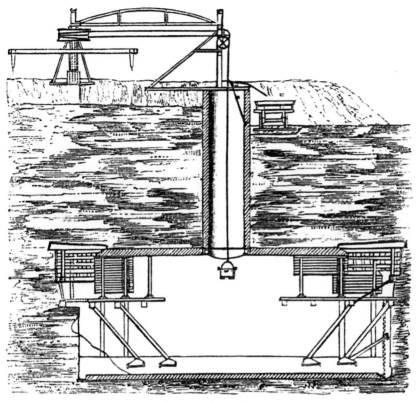

8.7 Longitudinal
section of
Primrose Hill
under
construction
(S. C. Brees,
*Illustrated
Glossary of
Practical
Architecture
and Civil
Engineering,*
1852)

Longitudinal Section of Tunnel.

Timbering of ordinary strength was insufficient to support the 26ft-diameter excavation at its maximum depth of 68ft. Mortar began squeezing out of brickwork joints, and the inner edges of the bricks were crushed.[47] In March 1835 Stephenson modified the design and increased the arch and invert thickness to 27in and 18in respectively (see Chapter 11).[48] With heavier timbering, work then proceeded satisfactorily, albeit with some fatalities in the autumn of 1835, and the tunnel was completed in January 1837.[49] It was felt that the pressure exerted by the ground was in some inverse proportion to its internal friction, and might be related to the slope found necessary in open excavation.[50] The more general view, however, attributed the high pressure to swelling of the clay when exposed at depth, and it is now known that full overburden pressure can be developed in London clay within two weeks.[51]

The 1650-yard Watford tunnel had six working shafts, 8ft in diameter lined with 9in brickwork, and with 3ft 6in diameter airshafts 50 yards from each end. The arch and side walls were two bricks thick, whilst the invert was one and a half bricks.[52] There was a minor collapse in November 1834, and

47 Letter, Robert Stephenson to Richard Creed, 25 March 1835, **PRO**, RAIL 1008/91.
48 He introduced paving bricks, see Burn. Also Laxton.
49 Op. cit. (n. 13), 11 January 1837.
50 Lecount (1839a), pp. 32–3.
51 Skempton, A. W. discussion on tunnel linings, *ICE Journal*, **20**, 1943, pp. 53–6.
52 Simms, pp. 28–31.

Stephenson's initial assessment, proving correct, was dismissive.[53] There were further, fatal accidents, the most serious in July 1835 resulting in ten fatalities.[54] The tunnel was driven through soft chalk 'much saturated with water',[55] and problems were compounded when the shaft 'near the observatory' was opened out before the tunnel had been fully supported at the base. Veins of sand compounded the problems, as also at Linslade, and much masonry work was required to support the tunnel and the shaft.[56] Construction continued to prove difficult, and there was another serious collapse in November 1835, probably due to the arch lining being incomplete when work halted for the weekend.

Beechwood tunnel, 302 yards long, was driven through rock and marl. Problems arose from lime in the brickwork, which was acted upon by water causing the bricks to decay.[57] Within three years Stephenson instructed that it should be relined with 9in Staffordshire blue bricks, secured to the original lining, with drainage channels chased into the latter.

The construction of the 2398-yard Kilsby Tunnel between 1835 and 1837 was significant in the history of civil engineering. It involved the first major application of pumps for groundwater lowering, and Stephenson was the first to observe and explain the flow of water through sand to a pumped well. These firsts are indicative of his resourcefulness as an engineer, as well as the difficulties presented by the construction of the tunnel.

The railway passed through a ridge in the Northamptonshire uplands (Fig. 8.8) at a maximum depth of 132ft. It was 27ft 4in high and 24ft wide, with a 27in brick lining. Two 50ft-deep investigation boreholes, near each end of the proposed tunnel, revealed hard clays of middle lias formation. After the line of the tunnel had been staked out, four trial shafts were sunk. They proved up to 26 feet of boulder clay and glacial gravel over the lias clays, with occasional thin layers of limestone. A considerable quantity of water issued from the deeper rock layers, which proved to be a nuisance during construction. A shorter tunnel could have been made to the east, but previous borings there had shown 'quicksand' and Stephenson chose the Kilsby line as an alternative route.[58] It was therefore ironic that the presence of quicksand at Kilsby was unknown when the tunnel contract was let to Joseph Nowell and Sons in May 1835.[59] The trial shafts had just missed a sand-filled buried 'valley' extending well below the water table.

The contractor began by sinking working shafts from which the tunnel would be driven.[60] The first four of these, in the middle and northern parts of the ridge,

53 Op. cit. (n. 11), 27 November 1834.
54 Op. cit. (n. 16), 19 August 1834, 17 July and 8 November 1835.
55 Dempsey (1855), p. 79.
56 Conder (1868), pp. 27–8, and Conder (1983), pp. 16–17.
57 T. M. Smith, 'An Account of the repairs done to the Beechwood Tunnel, upon the London and Birmingham Railway', *Proc. ICE*, **I**, 1841, pp. 142–3.
58 Hadfield. Also Stevens.
59 Op. cit. (n. 16), p. 312. This account is chiefly based on extracts made by the late L. T. C. Rolt, from engineers' letters and reports in **PRO**. See Rolt. Professor Skempton was grateful to Mrs Sonia Rolt for the loan of these notes. Further information is taken from Lecount (1839a). Detailed drawings of the tunnel were published in Simms, plates 38–47.
60 Op. cit. (n. 12), 30 July 1835.

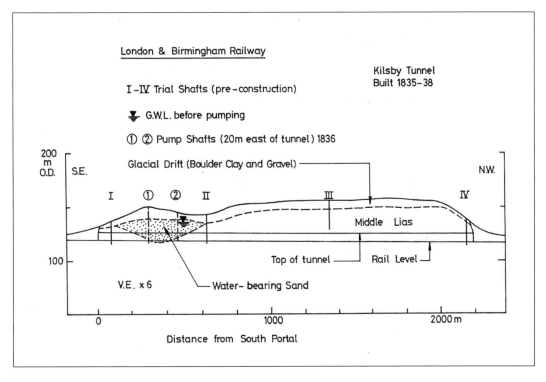

London & Birmingham Railway

Kilsby Tunnel
Built 1835–38

I–IV Trial Shafts (pre–construction)

G.W.L. before pumping

① ② Pump Shafts (20m east of tunnel) 1836

200 m O.D.

S.E.

Glacial Drift (Boulder Clay and Gravel)

N.W.

I   ①   ②   II   III   IV

Middle   Lias

100

Top of tunnel — Rail Level —

V.E. x 6

Water–bearing Sand

0   1000   2000 m

Distance from South Portal

8.8 Section of Kilsby tunnel (Prof. A. W. Skempton)

proceeded without trouble, but a shaft 500 yards from the south end encountered the sand.[61] Six investigatory borings demonstrated that a major problem existed, as the tunnel would have to pass through some 380 yards of the sand that 'boiled' up into the shaft as fast as it could be removed. At its lowest point, it descended 6ft below rail level.[62] Frank Forster undertook borings along another alignment, but this was no better.[63] The directors were alarmed at the threatened delays, as well as the cost implications, and a deputation was sent to inspect the works in November 1835.[64] Further inspections followed on a monthly basis.[65]

Drainage of the sand by one or more headings was the traditional solution and, after discussions with the contractor, it was decided to use a driftway and additional engines and working shafts.[66] In mid-October, however, on account of the great depth of groundwater, Stephenson advised a radically different method of dealing with the problem, requiring the purchase of two large pumping engines.[67] The first 20hp engine was erected in December–January, and the sinking of a 12ft-diameter shaft with its two pumps started early in February 1836. In the same month the driftway had to be

61 Birmingham Committee Minutes, London & Birmingham Railway, **PRO**, RAIL 384/67, Minute 242.
62 Ibid., Minute 282, 6 November 1835. The 'valley' itself appears to be a pre-glacial feature of a landscape differing greatly from the present topography. Lecount (1839a) recognized the sand as 'diluvial', not belonging to the lias formation.
63 Op. cit. (n. 61), 20 November 1835.
64 Op. cit. (n. 61), 20 November 1835.
65 Op. cit. (n. 61), 20 November and 18 December 1835, and 22 January 1836.
66 Op. cit. (n. 12), 22 and 28 December 1835.
67 Ibid.

abandoned after a sudden inrush of sand.[68] The situation was complicated by Nowell's illness and death, and his sons gave up the contract as they lacked funds to continue.[69] Thereafter the works were carried on by direct labour, supervised by the assistant engineer, Charles Lean, reporting directly to Stephenson.[70]

In March 1836 the directors accepted Stephenson's further recommendations. A railway was constructed over the ridge, and additional shafts sunk to speed up draining and tunnelling by increasing the working faces.[71] As groundwater was lowered, so the first pumping shaft was slowly deepened and lined with wooden 'tubbing'. Reduced to 9ft diameter in its lower half, the shaft reached the bottom of the sand, close to rail level, in September. The second pumping engine was in action from July and the shaft reached the bottom in October.

Headings were then driven from the pump shafts towards the working shafts in the sand. The working shafts were started in November, and tunnelling operations recommenced in December 1836 after nearly twelve months of pumping. In that period, the groundwater level on the line of the tunnel had been lowered 60ft. The steady success in lowering the water table was, however, followed by a fresh influx, the only recourse being additional pumping and working shafts, and the purchase of more engines.[72]

The two main pump shafts were 185 yards apart, just to the east of the tunnel (Fig. 8.9). Referring to observations made during the groundwater lowering process, Stephenson later wrote:[73]

As the pumping progressed, careful measurements were taken of the level at which the water stood in the various shafts and boreholes; and I was soon much surprised to find how slightly the depression of the water level in the one shaft influenced that of the other, notwithstanding a free communication existed between them through the medium of the sand, which was very coarse and open. It then occurred to me that the resistance that the water encountered, in its passage through the sand to the pumps, would be accurately measured by the angle or inclination which the surface of the water assumed towards the pumps, and that it would be unnecessary to draw the whole of the water off from the quicksand, but to persevere in pumping only in the precise level of the tunnel, allowing the surface of the water flowing through the sand to assume that inclination which was due to its resistance.

If this view were correct it was evident that no extent of pumping whatever would have affected the complete bed of sand. To test it, therefore, boreholes were put down at about 200 yards from the line of tunnel, when it was clear that, notwithstanding pumping had been going on incessantly for twelve months, and for the latter six

68 Ibid., 10 February 1836. Also op. cit. (n. 61), 26 February 1836.

69 Skempton (2002), pp. 490–3. Also op. cit. (n. 61), 25–27 February 1836.

70 Op. cit. (n. 12), 25 February and 14 May 1836. Also op. cit. (n. 61), Minute 481.

71 Op. cit. (n. 12). Also op. cit. (n. 61).

72 Op. cit. (n. 18).

73 *Mr. Stephenson's Second Report to the London, Westminster and Metropolitan Water Company*, London, 1841. Stephenson is here principally concerned with pumping from the chalk, and later refers to the 'cone' of depression around a pumped well. This he had observed in a full-scale experiment at Watford, as also in the Kilsby groundwater-lowering operations. Lack of interference with neighbouring wells was a vital factor in the use of the chalk aquifer; an effect hitherto not clearly understood (see Chapter 12).

8.9 Kilsby tunnel drainage pumping gear (J. C. Bourne, 1839)

month of this period at the rate of 1,800 gallons per minute, the level of the water in the sand, at a distance not exceeding 200 yards, had been scarcely reduced. The simple result, therefore, of all the pumping, was merely to establish and maintain a channel of comparatively dry sand in the immediate line of the intended tunnel, leaving the water heaped up on each side by the resistance which the sand offered to its descent to that line on which the pumps and shafts were situated.

The mathematics of the flow to a pumped well had to await the attention of later engineers, but the general principles involved could not be more clearly expressed. Professor Boyd Dawkins was later to observe that 'it is difficult to decide which is the more admirable, the scientific method by which Stephenson was able to arrive at the conclusion that the cone of depression was small in range, or the practical application of the results'.[74]

Pumping continued throughout the period of construction to maintain the lowered groundwater level, allowing tunnelling to proceed from the working shafts (Fig. 8.10). The tunnel was completed in June 1838, at a cost exceeding £320 000. Upwards of 1300 men and 200 horses had been employed at any one time; 25 million bricks were used in the tunnel lining and the two 60ft-diameter ventilating shafts (Fig. 8.11).

The Euston extension line and retaining walls

Retaining walls, forming ring walls to tunnel portals and bridge abutments, were stable and, at first, so were the 18–22ft-high walls, nearly a mile in length, on the Euston extension line. By 1843, however, the west wall had become badly tilted, and parts actually failed. Along with Kilsby tunnel, this remarkable example of progressive softening in brown London clay ranks among the classic geotechnical case records in railway history.

74 Boyd Dawkins, 'On the Relation of Geology to Engineering', *Proc. ICE*, **CXXXIV**, 1898, pp. 254–77.

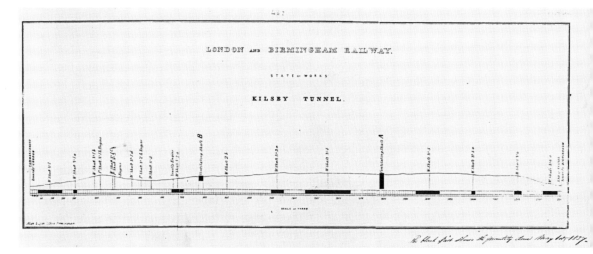

LONDON and BIRMINGHAM RAILWAY.

STATE of WORKS

KILSBY   TUNNEL.

8.10 Section of Kilsby tunnel showing progress of works on 1 May 1837 (Courtesy of Institution of Civil Engineers)

William and Lewis Cubitt undertook the contract for the work on the extension, supervised by Charles Fox under Robert Stephenson's direction. For the most part the line was constructed in cutting between the retaining walls and, for a length of 830 yards from Hampstead Road bridge to Park Street bridge, the excavation was entirely in brown London clay.[75] The walls, built in brickwork with a curved batter, had pilasters at 20ft centres, a concrete base to the footings at a minimum depth of 4ft below ballast level, and counterforts 4ft wide mid-way between the pilasters (Plate 12).

The walls south of Park Street bridge were built in front of a steep face excavated in the London clay. The specifications called for 'the space at the back of the walls to be well punned with clay' and stipulated that 'the face of the Excavation shall in no case be carried on more than 40ft in advance of the completed Retaining Wall'.[76] This took into account the temporary stability of the cut face, which had a depth of about 26ft to the heel of the wall. The whole contract, including seven bridges over the 'Grand Excavation' and a notable iron bridge over the Regent's Canal, was completed within sixteen months.[77]

Stephenson would not have contemplated undue economy in such important structures, and the walls were conservative in design.[78] After a few years, however, the west wall began tilting and, in the winter of 1842–1843, the movement accelerated by upwards of a foot at the top. In the worst section, halfway along the cutting, serious damage occurred, and in March 1843, the wall was propped by heavy timber shoring. As a trial drainage scheme, three 3-inch diameter holes were drilled through the wall in each of

75 The depth of brown London Clay is taken from investigations of the present wall on the west side about 100m south of Park Street. This wall was built 1901–1902 for a widening and deepening of the cut; see H. Q. Golder, 'Measurement of Pressure in Timbering of a Trench in Clay', *Proc. 2nd Int. Conf. Soil Mech.*, 2, 1948, pp. 76–81. Ten bays of the original wall can still be seen immediately south of Park Street bridge.
76 Brees (1837).
77 Lecount (1839).
78 Sections of the wall as built are illustrated in Brees (1837) and Dempsey (1855). They differ only in minor details from the contract drawings of 1835, two of which are in **ICE**.

three bays and into the clay. They were 6ft to 8ft long, and lined with perfo-rated iron pipes.[79]

He approved a further trial with five borings in each bay of between 12ft and 15ft length. The results proved so satisfactory that thirty more bays were drained between October and December. Robert Dockray supervised the remedial works. In August the company received permission to purchase a 150yd-long narrow strip of land between Stanhope and Crescent Place bridges where the wall was to be rebuilt.[80]

Stephenson also decided that, independent of the drainage system, 58ft-long cruciform-section cast-iron girders, spanning between the pilasters, should be inserted along the whole length between Hampstead Road and Park Street. Abutment plates were bedded against the walls in quick-setting Roman cement.[81] Ninety-six girders, braced longitudinally at the crown, and each weighing about 7 tons, were placed in position before June 1844 (Fig. 8.12).[82] Although little or no forward movement of the foundations occurred, timber struts were added as a precaution.

8.11 Kilsby tunnel ventilating shafts (J. C. Bourne, 1839)

79 Thomas Hughes, 'Description of the Method Employed for Draining some Banks and Cuttings on the London and Croydon, and the London and Birmingham Railways; and a Part of the Retaining Walls of the Euston Incline', *Proc. ICE*, **IV**, 1845, pp. 78–82.

80 C. W. Pasley, 'Report on an inspection of a piece of land near the Euston Square station', 9 August 1843, *Reports … of the Railway Department*, 1844, pp. 172–4, with a plan of the retaining wall between Stanhope and Crescent Place bridges. Vaults were to be constructed behind eight of the 23 bays in this length; they are shown in section by G. D. Dempsey, 'Description of the mode adopted for repairing and supporting the western retaining wall of the London and Birmingham Extension Railway', *Papers on Subjects connected with … the Corps of Royal Engineers*, 7, 1845.

81 Dempsey, op. cit. (n. 80), pp. 160–4.

82 Girders installed before Professor Hosking read a paper to the ICE in June 1844; but the timber struts appeared not yet to have been placed. The latter were detailed by Dempsey, op.cit. (n. 80).

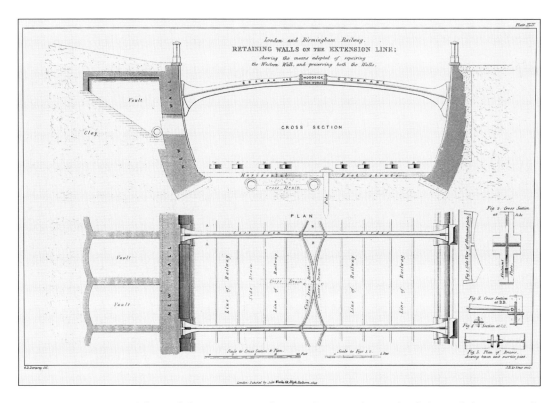

London and Birmingham Railway.
RETAINING WALLS ON THE EXTENSION LINE;
shewing the means adopted of repairing
the Western Wall, and preserving both the Walls.

8.12 Retaining
walls and girders
on the Euston
extension
(G. D. Dempsey,
1845)

Through his recommendations for remedying the failure of the west wall, Stephenson had made further significant contributions to the understanding of soil mechanics. The 26ft cut face of the London clay, at approximately 70°, had stood unsupported for a few weeks. The temporary nature of its stability was clearly recognized, however, and Stephenson had decided on 3:1 slopes for the approach cuttings to Primrose Hill tunnel. When the walls were built they were subjected to only a small pressure developed by punning the clay backfill that was still self-supporting.

Six years later the earth pressure increased to cause failure, this being a good example of the softening effect in fissured clay, as elucidated by Charles Gregory.[83] This was accepted by Stephenson, who, in the discussion on the paper describing the drainage pipes, commented that the walls were designed before he had attained experience of London clay, and that 'On examination it was found that … water, penetrating through the fissures, accumulated against the wall and reduced the clay to a semifluid state, increasing its mobility and reducing the cohesion, until it forced forward the retaining wall'.[84]

He added that the ground sloped up to the west, which probably explained why the wall failed on that side, and concluded that the usual wedge theory of earth pressure was not applicable when clay softened to a 'semifluid' condition. By all accounts the drainage pipes released an appreciable, but variable

83 Op. cit. (n. 36).
84 Robert Stephenson in discussion on paper by Hughes, op. cit. (n. 79), pp. 83–5.

amount of water. This indicated significant opening of fissures in the clay, following stress release on excavation of the cut face.

Conclusion

Though Robert Stephenson experienced considerable troubles of a geotechnical nature, these were in the context of a project of unprecedented magnitude both in scale and number of works involved. Some of the problems could not have been foreseen; all were satisfactorily solved, and many of the huge cuttings, embankments and viaducts never gave any trouble at all.

The impact of the London & Birmingham Railway can be likened to the works of John Smeaton, whose published record had guided the previous generation of engineers. The drawings and specifications formed major parts of Brees's *Railway Practice* and Simms's *Public Works of Great Britain*, which were available as a model to all civil engineers, providing 'time-saver' standards for the railway age. Stephenson also made the material freely available to Isambard K. Brunel for his planning of the Great Western Railway.[85]

G. D. Dempsey's papers on railway engineering for the Royal Engineers were based heavily on London & Birmingham practice, and were subsequently published as a monograph. Practical experience of the construction of cuttings and embankments was reflected in papers and discussions at the Institution of Civil Engineers and elsewhere, while the illustrations of J. C. Bourne, and the texts of Thomas Roscoe and Peter Lecount provided vivid images of the construction of the line. Neither Joseph Locke nor Isambard K. Brunel served as such as exemplars to the profession.

85 Jeaffreson, I, p. 213. Also, Robert Stephenson, report on works on Birmingham Division, Engineers' Reports, London & Birmingham Railway, January 1837, **PRO**, RAIL 384/103.

9

Railway building

Mike Chrimes and Robert Thomas

Robert Stephenson ... one talisman of our success

James Berkley, 1860[1]

After completing the London & Birmingham Railway, Robert Stephenson's reputation for railway-building achievement was high, but as one of the country's leading consulting engineers, he had all too little time for direct involvement in subsequent railway-building projects. The scale of his commitments necessitated a reappraisal of his role of 'Engineer-in-Chief', and meant he had to delegate his work and concentrate his efforts where he felt it was most needed. He had already gained considerable experience in delegation and learned the essential prerequisites of communication and motivation. Successfully harnessing this experience with the many railway construction projects was to be the hallmark of his achievements. His associates, both in the Westminster office and in the field, were competent, reliable and well motivated, with good communication skills. They generally formed a loyal and devoted team.

Stephenson provided leadership to his associates as they developed experience in overseeing route surveys, structural design, cost estimation and contract preparation. They also developed the requisite skills for negotiating with contractors, monitoring their progress and rectifying problems, together with record-keeping that helped to hone their expertise in project control. The application of these skills, both in Britain and overseas, kept the Stephenson team in the forefront of railway-building activities that ranged from small contracts with often inexperienced contractors to major projects, often dependent upon the financing skills of the larger contractors.

1   J. J. Berkley, 'Thul Ghat Railway Incline', Bombay Mechanics Institute, 1861.

Project management and delegation

The extraordinary number of projects and the attendant volume of work that Robert Stephenson undertook from 1839 required both a high dependence on delegation and effective administration. The success of his railway-building projects therefore depended on his selection of senior and junior associates, and upon their talents and continued motivation during intense periods of surveying and building.

The method of delegation employed by Stephenson can best be compared with that of Thomas Telford (1757–1834), who managed a similar range of work over the British Isles. Telford used regional correspondents and representatives, mostly paid as resident engineers by clients, together with a small office staff of experienced engineers and pupils, and was continually employing roving surveyors to view road and canal routes.[2]

In addition to George Bidder, who maintained his office in the Westminster practice, Stephenson's senior associates based around the country included Thomas Harrison, John Birkinshaw, Frederick Swanwick and Robert Dockray. After completion of the Manchester & Leeds Railway, Thomas Gooch rejoined Stephenson and Bidder at the height of the mania, responsible for lines in the Midlands and North. Other, more junior associates were required to follow the projects as the railway network expanded both in Britain and overseas.

During the recession years between 1839 and 1842, Stephenson took an active involvement in supervising the building of the several routes to which he had been appointed. As consultant to the London & Birmingham Railway, he was contracted to provide engineering services for a mileage-based fee, a third of which went to Robert Dockray, who had everyday charge of its civil engineering. Whilst the board generally expected him to liase with Stephenson, Dockray was a most able engineer, being entirely responsible, for example, for the arrangements at Curzon Street station, Birmingham, in 1841–1842.[3] He did much of the detailed research on issues such as permanent way, and later provided parliamentary support for a number of the branches.

The London & Blackwall line illustrates how, having replaced William Cubitt as engineer, Stephenson developed his working relationship with his clients and associates. The directors regarded him as the key figure, even though George Stephenson maintained a close involvement as a consultant. Responsibility for building the line was largely delegated to Bidder, who appeared before the Board and Engineering Committee throughout.[4] As contracts progressed three assistant engineers were appointed, Henry Austin, A. Moser and John Hart. Whilst Bidder and George Stephenson signed the

2 Skempton (2002), *passim*.
3 Whishaw (1840). Also, contract drawings and specifications, Curzon Street Station, **NRM**, DS/101 and 106.
4 Clark (1983).

regular engineering reports, and maintained a connection with the line after its opening, Robert Stephenson maintained overall supervision.[5] A decision on tenders for wrought iron rails, for example, was deferred in his absence,[6] and Bidder stated that contract drawings had to meet his approval.[7] It was Stephenson who decided when the line was safe to open.[8]

From 1839 Robert Stephenson took over responsibility for completing a number of lines that were already under construction, including some of his father's projects. These included the Preston & Wyre Railway, for which James Routh was resident engineer, and the Birmingham & Derby Junction Railway, with John Birkinshaw as resident engineer. The North Midland Railway was the most important, for which he had already attended several of the early meetings with his father.[9] Many of the contracts were already let, with Frederick Swanwick the competent 'assistant engineer'.[10] He was assisted by Alexander Ross and Charles Liddell, with Thomas Dyson as resident engineer for the northern half of the works.[11]

In 1839, when Stephenson became engineer-in-chief of the Northern & Eastern Railway, in succession to Walker and Burges, he sorted out the organization and identified some improvements to the original line.[12] Bidder managed the project for him, and dealt with the company on routine matters, with the experienced resident engineer Michael Borthwick retained by Stephenson.[13] On the five-mile branch to Hertford and Ware, Bidder was almost entirely responsible, providing the parliamentary evidence, and in February 1841 the directors noted that, owing to pressure of other work, Stephenson had to withdraw as engineer.[14] Although he maintained his overview of the railway's progress, presenting estimates for the Newport extension in February 1843, the contractor, Samuel Peto, later wrote that it was Bidder and George Stephenson who generally acted as engineers.[15]

Although Stephenson and his father played such a prominent role in the promotion of the Yarmouth & Norwich Railway, pressure on his time meant that Bidder and James Routh gave engineering evidence in support of the Bill.[16] Stephenson was appointed engineer-in-chief in June 1842,[17] but again

---

5 London & Blackwall Railway, Ninth Half-yearly General Meeting, 26 February 1841, Report of Directors and Engineers.
6 Minutes of the London & Blackwall Railway Company, **PRO**, RAIL 385/1, p. 344.
7 Op. cit. (n. 6), p. 250.
8 Ibid., 29 April 1840, p. 440, and 17 June 1840, p. 456.
9 Minutes of the North Midland Railway, **PRO**, RAIL 530/1, *passim*.
10 Ibid., 23 September 1836.
11 Op. cit. (n. 9).
12 Northern & Eastern Railway, Half-yearly Reports of Proprietors, 20 August 1839 and 20 February 1840, **PRO**, RAIL 541/1. (Robert Stephenson estimated cost at £700 000.) Also **PRO**, RAIL 541/3, 8 and 13 August 1839.
13 **PRO**, RAIL 541/3, 5 March and 23 April 1840, and **PRO**, RAIL 541/1, 2 April 1840 and 18 February 1841.
14 **PRO**, RAIL 541/1, 13 August 1840 and 18 February 1841. Also *RT*, **IV**, 6 March 1841, p. 304, 10 April 1841, p. 422, and **V**, 5–8 October 1842, pp. 1045–9.
15 Clark (1983), p. 151. Also Minutes of Evidence of G. P. Bidder, *Report of Gauge Commissioners*, 1846, p. 197.
16 *RT*, **V**, 14 May 1842, pp. 513–4, and 11 June 1842, p. 620.
17 *RT*, **V**, 2 July 1842, p. 694.

9.1 Thomas Elliot Harrison
(1808–1888)
(Courtesy of Institution of
Civil Engineers)

he delegated project management to Bidder, who represented him at the first general meeting[18] and again a year later.[19] It was not until the end of January 1844 that Stephenson inspected the line, prior to its opening that May.[20]

From 1840 Stephenson became responsible for the completion of the West London Railway, linking the London & Birmingham and Great Western Railways with the Kensington Canal and Thames Navigation.[21] Bidder assisted him, but Stephenson appears to have been largely responsible, with George Berkley's assistance, notably on the design of the stations.

In 1841, in taking over as engineer for the Great North of England Railway, Stephenson had recommended the abandonment of its proposed northern extension, as being too expensive. The creation of George Hudson's replacement Newcastle & Darlington Junction Railway, for which Thomas Harrison (Fig. 9.1) had undertaken the survey, amounted to just over 25 miles of new construction. In February 1842, he had showed the Railway Inspector, Maj.-Gen. Pasley, the route and satisfied him of its suitability.[22]

In July 1842, Stephenson was: 'appointed Engineer-in-Chief to the Company and Mr Thomas E Harrison his Assistant Engineer' and it was resolved 'that a salary of £1,200 per annum be paid to Mr Robert Stephenson for the services of himself and his Assistant Engineer including all travelling expenses.'[23] John Arrow and Robert Hodgson were appointed sub-engineers. Stephenson delegated full responsibility to Harrison and, as construction proceeded, the latter received regular praise. At a special meeting of the

18 *RT*, **V**, 20 August 1842, pp. 848–9.
19 *RT*, **VI**, 9 September 1843, pp. 980–1.
20 *RT*, **VII**, 3 February 1844, p. 113, and 17 February 1844, pp. 170 1.
21 *RT*, **IV**, 10 April 1841, pp. 402–3.
22 Report(s) of Maj.-Gen. Pasley relating to the Darlington & Newcastle Junction Railway, 22/28 February 1843, *RT*, **VI**, 22 April 1843, pp. 477–8.
23 Minutes of Newcastle & Darlington Junction Railway, 7 July 1842, **PRO**, RAIL 772/3.

company in April 1844 Hudson reported: 'Too much credit could not be due to Mr Harrison for getting the works in so forward a state.'[24]

In spite of his extensive involvement with the South Eastern Railway in the 1840s, the only route that the Stephenson team built was the Maidstone branch. As principal engineer Bidder supervised the building programme and attended most of the shareholders meetings. However, Stephenson spent much time in late 1842 on the design of Maidstone Bridge. The resident engineer for the branch was Peter W. Barlow,[25] William Cubitt's senior resident engineer on the main line.

The railway 'mania' during the mid-1840s placed extraordinary demands on Stephenson and his associates that required a broadening of the proven delegatory approach to project responsibility. Stephenson's time was so taken up with the broader strategies and tactics for railway development – particularly the preparations for, and attendance at, parliamentary committee hearings – that he became ever more reliant upon Bidder and the other senior associates.

Responsibilities within the Westminster office for extensions to the London & Birmingham and its associate railways varied from job to job. Stephenson nominated the resident engineers and other supervisory staff for the Northampton and Peterborough branch.[26] Bidder and other associates helped in the preparations. Resident engineers were appointed with specific responsibilities for two of the contracts, but Bidder 'who represents me generally on the … works' was nominated by Stephenson to direct the third.[27] In fact Bidder was placed in overall charge, with the help of three assistants: James Berkley, George Bruce and Henry Swinburne.[28]

Whilst Stephenson was the engineer for the Coventry and Leamington line, absorbed into the London & Birmingham in April 1843, Dockray undertook all the works including the station designs.[29] Edward Dixon assisted Dockray with preparations for the other London & Birmingham branches, including the Nuneaton and Coventry line and the 14¼-mile Rugby and Leamington line, whose resident engineer was Dixon's former pupil, William Doyne (1823–1877).[30] Charles Liddell managed the 35-mile Rugby and Stamford branch.[31]

On the Midland Railway from 1844, Stephenson's responsibilities were similar to those for the London & Birmingham company. Whilst William Barlow took over the routine duties,[32] Frederick Swanwick (Fig. 9.2) was put in charge of newly

24 *RT*, **VII**, 13 April 1844, p. 429.

25 Skempton (2002), p. 41.

26 *RT*, **VI**, 21 January 1843, pp. 50–2.

27 Letter, Robert Stephenson to the London & Birmingham Railway Board, 12 July 1843, **PRO**, RAIL 1008/90.

28 G. . Bidder Minutes, op. cit. (n. 15). Also C. W. Pasley, Report to Board of Trade, 29 May 1845.

29 *ILN*, 14 December 1844, p. 372. Also Michael Robbins, 'R. B. Dockray's Diary I – III', *JTH*, 7, 1965/6, pp. 115–19 and 149–56.

30 *Proc. ICE*, **LII**, 1875/6, pp. 270–3, and Obituary to Edward Dixon, *Proc. ICE*, **LIV**, 1877/8, pp. 280–1. Also Minutes of Rugby & Leamington Railway, **PRO**, RAIL 589/1.

31 Robbins, op. cit. (n. 29).

32 Midland Railway Board Minutes, 2 July and 10 September 1844, **PRO**, RAIL 491/13. His salary was raised to £700 p.a. when he took over responsibility for the Birmingham & Gloucester Railway on 10 August 1845.

9.2 Frederick Swanwick
(1810–1885)
(Courtesy of Mrs Brenda Tyler)

projected lines.[33] Stephenson divided responsibility for the preparation of drawings and specifications, and project management varied according to the project. In August 1845 he was asked to survey and report on nine extensions and branches.[34] Five of these routes were Swanwick's responsibility,[35] although the Board Minutes suggest it was Stephenson who let the contracts.[36] The extent of Swanwick's independence is indicated from a letter to him by George Berkley:[37]

I am desired by Mr Robert Stevenson [*sic*] to request you to send him as soon as convenient a plan and section of all the prospected lines of railway on which you are engaged under him ... a schedule of the prices you propose to apply to the quantities of each description of work and any remarks thereon which may think proper.

Charles Liddell also continued his involvement with new routes for the railway, including the Syston and Peterborough line in 1844–1845.[38] In July 1846 he was put in charge of the doubling and extensions of the Leicester & Swannington line, for which he had carried out surveys the previous year.[39] He continued to describe himself as an assistant to Stephenson when giving evidence on the Leicester and Hitchin line in 1847.[40]

33 Barnes, p. 84.
34 Op. cit. (n. 32), 10 August 1845.
35 Obituary of Frederick Swanwick, *Proc. ICE*, **LXXXV**, 1886, pp. 404–6.
36 Midland Railway Board Minutes, 4 January 1847, **PRO**, RAIL 491/14.
37 Letter, George Berkley to Frederick Swanwick, January 1845, Swanwick collection, **ICE**, SWA/1.
38 Op. cit. (n. 32), 8 March, 5 May and 10 June 1845. Also Midland Railway, Minutes of Syston and Peterborough Committee, **PRO**, RAIL 491/320.
39 Op. cit. (n. 32), 7 October 1845, and op. cit. (n. 36), 25 July 1846.

Stephenson's responsibilities for the York & North Midland Railway included building the extension lines to Scarborough and Pickering in 1844–1845. John Birkinshaw moved up from Birmingham to be his resident engineer for these and the extensions to Hull, Harrogate, Filey and Bridlington. The Leeds & Bradford Railway and its extensions were delegated to Thomas Gooch, assisted by Francis Young, John Forsyth and Charles Cawley.[41]

Under Stephenson's direction, Thomas Harrison undertook the building of the Newcastle & Berwick Railway. From July 1845, there was a rapid programme of work and the bulk of the route was completed in two years. Building supervision of the 'High Level' Tyne bridge was undertaken by Robert Hodgson, the resident engineer, and John Hosking the inspector, under Harrison. Similar care was taken with the Royal Border Bridge, where George Bruce was the resident engineer.[42]

With his appointment as engineer-in-chief of the Chester & Holyhead Railway in July 1844, Stephenson undertook a more prominent role in its construction than with other lines.[43] He attended shareholders meetings, and regularly corresponded with the company. Alexander Ross was appointed as the principal engineer reporting to Stephenson, assisted by Hedworth Lee at the Chester end and Frank Forster between Conway and Holyhead. On occasions, particularly early on, Ross attended board meetings. The design and construction of the Britannia Bridge occupied much of Stephenson's attention, and meant that he had to rely on his support staff to get on with other affairs (see Chapter 10).

Although Stephenson was appointed as engineer-in-chief of the Trent Valley Railway in July 1845, his role was largely that of consultant, with George Bidder and Thomas Gooch appointed as engineers for the project (Fig. 9.3).[44] Most of the survey work and management was undertaken by Gooch, 'the actual line being allocated to me'.[45] He was referred to by the chairman as 'that clever young man', but he was not alone, and credited Forsyth and Young for their help.[46] The same triumvirate of Stephenson, Bidder and Gooch was also responsible for building the North Staffordshire Railway, although Stephenson's involvement was minimal, Bidder again being principal engineer.[47] Forsyth, helped by James Berkley, acted as resident engineer.[48]

40 Barnes, p. 84.
41 Charles Cawley Obituary, *Proc. ICE*, **L**, 1876/77, pp. 175–7. Also Thomas Gooch, autobiography, **ICE**.
42 G. B. Bruce, 'Description of the Royal Border Bridge over the River Tweed on the York, Newcastle and Berwick Railway', *Proc. ICE*, **X**, 1850/1, pp. 219–33.
43 Board Minutes, Chester & Holyhead Railway, **PRO**, RAIL 113/3.
44 *RT*, **VII**, 13 April 1844.
45 M. Robbins, 'Thomas Longridge Gooch 1808–1882', *TNS*, **56**, 1984/5, pp. 59–69. Also Gooch, op. cit. (n. 41).
46 *RT*, **IX**, 14 March 1846, pp. 370–1.
47 *RT*, **XIII**, 9 February 1850 and Gooch, op. cit. (n. 41). Also Clark (1983).
48 Hollick.

9.3 Cutting the first sod on the Trent Valley Railway by the Prime Minister, Sir Robert Peel, 13 November 1845 (*Illustrated London News*)

In Ireland, the directors of the Londonderry & Enniskillen Railway obtained Stephenson's and Alexander Ross's services in 1845, shortly after the act was passed.[49] Ross undertook the bulk of the work, but Stephenson was required to be concerned in arbitration between the company and their contractor.

Stephenson's work for the railways between Shrewsbury and Birmingham brought him back into contact with George Buck's former pupil, William Baker.[50] Under Stephenson's direction, Baker managed the extensive and politically difficult Birmingham, Wolverhampton & Stour Valley and Shrewsbury & Birmingham Railways, and a section of the Shropshire Union Railway. Baker belonged to a new generation of engineers who were to dominate civil engineering in the third quarter of the century, having assimilated Stephenson's delegatory approach. Dockray later contrasted his own attention to detail, no doubt required by Stephenson's *modus operandi* in the 1840s, with that of Baker:

his system is very different to mine – he leaves far more detail to his assistants than I did and only troubles himself with the supervision. I think he is right in this, it leaves his mind free to grapple with the salient points and his strength is not frittered away in doing that which his subordinates quite as well can perform. The inference I should draw from this is that I am better fitted out for a second rather than a first place – my pleasure in detail seems to point to this – but after all perhaps it is an accident, I had to

49 Report of Robert Stephenson and Alexander Ross, *RT*, **VIII**, 30 August 1845.
50 Memoir of William Baker, *Proc. ICE*, **LV**, 1879, pp. 315–7.

arrange the detail, and gradually got into the habit of seeing to it myself; Baker finds the detail ready made as it were to his hand.

Following Stephenson's death, Baker succeeded as the engineer for the London & North Western Railway, which Dockray noted:[51]

An important change has been made in the duties of the Resident Engineer. His duties are now confined solely to the construction of new works of a large scale and extend over the whole of the line, so that he is in effect the Engineer of the line …

Apart from his foreign visits, the reason for Stephenson's lack of involvement in lines such as the Buckinghamshire Railway in the late 1840s was because of the depth of his great engineering challenges, such as the major bridge crossings. Stephenson hardly appeared before the board, and Dockray undertook the bulk of the work, aided by Dixon and possibly Liddell.[52]

Stephenson's overseas railway building projects required not only his reliance on delegated responsibility, but also his ability to come to terms with the very different requirements for route approval and design in each country. He directed William Hoppner and Robert Townshend to undertake the survey of the Leopold Railway between Florence, Pisa and Livorno.[53] They dissented from the findings of the local commission and recommended the route following the Arno Valley, which Stephenson approved. Under Hoppner's and Townshend's supervision, as his resident engineers, the line was built in sections over six years, between 1842 and 1848, including the 96-foot span trussed-girder bridge across the river Arno (see Chapter 10).[54] Stephenson helped to organize the procurement of material on the most favourable terms, using appropriate engineering staff.[55] Wild, for example, tested ironwork before this was exported. Later supervision was by Townshend and William Bray (1811–1885), who may have acted as contractor on the first section.[56]

Stephenson's responsibilities in Belgium were limited to consulting work, as Belgian resident engineers largely supervised the building of the concessionary lines,[57] although Peter Henderson (1813–1904) does appear to have prepared many of the drawings for the West Flanders Railway.[58] The contractor, Lewis Cubitt, acted as resident director for the Sambre & Meuse Railway.[59]

51 Robbins, op. cit. (n. 29), entries for 7 September 1853 and 9 January 1860, pp. 3–4.
52 Minutes of Buckinghamshire (and Brackley) Railway, **PRO**, RAIL 85/1, 86/1 and 86/2.
53 'Carta Topograficia della Strata Ferrante', Leopolda, 1841, in **ICE**, Starbuck Collection, 29. Stephenson's report is reprinted as: 'Relazione e stima del sig Roberto Stephenson di Londra (1839)', *Annali Universali di Statistica*, **69**, 1841, pp. 227–45. Also Briano, pp. 77–84.
54 Jeaffreson, II, p. 55.
55 *CEAJ*, 4 June 1841, p. 211.
56 Obituary of William Bray, *Proc. ICE*, **LXXXIV**, 1886, pp. 439–41.
57 *Annales des Travaux Publics de Belgique*, 1–11, 1840–1851, give details of appointments of Belgian state engineers.
58 Henderson began on the Stockton & Darlington Railway in the late 1820s, before working for the Great North of England Railway, and in 1844 was in the USA, **ICE**, Membership records.
59 *RT*, **IX**, 4 July 1846, pp. 917–9.

For the Scandinavian railway systems, Stephenson delegated responsibility for survey and construction work to Bidder.[60] In Norway, Thomas Greenwell acted as the resident engineer for the Norwegian Trunk Railway, with four Norwegian engineers, including the military engineer Johan Raeder, and Carl Pihl, who had worked in Stephenson's office.[61] In Denmark Bidder was the engineer-in-chief for Brassey, Peto and Betts' Royal Danish Railway concession, assisted by George Robert Stephenson, who undertook detailed engineering design and monitoring.[62]

In Egypt, Stephenson's management model was the familiar British one for the Cairo and Alexandria Railway, with Michael Borthwick as principal engineer supervising two teams north and south of Kafr el-Zaiyat on the Nile.[63] The resident engineers were Henry Rouse based in Alexandria, and Henry Swinburne based in Cairo.

As chief engineer of the Great Indian Peninsula Railway, James Berkley was assisted by two experienced associates, C. B. Kerr and R. W. Graham.[64] In 1854 the engineering management structure was radically changed as work began on the Kallyan extension, with a more formal bureaucratic structure.

It is thus clear that Stephenson obtained his reputation for extraordinary achievement as a railway civil engineer through effective delegation of responsibilities to a team of reliable associates. As the railway network grew rapidly during the mania years, and spread further afield beyond the British shores, each principal and resident engineer took on increasing responsibilities, whilst maintaining referral to Stephenson and the resources of the Westminster practice.

Surveying and contract preparation

All the Stephenson associates were well versed in surveying, parliamentary submissions and contract preparation. His own opportunities to walk the routes, as he did so conscientiously on the Birmingham line, were restricted by pressure of work, although India was the only place that he did not visit among his many construction projects.

His arrangements for the survey of the Yarmouth & Norwich Railway provided an insight into how he approached the assessment of a new route in an unfamiliar part of the country, against the background of so many parallel commitments:[65]

60 Clark (1983).
61 Cranfield, pp. 1–7. Also Owen, pp. 1–18.
62 Clark (1983), Chapter XIX. Also Peto, p. 23.
63 Jeaffreson, II, pp. 173–9. Also Wierner (1932) and Helong (1977).
64 Correspondence and records, Great Indian Peninsula Railway, **OIOC**. Also, Indian Council of Historical Research, *Railway Construction in India*, 3 vols, New Delhi, 1999. Also Davidson (1868), Sharma (1990), pp. 8–24, and Kerr (1995).
65 Robert Stephenson Report, 19 April 1841, *RT*, **IV**, 27 November 1841, pp. 1231–2.

Gentlemen, ... I took the earliest opportunity my engagements would allow to examine carefully the country between Norwich and Yarmouth.

In the first instance I laid out the line by the assistance of the ordnance map, in which the features of the country are so accurately delineated, that I had scarcely a doubt as to the expediency of the line I had selected. I then sent down two of my assistants to examine the locality, and report to me whether any, and what natural impediments existed to the construction of the line along the Valley of the Yare. Their Report being favourable, I at once gave orders for proceeding with the survey and section, and the plans were accordingly deposited on the 1 March last, in compliance with the Standing Orders of the Houses of Parliament ...

In the early 1840s, Stephenson was responsible for many of the surveys, contract drawings and specifications, for example on the Northampton and Peterborough branch of the London & Birmingham Railway. He walked along the Chester & Holyhead Railway route in December 1844 and suggested alterations to the levels to provide for bridge crossings of the mineral tramroads near Flint. Alexander Ross prepared detailed surveys and estimates, however, and together with George Stephenson, provided engineering evidence.[66]

On the Midland Railway and its predecessors, Frederick Swanwick and Charles Liddell undertook surveys and contract preparation, assisted by Thomas Dyson and William Barlow.[67] George Stephenson and George Buck had first surveyed the Syston and Peterborough route in 1844,[68] but Liddell finalized the survey work, aided by Joseph Colthurst (1812–1882).[69] They met extreme opposition when fighting broke out at Saxby Bridge between the surveying party and the Harborough Estate workers.[70]

Stephenson's Newcastle & Darlington Junction Railway route deviated from the original Great North of England alignment. In February 1842, when he was unavoidably detained, Thomas Harrison, who had already investigated the route independently of Stephenson,[71] satisfied the Board of Trade Inspector, Maj.-Gen. Pasley, of its suitability.[72] With the support of Harrison and his staff, Stephenson also organized surveys of the Newcastle & Berwick route, including some deviations from George Stephenson's original alignment from the 1830s. The Board of Trade favoured the route because of its convenience and ease of engineering.[73]

Thomas Gooch graphically described the pressure of work incurred in preparing plans and levels by the end of November parliamentary deadline:[74]

---

66 Board Minutes Chester & Holyhead Railway, 12 December 1843, 2, 10 and 11 January, 23 February, 11 March, 1 and 15 April 1844, **PRO**, RAIL 113/37.
67 Williams. Also Barnes.
68 Paid 100 guineas 25 July 1846, Midland Railway Board Minutes, **PRO**, RAIL 491/14.
69 Obituary of Joseph Colthurst, *Proc. ICE*, **LXXIII**, 1882, pp. 356–8.
70 P. A. Stevens, 'The Midland Railway's Syston and Peterborough Branch', *JRCHS*, March 1972, pp. 1–9.
71 *4th report on Railway Communications between London, Edinburgh and Glasgow*, 1841.
72 Op. cit. (n. 22).
73 'Newcastle and Berwick Railway', *RT*, **X**, 31 July 1847, p. 979.
74 Gooch, op. cit. (n. 41).

I may just state, that from the 9 of October to the end of November, in all 52 days, the following was the proportion of each day devoted to work:

11 [days] working all day & all night

11 ditto & up to 1 to 5 in the morning

15 ditto & up to 11 or 12 at night

15 ditto working all day (ordinary days)

… The chief inconvenience I felt from the excessive night & day work on these occasions was a considerable swelling & pain in the ankles … I had just seen the last of my plans off to be deposited; when, as I turned to reenter the office of Mr Chiffins [sic] in Southampton Row Holborn, where much of the work had been done, I suddenly found that it was with considerable difficulty I could walk.

For his overseas projects Stephenson relied on his associates to review routes and report accordingly. Bidder carried out a preliminary review of the Norwegian Trunk Railway route,[76] and Stephenson then arranged for John England (1813–1882), working with Johan Raeder, to make a detailed survey.[77] Their route, costed by Bidder at £420 000, formed the basis of Stephenson's final report.

Although Borthwick's first surveys of the Cairo to Alexandria line had identified a route skirting the desert on the west bank of the Nile, Stephenson had followed the Pasha's wishes with the selected route across the delta. The French, notably Lemoyne, criticized the route with its expensive bridges and some difficult terrain with possible negative impact on agriculture. Most of the concerns over topography and agriculture proved groundless, however.

John Chapman, the manager of the Great Indian Peninsula Company, supervised the early surveys for the first 170 miles of line from Bombay, conducted by George Clark and Henry Conybeare.[78] The surveys highlighted the problems presented by swampy ground in the 'Concan' plain along the Malabar Coast, and the 'Ghat' mountain range 80 miles inland from Bombay.[79] On James Berkley's appointment, he undertook a detailed survey for an initial route to Thana. While work proceeded on this first section, he carried out surveys on the extension to Kallyan, which involved two tunnels and a major viaduct across the Tanna river. The crossing of the Ghats was to incur some of the steepest gradients hitherto tackled for railway routes. Berkley's extensive surveys soon ruled out the previously favoured routes, and it was not until 1856 that the route for the Thul Ghat line was sanctioned, the

75 Cheffins was paid £250 for parliamentary surveys, Trent Valley Railway Board Minutes, 26 October 1844, **PRO**, RAIL 699/1.

76 Clark (1983), Chapter XVIII.

77 Obituary of John England, *Proc. ICE*, **LXX**, 1882, pp. 415–17.

78 *RT*, **VIII**, 15 November 1845, p. 2226.

79 **OIOC**, Chapman collection, E/234/54 and E/234/78. **OIOC**, L/PWD/3/245. **OIOC**, 31478L/ RWD/2/43. Also Indian Council of Historical Research, vol. 1, p. 227.

final route not being agreed until Stephenson had judged the alternatives in January 1858.[80]

The Stephenson rail routes in Britain were demanding in their requirements for surveying, but the increasing availability of Ordnance Survey maps, and access to local land agents wherever possible, meant that local knowledge was usually available to guide the engineers. The associates supervised levelling, drawing and estimation, but in the more remote areas overseas were obliged to begin with route surveys. Although there is no evidence that Stephenson and his team pioneered new surveying techniques, routes such as those in India meant of necessity that they made a major contribution to contemporary mapping.

Engineering design

The simple view of the Stephensons' railway practice would be to characterize their 'first class lines' as being based on heavy earthworks to produce minimum gradients for efficient working of locomotives.[81] Their notable structures of masonry and cast iron gave them an aura of permanence. There was, however, more to the Stephensons than heavy civil engineering and locomotive traction, and it is clear that there was a spirit of compromise, with an awareness of the need to balance cost against engineering ideals. This can be seen in the routing of the North Midland Railway to avoid prohibitively expensive earthworks, with Sheffield missed off the main line.

Robert Stephenson had a conservative approach to engineering design. He frequently preferred a proven solution to innovation, and would recommend what he felt best suited the circumstances on a short-term basis. Perhaps this was in part to avoid the criticisms associated with expenditure on the London & Birmingham line, matched with a realistic appreciation of the financial standing of many companies in the mania years. Thus, wherever he considered appropriate, he adopted single track, extensive use of timber for bridges, and meandering and undulating routes.

Whilst Stephenson directed overall design policy, often dictated by clients' demands, his design input had to be selective, given the pressure on his time. He relied on his associates to carry out basic research, but the scale of his practice meant that his office team were able to call upon a vast range of experience on subjects such as permanent way and bridge designs. Both in the office and the field, detailed bridge-design work, even in cases such as Britannia, Conway and Newcastle, was largely left to his associates.

Although innovative in some ways, Stephenson was not a leader in permanent way development compared to the initiatives of Joseph Locke, and the important contributions of Brunel, Vignoles and Barlow. For the London &

80 Davidson.
81 Whishaw (1837/8).

9.4 Greaves's
cast-iron 'pot'
sleepers
(Minutes of
Proceedings
Institution of
Civil Engineers)

Fig. 3.

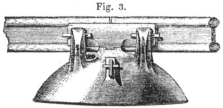

Greaves' and Douglas' fish-joint Chair and Sleeper.

Fig. 4.

Greaves' surface-packed Sleepers, with Douglas' fish-joint Chairs.

Fig. 5.

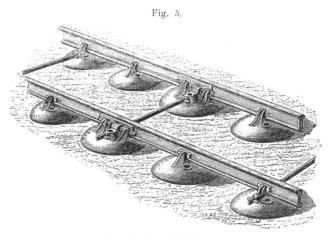

Greaves' surface-packed Sleepers.

North Western Railway, he delegated permanent way research to Robert Dockray, who presented alternative sections in January 1850 and, after trials, recommended removing the stone blocks from all the company's lines.[82] Stephenson, who had access to information on the suitability of permanent way on other railways, approved this policy, and railways using his recommended permanent way were probably the most extensive in the late 1840s. He did not freely adopt patented systems, and generally advised against change from trusted systems. Overseas, however, his lines adopted track forms to suit local circumstances. In Egypt, the shortage of local timber and ballast, as well as the climate, led him to adopt Greaves' cast-iron 'pot' sleepers for the permanent way (Fig. 9.4).[83]

The Stephensons' use of cuttings and embankments on the Birmingham & Derby Junction Railway's direct line to Birmingham, for example, meant that gradients were never more than 1 in 396.[84] On the North Midland Railway this

82 Robbins, op. cit. (n. 29).

policy led to 9.5 million cubic yards of excavation, 200 bridges and seven lengths of tunnelling totalling 2.5 miles.[85] The most challenging works were at Bull Bridge (Fig. 9.5), where an iron trough aqueduct was designed by Alexander Ross to carry the Cromford Canal over the railway, and Ambergate Tunnel.[86] This was driven beneath 'an inclined bed of wet shale, as slippery as soap'. To withstand the pressure, an elliptical tunnel was constructed of millstone grit blocks. These started to splinter under the pressure, and some of the hillside had to be removed, the shale drained, and additional iron ribs added to reinforce the lining.

Branch lines were different, however. The South Eastern Railway's single-track Maidstone Branch meandered along the Medway with only minor road crossings, often of timber.[87] On the Northampton and Peterborough branch the slopes of cuttings and embankments were steeper than on the main London & Birmingham line, though of relatively little depth or height, no

9.5 Bull Bridge, North Midland Railway: the Cromford Canal crossed the railway which crossed the river Amber (Elton collection, Ironbridge Gorge Museum Trust)

83 W. B. Adams, 'The Construction and Durability of the Permanent Way of Railways in Europe, and the Modifications most suitable to Egypt, India, etc.', *Proc. ICE*, **XI**, 1851/2, pp. 252–3, and Robert Stephenson, discussion 'On Railway Management', ibid., p. 461. Also, W. B. Adams, 'The varieties of permanent way, previously used, or tried, on railways, up to the present period', *Proc. ICE*, **XVI**, 1856/7, pp. 245–6, with discussion by G. P. Bidder, ibid., p. 287, and E. Price, discussion 'On the Laying of the Permanent Way of the Bordeaux and Bayonne Railway, through the Grandes Landes', ibid., p. 381. Also, Discussion 'On the Permanent Way of the Madras Railway', *Proc. ICE*, **XVIII**, 1858/9, pp. 434–5.

84 Whishaw (1837/8), pp. 10–13. Also Birmingham & Derby Junction Railway Minutes, **PRO**, RAIL 36/1 and 36/2.

85 Williams. Also Barnes.

86 Letter, George Tate to Hugh Ross, 30 September 1862. Use of wrought-iron trough confirmed in Butterley furnace ledger 'E' p. 95, **DRO**.

87 Drawings, Network Rail Plan Office, Waterloo Station.

9.6 Melbourne
viaduct on the
Warwick and
Leamington line
(*Illustrated
London News*)

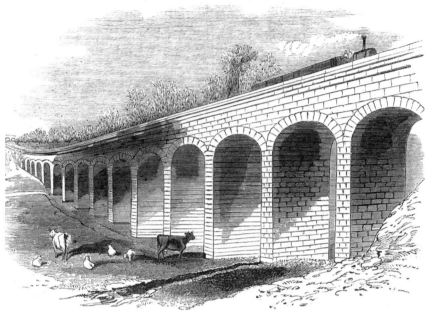

MELBOURNE GRANGE VIADUCT.

slips being noted at the time of opening. This steepness would have reduced land and construction costs, and the circuitous route along the Nene valley was similarly intended to minimize engineering costs, and maximize traffic between the small towns on the route.

Stephenson's team gained much practical experience in soil mechanics. Edward Dixon helped supervise work on the Nuneaton and Coventry line, which suffered deep clay slips in cuttings.[88] It also had bridges incorporating timber to help adjustment for mining subsidence. The Buckinghamshire Railway had heavy earthworks which included several long embankments that could be tipped at one end only, and Dockray concluded that such work should be avoided in future projects.

On several later railways Stephenson introduced some substantial structures to avoid costly earthworks. On the Warwick and Leamington branch the principal works were the 17-span Melbourne Viaduct in brick with stone facings, and the nine-arch viaduct over the Avon (Fig. 9.6). It was designed for single track, with no major earthworks to reduce gradients.[89]

Although Stephenson oversaw the development of iron bridges, detailed designs were delegated to his associates. When the London & Blackwall line was extended to Fenchurch Street in 1840–1841 it was George Bidder, together with George Phipps (then working for the ironwork fabricator), who detailed the trussed girder bridge over the Minories (Fig. 9.7).[90] In late 1842, however, Stephenson himself spent much time on the design for the Maidstone Bridge for the South Eastern Railway. It is likely that he advised on

88 Robbins, op. cit. (n. 29).
89 *RC*, 27 February 1845.
90 London & Blackwall Railway Minutes, **PRO**, RAIL 385/1.

MINORIES VIADUCT.

9.7 Trussed girder bridge over the Minories on the London–Blackwall Railway (*Illustrated London News*)

the replacement of the Wharfe bridge at Ulleskelf by a trussed girder bridge for the York & North Midland Railway in 1843, although Thomas Cabry was credited.[91]

George Bidder undertook the design of a number of bridges for the lines delegated to him. On the Norwich & Brandon Railway he designed three swing bridges, making use of cast-iron piles that he also employed on a bridge at Peterborough.[92] On the Rugby and Leamington line, William Doyne designed a wrought-iron lattice girder bridge across Honingham cutting, independently of the Great George Street office,[93] and went on to establish a reputation for his understanding of truss bridges.[94] Alexander Ross was responsible for detailing the bridges on the North Midland and Chester & Holyhead Railways, mostly masonry structures.[95]

Economy dictated Stephenson's use of timber for a number of major bridges and viaducts. The designs were generally functional, and did little to advance the use of timber as a structural material, with no evident exploration of the many truss types then being used in the USA and on the ontinent, or even the variety displayed by Brunel and Locke.[96] A number of timber bridges were erected, for

91 Lewis.
92 G. P. Bidder, 'Swing Bridge over the Wensum', *Proc. ICE*, **V**, 1846, pp. 434–7.
93 'Description of a wrought iron lattice bridge, constructed over the line of the Rugby and Leamington Railway', *Proc. ICE*, **IX**, 1849/50, pp. 353–9.
94 *Proc. ICE*, **XI**, 1851/2, p. 1 and **XIV**, 1854/5, pp. 460–3.
95 A drawing in the Network Rail office in Manchester signed by Ross is stylistically very similar to extant drawings of the North Midland Railway in **NRM**.

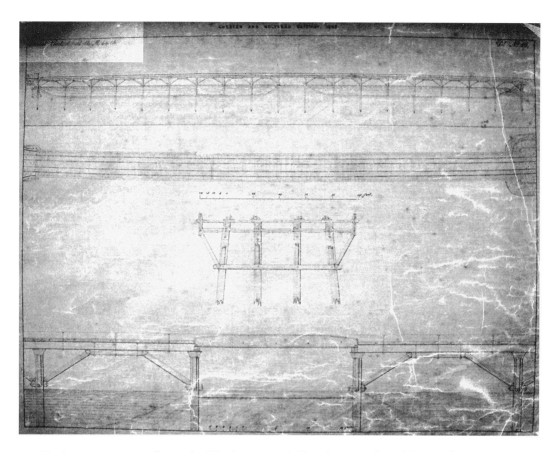

9.8 Timber viaduct on the Chester & Holyhead Railway (Courtesy of Network Rail)

example, on the Northampton & Peterbororough and Warwick & Leamington branches, whilst the Whitehaven & Furness Junction Railway crossed the river Duddon on a timber viaduct near Foxfield.[97] They were also to be found on lines better known for their iron structures, such as the Chester & Holyhead line (Fig. 9.8).[98] On the Newcastle & Darlington Junction Railway, lengthy timber viaducts were erected at Shincliffe, as well as at Cossop and Sherburn (Fig. 9.9). The latter, 670ft long, was described as 'one of the cheapest viaducts yet made'.[99] The 95-mile Newcastle & Berwick Railway opened in 1847–1848 with temporary timber viaducts over the Tweed and Tyne, and with temporary timber crossings of the Blyth and Wansbeck.[100]

Whilst much of the Newcastle & Berwick line can be attributed to Harrison, Stephenson made significant contributions to the major structures, particularly the bridges across the Tyne (Plate 13) and Tweed. He had been

96 J. G. James, 'The Evolution of Wooden Bridge Trusses to 1850', *Inst. Wood Sci. Jnl.*, 1982, pp. 116–35 and 168–93. Also L. G. Booth, 'Laminated Timber Arch Railway Bridges in England and Scotland', *TNS*, **44**, 1971/2, pp. 1–22, and L. G. Booth, 'Timber works', in A. Pugsley (ed.), *The Works of Isambard Kingdom Brunel*, 1976, pp. 107–35.

97 Gradon.

98 Drawings of Chester & Holyhead Railway, Network Rail office, Manchester.

99 'Timber Viaducts', *Art*, NS **1**, 1845, pp. 176–9.

100 *RT*, **X**, 31 July 1847, p. 1949.

9.9 The
Sherburn timber
viaduct on the
Newcastle &
Darlington
Junction Railway
(*Illustrated
London News*)

TIMBER VIADUCT ON THE DARLINGTON AND NEWCASTLE RAILWAY.

rigorously examined about the crossing of the Tyne by Parliament in May 1845, and the 'bowstring' bridge was one that had been frequently adopted by the practice (see Chapter 10).

Stephenson often concerned himself with best practice in bridge foundations. On the London & Blackwall line, concrete was substituted for 'puddled ballast' for the viaduct foundations, in keeping with the best London & Birmingham Railway practice.[101] He later considered the design of the 40ft-deep foundations for the 'High Level' bridge. Timber piles were used, driven to rock through silt and quicksand, with roman cement concrete placed between the piles. He recommended the use of a Nasmyth steam pile-driving machine,[102] and advised that the piles should be load tested *in situ* up to 150 tons. Construction was delayed because of the effects of the tides on the hydraulic profile in the sand, which affected the resistance of the ground to pile driving. Stephenson took similar care with the Royal Border Bridge at Berwick, where piles were driven to rock at depths of 40 feet through very dense gravel, again using a Nasmyth pile-driver. The bridge formed part of a one-mile contract with earth embankments built up from side cuttings to provide cheap approaches (see Chapter 11).[103]

Stephenson was much involved in developing the design of the tubular bridges on the Chester & Holyhead Railway (see Chapter 10). Although he was heavily dependent on Ross and Fairbairn for producing the drawings, as leader of the team he could scarcely have shown more commitment. The

101 Op. cit. (n. 7).
102 Jeaffreson, II, p. 88.
103 Op. cit. (n. 42).

failure of the Dee Bridge in May 1847 revealed the extent to which he had relied on his associates to produce 'routine' designs, and the stress under which he operated. It also revealed the confidence in him by the railway's board, as he was allowed to proceed with other major bridges in his charge. Indeed they accepted his refusal to allow a full-time Government inspecting engineer on the works in July 1847.[104] The opening of the Trent Valley line was delayed following the Dee Bridge failure, which necessitated the strengthening of the line's several trussed girder bridges. Although Gooch had done all the original calculations, Stephenson became closely involved in the strengthening work.[105]

The designs for Stephenson's overseas railway projects developed the experience gained on the British lines. The Leopold Railway in Tuscany was best known for the use of trussed beam girder bridges (see Chapter 10).[106] Many of the viaducts on the line were of timber, however (Plate 14), and a major work was the tunnel at Mount Carioso, completed in 1845.[107]

The 40-mile Norwegian Trunk Railway, with a maximum gradient of 1 in 40, was, against his better judgement, the steepest that Stephenson felt could be worked by locomotives.[108] Under the terms of the concession the railway was to be built to a 'good European standard', with stone or shingle ballast. The gradients were an attempt to minimize construction costs, as was the extensive use of timber for bridges, and the use of lower weight, 60lb/yard, rails than was normal in Britain. Otherwise the specification generally followed British practice, although longitudinal timber sleepers were used because of concerns about cross sleepers and chairs in frozen ground.

For the Cairo–Alexandria Railway in Egypt, detailed design work for the tubular bridges across the Bahr el-Shebin Canal at Birket el-Saba, and the Rosetta and Damietta branches of the Nile at Kafr el-Zaiyat and Benha, was undertaken by Charles Wild and George Robert Stephenson (see Chapter 10).[109] The bridge contractors made important contributions to the designs, however, the machinery for the swing spans at Benha (Fig. 9.10) and Birket el-Saba being designed by James Wilson for Grissells, who supplied the ironwork for both crossings, and who had already worked with Stephenson's office on similar spans in East Anglia. All the bridges and landing stages were supported on Mitchell's screw piles, and concrete-filled iron cylinders on John d'Urban Hughes's system. Hughes supplied the designs for Stephenson.

Although largely completed after his death, the Great Indian Peninsula Railway was one of the largest schemes with which Stephenson was associated.[110] The scale of the work, and communication difficulties, must have

104 Baughan, pp. 108–9.

105 'Trent Valley Railway', *Report of the Commissioners of Railways*, 1848, Appendix 17.

106 Commissioners ... into the application of iron to railway structures. London, 1849, 1, pp. 332–40 and 413–15; 2, Appendix 4, Plates 2 and 3, and Appendix 9, Plates 1.

107 *RT*, **VIII**, 1845, p. 992.

108 Owen, pp. 1–18.

109 C. Wild, 'Die Aegyptische Eisenbahn von Alexandria nach Kairo', *Allgemeine Bauzeitung*, 1853, pp. 168–71, plate 562. Also Jeaffreson, II, p. 179, Wierner (1932) and Helong (1977).

110 J. J. Berkley, paper on the Bhore Ghat railway incline to the Bombay Mechanics Institute, 1857, Bombay, 1858.

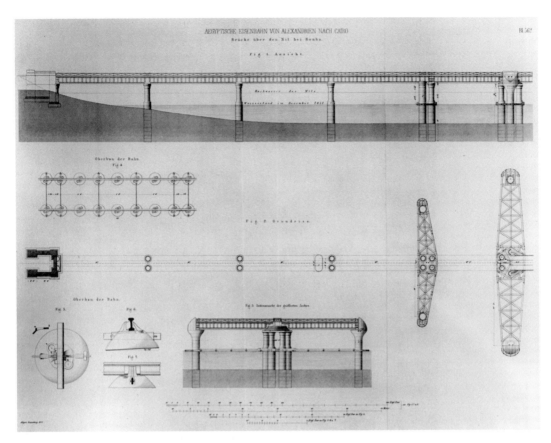

precluded use of the Great George Street offices for design work, as had been possible with other overseas projects. It was necessary to adjust to the methods of the Indian labour force and adopt locally available materials. Although native timber was generally used for sleepers, most permanent way was imported, including iron pot sleepers as employed in Egypt. Above all, despite the use of a broader gauge, it was built throughout on the model of '… Mr Robert Stephenson's English lines … plain, substantial and durable'.[111] Thus heavy engineering work, to minimize gradients, was preferred to lightweight materials and structures that might have provided short-term economies, but would not in the long term have sustained the heavy traffic anticipated.

9.10 Benha tubular and swing bridge over the river Nile on the Alexandria–Cairo Railway (C. Wild, *Allgemeine Bauzeitung,* 1853)

Architecture

Stephenson's personal contribution to railway architecture was limited, the design of stations and other structures being generally entrusted to architects, a division of responsibility typical for the time. Joseph Locke, for example, frequently worked

111 J. J. Berkley, 'On Indian railway: with a description of the Great Indian Peninsula Railway', *Proc. ICE,* **XIX,** 1859/60, pp. 586–624.

9.11 Chester station (Elton collection, Ironbridge Gorge Museum Trust)

with William Tite, and John Rastrick with David Mocatta on the Brighton railway.[112] Even Isambard K. Brunel, whose attention to architectural matters was atypical, cooperated with Matthew Digby Wyatt at Paddington Station.

Stephenson collaborated closely with Francis Thompson, who had first come to his attention on the final stages of the London & Birmingham project.[113] Thompson was best known for his work on the North Midland and Chester & Holyhead Railways, again reflecting Stephenson's delegatory approach to project management. Thompson could develop his own designs, but overall responsibility for location and layout lay with Stephenson. In East Anglia, Stephenson's presiding role led to Thompson's appointment as architect of many of the stations. Thompson was responsible for the architecture of Chester station (Fig. 9.11), assisted by Charles Wild. He was also responsible for the architectural treatment of the Britannia Bridge towers, and the Royal Border and High Level bridges.[114]

Robert Dockray undertook station designs and other works on the Warwick & Leamington line.[115] Often architect appointments were made at board level, such as William Livock for the stations on both the Northampton & Peterborough branch and the Buckinghamshire Railway,[116] Sancton Wood in East Anglia[117] and George Andrews for Hudson's lines in the north.[118] George Andrews undertook the design of the main stations at York and Gateshead (Fig.

112 R. Thorne (ed.), 'Iron Revolution', RIBA exhibition, 1990.
113 O. Carter, 'Francis Thompson an Architectural Mystery Solved', *Backtrack*, 1995, pp. 213–18.
114 Obituary, Hamilton Edward Harwood, pupil of Thompson, *Proc. ICE*, **XXXIV**, 1873, pp. 313–14.
115 Robbins, op. cit. (n. 29).
116 G. Biddle, 'The Railway Stations of John Livock', *JRCHS*, **31**, 1993, pp. 61–71, and 32, 1996, p. 141.
117 Simmons and Biddle.
118 M. J. Minett, 'The Railway stations of George Townsend Andrews', *JTH*, 2nd series, **7**, 1965/6, pp. 44–53.

9.12), on the Newcastle & Darlington Junction railway, using iron roof structures modelled on Fox's work at Euston. Stephenson's involvement in the design of Newcastle Central station seems to have been minimal, and his only contribution was to determine the layout, in conjunction with Thomas Harrison and Peter Tate (1792–1879) of the Carlisle line.[119] The station design was undertaken by John Dobson,[120] the well-known Newcastle architect, who was also involved with the Carlisle line.[121]

Stephenson's close association and working relationship with Francis Thompson and other leading architects resulted in some fine designs for stations and other buildings around Britain. The more limited opportunities for architectural work overseas, however, relied on the services of local practitioners, who provided designs appropriate for each location.

9.12 Part of the former Greenesfield station, Gateshead, c.1906, showing the type of girders first used at Euston station (Ken Hoole collection, North Road Museum, Darlington)

Contractors and contractual arrangements

Robert Stephenson had met with mixed success with the contractors on the London & Birmingham Railway. Although most contracts had been let by open tender, the lowest tenderer was not always accepted, as the financial strength of the contractor was more important. The size of contract had been in part governed by expectations of contractor resources, and selective invitations to tender had been sought from reliable firms for the most difficult contracts. In certain cases this process had been vindicated, but some

---

119 Donaldson, and Newcastle & Berwick Railway Board Minutes, 1 October 1845, **PRO**, RAIL 506/1. Also Rennison (2000/1), pp. 203–33.
120 Addyman and Fawcett.
121 Board Minutes, op. cit. (n. 118), 1 June 1846 and 19 March 1849.

contractors had failed to meet these expectations. This might have encouraged a cautious approach by Stephenson and his clients to the size and letting of subsequent contracts, although the success of some contractors, such as the Cubitts, had demonstrated that well-financed contractors could perform well.

There was an optimum size of contract for which documentation could be prepared with the engineering staff available, and which could be let relatively quickly and regularly to enable work to proceed in a planned manner. The London & Birmingham experience revealed the difficulty of resourcing this process. Stephenson had been generally understanding and prepared to recommend generous handling of contractors facing genuine financial or engineering problems. He recognized the need for the railway to provide plant, such as locomotives, to speed up construction. He also developed methods of detailed estimating and record-keeping to monitor progress. The majority of the lines he took over from 1839 had similar contractual arrangements, and some met with similar problems.

The contracts for the London & Blackwall Railway were let out slowly, and in short lengths. The first was let in August 1838, and the next two, to Thomas Jackson and Grissell & Peto, by the end of the year.[122] J. J. Bramah supplied the ironwork for the bridges over the Regents Canal. The fourth contract was let to Samuel Peto later that spring, again by selective tender, for which Stephenson himself was involved in the negotiations.[123] He recommended writing to selected manufacturers inviting tenders for the stationary engines,[124] the contracts for which were obtained by Maudslay, Son & Field and a Mr Barnes.[125]

There were seven relatively small contracts for the Preston & Wyre line, which did not anticipate developments in contract practice.[126] Stephenson insisted on close supervision, his progress reports detailing the total estimated volume of earthworks carried out and remaining.[127] Despite good administration, E. W. Morris, an experienced contractor, became embroiled in a legal dispute with the company, partly due to a deviation from the original line, to facilitate construction, after work had begun.[128] To speed the line's opening, a piled structure was substituted for 1200 yards of solid earthwork in the Wyre embankment, based no doubt on the Wolverton experience.

Many relatively small contracts had already been let before Stephenson took over responsibility for the North Midland and the Birmingham & Derby Junction Railways.[129] Their timing suited their complexity, and also the

---

122 Op. cit. (n. 6), pp. 250 and 270.
123 Ibid., 16 January and 13 March 1839, p. 303.
124 Ibid., p. 201.
125 Ibid., p. 228.
126 Contractors: Stanton, Tomkinson, Morris.
127 Robert Stephenson, Reports to Directors of the Preston & Wyre Railway, 1839–1840, **PRO**, RAIL 1080/90.
128 'Morris vs Preston and Wyre Railway Company', RT, **IV**, 21 August 1841, p. 380.
129 Minutes of Birmingham & Derby Junction and North Midland Railways, **PRO**, RAIL 36/1 and RAIL 530/1, *passim*.

engineering staff's capacity to provide drawings and specifications. The McIntosh family secured several short-length contracts on the North Midland line, but, given its impressive career as a public works contractor, failed to benefit from its large resources.

It was originally intended to let the Northampton to Peterborough branch contracts on a lump-sum basis, presumably to avoid the cost overruns incurred on the main London–Birmingham line, but the traditional method of procurement was preferred, in three lots in February 1844;[130] two to John Stephenson, the other to Brogden. John Stephenson's success, following that on the Liverpool & Manchester and North Midland lines, was an example of a contractor commanding increasing resources. Acting as arbitrator, Stephenson was fair and pragmatic to a legitimate claim from the ironwork contractor regarding the supply of rail chairs arising from an error in the original tender.[131]

Events on the Midland Railway's Syston to Peterborough branch were reminiscent of the London–Birmingham saga.[132] The lowest tenderer chosen for the first two contracts was Worswick, who immediately realized he had made errors in his estimates. Despite this he was given the third contract, for Oakham, which included Manton tunnel. He had to be continually warned about his dilatory progress, although he fared better than Wykes, Porter and Crick, who had to be relieved of the Manton–Stamford contract. It was only the last contract, from Melton to Oakham, let to Dyson, which proceeded at all satisfactorily.

From the mid-1840s contractors were able to undertake larger contracts, and even finance schemes, most notably abroad. Stephenson recognized increasingly that they were capable of much that was formerly the preserve of the engineer. However, perhaps at his clients' insistence, small contracts and improvident contractors continued to feature in his works. He developed a good working relationship with Samuel Peto, although perhaps not as close as that of Locke and Brassey. As financier and contractor, Peto was prominent in the railways of East Anglia (Fig. 9.13). He attributed an incident on the line between London and Cambridge to his excellent working relationship with Stephenson, who[133]

expressed his dissatisfaction with a wooden bridge. The contractor saw the Resident engineer, Mr Borthwick, who said he was the one to blame, and at Mr Peto's request gave him a drawing of an iron bridge of the type intended by the chief. On the final inspection Stephenson found an iron bridge substituted and said: 'I never ordered this. Why have you done it?'

Peto replied that by the terms of the contract the work was to be executed to the satisfaction of the engineer-in-chief, and he felt he could not leave a bridge standing with which Stephenson was dissatisfied. Stephenson warmly expressed his pleasure, and said that was the way in which he liked to be met …

130 *RT*, **VII**, 24 February 1844, p. 240.
131 Letter, Robert Stephenson to Richard Creed, 13 February 1844, **PRO**, RAIL 1008/90.
132 Op. cit. (n. 70).
133 Peto, pp. 17–18.

9.13 Sir Samuel Morton Peto
(1809–1889)
(Courtesy of Institution of
Civil Engineers)

Both Peto and Bidder became directors of the Yarmouth & Norwich Railway. Peto boasted he was carrying out £1.5 million-worth of contracts for Stephenson at that time, and all would be to price. Stephenson remarked on the completion of Peto's work on the Eastern Counties Railway in June 1848:[134]

In thus giving my final decision on these heavy contracts [amounting to over £1.1m] I find it my duty to state that many large and unforeseen contingencies have occurred and have required the greatest energy on the part of Mr Peto, and it affords me satisfaction to add my testimony to the willing and unflinching manner in which they have been met.

There is an element of hyperbole in this; the Norwich & Brandon line cost about £12 000 a mile, about half of some of Stephenson's other lines.

If this work with Peto typified the emerging role of the contractor in railway promotion, Stephenson's contemporary work with his north-eastern clients harked back to the previous decade, in terms of the size of its contracts, although in their engineering organization these were perhaps the most impressive with which Stephenson was involved.

Once the deviations to the Newcastle & Darlington Junction Railway had been authorized, the remaining contracts were let in May 1843. Progress on the line was remarkable, particularly the speed with which the deviation contracts were let. The *Yorkshire Gazette* reported 'The Royal Assent was only obtained to this Act on the 11th day of April last, and yet within the brief space of four weeks everything has been so determinedly pressed forward that the contracts for every yard of the land have been let. We believe there is no parallel to this in railway history.' As resident engineer, Thomas Harrison was undoubtedly responsible for the detailed preparations that resulted in such good progress being achieved.[135] Rapid progress under Harrison's supervision also typified the contracts on the Newcastle & Berwick Railway.

134 Ibid., p. 22.

However, such preparedness was in contrast to Stephenson's experience on the Chester & Holyhead Railway, where the volume of work in preparing drawings and specifications had led to contract delays. Stephenson was asked to prepare drawings and specifications in September 1844 with a view to begin letting contracts in January 1845.[136] However, on 15 November Captain Moorsom, the resident director, wrote to George King, the company secretary: 'I have written to Mr Stephenson to urge on the Contracts, but you cannot get Engineers to attend to these matters till after the 30th ... and every man is now at double pay.'[137] All Stephenson's staff were engaged in preparing plans by the end of November for the next parliamentary session, and the first contract documents were not ready for tender until February 1845.

The contractors were all well established, with Thomas Brassey and William Mackenzie securing two contracts, let on a traditional model.[138] Contracts were phased between February 1845 and July 1847, although letting the most difficult first was unattainable, as the location and form of the Menai crossing had yet to be fixed. Stephenson's active involvement in the tendering process led him to advise against Evans's and Harding & Cropper's tenders as they had sufficient on hand 'according to their means'. He recommended acceptance of Thomas Jackson's tender for Bangor without competition.[139]

Stephenson had gained much more confidence in the contractors, as demonstrated by his recommendation that all the Anglesey contracts should be let to Edward Betts, with whom he had previously worked on the South Eastern Railway's Maidstone Branch.[140] This confidence led him to exceed his authority by allowing more time to complete the Anglesey contracts whilst awaiting the completion of the Britannia Bridge. On the instructions of the board, however, he had to urge Betts to complete, who responded very positively.[141] Construction proceeded smoothly, with the contractors generally meeting targets, although Mackenzie was rebuked for using the permanent rails for contractors' traffic.[142]

During the mania of the mid-1840s, the demand for railway construction led to contractors of insufficient funds being selected for some lines. Economy affected the choice of Thomas Burton as contractor for the 35-mile single-track Rugby–Stamford branch. This resulted, as Dockray observed, in 'the contractors not being men of sufficient means, and I suspect that they were not judiciously treated, the consequence has been a general failure amongst

135 *RT*, **VI**, 20 May 1843, p. 572, and **VII**, 17 February 1844, pp. 188–190, and 10 August 1844, pp. 870–1.
136 Baughan, p. 56.
137 Ibid., p. 57.
138 Chrimes et al.
139 Baughan, p. 58.
140 *RT*, **VI**, 23 September 1843, p. 1041.
141 Letters, Robert Stephenson and Edward Betts, January 1846, **PRO**, RAIL 1008/90.
142 Letter, Robert Stephenson to George King, May 1847, **PRO**, RAIL 1008/90.

them, and much litigation. The works are however well executed and are highly creditable to the engineer, Mr Liddell.'[143]

This was in marked contrast to the growing number of major contracts undertaken by the larger contractors, such as Brassey and Mackenzie. Contractual arrangements on the North Staffordshire Railway, for example, were let in six large lots, the first three in September 1846,[144] including Brassey with the largest 46-mile stretch,[145] and the remainder from July 1847.[146] Progress was rapid encouraged by liberal advances by the Company. Opening was phased from April 1848 and the line fully opened in July 1849. Such rapid progress would not have been possible in the mid-1830s, a testimony to the organization of the contractors rather than the engineers. Brassey also took on the 61-mile Buckinghamshire Railway, which was then typical of his enterprise,[147] and he also built the entire Trent Valley line with his partners Mackenzie and John Stephenson.[148]

The Shrewsbury & Birmingham Railway was let in three small contracts between Wolverhampton and Shrewsbury, the final section being the joint venture with the Shropshire Union Company. The heaviest works were the bridge over the Severn near Shrewsbury, where Brassey was the contractor, and earthworks at Shifnal and Haughton.[149] Progress was delayed by adverse weather conditions in the winter of 1847–1848,[150] and although the contractor, McCleod, tried to expedite work on the 471-yard Oakengates tunnel, where the navvies worked night shifts, he was penalized for working too slowly.[151] Relations with William Hoof, the other main contractor, were better, and generally progress was rapid and within the £1m estimates. Work on the Stour Valley Railway was also let in three lots between Bushbury and Birmingham New Street. George Wythes was the contractor, and initial progress was rapid, with William Baker reporting that the Birmingham tunnel was one-third completed in August 1847.[152]

Stephenson was respected as a fair arbitrator, but was caught up in an extraordinary dispute with the construction of the Londonderry & Enniskillen railway. The first contracts had been let to James Leishman,[153] with whom Ross had long been acquainted, but who was also involved as a leading shareholder. Although Stephenson's and Ross's estimates had been subject to open parliamentary scrutiny, progress was hampered by the company's inability to raise funds from its shareholders, and pay for work carried out.

143 Robbins, op. cit. (n. 29), p. 6.
144 *RT*, **IX**, 26 September 1846, p. 967. Also Hollick.
145 *RT*, **X**, 27 February 1847, p. 272.
146 *RT*, **X**, 10 July 1847, p. 892.
147 Op. cit. (n. 52). Also Mackenzie collection, **ICE**.
148 Helps (1872). Contract with Mackenzie, Brassey and Stephenson, **PRO**, RAIL 699/3.
149 *RT*, **XI**, 26 February 1848, pp. 228–9.
150 Robert Stephenson and William Baker, Half yearly report to the ... Shrewsbury and Birmingham Railway, 21 August 1848, *RT*, **XI**, 2 September 1848, p. 940.
151 **PRO**, RAIL 45/1, May 1849.
152 Christiansen.
153 Engineers' report, 3 March 1846, *RT*, **IX**, 18 March 1846, p. 404. Also Skempton (2002), pp. 418–21 and 403, and Frank Smith files, **ICE**.

The line should have been completed from Londonderry to Strabane by September 1846.[154] However, some Irish shareholders opposed calls on the shares, alleging that Ross was financially involved with Leishman, precluding fair competitive tendering and with prices above a norm for Ireland.[155]

The directors insisted on Stephenson endorsing Ross's approval of Leishman's tender,[156] but shareholders remained dissatisfied. The relationship between engineer and contractor was thus put to a strong test. Stephenson relied on Ross, and Leishman was a contractor he felt was also reliable. Without Leishman's offer to build the line it is unlikely it would have begun at all. Indeed such financial arrangements with contractors became commonplace in the 1850s. Stephenson was obliged to arbitrate on the claims.[157] Both he and Ross had withdrawn as engineers by the time of his report in January 1848, which was a strong rebuttal of all critics and supported Leishman's contract price.[158] Ultimately, arbitration by Joseph Locke settled Leishman's claims for payment, but he had to settle for more than half in debentures from the cash-strained company.[159]

The classic British model of chief engineer, resident engineer and assistants, supervising contracts let in several lots by competitive tender, was exported abroad, most notably to India. Although on a larger scale than in Britain, the Stephenson team made the system work more successfully than other engineers. On his advice, Stephenson's clients often let contracts on a selective tendering basis. He even contemplated lump-sum rather than admeasurement contracts; in the latter, the scope for contractors to pursue claims for extra work was apparently much higher, and might have required more engineering staff to measure the work done.

Stephenson's role in Belgium was limited to appointing contractors and reviewing construction progress for British shareholders, as the state's engineers had largely determined the routes. This second phase of railway development, being largely on a concession basis, fostered an alliance of British financiers, engineers and contractors typified by William Mackenzie.[160] The resident engineers safeguarded the concessionaire's interests, but the ultimate decisions about the safety of the line lay with the Belgian Government. It appointed engineers to inspect the works that ultimately became State assets. A number of the concessionaire shareholders were themselves contractors and, as work progressed, any payments due were subject to a deduction to cover their share calls.[161] Mackenzie and Brassey were among the shareholders on the

154 Londonderry and Enniskillen Railway – General Meeting, *RT*, **IX**, 29 August 1846.
155 Mackenzie collection, **ICE**. Also Brooke, *passim*.
156 *RT*, **X**, 23 October 1847, pp. 1340–5, and *RR*, **V**, 15 January 1848, pp. 56–7.
157 *RT*, **X**, 23 October 1847, pp. 1340–5, and 25 December 1847, pp. 1558–61. Also, *RR*, **V**, pp. 15–16.
158 *RR*, **V**, 15 January 1848, pp. 56–7.
159 *RR*, **V**, 29 January 1848, p. 97, 4 March 1848, pp. 216–17 and 9 September 1848, p. 247. Also *RT*, **XI**, 2 September 1848, p. 950.
160 Webster. Also Chrimes et al.
161 *West Flanders Railway*, Report of G Stephenson, etc. ..., London, 1845, pp. 9–13. Also *RT*, **IX**, 4 July 1846, p. 917.

Tournai–Jurbise/Landen–Hasselt concession, but were hard pressed by the political and financial events of 1847–1848.[162]

Stephenson's role in Scandinavia was largely as a facilitator, working closely with Brassey, Peto and Betts to develop consortia with concessions to build railways in Norway and Denmark.[163] In this context his role as an arbitrator and independent consulting engineer was important in providing the traditional British separation between client, engineer and contractor. Bidder was free to act as engineer for the concessionaire-contractors.

The contract for the Norwegian Trunk Railway was undertaken by Thomas Earle and George Merrett, who were experienced, if not major British contractors.[164] Under the terms of the concession the railway was to be built to a 'good European standard'. The contractors were to operate the railway and maintain it for five years against a £60 000 deposit. Forty British workers trained the largely Norwegian workforce.

The Norwegians appointed a commission to supervise the concession, which was financed jointly by Norwegian and British interests. However, the cheap form of construction occasioned criticism from the Commission, who felt it represented poor engineering, rather than an attempt to keep to a limited budget. Partly because of this dissatisfaction, Earle and Merrett gave up their contract in February 1854, and the construction period was extended until August that year. Stephenson acknowledged some of the criticism of the construction standards, but recommended that the £60 000 deposit would suffice to remedy all eventualities.

The agreement that Stephenson had brokered specified that, in the event of any disagreement with the Norwegian authorities, the matter would be referred to him for arbitration. In 1856, the Norwegian directors expressed some dissatisfaction about the railway, and a survey was undertaken by a young military engineer, Lt. Jess Engelstad. He reported that parts of the line did not meet the anticipated standard, suggesting it did not compare well with other European lines. He specifically complained about substandard rails, poor ballast, subsidence, and the lack of preservative treatment for timber sleepers and viaducts. There was also an expectation that, buoyed by a successful first two years of operation, more locomotives and rolling stock could be provided to meet the growing traffic needs.

Stephenson arranged to visit Norway but, before he departed, a Norwegian deputation, including Engelstad, visited London to seek further investment in the line and rolling stock through arbitration.[165] Stephenson expressed 'strong indignation' by the implication that he had allowed a substandard railway to be built.[166] 'Not one word of that Report shall have my consideration, – it is perfectly despicable.' His angered response, which caused the young Engelstad

---

162 *Tournai–Jurbise*, etc., reports and correspondence, Mackenzie Collection, **ICE**.

163 Helps (1872). Also Peto.

164 Owen, pp. 1–18.

165 Letter, Robert Stephenson to Mr. Pim, London, undated but August 1856, **Stephenson**, Folder 18.

166 Arbitration evidence 'Re The Norwegian Trunk Railway Before Robert Stephenson Esq. M.P.', London, September 1856, **ScM,** GPB1/3/3f, pp. 17–21.

13 High Level Bridge over the river Tyne, York, Newcastle & Berwick Railway (Courtesy of Institution of Civil Engineers)

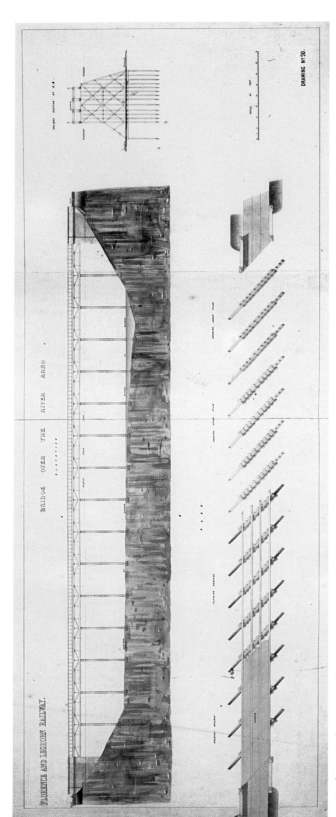

14 Timber viaduct over the river Arno on the Florence–Leghorn Railway
(Courtesy of Archivio di Stato, Firenze)

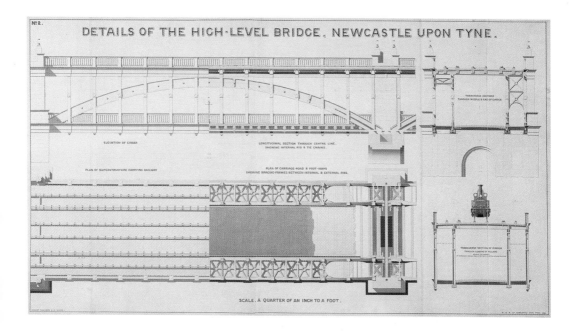

DETAILS OF THE HIGH-LEVEL BRIDGE, NEWCASTLE UPON TYNE.

15 Details of the Newcastle High Level Bridge drawn by R. Hodgson, the resident engineer (Courtesy of Institution of Civil Engineers)

16 Trussed girder bridge carrying the Northern & Eastern Railway over the river Lea at Tottenham (private collection)

17 Fabricating tubes for Britannia Bridge
(Elton collection, Ironbridge Gorge Museum Trust)

18 Floating second tube for Britannia Bridge
(Elton collection, Ironbridge Gorge Museum Trust)

19 John Lucas's painting of the conference at Britannia Bridge.
Standing, left to right: Admiral Moorsom, Latimer Clark, Edwin Clark, Frank Forster, George
Bidder, Mr Hemmingway, Captain Claxton, workman, Alexander Ross.
Seated, left to right: Robert Stephenson, Charles Wild, Joseph Locke and Isambard K. Brunel.
(Courtesy of Institution of Civil Engineers)

20 Wolverton
Viaduct west
side, the 1837
façade, London
& Birmingham
Railway (Ted
Ruddock)

21 Primrose Hill Tunnel south portal, London & Birmingham Railway
(J. C. Bourne, 1839)

to withdraw, included a sharp reminder to the delegation that they would not have had a railway at all but for his endeavours six years earlier. He did however rule that £1925 of the concessionaires' caution should be used to remedy some defects, such as the viaducts. Stephenson's arbitration was accepted, and the five-year contract term ran until the summer of 1859.

With the building of the Cairo and Alexandria Railway in Egypt Stephenson had become experienced in managing overseas projects, and with his team of experienced engineers on site, the main priorities were ensuring he was paid, and the logistics of delivering material to Egypt.[167] The contractor, Edward Price, who had agents based at Gabbary (Alexandria) and Bulaq (Cairo), began work at both ends and devised a rapid method of track-laying on the 'Greaves' system. By 1854, 104km had been completed to the Nile, and temporary river crossings were set up while the main bridges were built. Stephenson's visit to Egypt at the end of 1856 allowed work to begin, under John McLaren, on replacing the Kafr el-Zaiyat ferry with the tubular swing bridge, completed in 1859.

For the Great Indian Peninsula Railway a contract was signed in April 1851 with William Faviell, well known to Stephenson, to construct the initial 21-mile section to Thana. Construction proceeded on the British model, with locomotives used to move ballast and other materials, and the line, opened in April 1853, was completed for 2 per cent less than the estimates, and ahead of time.[168] This encouraged the company to persist with the British contract system, which contrasted with the departmental system familiar for most Indian Public Works Department contracts, where government engineers managed the labour as well as providing the design.[169]

Further shorter contracts followed for the Kallyan extension, but it was not until 1856 that the challenges of crossing the Ghat mountains were resolved (Fig. 9.14). The Thul Ghat incline contract was successfully undertaken by Wythes and Jackson, although their agent's work, frequently condemned by Public Works Department engineers, was heavily mechanized to deal with labour recruitment problems. The extraordinary difficulties on the Ghat routes led to the failure of several British contractors. The 15-mile contract up Bhore Ghat, for example, was let to Faviell, who pursued a low-pay policy and found it difficult to find a workforce, ultimately giving up the contract. In contrast the Parsee contractor, Jamerji Naegamwalla (1804–1882), was remarkably successful, completing one contract in the face of Berkley's scepticism.

At times over 100 000 men were employed on its construction, including over 30 000 on the Thul Ghat incline. There were appalling problems of disease amongst the workforce, and logistical problems such as the supply of water, and the death toll from disease and the poor working conditions in the remote areas was high.[170] In spite of this, the completion of the line was a triumph for Berkley and the contractors.[171]

167 Wierner. Also Helong.
168 Sharma, pp. 48–50.
169 Kerr.
170 Ibid.
171 Op. cit. (n. 110 and 111).

9.14 Nath-ha-Doonghur railway viaducts and mouth of tunnel no. 22 on the Bhore Ghat incline of the Great Indian Peninsula Railway under construction (Courtesy of Institution of Mechanical Engineers)

The contrast between the contractual arrangements on the London & Birmingham line and the Grand Trunk Railway in Canada, at the two ends of Stephenson's career, could not have been greater. On the London & Birmingham, Stephenson's concern was to find contractors who were reliable and financially secure, whereas the Grand Trunk contractors, Brassey, Peto, Betts and Jackson, presented themselves as the means whereby the railway would be built. Their reputation provided British investors with some confidence in financing a major railway at a time when the Canadians were despairing of being able to provide the railway infrastructure necessary to develop their economy.

The pivotal role of contractors in railway promotion had developed through the 1840s as the more successful contractors accumulated fortunes of several hundred thousand pounds.[172] A London visit by a member of the Canadian Assembly, John Ross, led to his meeting William Jackson MP, a personal friend of Thomas Brassey, which promoted the interest of his consortium in a major rail route between Toronto and Montreal and on to the United States, a massive 1100 miles of route.[173] The leading role of the contractors in the enterprise was one with which Alexander Ross was at ease, but which fitted uncomfortably on the shoulders of engineers such as the Shanly brothers, also working on the line, brought up in the Smeaton–Telford tradition.[174]

Although confident in the contractors, investors were concerned about the unprecedented scale of the Victoria Bridge (Fig. 9.15), and criticisms about its

172 H. Pollins, 'Railway Contractors and the Finance of Railway Development in Britain', *JTH*, **3**, 1957/8, pp. 41–51 and 103–10, and P. L. Cotterill, 'Railway Finance and the Crisis of 1866: Contractors Bills of Exchange, and the Finance Companies', *JTH*, NS **3**, 1976, pp. 20–40. Also Chrimes et al.

173 Currie.

174 White, pp. 62–102.

practicability in the short Canadian construction season, which prompted Stephenson to be called in. Fabrication of the bridge components was carried out in Brassey's newly established Canada Works in Birkenhead. Construction of the bridge was facilitated by innovations suggested by North American subcontractors such as Benjamin Chaffrey, who recommended the use of cribs rather than caissons, introduced centrifugal pumps and steam-powered derrick cranes.[175] As Stephenson himself remarked in Canada in 1853, 'the contractors left even the engineers themselves little more than the poetry of engineering.'[176]

9.15 Victoria tubular bridge across the St Lawrence River on the Grand Trunk Railway (J. Hodges, 1860)

The contractors had eight engineers on site, and Stephenson's attitude to their work is reflected in his report on changes to the design which they initiated: 'I am actuated by the feeling that the engineers would not be justified in controlling the contractors in the adoption of such means as they might consider most economical to themselves, so long as the soundness and stability of the work were in no way affected'.[177] This is the thinking of a mature engineer operating in a very different world from the 1830s, used to delegating and trusting both his subordinates and the contractors with whom they worked.

Construction costs

Although Stephenson insisted on thorough record-keeping for projects, financial overruns were an ongoing feature among early lines, and some later projects.

175 Hodges.
176 Helps (1872), p. 21.
177 Hodges.

Whatever the particular circumstances, there were often unforeseen engineering difficulties to complicate matters. Record-keeping on the Birmingham & Derby Junction Railway, for example, had been thorough but served to illustrate the inadequacy of the original estimates. In February 1842, shortly before the line's opening, Stephenson showed that the overall costs of £24 000 a mile were not excessive, possibly in part due to the use of timber for many of the bridges.[178]

Some cost overruns had been due to the Tame Valley deviation, which added four miles to the route, but this could not explain the costs being 20 per cent ahead of estimates. Of this 5 per cent was attributable to acquisition of land, but much of the rest was due to the costs of stations, particularly Lawley Street, Birmingham, and provision for handling additional traffic. These had earlier been a feature of the cost overruns on the London & Birmingham Railway, and can be attributed to the lack of experience in catering for traffic. The latter railway was still improving Curzon Street station in Birmingham at this time, and experience had not been accumulated in parliamentary estimates.

In contrast, the York & North Midland Railway extension lines to Scarborough and Pickering were built in under a year at a cost below £6000 per mile.[179] Similarly, the Yarmouth & Norwich Railway, opened in April 1844, had been completed in about twelve months at a cost of £200 000, well ahead of schedule. This was a tribute to Peto's organization and the simplicity of the route.[180]

Branch lines offered the prospect of economies. Efforts were made to keep the single-track Northampton and Peterborough branch within the £500 000 estimate, of which £370 000 was for engineering costs excluding stations.[181] The circuitous Nene valley route was intended to minimize engineering costs, and maximize traffic between the small towns on route. The Warwick and Leamington branch was largely completed in eighteen months at a cost of £170 000, a very economic rate for the near nine-mile Coventry–Emscott stretch.[182]

Financial issues affected the progress of some of Stephenson's lines, notably the Chester & Holyhead Railway, for which a cash crisis loomed during the 1847–1848 recession.[183] The opening of the first section to Rhyl was delayed until the whole section could be opened to Bangor in May 1848. At a time when work on the Britannia Bridge was well in hand, the Board was trying hard to raise funds. Stephenson was obliged to take shares in lieu of payment, and in 1850 Samuel Peto came to the rescue of the Company.[184] The cost overrun on the Britannia bridge – at £674 000 more than three times the estimate – was the chief question mark over the undoubted engineering triumph.

178 Report of Robert Stephenson to the Directors of the Birmingham & Derby Junction Railway, 14 February 1842, **PRO**, RAIL 36/1, p. 64. Also Dempsey (1845–1847), pp. 93–5 and plate xviii.
179 Tomlinson, p. 418.
180 *RT*, **VII**, 17 August 1844, pp. 926–7.
181 *RT*, **VI**, 21 January 1843, p. 63, 15 April 1843, pp. 436–9, 6 May 1843, pp. 512–15 and 29 July 1843, pp. 813–14.
182 *RT*, **VII**, 21 December 1844, p. 1499.
183 Evans.
184 Baughan.

Stephenson went to extraordinary lengths to pursue an inexpensive line for the Norwegian Trunk Railway.[185] Severe gradients and extensive use of untreated timber minimized construction costs, against which was set the cost of the 188m-long Loken tunnel driven through clay. When he made his final visit, for the last inspection and handover, he awarded £2800 against the concessionaires, and a further £7500 for additional work on the Strommen branch line. He stated that the line, which at £10 700 a mile had cost about a third of the average in Britain, was 'the cheapest line of Railway that has ever been made'.

Although Stephenson got some of his railway estimates quite wrong, many of the lines built under his guidance after 1839 were economic and to budget. The expensive works, like the Britannia and Victoria bridges, grabbed the headlines but were unrepresentative of the bulk of his work. Whether credit for the latter belongs to Stephenson or others like Harrison and Peto is less clear. Despite the obvious problems of working overseas with limited knowledge of local costs, the Stephenson team achieved some notable successes. The early work on the Great Indian Penisula Railway, for example, was completed for 2 per cent less than the estimates, and ahead of time.

Conclusions

At the banquet in his honour at Newcastle Central Station in July 1850 Robert Stephenson remarked:[186]

No one felt more intensely than he did the value of the assistance which he had derived from those who had been associated with him for some years past. If they would read the biographies of all their old distinguished engineers, they would be struck with the excessive detail into which they had been drawn ... but since then a change had taken place, and no change was more complete. The principal engineer now had only to say let this be done, and it was speedily accomplished, such was the immense capital, and such the ample resources of mind which were immediately brought into play. He had himself, within the last ten or twelve years, done little more than exercize a general superintendence; and there were many other persons ... to whom the works ... ought to be almost entirely attributed. He had had little or nothing to do with many of them beyond giving his name, and exercizing a gentle control in some of the principal works.

Reinforcing this view, Stephenson had written an interesting letter to Fairbairn along similar lines at the time of the fabrication of the tubes for the Conway Bridge:[187]

I am much gratified at your resolution, to devote a considerable portion of your time to looking the tube builders up, and getting a good job made of the whole affair. I do not think that a large proportion of your time is at all necessary. Two or three days a

185 Owen, pp. 1–18.
186 Jeaffreson, II, pp. 167–9.
187 W. Fairbairn, pp. 146–7.

fortnight is, I am sure, all that you will need give up to it; what would be most valuable is a regular periodical visit, so that the progress may be narrowly watched and advantage taken of every new continuation as it occurs ...

He clearly did not expect an engineer of Fairbairn's stature, any more than himself, to be engaged all the time. Delegation and gentle control were the key.

This brief survey of Stephenson's railway projects supports that view. He relied on his associates, who rarely let him down, and who generally deserve the larger credit for getting things done. They regarded him as their 'Chief'. Stephenson helped to develop a system for railway construction relying on delegation and cooperation with client and contractor, which enabled a network of railways to be built across a large portion of the globe in his lifetime.

Some of these lines involved some of the greatest civil engineering achievements of the early Victorian age. This distinguished Stephenson from Joseph Locke, who epitomized the predominant practice of the age, successfully managing a range of projects for clients all over Europe but without any eye-catching structures. Locke generally worked to estimates, but partly because of greater engineering challenges, Stephenson never acquired this reputation. Neither Stephenson nor Locke, however, attempted the tight control and attention to detail that characterized the work of Isambard K. Brunel. Locke led the trend in 'hands-off' engineering, but Stephenson showed a relaxed approach, and despite occasionally appearing conservative with issues such as gradients and permanent way, seems to have got his level of control on construction projects about correct.

Stephenson retained a strong allegiance to his clients, the boards of directors who appointed him.[188] Where appropriate, he provided engineering designs to suit his clients' limited resources, with single track and light engineering structures, such as the extensive use of timber bridges. He attained something of a reputation for his projects running over time and budget, which was partly a consequence of the lack of experience with heavy engineering in the early period of railway construction. Some criticism is indeed due. The estimates for the Britannia Bridge were unrealistic because the original suspension bridge, of much more economic construction, had cost more than £180 000. However, estimating improved through the 1840s with experience and the increased capacity and resources of contractors.

Stephenson was conservative on project organization, and did not lead the trend, which developed through the 1840s, towards letting works to major contractors. Indeed, many of the companies persisted in using a system of short-length contracts and undercapitalized contractors when other methods of procurement had become more common. Stephenson took on more work than he could manage, and he and Bidder were dependent upon Thomas Gooch in the mania years. Staffing in the Great George Street office was limited, and when lines progressed rapidly it was generally through sound preparations by the resident engineers. Innovation was often the work of others, and probably the consequence of time for reflection he could rarely afford.

---

188 *RT*, **XIII**, 2 March 1850, p. 212.

Stephenson and his team modified and advanced the design of railways, and spread their knowledge over four continents. The most spectacular advances were in the area of iron bridges. In India, Stephenson had direct influence on a railway he never visited and which he never directly managed or contributed to detailed designs. He made crucial decisions about the route over the Ghats that the resident engineers could never have carried without his support. This debt, acknowledged by James Berkley in a paper published after Stephenson's death, is made even more explicit in his account of the Thul Ghat incline presented in Bombay in 1860. He wrote of Stephenson as 'one talisman of our success', and continued:[189]

It was mainly upon the favourable report of Robert Stephenson that Government resolved to take the bold step of introducing railways into this country … It was Robert Stephenson who created the large professional establishment by which our designs and works are being accomplished. He it was who, with the able aid of George Berkley … adopted and pursued those vast supplies of mechanical appliances which the British Isles have contributed to our wants. By his influence, and the shelter of his prestige, we were able to find eminent contractors to undertake the execution of our extensive works; and it was to his counsel the Government appealed with confidence in any doubt or difficulty that beset the prosecution of our plans.

Stephenson's legacy was to have provided engineers capable of arranging such a major project, extending ultimately to 1114 miles of railway, at a cost of £10 000 a mile.

Stephenson's greatness was not as a superhuman attempting everything in his railway projects of the 1840s and 1850s. He recognized the time for such a role, if it had ever existed, had passed. Some among his associates, such as William Baker, easily followed this lead. Others were content to support the 'Chief', but others felt cheated of credit, notably William Fairbairn. Stephenson was not the only leading engineer to be affected by issues of professional jealousy. Brunel's sons became concerned at the way in which his assistant, Brereton, presented his responsibilities for the Saltash Bridge at the Institution of Civil Engineers.[190] Sir John MacNeill became embroiled in a dispute over credit for the Boyne viaduct, and, referring to the role of his assistants, made a striking comparison to Stephenson:[191]

[others] had no more to do with my original design in 1844, or with its improved realization in 1851, than any assistant Stephenson availed himself of.

Several associates, such as Thomas Harrison and Charles Liddell, had struck out independent careers in Stephenson's lifetime. Stephenson's delegatory approach encouraged it, and this approach in his work on bridge design is considered in the following chapters.

189 Op. cit. (n. 1).
190 Information from Derek Portman, based on his research for a biography of Henry Marc Brunel, **Brunel**.
191 J. Byrne, 'Sir John MacNeill', paper to conference, *Some Aspects of the Industrial Heritage of North-East Ireland*, Dublin, 2000, published by Industrial Heritage Association of Ireland, 2002, p. 11.

10

Iron railway bridges

James Sutherland

The opening of this magnificent structure, looked forward to with so much interest, came off this day at dawn, with the grandest success … Three engines, 200 tons of coal and 30 to 40 packed railway carriages passed through saluted by a wild burst of 'Rule, Britannia' from an array of Liverpool seamen on the towers, and so to Holyhead at the rate of 35 miles an hour

The Times[1]

The opening quotation records the passage of the first train through the Britannia Bridge and thus the completion of the route to Ireland (Fig. 10.1). This was the climax of Robert Stephenson's twenty-year involvement with iron bridges, and appropriately he was driving the train. Within the span of his career, there were momentous changes in materials and structural forms. Wrought iron replaced cast iron as the dominant structural material while structural design shifted from uncertain, but often creative, empiricism to a rigidly academic elastic theory. In this period there was an enormous burst in the use of structural iron, mainly brought about by the railways. Also engineering was first established as a discipline at university level in this period.

Not only did Stephenson live through these changes but, more than any other engineer of his time, he was at the centre of virtually all of them. Between 1830 and 1838 he and his team were responsible for designing and building the multiplicity of bridges on the London & Birmingham Railway, the most innovative of which were in iron. He was subsequently responsible for a whole range of iron bridges on other railways in the 1830s, 1840s and 1850s. Among the outstanding examples were the Newcastle High Level Bridge, built in 1845–1849, and the Britannia and Conway Tubular Bridges of 1845–1850. Overall this was a story of great success, but not everything went smoothly.

The final triumph of the Britannia and Conway bridges was marred by the gargantuan quarrel between Stephenson and William Fairbairn. However, Stephenson's blackest moment came in May 1847 when, at the most crucial stage of the work on these great structures, his Dee Bridge at Chester collapsed with a train on it. Although clearly shaken by the disaster and its aftermath, Stephenson not only saw his other larger bridges carried to a triumphant

---

1 *The Times*, 6 March 1850.

10.1 The Britannia Tubular Bridge (Elton collection, Ironbridge Gorge Museum Trust)

conclusion but he continued to be variously involved in the construction of iron bridges, such as the tubular bridge over the river Aire at Brotherton, the three tubular bridges in Egypt and one, by far the longest and again tubular, the Victoria Bridge over the St Lawrence at Montreal.

Each of these structures deserves more detailed research than it has had to date,[2] and this chapter may do no more than set the scene for this. In relation to Stephenson's career the story of these bridges may be divided into two eras. From about 1830 to 1848 there was the cast-iron era and then the wrought-iron one, which extended from 1845 to Stephenson's death in 1859, though continuing in other hands until nearly the end of the century. Inevitably such eras overlap, and 1847–1848 must have been almost unbearably traumatic for Stephenson, who also had heavy responsibilities in other fields.

The cast iron bridge era: c.1830–1848

The introduction of railways brought in a completely new layer of transport arteries superimposed on the existing layers of roads and canals or navigable rivers, entailing a vast number of bridges and tunnels. For instance, on the London & Birmingham Railway there were some 2½ bridges per mile on the 112.5 miles, making a total of about 280.[3]

In the eighteenth century, conflicts of level occurred between roads and waterways, but with the introduction of railways these conflicts multiplied.

2 Addyman and Fawcett (1999) is a worthy exception.
3 Whishaw (1840), p. 225.

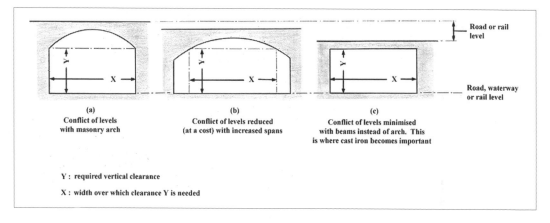

(a)
**Conflict of levels
with masonry arch**

(b)
**Conflict of levels reduced
(at a cost) with increased spans**

(c)
**Conflict of levels minimised
with beams instead of arch. This
is where cast iron becomes important**

Y : required vertical clearance

X : width over which clearance Y is needed

For economy, railway tracks needed to be as near to ground level as possible and low gradients were essential, especially on the early railways. To give the required clearances, which had to be maintained over the full span, bridges with minimum structural depth were needed. In such cases a flat, or nearly flat, soffit to a bridge deck became essential.

10.2 Conflict of levels

This problem of levels, bridge headroom and the distance over which this headroom was needed are illustrated in the accompanying diagram (Fig. 10.2). When the railway was on the upper level at a crossing, raising an arch to give the required clearance below could lead to enormously increased embankment costs on either side (Fig. 10.2(a)). Equally, if the railway was in a deep cutting in an urban area, the excavation and retaining walls to allow existing streets to cross over it could be expensive with an arch. Increasing the span of the arch was costly even if feasible (Fig. 10.2(b)). What was needed in these situations was a form of bridge with a minimum structural depth and a level soffit over the full span (Fig. 10.2(c)). This is where iron was crucial.

In 1830 the available structural forms were the arch bridge, the simple beam bridge or the suspension bridge, while materials were masonry, timber and cast iron. Where there was no conflict of level, arches in masonry or iron were ideal, even for spans well over 100ft, while timber, once strutted, was as restrictive as arched masonry. Where a slim level deck was needed cast-iron beams had just recently been proved feasible for railway loads, but only for spans below 30ft.

At first the suspension bridge must have seemed the answer for the longer railway spans with headroom problems. However, the first railway suspension bridge, built in 1829–30 by Capt. Sam Brown to carry an extension of the Stockton & Darlington Railway, was a failure. Stephenson reported:[4]

It was fearful when the engine went on it … I do not say that from having seen it myself, but I have heard it stated that when the engine and train went over the first time, there was a wave before the engine of something like 2 feet, just like a carpet.

The bridge had to be propped immediately and was soon replaced. Suspension bridges for railways have been damned in Britain ever since. Thus, where

---

4 *Report of the Commissioners Appointed to Inquire into the Use of Iron in Railway Structures* (subsequently referred to as 'Royal Commission'), 1849, p. 340, para. 936.

TYPE OF BRIDGE	FUNCTION	SITUATION	GIRDER OR ARCH SPAN (feet)	NOTES
Hodgkinson cast-iron beam or girder	Rail over farm or estate	Seven bridges mainly through new embankments	10-22	
Hodgkinson's research showed cast iron to be about six times as strong in compression as in tension. Thus bottom (tensile) flanges of girders larger as shown above. Spans were limited to about 30 feet in the mid 1830s	Rail over Road	Leighton Buzzard Wing Wolverton Rugby Denbigh Hall Stonebridge	16.25 21 3 x 20 24 30 24	Due to the severe skew this bridge became virtually a tunnel with a span at the limit for Hodgkinson beams
	Rail over canal	Wolverton Blisworth	31 30	
	Road over railway	Wriothesley Hampstead Road Park Street Harrow Road Kilburn Old Stratford	26 2 x 25 2 x 25 28 28 28	See Fig. 10.5 (one of several bridges with arched soffits to Hodgkinson beams)
Bowstring (tied arch)	Rail over canal	Regent's Canal Long Buckby	50 69.5	See Fig. 10.7 (a solution for longer spans with critical problems of headroom)
Composite tied girder	Road over railway	Lutterworth	64	See Fig. 10.8 (a simpler solution for longer spans and less critical headroom
Cast-iron arch	Rail over canal	Nash Mills Box Moor Seabrook Blisworth	66 66 66 66	See Fig. 10.4 (a true arch solution where there was ample headroom)
Opening (sliding)	Rail over branch canal	Weedon	8	

10.3 Iron bridges on the London & Birmingham Railway

a slim level deck was essential, Stephenson had nothing to start from but the improved form of the cast-iron beam developed by Hodgkinson, and then only for limited spans. New thinking was vital.

The London & Birmingham Railway

About thirty bridges were built in iron on the London & Birmingham Railway,[5] little more than one-tenth of the total number of crossings, the rest being masonry arches. The majority of the iron bridges (Fig. 10.3) were based on cast-iron beams of the Hodgkinson type but there were also some tall elegant arch bridges in cast iron where the railway crossed and re-crossed the Grand Junction Canal at angles so skew as to be scarcely conceivable in masonry, quite apart from the difficulty of building in masonry over a working canal (Fig. 10.4). In addition to these beam and arch bridges, two important new forms in iron were introduced, together with a small iron sliding bridge carrying the tracks over a branch of the Grand Junction Canal

5 Information largely from Returns and Plans of Iron Bridges, 1847, **PRO**, MT8/1 and 2.

10.4 Nash Mill
Bridge over the
Grand Junction
Canal
(J. C. Bourne,
1839)

to the Government Ordnance Depot near Weedon.[6] This could well be claimed as the first movable railway bridge in the world.

There was a pronounced emphasis on appearance in the design of these structures, something that was lost in later iron railway bridges. This was especially noticeable on those in prominent positions, such as the Hampstead Road and Park Street bridges over the cutting north of Euston Station. Here the beams were formed into the shape of shallow arches, but they were still beams of the Hodgkinson type, deeper in section at mid-span and with end fixings clearly not intended to take any arch thrust (Fig. 10.5).[7] The false arch form was further emphasized on the fascia beams. The architectural emphasis reached a climax with an elaborate Jacobean treatment in masonry of an iron girder bridge carrying the railway over a road in Rugby (Fig. 10.6). Reputedly this was designed by Stephenson personally and built with a contribution of £1000 from Rugby school towards its embellishment.[8]

The two new bridge forms on this railway were the one carrying the tracks over the Regent's Canal and the Lutterworth Bridge near Rugby. They merit some description in their own right because of their possible influence on later structural thinking. The need for a slim bridge was particularly critical when carrying the railway over the Regents Canal. Not only did the canal company require a span of 50 feet with full clearance over this length, but at the same time, to suit local conditions, the rail tracks needed to be as low as possible. The span was well beyond that then thought feasible with cast-iron beams, and clearly something wholly new was needed.

6 Capt. Jebb, 'Description of a drawbridge on the London and Birmingham Railway at Weedon', *Papers on subjects connected with the duties of the Corps of Royal Engineers*, vol. III, 1839.

7 Simms (1838), Plate 8.

8 Bourne, p. 24.

10.5 Park Street Bridge, north of Euston Station, showing arch-shaped Hodgkinson beams (F. W. Simms, 1838)

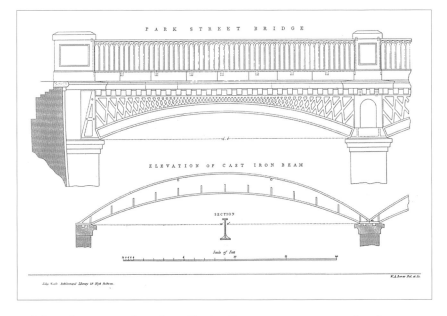

The solution, attributed to Charles Fox, was to use pairs of tied cast-iron arches spanning over the canal, with the bridge deck hung from the arches rather than supported on top of them (Fig. 10.7).[9] Thus the critical depth of the construction depended on the clear distance of only 24ft between the arches rather than that of the arch span, which, with this form, could be almost unlimited. The arch ribs, wholly in compression like the voussoirs of a masonry arch, could be cast in convenient lengths, while joints in the tie rods could easily be forged. The absence of any horizontal thrust on the foundations was a further advantage of the tied arch.

The idea of wrought-iron tie rods as auxiliaries to cast-iron beams was not new, but here the rods and the arch ribs each performed a primary function appropriate to its properties; that is, with the cast iron acting wholly in compression and the wrought iron in tension. This was an elegant and creative response to a new problem.

In today's parlance this was a bowstring girder bridge, but in the literature of the time when it was built, it was more likely to have been called a suspension bridge. The structural idea can be traced back at least to Verantius in the seventeenth century,[10] but the way in which it was used on the London & Birmingham Railway may well have been thought up from scratch.[11] A similar railway bridge, though with the greater span of 69ft, was built where the London & Birmingham Railway crossed over the Grand Junction Canal at Long Buckby Wharf.

9 Whishaw (1840), p. 225. Also plates in Simms (1838) say 'C. Fox direxit' bottom left.
10 Faustus Verantius, *Machinae Novae,* Venice, c.1616.
11 The arched iron aqueducts such as the Almond Feeder to the Scottish Union Canal (1820–1821) and the later Stanley Ferry Aqueduct were not bowstrings but designed as arches thrusting against abutments with the trough suspended. A small true iron bowstring of 1820 has been attributed to Ralph Dodd.

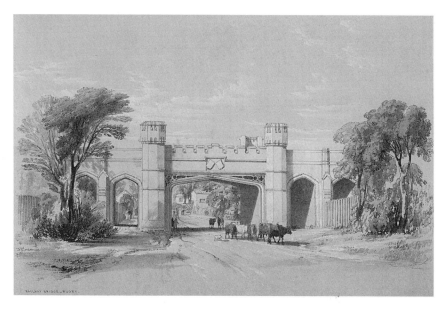

10.6 'Jacobean' iron bridge at Rugby (J. C. Bourne, 1839)

The other unusual iron bridge on the London & Birmingham Railway was the Lutterworth Bridge (Fig. 10.8), carrying the road from Banbury to Lutterworth at a skew angle of 30°. This bridge, again depending on wrought-iron ties with cast-iron ribs, was similar in its action to the bowstring girder but different in form. Outwardly it consisted of simple cast-iron girders spanning the then seemingly impossible skew distance of 64ft. However, these were not simple castings but composite structures closer in action to trusses or tied arches. The 'beams', like something escaped from a beam engine, each consisted of cast-iron ribs bowed upwards and the wrought-iron ties sagging an equal amount downwards, the two being kept apart by pierced cast-iron web plates. Even if curious to look at, these structures made good engineering sense.

Alas, all the original iron bridges on the London & Birmingham Railway have either been replaced or encased in concrete.

The next generation of cast iron bridges

The lessons of the London & Birmingham Railway were applied to subsequent lines. The Hodgkinson iron beam – within its span limits – became almost universal where masonry arches were not practicable. The span limit continued to creep upwards, reaching about 40ft by the mid-1840s.[12] Also, instead of a single beam under each rail, the later beams tended to be in pairs bolted together with the rail mounted on a timber block between them.

Fox's bowstring girders could meet virtually any situation where a longer span with a slender deck was needed; for example, on the Manchester and Leeds Railway, with spans of up to 102ft.[13] They reached their climax on the

12 Op. cit. (n. 4), p. 266.
13 Rennison (1980/1), pp. 192–3.

10.7 Bowstring
girder bridge
over the Regent's
Canal
(J. C. Bourne,
1839)

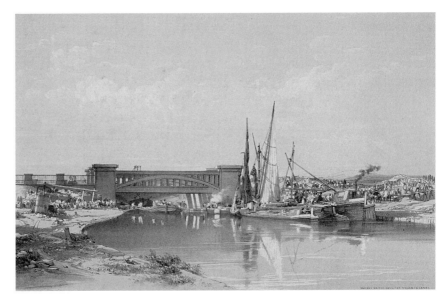

Newcastle High Level Bridge. Although there was no new principle in the
structural form of this bridge, since it followed Charles Fox's thinking of more
than ten years earlier, it was on a vastly greater scale than heretofore. Its six
spans, each of 124ft clear, carried the railway 100ft above the river Tyne.

For lateral stability the earlier bowstring bridges had two arch ribs braced
together on each side of the tracks, with the bridge deck suspended from the
centre of the bracing. At Newcastle, with the three tracks on top of the arch
ribs, there was no problem with lateral stability and there was also space for a
twenty-foot road and two footways, all suspended below (Plate 15).[14] The
whole design has a pleasing air of logic and thoughtfulness, but who designed
it – Robert Stephenson or Thomas Harrison?

In October 1845 the directors of the Newcastle & Berwick and the Newcastle
& Darlington Junction Railways resolved that 'T E Harrison Esq. be requested to
prepare the plans for all the Bridges, including those across the Tyne and the
Tweed.'[15] However, Harrison wrote in April 1846 that 'The plans [for the High
Level Bridge] have been prepared under my direction: the designs are *not mine*,
but my friend *Mr Robert Stephenson's.*'[16] Stephenson, however, stated 'beyond
drawing the outline (he) ... had no right to claim any credit for the works ...
upon Mr Harrison the whole responsibility for their erection lies ....'[17]

Finally Stephenson was engineer-in-chief, Harrison was the principal engineer, with Robert Hodgson as resident engineer for the bridge. There is
evidence that Stephenson was much more than a titular head, however.
Perhaps because of the size of the bridge, he insisted on the ironwork
contractor, Hawks Crawshay, providing samples for tests of the iron they

14 Ibid., pp. 193–207.
15 Ibid., p. 190.
16 Letter written by Thomas Harrison, 24 April 1846, and printed in *Gateshead Observer*, 3 August 1850,
    p. 6. See Rennison (1980/81), p. 202, and Addyman and Fawcett, p.47.
17 *Newcastle Journal*, 3 August 1850, See Rennison (1980/1), p. 202, and Addyman and Fawcett, p. 47.

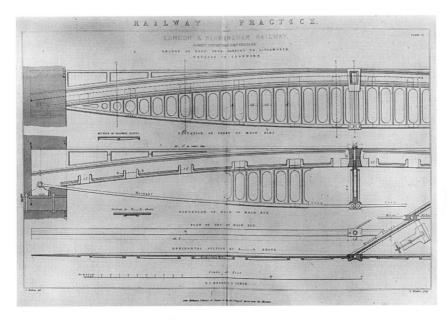

10.8
Lutterworth
Bridge
(S. C. Brees,
1839)

proposed using.[18] From the results of these tests, completed in February
1847, Stephenson was able to prescribe a cocktail of irons for the cast-iron
ribs. Later, when construction got under way, all castings were proof-tested
and so were the wrought iron ties. Once complete, each span was load-tested
with 700 tons.[19] Much of this was done after the failure of the Dee Bridge,
but whether planned before or not is uncertain.

The High Level Bridge was completed in June 1849 and opened by Queen
Victoria in the following September. Unlike most of the early iron bridges it
survives triumphantly today, although discreetly strengthened.

The trussed compound girder bridge

William Pole pointed out that bowstring girders, such as Fox's, were 'expensive and cumbrous'.[20] What everyone wanted was longer Hodgkinson cast-
iron beams, but the span was limited by difficulties in making large castings
and transporting them. Peter W. Barlow suggested the use of beams in
sections bolted together with special clamps to ensure the continuity of the
tensile flanges at the joints.[21] He seemed confident of their use for spans greater
than 50ft, but Stephenson does not appear to have used them.

The apparently ideal solution for spans beyond the limit of the simple cast-iron
beam emerged around 1840 and flourished, particularly within Stephenson's
circle. It consisted of iron beams each cast in two or three lengths and bolted

18 Ibid., p. 49 and Appendix 2(b).
19 Ibid., p. 55.
20 Jeaffreson, II, p. 47.
21 Op. cit. (n. 4), P. W. Barlow evidence, p. 309, and Appendix 1, Plate 7, South Eastern Railway,
    Ashford, Rye and Hastings Branch.

together, but now with tie rods of wrought iron on each side. In the Lutterworth Bridge the actions of the cast iron in compression and the wrought iron in tension were quite separate. In this new form of girder, the cast iron, although made in sections and jointed, was still seen as acting like a beam in bending but with the trussing 'helping' and thus perhaps calming any fears about the strength of the joints in the iron beams. To some extent these ties could be likened to the chains of a suspension bridge holding up the central part of the girder.

The ties needed to be anchored at the ends of the bridge, and clearly the higher the anchorages the steeper the slope of the ties and the greater the support to the girders. The most convenient place to anchor the ties was to the tops of the actual girders, but that would limit their slope. However, by increasing the depths of the girders at their ends, the slope of the ties could be made appreciably greater at very little cost. The resulting trussed girder also had the depth increased at the junction of the castings to give greater strength, as well as more space for bolts (Fig. 10.9).

In many ways the idea looked immensely attractive. Compared with the bowstring girder it was very simple and, with two support systems in parallel, the bridge must surely be safer than with simple jointed cast-iron beams? It seems that not much thought was given to what exactly happened to the tension in the tie rods at their anchor points above the tops of the beams. The presence of the trussing gave engineers the confidence to use jointed cast-iron beams for spans of 60, 70 and even 100ft. Furthermore, with the raised ends to the ties, the castings would not need to be deeper than for spans of about 40 to 50ft.

To the railway engineer these 'trussed compound' girders were an absolute blessing. Used in pairs, one on each side of a track, they fulfilled the function of Fox's bowstring girders much more simply and cheaply. Moreover, with the load carried on the bottom flanges of the beams the effective thickness of the bridge was reduced to an absolute minimum.

It is not certain who thought up the idea of these trussed girders. William Pole attributed the first use of these beams to George Bidder, saying:[22]

The first trussed compound girder, of 60 feet span, was erected by Mr Bidder, in conjunction with Mr Stephenson, for carrying the Cambridge Branch of the Great Eastern Railway (then called the Northern and Eastern) over the river Lea near Tottenham [Plate 16]: others followed on the same and other lines, one of the best known being that over the Minories, on the Blackwall Railway.

Bidder himself said in April 1847, just a month before these girders were discredited following the collapse of the Dee Bridge, that he had 'proved the system of tension rods in one of the first bridges on this principle', going on to refer to the Lea and Minories bridges.[23]

In the same discussion Charles Vignoles said he had used such girders in 1831 for bridges of 45ft span on the North Union Railway over canals in Lancashire. In several details this statement is at variance with other records of

22 Jeaffreson, II, p. 48.
23 *Proc. ICE*, **VI**, p. 220, 20 April 1847.

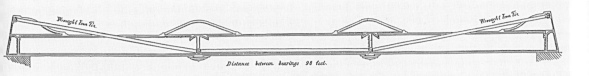

the iron bridges on the North Union, and it looks like a loose claim for credit, which Vignoles may have had reason to keep quiet about later.[24] As a means of adding to the security of cast-iron beams he used round bars, which may well have been straight and fixed near bottom flanges of his beams, a technique which had been used elsewhere without the concept of trussing. On balance it seems more likely that the idea of the trussed compound girder came from Bidder or one of his colleagues around 1840 than from Vignoles in 1831.

Large numbers of these trussed compound girder bridges were made in the 1840s, generally with spans of 50 to 70 feet.[25] Stephenson and his associates were the dominant users. Amongst other examples, there were two on the Northern & Eastern Railway, four on the York & Newcastle, several on the York & North Midland, one of three spans replacing the inadequate suspension bridge on the extension of the Stockton & Darlington Railway, and six on the Trent Valley Railway. However, the greatest of all was over the river Dee on the Chester & Holyhead Railway. Stephenson was also working on three such bridges of almost the same span as the Dee Bridge for the Leopold Railway between Florence and Leghorn. Other engineers employing this form of girder included John Hawkshaw, W. H. Barlow and John Fowler. The use of such bridges was increasing up until the collapse of the Dee Bridge on 24 May 1847.

10.9 The ultimate development of the trussed compound girder as used over the river Dee (Board of Trade report)

The collapse of the Dee Bridge and the inquest

The Chester & Holyhead Railway crossed the river Dee at a considerable skew, and the first form of bridge considered had five oblique arches in masonry. Because of foundation difficulties this was changed to three sets of trussed compound girders, each with a span of 98ft, unprecedented for this type of structure. At the time of the collapse the bridge was only being used, under agreement, by the Shrewsbury & Chester Railway and for construction traffic on the Chester & Holyhead line. It was unfortunate that it was a Shrewsbury & Chester train that was on the bridge when it crashed. This inevitably resulted in a fierce battle at the inquest between the engineers to the two railways.

24 Returns & Plans of Iron Bridges, **PRO**, MT8/1 and 2 records four iron bridges on the North Union line, one arched spanning 50ft and the other three beam bridges spanning 26 to 32ft; only one of the beam bridges being over a branch canal, the other two being over roads in Wigan. Tie rods of 1.75 to 2.2 inches diameter are mentioned, but not their shape. Regrettably no drawings of these have come to light.
25 Paul Sibly, 'The Prediction of Structural Failures', PhD thesis, University College, London, 1977.

10.10 Dee
Bridge disaster,
24 May 1847
(*Illustrated
London News*)

THE LATE RAILWAY ACCIDENT, AT CHESTER.

SCENE OF THE LATE RAILWAY ACCIDENT, AT CHESTER.—DILAPIDATED SPAN OF THE DEE BRIDGE.

The question first debated was whether the derailment of the train broke the girder or whether the girder simply collapsed under the weight of the train. Curiously, the heaviest part of the train, the engine, survived. It was reported that the driver, feeling the bridge sinking, opened up the steam and just got clear before the coupling broke and the tender and carriages fell into the river with the loss of five lives (Fig. 10.10).[26]

The accident caused a major sensation, with far wider implications than those immediately involved. Not only was the trussed compound girder discredited but, in the eyes of the public, so were all iron bridges. Furthermore the almost god-like image of the great railway engineers was badly tarnished.

In his report to the directors of the Chester & Holyhead Railway, made a week later, Stephenson maintained that the collapse must have been due to a derailment, arguing this from damage to the masonry of the abutment and to the tender. He repeated his conviction at the inquest in early June 1847, prefacing his evidence with a statement of his position: 'I am principal engineer of the Chester and Holyhead Railway Company; I approved of the design of this bridge, which was made by other parties in detail'.

Much to his credit, and perhaps wisely, Stephenson did not bring any of his staff or associates into the proceedings but faced the court wholly on his own, although, as reports indicated, not without considerable signs of distress. His rival railway engineers, Joseph Locke and Charles Vignoles, supported him in his opinion that the collapse was due to a lateral blow following derailment, as did Thomas Gooch, then working with him on the Trent Valley Line.

26 Report by Capt. Simmons on the fatal accident on 24 May 1847, by the falling of the Dee Bridge.

Against this powerful group, Henry Robertson, the engineer to the Shrewsbury & Chester Railway, maintained that the broken girder failed under load due to its weakness. The report by James Walker and Capt. Simmons to the Commissioners of Railways concluded that the bridge would have been adequate if the trussing and the cast-iron beam had acted together but that this joint action was difficult to achieve and should not be relied on. They added that neither was adequate on its own.

One factor supporting the argument for a failure under vertical load was a layer of broken stone over the timber deck of the bridge to protect it from fire from the engines.[27] The collapse was under the first train to cross after this layer had been laid.

Gen. Pasley, who as Inspector General to the Board of Trade had passed the bridge as safe in October 1846, now stated that he was opposed to this form of iron trussing and virtually admitted that he had approved the bridge because of the number of apparently successful ones already built. This may explain why he as well as Stephenson appeared so agitated at the inquest.[28] However, what Pasley went on to say was much nearer to sense than anything from those who advocated the trussing. Amongst his other remarks about the form of the bridge Pasley said: 'I consider that the tension bars are of very little use; indeed the tension bars are connected with the girder alone forming part of it and have no independent support.'

Here he was approaching the nub of the problem. The structure was like a suspension bridge without back stays. Pasley finally came out with the opinion that the girder broke due to the weight of the train and the added stone. This view became increasingly clear as the inquest continued. Although manslaughter had been considered, the jury finally brought in a verdict of accidental death on the victims. They added their opinion that the strength of the broken girder was 'insufficient to bear the pressure of quick trains passing over it and that the eleven remaining girders were equally dangerous', further adding that

… no girder bridge of so brittle and treacherous a material as cast iron alone, even though trussed with wrought iron rods is safe for quick or passenger trains and we have it in evidence before us that there are upwards of one hundred bridges[29] similar in principle or form to the late one over the river Dee, either in use or in course of being constructed on various lines of railway. We consider these unsafe more or less in proportion to the span; still all unsafe

The jury went on to recommend an inquiry into 'the merits or demerits of these bridges' and to establish their safety in the future. It was inevitable that some broader investigation would follow.

27 Report to the Commissioners of Railways by Mr. Walker and Capt. Simmons R.E. on the fatal accident on the 24 day of May 1847, by the falling of the Bridge over the river Dee, on the Chester and Holyhead Railway.
28 Conder (1868), p. 144.
29 Possibly an exaggeration. Sibly and Walker (1977), p. 192, say 'about 60 structures'.

In August 1847, just three months after the collapse, a Royal Commission was set up:[30]

To inquire into the conditions to be observed by engineers in the application of iron to structures exposed to violent concussion and vibrations and … it shall endeavour to ascertain such principles and form such rules as may enable the Engineer and Mechanic, in their respective spheres, to apply the metal with confidence …

Stephenson was much opposed to imposing rules – as were others, including Brunel – and, to the relief of the engineering profession, the commissioners did not lay down any specific criteria governing the building of iron bridges but made some useful suggestions, and in 1849 published the results of all the research they had initiated or collected.[31]

Historically the great value of the commission's report lies in the verbatim replies given by some of the most distinguished engineers of the time to searching questions put by the commissioners. Those consulted included Stephenson, Brunel, Locke, Fairbairn, Rastrick, Fox, Gooch, Hawkshaw and both P. W. and W. H. Barlow together with prominent contractors. Stephenson's replies show a deep involvement in the technicalities of iron bridges and must dispel any idea that he was so busy as a planner and construction manager that he had neither the time nor the temperament for the detailed technology of his railways.

The point missed on the Dee Bridge, and on its predecessors, was that with ties of this type any upward bending of the beam due to tension in the ties would be counteracted and nearly cancelled by the horizontal pull on the end fixings, which would bend the beam downwards. Although an oversimplification, it is hard to avoid the conclusion that the strength of these compound girders effectively depended on the strength of the cast iron alone, with the trussing adding little, except a false sense of confidence. One might ask why the earlier trussed compound girder bridges apparently worked so well. Perhaps engineers increasingly relied on the ties, as the beams became ever more slender and the spans greater. Whatever the thinking, the crunch came with the Dee Bridge.

There were so many unfortunate features of the Dee Bridge that it is not possible to say with certainty which one, or which combination, was fatal. Not only were the spans greater than any previous bridges of this type, but the girders were notably slender and highly stressed in bending as well as subject to twisting due to the eccentric application of the load. The addition of the protective layer of stone, increasing the static load by about 25 per cent, was probably the last straw.

The one witness who was actually looking at the bridge when it failed said in evidence at the inquest that he observed a crack opening up in the middle of the girder when the engine and tender were at about the middle of it. He was

30 Op. cit. (n. 4), p. vii.
31 Ibid., Stephenson on rules, p. 339, Clauses 925–9.

certain that the crack opened from the bottom.[32] This points to a simple failure in bending.

Without the collapse of the Dee Bridge, how long would it have taken for the fallacy of the trussed compound girder to emerge, and how many more such bridges would have been built? It is hard to believe that a similar disaster would not have happened somewhere else. Did the collapse of the Dee Bridge prevent something worse? If one of the bridges on the Florence to Leghorn railway had collapsed with a large loss of life, the international implications could have been horrendous.

Today it is easy to see the primary fault in the concept and to realize that the Dee Bridge was more vulnerable than most, if not all, of its predecessors. However, until there is a failure, misconceptions can all too readily be repeated on an increasing scale, the designer in each case relying largely on the success of the previous examples. Stephenson, Bidder and others must have derived comfort from the apparent strengthening effect of screwing up the ties without looking deeply enough into what was happening.

Although at the inquest Pasley was one of the first to acknowledge the faulty thinking, Stephenson himself, in evidence to the Royal Commission, admitted to 'a certain degree of oversight', saying in relation to the action of the ties on the beam, 'The fulcrum was below the line of thrust and increased the tension of the bottom and correspondingly increased the compression of the top by adding to it'. It is not clear how soon he realized this or who enlightened him.

It would be wrong to blame a single individual for the misconception over the behaviour of these girders. This was a case of group myopia suffered by a large tranche of the most distinguished engineers of the day. There is an interesting near-parallel to this mass blindness in the 1960s when multi-storey housing schemes based on large panels of precast concrete were introduced into Britain. The engineering profession accepted the apparent benefits and used these systems on an increasingly wide and daring scale, assuming, without too much thought, that they had been fully proved in France, Denmark and elsewhere. It was only after the dramatic failure at Ronan Point that engineers woke up to the unsound nature of the whole concept and the way in which it was being extended.

Action following the Dee Bridge failure

After the collapse of the Dee Bridge some decisive action was vital. All trussed compound girder bridges had become suspect, but it would have been unthinkable to close every railway route depending on these, awaiting the results of a long investigation. Action was fast. All the spans of the Dee Bridge were propped with timber, as doubtless were those on other compound trussed girder bridges which could not be justified as simple beams without

---

32 Thomas Jones's evidence at the Adjourned Coroner's Inquest, *Chester Chronicle*, 18 June 1847.

ties. Stephenson and his associates also worked quickly to find a long-term solution.

Instead of abandoning the suspect girders completely, it was decided to bolt extra castings on top of them, roughly doubling their structural depth, and at the same time to lower the ends of the tie rods to a level well within this increased depth. The man who saw most clearly what to do appears to have been Charles Heard Wild, a clever young engineer working for Stephenson. Wild certainly tested the efficacy of this remedial work and, at Stephenson's request, explained this and his tests to the Royal Commission, emphasizing the need to put a positive tension in the ties because 'applied in a neutral state they are of very little practical use.'[33] His figure was five tons per square inch applied tension.

The full remedial work on the Dee Bridge and the development of Stephenson's bridges for the Leopold Railway were going on closely in parallel, but it is not known exactly how far construction had gone when the Dee Bridge failed.[34] However, from the evidence to the Royal Commission it is almost certain that the girders for the bridges over the rivers Ombrone and Bisenzio were intended to be virtually identical to those over the Dee, but two feet shorter. Stephenson modified their designs in response to the Dee Bridge failure. The Royal Commission Report showed the final form of these two Italian bridges (Fig. 10.11). Referring to this figure, Stephenson said in evidence in March 1848:[35]

This shows the mode in which the girders on the Dee Bridge plan have been repaired by introducing three upper castings, corresponding in some measure with the lower ones; in fact it is a substitution of a continuous series of castings instead of local extensions.

He was making it clear that this was a remedial scheme using existing castings, whether the bridges had been fully erected or not.

The bridge for crossing the river Arno, also on the Leopold Railway, was an even more sophisticated design comprising trussed compound girders with full-depth segmental castings and tensioned bars fixed horizontally below.[36] This whole design probably dates from after the Dee Bridge collapse.

By this time the trussed compound girder was beginning to make good sense. What is more, Wild (assuming it was all his idea) had hit on and was using the important principle of prestressing, which then seems to have lain dormant until it was 'invented' by Freyssinet in relation to concrete in the 1920s.[37]

---

33 Op. cit. (n. 4), pp. 348–50, Clauses 1075–1116.

34 The early records of the Leopold Railway appear to have been lost in a fire in the Florence archives during the 1939–1945 war. Personal letter from Vittorio Nascè of Politecnico di Torino to the author, 30 April 1985.

35 Op. cit. (n. 4), p. 345, Clause 1039 and drawing, Appendix 4, No. 3.

36 Op. cit. (n. 4), p. 345, Clause 1041 and drawing, Appendix 4, No. 2.

37 Eugene Freyssinet, 'The Birth of Prestressing', translated for the Cement and Concrete Association from Travaux, 1954.

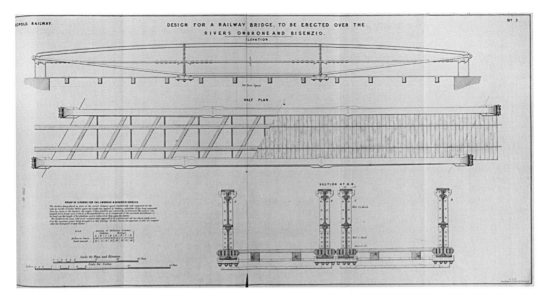

10.11 Bridge
design for
crossing the
rivers Ombrone
and Bisenzio;
also showing
the proposal for
strengthening the
Dee Bridge
girders
(Report on
Application of
Iron to Railway
Structures)

The bridges for the Leopold Railway were the last trussed compound girders to be designed. Even though by 1848 engineers understood how to make them logical and safe, this form of girder was totally discredited, along with its main material, cast iron. Trussed compound girders were no longer needed, however, as in parallel with their final flowering in the second half of the 1840s, another structural form, the tubular girder, was being developed for longer-span bridges, this time all in riveted wrought iron without the stigma of brittleness associated with cast iron. Stephenson and his team were again at the centre of this new development.

The wrought-iron bridge era: 1845 to Stephenson's death in 1859

Rolled wrought-iron plate was commercially available from the mid-eighteenth century and from the 1770s was used for making steam boilers, from the 1780s for canal boats and then in the early nineteenth century for seagoing ships, the plates in each case being formed into thin-shell structures by riveting. The introduction of rolled angle and 'T' sections, following Henry Cort's invention of grooved rollers, patented in 1783, made it possible to stiffen flat iron plates and ultimately to build up heavy structural sections in wrought iron.

There was a real advantage in using stiffened wrought-iron plate for ships and it was in shipbuilding that the technique of bending and riveting the material was developed, mainly in the 1830s. William Fairbairn became one of the principal exponents of iron shipbuilding, and his *Lord Dundas* canal boat of 1831 has been suggested as the first vessel to incorporate angles and 'T' sections with flat plate.

There was much less incentive to introduce riveted wrought iron into bridges and industrial buildings. On dry land cast iron, scarcely suitable for ships' hulls, satisfied virtually all the structural needs that were not already met with timber and masonry. Also, cast iron was less expensive than wrought iron. There were some experiments with riveted wrought iron for bridges in the early 1840s, such as that built over the Pollock & Govan Railway, a 30ft span just on the limit of cast iron at that time.[38] Also Stephenson said that he had made a design for a cellular bridge deck in wrought iron in the same year for the Northern & Eastern Railway.[39] In 1845 riveted wrought iron came into its own for land-based structures when it met the unprecedented demands of the Britannia and Conway Tubular Bridges.

The design of the Britannia and Conway bridges

The route to Holyhead posed major problems in getting the railway across the river Conway and over the Menai Straits to Anglesey. The act for the Chester & Holyhead Railway was passed in July 1844 and it was then up to Robert Stephenson as engineer-in-chief to work out how to make these crossings. The 400- to 500-ft clear spans needed were overwhelming by the railway standards of the time, even with a pier founded on the Britannia Rock in the middle of the Straits. With suspension bridges dismissed as unsuitable for railways, cast-iron arches were then considered, even though the spans would have been well beyond that of any existing cast-iron bridge.

At this point the Admiralty intervened, insisting on a headroom of 105ft over a minimum 450ft span for the passage of sailing ships at the Britannia crossing.[40] This demand for the full-width headroom was similar to that made at the canal crossings on the London & Birmingham Railway, but on ten times the scale. At this stage the outlook must have looked bleak for Stephenson. He was committed to taking trains to Holyhead but there was no proven means of doing so.

Stephenson next considered a solid wrought-iron tube, or possibly a stiff lattice cage, big enough for a train to pass through, to be built with the aid of suspension chains, originally thought necessary for auxiliary support (Fig. 10.12). It seems that the idea of a solid-walled tube soon took over from the lattice cage. Even if the tube could not be made strong enough to span on its own, it could be certainly be made stiff enough to avoid the severe deflections found with the railway suspension bridge at Stockton.

Shipbuilding had clearly shown the way of building the tubes. William Fairbairn (Fig. 10.14) was one of the main proponents of riveted wrought iron and, although Manchester-based, he had set up a shipyard in 1835 on the Thames at Millwall. What better person to consult about riveted iron? In April 1845 Stephenson consulted Fairbairn, who was enthusiastic and quickly became part of Stephenson's team.[41]

---

38 Dempsey (1850b), pp. 44–5.
39 Clark (1850), p. 25, and not built as such; probably just a sketch remembered later.
40 Clark (1850), I, plate opposite p. 80.
41 W. Fairbairn, p. 2.

10.12 Britannia Bridge with auxiliary chains as first proposed (Elton collection, Ironbridge Gorge Museum Trust)

The first task was to prove the feasibility of the tubes as beams, if only as chain-assisted ones. To Fairbairn's mind this meant model tests. In agreement with Stephenson he had wrought-iron tubes of circular, elliptical and finally rectangular section made in his shipyard at Millwall, and the testing of these started in July 1845. The next task was to find a 'formula' to relate such tests to the behaviour of the full-sized tubes. For this, Eaton Hodgkinson was brought into the team in August 1845, and he first visited Fairbairn on 19 September to see and discuss these tests. On the following day Fairbairn sent Stephenson sketches of tubes with cellular tops to resist crushing.[42] Whether this was Fairbairn's idea or whether it derived from his discussions with Hodgkinson is not clear.

Thus Stephenson, then only 42, but already with a wealth of general railway experience, was teamed with two older men, one the leading practical exponent of wrought iron and the other a much-respected theorist and experimenter in iron. In addition there was a fourth key man, then still in the background, but destined to play an increasingly important part. This was Edwin Clark, Stephenson's able and faithful resident engineer on these bridges, whose role far exceeded that which his title implies. It would be difficult to imagine another group better qualified to achieve the seemingly impossible. The time chart (Fig. 10.13) outlines the development of the design of the tubes and the course of construction of the bridges, but gives no idea of the scale of the physical and personal problems involved.

On 9 February 1846, seven months after the start of tests for the tubes, Stephenson, Fairbairn and Hodgkinson made separate reports to the directors of the Chester & Holyhead Railway.[43] Fairbairn's report was dominated by tables of the results of his tests and exuded confidence in the proposed bridge. Hodgkinson gave formulae, together with the results of further tests on tubes, which he had carried out that January and which showed greater strengths

42 W. Fairbairn, pp. 15–17. Original letters in **ICE**.
43 Clark (1850), pp. 135–54.

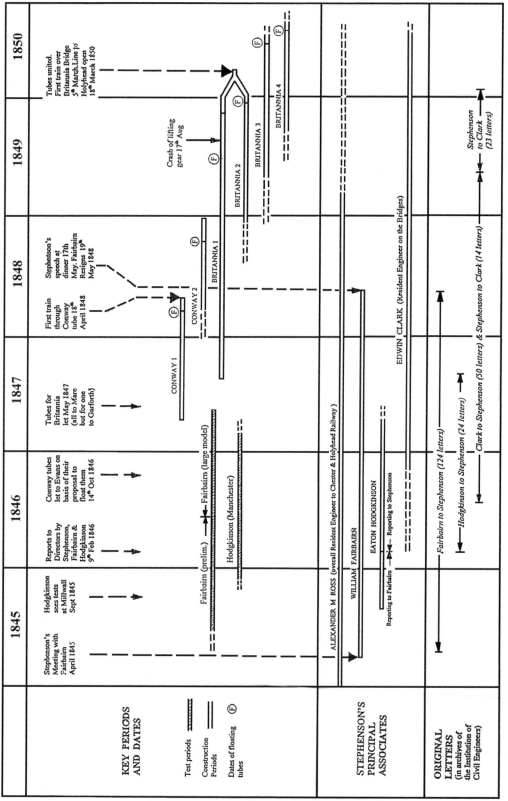

10.13 Time chart of the design and construction of the Conway and Britannia bridges

10.14 Portrait of William Fairbairn
(1789–1874)
(W. Fairbairn, 1877)

than the equivalents by Fairbairn. Even if these technical reports were bewildering to the directors, Stephenson's own report was a masterpiece of clarity, confidence and diplomacy. Of the three shapes considered for the tubes, the rectangular one was most favourably received. However it was clear that more tests were needed.

A dominant issue in the reports was whether it would be necessary to keep the chains as part of the permanent bridge. Fairbairn, possibly because he had an image of how well iron ships behaved, was strongly against their retention. Stephenson appeared to be open-minded on this, saying that if chains proved necessary they must be attached in such as way 'as to preclude the possibility of the smallest oscillations.' Memories of the failure of the suspension bridge at Stockton, although in no way Stephenson's problem, must have been strong. Eaton Hodgkinson, the cautious academic, ended his report by saying 'I would beg to recommend that suspension chains are employed as an auxiliary, otherwise great thickness of metal would be required to produce adequate stiffness and strength.'

The reports were read out at a meeting of the Board and the result is well summed up in the following letter written by Fairbairn to Hodgkinson three days after the meeting:[44]

My dear Sir,   Ipswich, Feb 12 1846

This is the first moment I have had to spare since the meeting of the Chester and Holyhead Railway – Mr Stephenson on that occasion exhibited a very beautiful design of the proposed bridge and after the different reports were read, it was ultimately resolved to build the Bridge.

It was further resolved that we should continue the experiments until all ambiguities were cleared up and that another tube of larger dimensions –about 1/6 the size of the Bridge – should be made as near the proportions as possible or as you and myself may decide.

44 Letter in private collection.

From this you will observe that we are all committed either with or without chains in the construction. On my return I will tell you more about it and remain in the meantime

Yours [illegible]

W Fairbairn

The letter records both the go-ahead from the Board and illustrates the degree of cordiality between Fairbairn and Hodgkinson. This was not to last.

The development of the design

Some years earlier Hodgkinson had established that cast iron was six times as strong in compression as in tension so it was surprising that the preliminary tests showed that the reverse appeared to be the case with wrought iron. Many of the tubes tested, the rectangular ones in particular, failed in compression at the top of their sections well before the expected tensile strength of the material was reached at the bottom. In the words of Stephenson's report to the Board: 'the power of wrought iron to resist compression was much less than its power to resist tension.' There was an error in the thinking here but an understandable one. The real problem was not the basic properties of wrought iron, but the buckling of thin plates of any material under compression. With the chunky cast-iron sections that engineers were used to, this had not previously been a problem.

In March 1846, just a month after the presentation to the Board, signs of strain between Fairbairn and Hodgkinson began to emerge. Until then Hodgkinson had communicated solely with Fairbairn, who had introduced him to the project, but he was increasingly unhappy about his position and clearly resented the fact that he had not been controlling the tests from the beginning. In a long letter to Stephenson, Hodgkinson expressed his concern about some of the opinions in Stephenson's report to the Board. He saw these as an interpretation of Fairbairn's opinions and indirectly, but not necessarily correctly, of his own. He thought that Fairbairn's tests at Millwall only 'furnished valuable introductory information', which might be proved wrong later. Hodgkinson then explained that he was not sure that, as stated by Stephenson, the form of the tube and the distribution of the metal had been finally determined. He wanted more tests, adding for emphasis that the rectangular form had not yet been indisputably shown to be the best, although he thought so for his own reasons.[45]

The correspondence is not complete, but much of it is reproduced in Fairbairn's book[46] and there are other letters in the Institution of Civil Engineers. Hodgkinson became quite emotional in statements like: 'I do not wish to

---

45 Letter, 10 March 1846, **ICE**, ECLB/94, and W. Fairbairn, pp. 55–7.
46 W. Fairbairn, pp. 1–169.

exclude Mr Fairbairn, except from taking the lead in those matters which his want of education and experience render him utterly incapable of.'[47]

Stephenson remained calm and wrote to Fairbairn saying:[48]

Mr Hodgkinson is getting nervous and has forwarded me some strictures upon what has already been done. I have this day written to him, giving him an unqualified assent to his undertaking any reasonable series of experiments that he may deem advisable for clearing his mind … he appears to wish to have them under his control. I am sure that you have no objection to this: I have none whatever.

Writing to Hodgkinson at the same time Stephenson said:[49]

I trust … that you will consider the scientific and experimental investigation under your own control, as I am far from wishing you to act as second either to Mr Fairbairn or myself in this department of the enquiry.

It is not certain whether, at this stage, Stephenson was just humouring Hodgkinson or whether he saw a major technical problem or a real difficulty with Fairbairn. Whatever his thoughts, one must admire his diplomacy. The upshot, as Fairbairn noted in his book, perhaps a little bitterly, was that 'from this time to the completion of the first Conway tube, there was no communication of the slightest importance made to me relative to Mr Hodgkinson's proceedings'.

Fairbairn may have feared that his authority was slipping. Hodgkinson, the academic he had recommended to Stephenson just to provide a 'formula', was now starting to control too much of the action. Responsibilities needed to be defined. For Fairbairn this was done, although at whose instigation is uncertain, at a board meeting on 13 May 1846 when, amongst other things, it was resolved that Fairbairn was to 'superintend the construction and erection of the Conway and Britannia Bridges in conjunction with Mr Stephenson' and 'with Mr Stephenson to appoint such persons as are necessary, subject to the powers of their dismissal by the Directors.' Fairbairn was also empowered to certify payments to contractors. There is no mention of design here. It seems that Fairbairn was just to manage the actual construction.

Fairbairn was in many ways an imaginative entrepreneur and a natural designer, with a strong intuitive feeling for the way structures behave. He combined these qualities with great confidence in his ability, but possibly he was a little naive. His contribution to the actual design of the bridges, and certainly to their detailing, was considerable.

Hodgkinson's formal status is less clear, but his contribution to the design of the bridges was also very large. He was recognized as an able and widely consulted theorist. Although highly intelligent, Hodgkinson seems to have been a bit pernickety and touchy. From an academic point of view he was right to be cautious in reporting to the Board, but that was no way to get a new and daring project off the ground. Fairbairn had few inhibitions and, even if

47 Letter, 18 March 1846, **ICE**, ECLB/96.
48 Letter, 14 March 1846, in W. Fairbairn, p. 58.
49 Letter, 16 March 1846, in W. Fairbairn, p. 62.

Stephenson had inner doubts, he may have sensed that nothing short of a great show of confidence would carry the Board members. With such different temperaments some friction was inevitable.

As well as the Britannia and Conway Bridges, Fairbairn was concurrently working on what came to be known as 'tubular' wrought-iron bridges, a different type of structure, consisting of built-up girders with tubular tops – the concept of a train in the tube now lost.

To show how much of an entrepreneur Fairbairn was, one only needs to look at the proposition he made to Stephenson in February 1846 for the Dee crossing: (Fig. 10.15)[50]

Since your departure yesterday I have been thinking about your Bridges across the Dee ... What I propose would be three hollow beams each of them in depth one-fifteenth the span and composed of plates as per annexed section [Fig. 10.15]. From the experiments already made it will be easy to determine the thickness of the plates requisite for Bridges of this kind varying from 60 to 120 feet span. I think they will be strong and cheap and provided we attach a line of hollow plates as **a a** in the form of an arch, well riveted on each side, we may reasonably calculate on the required amount of rigidity and strength.

These beams, with their cellular wrought-iron tops to resist compression, look very sound and in form must have been offshoots from the tests for the Britannia and Conway Bridges. Whatever Stephenson's immediate response to Fairbairn's proposal, his own idea of using trussed compound girders prevailed. The first two of Fairbairn's tubular wrought-iron bridges are thought to have been for Charles Vignoles on the Blackburn, Darwen & Bolton Railway in 1846–1847.[51] If Stephenson had accepted Fairbairn's proposal, it is virtually certain that the collapse of the Dee Bridge would have been avoided and thus, through Fairbairn, he would have been spared a major embarrassment.

A bridge over the London & Birmingham Railway at Chalk Farm, reported as conceived by Stephenson in July 1846 and finished in March 1847, was another early example of the tubular type. However, it had cast iron at the tops of the beams instead of wrought-iron tubes. Clark claimed it as a 'first' but it is most likely to have derived from Fairbairn's thinking.[52]

On 7 April 1847 Fairbairn applied for a patent for 'Improvements in the Construction of Iron Beams for the Erection of Bridges and other Structures'.[53] This was to have been a joint patent with Stephenson, but Stephenson declined to be involved.[54] The illustrations in the patent specification show two sections through a 'tubular' girder, one with rectangular cells in wrought iron at the top and the other with cast iron at the top. The inclusion of the cast-iron top supports the idea that Fairbairn and Hodgkinson had a

50 Letter, 4 February 1846, **ICE** (42) and W. Fairbairn, pp. 27–8.
51 Fairbairn evidence to Royal Commission, op. cit. (n. 4), pp. 322.
52 Clark (1850), pp. 524–5.
53 Patent No 11,401.
54 Clark (1850), pp. 812–3.

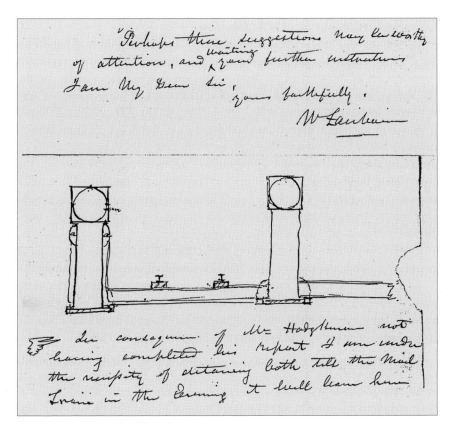

10.15 Part of
Fairbairn's letter
to Stephenson of
4 February 1846
proposing a
tubular wrought-
iron bridge over
the river Dee
(Courtesy of
Institution of
Civil Engineers)

substantial influence on the Chalk Farm Bridge, but by the time the bridge
was publicized Fairbairn's name was unpopular in the Stephenson circle.[55]

On 10 June 1847, two weeks after the Dee Bridge disaster, Fairbairn wrote
to Stephenson, criticizing the principle of the trussed cast-iron girder bridge,
and re-offered his wrought-iron 'tubular girder' bridge.[56] This was possibly
well-meaning but hardly tactful. Subsequently many bridges with twin or
triple girders were built following Fairbairn's tubular principle, which was
really the precursor of the simple plate-girder bridge.

The next stages in the development of the Britannia and Conway bridges
are difficult to untangle. Contemporary published accounts were slanted and,
as Fig. 10.13 shows, the surviving correspondence is far from complete.

Fairbairn made the suggested ⅙ scale (75ft) model tube with a cellular top
and this was tested progressively, with repairs and local strengthening wherever it failed. These tests went on from July 1846 to April 1847. In the meantime Hodgkinson was carrying out a number of tests in Manchester on smaller
tubes as beams, as well as on the basic properties of iron and, in particular, on
the resistance to compression of riveted tubes of different forms. The results of
these were reported to Stephenson but not to Fairbairn – as he complained.[57]

55 R. B. Dockray, *Proc. ICE*, **VIII**, pp. 169–70, 13 March 1849.
56 W. Fairbairn, pp. 148–51.
57 W. Fairbairn, pp. 54–5.

However, there clearly was communication.

In September 1846, when Fairbairn and Hodgkinson presented papers on the Britannia and Conway Bridges at the British Association, there were two rows of cells at the tops of the beams, and on that occasion credit for the cellular tops of the tubes was openly disputed between the two men. There were to be other disagreements.

Much of the design and all the final detailing of the Britannia and Conway tubes seems to have been undertaken by Fairbairn, who signed the contract drawings, with the results of Hodgkinson's research fed in. However, the antagonism between the two appeared to continue, as exemplified in Clark's letter to Stephenson in October 1846: 'I have seen Fairbairn and Hodgkinson and commenced my mediative commission with little success so far. They continue to hate each other most enthusiastically.'[58]

Later Clark wrote to Stephenson about getting Hodgkinson 'in a good humour, which is easily done by a little salve applied to his vanity bumps'.[59]

As the development continued, so did the wrangles. Fairbairn clearly wanted to halt Hodgkinson's experiments, which he thought irrelevant. Stephenson was sympathetic to Hodgkinson but had to control his scientific enthusiasm. Writing to Clark in March 1847, Stephenson said:[60]

Tell him [Hodgkinson] if I had my own way he should go on experimenting until the last day, but I am driven by many considerations to put an end to them now but I will go into the consideration of any suggestions he may have to make regarding two or three additional experiments when I come down.

The idea of having two layers of cells at the top of each tube and one at the bottom gave way to single layers top and bottom. Next, following a particularly successful test, Hodgkinson proposed adding a certain amount of cast iron to the tops of the tubes. Clark passed on this idea with qualified enthusiasm to Stephenson in February 1847.[61] At the same time Fairbairn, who had got wind of this, wrote to Stephenson objecting strongly.[62] Stephenson told Clark that the orders for plate must not be held up but did not totally dismiss the cast-iron idea for the future.[63]

Somehow out of an uncertain combination of tests and theory the final form of the tubes emerged (Fig. 10.16 and Plate 17) and their strength as beams was established, the theoretical understanding seemingly scarcely ahead of the practice.

Because of the incompleteness of the correspondence, details of proposals, problems and uncertainties come through in a disjointed way. However, what the letters show quite conclusively is that Stephenson was personally involved in almost every detail of the design of these bridges.

58 Letter, 28 October 1846, **ICE**, ECLB/3.
59 Letter, 2 March 1847, **ICE**, ECLB/12.
60 Letter, 1 March 1847, **ICE**, ECLB/10.
61 Letter, 25 February 1847, **ICE**, ECLB/8.
62 Letter, 27 February 1847, in W. Fairbairn, pp. 139–42.
63 Letter, 1 March 1847, **ICE**, ECLB/10.

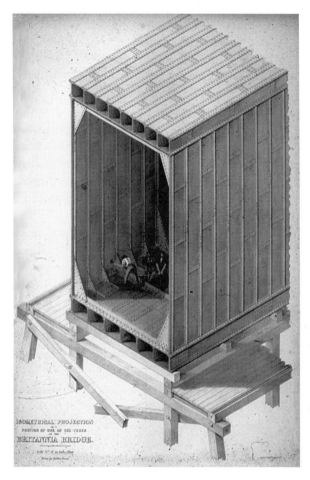

10.16 Isometric view of tubular bridge showing cellular construction (E. Clark, 1850)

Given all his other commitments and with the shadow of the Dee Bridge failure hanging over him after May 1847, the pressures on him must have been enormous. Clark kept him in close touch and one gets the impression that he was a great comfort, increasingly relied upon and always on Stephenson's side.

The erection of the Conway and Britannia bridges

On 15 July 1846 Fairbairn wrote to Stephenson proposing 'after a careful and deliberate consultation with Mr Clarke' [*sic*] to seal the ends of the Conway tubes, float them into position and jack them up to the required level.[64] On 18 July he wrote again suggesting making the tubes on a line of barges in a basin and then floating them out in the dry.[65] On 20 July Stephenson replied, stating that he had already discussed the idea of floating all the tubes with Alexander Ross and saying:[66]

64 W. Fairbairn, pp. 90–1. Original in **ICE**.
65 W. Fairbairn, pp. 92–3. Original in **ICE**.
66 W. Fairbairn, p. 94.

After much consideration, I felt that, although practicable, the risk of accident was so great, and the consequences of any miscarriage so serious, that I abandoned it, and resorted to the chains. The tidal current both at the Conway and at the Menai Straits is very rapid and would render the management of such a mass as a tube and pontoons extremely difficult and precarious.

The change of heart, from piecemeal fabrication and launching the tubes with cables back to building them locally, floating them and jacking them up, must date from the Board meeting on 14 October 1846. At this meeting William Evans, who was already the contractor for the masonry at Conway, gave a price for constructing the Conway tubes on the spot, providing all workshops, pontoons and other equipment and raising them into position.[67] This was accepted. Stephenson was terrified of the floating and let go of his feelings a little later in a letter to Clark saying: 'My doubts and fears will never end until the floating is actually finished. Turn it what way you like it is a frightful operation.'[68]

Fabrication of the first Conway tube started in 8 April 1847 and by 1 May 1848 it had been floated out, raised, load-tested and passed for traffic (Fig. 10.17). After the opening of this first tube Fairbairn resigned, though not for the first time. According to Clark he had offered to resign soon after May 1847 because of a disagreement over charges and the assigning of contracts, but Stephenson had persuaded him to change his mind.[69]

On 16 May 1848 Fairbairn wrote to Stephenson saying: 'the object for which I was engaged has now been attained', adding that 'the rest of the work on the bridges was routine which could be left to Edwin Clark.' He went on to say 'I shall however, as heretofore be much guided by your opinion on these matters.' On 19 May he wrote to Stephenson again saying that he had finally decided to resign. Not having an immediate reply he wrote on 22 May to the directors of the Chester & Holyhead Railway formally asking to be released from his appointment. It is broadly thought that Fairbairn resigned because he was not being given enough credit for the design of the bridges. Certainly at a dinner on 17 May 1848, celebrating the opening of the Conway Bridge, Stephenson had made a speech marked by surprising self-adulation and with niggardly acknowledgment to Fairbairn and Hodgkinson, even claiming to have introduced the cellular flanges, a claim already being disputed between Fairbairn and Hodgkinson.

Had Fairbairn read too much into his appointment by the Chester & Holyhead Railway to 'superintend the construction and erection of the Conway and Menai bridges, in conjunction with Mr Stephenson', taking this as meaning that he was joint engineer, level with Stephenson, on these bridges? Stephenson was engineer-in-chief for the whole railway, and it is hard to see how Fairbairn could have been anything other than a consultant or associate on part of it, however important that part. That does not mean that

67 Clark (1850), p. 807.
68 Undated letter, **ICE**, filed between 4 November 1846 and 11 January 1847, ECLB/5.
69 Clark (1850), p. 812.

10.17 Conway Bridge with one tube in place (E. Clark, 1850)

Stephenson should not have been more generous in his credits to both Fairbairn and Hodgkinson. It is clear that their contribution to the success of the bridges was crucial and Fairbairn rightly felt harshly treated.

The reason for this dispute must date from well before Stephenson's speech on 17 May but, looking back today, it is hard to find the firm evidence of what went wrong. Fairbairn comes across as a naturally creative designer, a 'hands-on' man with a strong feeling for materials and the detailing of their forms, but with little understanding of hierarchies and the finer points of business etiquette. Stephenson was a thinker, a man of vision combined with exceptionally sound judgement and an understanding of organizations as well as of materials. Perhaps friction was unavoidable.

Having resigned, Fairbairn immediately wrote a lengthy and expensively produced book, giving his account of the construction of the bridges up to this stage and bitterly attacking Stephenson.[70] Even though Stephenson acted in an ungenerous manner, totally out of character compared with most of his known dealings, Fairbairn's reaction does seem extreme.

A riposte was inevitable. It came in another book, written 'under the supervision of Robert Stephenson' by Edwin Clark, which outdid Fairbairn in style by being in two volumes with a magnificent atlas of plates.[71] There has been a tendency to look on it as the true story of the bridges, how they were conceived

70 W. Fairbairn.
71 Clark (1850).

and how they were built. In many ways it is just that, but it is becoming increasingly clear that it is an arranged account with many uncertainties glossed over and, understandably, no great credit to Fairbairn.

As history the mathematical analysis is particularly suspect. On 18 March 1850 Stephenson wrote to Professor Airy asking if he could recommend 'an able mathematician to look carefully through the declinations that have been drawn and the conclusions that have been arrived at'. Two days later he followed this with another letter saying 'I have just fallen in with Mr Pole who is a thorough practical man and a good mathematician. With him I have arranged the matter I alluded to.'[72] Pole, who could not have been involved in any of the early decisions and uncertainties, and was abroad until 1848, wrote quite a large part of the book, which is virtually a textbook giving engineering understanding as at 1850, but with little or no indication of the early uncertainties on the tubes, and no idea of how near they had probably been to the limits of knowledge.

Fairbairn does not seem to get full credit for his initial suggestions of floating the tubes rather than launching them on chains. Elsewhere there is often a feeling of slant, as there had been in Fairbairn's book. However, Clark's book is always polite and the only direct criticism of Fairbairn is in Stephenson's introduction, where he alludes to 'the [unnamed] gentleman' who 'endeavoured to enhance his own claims by detracting from the credit ... '[73]

The dispute between Stephenson and Fairbairn rumbled on within the engineering profession with appreciable support for Fairbairn, as shown in the 1853 edition of Ure's *Dictionary*.[74] Here Fairbairn is described as the 'inventor' of the Britannia and Conway tubular bridges while Stephenson is shown as having 'claimed the entire merit ... and assigned to Mr Fairbairn in a very slighting manner the place of a mere after adviser.' This was corrected in the 1860 edition. This whole disagreement reflected no credit on either of these great men, but it is more regrettable now because it has confused the history of one of the greatest engineering achievements of all time. This is why the surviving letters (Fig. 10.13) are so valuable.

When Fairbairn departed in May 1848, Stephenson and Clark were left in isolation, as Hodgkinson had already withdrawn. The floating, guiding and raising of the first Britannia tube in the Menai Straits was even more hazardous than it had been at Conway. Although he remained in overall control, Stephenson brought in Capt. Christopher Claxton, who had recently returned Brunel's *Great Britain* from Dundrum Bay, to run the water-borne arrangements. Clark describes in detail the arrangements for floating the first Britannia tube on 20 June 1849 and the problems encountered in this and in raising it.[75]

For Stephenson, always inclined towards pessimism, the anxiety in this period must have been intense. His letters to Clark are full of worries and warnings and descriptions of things that might go wrong. Clearly he knew

72 **Airy**, RGO 6/372, folios 368–9 and 372.
73 Clark (1850), p. 36.
74 Hunt.
75 Clark (1850), Section VII, Chapters IV and V.

that he was sounding neurotic, because in a letter to Clark in July 1849 about the fixing of the heavy lifting cross-heads, he says:[76]

A fall of one of them upon the tube would be fearful. The stiffening at the end would be all smashed and the tube would wholly collapse & drop its middle into the stream. You will say I am always conjuring up awful difficulties & consequences – my answer to this is it is an important part of the duty of an engineer.

Stephenson was right to be concerned because on 17 August, after raising the first tube 24ft, the hydraulic cylinder on which the lifting depended broke, dropping the tube 8–9 inches onto the packing below, with the fractured end of the cylinder crashing on top of it. There was one fatality, and considerable damage that led to the manufacturer, Amos, becoming personally involved. The tube did not reach its final position until 9 November 1849. There were also worrying moments in floating each of the next two tubes (Plate 18), as Clark records, but since he makes no mention of the floating of the fourth tube, one assumes all went smoothly.

The letters from Stephenson to Clark in this period mention other disturbing factors, particularly Stephenson's deteriorating health. In July and early August 1849, when the first Britannia tube was being raised, he said he was not well enough to finish his chapter for Clark's book and was 'still under doctor's orders'.[77] Above all he wanted reassuring news from Clark 'by every post' of how the work on the bridge was progressing. To answer a friend's enquiry about his health at the time he remarked: 'I have not slept sound for three weeks.'[78] The stress it created may have caused long-term damage to his health. To Thomas Gooch he confided at the time of floating the Britannia tubes:[79]

It was a most anxious and harassing time with me. Often at night I would lie tossing about, seeking sleep in vain. The tubes filled my head, I went to bed with them and got up with them. In the grey of the morning, when I looked across the [Gloucester] Square, it seemed an immense distance across to the houses on the opposite side. It was nearly the same length as the span of my tubular bridge!

In October 1849 Stephenson was ordered to Windermere for a rest and he told Clark to write to him in Bowness, or, if he was too busy, to ask his brother Latimer to write with daily news. He wrote once from Bowness thanking Edwin Clark for his 'delightful little epistle' and saying that he 'had been low and suffering from a good deal of acute pain in the region of the heart' before receiving it, adding that 'you and the tube are constantly in my mind.'[80]

Apart from Stephenson's worries about the tubes and his health, there were money problems on the project, glossed over in the published accounts but passed on by Stephenson to Clark in December 1849 when he referred to a 'dismal day', discussing[81]

76 Letter, 20 July 1849, **ICE**, ECLB/68.
77 Letters, 31 July and 3 August 1849, **ICE**, ECLB/70 and ECLB/71.
78 Smiles (1862), p. 435.
79 Gooch papers, **ICE**.
80 Letter, 13 October 1849, **ICE**, ECLB/79.
81 Letter, 29 December 1849, **ICE**, ECLB/86.

... with directors without a sixpence in their coffers as to the propriety of letting the [second] tube remain at its present [partly raised] elevation in order to shame the government into lending some assistance to finish the line.

The sum needed was apparently £50 000, which they would otherwise have to try to borrow. 'If they do not succeed I don't know what instructions I may have to send you,' says Stephenson. In the same letter Stephenson bemoaned the 'infernal devil' who had misrepresented him in the Bangor papers, presumably in relation to Fairbairn. This letter ends with a postscript: 'Many a happy new year to you.' Money must have been found, because work continued.

Only once in his letters to Clark did Stephenson appear to lose his calm. In May 1849 he wrote:[82]

How could you for one moment entertain the idea of letting Mares [contractor] get the ropes for the pontoon experiments from London ... at least a fortnight lost beyond recovery ... going to be very serious ... you and Claxton and Wild must lay your heads together instantly to rectify it with the least possible loss of time.

Clark's long explanation was followed by an almost apologetic letter from Stephenson, and good relations were restored.

Some indication of Stephenson's state of mind during the floating and raising of the tubes is given by John Lucas, the painter of the famous group picture, *A conference at the Bridge...* (Plate 19). Lucas, who was present at the floating of the fourth tube, records Stephenson 'to outward seeming, as calm and immobile as his iron structure' but 'as his nerve tension increased with the suspense attending the carrying out of the complex movements, involuntary tears were to be seen trickling down his face.'[83]

The rapport between Stephenson and Clark comes through strongly in these letters, one-sided as they are, especially in the final group. Always friendly, their warmth increases and the tone becomes more informal, even avuncular on Stephenson's side. It is interesting to note that in November 1847 Stephenson had been addressing Clark as 'My dear Sir'. In February 1849 and thereafter it was 'Dear Clark'.

The last structural task on the Britannia Bridge was to connect all the tubes for each line to make two continuous beams each some 1500 feet long stretching over five supports. Up to this time virtually all beams or girders, including the Britannia tubes as first conceived, had been considered as simple spans. However it was known in theory,[84] and in the practical understanding of carpenters, that there was a real strengthening and stiffening effect with continuity over supports. At Britannia continuity was provided most ingeniously both for the self-weight of the tubes and all that they carried. The principle was shown in Clark's book, but it is not known who thought of the idea. Wild seems most likely. The indications are that it came quite late, because there is a letter of 18 November 1849 from Stephenson to Clark discussing,

82 Letter, 3 May 1849, **ICE**, ECLB/58.
83 Narrated by Lucas to his son Arthur Lucas, in Lucas (1910).
84 Moseley.

with some uncertainty, how much to raise the end of a tube before making the joint.[85] Certainly there are no signs of taking advantage of continuity in the detailing of the actual tubes.

All the tubes for the first line were in place and connected together by 4 March 1850, and on 5 March the first train, driven by Stephenson, proceeded ceremoniously through the tube as described in *The Times*. Passed by the Railway Inspectorate, the first tube was opened to public traffic on 18 March and the second one on 19 October 1850.

Following the completion of the bridges, Clark became engineer to the Electric and International Telegraph Company and went on to design many bridges and other engineering works. His friendship with Stephenson continued, as is shown in a letter sent by Stephenson in December 1856, when he was about to leave for Egypt. 'Dear Clark,' he wrote, 'Before embarking I cannot refrain from saying how much I felt your kindness in making such a long journey to see me off.'[86] Stephenson's will disclosed a bequest of £2000 to Clark, a sum probably around £150 000 today.[87]

Hodgkinson was appointed 'Professor of the Mechanical Principles of Engineering' at University College, London in 1847. His tests for the Britannia and Conway Bridges were published and he continued his active career in research and testing. Fairbairn also remained active in many fields, not least as a popular author of engineering books. Simple tubular girder bridges, as proposed by him to Stephenson for the river Dee, were built widely and were the progenitors of the ubiquitous plate girder railway bridges of the later part of the century. Both Fairbairn and Hodgkinson became members, and medallists, of the Royal Society.

After 1850, Stephenson was responsible for a number of other iron bridges but, owing to his increasing public commitments, he no longer gave them the intense scrutiny which every detail of the Britannia Bridge received. These later bridges include the 225-ft twin tubular bridge at Brotherton over the river Aire opened in 1850, which was mainly remembered for the dispute over the clearance to the trains and the decision to slice open the tops of the tubes and insert extra plates.[88] Edwin Clark is credited with the original design, but Stephenson is reputed to have paid for the widening of the tubes. Also there were the first two iron viaducts over the Nile at Benha and the Bahr el-Shebin navigable waterway at Birket el-Saba, designed by Charles Wild and George Robert Stephenson and built between 1853 and 1855. Each had a central swing section and multiple side spans of 80ft, surprisingly built in tubular form, but with tubes only six feet square and the trains running on top.[89] The third, larger, tubular bridge, across the Rosetta branch of the Nile, was also designed by Wild and George Robert Stephenson, and completed in 1859.

85   Letter, 18 November 1849, **ICE**, ECLB/83.
86   Letter, 1 December 1856, **ICE**, ECLB/91.
87   Robert Stephenson's will, **ScM**, GPB/5/12/1.
88   Tomlinson, p. 502.
89   C. Wild, 'Die Aegyptische Eisenbahn von Alexandria nach Kairo', *Allgemeine Bauzeitung*, 1853, pp. 168–71, Plate 562.

The largest of the later tubular bridges was undoubtedly the Victoria Bridge at Montreal, built between 1853 and 1859, almost two miles long, with the tubular section consisting of 24 spans of 242ft and a central one of 360ft. Stephenson played a central role in rallying support for the enterprise on the London markets but his engineering contribution was small. The detailed design work was carried out in the Westminster office by George Robert Stephenson, who went on to supervise its manufacture at the Canada Works in Birkenhead.

The cellular tops and bottoms of the tubes, which were such a feature of the Britannia and Conway Bridges, were not repeated on any of these later tubular bridges. Simpler ways of stiffening had been found.

Finally, between 1858 and 1859 there was the rebuilding of the Wearmouth Bridge at Sunderland with tubular arch ribs of wrought iron. Owing to Stephenson's declining health the work was largely carried out by George Phipps.

Conclusions on the tubular bridges

The tubular form of the Britannia and Conway Bridges was a brilliant concept to meet a seemingly impossible challenge, but today it is hard not to wonder whether this level of innovation was essential. In the National Railway Museum there is a mysterious drawing for the Britannia Bridge, dated 1845 and showing simple iron arches with a suspended deck (Fig. 10.18). Who made it and what happened to the idea? Could the bowstring girder, as used on the London and Birmingham Railway, have been developed for the vastly greater spans needed? Both these arched forms would have met the Admiralty's requirements at Britannia. However, such speculations are of limited value. Stephenson had a vision of a stiffened suspension bridge, while Fairbairn must surely have seen the bridges as like the hulls of iron ships. These two concepts then came together and a totally new bridge form was developed and proved at full scale in an amazingly short time. This also advanced structural understanding by one enormous leap.

The idea of a solid tube with the trains inside was short-lived and by the time of the Victoria Bridge in Montreal, some eight years after Britannia, it had become an anachronism. By then there were several forms of girder with open trussing to choose from, each of which would have been more economical. However by then Stephenson's personal interests were moving into different fields.

The superseding of the tubular form does not detract from the achievement of the Britannia and Conway bridges. The great Britannia tubes were like nothing that had existed before and it is no wonder that they caught the imagination of the public. They must have seemed as fantastic as space rockets a hundred years later and to watch them being floated out, like great ocean liners incongruously balanced above the water on almost submerged pontoons, must have been awe-inspiring (Plate 18).

What could have been more exciting than being on the top of the first Britannia tube, high above the water, with crowds, cannon and bands on the

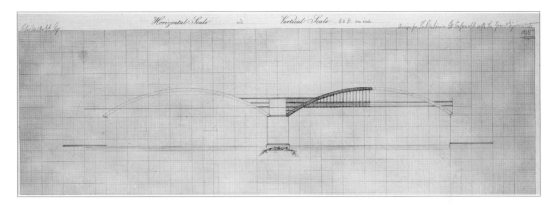

shore, while it was steered with cables through the strong current? To Stephenson, in charge, this operation was clearly terrifying, because he was personally responsible and his whole reputation depended on its success. For a young engineer like Wild, standing up there with Stephenson, Brunel, Locke and others, the floating must have been a magical experience, truly 'directing the great sources of power in nature for the use and convenience of man'[90] but with the added frisson of some personal danger. With all that talent on board, disaster, which came so close,[91] could have altered engineering history.

Postscript

The Britannia Bridge served its purpose well for 120 years until in May 1970 it was crippled by heat caused by the burning of protective roofing. The tubes sagged and when they cooled they split at the towers. They were deemed irreparable and the whole wrought iron structure was replaced. The Conway Bridge survives.

10.18 1845 proposal for arched bridge endorsed 'Design for the Britannia Br: Conformable with the Govern.t. Requirements' (National Railway Museum/Science & Society Picture Library)

90   Part of the Charter of the Institution of Civil Engineers, 1828.
91   Clark (1850), pp. 680–5. Also Rolt, pp. 311–14.

11

Masonry structures

Ted Ruddock

> A neat and elegant monument has been erected by the stonemasons to the memory of
> their deceased companions … [ten deaths in all] … It stands in the little churchyard of
> Llanfairpwllgwyngyll, which is close to the foot of the bridge on the Anglesey side
>
> Edwin Clark[1]

The masonry structures in the railway works for which Robert Stephenson
was responsible include bridges, viaducts, tunnels, earth-retaining structures, and buildings. The purpose of this chapter is to take an overview of
those structures, as far as possible in a chronological format, but focusing on
specific aspects of the story.

One focus is to seek clarification of the extent of Stephenson's personal responsibility with regard to individual structures for the design decisions, the writing of
specifications, and the control and supervision of construction, vis-à-vis the
contributions of other members of his staff and associates.

A second is to expose the context in which projects were undertaken, a
context chiefly defined by comparable works of other engineers and builders,
especially before his practice began, but also during its progress.

A third and related topic is to assess the degree of innovation, or the lack of
it, achieved in his works. Significant factors in this respect were:

1   The radically different loading of trains, compared with the earlier applied
     loads of horse-drawn vehicles and the weights of water and canal vessels
     applied to aqueducts. Railway loadings exceeded all earlier vehicle loadings
     both in weight and in strength of vibrations caused by their passage;
2   Rapid increase both in the scale of individual structures and in the overall
     quantity of construction, with the demands that it made on the available
     pools of labour, management and engineers; and
3   The broadening choice of structural forms, including increase in the use
     of varied arch forms and of skewed arch construction.[2]

---

1   Clark (1850), pp. 722–3.
2   Rolt, p. 248, named the construction of skew arches as 'Stephenson's most important contribution to civil
    engineering on the London and Birmingham' line. He may have been reading the strange reference in
    Conder (1868), p. 24, to Stephenson's 'development and practical construction of the theory of the skew
    arch' as meaning that Stephenson invented or was the first builder of skew arches. Whatever either of them
    meant, there is no doubt that skew arches were used by William Chapman in Ireland in the 1780s and the
    theory had been printed several times before the start of any designs for the London & Birmingham.

A fourth function of the overview is to give adequate description, by pertinent examples, of the construction materials, details and techniques that were used. Finally, an attempt is made to identify the bases and/or methods of design used for Stephenson's structures, in relation to contemporary writings on both the theory and the practice of masonry structural design.

Precursors

The precursors of the single-arch bridges built on the London & Birmingham Railway were hundreds of road crossings of the English canals constructed between 1760 and the 1820s, together with a few road-over-river bridges of larger scale. The ubiquitous bridges over the canals were built of both stone and brick, and competent means of construction for various curved wall shapes were well understood. There were a few skew arches and one or two descriptions in print of the difficult geometry needed for setting out of their courses. There were also a modest number of arched road bridges of sizes that compare with those of the largest bridges on the London & Birmingham Railway and later lines engineered by Stephenson.

Of straight span was, for instance, the bridge carrying Union Street in Aberdeen over the Dean Burn, built of granite of 130ft span, and completed in 1805.[3] Only under construction from 1827 to 1833 was Grosvenor Bridge at Chester, of several types of stone and 200ft in span.[4] Lee Bridge, a large arch of brickwork, one of several possible examples, and built both on the skew and with its road on a gradient, spanned the Birmingham Canal. It was designed by Telford, had a span of about 60ft and was completed in 1827.[5] Stephenson was also familiar with the skew single-arch over-bridge at Rainhill on the Liverpool & Manchester Railway, completed in 1829 under his father's supervision.[6]

The obvious antecedents to multi-span railway viaducts were the large aqueduct bridges built for canal companies from the 1760s onwards, and some multi-span road bridges built with horizontal roadways. Examples of the former were John Rennie's aqueduct over the Lune at Lancaster, finished in 1798, and of the latter his Kelso Bridge, completed in 1804.[7] Both were of five spans and built with voids in the spandrels between parallel walls that abutted against the extrados of the arches. They carried horizontal 'pavements' of stone slabs over which were laid the carriageway of the bridge and, on the aqueduct, the channel bed of the canal. The aqueduct structure also contained transverse wrought-iron tie-rods as an insurance against outward yielding of the sidewalls, a risk which would in due course be recognized also

3 Ruddock, p. 175.
4 Ibid., pp. 186–9.
5 Gibb, p. 306.
6 Biddle and Nock, p. 104, and Carlson, p. 103.
7 Ruddock, pp. 129–31 and 147–8.

in railway viaducts. The arches of Kelso Bridge were elliptical in shape, and those of the aqueduct were semicircles – both used in early viaducts by Stephenson and others, but with semicircles quickly becoming the most commonly used form. Acceptance of the influence on railway engineers of the earlier aqueducts is implicit in the inclusion of drawings of the Lune Aqueduct in Brees's 1837/1838 publications, with similar details of many early railway structures.[8]

Stephenson knew well the substantial Sankey Viaduct on the Liverpool & Manchester Railway, of nine semicircular arches each of 50ft span. It had been completed in 1830 across the wide valley that contained Sankey Brook and the St Helens Canal. It was built largely of brickwork but faced with stone,[9] thus using both the materials that were to be used, and sometimes similarly combined, in Stephenson's own practice. A further trio of railway viaducts also preceded his appointment and his beginning of design work on the London & Birmingham line, and as they were not very far from Newcastle he is likely to have seen or known details of them.[10] They are all near the Carlisle end of the Newcastle & Carlisle Railway. Two were begun in 1830, apparently designed by the line's engineer Francis Giles, and completed by 1834. Supervision of their construction was probably largely in the hands of John Blackmore (c.1801–1844). They were the Wetheral viaduct, which had five semicircular arches of span 80ft and maximum height 93ft, and Corby Viaduct of seven semicircular arches of 40ft span, 60ft in height; both built of Eden sandstone. The third was the Gelt Viaduct, which bears a plaque naming Giles as its engineer and its dates of construction as 1832–1835. It has three sandstone arches of 33ft span built on a 45° skew and maximum height of 64ft.

London & Birmingham Railway

From the date of Robert Stephenson's appointment as engineer-in-chief to the railway in September 1833, it is apparent that he was absorbed by the project. The first entry in his 1834 diary[11] says he was 'writing specifications, sketching plans' for the line. Most of the largest structures are mentioned in later entries, and work on many went on concurrently. For instance, as late as July 29, he wrote 'Brent bridge working drawings', presumably the final design work on that viaduct. He arranged the work of assistants in the office when he had to be away on visits to sites on the line or attending directors' meetings. But a letter written to Capt. Moorsom, the railway's secretary, in September 1834 seems to show that Stephenson was still under pressure to deliver the contract documents more quickly:[12]

8 Brees (1837 and 1838), Plates 67 and 68.
9 Biddle and Nock (1983).
10 Biddle and Nock (1983), pp. 54–5. Also Rennison (2000/1).
11 Robert Stephenson, Diary, **ScM**, 1947-135, entry for 27 January.
12 Letter, Robert Stephenson to Capt. Moorsom, 19 September 1834, **PRO**, RAIL 1008/91.

the whole of my time is now occupied in preparing plans of bridges, etc., with specifications for the contracts between Birmingham and the Sow. In a fortnight they will be
in a very forward state … the Committee may now reckon on my individual attention
to the Birmingham Contracts.

The section of the line mentioned probably involved about forty structures.
While assistants were vital for such rapidity in drafting, the major structures
on the line all engaged Stephenson's attention at some time. The assistants
who are named in diary entries are obviously men whose previous experience
equipped them to contribute to his design decisions: George Buck regarding
skew bridges and other things, Frank Forster about Weedon Viaduct, and
Thomas Gooch on various matters.

The structures on the railway are of interest firstly because they show us
Stephenson's earliest responses to the multiple choices set before him in
designing the structures of a major railway; and secondly because many of
them are readily accessible to external inspection. Most importantly, a
number of them are described in two contemporary books that print
detailed specifications of materials and construction, illustrated by comprehensive drawings.[13] The structures described include over-bridges and
under-bridges of a single span and of three or five spans, several also having
skew spans; also culverts, retaining walls, tunnels and viaducts. The arch
shapes in the viaducts included semicircular, segmental and semi-elliptical
examples (Plate 20).

Most of the surviving common under-bridges and over-bridges have red
bricks in the oldest (1830s) parts, but with alterations and/or re-facings more
often built with blue engineering bricks. In general, the use of stone was limited
to string courses, cornices, copings and other elevational features, but in a few
instances bridges, or at least their arches, were specified to be entirely of stone.
As some at least of these were of longer than usual span, it can be inferred that
stone was considered desirable for masonry which was more highly stressed,
though it was probably favoured also for bridges which were visually prominent.
The structural elements, chiefly the piers and arches, of viaducts on the line were
also generally of brick, as were retaining walls and the internal linings of tunnels
(Fig. 11.1). The portals, or facades, of the tunnels are all or partly of stone, and
some of them designed in pretentious architectural styles (Plate 21), which drew
some critical comment from engineering writers.[14] It is probable that architects
were engaged for the design of the portals, as was usual for station buildings.

As the whole of the main line from Camden Town to Rugby, first built of
two tracks, has been at least doubled in width, the original elevation of any
under-bridge (including viaducts) on that section as built by Stephenson can
only now be seen on one side at most. Knowledge of their interior structures
is only available from the published drawings. A considerable part of the

13 Brees (1838) and Simms.
14 For example, Whishaw (1842): 'The fronts of the Primrose Hill, Kilsby and other tunnels on this line
    are generally of stone, and some of them of far too elaborate design.' The Primrose Hill design was
    subject, for some reason, to approval by an architect to be named by Eton College.

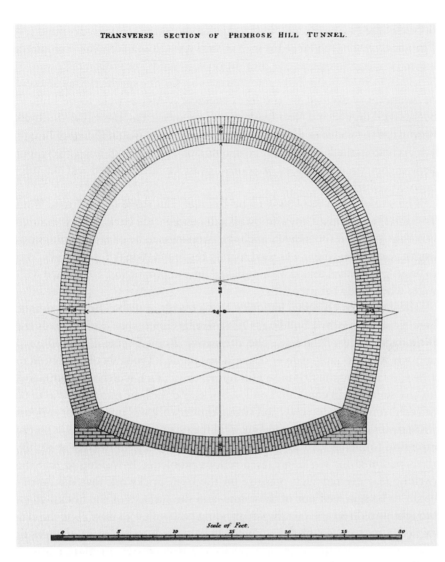

TRANSVERSE   SECTION   OF   PRIMROSE HILL TUNNEL.

Scale of Feet.

11.1 Primrose
Hill Tunnel
cross-section
(F. W. Simms,
1838)

published material depicts and describes works on the extension from
Camden Town to Euston that was decided on before much progress had
been made. This was a little less than one mile in length, almost entirely in
cutting, and built with breadth sufficient for four lines of track. Major
masonry walls were required to support the sides of the cutting and were
designed and built in brickwork, but it transpired that the potential pressure
on them from the ground behind them had not been understood (see
Chapter 8).

The specifications for the structures began with 'general stipulations',
which were followed by extra requirements relating to individual structures.
In the general stipulations, bricks on the faces were required to be 'malm-
bricks' of consistent form and colour.[15] Mortar was to be 'best burnt Dorking

15 A dictionary definition of 'malm-bricks' is simply 'best bricks'.

or other lime and river sand', well tempered in a pug-mill in proportions 1:3. The joints were not to exceed ¼ inch in thickness. Roman cement, if required, was to be mixed in one-to-one proportion with sand. For walls, bricks were to be laid in Flemish bond (but some contracts on the line specified English bond or 'whatever is decided by the local engineer'). Arches were to be built in concentric rings each a 'half-brick thick', meaning that the radial thickness was that of the width of the bricks, 4½ inches. Arches would therefore be 4½, 9, 13½, inches thick when made with one, two or three rings respectively. For skew arches the spiral lines of courses must be first marked out on fully boarded centring.

The stone, when used, was to be Bramley Fall stone (a sandstone from Yorkshire) and dressed smooth on all sides except 'the back', which ensured very thin joints on the facades, and every stone was to be of 2ft 6in minimum length. Concrete, which was used mainly for foundations of some walls, was to be of 'good gravel mixed with unslaked lime in proportion 5:1', mixed with water when ready for use.

The lime from Dorking, in Surrey, was a readily available, feebly hydraulic lime, good for normal building. Other similar limes were used towards the Birmingham end of the line. The alternative 'Roman cement' was adopted only where a very rapid gain of strength was needed. Probably the first need to arise was in lining the Primrose Hill tunnel (Fig. 11.1), which was contracted for and started with common London bricks and the lime mortar. It was to be driven through London clay, and strong timberwork was installed for support while the brick lining was built. But, as in the case of the retaining walls on the extension from Camden to Euston, the lack of existing knowledge about the clay's potential for swelling caused serious problems. It was found that the swelling clay exerted such pressure on the fresh brickwork that the mortar began to be squeezed out of the joints, and the surfaces of the bricks, when brought into direct contact, began grinding each other 'to dust'.[16] As the clay swelled, the diameter of the tunnel was being reduced. Urgent changes in materials were made, to stronger bricks and Roman cement mortar, which would set and gain strength very quickly and so avoid the damage to the bricks. The lining quickly gained strength enough to resist the swelling pressure of the clay. The thickness of the lining was also increased from 18 to 27in in some parts, and it was completed without further mishap, at a cost, however, of £280 000, compared with the initial contract price of £120 000.[17]

Further north, a use of masonry that was unusual, and perhaps unique, was devised to stabilize the most difficult parts of the long and deep cutting near Blisworth.[18] For most of its length the cutting was made to its full depth through limestone rock with steep side slopes of 1 horizontal to 4 vertical. Exploratory shafts, made before the contracts were written, however, showed that for lengths that added up in total to 1100 yards there was a thick bed of

16 Lecount (1839a). pp. 32–4.
17 Ibid., p. 34.
18 Simms, pp. 36–44 and Plates 20–37.

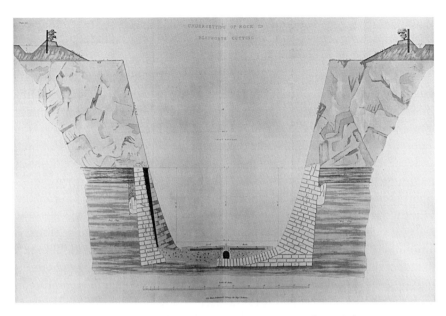

Section through wall   Section through buttress

clay under the limestone and above the proposed level of the bottom of the
cutting. Recognizing that the clay would compress under the edges of the
limestone, which would then crack, with risk of rock-falls on to the tracks, the
engineers designed masonry walls and buttresses (Fig. 11.2) to support the
edges of the limestone and retain the cut faces of the clay.

The material for the walls and buttresses was to be taken from the stone excavated while making the cutting in the limestone stratum. The stones were
required to be not smooth-dressed but 'rough nobbled', with the joints 'rustic'
and the courses in the faces to be at least 18in high and 'brought to a true though
rough bed'. Any 'backing', if necessary, should be at the engineer's discretion. The
maximum height of the walls and buttresses was expected to be 22ft, the walls
tapering in thickness from 4ft 6in at the bottom to 2ft 6in at the top, and the
overall plan dimensions of a buttress tapering from 9ft 6in × 6ft 0in at bottom to
4ft 0in × 4ft 6in at the top. The bottom of the cutting at rail level was to be 27ft
wide throughout, a few feet less than the top width of embankments on the line.

Masonry arch design for the London & Birmingham Railway

The London & Birmingham Railway structures themselves give important
indications of the principles and methods by which Robert Stephenson determined the necessary structural dimensions of his masonry bridges and
viaducts. It has already been noted that some retaining walls were unsuccessful
through the inadequacy of understanding of the behaviour of London clay.
The arch bridges and viaducts, however, fulfilled their purposes satisfactorily,
most of them for many decades, and some still carry today's traffic, of kinds
unheard of when they were designed.

Obviously Stephenson's educational experience must also have influenced his practice. When he attended the University of Edinburgh for about seven months in 1822–1823 he doubtless heard lectures on natural philosophy (physics including mechanics) by Professor John Leslie, and he certainly had access to the writings of others who had made mathematical studies of the theory of arches. It may be assumed that he had read theoretical treatments of 'the arch' from that of de la Hire in 1695, through Hutton in 1772 and at later dates up to 1812, leading to the books of Leslie's predecessor John Robison, and the contributions of Robison and others to major encyclopaedias published between 1805 and 1830.

Stephenson's mathematics prize from Leslie in 1823 was a copy of Hutton's 1812 book (Fig. 1.1).[19] The most accomplished British writer on the subject in the 1820s and 1830s was the Cambridge professor Henry Moseley. Two different authors who expressed high praise for Moseley made attempts to render the elements of his work usable by engineers in papers read to meetings of the Institution of Civil Engineers in 1846. Stephenson took part in both the discussions. He had read Moseley's published theory and described it, in broad agreement with other engineers present including Isambard Brunel and George Bidder, as 'highly scientific, and no doubt very beautiful [but] much too abstruse for the use of the practical man.'[20] He also remarked that 'old theories and formulae were looked upon [by himself] with much respect, and acting upon them, he had been generally successful'.[21]

Though both Robison and Leslie had serious contacts with leading engineers of their own periods, neither seems to have written a statement of arch theory which would lend itself to use as a method of determining the best forms or dimensions of arches for roads or railways. The likeliest meaning of Stephenson's phrase 'old theories and formulae' is that he had been using some simple 'rules of thumb'. Such rules had been written from as early as 1470,[22] and were certainly often used in the eighteenth and nineteenth centuries. A likely set for Stephenson to have known and used would have been those published by the French engineer, de Belidor, in 1752.[23] In summary, he set limiting structural proportions as follows:

for semicircular arches	span/pier thickness	maximum 6
	span/arch thickness	maximum 24
for semi-elliptical arches	span/pier thickness	maximum 5
	radius at crown/arch thickness at crown	maximum 12

Belief that the structural dimensions of the arches on the London & Birmingham Railway were assigned by such rules is encouraged by the general

19 Hutton: the first and longest tract being *The Theory of Bridges*, a revision of his first book published under the same title in 1772, and five others recording contributions by Hutton and others to bridge controversies from the 1750s to the early 1800s.
20 Discussion, p. 174, on paper, W. H. Barlow, 'On the Existence (Practically) of the Line of Equal Horizontal Thrust in Arches', *Proc. ICE*, **V**, 1846, pp. 162–82.
21 Discussion, p. 465, on paper, G. Snell, 'On the Stability of Arches….', *Proc. ICE*, **V**, 1846, pp. 439–77.
22 Alberti.
23 De Belidor, IV, Chapter 11.

evidence of pressure to complete designs quickly (see Chapter 8), as well as by the daunting complexity of Moseley's theory.

No serious breach of the Belidor rules is evident from a sample of the available dimensions of arch structures on the line. For over-bridges, which would be subject only to traditional loadings, arches of all three common forms – semicircular, segmental and semi-elliptical – were chosen. Such choices were presumably governed by the site constraints, including relative levels and alignments of road and railway, types of traffic, and the environment of adjacent buildings and topography. The spans were modest, normally no more than 30ft to span two tracks with necessary clearances. The ratio of span to arch thickness was generally within the range 10 to 20; but of two larger spans over wide cuttings, one had a ratio of 25. For another often-quoted structural ratio, span/rise of arch, the values varied from 2 (for semicircles) to 3.0–3.3 for ellipses, and about 5 for the two longer-span segmental arches.

The under-bridges, including viaducts, were going to be subjected to the unprecedented loading of moving trains, and of these five were of semicircular arches with span/pier thickness ratios of 2 to 6 and span/arch thickness of 10 to 17. One viaduct (Weedon) had segmental arches, span/pier thickness ratio 6, span/rise 3.9 and span/arch thickness 20. One (Wolverton) had elliptical arches (Plate 20), span/pier thickness about 6, span/rise 3.3 and span/arch thickness 18.[24] These figures show that nothing obviously adventurous was being attempted, but survival of the under-bridges and viaducts for many years under the loading of trains was at best still unproven. The best current practice was adopted, however, in all structures of more than one span, by putting no loose filling material in the spandrels, and building series of parallel walls under the individual rails (Fig. 11.3) which would ensure that the loads from wheels were shared between two arches and help to prevent elastic 'rippling' of the arches under moving loads. Moreover, thick internal masonry 'counterforts' were built to act similarly on the extrados of single arches and the end arches of viaducts (Fig. 11.4) and instructions were given that, when the arch was of ashlar, the counterforts should also be of ashlar with stones shaped to bond with the extrados of the arch.

Other masonry railway structures

Detailed facts about the masonry structures on other railways engineered by Robert Stephenson are more scarce than those quoted for the London & Birmingham Railway, but the number of masonry bridges and viaducts was very large. In the years immediately following the completion of that line, he was engineer or joint engineer for more than 160 miles of railway, including the 73-mile North Midland Railway and the 25-mile York & North Midland line. On the former there were 71 over-bridges and 133 under-bridges

---

24 The dimensions are derived from Brees (1838) and Simms, and, for Wolverton only, the author's measurements and Bourne.

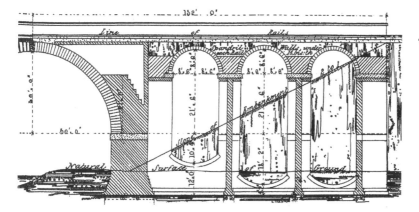

11.3 Sections
of Sow Viaduct,
London &
Birmingham
Railway
(S. C. Brees,
1839)

(including viaducts), and on the latter 31 bridges in all. The spans of the over-bridges on both lines were uniformly 30ft and their heights from rails to underside of the arches 16 or 17ft. Published dimensions and notes of the materials used in seven of the largest under-bridges show that the structural proportions were within the ranges for the London & Birmingham bridges.[25] Five of the seven had arches of more than 50ft span and one had a largest span of 90ft. Of five bridges for which the materials were stated, all were built with some mixture of brickwork and stone, the three main bridges on the York & North Midland line being apparently uniform in style, described as 'brick with Bramley Fall dressings' and all of their arches elliptical. They spanned the rivers Aire, Wharfe and Calder.

It would seem a safe assumption that 'ordinary' bridges and viaducts of masonry on later lines for which Stephenson was engineer, and probably on other lines where his associates held the main responsibility, were designed on principles, and with structural proportions, similar to those established in the years 1830–1840. This assumption can be tested using samples of the ninety contemporary drawings made to show geometrical details of all the bridges on the 48-mile eastern end of the Chester & Holyhead line, built in 1845–1849.[26] Abstracting data for ten over-bridges, five single-arch under-bridges and four viaducts, it may be shown that there is consistency in the structural dimensions and proportions, and reasonable consistency in the (unnamed) materials used.

Of the viaducts, three were built with segmental arches throughout, all of spans within the range 28 to 38ft and rise apparently standardized at about 7ft. Of the over-bridges all had spans of about 27ft, seven having segmental arches and two semi-elliptical, and again the standard rise of arches was about 7ft. All were designed to have stone facings of the arches, and the parapets and piers entirely of stone. Use of brickwork for the body of the arches was common and perhaps universal, but spandrels and wing-walls probably varied, most being either of brickwork or rubble masonry. Internal structures of the spandrels of

25 Whishaw (1842).
26 Drawings of bridges on the Chester & Holyhead Railway, in the keeping of Network Rail, North West Region, Store Street, Manchester.

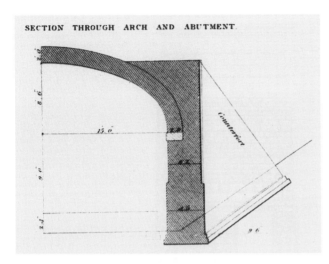

SECTION THROUGH ARCH AND ABUTMENT.

11.4 Counterfort to arch of bridge on the London & Birmingham Railway (F. W. Simms, 1838)

the viaducts were probably similar to those of the London & Birmingham viaducts (with longitudinal internal walls and voids), although less detail is shown on the drawings. Internal drainage of the spandrels is clearly drawn for all four viaducts. As this was a railway which engaged Stephenson's personal attention more than other British lines after 1840, the data give a valuable indication of his preferred practices in designing masonry bridges in his mature years.

Tall Viaducts

In contrast with his apparent use of empirical rules in deciding the forms and dimensions of arches, Stephenson and his associates regularly made quantitative estimates of force and stress in parts of masonry bridges which were subject to uniform (or axial) stress, and commissioned strength tests on bricks and stones for comparison. A small number of very high viaducts built in the late 1840s demonstrate his responses to the challenge of designing tall, relatively slender masonry piers. The structures concerned are the High Level Bridge at Newcastle, the Britannia and Conway bridges on the Chester & Holyhead line, and the Royal Border Bridge over the Tweed at Berwick. Only the last carries masonry arches, but its piers are broadly of the same type as the piers of the others which carry iron girders.

The Britannia Bridge being the most innovative because of its ironwork, Stephenson's personal involvement was greater than for the others, although his team of associates took more of the detailed design decisions. The resident engineer, Frank Forster, superintended the 'immense accumulation of masonry and scaffolding … the masonry being entrusted to the immediate supervision of Mr. T. E. Rawlinson, the resident clerk of works.'[27] There were five towers, the tallest in the middle of the straits being 221ft high and the others not much less. The middle one rose from a rock, which was exposed at low tide, to a plinth 25ft

---

27 Clark (1850), p. 551.

11.5 Tower
of Britannia
Bridge, elevation
and sectional plan
(E. Clark, 1850)

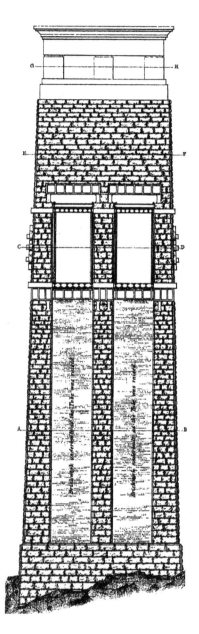

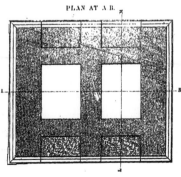

PLAN AT A B.

6in above the base. Up to the plinth level the two 'wells', or voids, which extended from the base up to the bottom of the iron tubes, were filled with rubble masonry. Above the plinth the wells were empty (Fig. 11.5).

The whole tower, like the other towers, was built with all faces battered, the thickness of the external walls tapering from 10ft 6in at the plinth to 8ft 0in at the top, while the internal dividing wall remained 8ft 4in thick all the way up, and the vertical walls which formed the backs of the recesses in which the ends of the tubes moved while they were being lifted, were uniformly smooth-hewn and 6ft 0in thick. The recesses were built up solid with brickwork below the rising tubes (Fig. 11.5). The middle tower contained almost 25 000 tons of masonry and the whole bridge 105 000 tons. A steam engine was sited on the rock at the base of the tower and drove hoists to raise the stones, frequently 8 to 10 tons in weight, working with 'travelling gantries for laying them over all parts of the tower with perfect ease'.[28] The timber scaffolding was of very heavy construction.

The general finish of the masonry was described as 'with a rough or quarry face', the stone being 'mountain limestone or Anglesey marble from quarries on the Island opened by the contractors'.[29] The internal work was of Runcorn sandstone, delivered by sea, and some brickwork. String courses, the 'campanile' tops of all the towers, and angles in the quarry-faced work were all dressed smooth.

Long consideration had been given to the style of the bridge, which when built was said by the architect, Francis Thompson, to be a mixture of Greek and Egyptian.[30] Practically, the horizontal stone courses of the 'campaniles' were aligned effectively with the edges of the tubes. There can have been little consideration of economy in the building of five towers to more than 60ft above the tops of the tubes. All the brickwork in the bridge was built with Roman cement and the mortar for the limestone building was a mixture of Aberthaw lime with chips of the same stone (and possibly dust) produced during the working of the stones.

For the Conway Bridge, Thompson adopted a medieval castle style to blend with the ruined castle nearby. The stone was the same as that used in the Britannia Bridge, finished with a quarry face up to the bottom of the tubes and smooth-hewn above that level. A fact of some historical interest is that the artist who made the plates of the Conway Bridge, which were published with Edwin Clark's classic description of the bridges, worked from photographs taken at the site, an early use of photography for an engineering publication.[31]

To carry its six iron tied arches the High Level Bridge at Newcastle required piers with maximum height, to the level of the railway tracks, of 140ft, the roadway being on a second deck about 18ft lower.[32] For most of their height the masonry piers were each divided into two columns 17ft × 14ft in plan. They

28 Ibid., pp. 542–3.
29 Ibid., pp. 539–40.
30 Ibid., p. 537.
31 Ibid.
32 Rennison (1980/1). Also Addyman and Fawcett (1999).

11.6 Pier of
High Level
Bridge, elevation
and sectional
plan
(Courtesy of
J. Addyman)

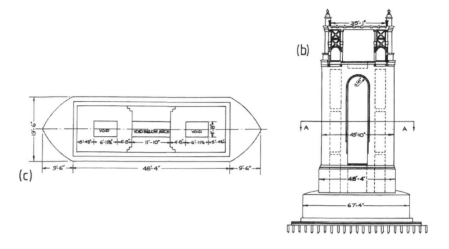

were joined at the top by an arch just under the road deck and at the bottom by
a base measuring 76ft 4in × 22ft 6in and resting on many piles at 2ft below low-
water level. There were also voids of plan area 7ft × 4ft 8in in each of the two
columns of each pier (Fig. 11.6), with rubble filling only up to about high-water
level. All the masonry was ashlar-built with stone from quarries at Heddon and
Corbridge, set in lime mortar but with external pointing of Roman cement.

While it is certain that Thomas Harrison was ordered by the railway directors in October 1845 to make plans for this and other bridges, including the
Tweed bridge at the England–Scotland Border,[33] Harrison himself later wrote
that 'the designs are not mine but my friend Mr Robert Stephenson's'.[34] The
masonry work, which included substantial arches in the approach structures,
was begun in January 1847 and was ready for the erection of ironwork to start
in July 1848.

The fourth viaduct with tall piers was the Royal Border Bridge, which
carried the twin tracks of the York, Newcastle & Berwick Railway over the
Tweed at Berwick.[35] It was all of stone except the barrels of the arches, which
were of brick, but stone-clad at the faces. There were fifteen arches over the
ground south of the river, with soffits up to 70ft above the ground, followed
by another thirteen over the river itself, standing much higher, up to almost
130ft above the river bed. It is the piers of the latter group that compare with
those of the High Level and Britannia Bridges. Stephenson spoke of having
'arranged the design' of the bridge,[36] but, as with the other tall piers, there is
little doubt that most of the detailed design work was done by others. Whilst
Harrison was engineer to the company, he probably delegated responsibility
at an early stage to George Bruce, who became the resident engineer and

33 Rennison, op. cit. (n. 32), p. 190.
34 Addyman and Fawcett, p. 47.
35 Bruce (1850/1), pp. 219–44.
36 Ibid., pp. 237–8.

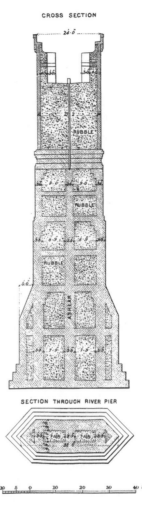

CROSS SECTION

SECTION THROUGH RIVER PIER

Scale of 30   5   0   10   20   30   40 feet

11.7 Masonry of
Royal Border
Bridge
(Ted Ruddock)

11.8 Pier of
Royal Border
Bridge, vertical
section
(G. B. Bruce
1850/51)

presented a full description of the whole project to the Institution of Civil Engineers in February 1851.[37]

The fifteen arches on land were completed well ahead of the remainder, a special thick pier being included at the northern end of the fifteen as an end buttress; some frightening collapses of strings of arches at the unfinished ends of viaducts were known to engineers and quoted in the discussion of Bruce's paper.[38] The paper gives details of construction provisions for the river arches, with deep cofferdams and piles driven to rock at 40 feet through very dense gravel, most of it done with a patent Naysmyth steam powered piling machine. A battery of pumps was also necessary to de-water the cofferdams. Bruce was unhappy with the quality of mortars in use at the time and settled, after some experimentation, for grinding the quicklime and mixing it dry with

37 Ibid.
38 Ibid. Reference was made in particular to the collapse in 1846 at Barentin in France of 28 spans of the unfinished viaduct. See D. Brooke, 'The Fall of Barentin Viaduct, 10 January 1846', *JRCHS*, **32**, 1997, pp. 363–6.

coarse sand, then storing it dry until just before it was required for use, when the water was added. For grouting he added some ground furnace slag to the mix.

The stones for the faces of the piers were all hewn smooth on four faces, for accurate fitting and thin joints, but the outside face left rough (Fig. 11.7), as on the Britannia Bridge. Similarly, each pier had two vertical voids, which were filled with 'a hearting of well grouted rubble', but at every 12ft a course of ashlar was laid right through the pier and the voids (Fig. 11.8). The structure's survival for one hundred and fifty years shows that this was a sound construction, but the combination of ashlar and rubble was strongly questioned in the discussion of Bruce's paper. Stephenson insisted that the construction was not mixing rubble with ashlar; the rubble being used only as a filler and weight-maker, the weight adding to the stability of the piers, but there being no bond (either intended or actual) between rubble filling and the ashlar face-work. He expressed a particular concern about the lateral thrust on piers that would result from any failure of the centring during construction of an arch.

In discussion of the stresses that would act on the stonework and the strength of the stone shown by tests, Stephenson spoke of his great anxiety, when the tubes of the Britannia Bridge were being raised, about the stress exerted on the masonry supporting the hydraulic presses that lifted the tubes. The stress was calculated to be 140 tons per square foot, but no crushing of the stone took place. In contrast, Bruce quoted the stress borne by the ashlar in the Border Bridge as a maximum of about 2 tons per square foot, and he understood that the maximum stress in the High Level Bridge piers was similar, but that stress of 20 tons per square foot was said to exist in 'the Victoria Bridge'. This was the fine viaduct on the Durham Junction Railway, crossing the river Wear near Washington, and designed by Walker and Burges for Thomas Harrison, engineer of the line. Completed in June 1838, it had four large arches with spans of 160, 144, 100 and 60ft.[39] Despite the large spans, the magnitude of the stress quoted is surprising. The stress at the base of the Britannia Tower at Menai was calculated to be 16 tons per square foot.[40]

The Victoria Viaduct at Montreal[41]

The masonry of the Victoria Viaduct across the St Lawrence River near Montreal was also limited to the piers, but its design posed very different problems from those of Robert Stephenson's other major bridges. Stephenson supported Alexander Ross's proposal to cross the river with a tubular girder

39 D. Bremner, 'Account of the Victoria Bridge…', *Proc. ICE*, **II**, 1842/3, pp. 97–9. Also Biddle and Nock, p. 44.
40 Clark (1850), p. 542.
41 Hodges. Also Jeaffreson, II, pp. 210–29.

bridge of many spans. The river was wide and surprisingly shallow, but with its bed bestrewn with very large rocks. The great need was to make the twenty-four piers resistant to the discharge of an enormous quantity of ice each spring, and to found and build them in working seasons which ran only from April or May to about the end of November.

Stephenson visited Canada in 1853 to see the site and consult the promoters before work began under Ross's direction. As consulting engineer for the project he wrote a long report in 1855, later printed in full, which shows that he had kept abreast of developments.[42] To minimize the enormous cost of the bridge it was determined that equal amounts should be spent on the two elements; the tubular spans, and piers and foundations. This equality was calculated to exist if there were twenty-four piers with spans between them of 242ft, except for a navigation span in midstream of 330ft. This was adopted.

For the piers, Stephenson asserted that the material and the way it was used, including the rough surface finish, were 'precisely similar' to those of the Britannia Bridge.[43] The ashlar exteriors (Fig. 11.9) were made of very large stones, each 5 to 20 tons in weight, and the interiors filled with rubble, which almost certainly in this case meant quarried stones of uncontrolled shape and size dumped into the hearts of the piers, compacted and grouted as a body. All the piers were founded on rock and were 90ft long and 23ft thick at the base. They were shaped as 'ice-breakers' with pointed nose

42 Hodges.
43 Ibid.

upstream and, from a little below the river's lowest water level, the nose sloped up at 45° to a height some 20ft above the highest (winter) water level. The face stones of the slope, up which sheets of ice would be forced by the current, and on which the sheets would break by their own weight, were bound and keyed into place by embedded iron bars. The ice-breaking slopes were covered up some forty years later when the original single-track line became insufficient and the tops of the piers were lengthened to support new girders carrying a second track. With some further adjustments, the piers remain in place and in use today.

Conclusions

As a general observation, it is clear that there was much less technical innovation in Stephenson's masonry structures than in his large iron girders. However, the quantity of masonry structures and the speed with which they were completed successfully, on his railway projects between 1830 and 1850, were astonishing when compared with the works of the busiest engineers of the previous generation, such as John Rennie and Thomas Telford. They bear witness to the strength of his leadership of the professional teams working on projects, and to his business sagacity in satisfying many clients. It is apparent that the technical basis of masonry design on many lines was simple, empirical knowledge from his own experience and published sources, supplemented by some tests for strength of the materials used. High standards of design judgement and of construction are evident in the success of all the structures in carrying the novel, pulsating loads of heavy trains for long periods, also in the adequacy of masonry piers of unprecedented height, and perhaps most notably in the ice-breaking piers of the Victoria Bridge over the St Lawrence River.

12

Water engineering

Denis Smith

The *dock* and *harbour engineer* requires the general and much of the special knowledge of the railway engineer ... The *waterworks* and *drainage engineer* must possess many of the qualifications of the railway and dock engineer, especially those which concern earthwork and masonry.

Sir John Fowler[1]

As Robert Stephenson's career as a consulting engineer developed from the early 1840s, he became involved with schemes for water supply to towns, main drainage, improvement and control of river regimes, fen drainage, docks, harbours and coastal works. His reports and contributions to discussions of papers read at the Institution of Civil Engineers produce a body of evidence testifying to his competence in these fields – spheres of engineering which have hitherto passed largely unnoticed in historical and biographical writing relating to Stephenson. For example, there is not a single reference to this part of his engineering work in the long obituary notice in the Proceedings of the Institution. However, it is not surprising that his unique contribution to the development of railway systems in Britain and abroad has overshadowed these other aspects of his career.

This chapter explores the extent and nature of Stephenson's involvement with water engineering and his contribution to the subject. His engagement with this field of engineering largely developed during the last twenty years of his life. Railway civil engineers were, in the normal course of their work, exposed to problems involving water management. Apart from river piers for bridges, they carried railways across fens and bogs and encountered difficulties with the stability of slopes in cuttings and embankments owing to the presence of water. This was done at a time before the development of scientific soil mechanics. The need for stable track foundations and drainage was an important aspect of their work. Water penetration into tunnel workings also resulted in expensive delays, most particularly in Kilsby tunnel on the London & Birmingham railway. In addition, railway engineering and harbour construction schemes were often linked projects in the nineteenth century, and Stephenson was naturally involved in both spheres.

1 Sir John Fowler's Presidential Address, *Proc. ICE*, **XXV**, 9 January 1866, pp. 214–15.

Following the railway construction boom the next great challenge of the nineteenth century lay in the field of public health engineering, and it is not surprising that Stephenson, and others, should engage in such issues as water supply and main drainage. His reputation and status in the railway field made the promoters of large-scale schemes in public health engineering keen to have Stephenson's name associated with their public works projects. He became consulting engineer to the Metropolitan Commissions of Sewers and was subsequently closely associated with Joseph Bazalgette's main drainage works in London. The scale of the expenditure and the complexity of the technical problems involved were eventually to give Bazalgette and other public health engineers something of the status of the eminent railway engineers. In this new field of urban water engineering, Stephenson was associated with Isambard K. Brunel, Sir William Cubitt, James Rendel, John Bateman (1810–1889) and Thomas Hawksley amongst others.

Dock and harbour schemes

Robert Stephenson's earliest design work in water engineering had been undertaken in 1824, when he first arrived in South America (see Chapter 1). Having arrived in the port of La Guayra on the Caribbean Sea coast of Venezuela he was asked to consider schemes for the harbour, including the relative merits of a breakwater or a pier. His report showed that he had rapidly gathered a great deal of information on the local characteristics of the seabed, weather conditions and even revenue statistics of imports and exports. He condemned the breakwater proposal as 'a dangerous experiment' and produced a design for a masonry pier constructed with local stone. The structure was to be 140 yards long with a top width of 24ft and would have cost £6000. His report included the placing of the stone blocks and he advised giving the pier 'a gradual slope on the seaward side, so that the waves might be completely broken'.[2] He did not stay to pursue the project, as he soon set off on his journey to Colombia on mining business.

Stephenson's first involvement in dock engineering as a consulting engineer was at Bute Docks, Cardiff, in 1840. In conjunction with Brunel, the scheme was in connection with the Taff Vale Railway Company and the landowner, Lord Bute.[3]

His next connection was with the Hull Dock development. The scheme for an extended dock system at Hull was promoted by three railway companies; the Hull & Selby, the York & North Midland and the Manchester & Leeds. The interaction between railway and dock companies was a common theme in nineteenth-century civil engineering. James Walker, engineer to the Hull & Selby Railway, reported in July 1834 to the directors saying: 'The distance from Selby to the Hull Dock Quay by the proposed plan, is under thirty-one

2 Jeaffreson, I, pp. 78–80.
3 Letter, I. K. Brunel to G. Bush, London, 11 February 1840, **Brunel**, Letter Book 2b, pp. 41–2.

miles.'[4] The Hull & Selby Railway opened in 1840. In September 1842 Stephenson returned to London from Cardiff 'where he had been examining the docks, and immediately on returning to Great George Street had a consultation about the Hull Docks'.[5] He made a report on the proposed dock development in October 1842,[6] and the scheme was made public at the railway's General Meeting in December of the same year.

In his report Stephenson said he was acquainted with the various plans that had been prepared for extending the dock accommodation of the Port and that he had 'thoroughly examined the locality'. He noted the contentious nature of the various proposals and said:[7]

When treating a question where large vested interest plays so powerful a part as is the case in the present instance, it is impossible to satisfy by abstract argument, or arrive at a result which shall obtain anything like general concurrence.

In respect of the precise site of the dock he wrote: 'In an engineering point of view I am unable to distinguish one part of the Foreshore from another.' He was unable at that stage to determine the cost of the proposed dock, neither had 'the precise Mode of Construction received from me that consideration which it requires before proceedings are taken in Parliament'. He had, however, given some thought to the question 'whether the application of cast iron for the Dock walls would not be desirable & economical & as far as I have proceeded in these calculations I am induced to think favourably of it'. Stephenson recommended that a survey be made immediately so that an application to Parliament could be based on it.[8] He concluded the report by saying:[9]

... that the position of the new Dock has had my most serious Consideration & I am thoroughly satisfied that to select any other site but the west foreshore would be to deprive the trade of Hull to a great degree of those advantages which can alone be developed by the Railway which if neglected at this moment may be iretrieveable.

Stephenson's next dock scheme was at Sunderland, adjacent to a district of high-quality coal. Nearly the whole of the trade of the port had been carried on in the tideway, although schemes for wet docks had been considered for some years.[10] However, none was built until 1838, when Brunel constructed a dock of about 6 acres on the north side of the river. Competition from the ports of Seaham, Hartlepool and the Tyne led, in 1845, to a proposal for a larger dock scheme, south of the River Wear. A prospectus for a company, with a share

4 Smith (1997/8), pp. 23–55.
5 Jeaffreson, I, p. 254.
6 'Report by Robert Stephenson. C. E., to the Directors of the Manchester & Leeds, York & North Midland and Hull & Selby Railways, re potential dock development on west foreshore at Hull', 20 October 1842, **PRO**, RAIL 770/15.
7 Ibid., p. 1.
8 John Clarke Hawkshaw, 'The Construction of the Albert Dock at Kingston-upon-Hull', *Proc. ICE*, **XLI**, 1875, p. 92.
9 Report, op. cit. (n. 6), p. 8.
10 John Murray, 'On the Progressive Construction of the Sunderland Docks', read 6 May 1856, *Proc. ICE*, **XV**, pp. 418–44. Dock schemes had been proposed by Dodd (1794), Jessop (1807), Stevenson [Edinburgh] (1829), Giles and Brunel (1831) and Rennie and Walker (1832).

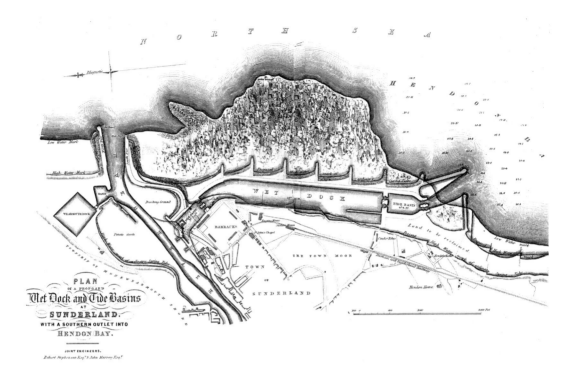

12.1 Wet dock
and tide basins
at Sunderland
endorsed with
the names of the
Joint Engineers,
Robert
Stephenson and
John Murray
(*Quarterly Papers
on Engineering*,
vol. V, 1846)

capital of £225 000, was advertised, with George Hudson as chairman and Stephenson and John Murray (1804–1882) as joint engineers.[11] Murray, a Scot, had been trained by William Chadwell Mylne before becoming engineer to Sunderland Harbour. In 1846 it was said that: 'Sunderland is indebted less to nature and more by art than the neighbouring port of Newcastle.'[12]

Stephenson later described the dock (Fig. 12.1) as built as having two or three points of interest:[13]

In the first place the site of the Docks was very peculiar, insomuch as they had been constructed on ground gained from the sea, by the action of groynes projected from the shore … In the second place, … the dams employed were novel in construction, and apparently cheaper than usual; they had been used with success in exposed positions, and seemed to have been more effective, than any others hitherto known. … In the third place, all the harbours on the north-east coast suffered, more or less, from the formation of bars across the mouths of the harbours themselves … the scouring power hitherto employed had not been very successful. The system used at Sunderland appeared to be better devised, and the results … superior to anything attained elsewhere.

Stephenson could reasonably adopt this style of detached appraisal as he ceased to be involved with the Sunderland Dock project once the act of parliament had been granted.

---

11 *RT*, **VIII**, 25 October 1845, p. 2069.
12 'Tidal Harbours Commission', Second Report of the Commissioners, 1846, p. xi.
13 Robert Stephenson, contribution to discussion following Murray's paper, op. cit. (n. 10).

In 1845 Stephenson teamed up with James Rendel to consider a greatly enlarged harbour for Margate. They submitted a Plan and Report to the Commission on the State of Tidal Harbours and requesting the 'favourable consideration of Her Majesty's Government'.[14] Little evidence has been found to add to this statement, except when George Robert Stephenson gave his Presidential Address to the Institution of Civil Engineers in 1876 he reminisced:[15]

As long ago as 1845 or 1846 it was proposed to construct a harbour of refuge near Margate, and it became my duty to accompany Mr. Rendel and Mr. Robert Stephenson to make an examination of the coast. Shortly afterwards an inspection of the east coast was made with a similar object; but though even at that time the traffic was so great as to arouse serious apprehensions, because of the want of maritime works, for securing the safety of the vessels engaged on that coast, the whole subject was permitted to lapse, and, so far as the east coast is concerned, to fall into oblivion.

From 1850, Stephenson increasingly took on the role of a respected independent consultant and arbitrator, the first consultation relating to the Grimsby Dock system. The Grimsby dock development was situated on the south bank of the river Humber, where there had been a small port since the medieval period. The fortunes of this isolated spot changed dramatically when the Manchester, Sheffield & Lincolnshire Railway opened from Sheffield in 1848. The company had bought out the Grimsby Haven Company in 1846, giving the railway company an interest in developing the port.[16]

By June 1850 Rendel's design for the Royal Dock was being discussed. At the railway's half-yearly General Meeting in June Mr Fosberry reported that in reference to the Grimsby Docks, there had existed a difference of opinion about the size of the dock – whether it should be ten acres or more – but 'Mr. Stephenson had been called in to guide them, and he had the greatest confidence in his opinion.'[17] In August the railway's chairman reported problems with the works at Grimsby and that the opinion of 'Mr. Stephenson, an independent engineer' as to whether any of the works in progress should be suspended for a time and that 'his opinion was decidedly that none of them should be stopped. [Hear.]'[18]

By mid-October 1850 there were further problems and it was resolved to refer to Stephenson the question as to 'the extent to which the Grimsby Docks, under all the circumstances of the Company, should be completed'. Stephenson made a report establishing conclusively:[19]

The inexpedience of diminishing the area of the Dock as the immediate saving would be much too small to justify the ultimate and permanent outlay, should it hereafter be thought advisable to carry out the Dock works in their integrity

14 Minutes of Tidal Harbours Commission, meeting 2 July 1845, **ICE**, Tait Room.
15 *Proc. ICE*, **XLIV**, 11 January 1876, pp. 1–17.
16 Bird, pp. 134–8.
17 *RT*, **XIII**, 29 June 1850, p. 626.
18 *RT*, **XIII**, 7 September 1850, p. 912.
19 *RT*, **XIII**, 12 October 1850, p. 1051.

Stephenson's growing reputation as an arbitrator on railway affairs had thus become extended into port engineering, and he was consulted by railway company directors where his opinion was valued regarding the work of their port engineer.

Stephenson was next asked to arbitrate on schemes regarding the development of Birkenhead Docks. In the early 1840s the Commissioners for the Conservancy of the River Mersey had become interested in constructing a dock on the west side of the river, opposite the Port of Liverpool. James Rendel submitted a scheme in October 1843 for two docks, the 'Morpeth' and the 'Egerton', on the site of Wallasey Pool. Rendel's scheme was authorized by act of parliament in 1844 and work began soon after.

The river Fender was diverted eastwards into Wallasey Pool and water was artificially impounded to form the 'Great Float' of about 150 acres. Rendel's scheme comprised the Great Float and a low-water tidal basin of about 37 acres with a depth of 12ft at low water, ordinary spring tides (OST). Ships would approach the dock from the Mersey through a 350ft-wide entrance. However, by 1847 the works were only partly executed and were described as 'all in unsatisfactory condition because of financial difficulties and the unsoundness of the original plans of J. M. Rendel'.[20]

Subsequently another plan by James Abernethy (1814–1896) was submitted. This scheme comprised the 150-acre 'Float', a half-tide basin of about 19.5 acres and an entrance basin of about 5 acres with a depth of 12ft at low water OST. In 1850 a plan was submitted to Parliament.

On 19 May 1851 the Mersey Conservancy Commissioners wrote to Stephenson soliciting his opinion on the relative merits of Rendel's and Abernethy's plans. Admiral Sir Francis Beaufort, Hydrographer to the Admiralty, was to be associated with Stephenson in this inquiry. Three main questions were submitted to Stephenson and Beaufort, namely:[21]

1   Which of the two schemes would be the least expensive in constructing the outer works?
2   Which would be the least expensive in working and easiest of extension?
3   Which would provide the greatest accommodation to the increasing commerce of the Port?

To help resolve these issues, Stephenson and Beaufort held the inquiry in Stephenson's Westminster office in June 1851, and the proceedings were published.[22] Many eminent engineers were involved in this inquiry.[23] Having received engineering support for Abernethy's plan from Sir John MacNeill,

20 J. Ellacott, 'Description of the Low Water Basin at Birkenhead', *Proc. ICE,* **XXVIII**, 1868/9, pp. 518–35.
21 Mersey Conservancy letter signed by Captain Geo. Evans, Acting Conservator, River Mersey, in 'Report of Robert Stephenson and Admiral Sir Francis Beaufort, 17 October 1851', p. 1, **ICE**, Tract fol. 5, (9).
22 Proceedings taken before Admiral Sir Francis Beaufort and Robert Stephenson, Esq., M.P., at 24 Great George Street, 7 June 1851, **ICE**, Tract fol. 5, (10).
23 These included Robert Stephenson, Sir John MacNeill, Sir John Rennie, J. M. Rendel, William Cubitt, Isambard K. Brunel and Captain Christopher Claxton, amongst others.

George Rennie, and Abernethy himself, and support for Rendel's scheme from William Cubitt, Isambard K. Brunel and William Radford, together with nautical support from Captains Claxton, Denham and Rowland (Principal Harbour Master of the Thames), Stephenson and Beaufort reported to the Conservancers in October 1851:[24]

> ... having regard to the works which are already so far advanced, it would be highly injudicious to introduce such a radical change in the original project, as that proposed by Mr. Abernethy; since all the evidence leads to the conclusion, that the expense would be increased, and its usefulness seriously impaired.

Under an Act of 1857 the Birkenhead Docks legally became part of the Port of Liverpool.[25]

An interesting epilogue to Stephenson's involvement with docks and harbours is provided by a letter he wrote to Brunel in October 1855:[26]

Dear Brunel

I enclose you the cards of two gentlemen who will call upon you if you will permit them professionally about the 8thth. of Nov – respecting the construction of some Docks which the Spanish Government wish to have made in the Phillipine [sic] Isles. Manilla [sic] I think. I shall be leaving for my Winter cruise about the end of next week – will you be at your office on Monday? Or shall I give you a call to morrow morning about 11 o clock.

Yours Sincerely

Rob Stephenson

Water supply schemes

The supply of water, and the development of technology applied to this subject, is one of the oldest themes in the history of engineering. The ingenuity required to capture water, to make it potable and to distribute it to communities over increasing areas has engaged some of the greatest military and civil engineers through the centuries. Several civil and mechanical engineers made the subject a lifelong study and became specialist consulting engineers. Robert Stephenson was not one of these, although he made an important contribution to the analysis and practice of the problems that arose in this field.

In the mid-nineteenth century London's water supply was in the hands of eight private companies, each supplying their own area.[27] In the 1840s and early 1850s interest developed in abstracting water from springs in the underlying chalk to augment the existing supply. The proposed schemes involved sinking boreholes into the chalk. The advantage claimed for this water source

24 Report, op. cit. (n. 21), p. 13.
25 Op. cit. (n. 16), pp. 284–8.
26 Letter, Robert Stephenson to Isambard K. Brunel, Westminster, 26 October 1855, **Brunel**, D.M.1306/48.
27 The companies, with their opening dates were, New River (1619), Chelsea (1723), Lambeth (1785), West Middlesex (1806), East London (1807), Kent (1809), Grand Junction (1811) and Southwark & Vauxhall (1845).

was the filtering action of the chalk and the consequent purity of the water abstracted – without requiring subsequent treatment. One of the principal sites explored was the Watford–Bushey area in Hertfordshire.[28] Watford stands on reasonably high ground formed of a ridge of gravel overlying the chalk. The river Colne crosses the town, dividing it from Bushey.

Stephenson was involved with two abortive schemes. The first was a scheme proposed by Mr R. Paten in 1840 for procuring water from Bushey by means of springs and boreholes. A provisional committee was formed for The London and Westminster Water-Works, with Stephenson as engineer. In 1840 he made a report to the committee, the quantity of water obtainable being obviously crucial:[29]

An attempt to fix positive quantities, by any line of argument, is naturally attended with considerable difficulty; ... In order to obtain positive evidence ... a well was sunk in Bushey Hall meadows, near the Colne, to a depth of about 34 feet.

The water rose in the well at 2.02 feet per second, yielding 1 091 000 gallons per day. Stephenson therefore concluded 'I trust I have now said enough to convince an unbiased person that there exists no difficulty, both in obtaining a supply of good water from the Springs of the Chalk, near Watford, and in conveying thence to London' and 'the advantages held out by the project ... consist in its being proposed to use spring water, already naturally filtered.'

However, early in 1841, one 'biased' person did intervene, anonymously, in a pamphlet consisting of a lengthy polemic against Stephenson and his proposals for the London and Westminster Company saying:[30]

Now with the highest opinion of that gentleman's talents as a *railroad* engineer, I must observe that the time he has devoted to the study and practice of that branch of engineering must have precluded the possibility of his having been able to obtain such experience in the construction of *water-works*, as to render his *opinions*, however ingenious, of equal authority with those he may give upon railroads ... If Mr. Stephenson had made himself acquainted with these *facts* before he gave his *ideas*, it would, I should suppose, have given those who are about to embark their money in this scheme more confidence – they may discover, too late, that *experience* in water-works, as in railroads, *may* be obtained at too great a cost.

Stephenson appears not to have responded to this attack.

Also in January 1841 a prospectus for The London and Westminster Water Company 'to be empowered by Act of Parliament' was published.[31] Stephenson was named as engineer to the company. As the year progressed, however, the company had expanded to become the London, Westminster & Metropolitan

---

28 Thomas Telford had, in 1834, produced a scheme for bringing water from the river Verulam at Bushey and conducting it by an aqueduct to a reservoir on Primrose Hill.

29 *Report to the Provisional Committee of the London and Westminster Water-Works*, 16 December 1840, p. 16, **ICE**, Tract, 8vo, 78 (No. 7).

30 *Observations on a Report made by Robert Stephenson, Esq., civil engineer to the proposed London and Westminster Water Company*, London, John Green, Newgate Street, 5 January 1841, **ICE**, bound volume marked 'London Water Supply'.

31 *RT*, **IV**, 16 January 1841, p. 71, repeated 23 January, p. 94 and 6 February, p. 157. The Company proposed a Capital of £600 000 in shares of £50 each.

Water Company. His second report, in which he developed his ideas about the water to be abstracted from the chalk, was published in August 1841. He linked his experience as a railway engineer to the problem, saying that he was well acquainted with the chalk between Watford and Tring, 'it having devolved upon me, in the course of my connexion with the London and Birmingham Railway, to sink a great number of wells in the chalk', and 'The Tring cutting … presents another forcible example of the constant and rapid absorption of water by the chalk.'[32] However, difficulties arose in raising the capital in the recession of 1842–1843 and this scheme did not materialize.

In 1848 attempts were made to renew the project, without success. In November 1849 a bill was sought to establish the London (Watford) Spring Water Company, but this was rejected by Parliament. Yet another attempt was made in the session 1850–1851 without success. In March 1852 the bill was again before Parliament, when Stephenson rose to say that:[33]

he had devoted a great deal of time to the examination of this project, and had given it his most serious consideration. He would not pledge himself to the allegations of the promoters of this Bill; he merely rose to assure the House that it possessed merits which ought to be discussed before a Committee. The result of his late investigation was to lead him to the conclusion that the proposal was well worthy consideration. No one was prepared to deny that the supplying of the metropolis with good water was most desirable; and on that ground the proposal ought to be examined by a Committee.

This was Stephenson's last public statement on this ill-fated project.[34]

Like most large industrial cities, Liverpool had, by the middle of the nineteenth century, a growing population and a problem of providing an adequate supply of water. During the first half of the century the water supply was in the hands of private companies who drew their water exclusively from wells sunk in the new red sandstone.[35] Stephenson was involved on two occasions with the Liverpool water supply; the first was in connection with the Corporation acquiring the water companies. In the parliamentary session 1846–1847, the Corporation obtained a bill authorizing them to purchase the works of the private water companies. These were purchased under arbitration at a cost of £622 000, with Stephenson acting as the arbitrator.

The second occasion was in 1850, when Stephenson was appointed engineer to report on 'the best plan for securing an adequate supply of water to the town of Liverpool'.[36] He was asked to 'inform himself upon the subject in all its bearings, by evidence, reports, or otherwise, so as to ensure that the views of

---

32 *Mr. Stephenson's Second Report to the Directors of the London, Westminster, and Metropolitan Water Company*, 24 August 1841, p. 5, **ICE**, Tract, 8vo, 78 (12).

33 *Hansard*, 3S, **120**, 25 March 1852, p. 81.

34 For a broader discussion of these issues see: B. C. S. Harper, 'The Chalk-Water Controversy in Early Victorian London', to be published in *TNS*.

35 Thomas Duncan, 'Description of the Liverpool Corporation Water-Works', *Proc. ICE*, **XII**, 1852/3, 19 April 1853, pp. 460–505.

36 *Report of Robert Stephenson, Civil Engineer, On the Supply of Water to the Town of Liverpool*, 28 March 1850, **ICE**, Tract, 4to, 49 (No. 19).

all parties may be elicited' and to report his opinion to the committee of four questions, namely:[37]

1   Whether a supply sufficient for the present and future needs could be obtained by additional borings, or otherwise, at the present pumping stations, and the cost involved.
2   Whether a sufficient addition to the supply could be obtained in the neighbourhood of Liverpool as recommended by Messrs. James Simpson and J. Newlands (the Borough Engineer) together with the cost.
3   Whether such supply could be obtained by means of the Rivington Works as recommended by Thomas Hawksley, and
4   'Under all the present circumstances of the case, what course is recommended to be pursued?'

The work was largely carried out, under Stephenson's direction, by his two associates, George Berkley and George Phipps. In his subsequent report Stephenson stated his view of the subject:[38]

To Liverpool, in particular, with its high commercial position, its large and rapidly increasing population, and its immense constructions for the purposes of trade, science and habitation, the advantages of a copious and permanent supply of good water can scarcely be over-rated. These prominent considerations, with many others easy to mention, have led me to approach the subject with anxiety, and to devote to it my best energies.

The Stephenson team first investigated the yield from the existing wells, the influence they had on each other and the way in which water was transmitted through the sandstone between wells. In March 1850 Stephenson personally supervised the sinking of a new 4-inch diameter borehole at the 'Windsor' pumping station. After a great deal of investigation he recommended the Rivington reservoir scheme, which was to be designed and executed under Thomas Hawksley.[39]

Another issue at Liverpool that engaged the attention of Stephenson was the question of the infiltration of salt water into the springs and wells. In his 1850 report he commented on the quality of the water:[40]

I shall not, I am sure, be expected to pronounce an opinion of the effects that may be produced upon the human frame, by the presence of salts held in chemical solution by the water obtained from the public wells and employed by the inhabitants of Liverpool for all domestic purposes. … But the general results sufficiently establish, that the progress of the salt-water into the wells is now very gradual, and where its existence has been proved at considerable distances from the River [Mersey], it would seem to be owing rather to accidental causes.

Speaking later in London he said 'At Liverpool, it was palpably demonstrated, that the increase of saline matters in the water, was in proportion to

37 Ibid., p. 4.
38 Ibid., p. 5.
39 Binnie, pp. 136–48.
40 Op. cit. (n. 36).

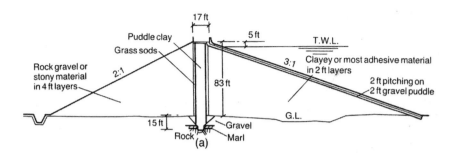

17 ft

Puddle clay
Grass sods

5 ft

T.W.L.

Rock gravel or
stony material
in 4 ft layers

2:1

3:1

Clayey or most adhesive material
in 2 ft layers

83 ft

2 ft pitching on
2 ft gravel puddle

G.L.

15 ft

Gravel

Rock

Marl

(a)

12.2
Rhodeswood
dam near
Manchester
(G. M. Binnie,
*Early Dam
Builders in
Britain*, 1987)

the proximity to the sea. In that case, it was a question, which was limited to a comparatively small area.'[41]

In the mid-nineteenth century Manchester's water supply was being augmented by the construction of a series of reservoirs high in the Longdendale valley to the north-east of the city. In February 1852, excessive rain set in motion an ancient landslip of about 40 acres, on ground that had given no previous indication of moving, and on which a contractor's village called 'New Yarmouth' had been built. The village moved six inches during the night of 6 February, seriously disturbing the wastewater weir and water-course of the Rhodeswood Reservoir (Fig. 12.2), then under construction.

John Bateman, the engineer to these reservoir works, admitted that despite all the experience he had, and his willingness to learn from failure as well as success, 'I am still far from having any decided view as to the best means of drawing water from a great reservoir.'[42] This was a major setback to the works at a time when the scientific understanding of the behaviour of soils was in its infancy. Bateman persuaded the city Council to invite Stephenson and Brunel to advise him 'as to the best course to be pursued to prevent further mischief'.[43]

In April that year Brunel, who apparently had heard nothing, wrote to Stephenson saying, 'What is doing in Manchester Water Works? Will not Bateman be waiting for us?'[44] However, Stephenson and Brunel reported to the Manchester Waterworks Committee in May 1852.[45] They both, in company with Bateman and several members of the Committee, visited the site on Saturday 27 March 1852 when

After examining the slips carefully … and having received Mr. Bateman's explanation of the means which had been employed, … we returned to Town in order to consider deliberately the subject, with the assistance of the plans and drawings, and the data which exist as to the position and state of the materials forming the hill side and the bottom of the valley.[46]

41 Robert Stephenson, contribution to discussion on the paper, Frederick Braithwaite, 'On the Infiltration of Salt-water into the Springs of Wells under London and Liverpool', *Proc. ICE*, **XIV**, 1854/5, p. 521.
42 Bateman.
43 Ibid., p. 168.
44 Letter, Isambard K. Brunel to Robert Stephenson, 24 April 1852, **Brunel**, D.M. 1306/44.
45 Copy letter, Isambard K. Brunel and Robert Stephenson 'To the Water Works Committee of the Town Council of Manchester', 5 May 1852, **Brunel**, private letterbooks, vol. 2, pp. 375–8.
46 Ibid.

The importance and the complexity of the case led Stephenson and Brunel to make a second site visit, after which each separately came to the view of 'the inexpediency of attempting to complete the construction of the work across the disturbed ground according to the original design'.[47] There was naturally a delay in the completion of the new design and eventually Stephenson and Brunel approved the measures adopted. In June 1854 Stephenson wrote to Brunel, saying:[48]

Dear Brunel

I cannot lay my hands upon the date or name of Reservoir when we were called upon by the Manchester water work Co. to advise with Mr. Bateman. If you can pray have the goodness to suggest a form for our account to go in – Had it not better be a joint one of 300 guineas. Put it into what shape you like and let me know.

Brunel also consulted Stephenson regarding the Crystal Palace water towers. The Crystal Palace, after its success in Hyde Park during 1851, was bought by the newly formed Crystal Palace Company, whose directors under-took the dismantling, redesign and removal to Sydenham in south London between 1852 and 1854. The new enlarged design required copious supplies of water to supply the ornamental fountains in the terraced grounds and the building's heating boilers, and for firefighting.

Two towers were proposed, each comprising ten floors, with a central brick chimney flue from the boilers and surmounted by a water tank. The design of the towers was first undertaken by Charles Wild, then Sir Joseph Paxton's assistant. Paxton expressed some anxiety about Wild's design and turned to Brunel for advice. Brunel wrote to Paxton in October 1853 saying: 'the attempt to support upwards of 500 tons at a height of 200 feet upon a cluster of slender legs with but a small base involves considerable difficulties'.[49] In November 1853 Brunel wrote to Stephenson seeking his views of the design:[50]

My Dear Stephenson,

I have been thinking a good deal over these water tower foundations and I have come to the following conclusions upon which however I should be very glad to be convinced that I am wrong. What do you say? The point is that the concrete founda-tion as we saw it is not to be depended upon … any bed of concrete in such a situation and for such a purpose should be made of hydraulic lime or cement and should extend over a greater surface and be carried to a greater depth than the present.

Unfortunately Stephenson's reply is not in the Brunel letterbooks, but Wild's partially built structure was demolished and replaced with two, more substantial, structures by Brunel. These survived the fire at the palace in 1936 and remained as prominent landmarks until they were demolished in 1941.[51]

47 Ibid.
48 Letter, Robert Stephenson to Isambard K. Brunel, 3 June 1854, **Brunel**, D.M. 1306/44.
49 Copy letter, Isambard K. Brunel to Joseph Paxton, 1 October 1853, **Brunel**, Private Letter Book.
50 Copy letter, Isambard K.Brunel to Robert Stephenson, 14 November 1853, **Brunel**, letter book 9, pp. 243–6.
51 Angus Buchanan, Stephen K. Jones, and Ken Kiss, 'Brunel and the Crystal Palace', *IAR*, **XVII**, 1994, pp. 7–21.

Stephenson and Brunel were also jointly consulted by the Glasgow water-works company. In December 1854 Stephenson wrote to Brunel from his Westminster office, saying, 'Can you come along here as Mr. Gale the Engineer of the Gorbals water works is here from Glasgow to give us his ideas on the whole question.'[52] The works were designed by John Bateman and J. M. Gale during 1853–1854, and Stephenson and Brunel were asked to comment on the proposed scheme. They reported to the Provost, Magistrates and Council in February 1855:[53]

In considering the very important subject which you have requested us to report upon, namely the supply of water to the City of Glasgow, and more especially the eligibility of the plan proposed by Mr. Bateman, for applying the waters of Loch Katrine to this purpose, we have had the advantage of considering the results of many previous enquiries. We have also personally inspected the localities, and have sought for, and received the fullest information from the parties to whom we applied for that information, and who we considered could assist us in the inquiry.

Glasgow City Council had asked Stephenson and Brunel to consider the whole question of various other projects and they approved Bateman's Loch Katrine proposal. The Corporation obtained their Act of Parliament in 1855 for this major scheme involving dams, a long aqueduct (comprising pipes, tunnels and bridges) and reservoirs at the southern end supplying the city by gravity. Work began in 1856 and the system was formally opened by Queen Victoria in October 1859.[54]

In water-supply schemes Stephenson was often consulted jointly with Brunel, and their involvement spanned nearly twenty years from 1840. This was the period when large towns like Liverpool, Manchester and Glasgow began to seek water supplies from remote sources: the scale of the engineering work grew dramatically, and a new generation of water engineers emerged.

Main drainage schemes

Robert Stephenson also became much involved with the major debate into London's main drainage proposals. The sanitary condition of London and the Thames had long given cause for concern and, from the 1830s, visitations of cholera brought matters to a head. The natural drainage channels on the north of the river flowed south into the Thames, and those on the south flowed northwards, and these streams discharged effluent into the Thames at low water. In an attempt to deal with the resulting problems on a larger scale, a series of six, short-term, Metropolitan Commissions of Sewers were established from 1848. The commissioners were appointed by Royal Warrant. The

52 **ICE**, 92: Stephenson R.
53 Copy letter, 'To the Honorable the Lord Provost, Magistrates and Council of the City of Glasgow', 12 February 1855, **Brunel**, private letterbooks, vol. 2, pp. 347–72.
54 J. M. Gale, 'On the Glasgow Water Works', *Proc. Institution of Engineers in Scotland*, **VII**, 1863/4, pp. 21–72. Also Binnie, p. 19.

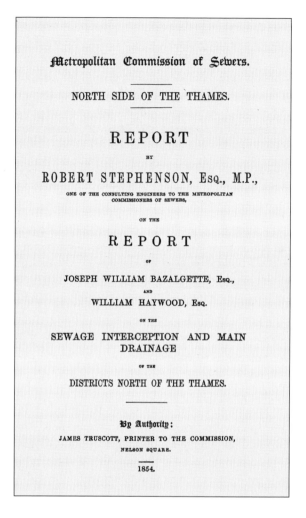

Metropolitan Commission of Sewers.

———

NORTH SIDE OF THE THAMES.

———

REPORT

BY

ROBERT STEPHENSON, Esq., M.P.,

ONE OF THE CONSULTING ENGINEERS TO THE METROPOLITAN
COMMISSIONERS OF SEWERS,

ON THE

REPORT

OF

JOSEPH WILLIAM BAZALGETTE, Esq.,

AND

WILLIAM HAYWOOD, Esq.

ON THE

SEWAGE INTERCEPTION AND MAIN
DRAINAGE

OF THE

DISTRICTS NORTH OF THE THAMES.

———

By Authority:

JAMES TRUSCOTT, PRINTER TO THE COMMISSION,
NELSON SQUARE.

———

1854.

12.3 Title page from Stephenson's report to the Metropolitan Commission of Sewers, 1854

third Commission, which became known as 'The Engineer's Commission', took power on 8 October 1849 and Stephenson was one of the commissioners.[55] One of the earliest of his specific involvements with sewer questions was recorded in a parliamentary debate on the Metropolitan Sewers Bill in June 1852. Sir Benjamin Hall rose to draw the attention of the Chief Commissioner of Woods to what he regarded as the excessive expenses of the Metropolitan Commission of Sewers that 'amounted to 25 per cent on the work done, besides the expenses of supervision and payment of damages'.[56] The work referred to was the Victoria Sewer, and Stephenson was stung to reply:[57]

The whole of the evils complained of in the construction and increased expense of the Victoria sewer was in consequence of the course pursued by the office of Woods and Forests. He went to the Chief Commissioner and endeavoured to induce him to

---

55 The other members were J. M. Rendel and Sir William Cubitt.
56 *Hansard*, 3S, **122**, 17 June 1852, p. 881.
57 Ibid., p. 883.

permit the sewer to be discharged into the Thames within the limits of Crown property; but that request was peremptorily refused. … This refusal made a large difference in the expenditure, and, worse than that, the foundations having been in the new line, a great portion of the sewer was now in a very dangerous state. Whether the responsibility of this rested on the late Chief Commissioner (Lord Seymour) or not, he would not undertake to say.

Lord Seymour replied that the Woods and Forests indeed had objected to the discharge through Crown property, but if they had agreed 'the effect would be greatly to deteriorate that property.' This epitomized the essential difficulty, in public works, of reconciling public good with private rights.

In June 1853 a Parliamentary Select Committee discussed a bill that proposed to establish The Great London Drainage Company with a view to bringing in private capital to finance the vast engineering works involved. Stephenson, as one of the sewer commissioners, was examined by the committee.[58] He was asked about the working practice of the commission, in particular whether he thought it advisable to separate the executive business from the details of considering rates and appeals. Stephenson agreed that it would be advisable, adding:[59]

It was felt by those who were then, like myself, professional men, that it was a waste of time, and interfered very much indeed with our arrangements, and I could not attend those appeals. If any engineering question was brought forward, then I made a point of attending, and so did Sir William Cubitt.

Towards the end of the questioning he was asked if the work of this Company were to be done under the supervision of the officers of the Sewers Commission, 'what amount of supervision would be necessary?' He replied:[60]

It is a difficult work, not an impracticable one; but it would require the greatest superintendence. I am not prepared to say that the work would fail when done, if done as it is proposed; but I should have some apprehensions if I was engineer of it, and I should make some experiment before I began it

This somewhat cautious reply may well have had some influence on the Select Committee, who subsequently dismissed the Bill. This distraction over, the Metropolitan Commission could resume their detailed planning of the interceptor sewer system. In December 1854 Stephenson and Cubitt produced a joint report on the drainage scheme to the Sewer Commissioners (Fig. 12.3).[61] Their report summarizes the series of experiments made by Frank Forster, Stephenson's former associate, in order to determine the best position of the outfall into the Thames on the north bank:[62]

58 In addition to Robert Stephenson the other engineer witnesses were Thomas Brassey, John Fowler, J. W. Bazalgette, Thomas Hawksley, William Haywood, Isambard K. Brunel and Sir William Cubitt.
59 Minutes of Evidence taken before the Select Committee on the Great London Drainage Bill, June 1853, 13 June 1853, **ICE**, Tait Room, p. 165.
60 Ibid., p. 159.
61 Report by Robert Stephenson and Sir William Cubitt upon Mr. Roe's Scheme, 11 December 1854, **ICE**, Tract 8vo, 108 (No 8).
62 Ibid., p. 34.

On the 13th July, 1851, a float was put into the centre of the river opposite Barking Creek two hours after high water. ... At low water the float reached 11¾ miles below that point and returned with the next flood tide to 1 mile above it

The experiments were repeated in August with similar results. This established that the discharge from the outfall at this point would not work its way back into central London – one of the prime requirements of Parliament! It is clear that Stephenson and Cubitt were aware of theoretical work on pipe flow characteristics done in Europe and in their report they commented that:[63]

No part of Engineering science has been more industriously investigated than the laws that govern the flow of water in pipes and open channels; and it is probably not too much to say, that the formulae which represent these laws rank amongst the most truthful that the professional man possesses. They have been the subject of laborious experimental investigation of the most elaborate character, and their results have been tested by the practical man under every variety of conditions, without their truth being impugned in the slightest degree.

However, in 1855, a Bill replaced the Metropolitan Commission with the Metropolitan Board of Works, which had jurisdiction over 117 square miles of London, north and south of the Thames. Now, for the first time, there was a capital-wide authority with the power and finances to implement the interceptor system of main drainage. The board took power on 1 January 1856 and Joseph Bazalgette, who had been engineer to the last commissions of sewers, was appointed engineer.

In 1858 the debate on the Metropolitan Board of Works enabling Bill began in Parliament, with the Chancellor of the Exchequer describing the Thames as 'That noble river, so long the pride and joy of Englishmen' which had 'really become a stygian pool, reeking with ineffable and intolerable horrors'.[64] Stephenson strongly supported Forster's proposed system of independent interceptor sewers on the north and south sides of the river, and continued his support of Bazalgette's development of the scheme, saying he 'believed that Mr. Bazalgette's plan was the best for the drainage'.[65] There was great debate, in Parliament and the press, about the position of the outfalls. and Stephenson contributed to the debate in Parliament:[66]

He thought the House was labouring under an error as regarded the question of outfall. They seemed to be under the impression that by adopting the intercepting system and fixing an outfall, they would be fixing themselves to a certain plan. That was not the fact, because provided they adopted the intercepting system, it was a matter of indifference whether the outfall was at Barking Creek or Sea Reach ... The only effective plan is that of the intercepting sewers; which if combined with embankment and wharfage of the Thames, would, I repeat, not only be remunerating for the outlay, but remove a stigma from London.

63 Ibid., p. 38.
64 *Hansard*, 15 July 1858, p. 1508.
65 Ibid., p. 1535.
66 Ibid. Also copy letter from Isambard K. Brunel to Robert Stephenson, regarding Metropolitan Sewers Commission, 1852, **Brunel**, Letter Book 7, pp. 175, 181–2 and 192.

The Board obtained its enabling Act in 1859 and work began. However, at this time various opinions still remained on the most appropriate engines and pumps required to lift the sewage into the outfall sewers. To resolve these issues Bazalgette convened a committee of engineers with wide experience in these matters, which comprised Robert Stephenson, Joshua Field, John Penn, Thomas Hawksley and George Bidder.

Stephenson, as an ex-commissioner of sewers and a consulting engineer to the commission, made an important contribution to the debate. His status in the engineering profession must have helped Government to have confidence in the proposed interception drainage system for London and to make the funds available for its implementation.

Stephenson was also involved with at least two other drainage schemes outside the Metropolitan Board of Works area. Stephenson's junior associate, William Lloyd, later wrote that he was involved with two drainage schemes for Stephenson, saying, 'In 1852 I undertook the drainage of Watford, which was duly implemented, and also reported on that for Banbury, which, however, was hardly ripe for execution, when other business of greater importance absorbed my attention.'[67]

Coastal, estuarial and river improvement schemes

Robert Stephenson and his associates undertook a considerable amount of river and coastal engineering. A major example arose with the building of the Chester & Holyhead Railway, which followed a route very close to the sea, and posed engineering problems with a variety of site-specific solutions. As engineer-in-chief, Stephenson had the choice of sea walls, cuttings, embankments, groynes, viaducts and tunnels, or a combination of these. In 1847, speaking in a discussion at the Institution of Civil Engineers, he said that he 'in common with all engineers, had met with difficulties in the construction of sea walls' and that details of the sea walls would be of interest to the Institution 'as much more was generally to be learned from failures than from successful works'.[68]

Part of Telford's Holyhead Road had already been carried round the promontory of Penmaenmawr, just east of Conway, and it was here that Stephenson faced particular difficulties. The twin-track railway was aligned on the seaward side of Telford's road and became, therefore, the first line of sea defence. The railway was carried on a terrace beneath the promontory at a level of 17ft above highest spring tides. The works included sea walls a mile and a quarter in length and a tunnel 693ft long (Fig. 12.4).

---

67 Lloyd, p. 40.
68 G. B. Wheeler Jackson, 'Description of the Great North Holland Canal, with an account of the Mode of gaining Land from the Sea by Polders, and of the Art of Building with Fascine work, and an Account of the Works at Nieuwediep', *Proc. ICE*, **VI**, 1847, p. 115.

12.4
Penmaenmawr
viaduct and
tunnel on the
Chester &
Holyhead
Railway
(lithograph by
G. F. Hawkins
after S. Russell,
1849; Courtesy
of Institution of
Civil Engineers)

Work began in the autumn of 1845.[69] The walls were divided into four lengths. The first was east of the headland and about 990ft long. The second, west of the headland, was the deepest and longest part, but was so severely damaged during a northerly gale in October 1846 that it was condemned. The third was of less depth than either of the former, whilst the fourth was originally designed as a dwarf wall, but owing to the heavy seas was eventually built of similar section to the other walls. After these setbacks the walls progressed rapidly during the spring and summer of 1846.

This section of line, with a tunnel through the headland, had been identified as a tricky length when the original route had been canvassed. The rock proved highly fissured, and the tunnel had to be lined for half its length. Stephenson's views of the problems encountered during design, construction, destruction, redesign and rebuilding were frankly expressed in 1851 after the line was opened:[70]

The first point to be solved in this case, was, whether it was better to make a long tunnel, or to construct sea-walls, or viaducts; very careful calculations were made, and it was decided, that the preferable course was to build retaining walls, with occasional short tunnels … He had, however, during the construction of the works, good reason to change his opinion; and he now believed, that if a long tunnel had been made in the first instance, instead of erecting artificial works to contend with the sea, it would have induced an economy of from £25,000 to 30,000 … it would be better to avoid walls altogether; they were difficult to manage, and there were no calculations which could be applied to them … in railway works, Engineers should endeavour, as far as possible, to avoid any necessity of contending with the sea.

Stephenson was also involved in several major schemes for the improvement of rivers, both tidal and non-tidal. Speaking in 1852, he said, 'The

69 Henry Swinburne, 'Account of the Sea-Walls at Penmaen Mawr, on the line of the Chester and Holyhead Railway', *Proc. ICE*, **X**, 1850/1, pp. 257–77.
70 Robert Stephenson in discussion, ibid., pp. 274–5.

subject of the treatment of rivers was one of great interest.'[71] He considered that the author had stated his views both boldly and generally but warned that

he must not, however, take it for granted, that the method which proved successful in one locality, would prove equally so, in another place, and under another class of circumstances. An Engineer having only obtained experience in a particular sphere of practice, and drawn his conclusions from the facts there observed, would soon find … how necessary it would be to modifiy his previous opinions.

This highlights the essentially site-specific nature of decision making in civil engineering, and Stephenson went on to refer to his own 'lengthened and somewhat varied practice' and observed that he had himself found it necessary to change his views several times on such subjects, having previously considered them sound.

Stephenson became involved with the river Nene in 1847. The drainage and reclamation of land from the fens goes back to Roman times, and many great engineers have been involved in such works in south Yorkshire, Lincolnshire and Cambridgeshire over the centuries. The Middle Level Fen, involving the rivers Nene, Witham and Ouse, all draining into the Wash, was the scene of some of the greatest engineering works. These were usually undertaken by groups of ad hoc Commissioners whose role was to identify a problem and engage consulting engineers to design and estimate the costs of the necessary works. The Commissioners would then raise the necessary finance and solicit Parliament for an enabling act.

The old course of the river Nene flowed eastwards from Northampton, passing to the south of Peterborough through March and Wisbech to the sea. The problems of making the river navigable from Northampton to Peterborough had been the subject of four acts of parliament in the eighteenth century.[72] The Nene outfall was designed by John Rennie (1761–1821) and work commenced in August 1827 and was completed in 1830 by Thomas Telford and Sir John Rennie.

The situation in the river remained unsatisfactory, however. At a meeting of the River Nene Improvement Committee held in Whittlesey Town Hall on 31 August 1847 it was confirmed that Stephenson would make a survey, report and estimate of the required works. The situation was complex, involving such issues as the irregular state and shallowness of the river, crowded shipping lying aground, the obstruction caused by the river bridge, and the drainage of the Waldersey and Redwood districts 'without the use of engines'.

Stephenson reported in January 1848,[73] saying that he had carefully studied 'the able Reports of the late Mr. Rennie, Mr. Telford and Mr. Chapman, and of Sir John Rennie; and the no less able Reports of Messrs. Walker and Burges on the Middle Level'.[74] With all this information and so much of it put into

71 Discussion following paper by William Alexander Brooks , 'On the Improvement of Tidal Navigations and Drainages', *Proc. ICE*, **XII**, 1852/3, p. 12.
72 Priestley, pp. 463–6.
73 *Report of Robert Stephenson, Esq., MP, on the Improvement of the River Nene and Wisbech River*, Westminster, 25 January 1848, **ICE**, Tract, 8vo., p. 232.
74 Ibid., p. 7.

effect, he said, 'I feel the subject is nearly exhausted.'[75] The new Nene Outfall had been satisfactorily completed but Stephenson clearly identified the main problem as being that 'The River Nene, from Peterborough to and through Wisbech, remains however nearly as it was in 1814'.[76] He considered the nub of the problem to be 'Cross Keys Bridge and Wisbech Bridge, with the tortuous and contracted channel through Wisbech Town'.[77]

One of Stephenson's recommendations was for a new cut (not a new suggestion) which would extend 'from Phillip's Brewery above the town to the Horseshoe Corner below it, and is about a mile and a quarter long'.[78] He ended his report with an estimate stating that:[79]

An outlay of £250,000 will eventually be required for the completion of the proposed works. The expenditure will of course be gradual, and may be extended over any convenient number of years, as the funds become available. I am scarcely informed enough to speak of sources of revenue, but from calculations made by others better qualified … there will … be sufficient to pay £12,500, the interest at 5 per cent. on the cost, and to leave £2,000 *per annum* for expenses and maintenance, which is an ample reserve in works of this kind.

However, Stephenson's proposed works were not executed; local interests were in conflict, personal differences intervened, and the funds required were large and no agreement could be made for sharing the costs.

In 1852 an act of parliament established the 'Nene Valley Drainage and Navigation Improvement Commissioners', who were empowered to construct works costing £150 000 to be completed by May 1857. It was the progress, or lack of it, of these works that drew Stephenson again to the river Nene. His last report on the Nene was made in 1858, in which he recapitulated the tangled web of events in this sorry saga of unrealized proposals for the improvement of the river.[80] It was a subject that he considered to be 'by no means free from embarrassment, and associated in my mind with many conflicting reminiscences'.[81] He died just over a year later and did not see his proposals implemented.

Writing in 1849, Robert Stephenson said of the Norfolk Estuary area:[82]

No district in England, perhaps, has had the services of engineers to such an extent, and for so long a continuous period, as the country abutting on the Wash, and its four

75 Ibid.
76 Ibid.
77 Ibid., p. 8. Cross Keys Bridge carried road traffic over the Nene outfall. The first bridge, in timber, was by Sir John Rennie in 1825. The bridge was rebuilt by Robert Stephenson as a wrought-iron swing bridge in 1850. In 1864 Stephenson's bridge was converted to dual road and rail use. The present bridge was built in 1897.
78 Ibid., p. 11.
79 Ibid., p. 19.
80 *Report of Robert Stephenson, Esq., MP,; G. P. Bidder, Esq.; and Geo. Rob. Stephenson, Esq. On the Improvement of the River Nene*, with a prefatory letter from Mr. Robert Stephenson, 31 July 1858, **ICE**, Tract, 4to, 41 (12).
81 Ibid., p. 3.
82 *Report of Robert Stephenson, Esq., C.E., on the Norfolk Estuary*, London, 26 May 1849, **ICE**, Tait Room, volume 'Norfolk Estuary Various' (No. 8).

tributary rivers, Ouse, Nene, Witham, and Welland, with their respective towns of Lynn, Wisbeach [Wisbech], Boston and Spalding; and in no other case that I know is the record so complete.

An Act of 1846 established the Norfolk Estuary Company and gave them powers to work on the outfall of the river Ouse into the Wash with the main objective of land reclamation. The 1846 scheme was prepared by Sir John Rennie. Questions arose about details of the scheme and delays in the work, and an Admiralty Inquiry was held at the Guildhall, Kings Lynn, in April 1849 at which the two engineering witnesses were Rennie and Stephenson as joint engineers to the company. Stephenson was questioned and agreed that Rennie's scheme was feasible and said that, moreover:[83]

it is the best method of improving the navigation, at the same time that it improves the drainage of the land, and also gives the shareholders the power of enclosing the land. … I do not think any other plan can be devised by which those three objects can be simultaneously obtained.

Mr Tycho Wing, who examined Stephenson at the inquiry on behalf of the company, said the Norfolk Estuary Company did not wish to be involved with drainage, saying, 'their object is to gain land, drainage is with them a collateral advantage.' But Stephenson insisted that the three elements must be considered together. When discussing the proposed new straight outfall of the Ouse, the question naturally arose about scour and possible siltation. In this case, Stephenson drew on his (and Rennie's) experience on the river Nene, which had remarkable similarities with the Ouse, saying:[84]

I want the new cut made for the purpose of doing three-fourths of the work for nothing, which I believe most firmly will be the case. … I think the circumstances of the Nene and the Ouse are so nearly alike in my estimation that you would be throwing away experience if you did not follow the same rule here which has answered so well there.

When questioned about the consequences on the regime of the river of decisions made, Stephenson expressed his view in general and philosophical terms:[85]

It is impossible to decide beforehand, or by any abstract calculations, what will be the effect of a change in the river. You cannot reason with very much certainty when you take it as a simple abstract question, but you know very well the direction or the tendency of anything you may do, and may approximate to the extent of the effect.

This clearly expresses the dilemma of the civil engineer in the mid-nineteenth century, half a century before hydraulic modelling was available. But, in answer to a question, he was clear on the specific issue of siltation in tidal rivers saying, 'There is more water running out than runs into a tidal river; consequently, you never can drive silt up a tidal river; it is an absurdity.'[86]

83 Evidence taken before Captain James Vetch, RE, and Captain John Washington of the Admiralty, in *Admiralty Inquiry: Norfolk Estuary Bill*, Guildhall, King's Lynn, 12 April 1849, p. 10, **ICE**, Tait Room, volume 'Norfolk Estuary Various' (No. 2).
84 Ibid., p. 12.
85 Ibid., p. 13.
86 Ibid., p. 15.

A month after the Admiralty Inquiry at King's Lynn, Stephenson presented his report to the Company.[87] The questions submitted to him were; can the interests of navigation and drainage be so combined with the reclaiming of land into one scheme beneficial to all, and is the estimate such that the prospect of remuneration would justify the Company to proceed? Stephenson said, 'The design is enclosed lands in North Lynn … giving at once a substitute for the tortuous and uncertain channel … Combined with this is the scheme for reclaiming land.'[88] In the report he restates and amplifies most of the views given to the Admiralty Inquiry, but adds some information about the issue of land reclamation:[89]

the rivers flowing into the Wash, have attained conditions necessary to equilibrium, or, in other words, that the action and reaction of the waters are all but equal; whence the deposit appears to accumulate slowly. But alter by art, or remove some of these conditions of equilibrium, and instantly new series of cause and effect come into play. Sandbanks may be shifted, and a more rapid increase of deposit may be made to take place.

Stephenson concluded his report by agreeing that the reclaiming of '9,000 acres is within easy compass' and with a slight increase in the estimate 'I feel quite justified in advising the promoters to proceed with their measure.'[90]

However, he was still required to give evidence to the Select Committee on the Norfolk Estuary Bill on 12 June 1849. The questions, on the whole, elicited answers similar to those given in the earlier inquiries. The questioner noted that the issue of the merits of a straight or circuitous outfall channel was mentioned for King's Lynn, to which Stephenson replied, 'Yes; it was raised, I thought, merely for the purposes of discussion.'[91] He was asked to confirm that the works must necessarily proceed gradually, to which he replied, 'Under any circumstances they must require a length of time to complete, for you only have as much as nature will assist you in doing.'[92]

Isambard K. Brunel was also involved with East Anglian clients concerned with the Norfolk Estuary works as they proceeded. In 1852, writing to Sir John Rennie, Brunel provided further evidence of his relationship with Stephenson:[93]

I have for several years been in frequent sharp conflict with my friend Stephenson (professionally) and that is the atmosphere that tests us most. And I have learnt to have a kind companion in him – I only trust this feeling is mutual – you and I have not been thus opposed.

87 Op. cit. (n. 82).
88 Ibid., p. 2.
89 Ibid., p. 5.
90 Ibid.
91 Ibid., p. 4.
92 Ibid., p. 5.
93 Copy letter, Isambard K. Brunel to Sir John Rennie, 25 March 1852, headed: 'Private', Brunel, Private Letter Books, vol. 8, p. 330. There is further correspondence between Brunel and Rennie on the Norfolk Estuary scheme.

Sir John Fowler, who was also involved with River Nene and other fen drainage topics, speaking in 1859 just after Stephenson's death said:[94]

at the present time the Ouse below and above Lynn was a complete river. The cut obtained by Sir John Rennie and the late Mr. Stephenson was certainly one of the finest engineering works in the country. The cut was two miles in length and from 600 to 700 feet in width, and a more successful result had never been obtained.

Stephenson was also consulted on a similar project in Holland. The Netherlands Land Enclosure Company was formed in 1852 with the object of reclaiming nearly 30 000 acres of submerged land in the Eastern Scheldt. The original share capital of the company was £500 000 and their engineer was Sir John Rennie. The capital was fully subscribed and enclosures of about 1500 acres began in the summer of 1852. However, these works were destroyed by a violent storm in February 1853. The directors consulted George Bidder, who inspected and reported in July 1853, advising a different method of working to that originally employed.

A new company chairman was appointed who suggested that Stephenson should accompany Bidder on a visit to the site. In August 1854 Stephenson and Bidder made their report, new capital was raised and the works were resumed. After further setbacks the scheme was gradually implemented and by 1868 land cultivation was improving, houses were built and the polder banks were sufficiently strong to resist the greatest storms.[95]

Ship canals

One of the distinctive, and important, characteristics of nineteenth-century civil engineering was the development of ship canals. These included the Caledonian (1822), the Gloucester & Berkley (1827), the Exeter (1829), the Suez (1869), the Amsterdam (1876), the Cronstadt (1878), the Corinth, the Manchester (1894) and the Kiel (1895). British engineers were significantly involved with these schemes and Robert Stephenson, in particular, staked a great deal of his professional reputation in discussing the technical and political issues surrounding the planning of the Suez Canal.

The desirability of a canal connecting the Red Sea and the Mediterranean through the isthmus of Suez had been discussed intermittently from the end of the eighteenth century. The French invaded Egypt in 1798 and the French engineers located the bed of an ancient canal and their survey suggested, mistakenly, a difference in level between the two seas of about 30ft. The British feared French domination in the Middle East and its consequences for their interests in India. The debate between Britain and France about the canal flared up again in the middle of the nineteenth century, leading to what

94 John Fowler in discussion of paper, R. B. Grantham, 'On Arterial Drainage and Outfalls', *Proc. ICE*, **XIX**, 1859/60, p. 101.
95 Clark (1983), pp. 208–11. E. F. Clark told the author that, on a recent visit to the Netherlands, he was informed that the original documents relating to this scheme no longer exist.

Lord Kinross described as 'a long spell of diplomatic warfare, fraught with abortive investigation and obstructive intrigue'.[96]

The debate about the technical issues was carried on by three engineers, Paulin Talabot of France, Alois de Negrelli of Austria and Robert Stephenson. Stephenson later wrote, 'In the year 1846 I was solicited by my friend, M. Talabot, one of the most eminent engineers of France' to investigate the practicability of an isthmus canal. Later, in 1858, an acrimonious public exchange of views ensued between Stephenson and Negrelli, who said:[97]

The only time I have ever spoken to Mr. Stephenson on this subject was on 30th November, 1846, at Paris, when we concluded a treaty according to which I was to undertake the exploration of the Bay of Pelusium and of the shore of Tineh. My friend Talabot took the levelling of the isthmus, and Mr. Stephenson the exploration of the Gulf of Suez.

This survey had been planned in January 1846 but was not undertaken. However, under Talabot's direction a corps of scientific engineers went to Egypt and undertook the levelling from September 1846 to January 1847. As a result it was found that there was no difference in level between the two seas. In December 1847, however, it was reported that Stephenson had arrived in Vienna, had several conferences with Negrelli and that 'They were expected shortly to set out together for Egypt'.[98]

Stephenson's contribution to the public debate during the 1850s was made by his speeches in Parliament and in reply to a letter published by Negrelli in the *Austrian Gazette*. In the House of Commons on 17 July 1857 a Member summed up the British attitude to the political factors affecting the Suez Canal by condemning the scheme as 'one which no Englishman with his eyes open would think it desirable to encourage'.[99] Lord Palmerston observed, ironically, 'As regards the engineering difficulties, I am aware that there is nothing which money and skill cannot overcome, except to stop the tides of the ocean, and to make rivers run uphill to their sources.'[100] Stephenson then rose, declined to comment on the political issues, and went on to say, perhaps not surprisingly:[101]

as an engineer he would pronounce it to be an undesirable scheme, in a commercial point of view, and that the railway (now nearly completed) would, as far as concerned India and postal arrangements, be more expeditious, more certain, and more economical than even if there were this new Bosphorus between the Red Sea and the Mediterranean.

This created an international reaction and, in August 1857, the International Scientific Commission on the Suez Canal published in Turin a critical analysis of Stephenson's comments.[102]

96 Kinross, p. xi.
97 Letter, Alois Negrelli to the Editor of the *Austrian Gazette*, Vienna, 10 June 1858, published June 1858. Also letter, Robert Stephenson to the Editor of the *Austrian Gazette*, July 1858, **ICE**, Tract, 8vo, 112, No. 9.
98 *RT*, **X**, 4 December 1847, p. 1498.
99 Jeaffreson, II, p. 148.
100 Ibid.
101 Ibid.
102 *Observations Sur Le Discours Prononce Par M. Stephenson, Ingenieur, Dans La Chambre Des Communes*, (17 July 1857 session), Commission Scientifique Internationale, by P. Paleocapa, Ingenieur, Turin, **ICE**, Tract, 8vo, 112, No. 8.

In Parliament just under a year later, on 1 June 1858, Stephenson went even further, saying:[103]

Even supposing its construction to be physically possible, which he, for one, denied, he was prepared to show that the engineering difficulties would render the scheme impossible. ... Instead of there being a difference of thirty feet in the height, however, it turned out that the two seas were on a dead level, and that no current whatever could be established ... if this channel were cut, and the water let into it, it would not be a canal but a ditch ... As far as the English engineers were concerned, he believed they all agreed with him to a man.

This brought a stinging reply from Negrelli, who wrote: 'It is requisite, ... to the interest of truth to expose the real facts of the case; and in so doing I feel it necessary to refresh Mr. Stephenson's memory.'[104] Another example of the vitriolic relationships between the English and French engineers was contained in a letter written in June 1858 by Charles Manby – at that time both Honorary Secretary to the Institution of Civil Engineers and London representative of Robert Stephenson & Co. His letter says:[105]

Suez Canal I have had Lesseps here bothering me & foaming at the mouth about the Cheif [sic] and the part taken by him relative to the Canal. We have, of course, ended by a row and the Frenchman will, also of course, try to get me into an epistolary discussion. At all events he has wasted a large part of my day which vexes me.

In August 1859 James Brunlees and E. B. Webb read their paper on an alternative scheme to the Suez Canal in which they said: 'We are of opinion that Mr. Stephenson's arguments are incontrovertible: they have been laid before the public, and there is no necessity to reproduce them here ... We propose to construct a SHIP RAILWAY between the two seas.'[106] This scheme was not built and the Suez Canal was opened, and welcomed in Britain, in 1869 – ten years after Stephenson's death. There can be little doubt that Stephenson's outright rejection of the Suez Canal scheme did detract from his reputation. His previous experience naturally led him to embrace the rival British railway project.

Contemporary with the Suez debate there were two papers read and discussed at the Institution of Civil Engineers on the proposed Panama Canal project. In December 1849 Robert Stephenson remarked that, although he was 'well acquainted with Carthagena and its neighbourhood, he had never been on the Isthmus'.[107] Nevertheless he had examined all the reports and 'saw nothing to deter enterprising men from undertaking the cutting of a ship canal'. He did, however, suggest that an inexpensive railway should first be made to enable the

---

103 Jeaffreson, II, pp. 150–1.
104 Letter, op. cit. (n. 97), p. 2.
105 Letter, Charles Manby to R. Stephenson & Co., Westminster, 8 June 1858, **IMechE**, IMS 171/5.
106 J. Brunlees and E. B. Webb, *Proposed Ship-Railway across the Isthmus of Suez*, 3 August 1859, pp. 6–7, **ICE**, Tract, 8vo, 112, No. 10.
107 Lt. Col. John Augustus Lloyd, 'On the facilities for a Ship Canal communication between the Atlantic and Pacific Oceans, through the Isthmus of Panama', *Proc. ICE*, **IX**, 1849/50, p. 79.

canal to be 'commenced at several points simultaneously'. He went on to remember that[108]

on returning from the Darien, in 1828, he met Mr. Trevithick, at Carthagena, and had been informed by him, that he had traversed the Isthmus three times ... and from this inspection Mr. Trevithick concluded, that the route by the river Chagres and the Rio Grande was the most feasible one, and that which ought to be adopted.

Seven years later, following a paper read by an American engineer in April 1856, Stephenson commented that he had[109]

spent some time in Columbia, and during his stay there, the late Colonel Lloyd explored the Isthmus; but the information collected by that gentleman, was insufficient to enable Engineers to form an opinion, whether an inter-oceanic canal, at that point was practicable ... Nothing could settle this question, but the co-operation of the Governments of Great Britain, France and the United States.

Stephenson considered that this paper had 'produced more intelligible information upon the subject, than had hitherto been given to the world'.

Robert Stephenson's opinion on the relative advantages of goods transport by canals or railways was explicitly stated in his Presidential Address to the Institution of Civil Engineers in January 1856, during his involvement with the ship canal question. He argued that nature opposed a limit to the number of craft using a canal:[110]

Every canal-boat has to pass a summit, more, or less abundantly supplied with water ... the extent of the traffic by this inland navigation must, therefore, be dependent upon the supply of water which can be commanded at the summits to be traversed. But, more than this, all canals are subjected to the vicissitudes of dry seasons ... and the frost of severe seasons, during which nature may compel a total cessation of traffic for several weeks. In comparison with these difficulties, railway communication has none; and hitherto, whatever barriers NATURE has opposed, SCIENCE has entirely surmounted.

The Serpentine, Hyde Park

The lake in Hyde Park was formed by constructing an earth dam, built in 1730–1731 by James Horne.[111] The work was promoted and the lake maintained by the Office of Works and their successors (Fig. 12.5), and by the middle of the nineteenth century the recreational lake was in a sad condition. The issue was discussed in Parliament during the summer of 1859 and was the occasion of Robert Stephenson's last speech in the House of Commons. He had spoken on the issue in the House on 4 August and again on 11 August, when he was described, on leaving a meeting of the Royal Society, as[112]

108 Ibid., p. 81.
109 Frederick M. Kelly, 'On the Junction of the Atlantic and Pacific Oceans, and the Practicability of a Ship Canal, without Locks, by the Valley of the Atrato', *Proc. ICE*, **15**, 1855/6, p. 417.
110 RS Presidential Address, *Proc. ICE*, **XV**, 1855/6, 8 January 1856, p. 152.
111 For a fuller account of the works see entry for James Horne in Skempton (2002), p. 341.
112 Jeaffreson, II, p. 252.

12.5 Serpentine
pumping station
in Kensington
Gardens
(G. M. Binnie,
*Early Victorian
Water Engineers*,
1981)

not looking well, nor was he animated with his usual flow of cheerfulness; and he left
the room early in order to take his seat at a debate in the House of Commons on
cleansing the Serpentine.

On 4 August the debate was opened by Sir Minto Farquhar, who described
the Serpentine as[113]

an abomination and a source of disease, instead of what it ought to be, an ornament to
the Park … not only did the drainage of the surrounding neighbourhood, but also
that from the Kensall Green Cemetery and the New Cemetery in the Harrow Road,
find its way into the Serpentine. This was most disgusting. During the last fifteen
years 3,963,689 persons had bathed in the Serpentine.

The government agency, The Office of Woods and Forests, had received a
report from Thomas Hawksley suggesting a plan for circulating the stagnant
water through filters and returning it to the lake. There was a variety of opinions about the best approach to dealing with the nuisance and Sir Morton
Peto thought it right to 'consult the first engineering authority in this country
– Mr. Robert Stephenson'.[114] Stephenson lived in Gloucester Square, just
north of Hyde Park, and had to pass the Serpentine daily on the way to his
office in Great George Street, and during the debate he said he 'was in the
habit of driving past it twice a day, and rode there occasionally for some
hours'.[115] Stephenson considered that the Serpentine was not in a condition to
cause offence but, nevertheless, remarked:[116]

With regard to Mr. Hawksley's plan, it was an engineering subject, on which he
trusted he might venture to give an opinion. Supposing, for the sake of argument, that

113 *Hansard*, 3S, **155**, 4 August 1859, p. 968.
114 Ibid., p. 969.
115 *Hansard*, 3S, **155**, 11 August 1859, p. 1346.
116 Ibid., p. 1348.

the state of the Serpentine was as impure as had been represented – though he distinctly said he did not believe that it was … the question was, what was the best mode of getting rid of the nuisance. … He believed there was only one efficient plan, and that was the one suggested by Mr. Hawksley; namely, that of pumping up a large quantity of water at one end, and so drawing it away from the other.

At this point Sir Joseph Paxton interjected, saying 'He does not do that' – at which Stephenson was rather rattled and replied:[117]

He does do it; and he could not pump water into one end of the lake without drawing it away from the other. It was impossible. He had great respect for his hon. Friend's opinion on matters of taste, but upon engineering matters he really must demur to give him the same confidence.

Paxton replied:[118]

He was the last man to put his opinion on any subject of engineering in competition with that of his hon. Friend who had last spoken and who was undoubtedly at the head of his profession; but he did not think this was altogether an engineering question. He (Sir Joseph Paxton) was quite satisfied that Mr. Hawksley's plan would not answer.

Hawksley's scheme was not implemented as it was replaced by Bazalgette's main drainage scheme. On this rather sad exchange Stephenson ended both his Parliamentary career and his involvement with water engineering matters – he had just two months to live.

Theoretical and experimental issues

It is clear that Robert Stephenson was as aware of the scientific background (such as it was) to his work in water engineering as he was in his railway work. By the mid-nineteenth century there was a growing body of work seeking to rationalize decision making in this difficult area of engineering design. Stephenson was aware of the work of European experimentalists, notably in France, on such issues as friction in pipe flow, and the resistance encountered by moving vessels in canals and at sea. He had practical experience of tide measurement, sediment transport and siltation.

Speaking in 1846 in the discussion of a paper on the resistance to moving bodies in fluids, Stephenson said, 'The object appeared to be, to ascertain the law of resistance with respect to large vessels, as deductions from the experiments on small bodies did not seem to apply.' The experiments being discussed involved a steam tug towing a vessel at low speeds, and Stephenson thought that 'a steam vessel contained within itself the best mode of trying experiments, by means of the indicator attached to the engines' and he thought this the better technique 'if the vessel was tried at various rates of

117 Ibid.
118 Ibid.

immersion, different speeds, and under circumstances that enabled deductions to be drawn'.[119]

When questioned in 1849 about the relative merits of confining an outfall
channel or reducing the length of the channel, Stephenson said:[120]

If you introduce the formula of Du Baat, which I believe is the one found to answer
the condition of rivers best, you will find that there the length is a most important
element in the formula; depth, I admit, is important *ceteris paribus*, but the length is
one of the most controlling elements in the velocity of a river, next to the hydraulic
depth. For instance, in the water-pipes of a town, it is found to operate.

Again, when discussing his work on the river Ouse in Norfolk he cited the
similarity between the Ouse and the river Nene, on which he had previously
worked, saying 'any theoretical doubt would not have weighed much, but here
was an experimental test of all the principles'.[121]

In 1855 he spoke during the discussion at the Institution of Civil Engineers
on a paper discussing experiments of the flow of water in pipes made by a 'Trial
Works Committee' directed by John Roe. Stephenson was severely critical of
the results, saying 'in this particular instance, it was almost unavoidably necessary, to examine into the scientific qualifications of the persons conducting these
extraordinary experiments, in order to arrive at an estimate of their value, or
rather, he must say, their utter worthlessness'. He went on to say:[122]

In the case of these experiments, it would have been more useful to have selected such
as could have been relied upon, with a view to applying to the accepted formula, any
correction that might be deemed necessary. The question was large and of much
importance; it had engaged the attention of some of the first men of the age, ... it
would be a benefit to science, to show that the discrepancies, assumed by the Board of
Health and others, did really exist, in order that a question of such vital importance in
the practice of Hydraulic Engineering, should be set at rest.

Stephenson brought to water engineering the same thoroughness and
insight that he gave to his railway work. He read carefully the reports on water
engineering projects submitted to him, and in giving evidence at inquiries
demonstrated that he was fully aware of the details. If necessary, he would visit
the site of a water project and even conduct on-site experiments. His work on
the interaction between adjacent boreholes at Liverpool and the infiltration of
salt water was masterful. He amassed a great deal of information on the regime
of tidal rivers and cautioned his colleagues to be aware of the dangers of
applying hydraulic rules generally in widely varying circumstances. His
support for the concept of the interceptor sewer system in London greatly
helped the Metropolitan Board of Works' application for their enabling bill,
and his personal status in civil engineering undoubtedly inspired confidence

119 John Mortimer Heppel, 'On the relation between the velocity and the Resistance encountered by
     bodies moving in fluids', 17 March 1846, *Proc. ICE*, **V**, p. 280.
120 Op. cit. (n. 83), p. 11.
121 Robert Stephenson evidence to Inquiry, ibid., p. 6.
122 James Leslie, 'Observations on the Flow of Water through Pipes, Conduits and Orifices', 6 February
     1855, *Proc. ICE*, **XIV**, pp. 290–1.

in the promoters of public health works and certainly facilitated the granting of government funding for these projects. In the Suez Canal debate it is somewhat difficult to understand his outright rejection of the project and his statement that the canal could not be built for engineering reasons. But it should be remembered the Suez question was one of considerable political complexity.

Water engineering represented an interesting diversification of Stephenson's consulting engineering practice in the latter part of his career, and in his obituary in the Proceedings of the Institution of Civil Engineers he was accurately described as 'a man of varied information, fond of winning others to his opinions.'

Bibliography

Addyman, John, and Fawcett, Bill (1999), *The High Level Bridge and Newcastle Central Station*, North Eastern Railway Association, Newcastle-upon-Tyne.

Alberti, L. B. (1470, English edition 1726), *Ten Books of Architecture*.

Allen, John S. (2000), *A History of Horseley, Tipton: Two Centuries of Engineering Progress*, Ashbourne.

Anon (1872), 'Joseph Pease, a Memoir', reprinted from *Northern Echo*, 9 February 1872, London and Darlington.

Anon (1982/3), 'Coalville 150', *Leicestershire Historian*, **3** (1), Leicester.

Bailey, Michael R. (1978/9), 'Robert Stephenson & Co. 1823–1829', *TNS*, **50**, pp. 109–38.

—— (1980/1), 'George Stephenson – Locomotive Advocate: The Background to the Rainhill Trials', *TNS*, **52**, pp. 171–9.

—— (1984), 'Robert Stephenson & Company 1823–1836', unpublished MA thesis, University of Newcastle-upon-Tyne.

—— (1986/7), 'Robert Stephenson and the Horseley Company', *TNS*, **58**, pp. 139–140.

—— (1989), 'Robert Stephenson & Co. and the Paper Drying Machine in the 1820s', *Bulletin of the International Association of Paper Historians* (Velp, Netherlands), **23**, pp. 6–11 and 51–66.

—— (1999), 'Decision-Making Processes in the Manufacturing Sector: The Independent Locomotive Industry in the 19th Century', unpublished DPhil thesis, University of York, Institute of Railway Studies.

Bailey, Michael R., and Glithero, John P. (2000), *The Engineering and History of Rocket*, London.

Barlow, Peter (1835a), *Experiments on the Transverse Strength and Other Properties of Malleable Iron – with Reference to its Uses for Railway Bars &c*, London.

—— (1835b), *Second Report Addressed to the Directors and Proprietors of the London & Birmingham Railway Co. Founded on an Inspection of, and Experiments made on the Liverpool & Manchester Railway*, London.

—— (2nd edn, 1837), *Report on the Weight of Rails, and Description of Chairs and Fastenings, the Distance of the Support and the Size of the Blocks, of the Liverpool and Manchester Railway*, London.

Barnes, Eric G. (1966), *The Rise of the Midland Railway, 1844–1874*, London.

Bärtschi, H.-P. (1983), *Industrialisierung, Eisenbahnschlachten und Städtebau*, Basel.

Bateman, J. F. (1884), *History and Description of the Manchester Waterworks*, Manchester and London.

Baughan, Peter E. (1972), *The Chester & Holyhead Railway*, vol. 1, Newton Abbot.

Beckett, Derrick (1984), *Stephensons' Britain*, Newton Abbot.

de Belidor, B. F. (1752), *Architecture Hydraulique*, IV, Paris.

Berridge, P. S. A. (1969), *The Girder Bridge: After Brunel and Others*, London.

Biddle, G., and Nock, O. S. (1983), *Railway Heritage of Britain*, London.

Binnie, G. M. (1981), *Early Victorian Water Engineers*, London.

Bird, James (1963), *The Major Seaports of the United Kingdom*, London.

Blackwell, Thomas E. (1860), *Report on the Grand Trunk Railway of Canada for … 1859*, London.

Booth, Henry (1830), *An Account of the Liverpool and Manchester Railway*, Liverpool.

Bourne, John C. (1839), *Drawings of the London and Birmingham Railway*, London.

Brees, S. C. (1837; 2nd edn, 1838), *Railway Practice: A Collection of Working Plans and Practical Details &c.*, London.

—— (3rd Series, 1847), *Railway Practice: A Collection of Working Plans and Practical Details &c.*, London.

Briano, E. (1976), *Stori delle Ferrovie in Italia*, Milan.

Britton, John (1839), 'An Historical and Descriptive Account', in Bourne, John C., *Drawings of the London and Birmingham Railway*, London, pp. 3–26.

Brooke, D. (2000), *The Diary of William Mackenzie*, London.

Brooks, Edward (1996), *Sir Samuel Morton Peto*, Bury St Edmunds.

Bruce, G. B. (1850/1), 'Description of the Royal Border Bridge over the River Tweed on the York, Newcastle and Berwick Railway', *Proc. ICE*, **X**, pp. 214–44.

Brunton, J. (1930), *John Brunton's Book*, Cambridge.

Burn, R. S. (1871, reprint 2001), *Masonry, Bricklaying and Plastering*, London.

Carlson, R. E. (1969), *The Liverpool and Manchester Railway Project, 1821–1831*, Newton Abbot.

Chaloner, W. H., and Henderson, W. O. (1955/7), 'The Manbys and the Industrial Revolution in France 1819–1884', *TNS*, **XXX**, pp. 63–75.

le Chatelier, Louis (1845), *Etudes sur la Stabilité des Machines Locomotives en Mouvement*, Paris.

Chrimes, M. M., Murphy, Mary K., and Ribeill, George (n.d. [1994]), *Mackenzie – Giant of the Railways*, Institution of Civil Engineers, London.

Christiansen, Rex (1973), *A Regional History of the Railways of Great Britain, vol. 7, The West Midlands*, Newton Abbot.

Clark, E. F. (1983), *George Parker Bidder The Calculating Boy*, Bedford.

—— (1998), 'George Parker Bidder and the Dee Bridge Failure', in Jarvis, Adrian, and Smith, Kenneth (eds), *Perceptions of Great Engineers II*, National Museums and Galleries on Merseyside, Liverpool.

Clark, Edwin (1850), *The Britannia and Conway Tubular Bridges* (2 vols + 3rd vol. of plates), London.

A Resident Assistant [Clark, Latimer] (1849), *General Description of the Britannia and Conway Tubular Bridges on the Chester & Holyhead Railway. Published with the Permission of Robert Stephenson*, London.

Clinker, C. R. (1954, republished 1977), 'The Leicester & Swannington Railway', *Transactions of the Leicestershire Archaeological Society*, Leicester and Bristol.

Cole, Henry (1884), *Fifty Years of Public Work*, 2 vols, London.

Conder, F. R. (1868, reprint 1983), *Personal Recollections of English Engineers … &c* (reprint editor, J. Simmons), London.

Corlett, Ewan (1975), *The Iron Ship*, London.

Cottrell, P. L. (1975), *British Overseas Investment in the Nineteenth Century, Studies in Economic and Social History*, London.

Cranfield, J. (2000), *The Railways of Norway*, London.

Currie, A. W. (1957), *The Grand Trunk Railway of Canada*, Toronto.

Davidson, E. (1868), *The Railways of India: with an account of their rise, progress, and construction*, London.

Dempsey, G. D. (1845–1847), 'Railways', in *Papers on Subjects connected with the duties of the Corps of Royal Engineers*, vols 7–9, London.

Dempsey, G. D. (1850a), *Iron Applied to Railway Structures, Comprising an Abstract of Results of Experiments Conducted Under the Authority of the Commissioners Appointed ... to Enquire into the Application of Iron to Railway Structures*, London.

—— (1850b), *Rudimentary Treatise: Tubular and Other Iron Girder Bridges, Particularly Describing the Britannia and Conway Tubular Bridges*, London.

—— (4th edn, 1855), *The practical railway engineer &c.*, London.

Dickinson, H. W., and Titley, Arthur (1934), *Richard Trevithick, The Engineer and the Man*, Cambridge.

D[ixon], W. (1925), *Intimate Story of the Origin of Railways [extracts from diaries of John Dixon and Edward Pease]*, Darlington.

Donaldson, T. L. (1859), *Handbook of specifications: or practical guide to the architect, engineer, surveyor & builder, in drawing up specifications & contracts for works and constructions ... 2 parts*, London.

Dow, George (1959), *Great Central, Vol. 1: The Progenitors 1813–1863*, London.

Elsasser, Kilian ('Konzept') (1997), *Kohle, Strom und Schienen: Die Eisenbahn erobert die Schweiz*, Luzern.

Evans, D. M. (1848), *The Commercial Crisis of 1847–1848*, London.

Fairbairn, Thomas (1849), *Britannia and Conway Tubular Bridges. Truths and Tubes on Self-Supporting Principles &c*, London.

Fairbairn, William (1849), *An Account of the Construction of the Britannia and Conway Tubular Bridges, &c*, London.

Fellows, Rev. Reginald B. (1930), *History of the Canterbury and Whitstable Railway*, Canterbury.

Fuller, Francis (1851), *Memoranda Relative to the International Exhibition of 1851*, London.

Gibb, Alexander (1935), *The Story of Telford*, London.

Giuntini, Andrea (1991), *Leopolda e il Treno Le Ferrovie nel Granducato di Toscana 1824–1861*, Napoli.

Gradon, William M. (1946), *Furness Railway; its Rise and Development, 1846–1923*, Altrincham.

Grundy, Francis H. (1879), *Pictures of the Past: Memories of Men I have Met and Places I have Seen*, London.

Guy, Andy, and Rees, Jim (eds) (2001), *Early Railways*, Newcomen Society, London.

Hadfield, Charles (1966), *The Canals of the East Midlands*, Newton Abbot.

Halsall, David A. (1976), 'The Chester & Holyhead Railway and its Branches', unpublished PhD thesis, University of Liverpool.

Hart, Brian (1991), *The Canterbury & Whitstable Railway*, Didcot.

Haskoll, W. Davis (1846), *The Assistant Engineer's Railway Guide in Boring*, London.

Head, Francis B. (1849), *Highways and Dry-Ways; or, The Britannia and Conway Tubular Bridges &c*, London.

Egyptian Railways Authority [Helong, M. A. M.] (1977), *Egyptian Railways in 125 years, 1852–1977*, Cairo.

Helps, Arthur (1872), *Life and Labours of Mr. Brassey, 1805–1870*, London.

Hills, Richard L. (1988), *Papermaking in Britain 1488–1988*, London.

Hodges, J. (1860), *Construction of the Great Victoria Bridge in Canada*, London.

Hodgkinson, Eaton (1852), 'Experimental Inquiries to Determine the Strength of Wrought Iron Tubes &c.', in *Supplement to Theory of Bridges*, London.

'Manifold' [Hollick, John R.] (1952), *The North Staffordshire Railway: A History of the Line &c.*, Ashbourne.

Hunt, Robert (ed.) (1853), *Ure's Dictionary of Arts, Manufactures and Mines*, London.

Hutton, Charles (1812), *Tracts on Mathematical and Philosophical Subjects &c*, London.

James, John G. (1980/1), 'The Evolution of Iron Truss Bridges to 1850', *TNS*, **52**, pp. 67–101.

James, John G. (1987/8), 'Some Steps in the Evolution of Early Iron Arched Bridge Designs', *TNS*, **59**, pp. 153–86.

Jeaffreson, John C. (1864), *The Life of Robert Stephenson, F.R.S.* (2 vols), London.

Jeans, James S. (1875), *Jubilee Memorial of the Railway System: A History of the Stockton and Darlington Railway &c*, London.

Jenks, Leland H. (1927, reprint 1963), *The Migration of British Capital to 1875*, New York and London.

Kerr, Ian J. (1995), *Building the Railways of the Raj 1850–1900*, Oxford.

Kieve, Jeffrey (1973), *The Electric Telegraph: A Social and Economic History*, Newton Abbot.

Kinross, Lord (1968), *Between Two Seas: Creation of the Suez Canal*, London.

Kirby, M. W. (1984), *Men of Business and Politics*, London.

Laffen, B. N. (1849), 'Notes upon the High Level Bridge at Newcastle', in *Reports of the Commissioners of Railways for the Year 1849*, Appendix 50, pp. 83–5, London.

Lambert, Richard S. (1934), *The Railway King 1800–1871*, London.

Lamalle, Ulysse (1953), *Histoire des Chemins De Fer Belges*, Bruxelles.

Landi, Pier L. (1974), *La Leopolda La Ferrovia Firenze–Livorno e le Sue Vicende (1825–1860)*, Pisa.

Lane, Michael R. (1980), *The Story of the Steam Plough Works*, London.

Laxton, W. (1839), *The Improved Builder's Price Book*, London.

Lecount, Peter (1836a), *An Examination of Professor Barlow's Reports on Iron Rails*, London.

—— (1836b), *Remarks on the Cheapest Distance for Railway Blocks*, London.

—— (1839a), *The History of the Railway connecting London and Birmingham &c*, London.

—— (1839b), *A Practical Treatise on Railways, Explaining their Construction and Management &c*, Edinburgh.

Lewin, Henry Grote (1925), *Early British Railways &c 1801–1844*, London.

Lewis, Brian (1994), *The Cabry Family: Railway Engineers*, Railway and Canal Historical Society.

Lloyd, William (1900), *A Railway Pioneer: Notes by a Civil Engineer in Europe and America from 1838 to 1888*, London.

Lucas, Arthur (1910), *John Lucas Portrait Painter 1828–1874*, London.

Maclean, John S. (1948), *The Newcastle & Carlisle Railway 1825–1862*, Newcastle-upon-Tyne.

MacDermot, Edward T. (1927), *History of the Great Western Railway* (2 vols, 3 parts), London.

Marshall, C. F. Dendy (1936), *A History of the Southern Railway*, London.

Marshall, William P. (1838), *Description of the Patent Locomotive Steam Engine of Messrs. Robert Stephenson & Co.*, London.

Medley, J. G. (ed.) (1866), *Professional Papers on Indian Engineering*, vol. III, Roorkee, India.

Moseley, Henry (1843), *The Mechanical Principles of Engineering and Architecture*, London.

Murray, K. A. (1981), *Ireland's First Railway*, Dublin.

von Oeynhausen, Carl, and von Dechen, Ernst Heinrich (1829, reprint 1971), *Railways in England 1826 and 1827* (translated by E. A. Forward, edited by Charles E. Lee in collaboration with K. R. Gilbert), Newcomen Society, London.

Owen, R. (1996), *Norwegian Railways*, Hitchin.

P[aine], E. M. S. (1861), *The Two James's and the Two Stephensons ... &c*, London.

de Pambour, Chev. F. M. G. (1836), *A Practical Treatise on Locomotive Engines upon Railways*, London.

de Pambour, Comte F. M. G. (1840), *A Practical Treatise on Locomotive Engines*, London.

Parnell, Henry (1833), *A Treatise on Roads*, London.

Passfield, C. (2001), *Construction of the Victoria Tubular Bridge*, Easton, PA.

Pease, Sir Alfred E. (1907), *The Diaries of Edward Pease*, London.

Perkins, P. (1985), 'The Building and Early Working of the First Norwegian Railway', unpublished MA thesis, Newcastle-upon-Tyne Polytechnic.

'H. P.' [Peto, Henry] (1893), *Sir Morton Peto: A Memorial Sketch*, London (private circulation).

Petroski, H. (1993), 'The Britannia Tubular Bridge: A Paradigm of Failure Driven Design',
    Structural Engineering Review, 5, No. 4, Oxford.
—— (1994), 'Success Syndrome: the Collapse of the Dee Bridge', *Civil Engineering*, 64,
    New York.
Pole, William (ed.) (1877), *The Life of Sir William Fairbairn, Bart*, London.
Priestley, Joseph (1831, reprint 1969), *Navigable Rivers and Canals*, Newton Abbot.
Rapley, John (1998), 'Fresh Perceptions of a Great Engineer', in Jarvis, Adrian, and Smith,
    Kenneth (eds), *Perceptions of Great Engineers II*, Liverpool, pp. 91–103.
—— (2000), *The Britannia Bridge 1845–1850*, Institution of Civil Engineers, London.
Rees, James [publisher] (1849), *An Account of the Grand Flotation of One of the Monster Tubes
    Over the Menai Straits, Britannia Bridge, June 20th 1849*, Carnarvon and Bangor.
Rennison, Robert W. (1980/1), 'The High Level Bridge, Newcastle: Its Evolution, Design
    and Construction', *TNS*, **52**, pp. 180–207.
—— (1998), 'The Influence of William Fairbairn on Robert Stephenson's Bridge Designs:
    Four Bridges in North-East England', *IAR* (Association for Industrial Archaeology), **20**,
    pp. 37–48.
—— (2000/1), 'The Newcastle and Carlisle Railway and its Engineers', *TNS*, **72**, pp. 203–33.
Richardson, Benjamin W. (1891), *Thomas Sopwith … with Excerpts from his Diary of Fifty-
    Seven Years*, London.
Robbins, Michael (1984/5), 'Thomas Longridge Gooch 1808–1882', *TNS*, **56**, pp. 59–69.
Rolt, L. T. C. (1960), *George and Robert Stephenson The Railway Revolution*, London.
Roper, Robert S. (1990), *The Other Stephensons: The Story of the Family of George and Robert
    Stephenson*, Rochdale.
Roscoe, Thomas, and Lecount, Peter (1839), *The London & Birmingham Railway &c*,
    London.
Ruddock, Ted (1979), *Arch Bridges and Their Builders, 1735–1835*, Cambridge.
Russell, John Scott (1865), *System of Naval Architecture*, London.
Ryall, M. J. (1999), 'Britannia Bridge: from concept to construction', *Proc. ICE*, **132** (2/3),
    132–43.
Sharma, S. N. (1990), *History of the Great Indian Peninsula Railway*, 2nd edn, vol. 1,
    Bombay.
Sibley, P. G., and Walker A. C. (1977), 'Structural Accidents and Their Causes', *Proc. ICE*,
    62, Part 1, pp. 191–208.
Sidney, Samuel (1846), *Gauge Evidence. The History and Prospects of the Railway System
    Illustrated by the Evidence Given Before the Gauge Commission*, London.
Simmons, Jack, and Biddle, Gordon (1997), *Oxford Companion to British Railway History*,
    Oxford.
Simms, Frederick W. (1838), *Public Works of Great Britain &c*, London.
Skempton, A. W. (1987), *British Civil Engineering Literature 1640–1840*, London.
—— (1996), *Civil Engineers and Engineering in Britain, 1600–1830*, Aldershot.
—— (ed.) (1981, reprint 1991), *John Smeaton, F.R.S.*, London.
—— (ed.) (2002), *Biographical Dictionary of Civil Engineers of the British Isles Vol. 1: 1500–
    1830*, London.
Smeaton, John (1812), *Reports of the Late John Smeaton* (4 vols), London.
Smiles, Samuel (1857), *The Life of George Stephenson, Railway Engineer*, London.
—— (1861), 'Life of John Smeaton', Part VI of Vol. II of *Lives of the Engineers*, London, pp. 3–90.
—— (1862), 'The Life of George Stephenson, &c.', Vol. III of *Lives of the Engineers*, London.
Smith, Denis (1997/8), 'James Walker (1781–1862): Civil Engineer', *TNS*, **69**, pp. 23–55.
Smith, S. (1992), 'The Development and Use of the Tubular Beam 1830–1860', in *History
    of Technology, 14*, London.
Sopwith, Robert (1994), *Thomas Sopwith, Surveyor: An Exercise in Self-Help*, Edinburgh.
Spencer, Herbert (1904), *An Autobiography* (2 vols), London.

Stephenson, Robert (1844), *Report on the Atmospheric Railway System*, London.

—— (1847), *The Double Gauge: Observations by Mr. R. Stephenson on Mr. Brunel's Report on the Double Gauge*, London.

—— (8th edn, 1856a), 'Iron Bridges', in *Encyclopaedia Britannica*, pp. 575–610, London.

—— (1856b), 'Our British Railways', Presidential address, *Proc. ICE*, **15**, pp. 123–54.

—— (1857), 'Résumé of the Railway System and its Results', in Smiles, Samuel, *The Life of George Stephenson, Railway Engineer*, London, pp. 477–512.

Stephenson, Robert, and Locke, Joseph (1830), *Observations on the Comparative Merits of Locomotive and Fixed Engines as Applied to Railways, &c.*, Liverpool.

Stephenson, Robert, Fairbairn, William, and Hodgkinson, Eaton (1846), *Reports ... upon the Experiments Made to Ascertain the Practicability of Erecting a Tubular Bridge Across the Menai Straits, for the Passage of Railway Trains*, London.

Stevens, Philip A. (1972), *The Leicester Line*, Newton Abbot.

Sutherland, R. J. M. (1963/4), 'The Introduction of Structural Wrought Iron', *TNS*, **XXXVI**, pp. 67–84.

Thestrup, Poul (1997), *På sporet 1847–1997: Dampen binder Danmark sammen*, Odense.

Thomas, R. H. G. (1980), *The Liverpool & Manchester Railway*, London.

Tomlinson, William W. (1914), *The North Eastern Railway Its Rise and Development*, Newcastle-upon-Tyne.

Turnbull, William (1847), *An Essay on the Air-Pump and Atmospheric Railway Containing Formulae and Rules for Calculating the Various Quantities Contained in Robert Stephenson's Report on Atmospheric Propulsion, &c*, London.

Tyson, S. (1978), 'Notes on the History, Development and Use of Tubes in the Construction of Bridges', *IAR* (Association for Industrial Archaeology), **2** (2), pp. 143–53.

Walmsley, H. M. (1879), *Life of Sir Joshua Walmsley*, London.

Warren, J. G. H. (1923), *A Century of Locomotive Building by Robert Stephenson & Co. 1823/ 1923*, Newcastle-upon-Tyne.

Watson, J. G. (1979), *The Civils*, London.

Weale, John [publisher] (1843), *Theory, Practice and Architecture of Bridges*, London.

Webster, Norman W. (1970), *Joseph Locke: Railway Revolutionary*, London.

Whishaw, Francis (1837; 2nd edn, 1838), *Analysis of Railways &c*, London.

—— (1840; 2nd edn, 1842), *The Railways of Great Britain and Ireland*, London.

White, R. (1999), *Gentleman Engineers: The Working Lives of Frank and Walter Shanley*, Toronto.

Whitting, Harriet A. (1917), *Alfred Booth, Some Memories, Letters and Other Family Records*, Liverpool (private circulation).

Wierner, L. (1932), *Egypt et ses Chemins de Fer*, Bruxelles.

Williams, Frederick S. (4th edn, 1878), *The Midland Railway, Its Rise and Progress*, Nottingham.

Wood, Nicholas (2nd edn, 1831; 3rd edn, 1838), *A Practical Treatise on Rail-Roads &c*, London.

Young, Robert (1923), *Timothy Hackworth and the Locomotive*, London.

Index